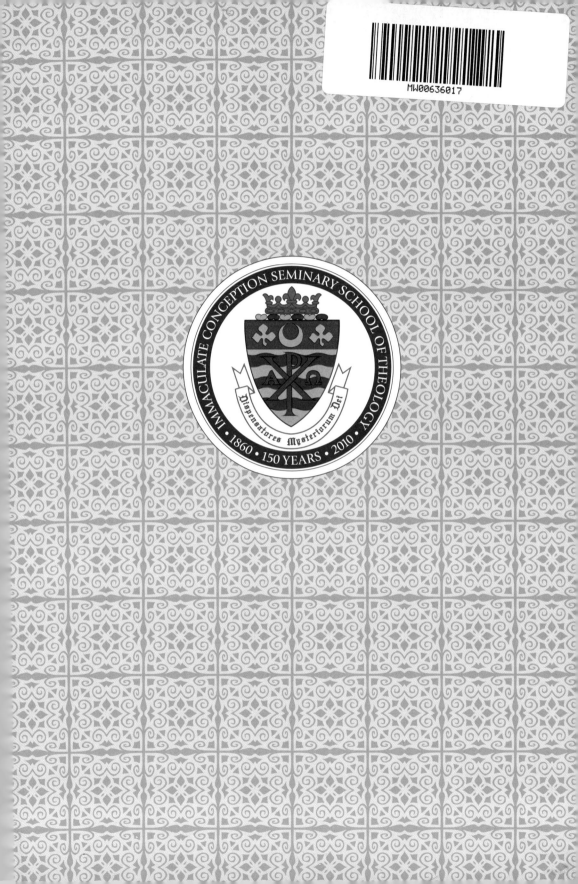

IMMACULATE CONCEPTION SEMINARY SCHOOL OF THEOLOGY

Dispensatores Mysteriorum Dei

· 1860 · 150 YEARS · 2010 ·

Cover illustration: "The Miraculous Draught of Fishes," cartoon for tapestry
by Raffaello Sanzio da Urbino (1483-1520), on loan from the Royal Collection
to the Victoria and Albert Museum.

This book was designed by art270, Inc. of Jenkintown, Pennsylvania.
The main text of the book was set in Adobe Garamond.

The book was manufactured in the United States of America
by Toppan America of Somerset, New Jersey.

Published by Immaculate Conception Seminary
400 South Orange Avenue
South Orange, New Jersey 07079

Library of Congress Control Number: 2010927213

ISBN: 978-0-615-36403-2

To
Monsignor Robert F. Coleman
Doctor of Canon Law
Rector and Dean
Without whose support and encouragement
this book would not have been possible

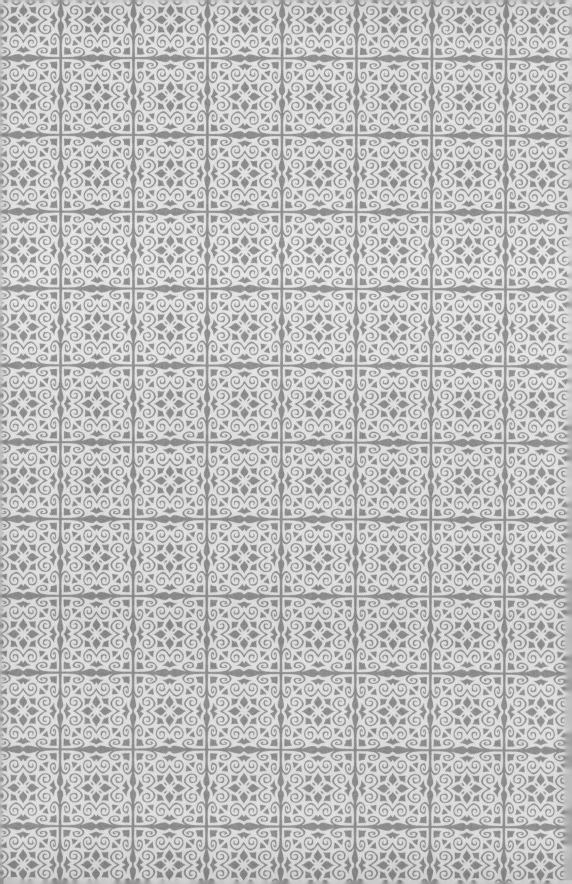

Table of Contents

Part III: The Major Archdiocesan Philosophical-Theological Seminary
of the Immaculate Conception at Darlington, New Jersey
TOWARD THE CENTENNIAL 1939-1960

Part IV: The Major Archdiocesan Philosophical-Theological Seminary
of the Immaculate Conception at Darlington, New Jersey
CRISIS AND CHANGE 1961-1982

Part V: Immaculate Conception Seminary School of Theology,
Seton Hall University
AFFILIATION AND RELOCATION 1982-2010

Part VI: Immaculate Conception Seminary School of Theology,
Seton Hall University
MOVING INTO THE FUTURE 2010

Introduction

To a traveler sailing on the Nile, gazing at the monuments of the pharaohs, 150 years might seem to be no more than a blink of an eye. Even in the history of a Church that measures time in centuries, a century and a half does not appear to be so long a time. In the life of the Church in the United States, it is quite a different matter.

Most of the seminaries established in the U.S. since the first in 1791 have disappeared. Simply to have survived is an accomplishment. To have prospered and thrived is an astounding feat.

The story of Immaculate Conception Seminary reflects the history of the United States and the history of the Catholic Church in this country. I do not know of any other seminary north of the Mason-Dixon Line that had a rector who was a veteran of the Army of the Confederate States of America. All seminaries have faced financial crises, but what other seminary was on the brink of sale by its bishop not once or twice, but on three separate occasions?

Like all seminaries, it has alumni who became bishops. But it also is a seminary that has produced chaplain heroes who have received the Medal of Honor and a unique Congressional Medal of Valor in two twentieth-century wars. One of the seminarians who passed though its halls, but was never ordained, received the Presidential Medal of Freedom, an award also conferred on Pope John Paul II.

I have tried to give the reader a glimpse of the ever-changing life of Immaculate Conception Seminary's students, faculty, and staff. It has been at one time or another a school with a dozen or more seminarians within a small college, an enclosed monastery-like institution with more than 300 seminarians, and finally a seminary and school of theology educating seminarians and lay men and women on the campus of a major university.

In each of these incarnations, it has maintained its central mission of training men for the priesthood of the Catholic Church as it has adapted to the needs of the Church and the realities of the times.

Mirroring its development, it has been known by a series of names, some simple, some rather cumbersome. In nineteenth-century national Catholic directories, we find it called the "Diocesan Seminary" and the "Ecclesiastical Seminary." Eventually it becomes "Immaculate Conception Seminary." In the twentieth century, reflecting the grandeur of the Darlington estate, it is the "Major Archdiocesan Philosophical and Theological Seminary of the Immaculate Conception." In the 1970s, it varied its name from year to year, occasionally called the "Darlington School of Theology" in its catalogues. As it moved to Seton Hall in 1984, its official name, reflecting the past and the present, was the "Darlington Seminary of the Immaculate Conception School of Theology and Pastoral Ministry of Seton Hall University"—

too long for letterhead. For this reason, throughout this book, I refer simply to "the seminary."

In its first century, the distinctions among college seminarians, philosophy students, and theology students were rather vague. Theology students clearly were "seminarians" and wore a cassock and followed a rather strict rule. Students studying philosophy sometimes were called seminarians but often were referred to in seminary documents as "ecclesiastical students" or "church students." First- and second-year college students were sometimes called simply "aspirants to the priesthood." This often-confusing nomenclature and the murky distinctions among these groups make it almost impossible to separate what today are much clearer administrative units. In 1911, Seton Hall's high school and college departments were designated the "preparatory seminary" of the diocese of Newark, New Jersey, but it was only in the 1940s, at the gentle prodding of the Holy See, that administrative distinctions became clear. As a result, this history is a story of high school, college, philosophical, and theological education.

While this is an "institutional history," it also is a history of people—and of a people, the Catholic people of the diocese and archdiocese of Newark and the dioceses and religious communities that the seminary serves. While it recounts the policy and administrative decisions and actions that have shaped the story, it also tries to give the reader a glimpse into the personalities that have shaped it as well as the lives of the seminarians, faculty, and staff that incarnated it.

The personalities often jump out at us and cause surprise and consternation. Father McQuaid resigns in a huff and runs to New York, but he comes back. Bishop Corrigan opens the coffers of the family fortune to save a bankrupt college and seminary. Mary Gwendolyn Caldwell haughtily sniffs that Seton Hall is a "broken-down college" and sends her money for a new Catholic university to Washington rather than to South Orange. Will Durant enters the seminary with the hope of creating a fifth column to bring the Church to socialism. Bishop Walsh enlists Democratic Party boss Frank Hague to raise money for the new seminary at Darlington. Seminarians of the late 1960s gather confreres from across the United States to demand more reforms in the Church. In one day, seminarians and faculty decamp from Mahwah and move to South Orange—in the middle of the semester. Seminarians of every era plan, plot, and conspire to evade whatever rules they deem restrictive or inconvenient.

I hope that the reader will not only enjoy this book but will appreciate the sacrifices made by so many people over the last 150 years to ensure that Immaculate Conception Seminary's mission to the Catholic Church has endured and prospered.

Foreword

By Christopher J. Kauffman

Catholic Daughters of the Americas
Professor Emeritus of American Catholic History
at The Catholic University of America

Monsignor Robert J. Wister has written perhaps the most extensive and detailed history of any Catholic seminary in the United States. It is principally an internal story with many remarks on context. For instance, he informs the readers of the various stages of immigration by noting the ethnic backgrounds of the seminarians themselves. The Irish originally dominated and from 1880 to 1920 European immigrants from Italy and Eastern Europe followed. In more recent times, Latinos, Africans, and Asians entered the seminary. There were also several religious communities and dioceses that sent their young men to the seminary.

Wister has a strong command of the primary source material such as correspondence between rectors and bishops, rectors' reports to the board of deputies (later trustees and overseers), and biographical material on many members of the faculty. He has consulted works related to the history of theological education from books, articles, journals, newspapers, and dissertations. Wister obviously spent many hours in archives, where he found materials never previously researched by scholars.

For example, in a later chapter evincing modern trends, Wister cites the Vatican approval of the study of psychology and psychological testing of seminarians. This approval occurred as late as 1955, about thirty years after Catholic colleges and universities had established psychology departments. Though he cites Henry J. Beck's centennial history of Immaculate Conception Seminary, he relies upon primary sources and goes beyond Beck. Wister himself published five articles related to this book, with titles such as "Theological Education in the Seminaries" and "The History of the Office of Rector in Roman Catholic Seminaries."

He focuses—most helpfully—on curriculum development throughout the years, and includes lists of textbooks, manuals of dogmatic and moral theology, ecclesiastical history, and canon law. In each section of this work, Wister lists the faculty, their academic backgrounds, and the courses they taught. In addition to academic development, the book devotes significant attention to human, pastoral, and spiritual formation in seminary training. He is particularly good at exploring the rules, customs, and daily schedules of the seminary, giving an inside view of its daily life in various eras.

The seminary was besieged by several fires, necessitating the construction of new buildings. Wister adeptly describes these building projects, from their architectural renderings to their completion. Readers are treated with celebrations marking significant events and anniversaries and of the seminary. He even notes some of the toasts to important guests and describes the menu of a festive meal concluded with café noir and cigars!

Wister's methodology is evident. He allows the cast of historic characters to speak for themselves through extensive quotes, rather than inserting his own comments into the narrative, and he skillfully paraphrases comments of the many figures in the history. Father Bernard McQuaid, the first head of the seminary, often labored on its farm, which yielded enough food for the meals of the seminary and the adjacent Seton Hall College. McQuaid is described as wearing a "high hat rather worse for wear" and clothes dusty "from working on the farm."

In 1915, the Holy See established the Sacred Congregation for Seminaries and Universities, and two years later the Revised Code of Canon Law was published. Rome now dictated extensive rules for seminary life, a list of offices to be filled, and a detailed daily schedule for all seminarians to follow. Rome even prescribed aspects of the curriculum. So significant were these Vatican-imposed changes to the way of life within the seminary that the seminarians were expected, in the words of the contemporary rector, to "recognize and venerate the person and authority of God as manifest in the rule and directions of seminary authority." Wister relates one rule directing students' rooms to be free of photos or art; he reports that "this present writer violated this rule and was ordered to remove a portrait of Paul VI from his desk."

In spring 1927, Immaculate Conception Seminary moved to a remote rural area—and became known as the Major Diocesan Philosophical-Theological Seminary of the Immaculate Conception at Darlington—in accord with the trend at the time toward areas safely removed from the secular influences of city life. In 1929, the constitutions and rules of the seminary were approved with only minor changes from the previous rule of 1917. The rector in 1929 told the seminarians "to bring your own mind, your own will to the directives of your superiors: to direct your consciences to the spiritual director and your confessor: for your intellectual development to the viewpoints of your professors and the textbooks, and your deportment to the rector and his subordinates." This triumphant style of authority in seminaries was also evident in the rules of religious women and men by which the obedience to the authority of the superior was tantamount to conforming to the will of God.

I consider the 1950s as having introduced developments which presaged the changes to come in the 1960s. The liturgical movement based upon congregational participation was gaining momentum in the 1950s; by mid-decade Pope Pius XII had deleted the traditional fast for receiving communion thereby allowing for Sunday Mass on Saturday evening vigils. At the same time, high school and college textbooks in religion were emphasizing the life of Christ and its significance in liturgical reform.

These developments fostered an incarnational spirituality, implicitly undermining the negative anthropology embedded in the rules and customs of the seminary. Immaculate Conception Seminary did not adopt some of these developments until the mid-1960s.

Monsignor George Shea, who became rector in 1961, considered those who were promoting renewal to be engaging in "self-indulgence." Wister notes that Shea remarked, "Seminarians do a lot of reading and in that way get ideas and become dissatisfied with the seminary program." It was not until 1965-66 that students were allowed to study in the library rather than in their rooms. Wister writes of "the many changes [which] were introduced … at a rapid pace: frequent concelebrations, Mass facing the people, increased singing at Mass, occasional group Masses."

It seems apparent to me that the seminary subculture was dissolving. For example, Wister describes the rule of the late 1960s as composed of 11 "formative directions, 12 specific directives, and lengthy seminary customs"—replacing the old rule of 77, the violation of which could mean suspension or dismissal. Seminarians reflected the general trends of student activism in colleges and universities such as striving for participation in the governance of universities and engaging in pro-civil rights and anti-war protests.

Immediately before the end of the Second Vatican Council, Darlington seminarians joined the organization of the Northeast Seminarians Study Conference, and two years later they sponsored a meeting of the conference at Seton Hall University. Wister reports that many local newspapers covered the event: "Almost immediately the press exploded with banner headlines: 'Seminarians want optional celibacy,' 'Seminarians, sisters take anti-war stance,' 'Seminarians in rumble: Ivory towers crumbling.'" The conference also resolved to allow non-Catholic Christians to "take communion at Masses during Unity Week next year."

Shea was not only alienated by the seminarians' conference but was disappointed with the faculty as well. He was particularly concerned that both groups were taking an end run around the rector and going directly to the archbishop. He tendered his resignation because he no longer had "the self-confidence or the stamina to cope with the relentless problems of the seminary." He was replaced by Monsignor William F. Hogan, who is said to have embraced the post-conciliar changes. Despite Hogan's sympathy toward recent reforms, seminarians and faculty still wrote directly to Archbishop Thomas Boland requesting specific programs and projects, such as supporting Cesar Chavez's farm workers, boycotting lettuce, and joining anti-war protests against bombing Cambodia.

Throughout the archdiocese, many priests and laity criticized the radical views of the faculty and seminarians, alleging a lack of spirituality and self-control. These and other criticisms led to Hogan's resignation. He was replaced by Monsignor Harold P. Darcy, who consolidated the post-conciliar changes and strengthened "traditional elements, such as community liturgy and conferences by the rector and spiritual director." Darcy led the seminary toward the State of New Jersey's approval of the master of divinity degree (M. Div.) for the seminarians and the master of arts (M.A.) for others. Eventually these degrees became very popular among large groups of religious and laity, who over time transformed the character of Immaculate Conception Seminary.

Peter Leo Gerety became archbishop of Newark in 1974 and was a distinctively post-Vatican II leader. He allowed the faculty and the new board of trustees to provide input on the selection of the rector. The faculty proposed two candidates, and Monsignor Edward Ciuba, professor of sacred scripture, was chosen as president/rector, as the title had recently been changed. Gerety was pleased to appoint him to a five-year term. According to Wister, Ciuba saw the seminary as having a new role in the contemporary Church. It became a theologically and spiritually vigorous resource center to which sisters and laity of the archdiocese of Newark—and beyond—sought sound preparation for ministry.

The 1970s witnessed a polarization within the Church; cultural wars flared over issues such as clerical dress, communion in the hand, and the role of social ministry in priestly formation. In reaction to change, many seminarians preferred traditional private devotions within a pious atmosphere free from the distractions and concerns of the larger society. Ciuba, supported by the archbishop and trustees, viewed the source of this "new conservatism" as the result of a "lack of personal development and maturity." He feared that this "would produce candidates unwilling and unable to function in the contemporary or future Church."

The financial status of the archdiocese of Newark had become so fragile that the budget of the seminary was severely affected. In 1976-77, the chancery's subsidy to the seminary drastically decreased. Wister narrates in detail the resolution to the crisis: affiliation of the seminary with Seton Hall University. He prefaces the narrative of this transformative event with this remark: "Many seminaries did not survive the severe drop in investments during these years [1972-1984]. Immaculate Conception not only survived but managed to transform itself as an institution that preserved the integrity of priestly formation and expanded its mission to offer professional and pastoral education and formation to the laity."

The institution became Immaculate Conception Seminary School of Theology of Seton Hall University. New tensions arose surrounding the relationship of the seminary and the university. The story of the long, drawn-out negotiations of the many issues involved is often dramatic.

I close this foreword that I may yield to the author's masterly historical narrative, including later eyewitness accounts of the administrations of Archbishop Gerety's successor, Archbishop Theodore McCarrick—who wrought significant changes in the 1980s and 1990s—and of his successor, Archbishop John J. Myers, the presiding shepherd of the Church of Newark, who continues to take an active part in the life of the seminary under his care and direction.

Acknowledgments

In Fall 2004, as I was discussing my impending sabbatical, Monsignor Robert Coleman, rector and dean of Immaculate Conception Seminary School of Theology, asked me if I would consider devoting the sabbatical to writing a history of the seminary to commemorate its sesquicentennial in 2010. I had been thinking about this as a possible project for several years, and I immediately responded positively to Monsignor Coleman's suggestion. In the subsequent years, he has been the major source of encouragement and support for this project. I am grateful to Immaculate Conception Seminary and to Seton Hall University for granting me the sabbatical time without which this task never would have been accomplished.

Almost all of the resources for this history are in the archives and special collections department of Seton Hall's University Libraries. Alan Delozier, director and university archivist, and Kathleen Dodds, archival assistant, shared their thorough knowledge of the archives with me and provided invaluable assistance. One of the great challenges I faced was the processing of the seminary archives. In this I enjoyed the able assistance of Reverend Michael Barone and Travis Lawminster.

Monsignor Francis Seymour, archivist of the archdiocese of Newark, was always available for date-checking and fact-checking. His knowledge of the history of the archdiocese of Newark, especially of its priests, can only be described as encyclopedic.

I also am most grateful to Monsignor Raymond Kupke, archivist of the diocese of Paterson and adjunct professor of Church history at the seminary, not only for reading the text as it emerged through the years, but for offering valuable suggestions. I owe equal gratitude to Greg Tobin, the senior adviser for communications at Seton Hall (and a lay ICS alumnus), for his many stylistic recommendations and editing skills.

Archbishop Peter L. Gerety and Cardinal Theodore E. McCarrick read the sections dealing with their years as metropolitan ordinaries of Newark. Archbishop Gerety asked for one small addition, and Cardinal McCarrick said the text was fine. Archbishop John J. Myers, our shepherd since 2001, read the text as it developed and peppered me for more details about events and personalities. I am grateful to have had the opportunity to talk with these bishops who have had a major impact on the history of the seminary.

The former rectors of the seminary, Bishop John Flesey and Monsignors Edward Ciuba, Richard Liddy, and Robert Harahan, generously gave of their time and culled their memories, correcting errors and adding information not available in printed form. Monsignor James Cafone, former vice rector, was equally generous and informative.

The following provided valuable information, recollections, and anecdotes that helped give life to this story: Dr. Peter Ahr, Monsignor Emmanuel Capozzelli, and Fathers Alfred Celiano, Thomas Guarino, Peter Lennon, Richard Nardone, and Gerard Sloyan.

A book of this size requires the assistance of many people to bring it to completion. My thanks go to these "hidden collaborators." Meredith Hale, our eagle-eyed copyeditor, uncovered and corrected many typographical and stylistic errors. Paul Kocak served as the proofreader. Michael Begley of Toppan America expertly guided the production and manufacture of the book. Our graphic designer, Dianne Mill of art270, applied her fine talents and skills in the final design process.

Mrs. Kathleen Childers, assistant to the rector and dean, graciously, patiently, and efficiently photocopied the various drafts.

I cannot express my thanks enough or often enough to my fellow seminary faculty members, colleagues who are not only a source of encouragement but also of inspiration.

Finally, I apologize for any errors and assume responsibility for them.

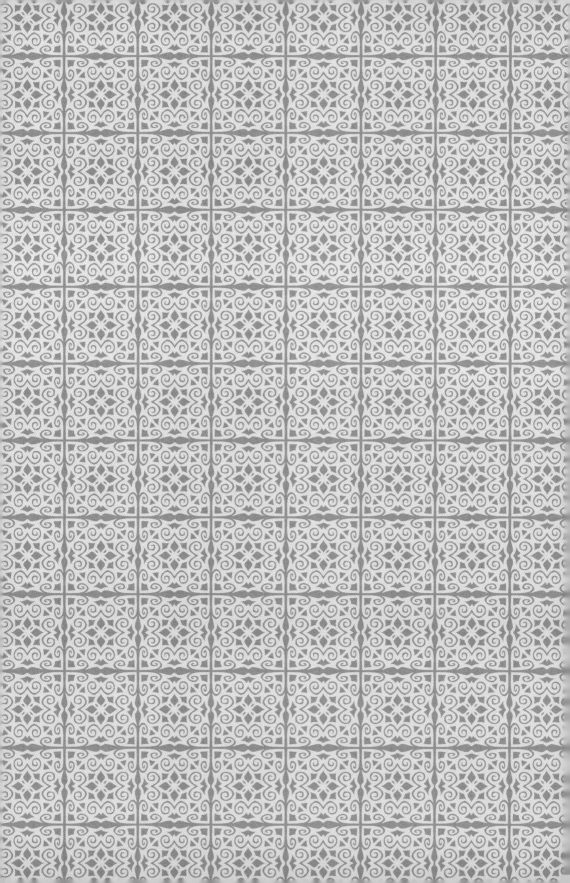

c. 1872. Faculty and seminarians on rear steps of seminary building. Second row, third from right: Reverend James Corrigan, director of the seminary. – Archives of the Archdiocese of Newark (AAN)

The Early Years at Seton Hall

When Bishop James Roosevelt Bayley founded Seton Hall College in Madison, New Jersey, in 1856, his plan included a seminary, which began when the college moved to South Orange in 1860. Throughout the early years of both institutions, the driving force was Father Bernard McQuaid, college president and seminary director and later the bishop of Rochester. When the Elphinstone Mansion, which housed the seminary, was destroyed by fire in 1863, the new seminary building, completed in 1867, carried a debt that would burden both college and seminary for a half century. The seminary and college, in then-rural South Orange, provided much of its own food from a small farm. The life of the seminarians was rather strict but was moderated by the proximity of the village of South Orange.

Bayley's successors, Bishops Michael Corrigan and Winand Wigger, struggled to maintain both institutions, although tempted three times to sell them off. The seminary enrollment remained modest throughout the 19th century, but began to grow in the first quarter of the 20th century. The faculty members rarely numbered more than a half-dozen, each teaching a great variety of disciplines. The most interesting seminarian of the period was Will Durant, who entered the seminary with the intention of converting the Catholic Church to socialism.

The Third Plenary Council of Baltimore in 1885 brought improvements to the seminary program and curriculum, and the 20th century brought a series of interventions in seminary life that provoked Bishop O'Connor to move the seminary to the rural Darlington estate in Mahwah, New Jersey.

Right Reverend James
Roosevelt Bayley (1814-
1877), first bishop of
Newark (1853-1872),
founder of Seton Hall
College and Immaculate
Conception Seminary.
– AAN

Right Reverend
Bernard John McQuaid
(1823-1909), first
president of Seton Hall
College (1856-1857,
1859-1868) and first
director of Immaculate
Conception Seminary
(1860-1862). – AAN

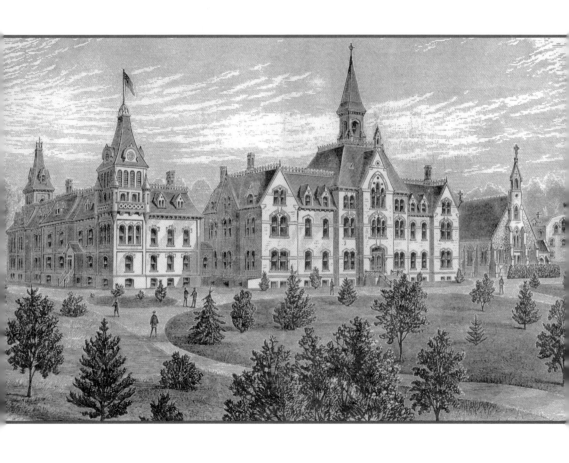

1867. Left, the College Building, expanded in 1863; center, the Seminary Building, completed in 1867; right, the Chapel, built in 1863. – AAN

Reverend Januarius De Concilio (1836-1898).
First professor of theology at the seminary,
major editor of the *Baltimore Catechism*.
– AAN

Right Reverend Michael Augustine Corrigan
(1839-1900), second bishop of Newark
(1873-1880), president of Seton Hall
College (1868-1877), director of Immaculate
Conception Seminary (1864-1868).
– Joseph M. Flynn, *The Catholic Church in New
Jersey*, New York: 1904.

1870s. Seminarians on
the chapel steps. – AAN

1880s. Seminarians, college
students, professors on
the front steps of the
seminary building. – AAN

1900. The seminary chapel. – AAN

The Faculty 1923-1924. The seminary and college faculty. Bottom row, left to right: Reverends J. J. Sheerin, J. H. Hewetson, and J. C. McClary, Monsignor Thomas H. McLaughlin (rector and president), Reverends J. J. Dauenhauer, W. A. Griffin, and T. J. Burke. Second row: Reverends T. J. Duffy, J. M. Walsh, J. A. Hamilton, T. A. Boland, M. A. Mechler, Charles Demjanovich, and M. F. Donnelly. Third row: P. J. McLaughlin, P. J. O'Neill, E. J. Kenny, F. C. L. Shreiner, A. F. Marquier, and E. L. Jennings. Top row: J. J. Prefladisch, R. A. Saner, and E. F. Magnier. – AAN

Right Reverend
Winand Michael Wigger
(1841-1901), third bishop
of Newark (1881-1901).
– AAN

Monsignor Thomas H.
McLaughlin (1881-1947),
president of Seton Hall
College (1922-1933);
rector of Immaculate
Conception Seminary
(1922-1938). – AAN

1938. The new Immaculate Conception Seminary at Darlington. – AAN

An Ascetic Life in a Manorial Setting

The move to the splendid isolation of the 1,500 acres of the Darlington estate initiated a period of growth and expansion that would peak in the 1960s and finish in the turmoil of the post-Vatican II years. For the first 40 years at Darlington, the seminary was akin to a cloistered monastery, a world unto itself. In the 1970s, it shook off its monastic constraints and extended its mission to the wider world of general theological education and the preparation of lay ministers.

Initially, the growing seminarian and faculty population was cramped in the Macmillan Mansion and the rather run-down Darling family summer home, grandiloquently named the Saint Thomas Philosophy House. Bishop (later Archbishop) Walsh raised over $1 million to erect a magnificent complex to house 300 seminarians and faculty attached to a splendid Gothic Revival chapel.

Until the 1940s, the seminary continued the tradition of maintaining a farm, and the vast property was like a national park for seminarian hikers, with indoor and outdoor sports facilities. Rarely were the students allowed to venture past the property lines. They did so under penalty of dismissal. In the late 1960s, as the Church changed, everything at Darlington began to change. Clerical garb was optional and rare. Seminarians left the property at will and on pastoral assignments. Their number decreased. As the world outside the seminary changed, the world within was transformed. Pastoral training programs were initiated and academic programs were changed at a dizzying speed. A financial crisis within the archdiocese of Newark and changing pastoral directions meant that the Darlington years would come to an end.

October 12, 1926. Dedication of new seminary at Darlington, New Jersey, and the celebration of the golden jubilee of Bishop O'Connor's ordination. Seated: Right Reverend John J. O'Connor (1855-1927), fourth bishop of Newark (1901-1927); second from left: Monsignor Thomas H. McLaughlin, president of Seton Hall College (1922-1933), rector of Immaculate Conception Seminary (1922-1938). – AAN

Monsignor Charles
Demjanovich (1899-1976),
known as "Father
Charles." – AAN

November 8, 1936. Most Reverend Thomas J. Walsh (1873-1952), fifth bishop of Newark
(1928-1937) and first archbishop of Newark (1937-1952), accompanied by the seminary choir,
opens the campaign for the new seminary broadcasting an appeal on radio station WOR. – AAN

Top: 1931. The chapel in the ballroom of the Macmillan Mansion. The altar is set in the fireplace. – AAN

Above: 1927. The Macmillan Mansion, Immaculate Conception Seminary (1927-1984). – AAN

September 26, 1937. Most Reverend Thomas J. Walsh lays the cornerstone of the new seminary at Darlington. – AAN

1948. The United States postage stamp issued to commemorate the "Four Chaplains." Reverend John P. Washington is second from the right. – AAN

1940. Chapel of Christ the King at Darlington. – AAN

1941. The seminary choir at Darlington. – AAN

Left to right: Monsignor Joseph Brady (1904-1961), rector (1955-1961); Most Reverend Thomas A. Boland (1896-1979), rector (1940-1947), second archbishop of Newark (1953-1974); Monsignor Thomas Powers (1899-1962), rector (1950-1955). – AAN

April 3, 1962, the seminary centennial lecture was delivered by Reverend Cyril Vollert, S.J. Left to right: Father Vollert, Monsignor George Shea (1910-1990), rector (1961-1968); Most Rev. Thomas A. Boland (1896-1979), rector (1940-1947), second archbishop of Newark (1953-1974). – AAN

1961. The seminary faculty. Left to right, front row: Reverends William Hogan, John Koenig, Joseph Manz, Joseph Przezdziecki, and Stanley Adamczyk; second row: Monsignors John Cassels and George Shea (rector), Most Reverend Thomas Boland, Monsignors George Baker and Henry Beck; third row: Reverends Russell Ruffino, Carl Hinrichsen, Leo Farley, James Turro, James Finnerty, Robert Hunt, and Donald Zimmerman, Professor Joseph Murphy. – AAN

Top: Early 1960s. The seminary dining room. – AAN

Above: 1950s. Tobogganing over the infamous "honey pots." – AAN

Top: 1960s. Seminarian volleyball game. – AAN

Above: Early 1960s. Tug o' war. – AAN

1970s. Christ the King Chapel at Darlington after the renovations of 1973. – AAN

Early 1960s. The "cycle classes" in the ballroom of the Macmillan Mansion, now called the "Magna Aula." – AAN

1970s. Reverend Leo Farley conducting class for lay students and sisters. – AAN

1984. The faculty at Darlington. Front row, left to right: Reverend George Reilly, Sister Margaret Kirby, S.C., Reverend Stephen Feehen, Sister Agnes Mallner, O.S.U., Reverends Charles Gusmer, Joseph Masiello, Arthur Serratelli, and Donald Zimmerman. Back row, left to right: Monsignor Edward Ciuba (rector), Reverends Frank DeDomenico, Richard Asakiewicz, Joseph Kukura, James Turro, and Robert Harahan, Monsignor John O'Brien, Reverends Thomas Guarino and Robert Wister. – AAN

June 7, 1975. The first commencement ceremony at Darlington. Monsignor Thomas Fahy, president of Seton Hall University was awarded the seminary's first honorary doctorate. Left to right: Monsignor Edward Ciuba (born 1935), rector (1974-1985); Reverend Stanley Adamczyk, academic dean; Most Reverend John J. Dougherty, auxiliary bishop of Newark, president of Seton Hall University (1959-1969); Most Reverend Peter Gerety (born 1912), archbishop of Newark (1974-1986); Most Reverend Joseph A. Costello, auxiliary bishop of Newark; Monsignor Thomas Fahy, president of Seton Hall University (1970-1976); Monsignor John F. O'Brien (1915-1997), vice rector (1960-1980).

1986. Reverend Thomas
Guarino lecturing. – AAN

Transition and Relocation

While on the surface all was tranquil, and all appeared to be in agreement over
the sale of the Darlington property and the move to Seton Hall, many aspects of the
affiliation of the seminary and the university would not be worked out easily. Tensions
continued to simmer between the two institutions and it would be several years before
an adequate agreement was reached. This was attained, in no small part, as a result of
the recommendations of the Vatican visitation team in 1986.

The seminarians adjusted quickly and the program continued as at Darlington.
However, the very informal atmosphere of Darlington gradually became more structured
at Seton Hall. Now a comparatively small part of a large university, it was necessary for
the seminary to maintain a clearly distinctive character and identity. The dress code was
again altered and clerical shirts replaced polo shirts.

The program was adjusted to meet all new requirements of successive editions of
the *Program of Priestly Formation*. The most significant change was in the composition
of the student body itself. The demographic changes in the Church in New Jersey
and the sending dioceses were reflected in the presence of increasing numbers of Latino,
Filipino, Korean, African, European, and Vietnamese seminarians. The seminarians
of the Neo-Catechumenal Way and increasing numbers of students from religious
communities added a further dimension. The growing presence of lay students was
evidence of the increasing variety of programs, in particular, the introduction of
a four-year bachelor of arts degree in Catholic theology and the new Institute for
Christian Spirituality.

1987. Lewis Hall, the seminary residence building at Seton Hall Universty.

June 13, 1983. Groundbreaking for construction of the seminary at Seton Hall. Left to right: Dr. Edward d'Alessio, president of Seton Hall University; Monsignor John Petillo, chancellor of Seton Hall University; Most Reverend Peter Gerety (born 1912), archbishop of Newark (1974-1986), Monsignor Edward Ciuba, rector (1974-1985). – AAN

Monsignor Richard Liddy, rector (1985-1990). – AAN

1986. Reverend Arthur
Serratelli instructing a
seminarian. – AAN

1986. Seminarian library
discussion group. – AAN

1987. The Apostolic Visitation. Left to right: Reverends Cornelius McRae and William Froehle; Monsignor Richard Liddy, rector (1985-1990); Most Reverend George Wirz, chairman of the visitation; Reverends William Fay and Paul Harmon, S.J. – AAN

1986. Reverend John Russell, O.Carm, lecturing. – AAN

1991. Visit of Dom Helder Camara (1909-1999), retired archbishop of Olinda and Recife, Brazil. Left to right: Reverend Thomas Peterson, O.P. (1929-2000), chancellor of Seton Hall University (1990-2000); Most Reverend Theodore E. McCarrick (born 1930), archbishop of Newark (1986-2000); Archbishop Camara. – AAN

1984. Celebration of Mass in the Seminary Chapel of the Good Shepherd showing the original design of the chapel. – AAN

1990. Most Reverend Theodore E. McCarrick celebrates Mass in the Seminary Chapel of the Good Shepherd. – AAN

2009. Seminarians at
the March for Life in
Washington, DC. – AAN

Stability, Renewal, and Growth

At the completion of its first 150 years, the seminary had become an eight-year academic institution, offering undergraduate and graduate theology programs. Lewis Hall, built in 1984 to house the resident seminarians and renewed and renovated over the years, is not only at capacity but overflowing.

The seminary today, in its student body, reflects the demographic changes in the United States Catholic Church of today. Seminarians are well prepared to serve all Catholics, those whose ancestors came to this land generations ago and those who arrived in recent years from Latin America, Asia, the Pacific Islands, Europe, and Africa. Some seminarians will serve in overseas missions as members of the Neo-Cate-chumenal Way. Seminarians from religious communities will serve the Church in the United States and elsewhere.

The seminary continues to prepare lay women and men to assume leadership in the Church as lay ecclesial ministers and as educated Catholic leaders in society. Spirituality programs reach out to the Catholic people of the New Jersey-New York metropolitan areas.

Immaculate Conception Seminary looks to the future with faith and confidence as it continues to educate and prepare the next generation of the "Stewards of the Mysteries of God."

Top: 2005. Monsignor Thomas Nydegger, vice rector, addressing the seminary community. – Bill Blanchard

Above: 2007. Seminarians relaxing on the porch of Lewis Hall, the seminary residence building. – Roy Regaspi

Top: 2009. Seminarian Glenn Evers with guests of the Little Sisters of the Poor at St. Joseph's Home for the Elderly, Totowa, NJ. – AAN

Above: 2009. Seminarians line up for auto-graphed copies of Archbishop Myers' science fiction novel, *Space Vultures*. – Roy Regaspi

Top: 2008. Reverend Christopher Ciccarino lecturing. – AAN

Above: 2009. Most Reverend John J. Myers (born 1941), archbishop of Newark (2001-), presides at Mass in the Chapel of the Good Shepherd at the seminary. – Roy Regaspi

2009. Institute for Christian Spirituality planning session. Left to right: Deacon Patrick Cline; Sister Phyllis, director of ESL programs; Andrew Brenycz, library assistant; Deacon Matthew Dooley; Diane Carr, academic services; Dr. Gregory Glazov, professor of biblical studies. – AAN

2009. The resident seminarians at Immaculate Conception Seminary. – AAN

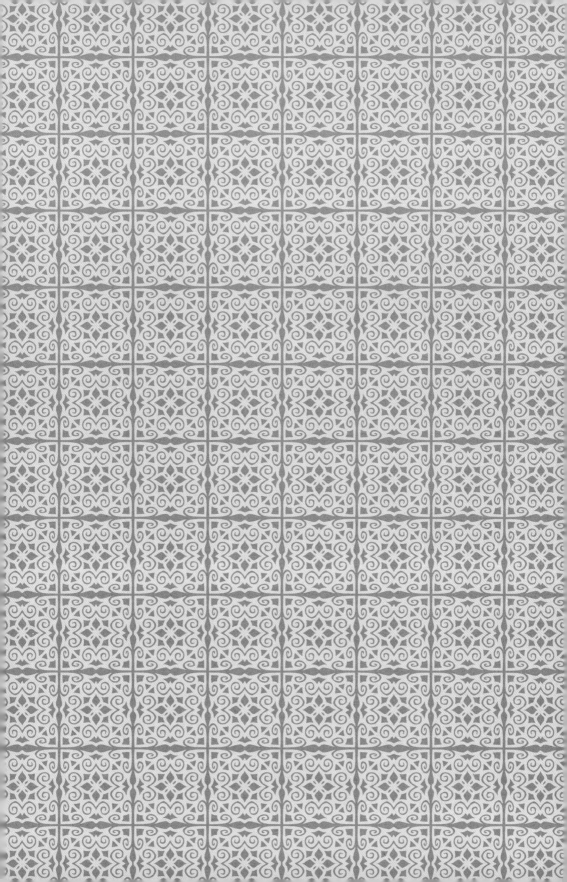

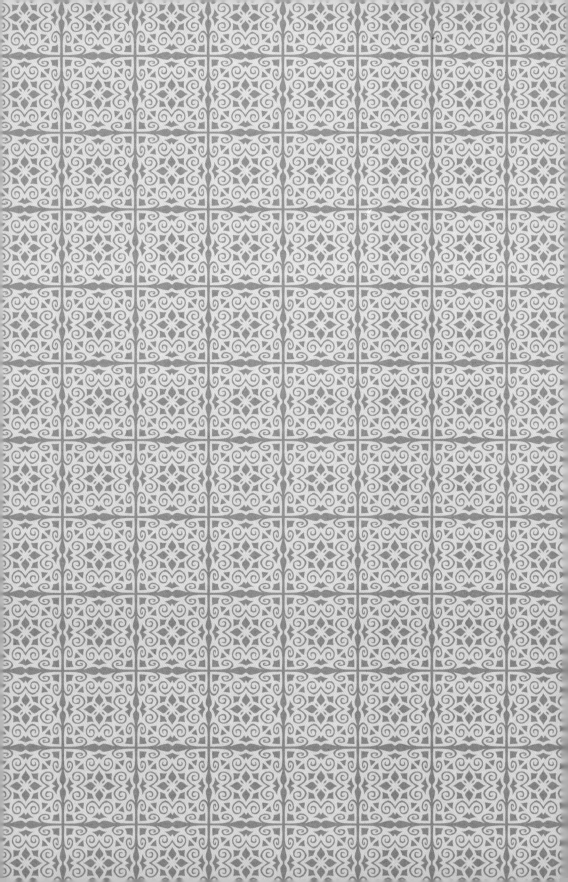

The Ecclesiastical Seminary at Seton Hall College

Vision and Realities —
Triumphs and Trials

1860–1927

Chapter One

Novarx in Nova Caesarea

> So, after careful investigation and timely consultation, by
> the fullness of our apostolic authority, we sever the entire
> state of New Jersey from the dioceses of New York and
> Philadelphia, and establish the territory we have thus
> separated as its own diocese properly so-called; and we
> place its episcopal see in the city of Newark, after which
> both the diocese and episcopal see will be named.
>
> —*Apostolici Ministerii*, Apostolic Letter
> Pope Pius IX, July 29, 1853

From 1808 until 1853, Catholic New Jersey had been divided into two parts,
the eastern section a part of the diocese of New York, the western a part of the diocese
of Philadelphia, Pennsylvania. The border roughly followed the colonial boundaries
of East and West Jersey. By decree of Pope Pius IX, it had a new integrity as a single
diocese encompassing the entire state.

The best estimates at the time count approximately 30,000 Catholics in the
new see. Most were concentrated in the northeastern portion of the state, in the
cities of Newark and Elizabeth and their environs, and in nearby Hudson County.
The remainder were scattered from the Delaware Water Gap to Cape May. They
were a diverse group. German, French, and Irish Catholics had settled even before
the American Revolution and continued to come in the years thereafter. In 1853,
the floodtide of the waves of the Irish immigration that followed the Great Famine
of 1840s Ireland already had begun to crest on New Jersey's shores.

To govern this new missionary diocese, the pope chose a young American of upper-class background, James Roosevelt Bayley.[1] Born in 1814, he first studied medicine but found his calling in the priesthood of the Episcopal Church, and was ordained in 1840, serving as rector of St. Andrew's Church in Harlem. Like a number of his confreres, probably influenced by the Oxford Movement, Bayley harbored doubts about Anglican claims, and resigned his rectorate the next year.

He traveled to Rome and, in spite of opposition from his family, he entered the Catholic Church in 1842. In doing so, he was following in the footsteps of his father's half-sister, Elizabeth Ann Bayley Seton. He was ordained a priest in 1844, and served as vice president of St. John's College, Fordham; pastor in Staten Island, New York; and secretary to Bishop John Hughes.[2] On October 30, 1853, he was consecrated the first bishop of Newark by Archbishop Gaetano Bedini in the old New York cathedral on Mott Street.[3]

Two days later, leaving behind the urban and academic environment that had been his life, the 39-year-old bishop crossed the Hudson River, debarked on the shores of his new diocese, and took the train to Newark. The train chugged into Newark where "thousands and thousands" welcomed him and, led by three brass bands, escorted him in an impressive procession to St. Patrick's Church, which had been designated the cathedral.

After the ceremony, Bayley was honored at a gala banquet provided by the rector of the cathedral, Reverend Bernard J. McQuaid,[4] who sold his horse and carriage to meet the expense. Many of the clergy had been concerned that such public Catholic demonstrations and open display might arouse Nativist feeling, always lurking beneath, and sometimes above, the surface and had complained to Bayley about McQuaid's plans. To Bayley's queries, McQuaid responded: "You are not bishop yet, and if trouble comes, then suspend me after you have taken possession of your cathedral."[5]

McQuaid was a familiar face to Bayley. The bishop had known him as a student during his time as vice president of St. John's College, Fordham. McQuaid, born in 1823, had a difficult, if not traumatic, childhood. His mother died when he was only four years old and his father remarried, only to die in an accident before McQuaid was seven. His "life with his stepmother had become such that . . . even to the day of his death, [he] could not shake off the bitter memories of the woman who abused him terribly in his childhood."[6] Fortunately, he was sent to the Prince Street Orphanage of the Sisters of Charity in New York, where the sisters provided his early education.

McQuaid then attended Chambly College near Montreal before going on to St. Joseph's Seminary at Fordham. Frail as a youth, he suffered a severe hemorrhage at Fordham but recovered after Father Bayley applied an "old-fashioned remedy."[7] Many years later, he referred to his early frailty, remarking that "sixty-three years ago friends expected to put me under the sod."[8] He was ordained in 1848, five years before the establishment of the diocese of Newark. Assigned to Madison, New Jersey, he thereby became a priest of the new diocese and, five weeks before Bayley's installation, was named rector of the newly designated Cathedral of St. Patrick in Newark.

Bishop Bayley quickly began to learn about the diocese and to assess its needs. He discovered that there were some 30,000 to 40,000[9] Catholics across the 7,400 square miles of New Jersey. Half of New Jersey's foreign-born population was in Hudson and Essex Counties.[10] The first church, St. John's,[11] had been established in Trenton in 1814, and the first in Newark, also St. John's, in 1828.[12] The number had grown to 33 churches and missions in 1853.[13] Appealing for funds in June 1854, Bayley described the situation in a letter to the Society for the Propagation of the Faith in Lyons.

> . . . the number of priests is not in proportion to the
> faithful; the diocese can count only on thirty-three
> clergymen to meet all its wants and demands. And what
> is most regrettable is that the state of New Jersey, having
> been regarded up to the present as an accessory rather
> than an integral and a permanent part of the dioceses
> of New York and Philadelphia, does not possess a single
> institution of learning or religion, so necessary to the
> establishment of religion.[14]

Bayley also begged the Roman Congregation for the Propagation of the Faith to give him two scholarships for seminarians from the diocese. The congregation agreed.[15]

Catholic education at all levels would be the cornerstone of Bayley's efforts during his episcopate in Newark. He moved swiftly not only to establish parochial schools, but, in spite of financial difficulties, to found a college and a seminary. One of the reasons for this ambitious undertaking was to improve the cultural level of Catholics in order to help eliminate prejudice, which the bishop knew well from his own Protestant background.

> Many of our Catholic immigrants have made fortunes,
> and if their children can be taught that in holding to
> their faith they can stand on the same level with
> Protestants, they will be able little by little to remove the
> prejudices which hinder the enemies of the Church from
> examining the truth of our holy religion.[16]

Bayley was continually concerned about the shortage of priests. Throughout the 1850s and 1860s he sought to obtain priests from abroad, chiefly from Ireland.

His successes were few. Many seminarians, whom he sponsored at great expense for a poor diocese, left before ordination. Some proved to be problems after ordination. Others asked to leave for another diocese after just a few years in Newark. Years later, he wrote that "for the most part, the only way by which we can hope to obtain [priests] is by taking those of our youth who give evidence of a vocation . . . and educating them ourselves."[17]

He often gave vent to his frustration.

> From what I see of persons who offer themselves for the missions whether as students or priests either in Ireland or on the continent, I am more and more disposed to depend on our own supply. These youngsters from Louvain, for instance, wrote to me for money to buy clothes, books, etc., as if they expected me to provide for the remainder of their lives. These are not the people who are to redeem Israel.[18]

> I am sick of taking priests from other dioceses or picking them up abroad and know no way of providing for our wants except by enlarging the number of our own students.[19]

Collegium Setoniense[20]

In 1855, Bayley purchased the property belonging to the Young Ladies' Academy conducted by Madame Chegary at Madison, New Jersey.[21] He named the new institution "Seton Hall" in honor of his aunt, Mother Elizabeth Ann Bayley Seton. This institution was to have a twofold purpose: the education of young Catholic laymen and the training of future priests. Bayley so described it in a letter to the Society for the Propagation of the Faith: "I have bought a property where I hope to open a college, in which young men of the diocese who give signs of a vocation to the priesthood will be trained."[22]

Charged with establishing this institution was 33-year-old Father Bernard McQuaid, still rector of St. Patrick's Cathedral in Newark. While the gentle and mild-mannered Bayley was the visionary father of Seton Hall and Immaculate Conception Seminary, McQuaid was the practical and hard-driving force behind their creation and their survival in the early years. McQuaid was a man who "knew no timidity."[23]

According to Joseph M. Flynn, in his 1904 history of *The Catholic Church in New Jersey,* "There is every reason to believe that success would not have crowned Bishop Bayley's efforts for the establishment and continuation of the college, had it not been for the indomitable energy and zeal of Father McQuaid."[24] The dauntless and indefatigable McQuaid hoped to have "30 to 40 students" when the college opened on September 1, 1856, but only five answered the first roll call. Among them was Leo G. Thebaud, who was ordained a priest eleven years later.[25] By the end of September, 20 more had registered.[26]

At Madison, Seton Hall, like most similar institutions of the era, functioned as what we today would call a combined secondary school and junior college: "Some of its students, Leo Thebaud among them, were, no doubt, thinking of the priesthood, and special attention may have been shown them. But there is nothing in the listings of courses and professors to indicate that theology was ever taught at Madison."[27]

The number of students at Madison remained stagnant at about 60.[28] The bishop's desire for a seminary there seemed impractical as Madison was rather distant from Newark and it would be difficult for seminarians to attend ceremonies at the cathedral. Bayley and the Seton Hall trustees decided to move the fledgling college to a site more accessible to Newark.

> One bright day in the early spring of 1860, Bishop Bayley and Father McQuaid were returning from a long drive over the Orange Hills from what had proved a fruitless search for a location for the new college; rather discouraged, they were driving slowly homeward over the South Orange and Newark turnpike, when Bishop Bayley's attention was attracted to a large white marble villa surrounded by superb grounds and stately trees. He turned to Father McQuaid and said "do you think that property can be purchased." "I don't know, but we'll try," answered the young priest with assurance and ready promptness. For Father McQuaid to will, was to accomplish, when he once set to work with a purpose in view, and despite several obstacles it was not long before the property was bought and the deed transferred to Bishop Bayley . . . on April 2, 1860.[29]

The main building, often called the Marble House, or the Elphinstone Mansion after its original owners, sat in the midst of 60 acres on which there were a farmhouse and stables. The property was situated on high rolling ground, one of the most elevated points between the Oranges and Newark. It was surrounded with well-kept lawns and fine shade trees and featured attractive winding paths throughout. The entire estate was purchased for $35,000, less than the original cost of the house alone.[30] A diocesan collection to defray the cost netted $8,273.96.[31] This early shortfall and consequent debt was a harbinger of future problems.

Knowing that more facilities would be needed for the college, McQuaid immediately began plans for a new building. On May 15, 1860,[32] Bishop Bayley laid the cornerstone for a three-story brick building with gables and dormers and a tall pointed tower, just southeast of the Marble House. Work progressed rapidly and on September 10, 1860,[33] 50 students entered the new Seton Hall at South Orange. Bayley explained to the diocese the reasons for the move in a circular letter to the clergy of the diocese.

> The object I have in view is to enlarge the present institution—to unite to it, as soon as possible, a theological school similar to that connected with Mt. St. Mary's near Emmitsburg—and by bringing it nearer to the episcopal city, to increase its usefulness and to render it more accessible to the clergy of the diocese, for retreats, conferences and other ecclesiastical purposes.[34]

He was determined to raise a significant amount of money and told the pastors: "On account of the importance of the object, and the need I have of as large a sum as possible, it would afford me gratification, if you would take up the collection yourself."[35] For this and future appeals, he would not receive unanimous cooperation from his priests.

Many early accounts of the history of Seton Hall claim that the college and the seminary were founded together and at the same time. A case may be made for this view by considering Thebaud, one of the first college students at Madison as a seminarian. Thebaud later is listed among the seminarians at South Orange and was tonsured there. While he may have had the priesthood as his goal in those early years, and may have taken philosophy courses, we have no record of any seminary program before 1860. Thebaud was an aspirant for the priesthood but not a seminarian in any formal sense.

While it was Bayley's intention to found both a college and a seminary, the resources at Madison were not adequate to the purpose. In his May 16, 1860, circular letter, he spoke of establishing a seminary "as soon as possible." Writing to the Society for the Propagation of the Faith in Lyons in August 1860, the bishop described Seton Hall as "un collège diocesain et seminaire préparatoire."[36] These documents make it clear that however good the bishop's original intention may have been, there was no seminary or theological school at Madison. The seminary began at South Orange.

Chapter Two

The Ecclesiastical Seminary

September 10, 1860, may be considered the date of the establishment of Immaculate Conception Seminary: "For the first time a division was made between the lay collegians, who occupied the college building, and the ecclesiastical aspirants, who took up residence in the marble villa, henceforth called the Seminary."[1]

That a seminary was functioning at this time is indicated by an August 27, 1860, letter to Bayley from Father William McNulty of Madison, who wished to send a priesthood candidate to the seminary at Emmitsburg, Maryland, "unless you [Bayley] and Fr. McQuaid prevent me by taking him to Seton Hall." McNulty was concerned that some "disadvantages shall attend the education of the seminarians for a year or two,"[2] indicating that the seminary was in the process of establishment.

Further evidence that the seminary was functioning in 1860 comes from Bayley's 1862 report to Rome. After apologizing for not bringing the report in person due to the "difficult condition of affairs in our country"—by which he meant the Civil War—he reported that the diocesan college had a seminary joined to it and that the seminary was in its second year with ten students following the course of studies customary in all European seminaries.[3] The *Seton Hall College Catalogue* of 1861–62 gives further clarity, stating that "the college is conducted by secular priests of the Catholic Church. A number of lay teachers assist in the various departments. Other teachers and the prefects of discipline are supplied from the Ecclesiastical Seminary connected with the college."[4]

The *Catholic Directory* of 1865, in giving data about Seton Hall, concluded with the statement "the diocesan seminary is attached to the college."[5] In the 1872 *Catholic Directory*, a separate listing is given to the "Seminary of the Immaculate Conception, South Orange," the first time the seminary was so designated.[6] Throughout the nineteenth century the seminary commonly was called the "Seton Hall Seminary."

McQuaid and Bayley had major difficulties, financial and personnel. They had incurred significant debts and were scrambling to put together a faculty to teach a full college and seminary curriculum at the new site in South Orange. In the first academic year of 1860–61, the seminarians were under the care and supervision of Father McQuaid as president of the college. He did not assume the title of rector, although he functioned as such. There were few priests in the diocese with academic qualifications. Reverend Edward M. Hickey, who was ordained a priest on October 4, 1860, was entrusted with the vice presidency of the college and also served as prefect. Reverend Prudentius Gehin was received into Newark on October 15, 1860, from the diocese of St. Brieu in France, and immediately assigned to the college. Gehin, like many others adopted by Bayley into the diocese, did not stay long. He left for Mexico in 1861. But Bayley and McQuaid did not give up.[7]

While we can date the inauguration of the seminary as September 1860, we have no evidence that theology was taught until 1861.[8] Among the evidence is a copy of Perrone's *Dogma,* which is inscribed "L. G. Thebaud, September 1861." Thebaud was among the pioneer class that had entered Seton Hall in Madison in 1856. Together with Winand Michael Wigger, a future bishop of Newark, Thebaud was tonsured by Bayley in the small oratory in the seminary on December 20, 1861.[9] After studies at the seminary of Brignole-Sale in Genoa, Thebaud was ordained a priest in 1867.[10]

Earlier that year, on March 8, 1861, Seton Hall College received a charter from the state of New Jersey that granted the college, and by extension, the seminary as part of it, "the right and power of conferring the usual academic and other degrees granted by any other college in the state."[11]

The first professor of theology was Naples-born Reverend Januarius De Concilio, who taught at Seton Hall from 1861–62,[12] apparently using Perrone as his text. Father De Concilio did not remain long at Seton Hall. He was unhappy. In June 1862, the always-blunt McQuaid informed Bayley that "I do not expect that Father De Concilio will remain here another year. . . . Father De C. has got the kink in his head that his health is suffering, and it will not be possible to retain him; nor is it advisable to do so against his will."[13]

De Concilio left Seton Hall that year, or early in the next. He had a long career as a pastor, chiefly at St. Michael's in Jersey City, and continued his intellectual pursuits, authoring numerous books and articles. He was the primary author of the famous *Baltimore Catechism*. His later writings drew a good deal of attention when he speculated that the redemption of Christ also redeemed extraterrestrial beings elsewhere in the universe.[14]

De Concilio was the only professor of theology for the eight to 10 (we do not know the exact number) seminarians enrolled in Fall 1861. Shortly before he left, he was joined by Reverend Henry A. Brann, D.D. The 25-year-old Brann was the first student of the North American College in Rome to be ordained; while in Rome, he received the doctorate in divinity from the Propaganda Fide College. Brann's recollection of his welcome to Seton Hall gives us a wonderful picture of McQuaid's personality and of the college and seminary in their first years.

> Father McQuaid wore a high hat, rather the worse for wear, and clothes that were dusty, for he had been rambling over the college farm. . . . "Good morning, father," said I. He paused a little before returning my greeting and then said: "Oh, I suppose you are Doctor Brann?" I told him I was. He then gave me a sharp patronizing look that took me in from head to foot. . . . "Well," said he, more civilly, "Come in. You will not find here the luxuries you have been accustomed to in St. Sulpice at Paris or in the American College at Rome. And I hope you will be happy in your new home." "Oh, I am sure of that," I replied, "for I love theology and study, and this is a beautiful place." "Well," said he, "come out and I'll show you my farm." Out we walked together. Pointing to a couple of gentlemen: "There," said he, "are some of *my* seminarians." A few paces further on, "There are some of *my* college boys," and he continued, "that's *my* man Simon you see yonder; here are some of *my* potatoes, there are *my* horses, over there *my* barn," and pointing at it, "there is *my* manure heap" . . . We entered the college. He showed me my room and then gave me a little lecture about Roman doctors and the Jesuits. He thought that the Roman doctors were too conceited and that the Jesuits could not teach as well as he could. "Seton Hall under my care," said he, "must above all things turn out young gentlemen." I agreed with him that it ought to do so, but felt that he was hitting me hard on the Roman doctor question and, as I was a pupil of the Jesuits, I did not like to hear them disparaged."[15]

Bernard McQuaid took pride in the farm, using its produce to reduce the cost of feeding hungry college and seminary students. McQuaid is said to have attributed the success of Seton Hall students in athletics to the excellent roast beef, homemade bread, and farm-raised vegetables with which the table was always abundantly supplied.[16] The farm was a rather fruitful enterprise. In 1869 it produced 242 bushels of oats, 200 bushels of corn, 550 bushels of potatoes, 1,000 bundles of stalks, a quantity of straw, and a sufficient supply of vegetables and milk.[17] Later, as bishop of Rochester, New York, McQuaid would continue to be interested in farming, establishing a vineyard to provide the diocese with altar wine.[18] There he built a cottage for his rest and recreation and oversaw the planting and the harvesting of the grapes.[19]

The McQuaid–Brann Drama

Although very different personalities, McQuaid and Brann started out well enough together. "There was everything in the college to make one happy," Brann wrote.[20] McQuaid informed Bayley that "Dr. Brann is doing very well in the seminary. He has so much to do there that he can be of little assistance to me in the College." While never ascribing to him the title of rector, Bayley refers to Brann as "stationed at the college and has charge of the seminary."[21] McQuaid himself remained in actual charge of the seminary, adding, "I have taken two seminarians on trial and subject to your approval. One will not succeed, the other may."[22]

Brann seems to have functioned as a "director of seminarians," but clearly subject to McQuaid. Whatever authority Brann exercised was what McQuaid allowed to him. After teaching logic and metaphysics in the college and theology in the seminary, and serving as vice president of the college for two years, Dr. Brann suddenly left Seton Hall, an institution for which he was very well qualified.

Brann's departure may or not have been voluntary. In July 1864, Bayley called Michael Augustine Corrigan back from studies in Rome, telling the rector of the North American College that "things have occurred which make it absolutely necessary that Rev. Mr. Corrigan should come and take charge of my ecclesiastical students at the college."[23] What "things" had occurred remain mysterious. Brann claims to have been devastated and "begged to remain another year at Seton Hall offering my services for nothing."[24] He profusely apologized to Bayley for his behavior, writing "I was proud, sensitive, susceptible, and had always been a pet. I was spoiled, and expected to be made more of than I was."[25]

After Brann left the diocese and relocated to New York, Bayley refused to allow him to lecture in New Jersey, and in 1873 Bishop Corrigan renewed this prohibition. Brann protested vehemently.[26] A strange and bitter exchange of letters ensued, with Brann referring to Bayley as "one of the kindest hearted bishops in the country,"[27] and later as "a man of fickle nature and vacillating judgment, never having any confidence in his own word."[28] Corrigan bluntly told Brann, "You have no right to preach in this diocese without the consent of the ordinary; and the ordinary does not think it advisable to give that consent."[29] Brann dramatically replied, "Your prohibition galls me to the quick—*Et tu Brute*!"[30]

Father Brann also appears to have been accused of financial irregularities while at St. Cecilia's Church in Englewood, New Jersey.[31] Brann denied this, telling Corrigan that "you know the real cause why I left the diocese. Permit me to say that the cause assigned was never the real cause."[32] What it was remains unknown. Was it shenanigans of some kind, disagreements with McQuaid, lack of recognition, or just restlessness? Perhaps the answer can be found in a letter of Brann to Bayley, where he states that "there is a type of melancholy in my temperament."[33]

Eventually Corrigan relented and, in July 1878, wrote to Brann: "I have no objection to your preaching in this diocese according to your request recently made in Seton Hall."[34] This reconciliation was doubly fortunate for Brann. He could return in honor to New Jersey and, in 1881, Corrigan became his coadjutor archbishop. Time and maturity brought many of these quarrels to an end, and Brann became a highly respected priest of the archdiocese of New York and an ardent supporter of Seton Hall. Unfortunately, the college and the seminary lost an academically gifted priest.

Brann's later recollection of events shows the softening effects of time. A half century later Brann gave no indication of the depth of the quarrel and offered his version of events. He wrote simply that Bayley "was not pleased when he found out that during his absence in Europe I had left the diocese and gone to the Paulists. He wrote to me a letter, asking me to come back; but I remained with Cardinal McCloskey, who knew me in the American College and crossed the ocean with me on my way home from Rome after ordination in the Summer of A. D. 1862."[35]

He recalled McQuaid as "a strong character and a stubborn one when he was young. But, after some years in Rochester, experience with wills as strong as his own, and the greater knowledge he acquired from living among good theologians, broadened his mind and softened his character. The bishop who so often visited me in St. Agnes', New York, was a very different man from the priest I had known as president of Seton Hall. . . . Father McQuaid mellowed very slowly."[36]

Life in the Marble House

Bishop Bayley, with the seminary now functioning, albeit with a faculty that did not seem to last very long, brought home some of the students he was sponsoring at All Hallows in Ireland to finish at Seton Hall. In a letter, oddly dated February 30, 1862, he summoned John Daly and James A. D'Arcy to Seton Hall.[37] They joined the other seminarians in the Marble House, bringing their number to about 12.

We can only surmise the living, study, and prayer arrangements. Certainly it was rather makeshift. Washing was accomplished with pitchers and basin. Bathrooms were "outside." Groups of seminarians bunked together in the various rooms, probably the old servants' quarters in the dormered third floor. Some faculty lived there as well, and others probably in the college building. The buildings were heated by steam and lighted by gas.[38] One room served as a refectory, or dining room; another as a classroom. The small library may have been distributed among several rooms.

One of the larger rooms was set aside as an oratory and dedicated to St. Joseph. There the seminarians and faculty gathered for daily Mass; morning, noon, and evening prayer; and for conferences. On Sundays and holy days, they were joined at Mass by 70 to 80 collegians and the small Catholic community of South Orange, consisting of about 25 persons.[39] It must have been crowded. Bayley described it as so small it would "barely hold the celebrant, and the boy to serve Mass."[40] Yet all managed to "make do" and sacraments were conferred in the tiny oratory. On November 25, 1860, Father Hickey baptized two-week-old Julia McGee,[41] and on the following December 11, Bishop Bayley confirmed 12 students.[42]

While most of the seminarians were of Irish birth or Irish heritage, the collegians were a more cosmopolitan group. About one of four collegians was from overseas, in particular from Latin America, with most from Cuba. In addition, several states were represented in the student body.[43] The seminarians interacted with the collegians on a daily basis in sports and recreation. They also served as prefects in the college, monitoring study hours and the dormitories. This was often a formidable task in colleges of the mid-nineteenth century: "At Georgetown, Jesuit scholastics were known to carry weapons beneath their habits to protect themselves from unruly students."[44]

Some seminarians who held college degrees, including Winand Michael Wigger, later Newark's bishop, served as instructors in the college.[45] The cassock was worn most of the day, even at sports events. Exceptions were made when seminary students played on the college teams, such as the "Alerts" and the "Quickstep Baseball Nines," in competitions with other schools.[46] All this was in addition to their responsibilities to the horarium, their spiritual life and prayer, and their studies.

Among the seminarians, discipline was enforced by a prefect. One of these was Michael E. Kane. He was "the oldest of the seminarians, pious, studious and popular. But he never saw a violation of the rule and was not sharp enough for practical jokers."[47] From the beginning, seminarians found ways to evade rules and regulations.

Just as the college students, the seminarians were required to bring "at least twelve shirts, twelve pairs of stockings, twelve pocket-handkerchiefs, six towels, six napkins, three pairs of shoes or boots, and [a] napkin ring marked with his name" in addition to their cassock and biretta.[48] The seminary provided laundry service and bedding. The laundry and housekeeping were under the supervision of the Sisters of Charity.

The academic year began on the last Wednesday of August and ended the last Wednesday of June.[49] While the small faculty and students used the generally accepted manuals of the era for study, they also engaged in public defenses of theological and philosophical theses. The first such defense was that of James A. D'Arcy. He successfully sustained a number of theses in dogmatic theology before a panel that included Rev. Dr. McGlynn, Rev. Dr. McSweeney, Rev. Dr. Burtsell, and Rev. Dr. De Concilio. These formidable individuals played significant roles in the controversies that engulfed the American Catholic Church in the latter years of the nineteenth century. But evidently they did not frighten D'Arcy, considered "the cleverest seminarian of those years."[50]

Defenses and debates were taken very seriously, but were the occasion for pranks as well. On one occasion, Sebastian Smith, who later became a prominent canon lawyer, was pitted against Pierce McCarthy, a seminarian known as a practical jokester. McCarthy was appointed to defend a thesis and Smith to object. Smith studied hard and prepared all the objections he could find. McCarthy stated his proposition and proved it well. Smith, after an eight-minute oration, promulgated a complex syllogism, with a self-evident major. McCarthy simply replied, "Nego majorem." Smith was dumbfounded and protested: "Doctor, is that fair of him to deny my major when I have been a month preparing my syllogism?"[51]

Bishop Bayley attended many of these theological debates, noting on February 22, 1864, that he "visited Seton Hall—debate—very admirable one, which did credit to the young men."[52]

The small community of about 80 collegians, 12 seminarians,[53] and three or four faculty enjoyed 60 acres of woods, grass, tree-lined paths, and a farm. The college catalogue boasted that the neighborhood was "noted for its healthfulness. The Orange Mountains are recommended by physicians of New York, as the most favorable residence for consumptive patients within many miles of the city."[54]

Seminarians and collegians assisted in the work on the property. Father McQuaid made sure that all did their part. A rigid disciplinarian, he insisted on promptness and exactness in every detail. John Smith, the college general utility manager at the time, later said that Father McQuaid was the only boss he ever feared: "Always vigilant, no dereliction of duty ever escaped his keen eye, whether it occurred on playground, refectory, study hall, or chapel."[55]

The President Pouts

McQuaid was not one to be trifled with, even by his bishop. During Lent of 1863 a bizarre sequence of events unrolled. It was the equivalent of an ecclesiastical comic opera. Bishop Bayley wanted the seminarians at the cathedral for Holy Week services; Father McQuaid and the faculty wanted them at the seminary. Bayley ordered McQuaid to send them to the cathedral. McQuaid, in a fit of pique, handed the account books to Dr. Brann, the vice president, and stormed out of Seton Hall. He went to New York City where he arranged to become the assistant to his friend, Father Donnelly, the pastor of St. Michael's. The wise old vicar general, Father Patrick Moran, intervened and convinced McQuaid to submit to the bishop, return to Seton Hall, and allow the seminarians to go to the cathedral.[56] Bayley's only recorded comment about the incident is that the seminarians sang "the best *tenebrae* we ever had."[57]

For seminarians, Solemn Pontifical Masses, other episcopal events, and High Masses at Seton Hall were occasions of prayer and solemnity, and opportunities to perfect the details of ecclesiastical ceremonial. They also were a source of amusement; an amusement that they, of course, had to be discreet in expressing. McQuaid, Bayley, and Corrigan were very poor singers: "Bishop Bayley when he came to a high note rose on his toes, and when the note was a low one he leaned back on his heels."[58]

Chapter Three

A New Chapel

The number of students and the Catholic population of South Orange were increasing, and the small oratory was quite crowded. The cramped conditions led Bayley and McQuaid to build a chapel to accommodate many more students and local Catholics. McQuaid went to work to raise money. On May 24, 1862, he sent a circular to the priests of the diocese asking them to take up a special collection to pay for the chapel, noting that "the Diocesan Seminary is now connected with Seton Hall College." A chapel was needed because there was "no possibility of teaching practically the ceremonies of the Church, without suitable accommodations."

McQuaid could be both blunt and diplomatic at the same time. He told the pastors, "I need not say to you, Reverend and Dear Sir, that, previous to our Rt. Rev. Bishop's departure for Europe, I obtained his full approval of the step I am now taking . . . it would afford great pleasure to the bishop on his return, to find that in his absence, the priests had taken an interest in the Diocesan Seminary, and built the church."[1]

A year later, Bayley sent out his own circular letter telling the pastors, "Our diocesan college, and the seminary connected with it, as you know, are now well-established" but that "one thing . . . is needed to make them complete, and that is a suitable chapel." He described the chapel in the Marble House as "confined and inconvenient . . . never intended for such a purpose." Further, he echoed McQuaid and indicated the importance of training in ecclesiastical rituals for the seminarians: "Our seminarians have now no proper place in which to practice the ceremonies of the Church, which form so valuable and necessary a part of their ecclesiastical training." Perhaps to encourage cooperation, he added, "We need it also for the clergy, when assembled at the annual ecclesiastical retreats and for diocesan synods."[2]

Bayley was determined to build the chapel and sustain and improve his seminary and his college. Some of his priests were not as enthusiastic as he. Normally "gentle and winning . . . free from maliciousness and uncharitableness,"[3] he could, when dealing with recalcitrant clergy, act with firmness and decisiveness. When Father John Kelly, pastor of Saint Peter's in Jersey City, New Jersey, did not cooperate with the bishop's fund-raising request, Bayley shot off a blistering broadside at Kelly:

> Your conduct with regard to the seminary chapel, render it impossible for me to bear with this state of things for any longer—You did not even read my circular to your congregation. . . . The collection for the seminary chapel, is as you must have felt & probably intended by your utter neglect of my instructions in regard to time and manner of taking it up, an insult to me. Now I do not recognize the right of any pastor to stand between me and the people under his charge. . . . If you are unwilling to recognize this principle and act upon it for the future my advice to you is to resign your cure . . . and I will appoint some one as pastor of St. Peter's Church, who will cooperate with me in building up the college, seminary, sisterhood, and whatever other good works I may think best to undertake."[4]

On May 21, 1863,[5] less than three weeks after sending his circular letter, Bayley laid the cornerstone of Immaculate Conception Chapel, west of the seminary building. Father McQuaid preached and Bishop William McCloskey of Albany, later cardinal and archbishop of New York, attended.[6] The construction must have been rapid. Amazingly, the shell at least was ready for the December 19, 1863, ordinations of James D'Arcy and Patrick Cody, the first priesthood ordinations to take place on the Seton Hall campus.

To the several dozen Catholics who had worshipped in the small oratory of St. Joseph in the Marble House, the new chapel must have seemed a veritable cathedral. On July 4, 1864, the first marriage took place there when Father McQuaid presided at the wedding of Bernard Kaiser of New York and Mary Steve of South Orange. The first funeral from the chapel was that of the college registrar, Henry Howard Burgess, which was celebrated on November 2, 1866.[7]

The rough brownstone chapel was designed in Gothic Revival style by prominent Newark architect Jeremiah O'Rourke. About 100 feet long, it had a large sanctuary designed to accommodate ordinations and solemn ceremonies. Normally, a small chapel built in this period would have had a much smaller sanctuary, but the needs of the seminary required this design.

The now-familiar front entrance would not exist for almost a half century. Two side entrances provided access. The one on the west side was for the convenience of the residents of South Orange, who continued to attend Mass and receive the sacraments at Seton Hall until the establishment of Our Lady of Sorrows Parish in 1887 and the completion of its first church in 1889. Collegians and seminarians used the east entrance, which opened onto a path to the seminary and the college buildings. The chapel lacked a sacristy that was not added until more than 20 years later.[8]

Although the total cost is not clear, it appears to have been just over $8,000. That amount may have been just for the construction of the shell. Eight years later, its interior decoration complete under the direction of J. R. Lamb of New York, the chapel was formally dedicated. [9] It was then estimated to have a value of $25,000.[10]

Also in 1863, a stone building was erected east of the chapel to serve as an infirmary and residence for the Sisters of Charity who had charge of the domestic affairs of the college and seminary. McQuaid and Bayley had been instrumental in permanently establishing the Sisters of Charity in New Jersey. Sisters from the New York and Cincinnati, Ohio, branches of the sisters formed a new foundation, the Sisters of Charity of St. Elizabeth, with their mother house at Madison, on the former Seton Hall property. The Sisters of Charity continued to serve the seminary in a variety of roles, in particular overseeing the infirmary, kitchen, and housekeeping until 1970. One of the first sisters, Sister Josephus, a skilled nurse, served the seminary for more than 30 years, leaving behind memories of a dedicated and caring religious.[11]

In spite of the Civil War, the college and seminary moved ahead, the college increasing its enrollment, the seminary remaining rather static at about 10 or 12 students. In May 1864, the irrepressible McQuaid, frustrated by Bayley's refusal to allow him to become a chaplain to the Union troops in the Civil War, took it upon himself to examine the quality of the spiritual assistance received by the troops in the field and traveled to the battle sites in Virginia. It seems he had the patient Bayley's permission for this trip, as he wrote to the bishop accounts of his adventures.

In his ministry to the soldiers, he utilized unusual but effective methods of evangelization:

> Late in life Bishop McQuaid loved to tell his
> ecclesiastical students of his short trip to the relief of
> dying Catholic soldiers, and his eyes twinkled merrily
> whenever he related how he made a convert through
> whiskey. A wounded Protestant soldier, through a long,
> weary, sleepless night, watched intently how the Catholic
> priest ministered small doses of the liquor to a fellow-
> soldier in a critical condition from his wounds. Later
> he told Father McQuaid if it was his faith that taught
> him thus to care for his neighbor, he also wished to be
> a Catholic.[12]

The Reverend Doctor Corrigan

In the fall of 1864, Reverend Doctor Michael Augustine Corrigan returned from studies in Rome. The disagreements between McQuaid and Brann had led to Brann's departure from Seton Hall. For the next decade and a half, Corrigan would not only have a great impact on the college and seminary, but would ensure their survival. Just 24 years old, he had been ordained in Rome a year earlier and had earned his doctoral degree at the Propaganda Fide College just before his return home.

Corrigan was the son of a wealthy Newark grocer, liquor dealer, and tavern owner. The elder Corrigan had prospered in Newark and could afford to send Michael and his sister to tour Europe. Setting aside his trade as a cabinet maker, he entered into the grocery business and had successfully invested in Newark real estate, so that he could leave his sons a substantial patrimony. Grocery stores at this time also sold liquor. Because of the taint connected with drunkenness, the Corrigans did not like to discuss this portion of the origin of the family fortune.[13]

A frail child who developed into a brilliant and pious student, Corrigan received numerous accolades during his academic career in the United States and in Rome:"Corrigan's academic forte was an exceptional memory. Once he had written anything out, he would have it committed to mind."[14] While at the North American College, he did not get along well with the extroverted and athletic student prefect, Edward McGlynn. Later, as archbishop of New York, he would excommunicate McGlynn.

Corrigan knew that the spirited McQuaid would not be an easy superior and chafed under his domination at first. His mentor, Reverend William McCloskey, rector of the North American College, urged him to be patient and to "bear in mind [McQuaid's] many good qualities."[15] Corrigan apparently followed this advice. Over the years he developed a close friendship with McQuaid, and the two became central figures in the parochial school and Americanist controversies in later years. In Corrigan's case, at least, McQuaid overcame his dislike for "Roman doctors."

The new director of seminarians had high standards and the seminarians found him to be more exacting than Father Brann. Corrigan worried about their restiveness and defiance of rules. McCloskey advised him to learn "how to bend without yielding . . . let them storm away . . . then they are so astonished to see you taking it calmly. . . ."[16] In addition to directing the seminarians, Corrigan also taught dogmatic theology, sacred scripture, and Church history in the seminary, and metaphysics, history, and Latin in the college.[17]

The college enrollment grew during the Civil War to 95 in 1864.[18] The college building was therefore enlarged "to twice its original size" in 1865.[19] On June 24, 1865, the seminary reached an important milestone. In the Seton Hall Chapel, Bishop Bayley ordained three priests: Michael E. Kane, James F. Dalton, and Gregory J. Misdziol.[20] Kane and Dalton were the first to have completed the full four-year course of studies in the new seminary. The next year tragedy struck.

The Fire of 1866

"Near midnight, on Saturday, January 27th, when the temperature was at the freezing point, and sleet and snow lay on the ground, the college was roused by the cry, Fire! Fire! And in less than four hours all that was left of the once beautiful marble villa, was a smoking mass of ruins."[21] As soon as the fire was discovered, McQuaid dispatched a messenger by sleigh to the chief of the Newark Fire Department, who dispatched steamer No. 3. The chief ordered two extra horses attached to the steamer and they galloped off to the college.

The fire had originated in the third story of the Marble House, housing the seminary. The flames spread rapidly to the roof. The fire department arrived but it was too late to save the Marble House. Water was drawn from a neighboring brook and poured into it and upon adjoining structures, confining the fire to the Marble House. Faculty and students removed as much furniture, books, and papers as they could. Priests, professors, and students set to work with a will, and through their bravery and activity, some of the furniture and valuable books and papers were saved and the fire confined to the building in which it originated.[22]

Reverend George Hobart Doane,[23] chancellor of the diocese, heard of the fire early the next morning. He immediately drove in a sleigh from Newark to the Passionist Monastery in West Hoboken (now Union City), New Jersey, where Bishop Bayley was making a visitation. He informed the bishop of the destruction of the Marble House, and the two then went to South Orange to view the ruins. Upon their arrival, they found a very anxious Father McQuaid. Bayley, after learning that no lives were lost or injuries received, tried to ease McQuaid's nervousness by asking, "Father McQuaid, did they save my grandmother's blue arm chair?" McQuaid assured him the armchair was safe and Bayley replied, "That's good; we can build another college but could not replace my grandmother's arm chair."[24]

Not only was the blue armchair saved, but the quick action of students and faculty saved most of the furniture, books, and documents housed in the building. However, the dearth of documents regarding the history of Seton Hall in its early days probably is due to the loss of records in this and subsequent fires. Seventy-two hours later, Bayley sent out a circular announcing a diocesan collection modestly calling for a new building, "a plain and substantial structure."[25]

A Larger, Grander Seminary

McQuaid, with his accustomed energy, immediately set to construct a new and much larger edifice. Less than a week after the fire, on February 2, 1866, he sent a circular letter "To the Patrons and Friends of Seton Hall." Assuring his audience that a "larger, grander" building was needed, he immediately got to the point: "A little plain talk . . . The new building will cost $50,000." A dinner at the elegant Delmonico's Restaurant on Fifth Avenue in New York netted an additional $2,000. Bayley and McQuaid's efforts brought in almost $15,000.[26] Together with $19,000 in insurance payouts, and $4,000 in materials, McQuaid was ready to build.[27]

A month later, on March 2, 1866, the Seton Hall board of trustees approved the plans.[28] McQuaid had been very busy in the days leading to the trustees meeting. Fearing that Bishop Bayley, ever concerned about increasing debt,[29] would hinder his plans, the resourceful McQuaid entered into a conspiracy with Jeremiah O'Rourke, Newark's premier architect. In the words of Henry G. J. Beck, he perpetrated a "pious fraud."[30]

The architect provided drawings that included only the center portion of the building McQuaid planned. To the bishop's eyes it was out of proportion; it was too high and too narrow. McQuaid agreed with Bayley's wise observation and suggested widening it. Little by little the plans were modified until it suited McQuaid. O'Rourke even provided a plan that included an elaborate arched brownstone porte cochere for the seminary entrance and a five-story bell tower to be attached to the chapel.[31] These never were built, but they gave McQuaid the opportunity to "scale back" the plans and placate the bishop. McQuaid moved quickly. Just five weeks after the Marble House burned, architectural plans for its replacement, a structure more than twice its size, had been approved by the trustees and the bishop.[32] A year later it would be completed and open for use.

The new Immaculate Conception Seminary was a three-story American Gothic Revival building constructed of dressed brownstone quarried in Newark not far from the site of the present-day Cathedral Basilica of the Sacred Heart.[33] Its 54 rooms were furnished with wainscoting of walnut and ash, with floors of Georgia pine. Its broad entry led to a wide staircase. As the staircase divided, stained-glass windows depicted the Immaculate Conception, with St. Joseph and Mother Elizabeth Ann Seton on either side. Although Bishop Bayley approved the likeness of Mother Seton, his aunt, we do not know if he had any memories of her from his childhood. The stained-glass background to her portrait is so cut that three pieces of glass might be removed and replaced with a halo. Perhaps this was Bayley's prophecy of her eventual canonization. Despite her canonization in 1976, the window remains unaltered as a tribute to her nephew's foresight.

The main floor contained reception rooms, an apartment for the bishop, and another for the president of the college and the seminary. The priests of the faculty lived on the second floor, which also had an oratory. The third floor had accommodations for 30 seminarians.[34] There also was a classroom on this floor. The refectory was in the basement and there were two "ecclesiastical libraries" in the building.[35] Seminarians "shared a gaslight between desks. The floor was bare. Each student had his own washstand, bowl, and pitcher. If you roomed in the front [north] of the house, in the winter, you wore a bathrobe as you studied, and it was common to wake up and find ice in the pitcher."[36]

The new facility allowed the seminary to grow. In the 1866–67 school year there were 16 seminarians; when the fall semester began in 1868, the enrollment had increased to 26.[37] In 10 years Father McQuaid had established a college in Madison, moved it to South Orange, added a seminary, overseen the construction of a college building, enlarged that building, directed the construction of a chapel and a combination infirmary and sisters' residence, endured a fire, and replaced a house with a suitable home for the seminary. In September 1866, he was named vicar general in addition to his other duties.[38]

That fall, he accompanied Bishop Bayley to the Second Plenary Council of Baltimore, Maryland, where he served as the bishop's theologian and assisted in the drafting of legislation on bishops, priests, and seminarians.[39] By the next year there were rumors that he was being considered for the episcopate. On March 13, 1868, Father McQuaid was "called to leave the quiet shades of Setonia and go forth to labor in another vineyard"[40] as the first bishop of the newly created diocese of Rochester.[41] Bayley was unhappy to lose McQuaid. The previous year he complained to Rome that his departure would be "a great inconvenience to me and harmful to the whole diocese."[42]

The Right Reverend Bernard J. McQuaid, founding president of Seton Hall College and founding rector, in all but title, of Immaculate Conception Seminary, left behind two small but growing institutions. He had spent, in his own estimate, over $222,000 in his years at Seton Hall, a considerable portion of which remained as debt.[43]

Chapter Four

Life in the Ecclesiastical Seminary

Twenty-eight-year-old Father Michael Corrigan assumed the presidency of Seton Hall College and the "Ecclesiastical Seminary" on June 24, 1868.[1] Four months later he was appointed vicar general of the diocese as well. During his first year as president, Corrigan ordered the construction of new roads and walks, improved the drainage system, and enhanced the steam and gas equipment of the college. These and other improvements to the classrooms were needed, but they increased the debt of the institution. He also reorganized the college curriculum. Other than adjustments in the class frequency and schedule, this change did not affect the seminary.[2]

He named his 24-year-old brother, Reverend James H. Corrigan, ordained the year before,[3] as director of the seminary. Father James, as he was known to distinguish him from his brother, was rather frail. He had studied at the North American College but ill health forced his return before ordination.[4] Father James became the de facto administrator of the college when his brother Michael became bishop and retained the title of president. Eventually, in 1877, Father James was appointed president of the college, a post he held until ill health forced him to retire in 1888. He died in 1890.

The seminary faculty in 1868 included the Corrigan brothers; Reverend Louis A. Schneider, a former Jesuit who taught dogmatic and moral theology; and newly ordained 23-year-old Reverend Sebastian Smith, D.D., professor of sacred scripture, ecclesiastical history, and canon law. Schneider remained until 1873, Smith until 1871. Breaking the clerical teaching monopoly was the professor of Gregorian chant, James A. Völker, probably the seminary's first lay teacher.[5]

The 26 seminarians were under the guidance of a president, a director, and two professors, all but one under 30 years of age. This was not unusual. In the mid-nineteenth century, many American seminaries functioned with only two or three professors, many of them newly ordained.[6] They would teach all of the "sacred sciences," relying on standard manuals.

Three years later the number of seminarians increased to 29: six in fourth-year theology, one in third, three in second, and 10 in first theology. Two were in "the philosophy year," and seven in "the logic year"; these classes corresponded to the senior and junior classes of the college.[7] Seminarians were not admitted into theology unless they had a bachelor of arts (B.A.) degree with a heavy concentration in philosophy and classical languages. Those students who received this degree from Seton Hall had four years of college Latin and Greek and, in the third and fourth years of college, numerous philosophy courses.[8] As Corrigan noted in his 1876 report to the Holy See, the seminary was a six-year institution divided into theological and philosophical classes.[9]

The academic schedule was grueling. Seminarians attended class every weekday except Thursday. Forty-five-minute classes were conducted from 8 a.m. to noon with a 15-minute break. They resumed at 2 p.m. and ran until 6:45 p.m. with an hour's intermission at 4:15.[10] Normally seminarians had five or six periods per day. For many of the subjects, seminarians of all four years of theology were joined together in one classroom.

The courses were taught on a cycle. Over the four-year course, the seminarian would have taken all his theology courses, but in no particular sequence.[11] The undergraduates in philosophy followed Salvatore Tongiorgi's three-volume *Institutiones philosophicae.*[12] Based on books conserved in the seminary library, those studying theology used J. Perrone's two-volume *Praelectiones theologicae* for dogmatic theology, and Petrus Scavini's three-volume *Theologia moralis universalis.* In scripture the text was Joseph Dixon's *A General Introduction to the Sacred Scripture;* in canon law, Craisson's *Manuale totius juris canonici;* and the text for Church history was Henry Wouters' *Historiae ecclesiasticae compendium.*[13]

Most classes in the theological disciplines were conducted in Latin. Others, such as ecclesiastical history and canon law, were taught in English. Reliance on textbooks was such that classes did not require a great deal of preparation and, as we have seen, a professor often would teach quite diverse subjects. Instruction consisted in simply translating and explaining the text. This practice was not unusual; rather it was the norm of the time. Mid-nineteenth-century seminaries in the United States commonly "adhered to the tradition of reliance on theological manuals to impart a measure of theoretical and practical knowledge in those aspects of theology considered appropriate for ministry."[14]

In spite of what today would be disdained as "manual theology," the seminarians were encouraged, at least at the college level, to excel by the awarding of gold medals in various disciplines. As an added incentive, the medals were 14-karat gold.[15] Numerous medals were available to the college students, among them awards for German, penmanship, oratory, natural science, recitation, and good conduct. Medals in Christian doctrine, Greek, Latin, and philosophy were particularly attractive goals for the seminarians.[16]

The public defenses of theses and other disputations also encouraged academic success. Attention to study particularly was encouraged by the presence of the bishop as one of the examiners at semi-annual examinations. One year, Bishop Corrigan commented that the moral theology examination was "very satisfactory," while the responses in dogmatic theology were "not so good."[17]

Seminarians continued to serve as dormitory and study hall prefects, and some taught in the college. They supervised a diverse group of college students, including collegians from Spain, Mexico, Colombia, and Cuba, as well as from more than eight states.[18] In the 1870s one could find seminarians teaching geography, history, and bookkeeping.[19]

As they completed the college course, seminarians were awarded the B.A. degree. After two years of theology, they had the opportunity to receive the master of arts (M.A.) degree in theology.[20] While many seminaries of the time did not confer degrees,[21] Immaculate Conception Seminary granted them as a unit of Seton Hall College, which was chartered by the state of New Jersey.

Seminarians serving as college prefects and teaching in the college created a situation in which the customary isolated, monastic life of a free-standing seminary was difficult. The seminarians had the run of the 60-acre Seton Hall campus, including its fields and paths. Some helped in the farm, which continued in existence into the twentieth century. But only with permission could they leave the property either to go home or to visit the nearby village of South Orange. Yet their schedule as much as possible was like the European seminaries that Bayley had alluded to in his reports to Rome.

Their program was governed by a rule, of which unfortunately we have no copies. If we may judge by the rule for the college, it was rather strict, not uncommon in contemporary colleges. The college students were not allowed to leave the grounds without a teacher, and were forbidden to use tobacco. They could not possess any textbooks without the permission of their professors, or any other books without the permission of the president. No newspapers were allowed, except in the reading room. They were allowed to correspond only with their parents, but the president reserved the right to examine all incoming and outgoing letters.[22]

The director was their immediate superior, charged to "advance spiritual or rather ecclesiastical interests,"[23] the two apparently considered to be identical. The seminary year began in the fall with "an eight day retreat to reintroduce the seminarians to the routine of spiritual exercises in an atmosphere of solitude and recollection, preparing them for the forthcoming year."[24] The retreat was normally a silent one, with readings from spiritual books during the meals. During the school year, rising was at 5 a.m., with prayer and meditation in the chapel from 5:30 a.m., preparing for Mass at 6 a.m. According to the advice of their confessors, seminarians received Communion infrequently, no more than once a week, and normally on the first Friday of the month. In conformity with the liturgical calendar, Lent was a time of penance, the specific dietary regulations enforced by the seminary and the college.

Devotions in honor of the Blessed Virgin were common, especially the recitation of the rosary, in private and in common. Special devotions in honor of Mary would fill the calendar in May. In conformity with the times, spiritual exercises in honor of the Sacred Heart were popular. A contemporary photograph of the sanctuary wall of the seminary chapel of the time testifies to this, bearing a large statue of the Sacred Heart.[25] Confession was frequent, often weekly. The Mass was, except on special holy days, a low Mass. After Mass, there was time for breakfast and preparation for class that began at 8 a.m.

The morning was spent in class or teaching and proctoring the collegians. Noon was the time for prayer and a particular examination of conscience, followed by lunch and time for study and spiritual reading. Classes and other activities resumed at 2 p.m., continuing until 6:45. Then it was time to return to the chapel for prayer and the rosary, followed by the evening meal. The day ended with night prayer and a general examination of conscience. All of the chapel periods were overseen by the director or one of the priests who offered short sermons or commentary on the rule or on a specific virtue that the seminarian should consider in his examination of conscience.

The spirituality of the day is clearly shown in this excerpt from Reverend William F. Marshall's *A Sketch of Seton Hall College*.

> The students also carry away from the college precious
> memories of the Chapel of the Immaculate Conception
> of our Blessed Mother; of hours passed in prayer within
> its sacred walls where our dear Lord is imprisoned in the
> tabernacle of love, and where they so often received the
> Bread of Life; the devotion to the Sacred Heart there
> instilled into their souls, the first Friday mornings, when,
> in a body, they gathered round the communion railing;
> an Ave Maria or Litany sung at the May devotions,
> which particularly touched the young man's heart; a
> sermon preached that left its impress on the youthful
> mind;—all these are beacon lights in the uncertain future
> that opens for each year's class of graduates as they go
> forth into the world;—for the young priest, a bright
> star guiding upward and onward to the high-road of
> duty by the narrow path he has chosen; to the young
> man who goes forth to test his fortunes in the fickle
> world, a light that casts its reflex over the days of his
> youth, and bids him be true to the watchword of
> Setonia, "Hazard zit forward."[26]

Thursday was a free day for seminarians and collegians to catch up on their studies and to recreate. There was a gymnasium in the college building and opportunities for walks on the property. Sunday also brought a more relaxed schedule. The seminarians sang the high Mass in the chapel joined by collegians and, until the establishment of Our Lady of Sorrows Parish in South Orange in 1887,[27] the Catholics of the village.

Seminary life was interrupted at various times by the joyful celebration of ordinations. Faculty would evaluate candidates based on their external conduct, academic achievement, fidelity to the rule, and the faculty member's personal observations. In the early 1870s, tonsure was the first step, normally shortly after admission to the seminary. The minor orders of porter, lector, exorcist, and acolyte often were given together. The major orders—subdiaconate, diaconate, and priesthood—followed in third- or fourth-year theology, all received over the period of a few weeks, even a few days. This changed in May 1876, when Corrigan complied with instructions from the Holy See not to bestow all sacred orders in one week. From this time on, tonsure and minor orders were spread out over second and third theology, and major orders over a period of months in fourth theology.[28] While ordination to the priesthood normally took place in the cathedral, occasionally it was conferred in the seminary chapel. All other orders were received in the chapel.[29]

During the year, the seminarians attended and often participated with the collegians in monthly celebrations with "literary and musical entertainment," and with occasional concerts in the chapel. These were coordinated to coincide with St. Cecilia's Day, Thanksgiving, Christmas, Washington's Birthday, and St. Patrick's Day. These occasions were marked by students giving orations on a number of topics such as "The Invasion of Rome" in 1870, "Heroes of the American Revolution," "Ecclesiastical Councils as Guardians of Morality," and "Seminary Philosophy." Musical concerts included sacred music as well as Verdi, Donizetti, and Offenbach.[30]

On November 22, 1871, seminarians enjoyed a "Literary and Musical Entertainment" observing the Festival of St. Cecilia. The program shows an impressive combination of musical and oratorical skill for such a small institution. How much the various orations interested the students remains unknown.

PROGRAMME

Part First

Overture, Egmont........Beethoven

Orations

Impossibility of Universal Irreligion........B. J. Mulligan

Political Non-Intervention (Ancient and Modern)........E. B. Briggs

Baritone Serenade........Hatton

Oration

The Norman Conquest in English Literature........J. J. Brennan

Part Second

Valse........Strauss

Oration

Moral Influence of the Drama........P. McCabe

Solo and Chorus, "A Sailor's Life for Me"........Guglielmo

Orations

Party Spirit........M. J. Brennan

Catholicity and Great Minds........J. Sheppard

Chorus "Hail, All Hail!"........Offenbach[31]

Chapter Five

The Burden of Debt

While a large number of similar small seminaries had already failed,[1] the diocese of Newark was committed to the survival of its seminary and its college. Although the college tuition had risen from $225 to $400 in 1867, the diocese paid only $200 for each seminarian.[2] Bayley probably could not afford anything more. Five burses had been established by 1875, but these brought in relatively little income.[3] The diocesan collection for ecclesiastical students at home and abroad was an annual disappointment—only twice in this period rising above $7,000, and often falling well below $3,000.[4] Besides the seminary at Seton Hall, Bayley was supporting numerous seminarians overseas.[5]

Lack of cooperation from pastors and the resultant poor donations from parishioners were nothing new in the diocese of Newark. Just as Bayley had experienced difficulty in obtaining money for the erection of the seminary chapel, he could not convince pastors to raise the funds necessary for the support of the seminary and the ecclesiastical students overseas.

His circular letters to pastors were a continual lament. He even tried to shame the pastors: "In none of the parishes, with two or three exceptions, is the amount what it ought to be, and the sum total has not been one-half or even one-third of what it is in other dioceses no richer than our own."[6] This did not work, and he later wrote, "The collection last year fell off several thousand dollars."[7] The bishop's frustration was palpable: "I am almost discouraged from making another appeal to the clergy and people of the diocese, on account of the little success which has attended my last two earnest appeals for this purpose.

Showing his irritation, Bayley again compared the poor showing to that of other dioceses: "The collection for ecclesiastical students by subscription books, which has been so successful in other dioceses, seems to have been a comparative failure in ours. As yet I have received but one small return from the whole diocese."[8] This appeal seemed to work, for the next year he wrote, "The success last year in so many parishes, of the collection for ecclesiastical students of the diocese, by means of subscription books, proves that it may be equally successful in all, if the pastors would take an interest in the matter."[9] Discouraged but determined, Bayley also printed many copies of an undated form letter to remind pastors that they had not submitted the funds from the seminary collection.[10] A few years later, his successor would have no better luck, telling many pastors, "I beg to call your attention to the fact that the returns of the seminary collection in your parish have not yet been received. . . . Over 60 churches have yet to report."[11] At the time there were 120 churches and 28 missions in the diocese.[12]

The diocese and the college were in terrible financial shape. Bayley told Michael Corrigan, the college president, that he had "not been able to obtain as yet any of the money I expected, but as I am not likely to need much before the 1st of July, I send you a check for $2,000 with which I trust you will be able to get around the corner, tho' it brings me down pretty low. If I can back some of my loans I will let you have more. The deposit fund brings me in scarcely anything lately, as I have to pay out almost as much as I take in. I intend to pay it off entirely as soon as I can get things in order, but at present it is the only way I can keep afloat."[13] The college, the seminary, and the diocese had become, and for some time would continue to be, day-to-day, almost hand-to-mouth operations.

The situation was dire. Just after Corrigan assumed the presidency, the debt stood at $80,000. Three years later, by 1871, it had grown to over $121,000.[14] Since the college and seminary accounts were intermingled, it is not possible to know exactly how much of this deficit was due to the low seminary tuition of $200, half the college's new $400 charge.[15]

The seminarians, like the collegians, received the same quality of instruction, room, and board, but at a drastically reduced rate. At the same time, seminary faculty and seminarians provided instruction in the college at no additional cost. However, in all fairness, it is evident that the college's subsidy of seminary education contributed to the dire financial straits of both. This was the opinion of Father James Corrigan, director of the seminary, who saw the problems as having arisen from "the obligations incurred by the erection of the seminary edifice."[16]

The economic difficulties of Seton Hall and of the diocese of Newark took place against the background of healthy growth in New Jersey's economy. The Civil War had fueled New Jersey industry, and prosperity and economic expansion continued after its conclusion. In the decade of the 1860s New Jersey had greatly changed. At the beginning of the Civil War, New Jersey's population was about equally divided between farm and town. By 1870 there was a great increase in the town and city population. Cattle farms had given way to dairy farms and New Jersey had become the home of many corporations, large and small.[17]

While the state was prosperous, the diocese, with limited resources, had to contend with providing churches and schools for an increasing Catholic population that was mostly immigrant and poor. Seton Hall had to keep its tuition rather low lest it discourage all but the wealthiest Catholics.

Exhaustion and frustration took their toll on the leaders of Seton Hall and the diocese of Newark. Over the years the diocese had advanced to the college $36,000, which was gradually reduced by the support of the seminary.[18] Rumors began to spread that the diocese was contemplating cutting its losses at Seton Hall. On February 20, 1869, Bishop Bayley wrote to Michael Corrigan, "I have heard today a report that we intended to discontinue the college at Seton Hall, which may be of great injury to us if it becomes general. We will have to prepare a good strong circular to our old friends and present patrons before the end of the year."[19]

Because the tuition charged seminarians did not cover costs, Bayley also had taken the serious step of refusing to receive students from other dioceses into the seminary, rather than subsidize them as well. He gave those already enrolled their marching orders, allowing them to remain for just one more year. This decision meant that six students from the new diocese of Rochester would have to leave. McQuaid, now bishop of that diocese, was more than simply unhappy; he was enraged. In his letter to Bayley, he wrote that "to make matters worse your letter scarcely reached me when I was struck dumb at hearing that Dr. Brann had been appointed to a professorship at Troy [St. Joseph's Provincial Seminary]. I don't know what to do. I fear to seem to persecute him, and yet I can't bear the thought of having my students under his influence."[20] Fortunately for McQuaid, the "Roman Doctor" Brann declined the appointment to Troy.

A Bishop's Despair

Bayley was still trying to keep the college afloat, but he had mentioned rumors of the possible termination of the college only, and did not speak of the seminary. The following September, from Paris, he wrote to Michael Corrigan, "My great anxiety is about the college, but I rely on your prudence and care."[21] A year later, in Fall 1870, despondent over Seton Hall's finances, Bayley contemplated giving up on the college, selling it to the Christian Brothers, and moving the seminary to Newark.

Father James Corrigan gave Bayley multiple reasons why such a move and a sale to the Christian Brothers would be a mistake.[22] Father James' letter gives us many insights into the life and behavior of seminarians and faculty in these years. He reminded Bayley that South Orange was a "healthy" site, with spacious grounds "well adapted for the recreation indispensably required for young men so long and so much confined as seminarians must be."

The facilities were ideal and the chapel suited for a seminary. The rural character of South Orange also provided adequate isolation for seminarians, being "sufficiently out of the way of public thoroughfares to preclude too much visiting from outsiders, and consequently will keep the minds of the seminarians comparatively free from outside nonsense." Just as the isolation was beneficial for seminarians, it was of equal advantage for the professors, who "are not particularly liable to be interrupted in their studies by visitors, and consequently have more time to prepare the lessons for their classes. And if they do go out sometimes, it is only at night, and into the very best society."

Having stated the positive aspects of a seminary in South Orange, Father James bluntly put forth the problems that would occur were the seminary moved to Newark. It would be "unhealthy," and there would be frequent visits to the seminarians by friends or priests. In Newark there would be no place "suitable for the purpose of recreation and taking fresh air." This was not an exaggeration. Nineteenth-century Newark was notoriously unhealthy. The water supply was tainted, the streets filthy, and epidemics of smallpox and cholera were not infrequent. The city lacked open public spaces and parks. This woeful state of affairs is chronicled in a 1988 study by Stuart Galishoff, *Newark: The Nation's Unhealthiest City 1832–1895.*[23]

Father James was quite concerned about the seminarians going out for walks "for we do not live in a European city and in a Catholic atmosphere, where seminarians can go out without danger of being insulted and stared to death." Even more he feared that if they went out in parties of two or three, they would succumb to "the multitudes of occasions and facilities of visiting, drinking etc., which seminarians precisely because being seminarians together often times easily fall into." The seminarians also would "be exposed to make visits which no stringent laws or rules can prevent; for they can be kept secret" and be tempted to purchase "forbidden and dangerous articles." In the city it would be "impossible to prevent a good deal of news, talk, and scandal from crossing the threshold, and hence an immense source of distraction."

Father James equally was fretful about the deleterious effects of city living on the professors, believing "there would be visits of people and priests to the professors, which would take away a good deal of their time, and lessons would not be well prepared and seminarians not well taught, though there be the best will in the world."

Apparently worried that some of the professors might spend too much time drinking, he delicately expressed his concern that the "professors would more or less frequently visit their friends at all hours throughout the day as well in the night, and you will readily admit that the Newark Catholic society is not the most refined: hence the professors might some times come home in a state not overedifying to the seminarians." Father James probably had cause to worry about both seminarians and professors let loose in the wilds of nineteenth-century Newark. Rural isolation of both was his solution.

Strangely, for a city that had the stately St. Patrick's Cathedral and the grand St. Mary's German Church, Father James ended his list of the difficulties of a seminary in Newark with this remark: "For years to come there will be no suitable church in Newark for seminarians, hence ceremonies could not well be properly taught and practically learned." Having expressed to Bishop Bayley his manifold reasons for keeping the seminary at Seton Hall, he urged the bishop to keep "a college and a seminary, which certainly will not be at all a blemish, but rather a bright jewel in your mitre."[24]

For Sale!

The Christian Brothers genuinely were interested in adding Seton Hall to their educational apostolate. Father James huffed that Brother Patrick Murphy, president of Manhattan College, would not "be so willing to purchase the property if he did not expect to make by it."[25] Discussions clearly were already under way to sell Seton Hall College to the Christian Brothers of Manhattan College. The matter had been discussed at the 1870 meeting of the trustees on June 20, 1870, although nothing of the sort is mentioned in the minutes.[26] There had been a quiet cover-up. No one was to know. A dozen years later, regarding these minutes, Father James told the newly installed Bishop Wigger, "There is a part unrecorded at the request of Archbishop Bayley and that is the meeting which related to the proposed sale of Seton Hall in 1870 and 1871."[27]

It is interesting to speculate the course of events had Bishop McQuaid still been on the scene. Perhaps exaggerating, McQuaid later would complain that he had met with considerable opposition from Bishop Bayley in regard to Seton Hall, "considering how much difficulty I had to induce Bishop Bayley to let me begin, and how much greater difficulty I had more than once to keep him from breaking it up."[28] McQuaid's successor as president was just as determined as he to save the college and the seminary. Soon after assuming the presidency, Michael Corrigan had written to his predecessor, "I am now beginning to comprehend your all-absorbing interest in the college, which formerly I used to wonder at."[29]

Five years earlier, in 1866, there had been a slight bubble of interest about a possible sale of Seton Hall. The Second Plenary Council of Baltimore had discussed the possibility of a national Catholic university in the third chapter of legislation on Catholic education, entitled *De Universitate Literarum Fundanda*. While the fathers of the council postponed the project, they planned to "examine the matter more maturely hereafter."[30] There was some discussion with Father McQuaid at the time. He later recalled, "When the proposition was made informally to me in 1866, I laughed at it. I had labored and made great sacrifices to build up a great diocesan institution, never dreaming that so many children of the household stood ready to tear it down."[31]

Michael Corrigan was determined to save Seton Hall for the diocese of Newark. He was not alone; he was joined by his brothers, Father James and Joseph, a physician.

In March 1871 Bayley believed that a sale of the college to the Christian Brothers was the only alternative to closing. On April 12, 1871, Michael Corrigan, counseling "absolute secrecy," summoned the trustees to a meeting on April 18 "to consider the question of continuing the college as at present or of passing it over to a religious corporation, viz., the Christian Brothers."[32] At the meeting Michael Corrigan estimated the assets of the college at $263,000 and its debts at $125,000.[33] The Corrigan brothers then offered to provide the necessary capital to sustain the college. The Corrigans were among the wealthiest Catholics in New Jersey. Their father had died in 1867, leaving them a considerable fortune in real estate. It is estimated that Michael Corrigan's share was $100,000.[34]

Ten of the 13 trustees attended the meeting. The trustees suspected that Bishop Bayley might have signed a contract with the Christian Brothers.[35] As Michael Corrigan summarized in his letters, "Only one person [Father Doane, the chancellor of the diocese] was in favor of making over the college to the brothers, the other nine members . . . were strongly opposed to the plan proposed by the bishop. I presume, then, that we may consider the questioned as settled."[36] The Corrigan brothers had preserved the college as they knew it and administered it. Michael Corrigan continued to work on reducing the debt. Within six years it had been reduced to just over $84,000.[37]

The cost of educating seminarians continued to bedevil Bayley. In August 1871 he reported "upwards of 50 students [at Seton Hall and overseas], most of them at the expense of the diocese." Yet he was faced with a deficit of the past two years amounting to between $5,000 and $6,000.[38] The following month he "refused all applications from seminarians lately, because I can't pay for those we have got."[39]

He continued to focus on maintaining his own seminary, telling Corrigan from Rome, "I am sick of taking priests from other dioceses or picking them up abroad and know no way of providing for our wants except by enlarging the number of our own students."[40] In spite of his efforts and circular letters, the diocesan collection for the support of ecclesiastical students did not fail to disappoint.[41]

Life Goes On

In spite of the almost catastrophic financial crisis, life went on as usual for the seminarians. Bishop Bayley continued to come to the college to take part in the examinations of the seminarians, to celebrate ordinations in the chapel, and to attend the June commencement.[42] He was so insistent on being present at examinations that he would order them to be deferred if circumstances prevented his presence.[43] During Holy Week, the seminarians participated in the services at the Newark cathedral, and continued to take part in the cultural life of the college. Philosophy students participated in the Washington Birthday concert of 1870 and the junior exhibition on January 25, 1871.[44]

Bayley relied heavily on Michael Corrigan. In addition to his duties at Seton Hall, he was appointed vicar general[45] and, during Bayley's absence at the First Vatican Council in 1869–1870, he served as administrator of the diocese. While Bayley was in Rome, Corrigan dedicated the now-finished and decorated seminary chapel. Corrigan developed a reputation in the hierarchy as a person who was expert in canonical and moral questions and was often consulted by bishops. In 1871, he was considered for the vacant diocese of Cleveland, Ohio. More than likely, his mentor, William McCloskey, now a bishop in that province, had a role in this.[46] Bayley, however, objected to losing so valuable a priest, and protested against the nomination made "without my knowledge and consent."[47] But Newark soon would lose Bayley.

Chapter Six

The Right Reverend President

A year later, on July 21, 1872, Bayley was named archbishop of Baltimore. Reluctant to leave Newark, he remarked, "I am too old a tree to be transplanted."[1] Michael Corrigan, after serving as administrator of the diocese, was named bishop of Newark on February 11, 1873. At 33 years of age, he was the youngest bishop in the United States.

Bayley evidently had a great role in Corrigan's appointment as his successor. He considered Corrigan to have "learning enough for five bishops and sanctity for ten"[2] and, before the Baltimore appointment, had thought of asking Rome to make Corrigan his coadjutor.[3] The archbishop of Baltimore also offered the new bishop of Newark some rather genteel advice: "Never do anything today that can be as well done tomorrow—drink a little claret with your dinner. Study to be quiet and you will grow fat and do much good in your generation."[4] It is doubtful that Corrigan was able, or even inclined, to take this advice.

Bayley's caution regarding the clergy, "Don't let those exacting padres press you too much,"[5] probably was more cogent. Corrigan as administrator of the diocese had some experience of this pressure but he was genuinely moved by the initial response to his elevation. "The clergy of the diocese, young and old," he reported to McQuaid, "are exceedingly kind to me, and well disposed. It is a great consolation and a great spur to hard work."[6]

There was some bad feeling against Father George Hobart Doane, Bayley's chancellor, whom Corrigan named his vicar general, but McQuaid counseled him to go ahead with the appointment, no matter what any clique of priests thought. "Priests who want to control the nomination of bishops," he reasoned, "and then direct the government of their bishop have a great deal yet to learn, even though they studied in Rome."[7]

McQuaid probably was referring to a group of priests including Father Sebastian Smith, the prominent canonist. Smith had earned a doctorate at the Roman Sapienza University in 1868 and briefly taught scripture, ecclesiastical history, and canon law at the seminary, leaving in 1871.[8] Smith and other priests in Newark and elsewhere were concerned about what they deemed the arbitrary exercise of authority by bishops not constrained by all the bonds of canon law in a nation still regarded by Rome as "missionary." A year after Corrigan's installation, Smith published his *Notes on the Second Plenary Council*, which became a rallying point for the reformers.

Corrigan had few doubts about the proper relationships that should exist within the hierarchy. As he assured Monsignor Robert Seton, a frequent correspondent, "The rule is that the assistant must be under the direction and control of the pastor. The assistant must consequently learn to know his place."[9] So too with pastors. "This pernicious principle of p[ries]ts choosing their own field of labor must be quietly put down," he noted in his diary. "Bishops rule dioceses, not priests."[10]

Financial Troubles Again

A year after he became bishop, the country fell into a depression as a result of the financial panic of September 1873. In 1877, to counter falling enrollment, the college reduced tuition from $400 to $350, while seminarian tuition continued to remain artificially low at $200.[11] Even with this low tuition, Corrigan was forced to desperate measures. He ceased "to assume any responsibility for the education of students in the preparatory seminary."[12]

A year later, he privately told Bishop McQuaid that he was paying only for theologians.[13] He informed McQuaid, "On account of the hard times, we will be obliged to reduce the number of ecclesiastical students very considerably in order to keep out of debt. I worry a great deal about the college. It is feared that the year will be a disastrous one, with a large harvest of debt."[14] Whenever possible, Bishop Corrigan sought to have the student pay his own expenses.[15] These cutbacks affected enrollment at the preparatory and college level, but not the theologate. While the total number of seminarians dropped from 80 to 56 from 1877 to 1880, the number of theology students dropped only from 35 to 32 in the same period.[16]

Corrigan, with the help of his brothers,[17] was able to reduce the college's indebtedness further by obtaining a mortgage of $60,000 on the seminary building from the Misses Mary Eliza and Mary Gwendolyn Caldwell of New York. This restructuring lowered the interest rate from seven to five percent.[18] The faculty also was affected by the hard financial times. Their salaries were cut in 1879 and 1880 and finally restored in 1881.[19]

Corrigan acknowledged this sacrifice when he addressed the faculty in 1880, recording his words in the third person: "Justice compelled him to acknowledge publicly before the clergy the debt of gratitude he was under to the Rev. Professors of the seminary both for the spirit of self-sacrifice manifested by them in the dark hours of the panic, when they cheerfully and spontaneously waived the greater part of their too small salary, and for the advice, counsel and opinion so often asked and so readily given."[20] The faculty had acquiesced in a reduction of their salaries by one half; the bishop had taken no salary.[21]

As if these financial difficulties were not enough, disease struck the college and the seminary. The normal course of daily seminary life was interrupted in mid-March 1875 when an epidemic of enteric fever struck 30 college students and seminarians. It was caused by contaminated water from a pump near the college. The contamination had been caused by an old drain in the vicinity which leached contaminants into the water drawn by the pump. As Corrigan recorded, "This drain was connected with the old marble building, destroyed by fire in 1866, and the drain itself has not been used since 1860."[22] The college dug a new well on high ground in a distant part of the campus. The Newark health physician certified the new well water as pure and the sewage and drain systems of the campus as safe.[23]

Unfortunately, one of the "best and most promising" college students succumbed.[24] The stricken seminarians were allowed to go home, while the others remained. Several faculty members also became ill from the epidemic.

A shrunken number of seminarians assisted at Holy Week ceremonies in the newly consecrated St. Patrick's Cathedral, and a disappointed Bishop Corrigan noted that the ceremonies were "not as well conducted as we expected."[25] Studies were not resumed until April 19. While the college catalogues claimed that the semi-rural location of Seton Hall was a healthy atmosphere, four students had died during the 1860s. This may be ascribed to the various epidemics of the era, in particular typhoid, scarlet fever, and diphtheria. There would be an outbreak of scarlet fever in 1880. Fortunately, it was contained through quarantine of the affected students in the infirmary.[26]

While the college had a separate infirmary building, this structure unwisely also housed the toilets and bathing facilities.[27] Among other medicines, the infirmary had a long list of "homeopathic medicines against sundry indispositions" that were used to treat a wide variety of ailments from sore throats to severe falls. Among them were aconite, arnica, and belladonna.[28]

Father Salt, Confederate States Army, Monsignor Seton, Prothonotary Apostolic, and Archbishop Messmer

Residing at Seton Hall throughout his episcopate, Bishop Corrigan retained the presidency of the seminary and the college until 1877. His brother, Father James Corrigan, however, became the actual administrator of the college. Father James relinquished the directorship of the seminary in 1873 to Reverend William P. Salt. Until 1877, Salt exercised the directorship subject to Bishop Corrigan as president of the college and seminary. In 1877, when Father James Corrigan was named president of the college, Salt was designated as president of the seminary,[29] a post he would hold until 1890. Throughout the first decades of the seminary, there is often a confusing mix of titles and responsibilities.

Father Salt came to Seton Hall by a most circuitous route. Born in Brooklyn in 1837, he grew up in the small village of Bath in western New York. At an early age he was taken from school to work in his father's carpenter's shop, learning the trade. Essentially self-taught through reading in his spare time, he read law in the offices of a judge in Bath, supporting himself through carpentry and teaching. Although his parents were Baptists, he joined the Episcopal Church. Dissatisfied with law, he went to Arkansas to pursue studies for the ministry.

In 1861, when the Civil War broke out, he was unable to return north and entered the theological seminary in Camden, South Carolina. Shortly afterward, he was drafted into the Confederate Army and served three years in the Marion Artillery, adding volunteer chaplaincy to his regular service. After the war, he returned north and was ordained a deacon in the Episcopal Church. Not long afterward, when he became "convinced of the authority of the Catholic Church to teach . . . all doubt vanished; my duty was clear."[30] In 1867, he was received into the Catholic Church and began his studies at Seton Hall.

Sent to Rome by Bishop Bayley, he joined several other students at the North American College in volunteering to serve in the Papal Zouaves in defense of papal Rome against the forces of the Italian Risorgimento. Pope Pius IX gently turned down their generous offer.[31] Ill health forced his return and he was ordained in 1871. He immediately was appointed to the faculty and in his career he taught logic, ecclesiastical history, political economy, civil polity, Christian evidences, mathematics, physics, and chemistry.[32]

The 1870s saw several singular additions to the seminary faculty. The most colorful was the grandson of Mother Elizabeth Seton, Monsignor Robert Seton, P.A., who taught archaeology and pastoral theology for four years. Seton holds the distinction of being the first American monsignor. Born in Pisa, Italy, in 1839, he attended Mount St. Mary's College in Emmitsburg. He was the first student enrolled in the North American College in Rome. He then transferred to the Pontifical Academy for Noble Ecclesiastics, an institution restricted to the nobility in training for high diplomatic and curial posts.

There he was "educated in the preciosities of ecclesiastical diplomacy, whereby well-born and well-groomed sons of the Church are trained in the dove-like and serpentine arts necessary to outwit the children of the world."[33] He was ordained in 1865, one day after the death of Abraham Lincoln. His ordination was unusual, in that he was ordained *sui patronatus*. While remaining a priest of the diocese of Newark, he was, to some extent, a "free agent" who was not dependent on his bishop for salary or sustenance. This situation assisted him in his lifelong independence, and his wealth enabled his frequent travels. Pope Pius IX created Seton a papal chamberlain one year after his ordination. A year later, he raised him to the dignity of prothonotary apostolic with the right to celebrate Mass robed as a bishop several times a year. His elevation to this rank was communicated to Michael Corrigan in a letter from William McCloskey in Rome: "Seton comes to you in full pontificalia . . . Clear the track, ye lesser Urbs!"[34] Seton later would lament the proliferation of the monsignorial dignity in the United States as "ridiculously common."[35]

"A survival from another age,"[36] Robert Seton was born several centuries, or at least one century, after his time. His aristocratic bearing and often disdainful comments about lesser mortals earned him the reputation of a snob. While in Rome during the Civil War, a lady of Confederate sympathies grandly told him that she was a "Mason, of the Virginia Masons." His reaction was that "she stupidly believed that that must impress a Seton."[37] At the same time, he was a patriot and a loyal anti-slavery advocate of the Union cause. When he refused to attend a reception in honor of the newly minted emperor of Mexico, Maximilian, and his wife, Carlotta, the rector of the pontifical academy ordered Seton expelled. Pius IX saved him, reminding the rector that the pope had appointed Seton to the school and only he had the right to expel anyone, noting that Seton was his only American.[38]

Holding a doctorate in divinity, Seton clearly was credentialed to teach. Yet, upon his return from Rome in 1867, he was assigned as a curate at St. Patrick's Cathedral in Newark. He left after six weeks because he was "spitting up blood."[39] Bishop Bayley, his cousin, told him he would do nothing for him lest it appear as favoritism, and insisted that Seton remain in the United States.[40] He moved to the convent of the Sisters of Charity in Madison, where he remained, while lecturing at Seton Hall and serving on the board of trustees.

Fond of proclaiming his aristocratic heritage, Seton "possessed a family pride so extravagant at times that it led to eccentricities which made him an enigma even to his coreligionists."[41] A member of the Sons of the American Revolution, he wore the medal of this organization on his monsignorial robes.[42] His various eccentricities led Bishop Corrigan to write privately to Cardinal McCloskey, "He is odd, as you know, and peculiar in his ways, but knows how to maintain his dignity on occasion."[43]

From 1867 to 1876 Seton served as chaplain to the Sisters of Charity at Madison. In 1876 he was named pastor of St. Joseph's Parish in Jersey City. A recognized authority in archaeology, heraldry, and ecclesiastical etiquette, he was a frequent lecturer at the college and the seminary. Seton was an accomplished linguist and writer in Greek, Latin, Hebrew, French, Spanish, and German. He frequently sprinkled phrases from these languages in his many, usually gossipy, letters. Seton always felt he had been "passed over." Resigning his pastorate in Jersey City, he moved to Rome in 1902. He spent his time exchanging visits with curial officials and a myriad of dukes, duchesses, counts, and countesses.

According to Seton, Cardinal Rampolla, the secretary of state, believed that "sinister forces" had kept Seton from advancement. He claimed that Rampolla, on his own initiative, proposed him for appointment as titular archbishop of Heliopolis *in partibus infidelium*. Seton apparently forgot that he had asked Cardinal Gibbons to recommend him for a titular archbishopric.[44] On June 10, 1903, Pope Leo XIII finally named Seton archbishop. On July 20, the 93-year-old Leo died.[45] His funds depleted due to bad investments, Seton left Rome in 1914, traveled in Europe for several years, returned to the hospitality of the Sisters of Charity in Madison in 1921, and died there in 1927.

Reverend Sebastian Gebhard Messmer, born in Switzerland in 1847, was ordained for the diocese of Newark at Innsbruck, Austria, in 1871 and joined the seminary faculty that same year. He would remain at the seminary until 1889, during which time he taught scripture, canon law, dogmatic and moral theology, and liturgy.[46]

In Messmer's first years at Seton Hall, "he found considerable difficulty in expressing himself in English. . . . Not always conjecturing the right meaning of the word he wanted, he often made mistakes that were as laughable and which he enjoyed as well as anyone else."[47] Down to earth and congenial, his good humor was appreciated by the children of nearby St. Mary's Orphanage, which Messmer often visited.[48]

He left Seton Hall in 1889 to assume the professorship in canon law at the newly established Catholic University of America in Washington, DC.[49] Two years later, he was appointed bishop of Green Bay, Wisconsin, and in 1903, archbishop of Milwaukee. He died in 1930.

Another notable addition to the faculty was Reverend John J. O'Connor. He was born in Newark in 1855, graduated from Seton Hall College in 1873, studied at the North American College in Rome, continued his education in Louvain, and was ordained in Belgium in 1877.[50] He would become director of the seminary in 1891 and the fourth bishop of Newark in 1901.

Farewell

In the midst of these troubles, the seminary bade final farewell to its founder. Throughout these years, Archbishop Bayley, the founding bishop of the seminary and the college, continued to take a great interest in both institutions. He often visited, staying two weeks in July 1874, and a month during the summer of 1876. For several years, his health had been declining. In 1877, he went abroad hoping to restore his health. Seeing no improvement, he returned to America, but was so feeble that he stopped in Newark. On October 3, 1877, he died in the rectory of St. Patrick's Cathedral, with Bishop Corrigan reciting the prayers for the dying. At the time of his death, the seminary he founded had graduated over 50 priests.[51] Years before, he had the stones cut for his tomb, which he desired to be in a vault under the college chapel. This was not to be.[52]

In 1873, during a visit to the grave of his aunt at Emmitsburg, he had made the following request: "It is here I wish to be buried,—here at Mother Seton's feet I would lie; there is room enough. I want no monument, only a slab telling that 'Here lies a poor old archbishop. '"[53]

Bayley left behind his own *Rule of Life:*

- To make three-quarters of an hour meditation every morning

- To hear Mass every day when possible

- To make always a visit to the Blessed Sacrament in the afternoon, and an examination of conscience when possible

- To say the chapelet every day with a decade for the dead

- To make one-half hour's spiritual reading for my meditation each evening, and one-half hour of Scripture in the morning

- To consecrate my going to bed and my rising with the same religious exercises as in the seminary, being particular always to make an examination of conscience, an act of contrition and a prayer for a good death

- To guard against dissipation, to endeavor to keep a quiet recollection in God, elevating my thoughts to Him, an ejaculation to my dear Saviour and His Blessed Mother, to guard over my words and all my senses.[54]

Chapter Seven

Silver Jubilee

Seton Hall College's first quarter-century and the seminary's first two decades were guided by the founding bishop of Newark, James Roosevelt Bayley, and his successor, Michael Augustine Corrigan. Until 1868, they had the more than able assistance of Bernard J. McQuaid. In fact, it may be argued that, without McQuaid, Seton Hall, both college and seminary, would never have survived its first decades. The last two decades of the nineteenth century would see a new bishop at the helm of the diocese of Newark, and be a time of new crises, as well as a time of calm and consolidation.

But a silver jubilee in 1881 was a time to celebrate. The Silver Jubilee Dinner on July 14, 1881, was no small event. Administrators, professors, alumni, guests, and perhaps some lucky seminarians feasted on a meal typical of the Gilded Age.

SETON HALL COLLEGE
SILVER JUBILEE DINNER
JULY 14, 1881

Little Neck Clams
Sauterne

Spaghetti Soup
Vino de Pasto

Veal Patties . . . Sliced Tomatoes
St. Macaire

Lamb Cutlets...Peas...Cauliflower
Roman Punch

Ribs of Beef . . . Roast Spring Chicken
String Beans . . . Lettuce Salad
Cotes de Camblanes

English Summer Pudding
Verzenay

Assorted Ice Creams
Cake
Fruits
Cheese

Coffee and Liqueurs[1]

The sumptuous meal was followed by 11 toasts: to the college presidents, college trustees, theological professors, classical professors, alumni president, senior graduates, clergymen, merchants, lawyers, doctors, and junior graduates. Thus fortified, the men of the college and the seminary were ready to face the challenges of the next quarter-century.

They needed to be well fortified. The tumultuous years for Seton Hall had not ended. Just four years earlier, Father James Corrigan had reduced the charges for board and tuition in "view of the general depression of business."[2] The 1880s saw the departure of the last of the early pioneers, Bishop Michael Augustine Corrigan, and would bring renewed peril to the institution's existence, as well as academic renewal.

The Mysterious Selection of Winand Wigger

On September 28, 1880, Bishop Corrigan received word from Rome that he had been named titular archbishop of Petra *in partibus infidelium* and coadjutor archbishop of New York.[3] Rumors abounded about the succession to Newark.

It would prove to be a controversial and mystifying process. Four years earlier Corrigan had recommended four priests for the episcopate: George H. Doane, the vicar general; William P. Salt, the director of the seminary; Winand M. Wigger; and Patrick Smith (Smyth). In his comments, Corrigan was least complimentary to Wigger.[4] He also recommended the division of the diocese.[5]

After Corrigan left for New York, the rumors began to fly. McQuaid reported hearing that a group of priests were planning to petition the Holy See in opposition to the possible appointment of Father Doane and that the "young priests" at Seton Hall were organizing a counterplot in favor of Doane.[6]

Wigger's name surfaced in the rumor mill and others were mentioned as well. They included Bishops Francis Chatard of Vincennes, Illinois; Patrick Lynch of Charleston, South Carolina; and John Lancaster Spalding of Peoria, Illinois; Father Thomas Preston, vicar general of New York; and Father Michael O'Farrell of New York City. Spalding, according to McQuaid, had "written absolutely to Card. Simeoni that he would *not* leave Peoria, under any consideration."[7]

When the bishops of the province of New York met, they had two lists or "ternas" to compose, for it had been decided to divide the diocese of Newark and establish a new see at Trenton. The bishops placed Reverend Michael O'Farrell of New York City first on the list for Newark. O'Farrell was a former Sulpician and professor of dogmatic theology at the Grand Séminaire in Montréal. They believed that it would be beneficial to have as bishop a scholar who would look out for the interests of Seton Hall.[8] Reverend Winand Michael Wigger, pastor in Madison, was placed second, followed by Irish-born Reverend Patrick Smith of Newark. For Trenton, they put Wigger on the top of the list, followed by Father Doane and Irish-born Father Patrick MacSweeney of New York City.[9]

Priests who had studied in Italy did not hesitate privately to write to Propaganda Fide concerning potential episcopal appointments. Among them, two priests, who had been on the seminary faculty, supported Wigger's candidacy in letters to Propaganda. Januarius De Concilio called Wigger "the only one who deserves to be a bishop,"[10] and Sebastian Smith wrote that Wigger would be "pleasing" to the entire diocese."[11]

On July 7, 1881, the consultors of Propaganda Fide met to vote on the division of Newark and the nomination of the respective bishops. Presiding was Cardinal Pier Francesco Meglia. The questions they addressed were vaguely worded. Their report read as follows:

> Concerning the division of the diocese of Newark and erecting from it a new diocese in Trenton and the nomination of the respective bishops.
>
> To the first: all consultors responded affirmatively.
>
> To the second: eight consultors voted to place before His Holiness Father Wigger, two Father MacSweeney, five for Monsignor Doane. [The Trenton terna]
>
> To the third: nine consultors voted to place before His Holiness Father O'Farrell, five for Father Wigger, one for Father Smith. [The Newark terna]

On July 11 the general congregation, consisting only of the cardinals of Propaganda Fide, met and produced the final recommendation. Presiding was the Austrian-born Jesuit Cardinal Johann Baptist Franzelin. It reversed the order!

To the first: affirmative

To the second: Father Michael O'Farrell

To the third: Father Winand Wigger[12]

This document was signed by Pope Leo XIII six days later. Word reached Newark on July 19, 1881. What had happened? McQuaid was extremely upset by the transposition of the names. "Is this not a mistake? It is not our work,"[13] he exclaimed to Corrigan. Corrigan responded that it was not a mistake but that, according to Cardinal McCloskey, there was "outside influence upsetting the recommendations of the bishops."[14] Both Corrigan and McQuaid were concerned that Wigger's health was not up to the task.[15]

The most benign interpretation is that the vague wording of the questions voted on led to a mix-up. A more conspiratorial turn of mind leads some to believe that Cardinal Franzelin deliberately shifted the names to give the appointment to Newark, the larger see, to an American of German descent. This is the opinion of Joseph M. Flynn, author of *The Catholic Church in New Jersey*.

In 1904, Flynn, with more than a bit of anti-German bias, wrote, "The truth is that among the cardinals to whom the choice was referred was Cardinal Franzelin. With that racial loyalty which is characteristic of the Germanic family, perceiving that Doctor Wigger was first on one list and second on another, contended, and successfully, that the more important diocese should be assigned to him."[16] This is not impossible, considering that Wigger also had been on Corrigan's 1876 list of recommendations for the episcopate, but the motivation is only conjecture. Another, rather imaginative, explanation that circulated was that an influential unnamed Irishman in Rome, knowing that Trenton was the state capital, and presuming that it would be the more important see, arranged for O'Farrell to be sent to Trenton.[17]

As in all such appointments, some were pleased, others not. Doane expressed pleasure that he was not appointed, O'Farrell contentment that he would have a new diocese where he could arrange things to his own satisfaction.[18] Robert Seton was not happy, although he immediately congratulated the bishop-elect. He later wrote that Wigger "has many good points—as has *every* worthy priest—but had nothing special to recommend him for the miter—but the persistent determination of Abp. C[orrigan] and Bp. McQ[uaid] to keep *me* out." (Emphases his)[19]

Seton was blissfully unaware that he was on neither terna and that Corrigan and McQuaid were themselves quite discomfited with the appointment. Even after he had obtained a titular see for himself, Seton remianed angry. He complained that "it was a great outrage to set poor—however well-meaning—Bishop Wigger over the Newark—or for that matter any American diocese."[20]

On July 19, 1881, it was announced to the public that the diocese of Newark had been divided, the seven northern counties remaining to Newark, and the 14 southern counties forming the new diocese of Trenton. Reverend Doctor Winand Michael Wigger, pastor in Madison, had been named the bishop of Newark.

Right Reverend Winand Michael Wigger

Born in New York on December 9, 1841, Wigger attended St. Francis Xavier College in New York, and through that institution's relationship with St. John's College, Fordham, received the baccalaureate in July 1860.[21] He applied to the archdiocese of New York for admission to the seminary but was rejected because of his poor health.[22] He crossed the Hudson and applied to Newark, where he was accepted in September 1860. He was tonsured in the oratory of the Marble House on December 20, 1861, the first ordination to take place at Seton Hall.[23]

While in the seminary at Seton Hall, "he gave part of his time to the instruction and superintendence of the college boys" and "became an assistant professor of mathematics and English as well as prefect of study halls."[24] He later studied at the Brignole-Sale Seminary in Genoa, Italy, and was ordained there in 1865. He returned to Newark that year. Shortly afterward, he went back to Europe and obtained his doctorate in divinity at the University of Rome in 1869. At Brignole-Sale, Wigger acquired a fluent use of Italian, to add to the German he spoke from childhood, and the French he had acquired at St. Francis Xavier College.[25]

He was consecrated bishop of Newark by Archbishop Corrigan on October 18, 1881. The sermon was preached by Bishop McQuaid, who had preached at Corrigan's consecration in 1873, and would again at the consecration of John J. O'Connor as fourth bishop of Newark in 1901.[26] The day after his consecration Wigger visited Seton Hall, where he was met with an enthusiastic reception by the faculty, the seminarians, and the collegians.[27]

Wigger, like so many of his contemporaries preoccupied with the nineteenth-century obsession with valetudinarianism, enjoyed frail health. He suffered from frequent chest and throat ailments that his physicians attributed to "catarrh." As a remedy, they suggested he wear a beard to keep his throat warm. Wigger sported a very unusual beard that covered only his throat, leaving his face clean-shaven. In 1886, he received formal permission to wear this beard in a rescript from the Sacred Congregation for the Propagation of the Faith.[28]

Shortly thereafter he had an extended controversy with the former administrator, Father Doane, rector of St. Patrick's Cathedral. George Hobart Doane was the son of George Washington Doane, Episcopal bishop of New Jersey, a recognized "high church" leader and friend of John Keble and Edward Pusey.

Ordained an Episcopal deacon, Doane converted to Catholicism and was excommunicated by his father for "intending to submit himself to the schismatical Roman intrusion."[29]

His conversion was aided by Bishop Bayley, himself a former Episcopal clergyman. When Doane came to the St. Patrick's Cathedral rectory late one night and insisted on speaking to the bishop, their long conversation ended with Doane asking to be received into the Catholic Church.[30] Aristocratic in manner, Doane could be rather grand in his dealings with others. His returns to Newark from long European trips were greeted by torchlight processions of his parishioners leading him in his carriage from the train depot to his rectory. When named a domestic prelate, he celebrated a Mass of thanksgiving with the same music used for the coronation of Napoleon.

Wigger claimed that the bishop was the canonical pastor of the cathedral parish to whom the cathedral rector was subject. Therefore, Wigger reasoned, the income of the parish should go to him rather than to Doane. The matter reached the Propaganda in Rome where Cardinal Simeoni suggested conciliation, indicating to Wigger that his claim was not sustainable. Wigger backed down.[31]

Due to hard feelings aroused by this disagreement, it is understandable that Wigger did not want to reside at the episcopal residence on Bleecker Street, which was also the parochial residence of Father Doane as rector of St. Patrick's Cathedral. During most of the controversy, the bishop resided in Newark at 98 Bloomfield Avenue,[32] and later at another residence in Newark.

By 1883, he was seriously considering moving to Seton Hall, but had qualms of conscience about residing outside the cathedral city.[33] Apparently, Wigger was unwilling to be entirely guided by the example of Corrigan, who had lived at Seton Hall. Bayley, on the other hand, had resided at the cathedral rectory in Newark, occasionally staying at Seton Hall.[34] Wigger sought the advice of one of the seminary faculty members, Sebastian Messmer, professor of canon law. Messmer confidently stated that a bishop had full liberty to live anywhere within the limits of the diocese, and he assured Wigger that the priests of Seton Hall would "rejoice to have their beloved bishop and father in their midst. Nor would the Rev. Chancellor be unwelcome, especially to the professors of the seminary, who might possibly (!) find in him a new colleague & fellow teacher."[35]

In March 1883, Wigger took up residence in the bishop's apartment on the first floor of the seminary building.[36] There he received the clergy on Mondays and Wednesdays.[37] South Orange was a small country town in those days, and it was considered a healthy location, especially for a bishop who had a rather frail constitution.

Chapter Eight

When in Debt—Build!

In spite of debt continuing to pile upon Seton Hall, the Seton Hall Alumni Association, founded in 1879,[1] decided, at the suggestion of Father James Corrigan,[2] to mark the silver jubilee of the college's founding by erecting a new building, Alumni Hall. While most of the cost of the building was realized through fund-raising, it was not completely paid for.[3] Opened in 1884, Alumni Hall, designed by William Schickel of New York[4] and standing behind the seminary building, is a two-story building constructed of undressed brown sandstone.

Originally it was surrounded on three sides by an attractive porch with covered walkways called "piazzas," which unfortunately was removed in the 1980s. Its tall second story, graced with gothic windows, was used for literary and musical entertainments, and also as a gymnasium. In the 1890s, it was used for military drills by the Seton Hall battalion of cadets.[5] Later this floor would be adapted into a science laboratory and then a classroom. Currently, it houses the Chapel of the Good Shepherd of Immaculate Conception Seminary.

On the ground floor were two billiard parlors, one for the younger and one for the older collegians; a reading room and library; and a recreation room for the seminarians.[6] The seminarians raised funds to furnish their section through a raffle and an appeal to the clergy. They already had a billiard table provided by Monsignor De Concilio, but sought a piano and "gymnastic apparatus."[7] Today this floor is the administrative wing of the seminary, housing the offices of the rector, vice rector, and associate deans. "With the chapel on the west, and the college on the east, Alumni Hall faces the rear of the seminary, and, united to these buildings forms a spacious quadrangle, rendered attractive not only by the enclosing group of structures, but by the level lawn, gracefully diversified with flagged walks to the seminary, the college, the chapel and the infirmary. In this beautiful quadrangle the annual commencements are held, the ceremonies taking place in the open air, the broad piazza of Alumni Hall forming a stage for the graduates and the faculty."[8]

As beautiful and useful as Alumni Hall was, the fund-raising it entailed was not directed to reduction of the debt, and the shortfall only added to that debt. In New York, while the diocese of Newark still was vacant, Archbishop Corrigan wrote to Bishop McQuaid concerning the "expediency of active measures for reducing the indebtedness of Seton Hall," and suggested "an appeal for the seminary."[9] The fate of the college and the seminary remained intertwined. Ironically, while the seminary's reduced tuition added to the institution's financial difficulties, fund-raising for the seminary was considered more attractive than fund-raising for the college.

Shortly after his consecration, Bishop Wigger asked Father James Corrigan, the president, for an analysis of the financial status of Seton Hall. Father James did not mince words. The total debt was more than $120,000.[10] Half of this represented the $60,000 mortgage taken out for the construction of the seminary building.

The situation was aggravated by the college's subsidy to the seminary. Father James wrote that this reduced rate "does not cover the cost of board and maintenance. . . . In addition to this, large deductions are allowed for ecclesiastical students in the college department." In five years, these deductions amounted to almost $7,000, and "four ecclesiastical students, each for one year, were kept gratis." Their places filled by lay collegians would have brought in over $11,000.

An additional burden on the college was that "the seminarians have better accommodations and a somewhat better table than the collegians; whereas the salaries of the theological professors, the wages of servants attending to seminarians' rooms and clothes, the furnishing of their rooms, together with heat and light, are paid out of the college revenues." To remedy the situation, he urged "the increasing of the pension for seminarians, so as to be sufficient to cover the cost of their maintenance."

Another proposed solution that Father James suggested was diverting funds from the Sacred Heart Union, established for the support of the Denville Protectory, to pay off the debt on the seminary building. But he worried that taking these funds "might render the institution liable to the charge . . . that Seton Hall is in a bankrupt state, and is going a begging." Getting right to his major point, he said to the bishop, "The seminary is, par excellence, a diocesan institution, and it seems fair that aid be given from the diocese to get the seminary out of difficulty. The paying off of seminary debt does not appear to be justly the work of the college."[11]

Father James also brought up an issue that would remain until the seminary's move from Seton Hall in 1927—and reappear in a different form when it returned to South Orange in 1984: "Many regard with disfavor the present coexistence of our seminary and college, necessitating increased work and duties on the part of the seminarians." He went on to say, without giving specifics, that "the hard and manifold labor required of ecclesiastical students in former days, and their peculiar position then, have not gained much good will for Seton Hall."

It is clear there was a grave financial crisis and the cost of the seminary was a significant part of it. However, the reports in the trustees meetings do not give any accounting of how much was expended on the seminary or on the college individually. It would be difficult to create an accurate picture. As in the past, the seminary building also housed the college administrators and faculty and the college offices. Seminary professors and seminarians continued to teach in the college, and seminarians continued to act as prefects in the college. Without an audit that included the modern concept of contributed services, it is difficult to get an exact picture of the extent of the subsidy of the seminary.

It is difficult to imagine that Father James did not feel a sense of loss on the transfer of his brother, Michael, to be archbishop of New York. He told Wigger, "Neither my brother the archbishop nor myself founded Seton Hall, or contracted its large debt. Moreover, I have assumed more work than my position called for, since with the demands of the presidency, I teach English classes, instruction in which was formerly, with the exception of elocution lessons, the sole occupation of a lay professor, who received $1,000 a year for his services. . . . But I need not speak of myself when my brother as president from 1868 to 1877 did not take the salary due him; and when our clergymen in 1878 gladly allowed their salaries to be reduced to half of what they formerly received, in order to lessen expenses."[12]

For Sale Again?

Bishop Wigger's decision on the sale is not recorded but, as they often do, rumors filled the gap, this time about a possible sale to the Benedictines. In November 1882, Archbishop Michael Corrigan, Father James' brother, wrote to Bishop McQuaid, "While in Philadelphia last week, I was informed . . . that during the visit of Msgr. Wigger to St. Vincent's [in Beatty, Pennsylvania] in the summer, it was the common talk of all that he had gone there to offer Seton Hall to the Benedictines. . . . I hear the price fixed on Seton Hall is $200,000, i.e., including the burses in the debt, about $100,000 surplus over liabilities: a good record after all and one would say, a reason for *not* selling."[13] McQuaid responded, indicating that the rumors were not confined to Pennsylvania, but also current in New Jersey. He recounted that Reverend William McNulty suggested he not come to Paterson, "as the news of the sale of Seton Hall to the Benedictines might prove unpleasant." "A strange ending," he commented to Corrigan, "after all our labors and sacrifices for the diocese."[14]

In fact, the rumors were true. Archabbot Boniface Wimmer of St. Vincent's Archabbey in Latrobe, Pennsylvania, wrote to Abbot Alexius Edelbrock of St. John's Abbey, Collegeville, Minnesota, also in 1882, that "Seton Hall College was offered to me again recently." He turned down the offer because he believed that there was "nothing in it for us [and] we would not profit by it. Of course, the bishop wants to get rid of the college because it does not pay."[15]

Carl D. Hinrichsen, Wigger's biographer, takes a benign view of the issue: "Despite McQuaid's stricture, Wigger's willingness to sell Seton Hall College was no indication that he lacked interest in Catholic higher education. One of the reasons [for] Wigger's moving his residence to Seton Hall was to renew the prosperity of the college in which he took great interest."[16]

However, it is clear Wigger wanted to sell the college. It was so sensitive an issue that Wigger acted in utmost secrecy and carried out conversations with the Benedictines, leaving no "paper trail." In a similar manner, in 1870, Bayley had ordered that the trustees' minutes not contain any reference to the proposed sale to the Christian Brothers. In any event, a sale did not take place.

Seton Hall could not draw itself out of debt, with punishing interest rates draining its coffers. After the 1883 commencement, Wigger recorded, "On this occasion I first conceived the idea of raising $50 thousand by subscription for Seton Hall."[17] His efforts were unsuccessful and the college's indebtedness soon rose to over $110,000.[18]

Wigger also abandoned the annual seminary collection in 1885 "after much reflection and consultation with bishops and priests." He substituted a tax on each parish, considering this to be a more equitable method.[19] While this increased his revenues, it did nothing to ameliorate the financial difficulties of Seton Hall.

"Lady Bountiful"

In 1884, at the Third Plenary Council of Baltimore, a committee was established to take up again the possibility of establishing a national Catholic university. A *seminarium principale*[20] would be the nucleus of this institution. This project was spurred by Bishop John Lancaster Spalding's call to intellectual commitment in his address at the 1881 jubilee of the Milwaukee seminary in which he asserted, "You will not, therefore . . . misunderstand me when I affirm that seminaries such as these are and must remain, here and elsewhere, and should give the highest intellectual education."[21] The goal of the planners was first to establish a seminary and add other schools to form a proper university.

At this point, the fate of Seton Hall, college and seminary, would be determined by the wealth and whims of a young heiress. Mary Gwendolyn Caldwell was born in Louisville, Kentucky, on October 5, 1863, to William Shakespeare Caldwell and Mary Eliza Breckinridge.

Mary Gwendolyn grew up in New York City, where she attended the Convent of the Sacred Heart in Manhattanville as a teenager. She and her family converted to Catholicism in the early 1870s. At their father's death in 1874, she and her sister Mary Elizabeth (Eliza) inherited several million dollars. The terms of the will stated that the sisters should use one-third of their inheritance to assist the Catholic Church in becoming a prominent part of American society.

A friend of Peoria Bishop John Lancaster Spalding, Mary Gwendolyn offered a donation of $300,000 to the new Catholic university that the bishop advocated. Miss Caldwell directed that $200,000 be used for land and buildings and $100,000 for professorships. She was only 21 years old at the time.

Like many American heiresses of the era, she was desirous of a European title. She first was engaged to Prince Murat, son of the Napoleonic King of Naples. Upon the prince demanding in the prenuptial contract that one-half of Miss Caldwell's fortune should be settled on him, she wisely broke the engagement. She eventually married Marquis de Monstiers-Merinville in 1896. The marriage was celebrated by Bishop Spalding. In her later years, she renounced the Catholic faith, and died in 1909.[22]

Miss Caldwell favored a location in the South but had been persuaded that it was better to establish the new university in the North.[23] Her friend Bishop Spalding also favored a Southern site, in particular, Washington, D.C., which he considered "neither a northern nor a southern city."[24] He believed that it would be a mistake to buy a college like Seton Hall to start an absolutely new institution.[25]

The plenary council appointed a committee of bishops, priests, and laymen to oversee the preparatory work. Archbishop Corrigan was a member of this committee. On January 15, 1885, Wigger sent Corrigan data on Seton Hall's finances.[26] At the committee's first meeting on January 26, Eugene Kelly, a member of the committee and executor of the Caldwell estate, proposed that they buy Seton Hall College. Corrigan then read a letter from Wigger offering to sell Seton Hall for $250,000. The next day he reduced the figure to $200,000.

Wigger made it clear that he had not initiated the sale but that the proposition had come from Spalding. He emphasized that he did not have to sell and, were it not for the purpose of establishing a national university, he would never sell for so low a price.

The proposal was carried, and Corrigan and Spalding were appointed to persuade Miss Caldwell to support the purchase of Seton Hall.[27] On February 3, the *New York Times* reported that Seton Hall was the likely site for the new university.[28]

Cardinal Gibbons, the leader of the American hierarchy, also supported purchasing Seton Hall, where "the work of the University could be begun with little delay," unlike Washington, where "we would have to create everything." His only reservation was his concern that Seton Hall might be invaded "by the terrible Jersey mosquitoes."[29] His Eminence apparently considered the mosquitoes of Washington less troublesome than those of New Jersey. Miss Caldwell could not be so persuaded. She still preferred her original idea that the university be located in the South. Bishop Spalding, also favoring a Southern site, and probably fearing the loss of her $300,000 donation, agreed with her.

The project stalled, and Wigger lost patience. On March 23, he called on Corrigan to obtain Miss Caldwell's address. He told Corrigan that "he intended to write to her withdrawing his offer to dispose of Seton Hall. He had previously promised to allow the question to remain open until the 1st of May."[30] By this time, Corrigan was tired of the control Miss Caldwell was exercising on the process and sniffed to Gibbons, "We cannot be the mere obedient servants of any Lady

Bountiful."[31] Cardinal Gibbons hoped that Wigger would change his mind, but it was too late.[32]

Miss Caldwell had set her mind against Seton Hall, telling Spalding "that in taking Seton Hall it would be rather like continuing an old institution than founding a new one." She rather ungraciously added that she did not "wish to put her money in a broken-down college."[33] In May, in spite of a great deal of opposition from various bishops, the committee recommended that Washington be the site of the new university. "Lady Bountiful" had won.

It is interesting that Archbishop Corrigan, who just 15 years earlier pledged his family fortune to prevent the sale of Seton Hall to the Christian Brothers, now favored its disposal. More than likely, he saw it as a transition from a local college into a national university that would bring the university to the New York area and bring prestige to his former diocese.

Money Troubles Continue

Enrollment in Seton Hall College declined from 100 in 1884 to 80 in 1885. Over the same year, the seminary population declined from 35 to 30.[34] Apparently, the idea of a separate seminary surfaced again. In a confidential circular to the priests of the diocese, Father James said it was impractical to separate the seminary from the college. Such a move, he averred, "is, at present, not feasible on the score of expensiveness. At least $14,000 per annum would be required to exclusively conduct the Theological Department." Based on 30 seminarians, he must have estimated an annual cost of nearly $500 per seminarian. The diocese was then paying $200 per year. Father James noted that the college buildings had been paid for, but the seminary, the "best structure on the premises," still was encumbered with a debt of $60,000.

Lest he offend the priests, many of whom were alumni of the seminary, he emphasized that "these facts and figures are mentioned [not] to disparage the seminary or the seminarians. The seminary has had in many ways a salutary influence on the college, it has imparted certainly an admirable religious tone, and has given examples of living, active virtue. The seminarians have been most devoted workers for the welfare of the college. Their labors, which could not be repaid by silver or gold, are cordially appreciated and thankfully remembered." However, Father James Corrigan wanted to dispel "the impression . . . that the seminary has been, and is, the financial support of the college." In fact, quite the opposite was true. To avoid a crisis, he appealed to the priests to encourage young men to enroll at Seton Hall and, where possible, have the tuition paid by the parish.[35] But a crisis of another sort was to come.

The Fire of 1886

On March 9, 1886, at about 1 p.m., "while the students and professors were all assembled at dinner, the college was again aroused by the dreaded cry, 'Fire, fire!'"

The alarm had been raised by Henry Friend, the college shoemaker. The fire had originated in one of the third-floor dormitories of the college building and quickly engulfed the entire structure.[36] Help arrived quickly. The driver of the horse car on the South Orange Avenue route had seen the fire and smoke coming from the building and raced to the center of South Orange Village and roused the fire brigade.[37] The flames had spread quickly under the influence of a strong northwest wind. As reported in the *Newark Daily Advertiser*, "The students and the faculty turned out and organized a fire brigade, some removing valuable books and papers on the lower floors, while others took such means as were at their disposal to check the rapid advance of the fire. The lawn about the building was littered with such documents as could be removed."[38]

The fire had reached the adjoining seminary, but faculty, students, and seminarians had hung wetted blankets on the outer walls to prevent its spread. Reached by telegraph, the Newark Fire Department sent two engines. Their swift arrival brought the situation under control and "the firemen succeeded in checking the flames,"[39] saving the seminary building from damage. None of the students was seriously injured, but the entire college building, built in 1860 and doubled in size in 1863, was destroyed. Only the walls were left standing. According to the *Newark Daily Advertiser*, the loss was estimated at between $45,000 and $50,000.[40]

Makeshift arrangements immediately were set up to shelter the dispossessed college students. The upper floor of recently erected Alumni Hall was used as a study hall; the lower floor as a dormitory. College students who could not be accommodated there were housed in the seminary, where all now took their meals.[41] Classes for the seminarians resumed a week later; for the collegians, two weeks later.[42]

Father James Corrigan feared that it might be necessary to discontinue the college and to proceed with the seminary alone but, at an emergency meeting on March 15, 1885, the trustees adopted Monsignor Seton's proposal that the college be continued at least until June, and endorsed a motion that plans for the restoration of the college building be initiated.[43]

Father James quickly sent out a circular letter soliciting funds, in which he noted that the destruction was estimated at $35,000, with insurance coverage of only $18,000.[44] On June 1, 1886, the trustees approved plans for reconstruction. Remarkably, the building was ready for classes in January 1887 and for use as a dormitory in May, "care being taken that the plastering was thoroughly dry before the students were permitted to use the new sleeping quarters."[45]

The debt, over $120,000 in March 1886, was reduced to under $93,000 by June 1887.[46] The trustees set about reducing the debt further. They authorized paying off the $60,000 mortgage on the seminary building, obtained in 1879 from the Misses Caldwell. This five percent mortgage was paid by a $50,000 loan from the Mutual Life Insurance Company of New York and "the Right Reverend Bishop supplying the balance of $10,000."[47] By continuing to exercise careful financial controls, this Mutual Benefit loan was entirely paid off by 1895, at which time Bishop

Wigger remarked, "Treasurer's report showed that the mortgage had been entirely paid off. Thanks be to God!"[48] In that year, the net indebtedness of Seton Hall was less than $5,000.

Financial worries and the fire took a toll on Father James Corrigan. Never of robust health, he asked to be relieved of the presidency in late 1887. Bishop Wigger acceded to his wishes and offered him a parish, St. Mary's in Elizabeth, New Jersey. Father James had expressed concern to the bishop that a parish might be too much for him, telling the ordinary that he did not have sufficient acumen to manage the financial affairs of the parish, and that he had "insufficient theological knowledge," not having made a full course of studies due to sickness brought on by scrupulosity.

Physically and emotionally, he clearly was exhausted. Wigger kindly told him that he would assign him to a parish that had a talented and active assistant so that the difficulties Corrigan cited "will in a great measure be removed."[49]

He died in 1891, after serving as pastor of St. Mary's, Elizabeth for almost two years.

> The memory of "Father James" will long be cherished
> by the old alumni of the college and seminary. He was
> always the gentleman, courteous and condescending
> to the youngest as well as to the oldest scholar. Ever
> watchful of their intellectual advancement, he was
> equally vigilant with regard to their physical well-being,
> and deeply and sincerely sympathetic with them in the
> many trials incidental to college training. It was always
> an effort for him to appear stern, and the suppressed
> merriment was easily transparent through the frown
> which clouded his brow. And after the glories of
> commencement or ordination day none was more
> sincere or more hearty in his congratulations. This
> same kind and solicitous spirit accompanied him
> when he exercised but too briefly the active ministry
> in St. Mary's, Elizabeth.[50]

Father James' eulogist noted, "His piety was as real as it was unostentatious, and I need not tell the students of Seton Hall how devoutly he said the holy Mass, and I confess I was always inspired with a sense of awe when he performed the sublime act of consecration." He went on, in true nineteenth-century style: "Father James Corrigan had the primacy of Abel, the patriarchate of Abraham, the government of Noe, the order of Melchizedeck, the dignity of Aaron, the authority of Moses, the power of Peter, and the unction of Christ, and he used them well according to the limited years God granted him, and hence in that brief span he attained unto the perfection of Samuel."[51]

He was succeeded as president by Father William F. Marshall, while Father Salt continued as director of the seminary. Born in 1849, Marshall graduated from Chritenden's Law and Business School in 1866. After working in business, he returned to school and graduated from Mt. St. Mary's College in Emmitsburg, Maryland, in 1877. He then entered Immaculate Conception Seminary and was ordained in 1881. Due to his business and financial acumen, the main debt of the college, more than $121,000 in 1882, was cancelled by 1895, and the buildings "offered a free gift to the diocese of Newark."[52]

During his tenure numerous sports were introduced or improved, including the Alert and Quickstep baseball teams.[53] Marshall served as president of the college until 1897.

Chapter Nine

Stability at Last

Although the continuance of the college and the seminary were in peril due to financial difficulties, possible sales, and another disastrous fire, the life of the seminary was relatively tranquil.

While there had been stability in the administration from the beginning of the seminary, and this continued during Father Salt's 17-year tenure, the early years of the institution had been plagued by constant changes in the faculty. Beginning in the 1880s and continuing thereafter, the faculty would be characterized by longer service, giving the institution greater internal cohesion. Like their predecessors, the majority of professors in this period had studied in Europe—at Rome, Louvain, Innsbruck, and Brignole-Sale in Genoa. Many of them likewise had earned a doctorate in divinity.

Father Sebastian Messmer, who joined the seminary faculty in 1871, remained until 1889. Father John O'Connor came to the seminary in 1878 and remained until 1895, teaching metaphysics, dogmatic theology, liturgy, and plain chant. Reverend Denis J. McCartie, Bishop Wigger's secretary, taught scripture, canon law, moral theology, and ecclesiastical history from 1883 until 1892. Reverend Charles Mackel, after studies in Rome, lectured on dogmatic theology, philosophy, sacred eloquence, and sociology.[1] More than likely, Bishop Wigger's residence at the seminary, where he "maintain[ed] a general supervision over" the college,[2] had a positive influence, maintaining confidence, especially during the difficult 1880s.

Recruiting, training, and retaining college and seminary faculty were not easy tasks. Concerned that with the division of the diocese in 1881 the new diocese of Trenton might claim Father Marshall, who was a native of a town now in the new diocese, Father James Corrigan worried that priests assigned to an "institution" rather than a parish might be fair game for episcopal poaching. Marshall had valuable training in the business world, and Father James suggested to Bishop Wigger that he barter with the bishop of Trenton to allow a Newark priest to remain in Trenton "on condition that Father Marshall remain at Seton Hall." He went on to explain to the bishop that it was difficult to get "the right sort of man" for a position in the college or seminary, and equally difficult to get that man "to stay any length of time in a subordinate position and under the restraints consequent upon college and seminary life."[3] After consultation with canon lawyers, he was relieved to find that Marshall would remain at Seton Hall. Father James obviously recognized the talents of Father Marshall, who would later become president of Seton Hall College.

Father James later elaborated on this situation, praising the priests of Seton Hall as "devoted to their work and loyal to authority. . . unobtrusive . . . not fond of gossiping, plotting, and intriguing for their own advantage." He saw the life of a diocesan priest teaching in the college or seminary as a life of sacrifice. Most colleges and seminaries were staffed by religious priests whose vocation included a structured existence and a conventual style of living.

For the diocesan priest it is difficult to "follow the observances of a conventual life, while the weight of discipline would press at times as heavily on him as upon the seminarian or the collegian, so that, in some measure, he might as well be a member of a religious community," while "charge of souls on the mission is more in keeping with a [diocesan] priest's aspirations." On the personal level, the priest professors remain in a state of "subordination," sacrificing their personal freedom, while their "former pupils have become rectors of important congregations."[4]

While Father James sang the praises of the faculty, Monsignor Seton was less complimentary about the alumni. Writing to Wigger, he complained, "So long as Bishop Corrigan was in this diocese it was impossible to obtain redress against a Seton Hall priest, at least such is a common belief (in which I fully share) among the older pastors." He quoted a pastor who had said on his deathbed, "You will see what scandals these Seton Hall priests will yet give." Seton went on to declare that the Seton Hall priests "as a class . . . are ignorant, impudent, not given to study but much given to visiting around particularly in the society of girls, acquisitive of money, wanting in disinterested zeal, utterly wanting in a spirit of prayer, self-denial, and mortification."

The good monsignor was angered that his assistant did not regularly return from his day off before 7:30 p.m. and immediately report to him. He also alleged that his assistant drank too much.[5] Seton believed that the younger clergy should use "some of their 'days off' . . . to spend a few hours in the libraries of such places as Seton Hall, Saint Peter's College, or in the Benedictine monastery in Newark."[6] Seton considered himself superior to the general clergy, and to most of humanity as well. Always emphasizing his family background and aristocratic connections, he did not hesitate in his letters to refer to "the lower class of Irish people"[7] with regal disdain.

The Third Plenary Council of Baltimore

The Third Plenary Council of Baltimore, meeting in 1884, issued specific guidelines for seminary training in the United States. The stability of faculty and administration enabled the seminary to study and implement its directives concerning seminary education. The diocese of Newark and the seminary, through present and past professors, were well represented at Baltimore. Of course, Bishop Wigger attended, as did Father James Corrigan. Sebastian Messmer served as a secretary of the council. Sebastian Smith attended as Bishop Wigger's theologian and also was invited by Cardinal Gibbons to be one of the notaries.

Bishops from small and distant dioceses "borrowed" Newark priests to serve as their theologians. Januarius De Concilio, who later became one of the compilers of the *Baltimore Catechism*, went as theologian to the vicar apostolic of Nebraska. George Doane and William Wiseman went as theologians to the coadjutor archbishop of Santa Fe, New Mexico. Thomas Steffanini, C.P., was invited in his capacity as provincial of St. Michael's Monastery in West Hoboken (Union City), and Damasus Ruesling, O.S.F., as provincial of St. Bonaventure's Monastery in Paterson, New Jersey. Of course, Monsignor Robert Seton, America's only prothonotary apostolic, was invited by Archbishop Gibbons to be the chief notary.[8] Seton later complained that this was the only occasion on which his talents were recognized.[9]

The council's legislation[10] on seminaries required substantial programmatic changes. In July 1885, just after the failure of the possible sale of Seton Hall to the new Catholic University of America, Bishop Wigger and Father Messmer attended a meeting in Buffalo, New York, where a gathering of bishops, provincials, and professors drew up a new course of studies for American seminaries.[11]

The council, following the European educational system, called for a minor seminary course of six years, corresponding, in today's terms, to four years of high school and the first two years of college. The major seminary also was to be a six-year institution; the first two years of which, corresponding to the last two years of college, were devoted to the study of philosophy and the last four to theology.

The council emphasized the necessity of four years of theological studies. It was not uncommon, in particular in the western United States, for many seminarians to be ordained before the completion of four years of theology. Immaculate Conception Seminary, together with St. Joseph's Seminary in Troy, New York, and St. Charles Seminary in Philadelphia, followed a four-year program before the council.[12]

The council also required the appointment of a board of deputies, one deputy charged with temporal affairs of the seminary, another with spiritual affairs. In September 1887, Wigger named Father William Marshall, vice president and treasurer of Seton Hall, as deputy for temporalities, and Father Salt, director of the seminary, as deputy for spiritualities.[13] The council also made provision for spiritual direction for seminarians. At the seminary, spiritual direction was part of the duties of the director or rector of the seminary, an arrangement that would persist into the 1920s.[14]

The *Seton Hall Catalogue* of 1885–1886 took note of some of the changes immediately introduced. The course of studies was modified and the responsibilities of the seminarians to the college were altered as well.

> Among the changes in the diocesan seminary, two very important ones may be mentioned. First, lectures on the relation between faith and science, and the study of German have been added to the theologians' course. Secondly, in order to afford them ampler time, the seminarians have been exempted from teaching any class in the college except the catechism classes, and these are reserved for the theologians who have received holy orders.[15]

Seminary Life

Theological students, however, continued to serve as prefects of discipline until the early twentieth century. In the 1880s and '90s, as a rule, only senior philosophy students were admitted into the seminary, an apparent continuing violation of the desires of the Baltimore Council. The last catalogue to mention junior philosophers among the seminarians was that of 1878.[16]

The 1898 catalogue specifies an already existing policy, stating that "only those students who have completed the classical course of studies in Seton Hall College, or in some other institution of equal standing, will be admitted to the seminary as divinity students. . . . As a general rule, three or four students of the college are received into the seminary during their senior year and continue their college work until they are graduated."[17] There are always exceptions to all rules, and we should not be surprised to find that the handwritten *Registrum Alumnorum* of incoming seminarians indicates that two juniors were admitted in 1895.[18]

This practice was based on practical concerns. Often there was not enough room in the seminary building to house junior philosophers, so they remained in the college building. For much of its history, the seminary did not make a clear distinction between "minor" and "major" seminarians.

Since 1873, the policy that "graduates of the college, two years after they have finished their course of studies, may, on application, receive the degree of master of arts"[19] continued to be applied. Seminarians could apply for this degree at the completion of their second year of theology, but not all would receive it. For example, at the 1898 commencement, 13 students received the M.A., and six of these were seminarians. The seventh seminarian in second theology that year did not receive the degree.[20] In the 1898 Seton Hall catalogue and continuing until 1927, with some modification, the section on the seminary appears as the "Graduate Department: Diocesan Seminary of the Immaculate Conception."[21]

Class Instruction and Manuals

The curriculum, as it was developed in response to the Third Plenary Council of Baltimore, was, for the first time, given in detail in the 1898 catalogue. It remained virtually unchanged through 1926, with the unfortunate elimination of Hebrew.[22]

The emphasis was on dogmatic and moral theology, each taught five hours weekly for eight semesters. The seminarian of this era would have had the equivalent of 40 credit hours in both of these disciplines. An additional hour was set aside for a pastoral conference and cases of conscience. In addition, each week there was a disputation, in which students were assigned theses to defend.

Scripture and exegesis accounted for three hours weekly through eight semesters for a total of 24 credit hours. Canon law was taught one hour weekly for eight semesters, accounting for eight credit hours. Classes in both ecclesiastical history and Hebrew were held two hours weekly for four semesters, or for the equivalent of eight credit hours each. Plain chant included two instructions and rehearsals each week over eight semesters, or 16 credit hours, including what today is called a practicum.

The exact hours for instruction in sacred eloquence are not specified but included instruction in theory and an annual sermon before faculty. Liturgy was covered by special classes before ordination and, through the years, by practice for ceremonies. Latin and Greek proficiency would have been achieved during the college and philosophy years. The only changes made over the years to 1926 were dropping the requirement for Hebrew and adding one hour per week for liturgy in addition to the special classes before ordination.

The table below gives us an idea of the curriculum, which, in today's calculation, would include more than 140 credit hours.

Discipline	Credit Hours
Dogmatic Theology	40, weekly disputations
Moral Theology	40, weekly disputations
Sacred Scripture and Exegesis	24
Canon Law	8
Ecclesiastical History	8
Hebrew	8
Plain Chant	16, including rehearsals
Sacred Eloquence	Instruction in theory and practice sermons
Liturgy	Special classes before ordination
Latin and Greek	In college and philosophy

Monsignor De Concilio's *Elements of Intellectual Philosophy* replaced Salvatore Tongiorgi's *Institutiones philosophicae* for Logic, while Tongiorgi continued to be used in other areas of philosophy together with Louis Jouin's *Compendium logicae et metaphysicae*. In 1885 Nicholas Russo's *Summa Philosophica* was adopted and continued in use until 1923. In dogmatic theology, Perrone continued to be used into the 1880s together with Bernard Jungmann's *Institutiones theologicae dogmaticae*. Hugo Hurter's *Theologiae dogmaticae compendium* was also used. In 1897 Adolphe Alfred Tanquerey's *Synopsis theologicae dogmaticae* was adopted and continued to be the text until replaced by Pesch in 1922 or 1923. Tanquerey also was adopted in many other seminaries and "began the extraordinary influence it would have in American and European seminaries until the middle of the 20th century."[23] Tanquerey was appealing because of his readable, compact treatment of the theological issues and the simplicity of the Latin text.[24] Adolphe Tanquerey's influence would continue with the publication in 1930 of *The Spiritual Life*, which would be adopted by the seminary as a text and continue in use until the 1960s.

In 1931, a year before his death, Tanquerey wrote to Monsignor Thomas McLaughlin, then rector of the seminary:

> I deem it a great honor for me that my work on *Spiritual Life* has been adopted by your seminary as a text-book for ascetical and mystical studies, and I thank you heartily for having so kindly called my attention to it. I hope the book will give satisfaction to the Faculty and to the students. Should any correction be desired, be kind enough to let me know it, or let these *desiderata* be transmitted to Very Rev. A. Vieban, St. Charles' College, Catonsville, who is in charge of this volume for the United States.
>
> So far the book has been very successful in France and foreign countries. We like to keep it up to date with the good suggestions of the seminaries where it is taught.[25]

In moral theology, Scavini was replaced with A. Konings' *Theologia Moralis s. Alphonsi*. Bishop Corrigan's comment, "The professors in the seminary are delighted with it," was printed in later editions of the work. Konings continued in use until after the turn of the twentieth century. In scripture, Dixon gave way to Thomas Lamy's *Introductio in s. Scripturam* and then to Ubaldo Ubaldi's three-volume *Introductio in s. Scripturam*. In the late 1880s Ubaldi was replaced by R. Cornely's *Compendium introductionis in Libros Sacros*, which remained as the text until replaced by Gigot in the early 1900s.

In ecclesiastical history, Wouters had been replaced by John Alzog's *Manual of Church History* (in English translation). By the 1880s, the text was

A. Birkenhaeuser's *History of the Church*, which continued in use until 1940. The texts in canon law were Sebastian Smith's three-volume *Elements of Ecclesiastical Law* and his *Compendium juris canonici.*[26]

The use of the same manuals for decades produced a uniform instruction for several generations of priests. They naturally would have a sense that nothing changed or developed in Church teaching. A newly ordained priest would have had essentially the same education as those ordained 30 or 40 years earlier.

Wigger took an active role in seminary life. No student could be admitted without his approval, and he often personally interviewed the candidates.[27] He, like his predecessors, also participated with the faculty in the end-of-semester examinations of the seminarians.[28]

In 1882, shortly after his consecration, Wigger changed the system by which seminarians were recommended for ordination. In the old system, six weeks before ordination, the seminary director called the seminarians to orders. Wigger directed that the priests of Seton Hall pass judgment on the qualifications of the individual candidates, communicate this evaluation to Father Salt, the director, and then directly to the bishop, who reserved to himself the final decision.[29]

That same year, Father James asked Bishop Wigger to continue to hold the ordinations of priests and deacons at St. Patrick's Cathedral, rather than at Seton Hall, as had been done up to 1878. Sounding a theme that rings just as true today, he told the bishop that the young men to be ordained priests invited more people than the Seton Hall Chapel could accommodate. Father James wrote that at one of the last ordinations in the Seton Hall Chapel, "900 people had come to be present."[30] Since the Seton Hall chapel has a capacity of approximately 180, this must have been quite a scene.

Evaluation and Criticism

Henry G. J. Beck, the author of the seminary's centennial history, saw these reforms as well intentioned but of little positive effect.

> Surely the diocesan authorities were well advised to make the adjustments in the seminary course announced in 1885. The purpose was good; but the product was not good enough. It is the impression of the present writer that the deficiencies of the South Orange institution were inherent in the minute budget upon which it was conducted. Because this was so small, the seminary faculty were assigned collegiate and preparatory classes to the detriment of their preparation. Because of this, the seminarians were involved in activities not consonant with quiet study. Because of this, library facilities were never adequate to the seminary's needs. Unfortunately, this was a fault general in its day.[31]

Bishop Spalding of Peoria was much more acerbic in his criticism of the seminaries of the period. He saw the seminary as a professional training school that did a decent job of producing priests who could fulfill the tasks of parish ministry. However, he said that "to imagine that it can become the instrument of intellectual culture is to cherish a delusion." In his opinion, seminaries simply train, they do not "open the mind...give it breadth, flexibility, strength, refinement, and grace." He kept his fiercest denunciation for seminary textbooks, or manuals. These were "written often in a barbarous style, the subjects are discussed in a dry and mechanical way, and the professor, wholly intent upon giving instruction, is frequently indifferent as to the manner in which it is imparted."[32]

Changes at the Helm

At the beginning of the last decade of the nineteenth century, the seminary bade farewell to its longest-serving director, Father Salt. In a laconic telegram on October 7, 1890, Bishop Wigger was advised, "Father Salt is dead. Died suddenly at 7:30 this morning."[33] Father Salt was highly regarded by his colleagues and his bishops. In 1876, Bishop Corrigan had proposed him for the episcopate, writing that Salt "enjoys my confidence and esteem in a higher degree than . . . any other priest in the Diocese, on account of his solid common sense and unaffected piety."[34] In 1885, Bishop Wigger named Salt as his vicar general.[35]

Father Marshall, the president of the college, described him as a "careful, exact, conscientious, practical" teacher, possessing "a strong logical turn, a power of keen analysis, and great facility for condensation." He "struck straight at the heart of the subject, and never wearied his pupils with irrelevant discussions. He inspired a certain fear, but it was reverential, and was tempered with respect and confidence." Apparently he was stern. "It was thought by some that he lacked the gift of sympathy. It was not so. His sympathy was swift and tender, but, like all the deep-hidden currents of life, it flowed silently."[36]

Salt's *Rule of Life*, which stood on his desk and was published after his death, is indicative of the depth of his devotion and exemplifies the spirituality of the priesthood of the time.

> The perfections of God, of which the priest should
> be the image, are patience, wisdom, sweetness, charity,
> sanctity, strength, stability. The priest's life should
> be such that men will be induced by their example to
> imitate God in this life, while waiting in the hope of
> seeing and possessing Him in the future life. One object
> of the incarnation was to give man an example of the
> perfect life. This Our Lord did, and left His priests to
> continue the work of making known the perfections

of God, of rendering those perfections visible in
their lives.[37]

Joseph Flynn, in his 1904 book, *The Catholic Church in New Jersey*,
remembered Father Salt in true Victorian style: "The perfume of Father Salt's memory
is as sweet and fresh today as it was on the day he passed over the bridgeless river to
the longed-for valley of rest. The recollection of his gentle life is as grateful as the
breath of a melody, as wholesome as the hand of benediction."[38]

Father Salt was succeeded as director of the seminary by Father John J.
O'Connor. Born in Newark in 1855, O'Connor graduated from Seton Hall College
in 1873. Completing his theological studies in Rome in June 1877, he was too young
to be ordained, and went to Louvain for an additional year of study. It was there that
he was ordained a priest on December 22, 1877, at 22 years of age. He had served on
the faculty since 1878, teaching metaphysics, dogmatic theology, liturgy, and plain
chant. Affable and generally liked by the students, he is described as "a general favorite.
Everybody went to him who was in trouble and his advice was like a benediction
from heaven. He mingled freely with the seminarians and took a friendly interest
in our pastimes and field sports."[39] O'Connor would serve as director until, already
vicar general since 1892, he was appointed pastor of St. Joseph's Parish in Newark
in October 1895.[40]

Father Joseph Synnott, born in 1863, succeeded O'Connor in 1895.
He graduated from St. Francis Xavier College in 1882 and entered the University
of Innsbruck where he was ordained in 1886. After receiving his doctorate in 1888,
he returned to the United States. Shortly after his return he was appointed to the
seminary faculty where he taught scripture, Hebrew, moral theology, and canon law.

When Synnott assumed leadership of the seminary in 1895, he took the title
of "rector," the first to do so. Two years later, in 1897, he was appointed president of
the college. Synnott was the first to hold the titles of both rector of the seminary and
president of the college. His three immediate successors would continue this tradition
until, in 1932, Thomas H. McLaughlin relinquished the presidency, but continued
as rector. Synnott's appointment as president necessitated the creation of the office of
vice rector of the seminary, since Synnott retained the rector's office. Reverend Hubert
J. Behr, who had been ordained in Rome in 1893 and held the doctorate in divinity,
assumed this post. He held this post until appointed pastor of St. Michael's in
Elizabeth in 1901.[41]

Synnott also secured full recognition for the degrees granted by Seton Hall
from the State Department of Education in Rhode Island and the Board of Regents
in New York.[42] This recognition gave Seton Hall degrees the same standing as degrees
granted in these states. Seminary students who received their bachelor and master of
arts degrees from Seton Hall thereby possessed degrees that were recognized elsewhere
as well. This gave the seminary a status enjoyed by few other similar institutions in
the days before accreditation.

Just a few years later, the seminary and college were shocked by the sudden death of Father Synnott on March 16, 1899, after completing fewer than four years as rector and two as president. Flynn describes him as possessing "a rarely gifted mind, extraordinary industry, a charming grace of manner, extreme modesty, and a character firm as it was gentle. He was eminently fitted for his position, and it is certain, if God had spared his life, that far higher honors and graver responsibilities awaited him. . . . His too brief career was cut short by his untimely death."[43] Among the achievements of his short tenure as president was the erection of a new library (today's Marshall Hall).

Cannons Salute the Bishop

Perhaps the most noticeable change in the life of the college and seminary campus was the introduction of a corps of military cadets in 1893. Father Marshall had long been contemplating introducing military drilling and instruction into the college. Through the intervention of his friend, U.S. Senator James Smith of New Jersey, the War Department assigned an officer to instruct in infantry tactics and military discipline at Seton Hall. A company of cadets, divided into three battalions, in gray uniforms similar to those of West Point, became a campus fixture. Their drills and reviews certainly added a new spirit to the campus. Two three-inch guns and other munitions were stored in an armory on campus.

In 1894, Bishop Wigger missed the commencement ceremonies and attendant military exercises. He had been in Europe on his *ad limina* visit to Pope Leo XIII, and extended his trip to include a pilgrimage to the Holy Land. On his return on June 6, he debarked at Hoboken and was greeted by diocesan and Seton Hall officials. They took the train to South Orange and were met at the station by the cadets, under the command of Lieutenant Michael J. Lenihan.

> Michael Redding, the expert college farmer, and the
> bishop's faithful coachman, drove him to the college
> while the cadets formed a military escort. On arriving
> at Seton Hall another greeting was awaiting the good
> bishop from Rev. William F. Marshall, the president;
> at noon a salute of 14 guns was fired by the battalion,
> in honor of Bishop Wigger.[44]

The number 14 remains a mystery, especially as an even number of shots is considered unlucky. According to military custom, a major general is accorded a 13-gun salute; a lieutenant general a 15-gun salute. Perhaps Lieutenant Lenihan considered Bishop Wigger's episcopal rank somewhere in between. Or, perchance, someone miscounted. The military department was disbanded a few years later due to complaints of violations of church and state relations and dissatisfaction on the part of some of the Seton Hall administration.

Chapter Ten

A Century Turns

The end of the nineteenth and the beginning of the twentieth century saw significant transition for the seminary. Father Synnott's death in 1899 was followed by the appointment of Father John A. Stafford, S.T.L., as president of the college and rector of the seminary. Father Stafford, born in 1857, was ordained at the North American College in Rome in 1888. He was assigned to several parishes before his appointment as vice president of Seton Hall in 1893. He also served as professor of Latin and English. He became a pastor in 1897, but returned to Seton Hall to take up his new roles in 1899.[1] At the time, there were 32 seminarians enrolled.[2] The first decade of the new century would be an eventful one for the seminary.

Bishop Wigger, who had lived at the seminary for 20 years, died there on January 5, 1901, after a short illness. Wigger took great pride in his seminary and college. At his invitation, the first apostolic delegate, Archbishop Francesco Satolli, had spent several days at the seminary in October 1896, during which he was tendered a gala dinner.[3] Wigger died a poor man. "When I was only a simple priest, I was always more or less in debt. Only once did I succeed in laying by $100. In less than three weeks, all had disappeared. Since I have been bishop, things are worse even. My personal debts are larger than formerly. There is some comfort in knowing that I have not spent much on myself. I have never done that. The money has been given to others, generally in charity."[4] A few weeks before his death, he left the following note in his Register: "This morning I went to visit the Catholics in the Poor House of Newark."[5]

The Catholic population of the diocese had doubled during the 20 years of Wigger's tenure. In 1882, there were 145,000; in 1901, 290,000 Catholics. The number of priests also had doubled, from 131 to 265. There were 83 churches in 1882; 155 in 1901.[6]

Since the diocese had been established in 1853, the Catholic population of New Jersey had grown from about 30,000 to 362,000. Of this number, Newark accounted for 290,000, and Trenton, 72,000. Catholics in the diocese of Newark accounted for about 25 percent of the total population of its seven counties, just over 1.1 million.

Much of this growth was fueled by immigration. From 1890 to 1900, for example, the number of Catholics in Newark rose from 170,000 to 290,000. In that decade, the new immigration, especially from Italy, made a great impact on the diocese. In 1900, almost 432,000 of New Jersey's population were foreign-born; in 1910 this swelled to over 658,000, in 1920 to almost 739,000.[7]

The state of New Jersey had changed quite a bit as well. Industry was concentrating in the northern counties that comprised the diocese of Newark; the area around Newark was the most heavily industrialized. Among the great centers of industry were the Standard Oil Refinery in Bayonne, Thomas Edison's laboratory in West Orange, Singer Sewing Machines in Elizabeth, Western Electric in Kearny, Ward Baking Company in Elizabeth, several meat packing companies in Jersey City, and Ballantine and numerous other breweries in Newark. Nearby Paterson was the center of the nation's silk-producing industry, and Passaic boasted numerous textile mills.

In the jubilee year of the diocese, Thomas Edison produced the film *The Great Train Robbery*. The action took place in Paterson and the train was borrowed from the Lackawanna Railroad. By 1900 New Jersey had more railroad mileage in proportion to its size than any other state. Farming still was important in parts of northern New Jersey, but was shrinking, except for dairy farming in Sussex and poultry in Sussex and Passaic Counties.[8]

Priests Vote for a New Bishop

For the only time in the history of the diocese of Newark, the process of recommending candidates for the succession to the diocese officially included the priests. According to the decrees of the Third Plenary Council of Baltimore, when there was an episcopal vacancy, the consultors and permanent rectors of the diocese were directed to meet and to compose a terna of candidates.[9] This terna would be presented to the bishops of the province, who then composed their own terna.

Father John J. O'Connor, the vicar general, was elected administrator of the diocese by the consultors. A few weeks later he summoned the consultors and permanent rectors of the diocese to meet at the home of the metropolitan, Archbishop Corrigan, in New York. Their task was to select three names to submit to the bishops of the province who would consider them and forward them to the apostolic delegate with the episcopal terna.

Archbishop Corrigan presided over the meeting and the first ballot gave Father O'Connor six votes of the eleven cast. Monsignor Seton then arrived, late. Balloting was resumed and Father O'Connor received seven votes of twelve. His name was placed first on the list as *dignissimus*. Father Charles Kelly, a Newark diocesan consultor, was placed second. In third place, they designated New York auxiliary bishop John M. Farley. Afterward, the clergy were "entertained most hospitably by the archbishop."[10]

When the bishops of the province subsequently met, McQuaid was absent, returning from his *ad limina* visit. They considered the priests' terna, and unanimously retained O'Connor in first place. Kelly remained in second place with five favorable votes, and one negative. Bishop Farley asked that he not be considered since he was 59 years of age, which, he stated, was too old to assume an important diocese. In 1902, a year older, Farley overcame his qualms about age and succeeded Corrigan as archbishop of New York, and was made a cardinal in 1911. The bishops replaced him on the terna with Father Charles Colton, the chancellor of the archdiocese of New York.[11] Both ternas were sent to the apostolic delegate, Archbishop Sebastiano Martinelli.

After the appointment of an apostolic delegate to the United States in 1893, the delegate's recommendation was accepted in Rome in the overwhelming majority of appointments. During the period between the Third Plenary Council of Baltimore in 1885 and the promulgation of the Code of Canon Law in 1917, the consultors and permanent rectors had the right to present a terna to the bishops of the province. The delegates invariably took the opinion of the priests into consideration and recommended a candidate who appeared on both the priests' and the bishops' ternas. Such a man obviously enjoyed wide support within the diocese and would be appealing to the widest range of clergy.[12]

Martinelli, citing O'Connor's good reputation, his financial ability, and his place at the top of both ternas, recommended him to the Congregation for the Propagation of the Faith, which presented him to Pope Leo XIII for appointment as bishop of Newark.[13] In 1903, Colton, third on the bishops' terna, became bishop of Buffalo.[14]

Right Reverend John J. O'Connor, former seminary director and professor, was consecrated bishop on July 25, 1901, in St. Patrick's Cathedral in Newark. It was very much a Seton Hall event. O'Connor was a former professor and director of the seminary. Father Stafford, the college president and seminary rector, read the papal bull.[15] Archbishop Michael Corrigan, onetime president of the college and the seminary, was the principal consecrator of the new bishop.

Bishop McQuaid, founding president of both college and seminary, preached "in his usually eloquent and reminiscent style."[16] He now had preached at the installations of the second, third, and fourth bishops of Newark, and had hosted the installation of the first as rector of St. Patrick's Cathedral. The South Orange campus celebrated with a fireworks display that night.[17] O'Connor was tendered a formal reception by the college and seminary the following September 24.[18]

O'Connor only briefly resided at the seminary, moving to the newly purchased nearby former Kelly estate, just a few hundred yards from the seminary and the college. He remained closely connected to the seminary, visiting weekly and having his daily Mass served by the seminarians. Throughout his episcopate, he continued the practice of presiding at the seminarians' examinations as well.[19]

A Season of Jubilees

Breaking the seminary routine, there would be a series of observances, celebrations, and formal events over the following years. The joy of these events was tempered by the death, on May 5, 1902, of Archbishop Corrigan of New York. Michael Augustine Corrigan, together with Bishop Bayley and Bishop McQuaid, was one of the most important personages in the foundation and sustenance of the seminary and the college. Without his dedication and generosity, it is fair to say that both institutions may not have endured.

In 1902, yielding "to the importunities of his priests,"[20] Bishop O'Connor celebrated the silver jubilee of his ordination to the priesthood. The seminary offered O'Connor a musical tribute to mark the occasion. The 32 seminarians[21] must have possessed a great deal of musical talent. They provided a musical salute to the bishop that featured a glee club, a quartet, and an orchestra. These groups performed songs that included "Swiftly We Glide," "Chapel," "For all Eternity," "The Old Brigade," "Les Dames de Seville," and "Noel."[22]

The following year, the rector was invested as a domestic prelate, a rare honor in those days.[23] The year 1903 also marked the fiftieth anniversary of the establishment of the diocese. In his pastoral letter marking the occasion, O'Connor did not mention either the seminary or the college, but focused on appealing for funds to assist in the construction of the new Cathedral of the Sacred Heart, begun by Bishop Wigger just a few years before.[24]

The diocese, although growing, was stretching its resources. It also was stretching the generosity of its priests and people. In October 1903, O'Connor wrote to the priests, noting their generosity but lamenting the slow response of the laity to the appeal for the new cathedral: "As you are aware, the hopes entertained by the late Bishop Wigger of obtaining for the cathedral fund $100,000 every year by assessments and other similar means have proved futile. Six years have elapsed and only $332,000 have been received; and of this amount more than one-fourth has been subscribed by the priests of the diocese from their own personal income."[25]

The seminary again hosted an apostolic delegate, Archbishop Diomede Falconio, as part of the golden jubilee celebrations.[26] The seminarians, of course, participated in the golden jubilee Mass at St. Patrick's Cathedral in Newark on November 3, 1903. On that day, Bishop Bernard McQuaid, "the only survivor of all the clergymen who took part in the installation of Bishop Bayley 50 years before," delivered a one-hour-long sermon, rising to "the eloquence, dramatic force, and beauty of his early days of speaking."[27] In his sermon, he made the interesting statement that Bishop Bayley "established Seton Hall College to educate young men for the priesthood."[28] Strangely, he made no mention of the college as an educational institution for laymen.

After the Mass, the clergy adjourned to a banquet in the Krueger auditorium. There they enjoyed a banquet followed by the usual toasts. There was, however, a significant innovation, the toast "to the Immigrants of Today," offered by Reverend Andrew M. Egan. Father Egan praised the piety, the accomplishments, and the generosity of the immigrants who had established the diocese on a sound footing. He then praised the contemporary immigrants: Germans, Irish, Italians, Poles, and Slavs. He recognized that they did not have the advantage of the Irish in being able to speak English on their arrival in America.

He noted that some had strayed from the faith. But, urging patience with the difficulties of the contemporary immigration, he declared that "the multitude of the immigrants of today will carry on the same work in the cause of God and his holy religion as has been done in the past." Amid the usual triumphal recital of statistics of growth and success, Egan recognized that the diocese had grown but also had changed. It was already, in 1903, a mixture of many nationalities, no longer an Irish and German church.

This ethnic mixture was not reflected in seminary enrollment. Of the 59 students who entered the seminary from 1900 through 1905, 49 were of Irish heritage. The remaining ten included six of German, two of Polish, one of Hungarian, and one of Italian background.[29] The diocese made up for this by admitting foreign-born priests. In 1900, there were 20 German-born priests, 20 Italian, and five Polish.[30]

In 1904, the seminary was the scene of a reception for Bishop O'Connor and the rector on their return from Rome.[31] Just in case they missed out on one of the banquets, the Seton Hall Seminary Alumni Association celebrated its first annual reunion and dinner at the college on December 28, 1904. This gala event featured a menu suitable to such a distinguished gathering.

MENU
Blue Points, Deep Shell
Soup Jenny Lind
Olives, Salted Almonds, Celery
Sweetbreads, French Peas
Prime Porterhouse au Gras
French String Beans, Princess Potatoes
Roman Punch à la Setonia
Quail on Toast, Currant Jelly
Lettuce Salad
Ice Cream, Assorted Macaroons
Cheese, Crackers
Café Noir, Cigars[32]

Monsignor Stafford endeavored to improve both the intellectual and the athletic standards of Seton Hall in both college and seminary. In reporting the ceremonies of his 1903 investiture as domestic prelate, the *Newark Evening News* noted that Monsignor Stafford had a keen interest in athletics and that "seminarians as well as the collegians have experienced the benefits of these up-to-date methods."[33]

Apparently, the rector and president believed that the seminary and the college were so united that they should share the athletic abilities of their students. On October 20, 1904, the *Newark Evening News* reported that Seton Hall had won a football match over Fordham, 6–0. It described the match as a "bruising battle from the start . . . Magnificent team play on both sides . . . superb individual work."[34] The paper published the lineup but no one noticed that Seton Hall's team included Thomas Corr, a third-year theologian, right halfback; James Rutledge, a first theologian, at left; Andrew Clark, a second theologian, left tackle; and James Owens, first theologian, left guard.[35] Using graduate students in an undergraduate sports event surely strained the bounds of intercollegiate sportsmanship, but evidently did not bother Monsignor Stafford. It would not be until 1931 that Seton Hall's teams received the nickname "Pirates,"[36] but it may have already been deserved.

Stafford's interests ranged beyond athletics. An imposing series of lectures under the auspices of the DeSales Union included Dr. Brann's "Paradise of Dante," Dr. Kelly's "Medical Diagnosis," and the Hon. James Minturn's "Law and Lawyers."[37]

Finances, Yet Again

Although he endeavored to improve the athletic program and to continue to bring esoteric lecturers to the college, Stafford had other things on his mind. Seton Hall's rickety financial situation, the continual amassing of debt, and the discounts granted to seminary students irritated Stafford. The Newark *Sunday Call* later noted that the diocese was able to conduct its seminary at a cost of about $7,000 a year because of these discounts.

As Stafford's predecessors had complained several times, the college effectively was subsidizing the seminary and saving the diocese a significant sum of money. The constant mixture of funds, loans from the diocese, and subsidies to the diocese through discounts for the seminary made life difficult for any administrator. In addition, beyond the discounts for seminarians, the college gave the same discount to preparatory and college students who declared themselves "ecclesiastical students" with a desire to enter the seminary. This discount was significant. The tuition in the catalogue was $380, the ecclesiastical discount brought it down to $250.

After a painstaking audit, Stafford wrote to O'Connor on January 13, 1905, that there were "in the college 42 students, or about one-half the number registered who purpose to become priests, and who according an ancient tradition must be educated at the same rates as those who are actually in the seminary, namely $250 or $41.40 per capita less than the actual cost of their education and maintenance."

Stafford also raised an unusual idea, a diocesan subsidy—an idea that would not make the bishop happy.

Perhaps referring to McQuaid's remark concerning the college at the diocesan jubilee Mass, and a general apprehension among the clergy of the diocese, he wrote, "If I am not mistaken the college was founded as an *aid* to support the diocesan Seminary. If such be the fact it seems scarcely just to force the corporation as such to increase its debt in order that the seminarians and ecclesiastical students may be housed and fed and educated. When the college has lent all the *aid* in its power, the deficit it seems to me should be supplied by the diocese either by direct assessment on the various parishes or by any other means you and the diocesan council may suggest."[38]

Stafford asked the bishop at least to raise the seminary tuition for the 31 seminarians to $291.40, the actual cost per annum as he calculated it. The same day, in another letter, demonstrating the various problems he had to deal with on a daily basis, he told the bishop he was having difficulties with Father Mackel, the professor of dogmatic theology, who was demanding too much of the seminarians' time. "No professor has a right to a monopoly of a seminarian's time. Dogma, moral, scripture and history are all equally necessary to a well rounded seminary education."[39]

Chapter Eleven

The College Jubilee

The jubilee season continued. In 1906, it was the turn of Seton Hall College to celebrate its golden jubilee. The seminary also considered it to be its jubilee year, believing that the two institutions were founded simultaneously, a misapprehension that was not corrected until Beck's centennial history of the seminary in 1961. A major renovation was undertaken of the seminary chapel, which also served the collegians. The original belfry in the center of the façade was removed during the course of the summer of 1906 and a new entrance opened beneath it. The side entrance on the west, originally constructed for the convenience of the Catholics of South Orange, was closed and transformed into a chapel of the Sacred Heart. A cloister-like connecting passage was constructed linking the chapel to the seminary building.[1] The chapel already had been enlarged in 1887 by the addition of a sacristy to the rear of the building.[2]

The theme of the renovation was, not surprisingly, Marian. The chapel, like the seminary, was dedicated to the Immaculate Conception. Professor Ferdinand Baraldi and his assistants painted the ceilings in scroll designs, with a lily and the letters "AM," for "Ave Maria," as a centerpiece. The general color scheme was gold and light blue. The eight beatitudes were inscribed in gold between the rafters. A large painting of the Immaculate Conception was placed above the altar on the south wall of the sanctuary.[3]

The statue of the Sacred Heart, which had been installed on the rear wall of the chapel over the altar, was removed and possibly placed in the new Sacred Heart Chapel, located in the former west entry. The funds for the improvements and renovations were provided by the seminary alumni, who donated more than $3,000, and a $6,000 loan from Father Joseph H. Meehan, pastor of All Saints Parish, in Jersey City. Father Meehan also donated several of the stained-glass windows. Just over $9,000 was expended on these renovations. They took place concurrent with the changes to the structure of the chapel and the installation of new stained glass in the nave and in the chancel. Priests of the diocese contributed to the cost of the new brownstone passageway between the chapel and the seminary.[4]

Above the chancel arch, an ornate banner was painted reading *Ave Gratia Plena, Dominus Tecum* (Hail, Full of Grace, the Lord is with Thee). The wood altars were painted white and, in 1915, a new marble main altar was installed, the gift of Monsignor Isaac P. Whelan, rector of St. Patrick's Cathedral in Newark.[5]

> The Jubilee celebration took the form of an Alumni Day, held on Tuesday, June 12, 1906, with Mass for deceased alumni, a banquet, and a baseball game with Manhattan College [which Seton Hall won, 11–3], and then, on the 13th, commencement exercises in the Newark Theater, at which Bishop McQuaid of Rochester, first president of both college and seminary, delivered the address. Of the ten graduates that day receiving their degrees, seven would enter the seminary in the fall.[6]

As part of the golden jubilee observance, the college sponsored a series of lectures in 1906. They were the typical and boring academic fare: "Robert Burns" by the Hon. William B. Curley and "Goethe's Faust" by the Rev. Dr. Henry A. Brann, long reconciled to diocese and college. However, there was an exception to the soporific norm, a lecture on "Submarine Navigation" delivered by a fascinating character and local hero, John P. Holland, the "Father of the Submarine."

Holland was born in 1841 in Liscannor, County Clare, Ireland. He joined the Christian Brothers but left due to ill health in 1873. While with the Brothers he kept up his interest in scientific experiments. He completed his first draft of a design for a submarine in 1859, a design he never radically changed. Inspired by the publication of Jules Verne's *Twenty Thousand Leagues Under the Sea*, he sought to turn the dream into a reality. In 1873 Holland joined his mother and two brothers in the United States. He took up teaching at St. John's Parish School in Paterson, New Jersey.

His early attempts to convince the United States Navy of the feasibility of his idea met with rejection. He later received financial assistance from the Fenians, who planned to build a submarine, to be christened the *Fenian Ram*, which, they hoped, would sink a British warship. This came to naught and Holland severed his connections with the Fenians and, in a complete about-face, sold his designs to England's Royal Navy. A later prototype successfully was launched in New York Harbor on St. Patrick's Day, 1898.

The United States finally bought the prototype in 1900, and it was commissioned on October 12, 1900, the first submarine in the U.S. Navy. Holland died on August 12, 1914, at the beginning of the great world conflict that would convincingly demonstrate the military effectiveness of the weapon he had done so much to create. He is buried in Totowa, New Jersey, less than one mile from where he launched his first submarine in the Passaic River. His lecture must have been a welcome change for all listeners.

Monsignor Stafford Departs

Taking Monsignor Stafford's plea for financial assistance into account, but not giving him the direct subsidy or tuition raise for seminarians he desired, O'Connor used the jubilee to send a circular letter to the clergy asking for a collection to benefit the seminary. O'Connor recounted the expenses of the previous decade: the renovation and re-plastering of the seminary, the construction of the new library, and a new heating system in both seminary and college. These expenses resulted in the debt of the college rising to $69,000.

Calling on the faithful "to testify by their generosity their appreciation of the great and noble work of educating young men for the priesthood," O'Connor wrote that "the seminary is the principal institution of the diocese and the one on which humanly speaking the perpetuation of our holy religion chiefly depends." He also reminded the priests that the improvements in the seminary also were "caused by the need of providing better accommodations for the clergy at the annual retreats." The collection realized over $30,000 but did not solve Seton Hall's financial woes.[7]

The appeal was for the seminary, not for the college. Apparently, the major interest of the diocese and of the presbyterate—and perhaps the bishop—was indeed the seminary and not the college, even though the buildings and renovations benefited both. It evidently was a marketing strategy as well.

Stafford was fed up with the situation. He was expected to manage an institution sponsored by the diocese but with no assistance from the diocese. Moreover, he believed he was being forced to run it in a way that he considered fiscally irresponsible. "If I happen to be in the way of a peaceful and satisfactory adjustment of the difficulties," he wrote, "I shall cheerfully resign the office with its onerous duties and grave responsibilities."[8] After the close of the jubilee observances, Stafford renewed his request to resign and be named to a parish. On January 7, 1907, O'Connor appointed Stafford pastor of St. Paul of the Cross Parish in Jersey City. Less than two years later, he transferred to St. Patrick's in Jersey City, where he died on January 21, 1913.[9]

The Seminary Grows and Life Goes on

Father James F. Mooney was appointed to succeed Monsignor Stafford as president and rector. Mooney was born in Brooklyn, New York, in 1864. He attended St. Francis College in Brooklyn, transferred to Seton Hall, and graduated in 1884. He attended the College of Brignole-Sale in Genoa, Italy, and was ordained to the priesthood there on September 21, 1889. Some years later in 1905, he enjoyed the unusual distinction of receiving the degree of doctor of divinity from Brignole-Sale after active service in the ministry. After several years in parish work, including the pastorate of St. Cecilia's Church in Kearny, New Jersey, Father Mooney returned to Seton Hall in 1902 to become professor of English and Latin in the college. In addition, he taught theology and canon law in the seminary, where he also served as vice rector. Dr. Mooney was serving in these capacities when appointed president and rector in 1907.[10]

Little or nothing in the seminary, other than the personalities, had changed since the academic reforms of the Third Plenary Council of Baltimore in 1885, while college finances fluctuated and finally improved. The lectures for the theology students, all four years together, still following the "cycle," were given in a classroom at the head of the stairs on the third floor of the seminary building, while those for the "senior seminarians," as those in philosophy were called, took place in the college classrooms.[11]

Unfortunately, seminarians still were engaged in many activities[12] other than study. Of the 42 theology students of 1909–1910, three served as prefects of discipline in the college, two as prefects in the high school, and two in the grammar school. In addition, a first theologian, Mr. William James Durant, A.B., taught French in the high school, English in the college, and served as college librarian.[13]

From recollections about their professors gathered by Henry G. J. Beck, we know that the seminarians saw Mooney as a man possessed of great self-assurance, but they also admired him for his full participation in their daily routine. He joined the community in morning meditation, and sometimes would call on a student to present the points which had been read the night before. They considered his grasp of moral theology to be superior. Later, when the Code of Canon Law was proclaimed in 1917, and it was impossible to obtain the text, Mooney would skillfully summarize the new canons.

A prominent professor in the 1900s was Reverend Cornelius Clifford. Clifford was born in New York in 1859 and entered the Society of Jesus in 1879. He did his theological studies at Innsbruck, Louvain, and at St. Benno's, Wales. He earned a doctorate in theology from Louvain and was awarded a Litt.D. from Columbia University in 1929. He was released from his religious vows in 1899, a year after his ordination. Accepted into the diocese of Newark, after serving three years in parochial work, he was assigned to the seminary in 1907, where he taught philosophy and Church history. According to Henry Beck, "During his two years at South Orange, Clifford brought insight into history and life into philosophy. His 'bless my soul' soon became a byword on the campus."[14]

In 1909, the Sacred Congregation for Religious decreed that secularized religious were forbidden to teach in diocesan seminaries,[15] and Clifford was assigned as pastor of Our Lady of Mercy in Whippany, New Jersey, where he died in 1938. From 1913 onward, he lectured in philosophy at Columbia University.[16]

In Beck's opinion, there was more than the Roman decree behind Clifford's departure.[17] He cites the editorial "Dunwoodie and Modernism," in the *Independent*, which specifically mentions Clifford's departure and refers to it as a "removal." The *Independent* stated that it was erroneous to assume that "the removal was required by a general rule as to the right of those to teach who had left the orders." Given the title of the editorial, one can only assume that Clifford was removed because of suspicions of modernism.[18] At the same time, at St. Bernard's Seminary, Rochester, in 1907–1908, the Rev. Dr. Edward J. Hanna, future archbishop of San Francisco, was under suspicion of modernism.[19]

Beck saw the departure of this gifted professor in the early 1900s as an example of what seminaries lost because they focused more on absorption of data than on training the intellect. He castigated the involvement of seminarians as prefects and teachers as taking them from their primary duty as students: "For students so occupied, collateral reading must have proven close to impossible. And even for others, an emphasis upon the text in class along with limited holdings of the library meant, in most instances, that their training was that of technicians. Brief contact with a man of Father Clifford's eminence called forth a response which, had he been spared to Seton Hall, might well have inaugurated a renaissance at South Orange."[20] There was no academic renaissance at Seton Hall or elsewhere in the seminary world.

"Manual theology" did not change, but some of the manuals did. Russo would remain the text in philosophy, and Tanquerey in dogma until 1923. Birkenhaeuser, adopted in 1887, remained the text in Church history until 1940. Andreas Meehan's *Compendium juris canonici* was adopted in 1904 and remained until replaced by the new Code of Canon Law in 1918. That year, due to World War I, copies of the code were difficult to come by and the rector, the only person who had a copy, dictated it to his class.[21] In 1905, Sabetti-Barrett's *Compendium theologiae moralis*, was replaced by Noldin's *Summa theologiae moralis*. Noldin, with revisions by Schmitt, had a very long run, lasting until 1956. For scripture, Cornely's *Compendium introductionis,* introduced in 1889, was replaced for a few years by Gigot's three-volume *Introduction to the Study of Sacred Scripture* and restored in 1909. With revisions by Merk, it continued in use until 1937. Michael Seisenberger's *Practical Handbook for the Study of the Bible* was also used from 1916 onward.

Chapter Twelve

Seminary Life: Father McWilliams and Will Durant

We are fortunate to have rather colorful portraits of seminary life in the early 1900s from two seminarians of the time. They both were seminarians during the rectorate of Monsignor Mooney, although their years did not overlap.

One was Monsignor Leroy McWilliams, legendary pastor of St. Michael's Parish in downtown Jersey City, then a bastion of Catholicism and a city where there was little distinction between church and state. In Jersey City, until the middle of the twentieth century, "You were born a Democrat and then baptized a Catholic" and remained both until your death. According to local lore, longtime Jersey City mayor and boss Frank Hague, to a query from President Franklin D. Roosevelt concerning the number of votes he would receive in the next election, responded unhesitatingly, "How many do you want?"[1]

McWilliams' reminiscences are gathered in the book *Parish Priest*, written by Jim Bishop and published in 1953. His genial stories of a world in which the priest was a prince among his people and served them with love and dedication are filled with Irish wit, and sometimes telling commentary, regarding his seminary days of 1915–1918.

As an ecclesiastical student in the college, McWilliams participated in many sports, as a player and as a manager. He enjoyed football, baseball, and diving. Too short to be a significant player, he managed the basketball team. The athletic ethics condoned by Monsignor Stafford had not left the campus, but this time the future Pirates were found out.

McWilliams remembered "arriving in the gymnasium just before a basketball game with New York University, and there stood a great star from St. Benedict's donning one of our uniforms. As manager, I protested, not only because it was unethical and plain dishonest, but because someone on the opposing team would be sure to recognize him. I was overruled. And someone from NYU did recognize the player, and for years afterward Seton Hall was blackballed by New York University."[2]

Our other source is one of the most prominent historians of the twentieth century, William James Durant. He spent several years at Seton Hall, as a teacher, a seminarian, and, after he left the seminary, as a teacher again for a brief time. Because of Durant's publicly professed agnosticism, the seminary long considered him a turncoat and a traitor. Yet he was rather positive about both his college and seminary experiences at Seton Hall. His most negative remarks were about himself and the strange mix of motivations that led him into the seminary. In any event, Will Durant remains the only Seton Hall professor and seminary student who, along with his beloved wife, Ariel, was awarded the Presidential Medal of Freedom.

The seminary's shame over Durant surfaced early in 1931 when Monsignor Thomas McLaughlin, rector of Immaculate Conception Seminary, received a letter from the secretary of the bishop of Boise, Idaho. He wrote, "William James Durant lectured in Boise recently and we have had many inquiries in regard to him. 'Who's Who' states that he taught Latin and French at Seton Hall from 1907 to 1911. (1) Will you kindly inform me if he was a seminarian? (2) Did he marry Ida Kaufman in 1913 outside the Church? (3) If he was not a seminarian was he a Catholic?"[3]

Monsignor McLaughlin's response may be described as apoplectic: "I would say that for me, Mr. Durant is a very painful memory." He described Durant as follows:

> [He was] of a very good Catholic family of rather humble circumstances, [who] secured his classical education at Saint Peter's College, Jersey City, N.J., through the kindly intervention of a good priest, now dead. He was regarded as a young man possessing great talent, though proud and self-assertive.
>
> After trying newspaper work for a while, he approached my predecessor, the late Monsignor James F. Mooney (who, by the way, was the priest who had assisted him with his education) seeking a position as a teacher at Seton Hall. He was an instructor in Seton Hall High School from 1907 to 1909. He was then accepted for Immaculate Conception Seminary, then located at South Orange, N.J., but withdrew from the latter in February 1911, though he continued to teach until the end of the scholastic year.

The good monsignor then denounced Durant and his recently published book.

> The hypocritical character of this man is now made manifest by his unfortunate book entitled "Transition" which we regard as a disparagement of everything we regard as sacred and holy. His representation of facts is misleading. It would appear that even while at Seton Hall he was already in league with the enemies of our faith, for scarcely had the school year of 1911 closed when he openly and publicly allied himself with the Communistic Ferrer School in New York City.

McLaughlin ended with a prayer that "Almighty God may give him the light to see the error of his ways."[4]

Transition: A Sentimental Story of One Mind and One Era, to which Monsignor McLaughlin refers, was published in 1927. Durant described the book as the story of "the evolution of a fairly typical rebel from utopian aspiration through a cynical despondency to some measure of reconciliation and good cheer."[5] Although autobiographical, Durant gave each character and many places fictitious names. He was "John Lemaire." Seton Hall was "South Hall." Saint Peter's College was "St. Paul's." Father Mooney was "Father Morley." It was far from difficult to read through this simple deception. McLaughlin surely was able to do so.

In *Transition*, Durant was rather kind to Seton Hall and laudatory of Father Mooney. McLaughlin's anger surely was caused by Durant's apostasy and excommunication for espousing socialist views and, even worse, for supporting the idea of "free love." This scandal brought shame on the college and the seminary, and grief to Durant's family. That Durant was regarded as a gifted writer, thinker, and intellectual surely made matters even more humiliating to the seminary. In his lifetime, Durant authored alone, or with his wife, 53 books.[6] He and his wife, Ariel, died within two weeks of each other in 1981. He returned to the Catholic faith at the end. In the words of William F. Buckley, Jr., Durant "followed the example of Voltaire, and confessed his sins to a priest."[7]

What Monsignor McLaughlin did not foresee was that Durant, in *Transition* and later in *Will and Ariel Durant: A Dual Autobiography*, published in 1977, would give us invaluable insights into and anecdotes about seminary life and people in the early twentieth century.

The Stealth Seminarian

Durant's friendship with Father James Mooney spanned more than a decade. Durant described Mooney as the "saintliest man I ever knew."[8] He continued, "In the spring of 1900 Father Mooney took me to the Jesuits at Saint Peter's College, Jersey City, and entered me into a contest for a scholarship. I was one of the winners—perhaps by merit, perhaps by Father Mooney's hint that I was sacerdotal material."[9]

While a student at Saint Peter's College, Durant took on Dr. Henry Brann, then a reigning Catholic apologist. Brann had delivered a lecture denouncing socialism and Marxian theory. Durant forcefully rebutted Brann in a letter to the Jersey City *Evening Journal*. The *Journal* published the letter on March 25, 1907. He concluded his letter, "If such attacks as that of Dr. Brann are all that the enemies of socialism can make, socialism has little to fear." The Jesuits ordered Durant to issue a retraction and an apology or be denied graduation. He refused, and they backed down.[10]

Durant's mother and Mooney clearly had hopes that Will would become a priest. While at Saint Peter's, Durant devoured every book he could and became a fixture at the Newark and Jersey City Public Libraries. His reading had led him to doubt his faith and this, together with visits to the Bon Ton Burlesque Theater in Jersey City, convinced him he was not material for the priesthood.[11]

He now believed in evolution and socialism, and he was losing his belief in God. He wrote, "As I relinquished my belief in heaven, I turned with religious fervor to faith in a socialist utopia."[12] He brought his doubts to Father Mooney, who counseled him that such lapses were common and urged him to "go to Mass daily, receive Communion frequently, and pray that faith would return."[13] Trying to restore his faith, he read Father Faber's devotional works, Cardinal Newman, and *The Imitation of Christ*, in both English and Latin.[14]

Although he enjoyed the burlesque house, Durant did not think highly of Jersey City, which he called the "most unfortunate city in the United States."[15] He could not understand why the great metropolis of New York had grown while, in his opinion, the better site on the west bank of the Hudson, "accessible by land to all the continent," had languished. "In place of that proud destiny the city of my first Alma Mater had become merely a railway terminus for New York, breathing the fumes of ten thousand locomotives that brought freight and passengers to the lordly Isle of Towers."[16]

In 1907, Mooney had become rector of the seminary and president of Seton Hall College. He arranged for Durant to teach Latin, French, and geometry at the college and to reside there as well.

While Durant wrote glowingly of the atmosphere of Seton Hall, he was less generous in his description of his fellow teachers in the college, finding them "a rather uninspiring lot. Some of them were encyclopedically ignorant; none of them had any of my passion for literature or philosophy. . . . Yet, these same men, unlettered as they appeared to me, were capable teachers."[17] Using pseudonyms, fortunately and mercifully, he described a rather colorful lot.

Some of the teachers stand out individually in my
memory: Cummings, who dressed like a millionaire on
fifty dollars a month; Zaccarelli, the fiery Italian, who
swore like a soldier despite my dubbing him "Cardinal,"
and who wished to kill us for laughing at his staccato
English; and timid old Daly, who indulged in alcoholic
amnesia once a week, and spent the other days worrying
whether Father Morley heard about it. I liked Zaccarelli
best, because I relish pride and passion in a man; but
the only one with whom I could have any stimulating
mental intercourse was Daly.[18]

Durant, together with a senior student bound for the seminary, conceived
"an idea worthy of the most imaginative lunatic." He would please his family and
Father Mooney by entering the seminary. He would pretend to have abandoned his
radical ideas, become a priest, and then work from within to lead the Catholic Church
in the United States to cooperation with the socialist movement.[19]

Durant described his entry into the seminary as "an act of hypocrisy,
generosity, idealism, and egotism. After two years I had had no success in recapturing
either the old piety or the old faith. . . . The idealism and egotism were inextricably
mixed, as they so often are. I took with Quixotic seriousness the mission I had
assigned myself, of working within the Church to ally it with socialism."[20]

They entered the seminary on September 4, 1909.[21] Durant never revealed
the name of his co-conspirator. He recalled his first year in the seminary as a happy
time. He described his fellow seminarians as "all fine men; they forgave my scandalous
acquaintance with non-Catholic literature, perhaps because they found me a helpful
partner in handball and tolerable in baseball."

The schedule was rigorous, "rising at five, hearing Mass before breakfast,
attending classes in theology, ethics, church history, and liturgy, continuing to teach
in the college, eating meals in silence, reciting the rosary together in the open air,
enjoying the daily periods of recreation, studying after supper till nine, murmuring
evening prayers in the chapel; going to bed at nine-thirty." He also noted, "I was so
tired that (though I do not trust the memory) I can't recall having any sexual desires
or fantasies while in the seminary. Perhaps those wise old theologians had put some
antiaphrodisiac in our coffee."[22]

Two Seminary Memoirs

Durant, however, called Seton Hall "a paradise." He recalled approaching
it "by wide gravel walks that ran apart and then came together before the entrance
of the administration building. Every inch of the walks was shaded by generously
spreading trees. To the right lay great fields of corn and wheat, which fed the college

tables; at the left was a spacious playground where happy lads were tossing baseballs, and the other paraphernalia of youth."[23]

The good Father McWilliams was much less lyrical. For him, Seton Hall was a "priest factory" and its appearance "far from impressive. . . . It was a three-story brownstone, and in its time it must have been a substantial edifice; but, in mine, I never wanted to live there forever."[24] Moreover, he considered the majority of seminary rules as "witless."[25]

The historian Durant described himself as "in the flowing cassock and the square biretta, looking a little more pompous and learned than before, walking with the consciousness of my augmented importance in the history of mankind." Like many other theology students at the seminary, he had additional responsibilities as a teacher in the college. He lamented that, unlike a salaried lay teacher, he "lost the privileges and emoluments of a professor." He recalled, "Instead of eating the cannibalistic meals that had been served at the teacher's table, I had to accustom myself to the ascetic diet of the seminarians' refectory." The refectory was in the basement.

The seminarians' accommodations drew the scorn of both Durant and McWilliams. They shared "small bare rooms" and lived on the third floor "directly under the roof, where we suffocated in summer and shivered in winter. . . . Many a day found the water in the wash-bowl frozen to the bottom. It required a great deal of religion to get out of bed on those icy mornings; and as I [Durant] had a little less than the others, I suffered accordingly. There was one room that was colder than all the others. We called it 'the freezer.'" And one sub-zero afternoon, someone hung a red ball outside the door and a sign that said, "Skating here today."[26]

With the other seminarians, Durant "rose at five, washed in a minute, dressed in two, and then hurried down to the chapel for first mass. Very often we stayed for a second mass, making an almost continuous hour on our knees. Every knee in the seminary was calloused with devotion, and almost every back was bent with the humility of prayer. Then we were free till breakfast time, which came at half-past-seven, and found us ravenous."

Monsignor McWilliams described the first hours of the seminary day with less piety than Mr. Durant.

> Your brain is still heavy with sleep, and you are trying to
> meditate as "Little Napoleon," the rector, walks up and
> down the dimly lit aisle, and you hope that he will not
> call upon you to explain the points of the meditation.
> Your relief is great when he does not call on you,
> and you know you are safe for at least one more day.
>
> The rector now goes over the whole meditation,
> extracting all the spiritual meat from it and making

pertinent remarks, or applicable remarks, about current affairs. Mass begins at 6:30. Other Masses begin at the side altars. You are careful to make your thanksgiving in the Mass that follows.[27]

Classes began at nine when all the seminarians "crowded into a little room on the top floor" for class, the "cycle." The first class was dogmatic theology, the professor, Father Thomas McLaughlin. Durant wrote that McLaughlin "had just returned from a long stay in Austria; and he combined with a Teutonic patience in study and teaching, a tendency to speak English with queer Teutonic idioms—ending every fifth sentence with 'the same.' But there never was a purer heart or a kinder one."[28] McWilliams' comments on McLaughlin were less generous. As was then and remains the custom today, seminarians genially nicknamed their professors.

> Father Thomas McLaughlin, a walking encyclopedia and the personification of respect for his superiors, was stout. So we called him "Slitz" [sic]—never, of course, to his face . . . his great gift was not teaching. His job was to blue-pencil assignments, and how that pencil whirled! No matter how good the work submitted Slitz lacerated the sentences until the papers looked like a cross section of the venous system of a frog. One day two of the local wits submitted, as papers, direct quotations from Ben-Hur and from Cardinal Newman. Sure enough—when they returned, Slitz had mangled the imperishable prose so badly that only surgery and a plaster cast would fit it together again.[29]

After the first class, the "seminarian professors" (both Durant and McWilliams fell into this category) went off to the college to teach. At eleven, Monsignor Mooney, the president and rector, held class in moral theology. Durant described him as "a teacher who quite came up to Nietzsche's ideal, of exacting much and praising little. He assigned huge lessons of the most abominable subtleties, and expected us to recite and discuss the lesson in Latin." Most had "a terrible time" of it, and learned to hate Latin. Even those quite proficient in Latin occasionally fell, to Mooney's great disappointment, and received a blistering rebuke. Mooney could turn to a student "like a dying Caesar to his Brutus, with the stern words: *Neque tu hanc rem melius studisti* (Neither have *you* studied this matter too well)." [30]

After these trials, it was time for 15 minutes of prayer in the chapel, the angelus, and then lunch in the refectory. According to Durant, "While the sinful business of eating went on in silence, a seminarian read Alzog's *History of the Church*, or some similar sedative." Finally, there was an hour of recreation. Billiards, chess, checkers, and the piano were available. Some played "handball or baseball with due seminarian dignity, holding up our black skirts as we chased the ball over the field."[31]

At two o'clock, it was time for ecclesiastical history, taught by Father John A. Duffy. He also taught rhetoric and was considered to be a most impressive speaker. But Duffy was sensitive and "anyone who asked a question risked being drawn and quartered because Father Duffy looked upon all such interruptions as a clever plot to trap him. The sarcasm that followed a question would scorch the paint on the classroom walls."[32] The Church would reward Duffy by making him bishop of Syracuse, New York, and later of Buffalo.

Among the other professors were Father Dauenhauer, who taught liturgy, Church history, and economics. He was "kind, genial, and a general favorite. . . . Yet he was never known to us by any other name than 'Dingle.'" Father Frank McCue was called "Baldy" because he wore a wig. McWilliams described, "His forte was the ability to simplify a problem. If, when you left his class, you didn't know the answer, it wasn't Baldy's fault. And he kept his simple poise to the end. As he lay dying, he summoned his old friend, Father Barret, and named the ministers he wanted at his funeral."[33]

Father Cloherty was regarded as "the best of all the teachers." A former Christian Brother, he studied for the priesthood rather late in life. "If any man could ever say, 'Teaching is my business,'" McWilliams recalled, "Father Cloherty was the man. Still, we called him 'Pop' all the time, but it was intended as a term of affection."[34]

Three o'clock began another hour of teaching in the college for those so chosen. Recreation came again between four and five. At five, seminarians walked the gravel paths beneath the trees and recited the rosary, and then went to the chapel for prayers. According to Durant, "This was one of the pleasantest parts of the day, for it gave us a chance to think of things we had had no time for during the other hours." Supper began at six, then study, meditation and final prayers in the chapel at nine, and lights out at 9:30.[35] Mooney adjusted the schedule a bit, introducing choral recitation of the rosary at 3:30 and, between five and six, spiritual reading and a conference by the rector.[36]

Thursday was a free day, but hardly a day for free exploration. McWilliams recalls that the "biggest treat we were permitted was to take a long walk with the prefect. . . . It was no fun. Still, when Thursday came, we marched two by two with the prefect up hill and down dale, not knowing where we were going or 'whyest.'"[37]

The Sunday schedule was lighter, but demanding. The seminarians "prayed twice as much as usual; but also we had an afternoon's holiday." The seminarians, after their early Mass, "knelt within the altar-railing, in . . . starched white surplices, to sing the High Mass in all the grandeur of its ritual." The dinner was better than on weekdays and without "the distraction of exciting literature." After lunch they could leave the property for three hours for walks in the neighborhood and the village: "We dressed in our finest black suits, our stiffest Roman collars, our shiniest boots, and our best derbies, and went out into the magnificent country that surrounded the college site." They returned at 5 p.m. for the rosary, followed by vespers, "a glorious ceremony for the eyes and ears."[38]

While Durant did not speak in any detail of the spiritual life of the seminary, other than describing the daily exercises, McWilliams showed a desire to grow in the spiritual life. "I learned that we cannot seek ourselves and expect to find God," he wrote. He admitted that he "needed a radical transformation of character, and the only way to find it was by self-renunciation, by living every moment according to the crucifying standards set forth by Christ in the Gospel."[39]

Frequent confession was one road to holiness. The seven priests at Seton Hall, college and seminary, served as confessors. Bishop O'Connor reported to Rome that seminarians confessed at least once weekly, all received Holy Communion several times a week, and many received daily. They participated in a spiritual retreat at the beginning of the academic year and another at the conclusion of the academic year. The bishop continued to preside at theological examinations.

In accord with canon law, tonsure and minor orders were conferred at the end of the second year of theological studies, subdiaconate at the end of the third, diaconate at the beginning and, for most, priesthood at the end of the fourth year.[40] For McWilliams, the cutting of hair at tonsure indicated that the "seminarian now bears the likeness of a crown of thorns around his head."[41] Not without humor, he referred to the promise of celibacy as "the putting on of the tin pants."[42] Each year, several fourth-year theologians were ordained priests in December.[43] McWilliams was among those ordained in December 1918. During the summer, seminarians were under the supervision of their pastors, who furnished the rector with a detailed report of their activities.

Farewell to a Rebel

When Durant decided to leave in January 1911, Mooney treated him kindly, and "as if to ease the transition for me and my parents he asked me to resume my former duties as a lay teacher in the college. I gladly agreed, for I loved Seton Hall."[44] He continued to teach until the end of the semester. Durant was grateful to Mooney whom he considered to have been "my greatest incentive to live an honorable life."[45] However, when he left, he noted, "In those final months we had drifted far apart, and now we seldom did more than exchange the courtesies of the day. . . . When we parted it was almost coldly, as if we understood, by some vague fatalism, that we would never see each other again."[46]

A year later, on January 7, 1912, Durant lectured at the Francisco Ferrer Association in New York on "The Origins of Religion" and "The Evolution of Sex, Homosexualism, Autoeroticism, and Malthusiasm." In his lectures, he stated that sex was one of the origins of religion, likening church steeples to phallic symbols. This was bound to draw the attention of authorities. A week later, he read a headline in the

Newark Evening News: "CENSURE FOR FERRER ALLY: Monsignor Mooney Says Arlington Man's Lectures Excommunicate Him." Durant believed that he had incurred an "episcopal excommunication,"[47] but this was not the case.

Mooney, concerned that Durant's former association with Seton Hall would be a cause of scandal, had told the newspaper, "These lectures which are being delivered by Mr. Durant constitute an apostasy from the Catholic religion and entail excommunication. Nevertheless Mr. Durant continues to act in his home town not only as a consistent, but even as a devout, Catholic."[48] His mother broke down; his father ordered him to leave the house. So ended Will Durant's association with Immaculate Conception Seminary.

For many years there was a legend among the priests of the diocese that, after Durant left the seminary, Monsignor Mooney locked the Seton Hall library, and left it locked until he retired—lest any other seminarian read himself out of the faith.[49]

Mooney, in spite of these sad and bitter words, always claimed Durant's affection. In his autobiographical work *Transition*, Durant wrote extensively about his early experiences. He gives us a wonderful word picture of the young Father Mooney during his days as pastor in Kearny, a glimpse into the personality of a rector and president that we lack for almost all other holders of these offices.

> He came to us from several years of graduate study
> in Italy; and though he had gone an Irishman, he had
> returned looking almost Italian,—dark and fiery and full
> of energy, like another Corsican. What a vivid picture he
> made as he galloped through the parish on his prancing
> horse! He rode like a gentleman born to the hunt.
> He had the small feet and hands of an aristocrat, and
> the alert and mobile face of a poet; yet in his thin lips
> and sparkling eyes there was an omen of anger and
> power which enabled him, despite his boyish stature,
> to dominate almost everyone who came into his life.
> We did not know then that a painful disease was weakening
> him, and shutting him out from that high career for
> which his energy and his intellect had fitted him. . . .
> He did not hurry through Mass like so many priests,
> who seem to be thinking of their postponed breakfasts
> when they are changing the bread and wine into the
> body of God; he gave us every word distinctly, so that
> the sonorous Latin became a stately chant as he
> pronounced it.[50]

McWilliams was laudatory of Mooney but not as hagiographic as Durant. He wrote that Mooney was "short and had large brown eyes and a distant dignity—a dignity that kept you at more than arm's length from him. He was more than a priest; he was a priestly priest. He was never a signpost, pointing the way; instead he walked the way of Christ, and everyone in Immaculate Conception Seminary knew it."

Mooney was a man possessing "a fine intellect, and he was an excellent grammarian." But he "lived a lonely, isolated life, and he built the walls which kept other people from him. You could respect him. You could feel a reverence for the ascetic life he had chosen. But he never encouraged you to like him. Those who did not like him complained that the Monsignor was on top of Mount Parnassus most of the time. Maybe. If so, he climbed it himself and elected to stay there."

Mooney did not fraternize either with the clergy or the laity, and when he was in company, he was ill at ease. Like Durant, McWilliams referred to Mooney's illnesses, noting that he "had a poor stomach . . . and many a night he suffered the pain in silence and read and read and read until the wee hours. Still, the next day, when he chose a walking companion from among the quaking students, the lucky boy almost always heard a wonderful dissertation on a book. As he walked he talked. And as he talked, he coughed. The cough sounded like 'pum-pum'; so, as you might guess, he was known to us as 'pum-pum Jimmy Mooney.' This wasn't intended to be derogatory. Far from it. When he approached, or started a tour of the corridors, he was always kind enough to render the warning 'pum-pum,' and, if anything was amiss, the boys were now alerted and had a chance to straighten matters out before his arrival."[51]

Chapter Thirteen

The Fire of 1909

Mooney faced greater difficulties than problem seminarians. The college mourned the passing of its last surviving founder, Bishop McQuaid, who died at the age of 85 on January 18, 1909. Then, on March 27, 1909, Seton Hall once again experienced a devastating fire. It began shortly after midnight in the basement of the college building. The flames spread rapidly. Fortunately, Austin Gibbon, professor of Latin in the college, returning to Seton Hall late that Saturday night, noticed a bright light in the basement of the college building. Upon investigation, he found the entire basement ablaze. He awakened Monsignor Mooney and Father McLaughlin, who immediately telephoned the fire department. They then raced to the dormitories and raised the alarm.

The prefects took charge and the students evacuated the building. According to the *Newark Evening News,* "Flames were already beginning to ascend through the corridors which were filled with smoke, and it was necessary to descend by means of the fire escapes. When the South Orange Fire Department arrived, the flames had made such headway that the Library building was threatened. Help was immediately summoned from Newark and Orange."[1] Under the direction of the seminarian prefects, the students organized themselves into groups and removed many of the books from the library, which adjoined the college building and was exposed to heat, smoke, and water. It was about 3 a.m. before the fire was brought under control.[2]

Durant leaves us a colorful recollection of his experience during and after the fire.

> I was alone in my room at the time, and did not awake
> till I heard rather unusual noises outside my door.
> "What the devil are you doing with that hose? Bring it

here, damn you!" "Hose"? And "devil"? And "damn"?
I passed from sleep into amazement. I peered out into
the corridor, and found it filled with firemen. Apparently
they were letting the building burn while they discussed
ways and means and displayed their vocabulary; it turned
out later that the fire-alarm had interrupted their weekly
exhilarations. I smelled smoke and whiskey, and heard
the shouts of seminarians and students on the campus
below. I dressed, hurried down into the open, and saw
that half the institution was in flames. I must have been
sleeping well, for a seminarian vowed that he had knocked
on my door to warn me.[3]

Durant was enchanted by the fire as "an esthetic spectacle." "It looks like
Hell, doesn't it?" he observed to a fellow seminarian. He realized his remark was
"frivolous and profane," and also inopportune. "While it yet echoed in my ears I
found myself looking into the stern face of Father Morley [Mooney] himself. In the
dark I had not noticed that he was directly in front of me. I bowed my head and
shrank into silence for the rest of the night."[4]

The college building, already burned in 1886, was destroyed. Only the walls
were left standing. The library suffered only slight damage. The seminary was untouched.
Most importantly, no lives were lost.

The next day saw chaos: "Straw hats, overalls, bandanna handkerchiefs
and other nondescript clothing were in evidence at the College this morning."
More fortunate students and faculty lent clothing to those who had lost everything.
"Permission to go home," reported the *Newark Evening News,* "was given to students
by Dr. Mooney who supplied the money for carfare. Trolleys and trains were filled
with students wearing clothing too large or too small, and misfit shoes but they did
not seem much concerned with their losses."[5] As in the case of the fire of 1886, the
facilities of the seminary were pressed into service to meet the emergency.[6]

A New College Building—Seminarian Laborers

Just a week after the fire, the trustees approved the construction of a new and much
larger college building.[7] Less than two months later, construction began and was
completed in April 1910.[8] The new building, named Mooney Hall, provided
administrative offices, classrooms, private student rooms, dormitories, a study hall,
and additional faculty quarters. The first floor of the old college building was
reconstructed and converted into an auditorium.

The seminarians were drafted to assist the masons and carpenters. They
"made cement, and hammered nails, and built chairs and desks, and painted walls
and floors, and for a month or two exchanged the intellectual for the practical life."

They did not complain: "After the minutiae of moral theology it was a pleasure even to hammer one's thumb." In fact they took pride in their work. According to Durant, "When the building was finished we looked upon it as our co-operative product." He later confessed that "to this day I pass it (safely anonymous) with a strange feeling of affection and pride."[9]

Slow and Steady Growth

The seminary grew quietly in the second decade of the twentieth century. In 1911, Bishop O'Connor officially designated Seton Hall's high school and college departments as the preparatory seminary of the diocese. He also prescribed that all aspirants to the major seminary must enroll, either as day students or boarders, at Seton Hall.[10]

In 1907 the seminary enrolled 35 students. The number grew to 58 in 1919. In a building designed to house 30, the conditions were quite crowded. In 1919, the trustees discussed an addition to the seminary that would house 70 students, but the matter "was laid over for the present."[11] That same year, in his quinquennial report to the Holy See, O'Connor mentioned the plans and the increase of numbers of seminarians: "It is necessary that the diocese provide a new [seminary] building. The number of students increases every year. We will begin a new building in the next year that will be sufficient for the number of students."[12]

At the 1920 meeting of the trustees, a motion was carried recommending "to the Right Reverend Bishop and to the consultors of the diocese that an assessment be levied by the bishop on all the parishes of the diocese in order to raise a sufficient sum of money to erect a new seminary building adequate to accommodate at least 100 seminarians and provide rooms for the professors."[13] The matter was to be discussed again at the next year's trustees meeting but any decision was postponed.[14]

After more than 14 years, Monsignor Mooney stepped down from the offices of rector and president on August 2, 1922. His health never had been good. He had endured a fire and overseen the construction of Mooney Hall and Bayley Hall, still fixtures on the Seton Hall campus. He had added a modern farm building as well, and liquidated the debt incurred by their construction.

To his great credit, he left the institution not only debt free for the first time in its existence, but miraculously operating in the black. The treasurer's report for 1920–21 reported receipts of $227,000, expenditures of $176,000, and a balance on hand of $51,000. The seminary had done little to contribute to this surplus, providing only $15,000 for the education of 58 seminarians.[15]

A Teutonic Irishman

With the departure of Monsignor Mooney, a new figure emerged on the scene. Thomas H. McLaughlin literally would rule the seminary for the next 15 years.

He would carry the nickname "Schlitz," given him by seminarians in his first years of teaching, throughout his time as rector and his reign as bishop of Paterson, New Jersey. McLaughlin was born in New York City on July 15, 1881. His family moved to Montclair, New Jersey, when he was 14, but he continued his high school education at St. Francis Xavier College in Manhattan, and graduated with a bachelor of arts degree in 1901.

Bishop O'Connor sent him to the Jesuit theological faculty at the University of Innsbruck, where he was ordained in 1904. After ordination, McLaughlin remained at Innsbruck to receive the doctorate in sacred theology in 1908. After several months in St. Michael's Parish in Jersey City, he was assigned to Seton Hall College as vice president, also teaching classical languages, English, and philosophy in the college, and scripture, dogmatic theology, homiletics, and canon law in the seminary. In August 1922, he was named president of the college and rector of the seminary. The next year he was invested as a domestic prelate.[16] He took this title seriously, on formal occasions wearing the purple stockings and silver-buckled shoes of his rank.[17]

Not one to waste time, within a year McLaughlin sent out a circular letter to the priests of the diocese appealing for $65,000 for new equipment for classrooms, laboratories, the library, the auditorium, and the gymnasium, as well as a new organ for the chapel. He described the college as a place where young Catholic men may "imbibe the spirit of truth, guided by faith, together with a proper appreciation of the sciences and literature, without danger of being contaminated by skepticism and the lack of solid religious conception so marked in many seats of learning without the pale of the Church's influence."[18] His appeal generated almost $53,000, while the improvements he undertook cost almost $80,000.

With regard to the seminary, McLaughlin had to fill several faculty positions. When he assumed the rectorate, there were just three priests on the faculty: Monsignor Mooney, his predecessor who soon would leave, Father Dauenhauer, and himself. In 1923, Reverend Thomas Aloysius Boland, S.T.L., and Reverend Thomas F. Burke, S.T.D., joined the faculty. Father Boland was assigned to teach scripture, canon law, moral theology, and ethics. Father Burke taught moral theology, canon law, and pastoral theology, and served as vice rector for two years. He became rector of the North American College in 1925. After 10 years, he was named pastor of Holy Trinity Parish in Hackensack, New Jersey, where he died in 1951.

Thomas Boland was born in 1896 in Orange, New Jersey. He completed high school studies at Xavier High School in New York and college studies at Seton Hall. He studied for the priesthood at the North American College in Rome, receiving the licentiate in sacred theology (S.T.L.) degree. In 1938 he was named chancellor of the diocese and, in 1940, auxiliary bishop and rector of the seminary. After seven years as rector, he became bishop of Paterson in 1947, then archbishop of Newark in 1953. He retired in 1974 and died in 1979.[19] When Boland was installed as bishop of Paterson in 1947, the printer put "S.T.D."[20] (doctor of sacred theology) after his name, although he had never received that degree. It so remained thereafter.

In 1925, Reverend Michael J. Whelan, M.A., was assigned as the seminary's first spiritual director and professor of ascetics. At the same time it was announced that two faculty members would serve as "ordinary confessors," although a seminarian remained free to choose any priest in the house as his confessor.[21] Whelan served in this post until his death in 1937.[22]

Reverend Michael E. Donnelly, M.A., born in 1897 and ordained at Louvain in 1923, joined the faculty that year to teach Church history and serve as vice rector. Reverend Francis J. Monaghan, D.D., born in 1890 and ordained in Rome in 1915, came to the seminary in 1926 as professor of dogmatic theology and metaphysics. After serving as president of Seton Hall from 1933 to 1936, he was named coadjutor bishop of Ogdensburg, New York, and died there as bishop in 1942.

McLaughlin had high expectations of his professors. In a 1925 conference for the priests he reminded them that the seminary was "the most important post in the diocese," and they were called to "personal sacrifice and service" and responsible to see that "ecclesiastical discipline is observed, [and] that the seminarians are correctly guided and taught." They were to observe priestly decorum "even in minutiae." Among the minutiae was the observance of silence in the corridors after the seminarians retired. He added that in all of this they always were to be "cheerful."[23]

Most professors served until they were assigned as pastors. Pastorates then were allocated according to a seniority system. When a priest's "turn" came, he was assigned to a parish. For most professors, this was considered to be a promotion. As Father James Corrigan had written, parish life was much more attractive than college or seminary life. This resulted in a continual search for qualified professors, which was not as difficult as it might seem. At this time an individual could teach many disciplines with only an M.A. or an S.T.L. degree. Such would not be the case in the near future.

Occasionally a professor ran afoul of the rector. Father Francis Mestice, who instructed the seminarians in Italian, made the mistake of bringing Italian newspaper clippings to the seminary to aid in his instruction. McLaughlin courteously reminded Father Mestice that "your reverence, with the laudable purpose of creating interest as well as instruction in the language, have [sic] brought newspapers to class. . . . Now according to the rules of the seminary NO newspaper or periodicals save those which have come thro [sic] the house are permitted to the seminarians."[24]

Mestice knew how to placate the rector. He explained to McLaughlin that he had not brought newspapers, only short clippings, clippings recounting the signing of the Lateran Treaty between Italy and the Holy See. He promised to restrict his reading material to *The Imitation of Christ,* the biography of Pope Pius XI, and the catechism compiled by Pope Pius X. He closed with the words: "Hoping that Your Reverence will rely [sic] full confidence in my teaching, as for the past, with a quiet conscience, I humbly kiss your right hand and with a true, filial obedience, I am, Very Sincerely yours in J. C."[25] The rector was appeased.

Seminarians

McLaughlin was a stickler for detail and expected the same of the seminarians. During one conference, he criticized the seminarians for "an attitude of negligence . . . in matters of neatness and ecclesiastical decorum . . . lateness . . . and table manners." Some of this criticism may have resulted from one of his surprise inspections of seminarians' rooms. The house prefect's journal notes the "inspection of rooms by the Rt. Rev. Rector and as a consequence a talk was given by him at 8 p.m." The next day, the prefect wrote that "seminarians cleaned their rooms."[26]

As the seminarians were about to depart for their Christmas vacation in 1926, McLaughlin reminded them of their spiritual duties and warned them that they were not to attend any parties except with their confreres, and they were to guard their speech and never to discuss ecclesiastical affairs with "outsiders."[27]

The rector occasionally was flexible. Seminarians sometimes were allowed to go shopping in the village, to play ball, and to attend college football games. A special favor was granted on January 24, 1925, when, "on account of the eclipse of the sun, the seminarians were allowed to stay in the recreation room till 9:35 p.m."[28]

Chapter Fourteen

A New Seminary—But Where?

It would fall to Monsignor McLaughlin to address the increasing number of seminarians and the resultant crowding. The trustees several times had advocated a new building for the seminary. Such an edifice not only would provide adequate quarters and classrooms for seminarians and faculty, but free the seminary building for the increasing needs of the college. At their 1921 meeting they discussed the location of such a new building and the amount to be expended. They wanted a building that would be "sufficiently large . . . to accommodate the number of seminarians required by the diocese in years to come." They further advised that "no expense should be spared" and "its appointments should be of the highest order of excellence."[1]

Four years later, in 1925, the trustees resolved to "empower" Bishop O'Connor and Monsignor McLaughlin "to secure the services of a responsible architect to draw plans and prepare specifications for a new building on the college property . . . to serve the purpose of the Diocesan Seminary of the Immaculate Conception . . . and to let contracts for the construction and equipment of the said building." They also resolved that financial support come from fund-raising from the diocese and from "the collection made throughout the diocese about seven years ago for the seminary building fund."[2] This fund contained almost $480,000.[3]

The architectural firm of Fanning and Shaw drew up plans that "envisioned a four-story, *E*-shaped building, with a 208 foot frontage and side wings of 112 feet, providing 141 single rooms for students. The center wing would have extended 144 feet and would have contained, on the second floor, a chapel to seat 162, and on the third floor, a single amphitheatre to seat 105 theologians, and two classrooms, each for 42 philosophers."[4] This plan, because of its single amphitheatre, condemned the seminarians to continue the "cycled" course in theology. It did not materialize for a number of reasons.

Roman Direction

The Catholic world and the seminary world had changed significantly in the preceding decades. The Church in the United States long had been a "missionary" institution, under the direction of the Sacred Congregation for the Propagation of the Faith, "Propaganda Fide." It was governed by its own particular law formulated in the provincial and plenary councils of Baltimore. Before the Third Plenary Council of Baltimore in 1885, seminaries, under the direction of the local bishop, had more or less followed the general Church law concerning seminaries drawn up at the Council of Trent and promulgated in 1563. After 1885, they sought to conform to the legislation of the Third Plenary Council of Baltimore that applied to seminaries. The seminary at Seton Hall adhered to this legislation rather assiduously.

The First Vatican Council in 1870 issued the dogmatic constitution *Pastor aeternus*, which stated that the Roman Pontiff possessed "episcopal and immediate" jurisdiction "not only in matters pertaining to faith and morals, but also in those pertaining to the discipline and government of the Church throughout the world."[5] The universal jurisdiction of the pope soon extended to seminary studies.

In 1879, Pope Leo XIII's encyclical *Aeterni Patris* directed seminaries throughout the world to follow the philosophy of St. Thomas Aquinas. In 1893, his encyclical *Providentissimus Deus* provided regulations regarding biblical studies. Leo XIII also was concerned about the inviolability of the internal forum, the "seal of the confessional." He called into question the then-current method of spiritual direction, in which rectors and faculty served as spiritual directors and confessors of seminarians.[6]

Popes Leo XIII and Saint Pius X greatly influenced Catholic spirituality and, thereby, seminary practice. Each strengthened Marian devotion and other forms of piety throughout their reigns.[7] Pius X radically changed eucharistic spirituality through several decrees on frequent reception of Communion. The most important of these was the decree *Sacra tridentina synodus*[8] of 1905. He also had a significant impact on seminary teaching, requiring in 1910 that all seminary professors take an oath against modernism.[9]

Pope Pius X transformed the American Church in 1908 by the apostolic constitution *Sapienti consilio*, which ended its "missionary" status. It no longer was subject to the direction of the Sacred Congregation for the Propagation of the Faith. Its business henceforth was to be directed to relevant offices of the Roman Curia.[10]

The most influential institutional reform of Pius X was the codification of canon law, begun with the motu proprio *Arduum sane munus* in 1904. The work of revision would not be completed until 1917 with the promulgation of the Code of Canon Law by Pope Benedict XV in the apostolic constitution *Providentissima mater ecclesia*. Two years previously, in 1915, Benedict XV had consolidated and strengthened papal oversight of seminaries in a new dicastery, the Sacred Congregation of Seminaries and Universities.[11] The Holy See, through the new congregation and the new code, would direct the future of seminary training.

Canons 1352 through 1383 codified much of the recent papal legislation on seminaries. They provided much more detailed norms than the Council of Trent. The bishop of the diocese remained responsible for the seminary's administration and its internal rules but always was to act within the framework of legislation from the Holy See. He was urged to visit the seminary frequently and to be familiar with all aspects of the seminary and its students. The code even enumerated the officers of the seminary: rector, vice rector, econome (or treasurer), and spiritual director.[12]

The code and later directives contained very specific regulations regarding the separation of the internal and external forums. Each seminary was to have a spiritual director who would have no other duties and readily be available to the students. The seminary also was to appoint two ordinary confessors. In diocesan seminaries, it was specified that the ordinary confessors be from religious orders. Additional extraordinary confessors, from the faculty if necessary, were to be designated as well.[13]

In order to safeguard the confidentiality of their relationship with the seminarians, the spiritual director and the confessors were not to take part in discussions concerning promotion to Holy Orders. The rector, for similar reasons, was not to engage in spiritual direction or to hear the confessions of seminarians, except in the most extraordinary circumstances.

The seminarian's daily schedule of prayer was delineated. There was to be morning and evening prayer in common, designated time for mental prayer, confession at least weekly, frequent Communion, an annual retreat, and a weekly spiritual conference.

The major seminary was to have a six-year program. The code prescribed at least two years of specialized philosophical studies, based on the philosophy of St. Thomas Aquinas, and four years of theological studies. In the two years of philosophical studies, the seminarians also were to study the vernacular language, Latin, Greek, history, natural sciences, and mathematics.

During the four years of theology, in addition to dogmatic and moral theology, the code required study of scripture, Church history, canon law, liturgy, sacred eloquence, and chant. A course in pastoral theology was to include instruction in hearing confessions, teaching catechetics, visiting the sick, and attending the dying.[14]

Following the code, several instructions from Rome spelled out its requirements with additional directives. In his motu proprio *Bibliorum scientiam*, Pope Pius XI required seminary professors of scripture to have degrees from Rome's Pontifical Biblical Institute. In instructions in 1926 and 1928, the Sacred Congregation of Seminaries and Universities required the introduction of courses in catechetics and in the theology, liturgy, and history of the Eastern churches.[15]

Rome Speaks to American Seminaries

In order to monitor and ensure compliance with its directives, the congregation issued the decree *Quo uberiore* in 1924, requiring bishops to submit triennial reports on all seminaries in their dioceses. The bishops were to list seminaries' faculty and their qualifications, textbooks, enrollment, course offerings, and extracurricular activities of seminarians.[16] After the first reports were submitted, the cardinals of the congregation made their observations known in a letter to the American bishops from the apostolic delegate, Archbishop Pietro Fumasoni-Biondi, on May 26, 1928.

The letter criticized preparatory seminaries that operated as day schools. These were to be converted to boarding schools so that the students "so easily led away by the bad example of others" might have their vocation "safeguarded more adequately." They were to be "day and night under the watchful care of responsible superiors."[17]

Major Changes in Seminary Life

The emphasis on a spiritual director was probably the most important portion of the congregation's observations transmitted through Fumasoni-Biondi. It left an imprint on seminary training that endures to this day. It established a new and autonomous office within the seminary structure and ensured the security of the internal forum.

The spiritual director was to be a person as competent in spiritual matters as the other professors were in their subjects. He was to have no other responsibilities in the seminary "since he must devote all his time to the things of God and of the soul." His major responsibility was to know the life and character of the seminarians so as to be able to give them prudent advice regarding their vocation. He was to dissuade from continuing those who were not called to priesthood and encourage *fortiter et suaviter* those who were called "to ever greater efforts toward perfection."[18]

The spiritual director was to assist the seminarians to develop their spiritual lives through examination of conscience and the development of habits of mental prayer. Mental prayer received special and detailed attention from the congregation. The spiritual director was instructed

> …not only to preach the need of prayer, but especially of mental prayer, and to teach students the method of practicing such prayer. He should select for them a suitable meditation book which all will use when they make their meditation in common in the chapel. At this exercise, too, he should assist personally. It is understood that, from time to time, instead of reading the meditation, he himself shall give an appropriate

meditation to the seminarians. If the spiritual director follows these rules he will succeed in establishing the students in the habit of daily meditation. And he will make secure his own work in their souls, especially for the time after ordination when his seminarians are thrown out into the many occupations and distractions which surround the work of the sacred ministry in the United States.[19]

The congregation also specified that Latin was not only to be taught but was to be the language of instruction and examination in philosophy, theology, and canon law. Canon law was to be given an important place in the curriculum and must be taught by a person with advanced training in this discipline.

Fumasoni-Biondi also found fault with seminarians developing athletic interests and skills beyond normal physical exercise. He disapproved of allowing the public to view athletic events in which seminarians participated. Moreover, he emphasized that the seminaries must ensure modesty in their bathing arrangements.

These instructions from Rome would influence the development of Immaculate Conception Seminary and all American seminaries in many ways. In 1925, three years before Fumasoni-Biondi's letter, Reverend Michael Whelan had been appointed the first spiritual director of the seminary. Mount St. Mary's Seminary in Emmitsburg, Maryland, where the same priest held the offices of president of the college and rector of the seminary, was directed to separate the offices in order to comply with the code.[20] Seton Hall and the seminary would soon follow suit.

The arrangements for ecclesiastical aspirants at the high school and college at Seton Hall clearly did not conform to the code and the subsequent directives. In Newark, there would be sporadic directives requiring those in the high school and college years to live at Seton Hall. Over the following years, additional regulations served to separate "church students" as much as possible from "secular students." No more would seminarians be able to serve as "ringers" on Seton Hall's sports teams. This situation would not be fully resolved until the establishment of the College Seminary at St. Andrew's Hall at Seton Hall University in 1973.

In Boston a similar arrangement had many pre-seminarians receiving training at the Jesuit Boston College, across the road from St. John's Seminary. The formidable Cardinal O'Connell was enraged that the congregation should criticize him and he frequently, at the Catholic University trustees meetings, denounced Cardinal Ernesto Ruffini, the prefect of the congregation.[21] Archbishop John Timothy McNicholas of Cincinnati faithfully reported O'Connell's fulminations to the apostolic delegate.[22]

Decision to Move

The Roman emphasis in favor of the isolation of seminary training led to the relocation of several seminaries at this time. The idea of relocation was not unique to Newark. Kenrick Seminary in St. Louis, Missouri, moved to a suburban area in 1916. Cincinnati's Mount St. Mary's of the West moved to Norwood, Ohio, in 1923. St. Mary's Seminary, the first United States seminary, moved to a new and expanded location in Roland Park, a Baltimore suburb, in 1925. In 1931, the Pontifical College Josephinum moved from Columbus, Ohio, to a semi-rural setting.[23]

Although *The Setonian* reported on May 21, 1926, that "plans for the new seminary are practically complete and it is hoped that work may soon begin on that building," Bishop O'Connor and Monsignor McLaughlin were moving in another direction.

At the direction of Bishop O'Connor, McLaughlin drafted a proposal outlining the rationale for a separation of the seminary and the college and for moving the seminary to "a place more removed from suburban congestion, preferably in Morris or Sussex Counties."[24]

His first reason was that such a move would be in conformity with "the regulation of the Code of Canon Law and the directives of the Congregation of Seminaries which demand a separation between secular and ecclesiastical students." The cost of a new building at Seton Hall would be at least $850,000 exclusive of heating, electric fixtures, and furnishings. Moreover, no location at Seton Hall "would ensure the privacy that would be requisite for proper seminary training." If the property purchased did not contain buildings adaptable for seminary use, he suggested that the plans for the seminary at Seton Hall be adapted and used on the new site.

McLaughlin believed that the separation of college and seminary was inevitable in order to have a seminary in line with canon law. In addition, Seton Hall needed the current seminary building to provide additional facilities to attract students who were not studying for the priesthood. Another advantage would be that a rural setting would provide a permanent residence for the seminarians, including during the summer, a "feature required by the Holy See."

The specific norms for philosophical studies influenced the decision as well. McLaughlin noted that "as the Holy See itself has pointed out, the course in philosophy required for the aspirant for the priesthood must be of a deeper and more intensive type than that for the educated layman and touches problems whose knowledge is not necessary for seculars."

He recognized the shortcomings of the often-criticized but long-standing custom of seminarians acting as prefects. With blunt honesty, he commented that "there is no use blinking [*sic*] the fact that the present method of student prefects is not ideal. For a whole year they are practically unable to center their attention upon their studies or spiritual training . . . they have not the poise to meet the situations that arise . . . they are only two years removed from the young men whom they are expected to govern and guide, and on account of the irregularity in hours at times necessitated by a prefect's duty, they are not able to respond and provide for their own spiritual advancement in a way that is desirable." Not surprisingly, given the situation at Emmitsburg, McLaughlin also suggested that although the offices of president and rector should remain united for a short period, they must be separated as soon as possible.

Finally, he hoped that at least 100 acres would be purchased so that "we would again be in a position to maintain cattle and perhaps produce certain staples that would accrue to the advantage of both institutions." He believed that the diocese could secure the land, erect the buildings, and provide water, light, and heat for about $600,000 to $700,000.

The Darlington Estate

Late in 1925, McLaughlin requested that the real estate firm of F. M. Crawley and Brothers of Montclair, New Jersey, search for a suitable site for the seminary. The search extended to Essex, Sussex, and Bergen Counties. McLaughlin personally was involved, minutely examining the possible sites. Crawley recalled that McLaughlin "proved to be one of the greatest mountain climbers and estate hunters that I have ever met in the forty years of my activity in the realty business."[25]

They settled on a large estate in Hohokus (now Mahwah) Township in the Ramapo Valley of Bergen County. Fifteen magnificent homes, built by wealthy New Yorkers, lined Ramapo Valley Road. The estate was known as "Darlington," after A. B. Darling, who had previously owned the property. The real estate firm obtained an option to buy the property without divulging the future use of the property.

The estate was graced by a Jacobean mansion built by George Crocker. Crocker had spent $2 million on the 75-room mansion that he began in 1901 and finished in 1907. It was considered by architectural critics of the time as "a magnificent residence . . . among the finest country houses of America."[26] The mansion was modeled on Bramshill, one of the finest examples of Jacobean architecture in England. Bramshill was built for King James I's eldest son, Henry, Prince of Wales, who died at age 18 in 1612, shortly after the completion of Bramshill. The Darlington mansion was designed by architect James Brite.

In 1912, L. R. McCabe commented in *Architectural Record,* "No private house in the United States, perhaps, is so rich in carvings wrought by hand out of solid wood. Many varieties of wood contribute to the rich, somber beauty and solidity of the whole; American quartered white oak, English oak, cherry, Circassian walnut, English walnut and California redwoods."[27]

Crocker lived in his home for only two years, dying in 1909. Darlington then was sold to Emerson McMillan, who had made his fortune in gas and power enterprises. McMillan resided there until his death in 1922. Due to a depressed real estate market, his estate sold Darlington for $685,000 to a development company that had plans to create the Darlington Golf and Country Club. Among the officers of the development company was Mayor Frank Hague of Jersey City. The company went into receivership after two months[28] and the McMillan heirs regained the property through foreclosure.[29]

The condition of the grounds; the size of the estate, more than 1,000 acres; a private reservoir free from pollution; the woods, lanes, hills, and river; and the inspiring aspect of the property impressed the bishop and the consultors. However, while the magnificent building had many desirable features, in other respects it was scarcely suitable as a permanent residence building for students, apart from the fact that only a very limited number could be accommodated.[30]

On May 26, 1926, the consultors visited the property and voted for its purchase.[31] On June 3 the diocese signed a contract with the heirs of Emerson McMillan, and their interest in the will was signed over to the diocese the next day. Seton Hall's board of trustees met on June 9 and ratified the actions. The trustees also affirmed that "the faculty of the Seminary of the Immaculate Conception, as well as the student body, constitute, in educational matters, covered by the charter of Seton Hall College, an integral part of said institution" and that the rector of the seminary shall be a member of the board of trustees of the college.

They further directed that the "seminary accounts be kept separate and distinct from Seton Hall College, according to the provisions of canon law." The seminary burses, amounting to almost $172,000, were transferred to the seminary account. The seminary account was a separate account within the diocesan civil corporation.[32] The title was closed on July 15, 1926, for a net purchase price of just over $478,000.[33] It was a cash transaction, the money already collected and at hand.[34] The sum of $275,000 had been collected for the new seminary in 1914, and $200,000 was advanced from diocesan funds.[35]

The diocese moved quickly to effect the transfer. On October 4, 1926, Reverend Charles C. Demjanovich, the procurator, took up residence in the building and was joined by Monsignor McLaughlin from Monday to Wednesday.[36] Demjanovich oversaw the alterations necessary to ready the buildings for occupation by the seminary. On October 12, 1926, the combined ceremonies of the dedication of the seminary and the celebration of Bishop O'Connor's golden jubilee of priesthood were celebrated at the new site.[37] McLaughlin considered the facilities transitional from the beginning "till such time as a proper ecclesiastical structure shall have been reared and ample chapel and administrative facilities provided."[38]

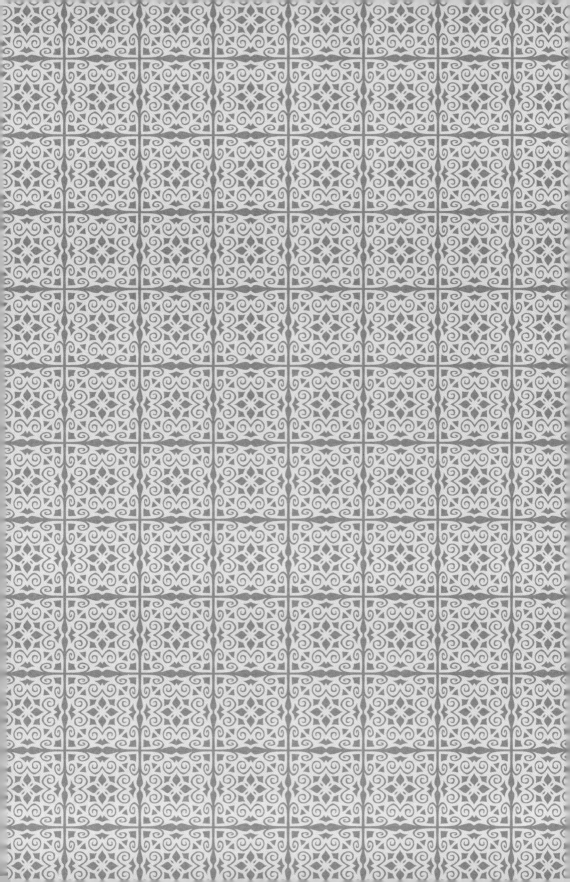

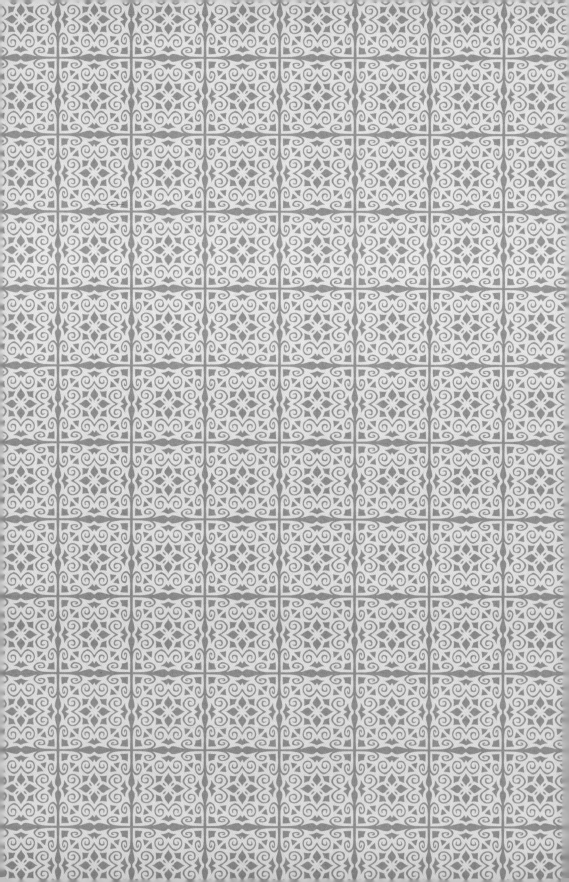

The Major Diocesan Philosophical-Theological Seminary
of the Immaculate Conception at Darlington, New Jersey

A New Beginning

1927–1938

Chapter Fifteen

The Move

The last days at Seton Hall were recorded by Monsignor McLaughlin.

> April 15: Last conference to seminarians at South
> Orange. General directions for way to Darlington and
> the proper spirit of entry therein.
>
> April 16: Seminarians left to go to cathedral to go to
> Darlington, Thursday, April 21, 1927.
>
> April 17: Took all seminarian registers and documents
> pertaining to seminary and new seal to Darlington, thus
> closing seminary at South Orange after 66 years in that
> spot. May God bless the seminarians and successors in
> new home.[1]

The pioneer group of 45 seminarians entered Darlington on April 21, 1927, at 3:30 p.m. Scarcely had the move occurred, when Bishop O'Connor died on May 20, 1927.

Nine of the 11 fourth-year theologians had been ordained on March 12. However, the ordinations of two other fourth-year theologians, Messrs. Kinsler and Neafsey, were deferred because of their procrastination in applying for diocesan insurance that reimbursed the diocese for their education. They were ordered to recall their invitations and went to Darlington until their ordinations on June 10, 1927.[2]

The property had been prepared for their arrival by Father Charles Demjanovich, the procurator, who had spent part of each week in residence at Darlington since October 1926.[3]

Initially, seminarians and faculty all moved into the Crocker Mansion. As one of the new arrivals put it, "We ate, slept, studied—and we were bawled out—all under one roof." Although there were not yet any recreational facilities, the seminarians were kept busy: "We did manual labor. We were assigned to till the fields, and cut the grass, and paint fences."[4]

Commuting

There was not enough room for all faculty and students in the mansion building. Furthermore, faculty members had teaching responsibilities in the college as well as the seminary, and the rector remained president of the college. This required the rector and some faculty to commute between South Orange and Darlington from April to June. Monsignor McLaughlin split his time between Seton Hall and Darlington. Father Michael Donnelly, now designated director of discipline, resided at Darlington and traveled to Seton Hall to teach history. Fathers Francis Monaghan, Thomas Boland, and Adrian Maine resided at Seton Hall and commuted to Darlington to teach their classes. Only Father Charles Demjanovich and Father Michael Whelan, the spiritual director, resided full-time at Darlington.

Over the summer, the former residence of Mr. A. B. Darling, after whom the estate and the area were named, was rehabilitated as a residence for philosophy students. Located "down the hill" from the Crocker Mansion on Valley Road, it was a rambling three-story nineteenth-century home with 27 rooms. The renovation cost $26,000.[5] The building that would house the philosophy students was grandly named the Philosophy House of St. Thomas Aquinas and dedicated on September 16, 1927. The gardener's house near the greenhouse was converted into a residence for the Sisters of Charity.[6]

Opening Day

With the St. Thomas House providing additional facilities, 84 students began the Fall 1927 semester. They included 23 senior philosophy students. There was not yet room for the junior philosophy class. The elegantly paneled, frescoed, and plastered rooms of the Crocker Mansion, graced with marble fireplaces, were transformed. The first floor now housed two classrooms: one for the "cycle" course for all theology students, and the other for the philosophy students. The mansion's library continued to function as such, as did the dining room, although with many more diners than ever anticipated by the original owners.

The ballroom, or Great Hall, 30 feet high, encased in Caen stone, with enormous Tiffany silver chandeliers and statues of cavaliers on the balconies, was rechristened the *Magna Aula*, and became the chapel. An altar was placed in the giant alcove before the grand marble fireplace. It was an appropriate place for a chapel. There was a built-in pipe organ and the windows were decorated with sixteenth- and seventeenth-century stained-glass vignettes.

The faculty, with the exception of the priests at St. Thomas House, together with the theology students, resided on the second and third floors. The accommodations required that, as at Seton Hall, several seminarians share a room.[7] By 1928, the entire faculty resided at Darlington, except for Monsignor McLaughlin, who continued to divide his time between Darlington and South Orange.

At the beginning of the Darlington era the faculty numbered six. The rector, Monsignor McLaughlin, taught education, catechetics, sociology, and canon law. Father Michael Whelan, the spiritual director, lectured on ascetics, pastoral theology, and apologetics. Father Michael Donnelly, director of discipline and later vice rector, taught Church history, liturgy, education, and plain chant. In teaching plain chant, he was assisted by seminarian Francis Ballinger. Father Francis Monaghan was professor of dogmatic theology and metaphysics. Father Thomas A. Boland lectured on moral theology, canon law, ethics, and pastoral theology. Father Demjanovich, the procurator, also taught canon law, history of philosophy, and accounting. New to the faculty was Father Justin J. McCarthy, ordained on April 16, 1927, after obtaining the licentiate in sacred theology in Rome. Over his career he would teach scripture, homiletics, English, classical languages, and education. After becoming spiritual director in 1937, he would also lecture in ascetics and religion.

Since the seminary now officially included a philosophical curriculum, undergraduate courses as well as graduate theological courses would be a part of the program. The two years of philosophy were considered the last two years of the Seton Hall program for the bachelor of arts degree.[8] Classes of 45-minute duration were held at 9, 10, and 11 a.m., and at 2:30 and 3:15 p.m. Thursday was a free day, and each school day had one or more periods free.

Constitutiones Seminarii Majoris Dioceseos Novarcensis

Just a month before his death, Bishop O'Connor approved the new *Constitutiones Seminarii Majoris Dioceseos Novarcensis*, the constitutions and rules of the seminary.[9] Slightly revised in 1929, it reflected the directives of the Sacred Congregation for Seminaries and Universities, together with the Code of Canon Law. It observed the letter of these documents and even went beyond with incredible attention to detail.

Monsignor McLaughlin's hand in its composition was evident, several rules bearing the notation *Consuetudines Oenipontani*, or "Innsbruck Customs." Various local customs also were integrated into the new rule. Now that the seminary was separate from the college, no seminarians were involved as college instructors or prefects, or subject to any other distractions. The rule literally covered every minute of the day.

In the opening conference after the seminarians arrived at Darlington on April 21, 1927, McLaughlin presented them with the rule and outlined his interpretation.[10] In his words, the purpose of the seminary was to enable "the student for the priesthood . . . to understand . . . that he is with the grace of God in the triumph over self interest, pleasure and gain, to be an apostle that is an ambassador of Christ, yea verily to be another Christ."

The seminary, he told them, "is not a college for seculars and the secular spirit, which smacks of ambition, ease, self interest." Such inclinations "must be torn out of the heart root and branch" and replaced with the "spirit of Christ, the spirit of humiliation, suffering, self denial, and general charity." The seminary is "not a place to have a good time," but rather a place to "subject yourselves to the will of God and those whom God through his Church has called to guide you."

He instructed the seminarians to "bury your own mind, your own will, to the direction and rules of your superiors; the direction of your consciences to the spiritual director and your confessor; the direction of your intellectual development and viewpoints to your professors and textbooks; your deportment to the rector and his delegates in all matters." For McLaughlin, there was no room for discussion because the rule was of divine origin: "It is the law, not the law of the individual rector, but of the Church, nay of God himself."

In entering the seminary, the students had left "the world" behind them.

> No one must bring into the Catholic seminary the
> viewpoint of the present age of revolt or independence
> because this is the very spirit which must be broken in
> the hearts of men if they would be saved. . . . The best
> means to this end is constant fidelity to rule . . . with
> subjection of will in thought as well as in deed. . . . Now
> the rule of the seminary properly viewed has this purpose:
> The submission of one's own judgment, likes, and
> dislikes to the will of ecclesiastical authority.[11]

"No rule should be taken lightly." McLaughlin specifically focused on the rule against visiting "stores or dwellings." He noted that "the world, hypocritical and pharisaic as it is, has always taken umbrage at social visiting of the clergy." He roared that such visits often are the occasion of scandal, "drink, and intercourse with young people of the other sex." Social visiting was a particular bête noire for McLaughlin. Like an absolute ruler dispensing decrees, he warned the seminarians: "Let it be distinctly understood that when evidence of this kind comes to my attention; no quarter will be shown."

Entering stores to purchase candy or snacks was an equally serious offense: "Visiting stores, especially to gratify the palate, is certainly a manifestation of lack of self control, and hankering after the flesh pots of Egypt." He ended by noting that, when the rule is kept perfectly, there will be "peace, happiness, joy in suffering and trial . . . then will Jesus pour forth his blessings and all will learn *quam bonum et jucundum habitare fratres in unum*."[12]

The schedule for class days left nothing out. The rule enjoined, "When the signal is given the student should immediately proceed to the next exercise." Thursday was a "day off." However, the hours and minutes were carefully assigned. Mornings included manual labor, choir practice, and mandatory weekly confession. In the afternoon, there was a mandatory two-hour walk followed by recreation for an hour and a half.

"You Keep the Rule and the Rule Will Keep You"

In introducing seminarians to the rule over the years, directors of discipline invariably invoked the motto "You keep the rule and the rule will keep you." The rule and the spirit behind it, similar to most American seminaries of the time, created an almost hermetically sealed world. All was provided 24 hours a day, seven days a week. Even food from "outside" was prohibited.

Only approved books and texts were allowed. In the early years at Darlington, group walks within the environs were allowed. Other than those occasions, seminarians could leave the property only for supervised visits to the cathedral for pontifical ceremonies, or to the hospital for medical emergencies, always in the presence of a "prudent companion." Minor illnesses were treated in the seminary infirmary or during the periodic visits of the seminary physician. Seminarians were trained to cut one another's hair, often with unfortunate results. They were isolated from world news by the prohibition of newspapers and magazines. Eventually radio and television would enter the seminary, but were restricted to news programs in the recreation rooms.

This rule and way of life would remain essentially unchanged for almost four decades. Only in the tumultuous years following the Second Vatican Council would any substantial changes be made. Then, the rule and the way of life it exemplified would disappear almost overnight.

HORARIUM

5:15 a.m.	Rising
5:35 a.m.	Morning Prayer
5:45 a.m.	Meditation
6:15 a.m.	Mass and Thanksgiving
7:00 a.m.	Order rooms
7:30 a.m.	Breakfast and Visit to the Blessed Sacrament, followed by moderate recreation
8:30–10:00 a.m.	Class or Study
10:00–10:10 a.m.	Recreation
10:10–10:45 a.m.	Class or Study
10:45-11:00 a.m.	Break
11:00–11:45 a.m.	Class or Study
11:45 a.m.	Preparation for Lunch
11:53 a.m.	Particular Examination of Conscience in Chapel
12:00 noon	Angelus and Lunch. After lunch spiritual reading in common and recreation
1:15–2:00 p.m.	Class
2:00 p.m.	Class or manual work
2:45 p.m.	Recreation (Friday, Stations of the Cross)
4:30 p.m.	Private Spiritual Reading
4:45 p.m.	Study
5:30 p.m.	Preparation for Dinner
5:40 p.m.	Rosary and Devotions
6:00 p.m.	Angelus and Dinner, followed by Visit to the Blessed Sacrament and Recreation
7:00 p.m.	Study
8:45 p.m.	Points of Meditation and Evening Prayer
9:00 p.m.	Return to rooms
9:15 p.m.	Lights out

Chapter Sixteen

Immaculatos ab Hoc Saeculo

Upon rising in the morning, the seminarians were to respond to the prefect's knock on their doors with the prayer *Deo Gratias*. They were obliged to make sure windows were closed, lights were turned out, and shoes and clothes in dressers and closets before leaving their rooms. Only with the permission of the director of discipline or the prefect could a seminarian enter another's room; in other circumstances they were to conduct any necessary business at the door. Violation of this rule and of many others rendered a seminarian subject to dismissal.

Possession of liquor, narcotics, games of chance, or engaging in commerce of any kind also rendered one subject to expulsion. Just in case an unforeseen offense might occur, the rule provided that any seminarian who was "refractory, incorrigible, seditious," or failed in his studies would be dismissed.

Seminarians would now spend most of the summer at the seminary, with the exception of a two-week vacation in June and another in September. While away from the seminary, they were to attend daily Mass and fulfill their spiritual devotions, give good example, and remain *immaculatos ab hoc saeculo*, untainted by this world. Upon return, their pastor would file a report on their behavior with the rector.

At the Third Plenary Council of Baltimore, the American bishops had opposed the idea of summer villas that kept students in the seminary almost year-round. However, Rome continued to advocate the idea.

The summer policy was solidified in 1935, when a letter from the apostolic delegate, Archbishop Amleto Giovanni Cicognani, warned bishops of the "endangering outside influences" of an unsupervised summer and reiterated the need for summer villas for seminaries. The delegate also lamented that seminarians, during the summer, would often obtain employment. He then listed occupations that were forbidden as "not in keeping with the dignity or spirit of their holy vocation."

Among the forbidden occupations were "a) positions in hotels, cafes, theaters, moving-picture houses, bathing beaches, billiard and pool parlors, etc; b) positions in shops and offices in which persons of the other sex are employed; c) positions of a political character; d) driving of taxicabs." No seminarian was to be allowed to take up any form of employment without the permission of the rector.[1]

Bishop Thomas Joseph Walsh, who succeeded O'Connor as bishop of Newark, assured the apostolic delegate that the Darlington seminarians spent eight weeks of the summer *in villegeatura* on a campus of more than 1,000 acres "entirely removed from influences which would adversely affect their vocations, and under a suitable regime."[2]

Reflecting on the ever-increasing restrictions on seminaries coming from Rome, Father John Fenlon of the Sulpician Seminary in Washington, DC, wrote in 1934:

> Their chief idea of [clerical] education seems to be to surround clerics with all sorts of safeguards and to keep the candidates for the priesthood, from childhood almost up to ordination, away from contact with their family and with the world. Perhaps that is the only way in which Italian boys can be turned into good priests. I think such a system of education has very decided defects. Men so trained can hardly have the manliness that is necessary for the priesthood. When they are released from that training, there is almost an inevitable reaction. Priests with such training do not know how to work among the people. I do not wonder that there is an estrangement between the Italian people and the Italian clergy and that Italian men have not much esteem for the clergy. . . .
>
> If our American clerical students are to be subjected to the same hothouse system of development, the results will be still more disastrous because of the greater freedom which American priests have, and I cannot help dreading the results if the Sacred Congregation of Seminaries imposes Italian ideals more and more upon American seminaries.[3]

Attain Solid Virtue

The purpose of the rule was not simply to maintain discipline and order in the seminary but to enable the seminarian "to acquire priestly perfection through the exercise of the virtues of charity, obedience, and self-denial."

Each year began with a six-day retreat. The first Sunday of each month was a recollection day, with additional spiritual conferences and exercises in addition to the Sunday Solemn Mass and Vespers. Exemplifying the devotional spirituality of the time, the schedule gradually over the years was amplified by novenas preceding major feasts of Our Lord, the Holy Spirit, the Blessed Virgin, and St. Joseph. The solemnities of St. Thomas Aquinas and St. Francis de Sales were observed with additional devotions. During the month of May, the Litany of Loreto was recited daily, and during October the rosary, litanies, and prayers to St. Joseph were recited before the Blessed Sacrament.

On the first Friday of every month, special devotions to the Sacred Heart included the recitation of acts of consecration and of reparation followed by benediction. On rogation days, the litanies were chanted in procession, often outdoors, before the community Mass. Since, during dry spells, the purpose of the procession was to intercede to end the drought, the seminarians referred to the procession as the "rain dance." The Church Unity Octave was celebrated from January 18 through 25, with the recitation of the prescribed prayers. The anniversary of the election of the reigning pontiff was celebrated with "suitable solemnities."

Christ the King Sunday, which would become the patronal feast of the seminary church, was celebrated with supplementary litanies and spiritual exercises in addition to the usual October devotions and Solemn Mass and Vespers. Seminarians often referred to endless devotions of that particular day as the "Mystical Marathon."[4]

Individual spiritual guidance was now the responsibility and burden of the one spiritual director for all seminarians. They were required to "report to the Spiritual Director for a spiritual visit at regular intervals according to schedule." How often this took place is unclear. As the number of seminarians increased, it became almost impossible for one man to offer adequate spiritual guidance.

Let His Senses Therefore Be Mortified

The virtues of obedience and modesty were exalted in the rule. Seminarians were to recognize and venerate "the person and authority of God" as manifest through the rule and the directives of seminary authorities. Toward one another they were always to exercise fraternal charity and refrain from back-biting and gossip, always giving good example. Seminarians were directed to address one another by their Christian names, refraining from nicknames.

Modesty required the seminarians to shun pride that "renders men enemies of God and odious to their fellows." They were not to "loiter in windows." They were always to walk quietly and with dignity, never waving their arms indecorously, rolling their eyes, or speaking with a loud voice. Silence was to be maintained in the corridors at all times and the "Great Silence" was in effect from evening prayer until after breakfast the next morning. To assure quiet in the building, they were obliged to wear shoes with rubber, not leather, heels.

Rome had directed that "care of the body should always be circumscribed by such precautions as Christian modesty demands, precautions which unfortunately the world often pays little attention to: for which reason the Church disapproves and condemns such practices."[5] To guarantee modesty, a dressing room was provided adjacent to the showers. In going from their rooms to the dressing room and from the dressing room to the showers, the seminarians were to wear bathrobes. The rule stated: "Neither the dressing room nor the shower room is a place of recreation. Silence must be maintained in both places at all times."

When at the lake, their swimming costume was to completely cover their upper body and reach *usque ad genua,* to their knees. The "bathing suit should have a top that covers back and front, and trunks of the style of gym shorts." For recreation "the student should have dark gray slacks and a white sport shirt with at least half sleeves."[6] In the rooms mirrors were placed so that they could reflect only the shoulders and face.

Mens Sana in Corpore Sano (A Sound Mind in a Sound Body)

Regarding dress, seminarians were to wear the cassock and biretta, and the zimarra (a heavy, ankle-length coat with a shoulder cape) in winter; a black suit and tie, and a hat, when away from the seminary. Each student was required to furnish his own personal clothing, toilet accessories, books, stationery, towels, and an inexpensive napkin ring clearly marked with the student's name. Their personal clothing included "sufficient light and heavy underwear for one year, one black suit, one black overcoat and hat, cassock, zimarra, serge biretta, three plain linen surplices, one dozen clerical collars, one black necktie, black trousers, sweater and cap, shoes, rubbers, umbrella, black raincoat, black book bag, and two laundry bags. . . . The cassock should be a Roman cassock, i.e., one with the buttons down the front and without the sash."[7] These garments always were to be clean and neat.

Seminarians were not allowed to introduce any items into their rooms, including electric bulbs other than those supplied by the seminary. Originally, they could have no personal pictures in their rooms, only a picture of Our Lord, the Blessed Virgin, or a saint. When the new seminary was completed, they were forbidden "to introduce into their rooms any article of furniture or any pictures or decorations beyond those supplied by the seminary." The present writer once violated this rule and was ordered by the vice rector to remove a portrait of Pope Paul VI from his desk.

At meals, seminarians sat in assigned places and waited on tables. They were urged to observe proper table manners and not to eat either too slowly or too quickly, never leaving scraps on the tablecloth. They were never to engage in frivolous conversation at table. Normally, meals were accompanied by spiritual reading, except for breakfast, which was in silence. They were forbidden either to remove any food from the dining room or to have any food in the rooms; any food received from outside was to be turned over to the rector. After meals, on the way to the chapel for prayer, the seminarians were to recite the lengthy Latin prayer, the *Benedicite*.[8]

Recreation was mandatory. In all sports, seminarians were to be governed by charity and priestly gravitas.[9] Rome had counseled seminary authorities that "sports are a means not an end in themselves . . . the seminary . . . has not been established to turn out athletes who are able to exhibit their skill and prowess before the public on the athletic field. Rather, the purpose of the seminary is to turn out athletes who will fight bravely the battles of the Lord."[10] Any gambling on the outcome of games was strictly forbidden.

While on recreation, seminarians were forbidden to go near the homes of the seminary's workers or places reserved for the faculty. On Thursdays, they were allowed to go on "grand walks" on the spacious grounds and, with the permission of the rector, to go beyond the limits of the property. Before and after these walks, they were to visit the Blessed Sacrament. At all times seminarians were counseled to avoid "particular friendships" and "exclusive groups."

On daily afternoon recreation periods, seminarians were required to spend the first hour of the period outdoors, except in inclement weather or when the temperature went below freezing. A bell would announce when the temperature was below freezing. No seminarian was allowed to take his recreation alone.

Clandestine Correspondence

Only for a grave reason was a seminarian given permission to use the telephone, and never was he allowed to receive a telephone call. Seminarians were required to place their outgoing mail in a special box for possible inspection by the vice rector. Incoming mail likewise was subject to inspection by the vice rector before distribution. Federal laws regarding mail did not apply within the bounds of Darlington. Any "clandestine correspondence" rendered a student subject to dismissal.

On the second Sunday of each month, Christmas, St. Stephen's Day, Easter, All Saints, May 30, July 4, Labor Day, and Thanksgiving Day, seminarians could receive family and friends from 2:30 to 5 p.m. in the library and the parlors.

Seminarians were prohibited from receiving or having in their possession any newspapers or journals, even Catholic ones. In the seminary library, students were appointed to catalogue and shelve books. All books without a religious or historical theme were prohibited. Only during study times were seminarians allowed to use the library.

The course of studies followed the prescriptions of the Code of Canon Law. A seminarian could absent himself from class only because of illness. Presence at liturgical practice or chant were not excuses to miss class. Seminarians were required to have personal copies of the Vulgate edition of the Holy Bible, the New Testament in English, *Missale Romanum, Liber Usualis Missae et Officii, The Imitation of Christ,* the *Code of Canon Law* (Latin), and the *Diocesan Statutes.* Seminarians in major orders were required to possess the *Officium Divinum;* other seminarians the *Officium Beatae Mariae Virginis.*

Bulletinarius—Bedellus, Praefectus, Praecentores

Seminarians were allowed to form several societies: the Apostleship of Prayer, which offered prayers for intentions of the Holy Father; the Society of the Propagation of the Faith, which raised money for overseas missions; and the DeSales Union, which organized sports and entertainment activities for the student body. Each organization was under the direction of a faculty moderator.

Students were appointed to various internal offices, called "house jobs." These positions were considered to be a singular honor. This allowed some seminarians to exercise a certain amount of authority and initiative, but always under careful scrutiny and supervision.

The "prefect of the house," under the director of discipline, assigned seminarians to duties in the dining room and in the first years at Darlington, as leaders of walks. He supervised the other prefects of groups of students, called corridor prefects and later *camerata* prefects. Seminarians were required to seek authorization for various privileges from the corridor prefect. These permissions included going to the library during study time and visiting at the door of another seminarian. All corridor prefects were to report these permissions and any infractions of the rule, such as tardiness, on the part of the seminarians under their supervision in a weekly meeting with the vice rector.

The sacristan, who reported to the procurator, was in charge of the running of the chapel and sacristy. It was his duty to inventory and care for vestments, sacred vessels, and other liturgical supplies.

The *bedellus,* or *bulletinarius,* who was supervised by the rector, had the duty of ringing a large bell to announce chapel services, the angelus, and the end of recreation. He used a smaller bell to announce the beginning and end of activities in the house. He also was charged with posting official announcements on the bulletin board.

The librarian cared for the cataloguing and shelving of the books in the library, as well as other duties assigned by the procurator. Students were allowed to use only the student library. Permission of the rector and the recommendation of a professor were required before a student could use the main library. In no case could he remove books or periodicals from this library.

The master of ceremonies, under the direction of the professor of liturgy, supervised the arrangement and practice of the various liturgical ceremonies of the seminary. The master of chant supervised the practice of singing the Gregorian chant for these ceremonies. He supervised the *praecentores,* who intoned the introductions to the various chants. The master of reading was in charge of assuring that readers in the refectory were properly prepared for both English and Latin readings, with special attention to the nuances of reading the *Martyrologium Romanum* that closed the evening meal.

In a manner very different from Seton Hall, the seminary had become a "world in itself."

Chapter Seventeen

A New Reign

The state of New Jersey was growing at an astounding pace. Since 1900, its population had more than doubled by 1930 to over 4 million.[1] In the same period, the 290,000 Catholics in the seven counties of the diocese of Newark had almost tripled to over 725,000, 27 percent of the total population. The number of priests, diocesan and religious, also had almost tripled, from 256 to 715. The 155 parishes had increased to 226 with 50 additional missions.[2] The restrictive anti-immigration laws of the 1920s had begun to slow this growth. The cities remained the centers of Catholic life but the suburbs were experiencing an increased Catholic presence. Just after the death of Bishop O'Connor, there were 65 students in the seminary and 227 attending Seton Hall College.[3]

On March 7, 1928, the appointment of the Right Reverend Thomas Joseph Walsh, hitherto bishop of Trenton, as bishop of Newark, was announced by the Holy See. Walsh was born in Parker's Landing, Pennsylvania, on December 6, 1873. After studies at St. Bonaventure's College and Seminary, he was ordained for the diocese of Buffalo on January 27, 1900.

Less than five months later he was named chancellor of the diocese, and seven years after that, he was assigned to study canon law in Rome. He enrolled in the Pontifical Roman Seminary, the Lateran, in June 1907 and received the doctorate *utriusque juris* on December 17, 1907. Six months later, on June 19, 1908, he received the doctorate in sacred theology. Upon his return to Buffalo, he again took up the duties of chancellor as well as pastor of the cathedral parish.

During his time in Buffalo, Walsh took great interest in immigrant groups, particularly Italians and Poles. He also devoted much of his energies to the Mount Carmel Guild, an association of volunteers who devoted their time to charitable works, including relief of the poor and catechetical instruction of the young. Walsh eventually would bring these interests and his phenomenal energy to Newark.

In May 1918, he was named bishop of Trenton. In his decade in Trenton, he focused on expanding parishes and establishing parochial schools. He also founded the Mount Carmel Guild in that diocese. His work on behalf of immigrants was exemplified by his support of the Maestre Pie Filippini, an Italian order of sisters dedicated to serving the needs of the immigrant Italian community.[4]

Walsh would direct his energy in Newark to the same areas as he had in Buffalo and Trenton: parochial life, education, immigrants, and social services. In addition, he would take a very direct role in the future and direction of the diocesan seminary.

It became clear very quickly that the seminary would be a major interest of the new bishop. Walsh visited his new see for the first time on March 26. His first stop was St. Mary's Hospital in Orange where Monsignor McLaughlin was hospitalized. McLaughlin told him of the crowded conditions at Darlington and Walsh told him that he would see to it that a new seminary would be erected.[5]

On May 12, 1928, shortly after his installation as bishop of Newark, Bishop Walsh visited Darlington to confer orders. The crowded conditions were evident. Less than two weeks later, on May 24, 1928, Walsh again visited Darlington to preside at the meeting of the board of deputies of the seminary. He was apprised that there were now 84 seminarians in residence. The facilities clearly were overcrowded in buildings that were not designed to serve as a residence for so many, much less to serve educational purposes. Together with the rector and the vicar general, Walsh "visited the grounds with a view to a new seminary."[6] So far, exclusive of the cost of the property, the diocese had expended more than $250,000 to make the buildings ready for occupancy.[7] At that same meeting, $16,000 was approved for additional repairs and $75,000 for current expenses. While the property and buildings were paid for, the expenses of running the seminary were not being met. The parish collection brought in only $40,000, leaving a deficit of $35,000. This problem would not go away in the coming years.

Walsh insisted on being informed of every detail of seminary life. Like McLaughlin, he expected his every word to be obeyed—immediately. In Walsh, McLaughlin had a firm supporter in enforcing discipline.

Contraband Candy

As he promised, Monsignor McLaughlin enforced the seminary rule "with no quarter." Having uncovered what he deemed severe violations of the rule, regarding visiting stores and purchasing candy that might lead to the "flesh pots of Egypt," he wrote to Bishop Walsh on December 1929:

Your Lordship,

It is extremely distasteful for me to approach again Your Lordship with a disciplinary matter in the Seminary . . . a seminarian by direction and command of his confessor revealed to me that he at the solicitation of two older seminarians, purchased not only the magazine mentioned but two others as well as other contraband (candy). This seminarian had been taken as a companion in accordance with the rule to the Suffern hospital, and while there had entered two stores. The seminarians have been warned with special emphasis about Suffern, because of the attitude of many of its inhabitants towards the Church.

I have felt that if such violations involving scandal were to continue with impunity discipline would be imperiled. Accordingly after consultation with Rev. Dr. Donnelly the Disciplinarian and Msgr. Whelan I have suspended the seminarian who brought the magazines into the house as well as those for whom they were bought. Together I have told them they may make application for re-entrance next fall. . . . The third I have swiftly dismissed. . . . I have prayed in this matter and it cuts me to the quick to take this action.

Yours obediently in Christ,
Thomas H. McLaughlin, Rector [8]

Bishop Walsh did not object to disciplining seminarians who purchased candy but he had even more serious concerns. The seminary rule prohibited the seminarians from possessing or drinking alcoholic beverages of any kind under pain of dismissal. After the end of Prohibition in 1933, Walsh decreed that not only should seminarians abstain from intoxicating beverages but that, "upon the eve of . . . holy ordination," they would "solemnly promise with the aid of divine grace and for the honor of my sacred ministry [to] abstain from all intoxicating and alcoholic beverages for the space of five (5) years." Alternatively, they could pledge "to abstain for life from all intoxicating drink and alcoholic beverages except beers and light wines."[9] Subsequent history shows that this was a futile gesture.

Receptions and "All-Day Rambles"

It cannot be known whether it was Walsh or McLaughlin who was the more eager to impose ever stricter rules on seminarians. In 1932, at the bishop's command, the rector promulgated the following rules: "1. There are to be no receptions on the occasion of ordination and First Mass; 2. Dinners following First Masses are allowed only in the rectory or else in the parents' home; 3. Hereafter all invitations must be submitted to the rector of the seminary before being sent to invitees."[10] It is not clear whether these rules were devised simply for disciplinary reasons or to avoid comments about elaborate parties during the Depression. In any event, they were draconian.

One year later, in 1933, McLaughlin recommended several changes to the rule, making it even more restrictive. He wrote to Bishop Walsh of his desire "to obviate certain abuses contrary to the spirit and rules of the seminary." These abuses had arisen in connection with the "All-Day Rambles," or all-day hikes taken twice each term by the seminarians on the vast Darlington property and adjoining estates. The most significant abuse was that the seminarians were eating at roadstands on the byways that intersected the Darlington property. Instead, he recommended that the hikes be limited to between dinner and 5 p.m.

However, during the summer session he was willing to allow the seminarians to take "at their own option and expense," and "with the approval of the Rector," a one- or two-day trip to a point of "religious, historic or scenic interest not in cities, e.g. Bear Mountain Reservation." Even though this favor was granted, the seminarians were busy during the eight-week summer session. They took classes in Church music, lives of the saints, Christian sociology, and sign language. They had lectures on special topics in moral and dogmatic theology and canon law, as well as on the diocesan statutes and faculties. Fourth-year students had classes on the administration of the sacraments, homiletics, and ecclesiastical bookkeeping.[11]

McLaughlin also was concerned about the Sunday visiting days. On successive Sundays, friends and relatives of each class were allowed to visit the seminary. This, in McLaughlin's eyes, had been abused "in spite of admonitions," with the "advent on practically every Sunday of large throngs with attendant disorder." He recommended that no lay visitors be allowed during the summer session and that during the school year visiting be terminated and replaced with a weeklong vacation at the end of the winter term. He eventually allowed one visiting day during the octave of Christmas. He also suggested that he prepare a "spiritual letter" to parents of the seminarians "explaining the purpose of the seminary and its rules so that they may cooperate in the preparation of their sons for the Holy State by removing obstacles."[12] The May 17, 1934, meeting of the deputies formally approved the elimination of all visitors for seminarians during their stay at the seminary.[13] Eventually, one visiting day was reinstated, namely one day within the octave of Christmas.

The Monsignor and His Lordship[14]

McLaughlin, a terror in his own right, knew he had to tread softly when dealing with Walsh. His advocacy of a winter break may have been occasioned by a contretemps two years earlier, in 1931. That year an anonymous seminarian dared to write directly to Bishop Walsh. Apparently, the vice rector was not effectively monitoring outgoing mail. He would never have allowed a letter to go out to the bishop. The poor benighted seminarian thanked the bishop for his Christmas gift to the seminary and his "fatherly interest" and then ventured to propose a request, "trusting that it will appear reasonable." He wrote on January 5, 1931:

> We believe, as you have stated, that it is sounder for us to celebrate Christmas in the seminary with the full ecclesiastical liturgy, than to spend it in the world. But due to our strenuous schedule, which extended solidly from September and even required classes between Christmas and New Year's, we trust that it is not an imposition upon you to request a reasonable rest at home at the end of this term.[15]

His Lordship was stunned at such a display of lèse-majesté. On January 7, Walsh, in a manner that only can be described as hysterical, exploded at McLaughlin in grand inquisitorial style.

> Any and every ecclesiastical student of the seminary who had any part in the composition, execution or transmission of this anonymous letter or who has or had any knowledge regarding the same is invited to confess privately his relative participation or knowledge to you within three days after the promulgation of this letter, and to accept and fulfill any relative penalty or penance that you may impose. If this invitation is accepted, and if it solves the case, you may make thereafter appropriate public announcement in the chapel without mention of names.
>
> If this invitation is disregarded, you are hereby directed to examine or have examined under oath by yourself and by the priests of your faculty—one priest suffices as an examining tribunal—each and every ecclesiastical student in the seminary as to his participation in or his knowledge of the anonymous letter in question. I further direct the submission to me of all evidence secured in this examination for adjudication and sentence.
>
> Please read this letter to the full student body.[16]

McLaughlin hoped that the passage of time would allow Walsh's wrath to simmer. Not placated, Walsh spoke to him again about the matter on February 9. McLaughlin brought the matter to the faculty on February 18. McLaughlin imposed only a slap on the wrist, hoping that Walsh might be conciliated. He wrote to the bishop, reporting the conclusions of the faculty.

> It was the unanimous mind that while the composition and sending of the anonymous request was most cowardly, disrespectful and ungrateful on the part of the seminarians concerned, it was felt that the young men at the time did not have a proper appreciation of nor did they fully realize the consequences of their act, that now they appear to be fully aware of the gross impropriety committed, that they have since sought to give good example, that the community at large do not know who they are and accordingly that they be permitted to receive the remaining minor orders with the other members of their class.
>
> It was suggested and all approved the suggestions that it would be appropriate for the two seminarians to send Your Excellency letters expressive of their deep sorrow and apology.[17]

As much as he was a strict disciplinarian, McLaughlin realized that the bishop's reaction was overdone and that any severe punishment for such an offense could have negative ramifications on both students and faculty. He also was wise to let time pass to cool the episcopal temper and to obtain unanimous backing from his faculty. Equally shrewdly, he wrote with appropriate obsequiousness. One can only imagine the atmosphere such an inquiry provoked among seminarians, and among faculty. In the end, Bishop Walsh approved McLaughlin's rather benign resolution of the heinous act.[18]

Chapter Eighteen

A New Seminary Building

With his customary energy, Bishop Walsh moved quickly to plan for new seminary buildings. On February 4, 1929, he appointed a "Committee for the New Seminary."[1] On April 19, the diocesan building commission recommended going forward immediately. In June, the services of architect Joseph Shanley were retained. By December, preliminary plans were drawn and a model executed. The plans called for a three-story, *E*-shaped building, with a chapel, six classrooms, an auditorium, a library, and a dining hall to house 275 students and faculty. The cost was estimated at between $2 million and $2.75 million.[2]

From the beginning the project was plagued with difficulties. Shanley proposed a site on the north side of the Ramapo River in spite of concerns that this part of the Darlington property might be impounded by the North Jersey Water Commission. This threat, and rising seminary expenses coupled with the exhaustion of the seminary fund due to unforeseen repair costs to the existing buildings, caused Monsignor McLaughlin to inform Shanley in January 1930 that the project was in abeyance.

During 1929, seminary current expenses had jumped to $99,682, and repairs to $22,700. At the same time, the receipts from the seminary collection were falling short of expectations. The deputies recommended that the seminary collection should include all monies taken on the Sunday specified, with the exception of seat money, surely a measure that would not be greeted with enthusiasm by the pastors of the diocese. The shortfall had to be made up by the diocese, and the seminary was accruing a significant debt to the diocese. The financial situation was exacerbated and would be continually worsened by the crash of the stock market in October 1929.

Success in attracting vocations was producing a desperate situation requiring what the board of deputies called "spiritual heroism in consideration of the inadequate housing facilities"[3] at Darlington. In spite of these difficulties, McLaughlin, in December 1930, composed a letter begging Walsh to move ahead on the construction of new buildings. The 84 pioneer seminarians had increased to 99. They were living five and six to a room and sharing woefully inadequate washing and toilet facilities. The congestion in the dining room was so bad that the rector described the atmosphere there as "very vitiated."

The situation could only grow worse, as the enrollment for the next year was estimated to grow to 116. This number did not include the junior-year philosophy students who still could not be accommodated at Darlington. McLaughlin lamented that he would have to put students into the temporary infirmary and close off unheated corridors and turn them into dormitories as the enrollment increased. The lack of facilities would put off into the future the goal of having all philosophy students at Darlington. Unless a new building was constructed, he foresaw rejecting applicants due to lack of room.

He estimated that the present need was for facilities for 106 seminarians, and in the near future, 250. Even before construction could begin it would be necessary to build a water purification plant, a sewage system, and new roads. If the site suggested by the architect was chosen, a bridge and additional roads also would be required. He never sent the letter. Walsh told him on December 18 that financial conditions were such that he "would not contemplate building at the present time" and ordering him "to devise a temporary expedient."[4] The only expedient was to squeeze the seminarians in as best as he could.

Walsh may have been discouraged, but he would not surrender, even to what was becoming the Great Depression. At the May 12, 1931, meeting of the seminary deputies, he instructed the rector to proceed with the plans for the new buildings to the point where precise estimates could be procured.[5] Shanley proceeded to produce more detailed plans and estimates. On July 13, Shanley produced new plans and a new estimate of $3 million.

The seminary building committee did not view the cost as too high given the $3 million recently expended for the new Baltimore seminary, and $4 million for the Detroit, Michigan, seminary.[6]

The impact of the economic downturn was daunting even for Bishop Walsh. The seminary deficit was increasing, despite "rigid economies." Diocesan collections for the seminary were not making up the deficit. Walsh then imposed an assessment on the parishes to raise $150,000 per year for the seminary. But at the deputies meeting on May 12, 1932, "McLaughlin reported that in view of the conditions of the times it had been thought to defer the continuation of plans for the new Seminary."[7]

Walsh watched each and every dollar. The architect Shanley, who had created extensive plans for the new edifice, asked for payment for his work up to that date. McLaughlin asked Shanley for an exact amount and informed him that he would take the matter of payment to the bishop. Walsh, annoyed that Shanley was asking for $24,000 for his services, instructed McLaughlin not to pay that amount.[8] Shanley continued to press for payment. He appealed to the apostolic delegate, who refused to intervene. Eventually, in 1935, he settled for exactly $7,842.75.[9]

A Donor Dies

The postponement was prescient. Walsh had been depending on a major gift to cover a substantial part of the seminary project. After his appointment to Newark, but before his installation, Walsh instructed Father John A. Duffy, later bishop of Syracuse, to approach Thomas J. Maloney, of Saddle River, New Jersey. Maloney, a director of Lorillard Tobacco Company, told Duffy that he would give "$150,000 now in stock, $100,000 when the seminary is begun, and $500,000 as a seminary foundation."[10] Meanwhile, Maloney and his wife donated land and funds to create Villa Marie Claire in Saddle River. Named after Mrs. Maloney, the villa served as a rest home and recuperative center for Catholic young women under the direction of the Sisters of St. Joseph of Peace.[11]

In gratitude for the Maloneys' generosity and their prospective gift toward the seminary, Walsh arranged for Maloney to receive the most prestigious honors that the Holy See could bestow. On October 30, 1929, Thomas J. Maloney was invested both as a Knight of the Grand Cross of St. Gregory the Great and as a Private Chamberlain of the Cape and Sword, while his wife, Marie Claire Maloney, received the Distinguished Merit Cross, Pro Ecclesia et Pontifice. After the installation, Walsh hosted the Maloneys and their guests at a formal luncheon.[12]

Walsh meticulously noted that the cost of obtaining these honors, including taxes and insignia, was precisely $2,637.61.[13] He surely considered this a good investment but his benefactions did not end here. Through Walsh's intercession, Pope Pius XI granted the Maloneys the rare privilege of having a private chapel in their home where Sunday Mass could be celebrated.[14] Both Mr. and Mrs. Maloney died in 1933. The diocese filed a suit objecting to the probate of Maloney's estate, resulting in a banner headline in the *Jersey Journal*, "DIOCESE SUES MALONEY ESTATE."[15] Eventually, the diocese received stock valued at $157,000 from the estate.[16]

Tight Quarters

As the years progressed, living conditions grew even worse. There was no room for the junior philosophy seminarians who remained at Seton Hall. The senior philosophy students lived three and four to a room in the old summer home of the Darling family, located across a highway near the Ramapo River. This grandiosely named St. Thomas House was devoid of indoor plumbing and any running water. Its heating system was makeshift at best. Every day they trudged up the hill to the Crocker Mansion for Mass, prayers, class, and meals.

The board of deputies meeting of June 6, 1935, would be the catalyst for decision. As Bishop Walsh presided, now Bishop-elect McLaughlin laid out the situation. The number of seminarians was happily increasing, but there was no place to put them. St. Thomas House was old and in need of constant attention. The Crocker Mansion was overcrowded. He suggested the construction of a "modest but respectable" temporary frame building on the site of the old greenhouse to accommodate 30 seminarians.

Bishop Walsh then led the members of the board on a survey of the mansion, St. Thomas House, and the greenhouse site. Upon returning to the meeting room, Walsh dismissed the idea of a temporary structure and declared:

> It is my judgment that if we build the right kind of
> residence building we have a seminary for all time . . .
> on the first floor a chapel, one or two general recreation
> rooms . . . accommodations for 150 single rooms,
> running water in every room, and one toilet between
> every two rooms like St. Anne's Villa at Convent Station
> . . . then have bathrooms in the basement . . . [and]
> include apartments for two or three priests.[17]

Not surprisingly, the deputies agreed with the bishop. In fact the enthusiasm of the moment carried them further. They resolved to construct a building with "at least 200 useable rooms, finishing 150 of these immediately . . . finishing . . . the others when necessity demands." They voted to include a chapel, and increased the number of suites for priests to four. The Crocker Mansion would become the administration and classroom building with suites for the officers of the seminary. The deputies also voted to secure the services of an architect.

Walsh appreciated the situation and the efforts of students and faculty to maintain good morale under such conditions. He saw a new seminary building as the only possible long-term solution. He told the deputies:

> The spiritual condition of the seminary and the
> seminarians is beyond criticism, and we may say that,
> this perfect condition is a manifestation of spiritual
> heroism in consideration of the inadequate housing
> facilities, and that the new seminary and improved
> housing conditions will absolutely guarantee the
> continuation of this perfect spiritual condition without
> heroism on the part of students.[18]

Moving Ahead

Walsh moved swiftly. The next day, June 7, he secured the services of the architectural firm of Fanning and Shaw of Paterson, New Jersey. A week later, in a conversation with McLaughlin, Walsh increased the number of seminarian rooms to 300.[19]

Sketches were submitted on January 9, 1936, and, on January 27, a joint meeting of the diocesan building and sites commission and the commission for the new seminary voted to go ahead with plans for the "New Seminary Residence Building and Chapel of the Immaculate Conception Seminary at Darlington, New Jersey, on the terrace site of the present green houses." On January 31, Walsh invited the clergy of the diocese to inspect the plans at the chancery office and to submit suggestions.[20]

Bishop Walsh engaged his friend, the Roman artist Gonippo Raggi, to supervise the decoration of the seminary chapel. Raggi, born in Rome in 1875, studied at the Art Institute of S. Michele in Rome. He came to the United States in 1904 at the invitation of Papal Marquis Martin Maloney to supervise the decoration of St. Catherine's Memorial Church in Spring Lake, New Jersey. Maloney had erected the church as a family tomb and in memory of his daughter, Catherine. Raggi drew Walsh's attention while he was bishop of Trenton. Raggi was related to several notable officials of the Roman Curia, among them Cardinal Lorenzo Lauri, a friend of Walsh's as well.

When Walsh became bishop of Newark, he not only encouraged Raggi to continue his work in the Newark diocese, but often directed pastors to give Raggi commissions. Raggi was internationally acclaimed as a portraitist. His ecclesiastical art, although often on a grand scale and quite attractive, was in no way original and normally consisted of copies of existing religious art. He provided murals for many churches and Church institutions in the United States and, in his last major work, Raggi supervised the decoration of the Cathedral Basilica of the Sacred Heart in Newark. He died in 1959.[21]

The Bishop's Association and New Technology

Bishop Walsh proceeded methodically but with determination and speed. He personally visited with all of the diocesan consultors and secured their agreement to a plan to raise $1.5 million, spreading $1 million over the parishes if necessary. On March 24, 1936, he contracted with the professional fund-raising firm of John McKeown to direct the fund drive. Bishop McLaughlin was assigned as chairman of the effort. The plan was presented to the clergy meeting of April 29, and the drive scheduled to begin in September. As a first step the deans, with the pastors, began a complete census of the Catholic population of their deaneries.

On May 10, a group of 46 leading laymen, under the leadership of Joseph M. Byrne, Jr., gathered at the seminary and took the first steps to form the Bishop's Association of the Laity to aid in the campaign. Each donor would be enrolled in this association. The campaign opened in September with a series of dinners in each deanery. The bishop presided at each dinner and addressed the gathering. These dinners resulted in pledges of more than $600,000.

Walsh formally opened the direct campaign on November 8, 1936, with a radio address on station WOR in Newark. The seminary *schola cantorum* provided musical selections for this broadcast. In his address, Walsh described the seminary as terribly overcrowded—so overcrowded that only one year of philosophy students was in residence. He explained, "There are now in residence at Darlington . . . 117 persons. This number of persons will continually and substantially increase every year. The eight priests and 56 students, 64 persons, have their crowded sleeping quarters in the mansion building, where the chapel, refectory, class rooms, dining rooms, library and all other service rooms are; 44 students are quartered in the farm house at the foot of the hill a mile and a tenth away; and nine students are quartered in another small residence three-quarters of a mile away from the mansion building." Walsh's distances were a bit exaggerated, but he always thought grandiosely. He went on, stating the need for "the immediate construction" of a new seminary "wherein to house, fashion and train during eleven months of every year for six years . . . our ecclesiastical students in canonical preparation for ordination to holy priesthood. . . . The minimum estimated construction cost of the new seminary building will be $1.5 million."[22]

On Christmas Day, just over a month later, the seminary broadcast the midnight Mass on the same station. The solemn pontifical Mass, featuring the seminary choir, was celebrated by Bishop McLaughlin. Afterward, McLaughlin received dozens of complimentary letters from places such as Idaho, Illinois, Oklahoma, Massachusetts, and Washington, D.C., as well as from the Canadian provinces of New Brunswick, Nova Scotia, Ontario, and Saskatchewan. Apparently, WOR had a very wide range for the day.[23]

Throughout the campaign, Bishop Walsh made use of the relatively new technology of radio to spread the message of the campaign for the seminary and of its successful conclusion. Pastors were instructed to inform their parishioners of the schedule of these broadcasts and encourage them to listen. It is more than likely that this sophisticated publicity aided in making such an ambitious campaign in the middle of an economic depression a resounding success. It also publicized the diocese's efforts to provide priests for its ever-growing number of faithful.

Evidently very proud of his radio addresses, Walsh ensured that they continued to reach appropriate audiences. On January 10, 1939, the bishop ordered that a recording of his radio address be presented in the auditorium of the chancery, directing that "everyone affiliated in any way, in the chancery building, should hear this recording."[24] Similarly, Bishop William A. Griffin, then the seminary rector, received a copy of the recording with very precise instructions. Griffin was directed to play the record "for the faculty assembled in globo or in smaller groups . . . for the entire household . . . for the priests assembled on occasion of the 'Day of Recollection' . . . on Saturdays and Sundays or occasions when groups come to the Seminary whether for the purpose of viewing the new buildings or to make enquiries, etc." Lest any mishap occur, and looking forward to the future, there also was enclosed "an especially prepared needle which will play 2,500 recordings perfectly."[25]

Chapter Nineteen

Fund-raising Success

A committee of pastors met and set quotas for each parish. Each parish organized canvassers, "a vast, devoted, loyal army of 12,000 authorized Catholic men and women, they themselves generous contributors,"[1] who visited each home in the parish to solicit pledges and membership in the Bishop's Association. They made their rounds from November 8 to 19. In 11 days, they secured pledges from almost 50,000 contributors, bringing the total pledged to over $1.8 million. Of this amount $500,000 was pledged by the clergy. Pastors were asked to contribute $1,000; curates $600, payable over two years. When the final report of the campaign was made in December 1941, nearly $1.7 million had been realized. This amount exceeded the total cost of construction and furnishings and campaign expenses.[2]

Bishop Walsh then moved to expand the Bishop's Association, adding branches for the clergy and religious. Clergy who already contributed would automatically become members; others were invited to apply for membership for an initiation fee of $300. Religious communities could obtain membership through the payment of $1,000 for the motherhouse or $100 for each house in the diocese. The Bishop's Association of the Laity would continue to enroll members for a minimum of $25.

The Bishop's Association now was the "Bishop's Association of Clergy, Religious and Laity." Walsh commissioned Professor Gonippo Raggi to create an impressive scroll to be presented to all who fully redeemed their pledges. The scroll was graced with a rendering of the new seminary and a portrait of Bishop Walsh.

In gratitude Walsh announced the bestowal of "superabundant and supreme spiritual privileges" on the members of the association. In a decree sent on January 27, 1937, to Bishop McLaughlin and "his successors *in perpetuum* in the office of Rector," he delineated these benefactions. It deserves to be quoted in full.

In perpetual attestation of our profoundest sense of gratitude and appreciation and eloquent recognition and perpetual remembrance of the purest charity and incomparable generosity of our benefactors, builders of our new seminary buildings, I hereby command you and your successor and successors in perpetuum in the office of rector of our major diocesan seminary of the Immaculate Conception, to have celebrated, beginning this current year 1937 A.D. and continue every year in perpetuum, at the major diocesan seminary aforesaid at Darlington at 9:30 a.m. a Solemn High Mass on the feast of St. Joseph, March 19th; and on the feast of Our Lord Jesus Christ the King, last Sunday in October; and on the feast of the Immaculate Conception of the Blessed Virgin Mary, December 8, for the intentions of and for the spiritual and temporal wellbeing and welfare of all the members of the three branches of the Bishop's Association for the Seminary; and on the Commemoration of All Souls, November 2, for the happy and eternal repose of the souls of all departed members and for the intentions of all living members of the three branches of the Bishop's Association for the major diocesan seminary.

I command that all the members of the Bishop's Association in its three branches for the major diocesan seminary shall be and shall remain in the daily prayers of the faculty and ecclesiastical student body of the major diocesan seminary of the Immaculate Conception hereafter and forever.

I command each and every ecclesiastical student in perpetuum ordained hereafter a priest for the diocese of Newark, and each and every ecclesiastical student in perpetuum ordained hereafter a priest under any canonical title from the major diocesan seminary of the Immaculate Conception, Darlington, to celebrate within thirty days after his ordination three low Masses for the intentions and for the spiritual and temporal wellbeing and welfare of all the members of the three branches of the Bishop's Association for the major diocesan seminary.

This decree shall be promulgated, read in its full text to the entire faculty and to the entire student body of the Major Diocesan Seminary of the Immaculate Conception in the seminary chapel immediately and again on the feast of St. Joseph, March 19, 1937 and annually thereafter on the feast of St. Joseph, March 19 in perpetuum.

> I am,
>
> Yours gratefully and devotedly in Christ,
>
> Thomas Joseph Walsh
>
> Bishop of Newark[3]

Listening to this letter and other similarly worded decrees every year, it is not surprising that seminarians nicknamed the bishop "In Perpetuum" and, given his long reign, "the perpetual Walsh."

Walsh "Encourages" Priests' Donations

While the campaign had been a success, the cooperation of the clergy was not as enthusiastic as public reports indicated. Walsh clearly was unhappy at the November 17, 1937, clergy conference. He reminded the clergy assembled, secular and religious, that they had received a $300 annual raise in 1928, and that this raise had continued in effect during the Depression. He also reminded the priests that he "had promulgated canonically and publicly" his judgment that each and "every priest, secular and regular, could afford to give and should give as a minimum gift, freely and promptly," the $300 salary increase for two years, or $600.

He expressed his annoyance that, "in many, many parishes," his directive that all pastors announce at Sunday Masses at the opening of the campaign the amounts of the pledges made by the pastor and assistants, "as an example and inspiration" to the people, was not obeyed. He further expressed his dismay that the attendance of priests at the six special pledge deanery dinners of the laity was "not numerous." The priests also were severely rebuked for not attending the cornerstone laying of the seminary the previous September 26, and for not, as directed, organizing "parish pilgrimages" to the cornerstone laying.

Walsh then presented the priests with the following "set-up," or list, which "shall be a progressive, certified, official, and permanent record."

Number of pledges made and paid in full—37

Number of pledges on which part payments have been made—425

Number of pledges made upon which no payments have been received—68

Number of clergy who did not sign or make a pledge—104

Walsh thanked those who had redeemed their pledges, and urged those who had not completed payment to do so before March 19, 1938. He also requested "the 104 priests who have no pledges to make pledges and to redeem their pledges on or before March 19, 1938."[4] To make sure that his will was made clear, a copy of his remarks was sent to all the priests of the diocese with pledge cards and a cover letter that, in appropriate cases noted, "You are listed in the group of the 104 priests."[5] Walsh also directed that the priests should hang their certificates in a prominent place in their rectories.

In response to this dunning letter, numerous priests explained why they were unable to pay what amounted to a personal assessment. Their plaints were rather sad. One, due to the poor financial conditions of the times, had been without a salary for a year and a half.[6] Another, whose brother had been killed in the Spanish Civil War, was supporting his penniless sister in Spain.[7] A third had unforeseen dental expenses and promised to pay as soon as possible.[8]

On November 22, 1937, Walsh issued a further decree commanding that all priests ordained prior to November 19 of that year and thereafter *in perpetuum* should become members of the Bishop's Association of the Clergy for the Major Diocesan Philosophical-Theological Seminary of the Immaculate Conception, Darlington, N.J., by the full payment of the membership fee of $300. Like all others, this decree was to be promulgated to "all actual or potential priests who may come under its application."[9]

Help From Mayor Hague

To ensure the success of his seminary campaign, Walsh did not hesitate to call in political favors. Mayor Frank Hague, the Democratic Party boss of Hudson County, and of New Jersey as well, was recruited to chair the campaign dinner in Hudson County and to "encourage" his followers to contribute. Hague himself contributed $15,000. He brought in an additional $52,000 from his chief lieutenants as well as from New Jersey corporations, including Standard Oil, Continental Can, Colgate-Palmolive, U.S. Gypsum, Lorillard, and National Grocery.[10] One of Hague's assistants, Harry A. Delaney, passed on contributions to the campaign from the warden of the Hudson County Penitentiary, the superintendents of the Jersey City police and fire departments, the chief of the Hudson County detectives, various fire department battalion chiefs, detectives from the prosecutor's office, and others who owed fealty to the mayor. Delaney, ever aware of security, wrote to Monsignor John McClary, the vicar general and pastor of St. Aedan's Church in Jersey City, that he would "mail checks to the rectory, and send cash by personal messenger."[11] In the Jersey City of that time, for various reasons, cash was utilized more than checks.

The Dream Becomes Reality

On April 9, 1937, the consultors approved the project; on April 16 the contracts were signed. The official groundbreaking took place on April 23. About 700 participated: clergy, seminarians, students from Seton Hall, and laity. The procession went from the chapel in the Crocker Mansion to the site of what would be the main entrance of the new residence building. The seminary choir sang the *Veni Creator;* the bishop addressed those gathered and turned over a spadeful of earth.

On September 26, 1937, the bishop presided at the laying of the cornerstones of the chapel and the residence building and delivered an address broadcast over radio station WOR. In his address, Walsh boasted that the campaign had exceeded its goals and invited further donations. [12]

The new complex would consist of a four-story, *H*-shaped residence building providing single rooms for 300 seminarians and 12 priests, offices for rector and procurator, reception and recreation rooms, a gymnasium, an auditorium, a kitchen, an infirmary, and a dining room for 400. A detached chapel, dedicated to Christ the King, was connected to the residence by an enclosed cloister walk.

As the seminary was under construction, Walsh received news that the Holy See recognized the growth of the Church in New Jersey and his achievements as well. Newark was elevated to metropolitan rank on December 10, 1937. The day before, the diocese of Paterson had been created, and on December 16, Thomas McLaughlin, the rector, was named its first bishop. At the same time, the diocese of Camden was established with territory taken from the diocese of Trenton.

A triple ceremony took place. The first, at Newark on April 27, 1938, brought the pallium to Archbishop Walsh; the second, at Paterson on the next day, installed Bishop McLaughlin in Paterson; and the third, at Newark on May 1, consecrated William A. Griffin as auxiliary bishop of Newark. On May 9, Griffin was named rector of the seminary. [13]

The newly created archdiocese of Newark was small in area, less than 500 square miles encompassing the counties of Hudson, Essex, Bergen, and Union. However, it embraced 645,000 Catholics, 185 parishes, and 21 missions served by 666 priests, diocesan and religious. The seminarians numbered 141 at Darlington and six in Rome and Louvain. [14]

By December 1937, the exterior construction was complete. Just a year after construction began, 141 seminarians took up residence on September 24, 1938, when now-Archbishop Walsh blessed the building. For the first time at Darlington, with the addition of the first-year philosophy students, all six years of the major seminary program were in place. The previous May there were 102 students on the roll. Of that number, 66 had names indicating that they were of Irish background, 17 Polish, nine German, five Italian, three Slav, and two Lithuanian. [15]

On December 8, the archbishop consecrated the Seminary Church of Christ the King and formally dedicated the seminary. In his sermon, Walsh thanked the many who had contributed to the campaign and reiterated the promised spiritual benefits *in perpetuum*, and reminded his listeners that there still was an opportunity to designate various furnishings in the chapel as memorials. He described the seminary as a place where "canonically committed and accepted ecclesiastical students aspiring to ordination to the Holy Priesthood are educated, trained, fashioned and proved."[16]

It was a full day. For the seminarians it began with rising at 4:30 a.m. They sang the penitential psalms at 5:40 a.m., a penance in itself.

The ceremonies began at 6 a.m. with the consecration of the chapel and its nine altars. Solemn Pontifical Mass at 9:30 was followed by four low Masses at half-hour intervals. An organ recital at 1 p.m. preceded the 2 p.m. canonical erection of the Stations of the Cross, which was followed by another organ recital. The last ceremony was Vespers, Benediction, and a solemn *Te Deum* at 5 p.m. Nothing was left out and the last hour was broadcast on the radio.[17]

At the series of services, 10 members of the hierarchy were present, together with priests, religious, and laity estimated at not fewer than 20,000. Seventeen hundred persons were served with dinner in the refectory and nearly 5,000 with buffet luncheon in another part of the building.[18] It was an event of truly biblical proportions, worthy of Archbishop Walsh.

Chapter Twenty

Pope Pius XI

During the years of transition from Seton Hall to Darlington, the Catholic Church was shepherded by Pope Pius XI (1922–1939). His initiatives in the area of devotions and spirituality, as well as in academic reforms, would have weighty influence on the seminary as it developed in its new home. He had taken as his motto *Pax Christi in Regno Christi* (The Peace of Christ in the Kingdom of Christ).

In the encyclical *Quas primas* in 1926, he expanded on the theme of reintegrating Christ into "lives, families, and public life."[1] In a gesture that rebuked the totalitarian regimes that had placed the state as the highest object of reverence, he established the liturgical feast of Our Lord Jesus Christ, King, setting it on the last Sunday in October. He linked devotion to the Sacred Heart of Jesus to the new feast of Christ the King by designating it as the appropriate day for the annual consecration of the world to the Sacred Heart. In 1928, in the encyclical *Miserentissimus Redemptor,* Pius raised the feast of the Sacred Heart to the highest liturgical rank.[2] These encyclicals stressed the necessity of atonement for sins through exercises of devotion that became traditions at the seminary.

Pius XI also made St. John Vianney the patron saint of parish priests. Known as the Curé of Ars, Vianney was a tireless confessor to whom troubled souls would unburden themselves. He had entered the seminary but was dismissed because of his lack of aptitude for learning. After private examination and instruction from his bishop, he was eventually ordained. According to historian Joseph M. White, "Among struggling seminarians his difficult pursuit of ordination was a source of consolation."[3]

The Sacred Congregations

Under Pius XI, the Sacred Congregation of the Sacraments issued directives that would require new policies in the seminaries. In 1930, this congregation was concerned over an increasing number of requests for declarations of nullity of ordinations due to outside pressure. In its instruction *Quam ingens ecclesiae*,[4] the congregation sought to protect the freedom of candidates for orders. Each candidate for minor or major orders was required to write out "in his own hand" a petition for reception of orders. In specific instances, the bishop could order a further investigation to ascertain the candidate's freedom.

This instruction was designed to protect seminarians from undue pressure from parents or relatives to seek ordination. So that seminarians would be aware, the congregation ordered that the instruction be read annually in seminaries, and that rectors bring the instruction to the attention of seminarians, discuss its provisions with officials and professors, and have sermons on the instruction.[5]

The Sacred Congregation of the Sacraments also was concerned over situations in seminaries that had developed as a result of Pius X's directives on frequent reception of Holy Communion. In seminaries, where the students attended daily Mass in a body, it was difficult for those who might wish to abstain from receiving Communion to do so without drawing attention. In a confidential instruction in 1938, the congregation emphasized that frequent Communion was optional and not obligatory, and seminarians were free not to receive Communion. It also urged that, in seminaries, a priest be available for confession before the community Mass so that members of the community could confess their sins so as to receive Communion worthily.[6]

Deus scientiarum Dominus

In 1931, Pius XI issued the apostolic constitution *Deus scientiarum Dominus*,[7] the most important and far-reaching document regarding seminaries since the 1917 Code of Canon Law. The apostolic constitution provided a charter for the Sacred Congregation of Seminaries and Universities in its direction of faculties that grant "ecclesiastical degrees." The constitution imposed stricter requirements for achieving degrees in the ecclesiastical universities. It ended the quick doctorates of theology and canon law that Roman universities conferred on the basis of written and oral examinations only six to 10 months after the completion of the ordinary seminary course. Doctoral degrees now required from two to five years of study and research.

Henceforth, in theology, a minimum of four years was required for the licentiate, and an additional year or more for the doctorate, which now required a dissertation entailing original research. In canon law, an additional two years after the seminary course was required for the licentiate and at least an additional year for the doctorate, which also required a dissertation.

In effect, the pope applied the academic standards of northern Europe and North America to the Roman universities. As White states, "The dissertation alone introduced the idea of research into theological study, with far-reaching consequences for bringing historical and critical methods into Catholic theology. The provisions of the constitution would have their impact in the training of theological faculties for seminaries."[8]

Deus scientiarum Dominus also highlighted the requirements of Canon 1366 of the 1917 Code of Canon Law that stated: "There should be separate professors at least for the following subjects: Sacred Scripture, Dogmatic Theology, Moral Theology and Ecclesiastical History."[9] From now on, seminary professors would be required to hold a doctorate in their specific field of instruction. The new seminary instructor, trained in the methods of research, was making the transition from apologist to scholar. The "old days" of professors with a general licentiate or a master of arts degree teaching "across the curriculum" soon would come to an end.

Pius XI's abiding interest in seminaries also was demonstrated in his 1935 encyclical *Ad Catholici Sacerdotii*,[10] a summary of all that was written on the priesthood and priestly formation. A major point of the encyclical was the emphasis on the priest as a participant in the action of Christ in the Church rather than as the sanctified loner of traditional literature. This encyclical had great influence on the spiritual formation of seminarians in the following decades. The apostolic delegate, Archbishop Amleto Giovanni Cicognani, requested that the encyclical be read in the seminaries and that the seminarians be given personal copies.[11]

In 1937, Cardinal Gaetano Bisletti, prefect of the Sacred Congregation of Seminaries and Universities, died, and Pope Pius XI assumed the office of prefect himself. He immediately ordered an apostolic visitation of all the world's seminaries to take place in 1938 and 1939. For more than a decade, seminaries had sent triennial reports to Rome. Now there would be a personal inspection to ensure that they were following the wishes of the Holy See.

Archbishop Cicognani, the apostolic delegate, announced the visitation to the bishops and informed them that he had been designated "apostolic visitor," and seven American bishops named as "associate visitors."[12] Unlike later visitations, this one was not announced publicly and was an internal and completely confidential Church affair.

Commenting on the visitation, Sulpician superior Father John Fenlon wrote, "The Congregation has a small opinion of the wisdom of hierarchies; all wisdom seems to be concentrated in the head of Monsignor Ruffini (Secretary of the Sacred Congregation of Seminaries and Universities), whose mind seems, (to himself at least) to mirror the eternal wisdom."[13]

The visitations usually lasted a day or two and were preceded by a detailed questionnaire requesting basic statistical information on the institution. Cicognani personally visited a number of seminaries and, where possible, gave them a chance to remedy problems before he sent his report to Rome.[14] Cicognani personally would visit Darlington.

Middle States Association

Pressures to achieve academic excellence also came from sources other than the Holy See. From the beginning of theological education at Seton Hall, the seminary was considered an integral part of the institution. Ever since the graduation of June 1866, seminary students had received the degree of master of arts from Seton Hall.[15]

In preparation for the move to Darlington, the Seton Hall trustees wished to continue this connection. In 1926, they resolved that the faculty and student body remain "an integral part" of Seton Hall. They repeated this decision in a resolution in May 1933, which separated the offices of rector and president.[16] Up until 1932, the *Seton Hall College Catalogue* would describe the graduate department of Seton Hall as functioning "in connection with the first and second year of study in the Theological Seminary at Darlington, N. J."[17] The long tradition of granting the M.A. degree to seminarians would end in that year.

Shortly after assuming the presidency of Seton Hall College in 1922, Monsignor McLaughlin began the arduous process of attaining academic accreditation from the Association of Colleges and Preparatory Schools of the Middle States and Maryland, known as the Middle States Association. In part, he was spurred by the experience of several Seton Hall graduates who, on applying to graduate schools, were told that their degrees would not be recognized because Seton Hall was not accredited.[18]

In November 1925, McLaughlin was notified that the Middle States Association had voted to defer action on Seton Hall's application. He also was informed that the association was hesitant to approve any M.A. degree granted by a college that had not yet had its A.B. degree approved.[19] Middle States had several concerns about Seton Hall: its insufficient library and laboratory facilities, the relationship of the college and the preparatory school, and the training and degrees of the faculty. Correspondence with Middle States continued over the next few years.

The Master of Arts Degree

Finally, in May 1932, Seton Hall received a visit from a representative of Middle States. The visitor, Professor George Gailey Chambers, of the University of Pennsylvania, noted that the M.A. degree now was given at the Darlington campus. He also criticized the holdings of the library at Seton Hall, noting that "there appears to be no recent large dictionary such as the *New International* or the *New Standard*." Chambers was very critical of the training of the faculty, most of whom had obtained their M.A. degrees through Seton Hall while they were in the seminary, and taught courses in a variety of fields. Regarding the M.A. degree, he reported that the areas of instruction "for the A.M. degree are philosophy, language, literature, social and natural science."[20]

This is surprising since most of the degree recipients were seminary students whose graduate studies were almost exclusively theological. The requirements as stated in the seminary catalogue of 1930–31 mention "students pursuing theological branches" and called for 24 graduate credits, proficiency in a modern foreign language, and an essay of 6,000 words. It appears that McLaughlin was raising the requirements. In McLaughlin's notes with his own corrections, probably prepared for the catalogue, we find a rather confused picture.

The notes state that applicants were required to prepare an article (changed to thesis) of 1,000 (changed to 3,000) words on a topic covered during the first two years of theology. All references were to be noted "in the margin" (crossed out). The fields are stated as "Dogmatic Theology with emphasis on the philosophical features, Moral Theology with emphasis on ethical problems, History, Sacred Scripture in its literary, linguistic, or archaeological features, Philosophy and its history." This line is entirely crossed out and "Philosophy, Science, Literature" are overwritten. Apparently, McLaughlin was trying to make the M.A. more palatable to the Middle States Association as evidenced in their report, which does not even mention theology as a discipline for the M.A.[21] It was too little, too late. He would not succeed.

McLaughlin raced to comply with Middle States requirements. He ordered new periodicals for the Seton Hall library as well as a copy of *Webster's New International Dictionary*.[22] The chairman of the Middle States Association, Adam Leroy Jones, went out of his way to give McLaughlin advice before the meeting of the association. He urged him to correct the practice of admitting inadequate students to the college, take steps to obtain better-trained faculty, reduce the size of classes, address poor salaries, and improve the science laboratories. He also noted that the "practice of the college in granting the degree of Master of Arts seems also to be open to criticism."[23]

McLaughlin scurried to find faculty, contacting the placement bureaus of Catholic University, Columbia, Yale, New York University, and the American Association of University Professors.[24] Over the summer, to the great amazement of Middle States, he hired twelve new faculty members, all with college teaching experience, seven holding doctor of philosophy (Ph.D.) degrees.[25]

McLaughlin quickly moved away from the problem of the M.A. degree, telling Jones that "we are not seeking any definite recognition for this degree at the present time."[26] The final Middle States report again mentioned the M.A. degree as an issue. The report described the degree as "apparently based on a part of the regular work in the theological seminary supplemented by a special essay. It appears to be awarded to all or nearly all of the theological students."[27] McLaughlin replied, offering to discontinue the M.A.: "It might be well to observe with regard to the A. M. degree that the college is willing to withhold giving this degree if the commission does not consider it proper for us to do so."

He then made some rather mystifying comments, definitely perplexing to a professor at the University of Pennsylvania.

> In the description, it might leave the impression that
> it was given to all theological students indiscriminately.
> This is not the case. On account of features connected
> with the clerical staff, we do not make any public
> record of theological students who fail. They simply
> are withdrawn without comment, so that all students
> who continue their studies and receive this degree have
> satisfactorily completed the work. In the seminary we
> do not rate failure. As already noted, they simply are
> withdrawn."[28]

In other words, seminarians who failed academically were told to leave the seminary. The Middle States Association, in its final report, informed McLaughlin that "while the Commission does not desire to be insistent in the matter, it did feel that it was not desirable for the college to grant an A.M. degree for work done entirely in the seminary."[29] In 1932, the Seton Hall master of arts degree was awarded to seminary students for the last time.

Chapter Twenty-one

Monsignor McLaughlin Goes to Europe

Pius XI's 1931 apostolic constitution *Deus scientiarum Dominus*[1] required that seminary professors have degrees in their specialty from ecclesiastical faculties, sometimes mistakenly called "pontifical" faculties. In 1932, at Walsh's direction, during his struggles with Middle States, Monsignor McLaughlin, together with Father Dauenhauer, sailed to Europe to investigate the various Catholic universities where the future professors of Immaculate Conception Seminary and Seton Hall College would be trained.

McLaughlin and Dauenhauer visited all of the Roman universities and *athenea*, as well as a wide assortment of possible residences for priest students in Rome. They did not limit themselves to Rome but also visited universities in Austria, France, Switzerland, Belgium, and England. For a variety of reasons, McLaughlin quickly eliminated the universities in France and England.

McLaughlin prepared a detailed report for Bishop Walsh, finishing while returning to the United States on the SS *Berlin*. One cannot help but feel that "Schlitz" felt quite comfortable on this liner. After expressing Pope Pius XI's "deep esteem" for Bishop Walsh and passing on the pope's blessings to all and sundry, as well as the regards of many Roman notables, McLaughlin got down to business.

Concerned with providing for the college as well as the seminary, he noted that the University of Fribourg in Switzerland and the University of Louvain in Belgium might serve as appropriate schools for training priests studying mathematics, languages, and science, as well as theology. Not surprisingly, he gave high praise to the University of Innsbruck, his alma mater.

In the end he concluded, "Rome remains the best place for theological, the only place for Canon Law and Scripture in their completeness. This however means first and foremost the Gregorian." He ended his report with a list of seminarians and recently ordained priests who should be sent to Rome, Innsbruck, and Louvain for studies in scripture, dogma, and canon law. [2]

New Professors Professionally Trained

As planned, Monsignor McLaughlin resigned the presidency of Seton Hall College on June 7, 1933, and was succeeded in that office by Reverend Francis J. Monaghan, of the seminary faculty.[3] McLaughlin was now able to devote his considerable energy exclusively to the seminary.

To succeed Father Monaghan, Reverend George W. Ahr was assigned to the seminary. Ahr, who had been ordained in 1928, held the doctorate in theology from the Propaganda University in Rome. In his time at Darlington, Doctor Ahr, as he was known even after he became bishop of Trenton, would lecture in dogmatic theology, metaphysics, oriental theology, and catechetics.[4]

During his visit to Europe, McLaughlin met with Newark students John Dougherty and John Tierney and arranged for them to pursue higher studies in Rome. Originally, Dougherty was assigned to study canon law, and Tierney scripture. The assignments were reversed before they began doctoral studies,[5] an intriguing turn of fate.

Tierney would die young as professor of canon law and director of discipline at Darlington. Dougherty would go on to be a highly regarded scripture scholar, often appearing on television, and to serve as president of Seton Hall University and as auxiliary bishop of Newark. Dougherty might have headed a diocese, had it not been for his opposition to the United States war in Vietnam. He told the present writer that Cardinal Francis Spellman had "blackballed" him for this reason.

In 1938, Fathers Henry G. J. Beck and Walter W. Curtis were sent to the Gregorian to pursue doctorates in Church history and moral theology respectively.[6]

Walsh and Educational Excellence

Bishop Walsh believed that an educated clergy was a pastoral necessity, in particular since the diocese sponsored both a seminary and a college. For Walsh, this could only be achieved by planning and commitment of resources. In the first 10 years of his reign, and that is the proper word, which roughly coincided with the first 10 years at Darlington, he transformed not only the physical structure of the seminary but also its program.

At home, in 1931, he established Aquinas House on the grounds of Seton Hall, as a residence for priests engaged in higher studies there or at universities in the metropolitan area. The majority of these priests would teach at Seton Hall, which now was required by Middle States to have professors trained in particular specialties rather than generalists.

Following Walsh's instructions, the seminary faculty asked students to indicate their personal areas of interest for potential graduate studies. The faculty members would then review and judge these requests based on their view of the students' abilities, and report to the bishop. In the 1940s, seminary students with particular aptitudes would spend their summers taking prerequisite courses at Seton Hall to insure their admission to graduate schools.

These studies were not limited to the "sacred sciences." Walsh wanted to have a cadre of professionally trained and degreed priests to teach in various fields in arts and sciences at Seton Hall as well. This careful long-range planning was typical of Bishop Walsh, as was evidenced in his well-planned seminary campaign. It well served the seminary and Seton Hall for decades to come.

The seminary followed a detailed process in making recommendations for further study. After the midterm examinations each professor was asked to compose a list of students in his subject who in his opinion had the qualifications to pursue higher studies. In 1939, 36 names from all six classes were recommended. Each of these was interviewed by the rector and vice rector together. From these a number were chosen. They were directed to consult with their professors and indicate whether they had an interest in graduate studies and what particular area appealed to them. Their qualifications and their area of interest were then discussed in a meeting of the faculty, and final recommendations were made to the archbishop.[7]

In 1943, Walsh extended this procedure to the seminarians in Seton Hall College in a decree entitled "Constitution of a Special Academic Commission in Seton Hall College."[8] This commission, consisting of the president of the college, the spiritual director of ecclesiastical students, and three other priests, was charged to ask each student, "Would you wish to teach in a high school or a college if you were an ordained priest?" If he answered affirmatively, his "piety, character, ability, personal appearance and disposition" were to be evaluated and the assessment of the commission sent to the rector of the seminary.

Strict Admissions Standards

That same year, Walsh formalized the process of recommending Seton Hall ecclesiastical students for admission to Darlington. In a decree regarding the "supremely important matter of the admissibility or inadmissibility of all students to the Major Philosophical-Theological Seminary," dated April 16, 1943, the archbishop outlined the procedure in minutest detail.[9]

All of the priest faculty of Seton Hall were to participate in an annual meeting in April for this purpose. They were to be given biographies of each candidate containing their academic and conduct ratings. The candidates were to be discussed as to "piety, disposition, character, integrity, ability, appearance, and vocation." Each priest then voted on each candidate, having been provided, at the archbishop's direction, with "paper and pencils for use of the priests in the secret balloting." There is no mention whether or not the pencils were collected after the meeting. "Upon the completion of this holy work, the meeting may recess for a period of not more than 24 hours to give the secretary the time to write the minutes." The next day, after the approval of the minutes, each priest was to sign them and they were to "be delivered within five days to the archbishop of Newark at the chancery office."[10]

The archbishop then wrote to the pastor of each candidate requesting his opinion according to a specified interrogatory. No student was to be accepted unless he had satisfactorily passed all his preliminary work at Seton Hall. The rector of the seminary personally interviewed each candidate. After receiving a doctor's report, the composite report was sent to the archbishop, and notice of acceptance or non-acceptance was sent to the candidate.[11]

The Master School of Modern Languages

Underlying all of Walsh's academic planning was a pastoral foundation. In 1930, he decreed the establishment of the "Master School of Modern Languages" at the seminary. Classes were held weekly in Italian, German, Lithuanian, Slovak, and Polish. In 1936 Walsh expended the Master School to ecclesiastical students in Seton Hall High School and College, adding Arabic, Armenian, French, Hungarian, and Spanish. In a lengthy decree, he described this program in detail. Its goal was that each and every future priest has a "salutary, comprehensive, and certified reading, writing, speaking knowledge of a second modern language." The students were expected to take the language of their heritage.

As Walsh put it, the "student of a blood [sic] having a national language shall select and pursue the course in his national language." Students could expect to be assigned to national parishes after ordination. Those of Irish or "American" background most often took Italian. What constitutes an "American" background is not indicated by the usually precise archbishop. In Walsh's legalistic and rather strange expression, the "student of a blood of an English-speaking nation may select and shall select and pursue the course in any of the aforementioned languages. The selection of the language shall be deliberate, as it is unchangeable."

Each student was ordered to "possess, hold, and use" a dictionary, a grammar, a Bible, and a prayer book in the language studied, and to practice discourses and sermons in the language. Ever a stickler for detail and direction, Walsh added, "May I recommend that every student look up every word in the dictionary signing the word looked up in every reference with the dot of a lead pencil. May I recommend that every student learn one new word every day during all his years of study."

The bishop was not going to exempt any transfer student in the high school from fulfilling the requirements of this program. Each and every transfer student had one year to catch up to his counterparts, "under penalty of perpetual ineligibility ipso facto incurred to adoption as an ecclesiastical student of the diocese of Newark or to admission to its diocesan seminary." [12]

Ideally, a newly ordained priest who had gone through the program from his first year of high school would have attained fluency in a modern language after twelve years of study. In spite of the draconian and legalistic tone typical of Walsh, the program had obvious pastoral benefits. Walsh did not forget the deaf, assigning Father Stephen Landherr, C.Ss.R., as professor of sign language. Father Landherr would serve until the 1970s, when he was replaced by Reverend John Hourihan.

In 1936, two seminarians were studying Lithuanian, eight German, 13 Polish, and three "Slavish." Seventy-two were studying Italian, five of them of Italian origin, the others of Irish or "American" backgrounds.[13] The number of seminarians of Italian background never equaled the need for service to the large Italian-American immigrant population. The Master School of Modern Languages would continue until the 1960s, when it was replaced by programs concentrating on Spanish.

Latin also was essential, as often stressed by Rome. By Walsh's command, lectures, recitations, and examinations in dogmatic and moral theology and in canon law were conducted in Latin. Philosophy students used Latin textbooks, but otherwise used English.[14]

Music

Bishop Walsh, following the instructions on sacred music of Pope Pius X, insisted that the seminarians be well trained in chant and be familiar with all other forms of sacred music. In 1932, at Walsh's behest, Professor Nicola A. Montani, a professional conductor and composer, was appointed professor of chant. Montani, born in Utica, New York, in 1880, received his professional training at the Conservatory of St. Cecilia in Rome. In 1914, he had been one of the founders of the Society of St. Gregory and, from 1915 to 1942, editor of its organ, *The Catholic Choirmaster.*

Under Montani's direction, the seminary choir attained what many regarded as professional quality, singing on various radio shows and recording several phonograph records. At the seminary, the music followed *The St. Gregory Hymnal*, edited by Montani, and was enhanced by pieces that the maestro composed specifically for the seminary. Among these was a multi-part setting of *The Divine Praises.*

Walsh also appointed Montani director of the archdiocesan Institute of Sacred Music. The institute provided training and advice for parish organists and choirs, and supervised annual "Demonstration Masses" that celebrated solemn Mass to a degree of musical and liturgical perfection rarely achieved.

Montani supervised the musical preparation for solemn ceremonies in Newark's St. Patrick's Pro-Cathedral and in the unfinished Cathedral of the Sacred Heart. The interior of Sacred Heart was decorated for several major occasions such as episcopal consecrations and the reception of the pallium when Newark was raised to the status of an archdiocese. These services can best be described as imperial.

Bishop Walsh had a special interest in ceremony and music. He insisted on the most elaborate liturgy and perfection in its execution. For Holy Week, Christmas, Pentecost, and other feasts, the choirs of Immaculate Conception Seminary combined with the choir of the Religious Teachers Filippini of Morristown and the Cathedral Singers. Professor Montani, a professional conductor and composer, directed the music.

On these occasions the pontifical Mass was celebrated with splendor rarely seen in this hemisphere. Bishop Walsh's entry into the cathedral, to a polyphonic arrangement of *Ecce Sacerdos Magnus*, was an event comparable to a Renaissance pageant. Two Papal Chamberlains of the Sword and Cape, one of them the artist Gonippo Raggi, escorted him. These chamberlains were arrayed in the military-style uniform of Knights of St. Gregory, gold-embroidered tunics, gold chains of office, and plumed hats and swords. Walsh was vested in an ermine cape over his magenta *cappa magna*, a long silk train. As many as six young pages, in costumes of silk and velvet, carried the train. The organ often was accompanied by an orchestra and combinations of Gregorian chant and polyphony filled the cathedral. The seminarians strove to be in the choir since these ceremonies gave them an opportunity to leave the strict confines of the seminary and its routine, even for a few hours.[15] Professor Montani remained at Darlington until his death in 1948.[16]

A New Integrated Curriculum

The issuance of *Deus scientiarum Dominus* in 1931, followed by Seton Hall's decision to cease to award the master of arts degree for work exclusively done at the seminary, provoked extensive changes in the Darlington curriculum and in its educational policies. Besides professors trained in particular specialties, Rome desired more thorough teaching in various areas.

In January 1938, McLaughlin announced to the faculty that a six-year curriculum in philosophy and theology would be prepared for submission to the archbishop.[17] In June 1938, Archbishop Walsh established a committee to review and expand the seminary curriculum and to coordinate it with the curricula of Seton Hall College and High School. The committee consisted of the faculties of the seminary and college and other priests who were officials of the archdiocese of Newark and the newly created diocese of Paterson.[18] The committee met though the summer of 1938 and, in September, Walsh approved the new seminary curriculum.[19] While the new curriculum included recommendations regarding high school and college religion courses, its chief accomplishment was the revision of the six-year Darlington curriculum. With the opening of the new seminary buildings, all six years finally would be at the same place.

The curriculum suggested that the two-year philosophy course at Darlington be increased to 32 credits from the 24 then current at Seton Hall. All other courses, English, education, etc., were made identical with those at the college, so that the Darlington students would be able to fill the requirements for the bachelor of arts degrees.[20] The seminary would continue for more than three decades to describe its philosophy curriculum as "an integral part of the College of Arts and Sciences of Seton Hall University."[21]

Chapter Twenty-two

Affiliation with the Catholic University of America

Walsh wanted a theology curriculum that would conform to that of the Gregorian University in Rome with a view to granting the licentiate in theology degree at Darlington.[1] His goal was to affiliate Darlington with a pontifical university. The revised theology curriculum was in accord with this purpose. In August 1938, Father Edward Coffey, S.J., of the Gregorian University met with seminary officials to discuss affiliation.

Both Walsh and McLaughlin regarded the Gregorian University as the best of the Roman schools. They were pleased when, in 1932, the North American College changed its policy of sending seminarian students to the Propaganda University and switched to the Gregorian. Monsignor Eugene S. Burke, a Newark priest and rector of the college, reported to McLaughlin at the time that the change was made without objection, save from the Secretary of the Propaganda.[2] However, this project would be put aside when the Catholic University of America (CUA) invited American seminaries to request affiliation with its pontifical theology faculty.

Contact had been made with Monsignor Joseph Corrigan, rector of The Catholic University of America in July and, on August 11, he appointed Monsignor Francis Lardone to act as his delegate.[3] On August 17 and 18, Monsignor Lardone met with Bishop Griffin and, on August 23, 1938, Archbishop Walsh signed an agreement entering into a temporary affiliation with CUA. The seminary ceded supervision over its theology courses to the university, in return receiving the right to have its own students qualify for admission with advanced standing in the university's licentiate in sacred theology program.[4]

On December 6, 1938, the Sacred Congregation of Seminaries and Universities approved the affiliation on a probationary basis. It would be confirmed for an additional five years in 1942. In 1947, it was declared to be permanent.[5] The program was much more selective and rigorous than that which granted master of arts degrees from Seton Hall in previous years. Only academically gifted seminarians would be selected to take part in the program, and take their last year of residence at the Catholic University campus in Washington, DC. It gave some, but not all, students an opportunity to receive a graduate degree for their four years of study.

At the time of the affiliation, Darlington was the first and only seminary to be so affiliated. An interesting and amusing sidelight on this question of affiliation occurred at the National Catholic Educational Association Convention in 1939. Monsignor Corrigan, rector of CUA, read a paper on the subject of affiliation of seminaries with the university and mentioned that Darlington was the only seminary so affiliated. A priest indignantly asked why Corrigan had not notified the bishops of the country about this possibility. Corrigan replied that he had notified all the bishops, but the archbishop of Newark was the only one who had taken advantage of the opportunity.[6] Once again, Walsh had moved swiftly and without hesitation. Until the end of the affiliation in 1958, 78 Darlington students achieved the licentiate in sacred theology.

A New Curriculum

From a pedagogical perspective, the most positive effect of the curriculum review was the reduction of the number of classes included in the dreaded "cycle." Previously, dogmatic theology, moral theology, canon law, scripture, and Church history all were taught as cycle courses throughout all four years of theological studies. The new program did away with this over a two-year period, ending in 1941. The rector reported, "The curriculum now calls for fundamental dogma and fundamental moral to be taught each year in first theology, the sacraments in dogma, and the two tracts on penance and matrimony in moral will be taught each year in fourth theology. The other tracts in dogma and moral will be taught in cycle in second and third theology."[7]

Henceforth, first-year and fourth-year theology classes were separated from the cycle, leaving a two-year cycle for second and third theology students. The only exception was Church history. There, first theology was separated from the cycle in 1943, and fourth theology finally in 1961.[8]

Faculty Transitions and Misunderstandings

In order to provide for this expanded curriculum, six priests were assigned to the seminary in 1938. Reverend John J. Tierney, ordained in 1932, had agreed to continue on to doctoral work during McLaughlin's 1932 visit to Rome. He returned with the licentiate in theology from the Gregorian University, and in canon law from the Lateran University. Illness had prevented him from completing the doctorate in both laws. Tierney was assigned as professor of canon law. Reverend Joseph P. Christopher, ordained a priest of the Rockford, Illinois, diocese in 1916 in Rome, where he earned the S.T.L. degree, held the doctorate in philosophy in classical languages from Catholic University, where he had been serving from 1919 to 1937. He was assigned to teach Latin and English. Reverend Daniel F. Meehan, ordained in 1929, having earned an M.A. from Columbia University, was assigned to teach English, although not to reside in the seminary.

In addition, three Benedictines were assigned for three-year terms as resident professors at the seminary. Father Albert Hammenstede, a native of Cologne, Germany, was ordained in 1901. Former prior of Maria Laach Monastery, he earned an S.T.D. degree at San Anselmo in Rome, and was assigned to teach liturgy and Church history. Father Damasus Winzen, a native of Hanover, Germany, was ordained at Maria Laach in 1923, and assigned to teach philosophy. He too held a doctorate in sacred theology from San Anselmo. Father Leo Rudloff, born in Dueren, Germany, and ordained at Gerleve in 1926, also with a doctorate from San Anselmo, would teach patrology and moral theology.[9] In 1952, Father Leo, by that time a United States citizen, became abbot of Dormition Abbey in Jerusalem, which the Israeli government would not have permitted otherwise.[10] Father Leo, scion of old German minor nobility, constantly reminded seminarians that his proper name was von Rudloff.[11]

The good monks were to have a rocky time at Darlington. In 1939, the monks addressed a letter to Archbishop Walsh questioning their roles and responsibilities, and their remuneration. They had no more success than the poor seminarian who asked Walsh for a week's vacation at Christmas. Walsh summoned them to a meeting with himself, the rector, vice rector, the procurator, and the chancellor and vice chancellor of the archdiocese.[12]

Walsh angrily demanded responses to the letter, phrase by phrase. In their letter the monks had said that they observed "a certain reservation" in the seminary, and explained this on the grounds that they were "only guests." Walsh demanded to know what they meant by that. They responded, "We stood apart from discipline and other matters which we felt were not our concern." To this Walsh thundered: "You three Reverend Benedictine Fathers have no administrative authority whatever in the seminary." This apparently was the point the monks were trying to make.

They also had asked for some additional time off and Walsh informed them that if they took more than the three weeks' vacation allotted to the diocesan priests of the seminary, their salary would be reduced proportionately. The monks also had asked for the "full payment" of the honoraria they received for parish work on Sundays. The seminary custom was to turn half of the honoraria over to the seminary treasury. Walsh told the monks, "I promised the Benedictine Fathers 50 percent of their earnings for services in parishes and 50 percent only."

At the end of the meeting, the archbishop gave his judgment in his typically legalistic manner.

I hereby conditionally release you from fulfillment of
your three years service pledge and promise as follows:
I hereby permit you three Benedictine Fathers,
individually and collectively to file in writing with the
Most Reverend Rector of the Seminary on or before July
1, 1939 as effective September 1st 1939 or on or before
July 1st 1940 as effective September 1st 1940 your
formal resignation or resignations of your professorship
or professorships in this our Archdiocesan Major
Seminary of the Immaculate Conception in
Darlington, N.J.

After this contretemps, peace was restored and the good Benedictines remained at the seminary for the remainder of their terms, except for Father Albert, who fell ill and resigned in 1940.[13] He then repaired to St. Meinrad Abbey in Indiana.[14]

The following year would see the addition of Reverend Walter W. Curtis to the faculty as professor of moral theology. Father Curtis, ordained in 1937, was completing his doctorate, but, due to the need for a second moral theology professor to align the courses with Catholic University, he was recalled from Rome early and would finish his doctorate several years later. He was consecrated auxiliary bishop of Newark in 1957, and named bishop of Bridgeport, Connecticut, in 1961.

Joining Father Curtis was Reverend George W. Shea. Ordained in Innsbruck in 1936, Father Shea continued graduate study there. When the Innsbruck theological faculty was suppressed by the Nazis in 1938, Shea went to Switzerland with the Innsbruck faculty. There, reorganized as the Pontifical Canisianum Academy, it conferred the doctorate in theology on him in 1939. He would become professor of dogmatic and fundamental theology and seminary librarian. Shea would serve as a chaplain from 1942 to 1946.

In 1940, Reverend Henry G. J. Beck, ordained in 1938, joined the faculty as professor of Church history. Beck had received the licentiate in theology from the Gregorian in 1938 and the licentiate in Church history in 1940. The closing of the North American College in 1940, due to the tensions of World War II, forced him to interrupt his studies and return home. He finished his doctoral studies after the war ended.

Apostolic Visitation

The diocese was now an archdiocese, its ordinary a metropolitan; the new seminary was completed and blessed, the curriculum revised in accord with Roman standards; new faculty trained at pontifical universities were on the staff; and the seminary was affiliated with the Catholic University of America. It was time to welcome Pope Pius XI's representative on an inspection tour.

On December 11, 1938, just three days after the elaborate dedication ceremonies, Archbishop Amleto Giovanni Cicognani, the apostolic delegate, returned to Darlington to conduct an apostolic visitation. The Holy See had directed Cicognani or his delegate to conduct such visitations of all the seminaries in the United States.

These visitations consisted of an official investigation of the seminary faculty and student body, records, buildings, equipment, forms, and curriculum. Before Cicognani's arrival, the seminary had prepared a detailed report including resumes of faculty, descriptions of the courses and curriculum, lists of textbooks, and the daily schedule of seminary life. In many ways, the process is similar to a visitation from an academic accrediting agency.

The visitation lasted from Saturday, December 10 through Monday, December 12.[15] It went off with clock-like precision. The apostolic delegate, accompanied by his secretary, Monsignor Joseph McShea, later the first bishop of Allentown, Pennsylvania,[16] was met at Newark Pennsylvania Station at 7:20 p.m. by the rector, Bishop Griffin, accompanied by Reverend Martin Stanton,[17] archdiocesan director of the Society for the Propagation of the Faith. They proceeded by car to the seminary and arrived one hour later. As soon as they departed Newark Pennsylvania Station, Father Stanton hastened to nearby St. John's Church to alert the seminary by telephone that the delegate did not desire the elaborate "liturgical visitation ceremony" that had been planned. He must have been fatigued by the train ride.

The official visitation began at 4 p.m. on Sunday. The delegate had spent most of Sunday at the Hackensack parish of his friend, the former rector of Rome's North American College, Monsignor Eugene Burke, where he celebrated Solemn Mass.

Returning to the seminary, the delegate interviewed the rector from 4 to 6 p.m. They discussed the entire personnel of the seminary: officers, professors, religious sisters, and lay help. Cicognani inquired regarding the board of deputies, the frequency of its meetings, and the role of the archbishop on the board.

The delegate asked very detailed and rather fussy questions regarding seminary discipline. He "inquired whether the seminarians leave the seminary grounds . . . their recreation . . . their games and reading." He also asked whether the seminarians were allowed to visit other seminarians' rooms and "whether there is an assigned place at table at which the same seminarian remains for the entire year or whether they may sit at any place at any meal." He was interested "whether the various nationalities were inclined to group themselves together and keep themselves aloof from others; on whether there were any cliques in the seminary" and whether smoking was permitted in the rooms.

Regarding the spiritual director, Cicognani asked about his character and "whether he gives his conferences with regularity . . . and . . . exemplifies his teaching in his own life." Regarding "temporalities," wise Italian prelate that he was, his major interests were the quality of the food and the continuing financial stability of the seminary.

The next morning, the delegate continued his interview with the rector. He was very interested in the extent to which Latin was used in lectures and exams. The rector informed him that since the seminary came to Darlington, Latin had been the language of the classroom and the examinations in theology, and Roman Latin diction was insisted upon. Training in chant was another interest of the delegate, and he was pleased to hear that four 50-minute periods a week were devoted to chant.

Cicognani also made inquiries concerning the sisters and suggested that they be given conferences twice a month.

The delegate thoroughly inspected all parts of the seminary, chapel, faculty and student rooms, recreation rooms, the kitchen, and the basement. He even went up to the roof to see the neighboring countryside. In the library, he took great interest in the periodicals available to the seminarians.

The delegate spent three days at the seminary, carrying on his work "with regulation, method and minute detail." Cicognani spent a total of two-and-a-half hours with the rector, and 20 to 30 minutes with each member of the faculty. He addressed the seminarians in the chapel at noon and told them he would meet with any seminarian who wished to speak with him.

After lunch and a siesta, he met with seminarians. They had been asked to volunteer to meet with Cicognani, but none did so. The vice rector then selected 12, wisely choosing students who represented the various nationalities, to meet with the delegate. He met with each for about 10 minutes.[18]

Roman Praise

In his report to the deputies, Bishop Griffin made particular note that no one was put under oath during the course of the Darlington visitation, remarking that "in some seminaries the Most Reverend Apostolic Delegate interviewed almost a hundred students and all under oath." With great pride, Griffin stated that the delegate's final word "was one of complete satisfaction and approval for the seminary, its faculty, its student body and its appointments."

Griffin expressed confidence that all met with Cicognani's approval. He reported to Walsh that the delegate told him to "inform Archbishop Walsh that I am greatly pleased with my visit to Darlington and that I would like to come back in the Spring, when the flowers here are all in bloom, to take a few days recreation."[19]

In July 1941, Cardinal Giuseppe Pizzardo, prefect of the Sacred Congregation of Seminaries and Universities, responded to the apostolic delegate's report in a letter to Archbishop Walsh. Cicognani evidently had been pleased and impressed. Pizzardo described his report as "not so much a recital of facts and observations but rather a eulogy of the Immaculate Conception Seminary."

He wrote:

> For the delegate recounts not only Your Excellency's
> vigorous determination and untiring efforts in
> making all the plans and preparations necessary
> for the accomplishment of so great an undertaking,
> he describes not only the unbounded generosity of the
> clergy and laity, the extent and charm of the seminary
> site, the beauty and convenience of the buildings
> erected, the huge sum of money collected and expended,
> but he likewise praises the prudence and vigilance
> of the superiors whom you have placed in charge
> of the seminary, the learning and skill of the professors
> and the lively interest of the students in their studies
> as well as their docility and amenability.
>
> What shows more clearly your vigilance and
> farsightedness is the organizing of the bishop's
> association which had for its object both the actual
> building of the seminary and its maintenance and
> development in the future.[20]

Pizzardo then praised the seminary's constitutions and rules, sent, like the entire report, in Latin. But apparently the cardinal could not restrain himself from adding some comments of his own, written with a fine Roman hand: "The typographical errors with which the copy attached to the report abounds should be carefully corrected in a new edition." He also asked Walsh to "erect a minor seminary properly so called."[21]

The Seminary Faculty

When the new seminary opened, it had a larger faculty than ever; 16 priests, one layman, for 141 students. Not all were resident; nor were all full-time. Many of the language professors were engaged in pastoral work and came to the seminary once a week for their class.

The affiliations with Seton Hall and with Catholic University necessitated an apparently complicated arrangement whereby the same professor often served on both faculties. Just as administrators often taught, faculty also had a variety of administrative responsibilities. Father Ahr, professor of dogma, served as sacristan, and Father Dougherty, professor of scripture, was librarian. This was typical of seminaries at the time and today as well.

The Seminarians

At the time of the dedication and the visitation, the 141 seminarians in the new Darlington represented, although not proportionally, the ethnic makeup of the dioceses of Newark and Paterson. Eighty, or 58 percent, were of Irish heritage. Thirty-five were of Polish or Slavic background, 14 of German background; only ten bore Italian names. There was a lone seminarian whose name indicated his French heritage and one more with a Dutch name.

The effects of the slowdown of immigration during World War I and the subsequent anti-immigration legislation of the 1920s were apparent. All but four of the 141 were born in the United States. Two of the four foreign-born were Irish who had been born in England, one was born in Italy, and one in Czechoslovakia.

The 137 American-born overwhelmingly were from the local area. One hundred fourteen were natives of the dioceses of Newark and Paterson. Nineteen were by birth from the neighboring dioceses of New York; Brooklyn; Trenton; Albany; Hartford, Connecticut; and Philadelphia. Two had been born in Ohio, in Toledo and Cleveland. One was from Springfield, Massachusetts. The only one not born in the northeast was from Lafayette, Louisiana.[22]

Chapter Twenty-three

The Seminary in 1938

The seminary, now in its new home at Darlington, was very tightly structured. These charts provide a skeleton that shows the results of years of planning and organization.

OFFICERS	TITLE
Most Rev. William A. Griffin D.D., LL.D.	Rector
Rev. Charles C. Demjanovich, M.A.	Procurator
Rev. Michael E. Donnelly, M.A.	Vice Rector
Rev. Justin J. McCarthy, M.A., S.T.L.	Spiritual Director
Rev. George W. Ahr, S.T.D.	Sacristan
Rev. John J. Dougherty, M.A., S.T.L., S.S.L.	Librarian
John C. Petrone, M.D.	Physician

Philosophy Department, Affiliated with Seton Hall College
For the conferring of the Degree of Bachelor of Arts

FACULTY	COURSES
Rev. Damasus Winzen, O.S.B., Ph.D.	Logic, Epistemology, Psychology, History of Philosophy, French
Rev. Leo von Rudloff, O.S.B., S.T.D.	Ontology, Cosmology, German
Rev. Joseph P. Christopher, M.A. (Oxon), S.T.L., Ph.D.	Latin, English, Italian, Roman Latin Diction, French, German for post-graduate work
Rev. Michael E. Donnelly, M.A.	Education

Rev. Justin J. McCarthy, M.A., S.T.L.	Religion
Rev. Daniel F. Meehan, M.A.	English
Rev. John J. Dougherty, M.A., S.T.L., S.S.L.	Hebrew, Biblical Greek
Rev. Albert Hammenstede, O.S.B., S.T.D.	French
Rev. Charles C. Demjanovich, M.A.	Slovak
Rev. Michael G. Kemezis, A.B., M.A.	Lithuanian
Rev. Joseph Jarumczuk, A.B., M.A.	Plain Chant
Rev. Boleslaus D. Moscinski, A.B., S.T.L.	Polish
Nicola A. Montani, K.C.St.S.	Ecclesiastical Music

Theological Department affiliated with the Catholic University of America for the conferring of ecclesiastical degrees

FACULTY	COURSES
Most Rev. William A. Griffin, D.D., LL.D.	Pastoral Theology
Rev. Albert Hammenstede, O.S.B., S.T.D.	Ecclesiastical History, Christian Archaeology, Liturgy, Rubrics, French
Rev. Thomas A. Boland, S.T.L.	Diocesan Faculties and Statutes
Rev. Joseph P. Christopher, M.A. (Oxon), S.T.L., Ph.D.	Italian, French, and Italian for students preparing for degrees
Rev. Charles C. Demjanovich, M.A.	Slovak, Ecclesiastical Accounting and Moderator of Missiology Seminar
Rev. Leo von Rudloff, O.S.B., S.T.D.	Moral Theology, Patrology, German
Rev. Justin J. McCarthy, M.A., S.T.L.	Ascetical Theology, Homiletics
Rev. George W. Ahr, S.T.D.	Dogmatic Theology, Catechetics
Rev. Damasus Winzen, O.S.B., Ph.D.	French
Rev. Michael G. Kemezis, A.B., M.A.	Lithuanian
Rev. John J. Dougherty, M.A., S.T.L., S.S.L.	Sacred Scripture, Sociology
Rev. Boleslaus D. Moscinski, S.T.L.	Polish
Rev. Stephen Landherr, C.Ss.R.	Sign Language
Nicola A. Montani, K.C.St.S.	Ecclesiastical Music[1]

1938 Curriculum

While it is clear that this is a very heavy load of classes, some of the classes, such as the modern language classes in the Master School, were not credit-bearing. Reverend James Kelley, president of Seton Hall College, was concerned that the large number of credits per semester would raise objections from accrediting agencies, but the seminary, even with some classes not bearing credits, went ahead with a very taxing program.[2]

Below is a summary of the seminarians' studies, as well as the hours per week of instruction for each class.

YEAR	HOURS OF INSTRUCTION
First Philosophy	
Ontology	4
Logic	8
Religion	4
Cosmology	8
History	4
Latin	8
Pedagogy	6
Hebrew	2
English	6
Eloquence	2
Modern Language	2
Chant	3
Total	**57; 20 in Philosophy**
Second Philosophy	
Psychology	4
Natural Theology	4
Religion	4
Pedagogy	6
English	6
Ethics	6
History	4
Hebrew	2
Eloquence	2
Greek	2
Latin	6
Modern Language	2
History of Philosophy	2
Chant	3
Total	**43; 12 in Philosophy**
Total for two years	**100; 32 in Philosophy**
First Theology	
Sacred Scripture	8
Fundamental Theology	10
Ascetical Theology	2
Patrology	2
Homiletics	2

Liturgy	4
Church History	6
Moral Theology	8
Modern Language	2
Eloquence	2
Chant	3
Total	**49; 8 in Dogma, 8 in Moral, 8 in Scripture**

Second Theology

Scripture	8
Dogmatic Theology	10
Ascetical Theology	2
Homiletics	2
Canon Law	6
Moral Theology	8
Christian Archaeology	2
Modern Language	2
Eloquence	2
Chant	3
Total	**45; 10 in Dogma, 8 in Moral, 8 in Scripture**

Third Theology

Scripture	8
Dogmatic Theology	10
Ascetical Theology	2
Liturgy	2
Canon Law	6
Church History	6
Moral Theology	8
Modern Language	2
Chant	3
Sign Language	2
Total	**49; 10 in Dogma, 8 in Moral, 8 in Scripture**

Fourth Theology

Scripture	8
Dogmatic Theology	10
Ascetical Theology	2
Liturgy	2
Archdiocesan Statutes and Faculties of Confessors	1

Pastoral Theology	4
Christian Sociology	4
Catechetics	4
Moral Theology	8
Modern Language	2
Chant	3
Sign Language	2
Total	**50; 10 in Dogma, 8 in Moral, 8 in Scripture**
Total for four years	**193; 38 in Dogma, 24 in Moral, 24 in Scripture**

In order to fulfill this very demanding curriculum, seminarians attended class five days per week. Each day classes were held for four 50-minute periods beginning at 8:15 a.m. Two days per week, one or two classes were held in the afternoon and chant on another afternoon.[3]

Their program used both Latin and English texts and manuals. Archbishop Walsh maintained control even of the textbooks, personally approving a change of the dogma text from Pesch to Hervé in 1943.[4] Below is a summary of the approved course material.

COURSE	AUTHOR	TEXT	YEAR
Pastoral Theology	Schulze, F.	A Manual of Pastoral Theology	1936–39
Fundamental Theology	Pesch, C.	Compendium Theologiae Dogmaticae	1936
Dogmatic Theology	Pesch, C.	Volumes I, II, III, IV	1936
Moral Theology	Noldin, H.	Summa Theologiae Moralis I, II, III	1937
Church History	Birkhaeuserr	History of the Church	1933
Logic	Hickey, J. S.	Summa Philosophiae Scholasticae	1933
Ontology	Hickey, J. S.	Summa Philosophiae Scholasticae	1933
Cosmology	Hickey, J. S.	Summa Philosophiae Scholasticae	1933
Psychology	Hickey, J. S.	Summa Philosophiae Scholasticae	1933
Theodicy	Hickey, J. S.	Summa Philosophiae Scholasticae	1933
Ethics	Hickey, J. S.	Summa Philosophiae Scholasticae	1933
Liturgy-Rubrics	Wapelhorst	Compendium Liturgiae Sacrae	1935
	Caronti	The Spirit of the Liturgy	1932
Pedagogy	Kelly, W.	Educational Psychology	1932
History of Philosophy	Glenn, P.	History of Philosophy	1932
Scripture	Pont. Bibl. Inst.	Institutiones Biblicae	1932
Ascetic Theology	Tanquerey	The Spiritual Life	1931
Archaeology	Marucchi	Christian Archaeology	1935
Religion	Herzog	God the Redeemer	1938
Hebrew	Davidson	Hebrew Grammar	1933

Greek	Nunn	Elements of New Testament Greek	1936
Sociology	Pope Pius XI	Quadragesimo Anno	
	Pope Leo XIII	Rerum Novarum	
Patrology	Cayré	Manual of Patrology	1937

In addition, other books were used by professors or assigned to students.

COURSE	AUTHOR	TEXT
Fundamental Theology	St. Thomas	Summa Theologiae
	Garrigou-Lagrange	De Revelatione
Patrology	Cayré	Manual of Patrology
Ascetic Theology	Devine	Manual of Ascetical Theology
	Pierce	Virtues and Vices
	Pourrat	Christian Spirituality
	Noval-Fernandez	Theologiae Asceticae et Mysticae
Cursus		
	Farge	Ordinary Ways of Spiritual Life
Dogmatic Theology	Pesch	Praelectiones
	Tanquerey	Praelectiones
	Hervé	Praelectiones
	Lepicier	Praelectiones
	Palmieri	Praelectiones
	Billot	Praelectiones
	Franzelin	Praelectiones
	Hugon	Praelectiones
Moral Theology	St. Alphonsus	Theologia Moralis
	St. Thomas	Summa Theologiae
	Vermersch	Theologia Moralis
	Wouters	Theologia Moralis
	Prümmer	Theologia Moralis
	Aertnys-Damen	Theologia Moralis
	Capello	De Sacramentis
Philosophy	Mercier	Varia
	Hugon	Varia
	Gredt	Varia
	Joyce	Varia
	Maritain	Varia
	Maher	Varia
	Boedder	Varia
Canon Law	Maroto	Institutiones Juris Canonici
	Chelodi	Jus de Persona
	Cicognani	Normae Generales

Ethics	Cronin	Science of Ethics
	Donat	Ethica Generalis et Specialis
	Cathrein	Philosophia Moralis
Scripture	Höpfl	Introduction Generalis
	Cornely-Merk	Compendium
Church History	von Pastor	Lives of the Roman Pontiffs
	Mann	Lives of the Roman Pontiffs
	Grisar	Luther

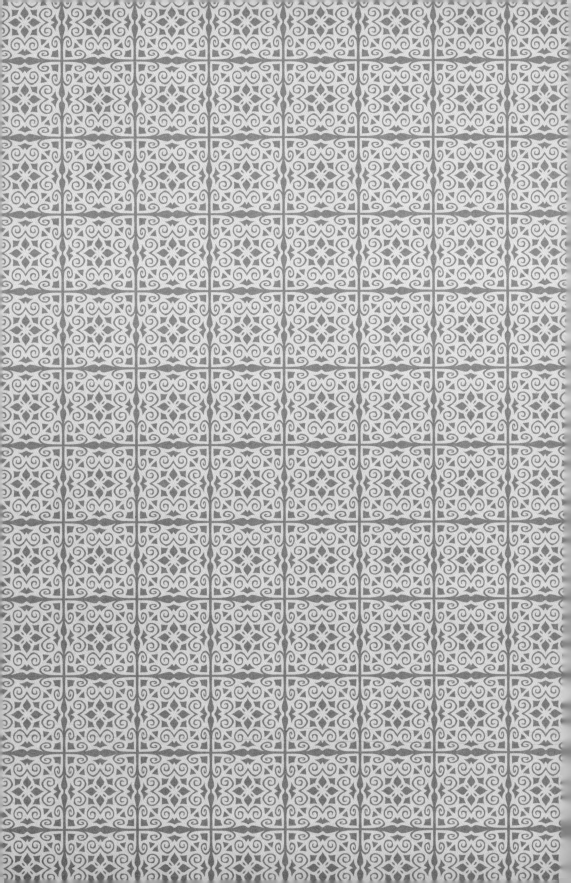

The Major Archdiocesan Philosophical-Theological Seminary
of the Immaculate Conception at Darlington, New Jersey

Toward the Centennial

1939–1960

Chapter Twenty-four

Mr. Henry G. Havemeyer

In addition to his normal duties, the rector of Darlington had to maintain good relations with the neighbors, many of whom were extremely wealthy and correspondingly demanding. The neighbor who consumed a great deal of Monsignor McLaughlin's time, and that of Father Charles Demjanovich as well, was Henry G. Havemeyer. Beginning in 1928, Havemeyer carried on a voluminous correspondence with the rectors of Darlington, chiefly with McLaughlin. Henry Havemeyer, president of the American Sugar Refining Company, occupied an estate adjacent to the seminary property. A man of considerable means, Havemeyer's offices were on Broadway in New York City, and he and his family summered in their cottage in Newport, Rhode Island. An active Catholic, he was a Knight of Malta and of St. Gregory. He was a man accustomed to having his way in all things.

Shortly after the arrival of Bishop Walsh in the diocese of Newark, Havemeyer petitioned him to confirm the permission that, according to Havemeyer, Bishop O'Connor had granted him to allow the Blessed Sacrament Fathers from Suffern, New York, to offer Sunday Mass in the chapel in his house at Darlington.[1] Walsh asked McLaughlin to investigate the matter and report back to him.[2]

McLaughlin uncovered a canonical muddle. There were no records of Bishop O'Connor giving permission for Mass in the Havemeyer home. However, the Blessed Sacrament Fathers recalled receiving such permission from Monsignor John Sheppard, administrator of the diocese while the bishop was in Rome in 1914 for his *ad limina* visit. They also had received permission from Cardinal Farley of New York, who may not have been aware that the Havemeyer estate was in the diocese of Newark. McLaughlin believed that Havemeyer had acted in good faith to provide Mass for his family and for about 30 local Catholics who would have found the trek to either

Suffern or Hohokus for Mass an arduous undertaking. He recommended to Walsh, given Havemeyer's status and good will, that he allow the weekly Mass to continue.[3]

Walsh decided otherwise. Havemeyer was angered by the bishop's decision, but his ire did not extend to Monsignor McLaughlin. McLaughlin appealed to Havemeyer to support one of Walsh's pet projects, the Mount Carmel Guild. Havemeyer replied, telling the rector that he had never heard of the Mount Carmel Guild, since he and his family now went to Mass in Suffern.

In May 1930, he told McLaughlin, "Had your appeal to this diocesan charity been made as a personal matter, without reference to the Right Reverend Bishop, I would have bent backward and gladly made an effort, even with the many calls upon my purse to do something to please you, but since you mention that it is 'dear to the heart of the Right Reverend Bishop,' it immediately makes me want to draw back. You must know, I have not the very kindliest feelings for the Right Reverend Bishop, in view of the manner with which he treated me."

A very incensed Havemeyer went on: "I cannot but feel that the Right Reverend Bishop will have to answer some day to Almighty God for his decision in denying me this privilege, which, as you must know, will not effect, in any way, the parish which you recently established in Darlington, as we all go to Suffern for church." Havemeyer closed by asking McLaughlin to visit him and his family at home.[4]

There is something strange about this entire episode. In 1935, Walsh sent to Havemeyer an apostolic indult by which Pope Pius XI authorized the celebration of Mass in his private chapel.[5] The brief was dated August 1, 1929,[6] six years earlier. In the indult, the pope noted that Walsh had been consulted by the Secretariat of State. According to protocol, the document was sent to Walsh. More than likely, Havemeyer had appealed to Rome without Walsh's knowledge. Havemeyer was not a man without influence in the archdiocese of New York to which he was rather generous. The Secretariat of State would, as a matter of course, have consulted the bishop.

Havemeyer did not know the privilege had been granted. In 1933, a close friend, Patrick Hamill, M.D., of Jersey City, asked Monsignor John C. McClary, the chancellor, to have the bishop reconsider the private chapel, noting that Havemeyer would have granted a $40,000 loan to the Darlington parish but was afraid it would appear that he was trying to purchase the chapel privilege.[7]

McLaughlin wrote to McClary that Havemeyer refused even to consider a contribution to the Darlington parish and would have nothing to do with it until the illness of the pastor in Suffern brought him to the Darlington parish. He asked to rent a pew, something no longer done in the diocese. However, the curate of the parish allowed him to do so and put a plaque with his name on the pew. Soon thereafter, he demanded that the time of the Sunday Masses be changed.[8]

During these six years, Walsh kept McLaughlin and his own chancellor in the dark about the papal indult. Had Walsh sent the indult when it was received, Havemeyer might have decided to be more generous to projects "dear to the heart of the Right Reverend Bishop."

Barking Dogs and Ringing Bells

Havemeyer's wife was ill, and the barking of the seminary dogs bothered her. He complained to McLaughlin. McLaughlin was surprised that the "police dog" kept near the dairy and chicken coop could be heard a mile away. Havemeyer corrected him, informing the rector, "From my house to your dairy is exactly .45 of a mile. On a still night or when the wind is from the south or southwest, or a foggy night, you can hear your Police Dog just as plainly as if he were two blocks away." To remedy the situation, Havemeyer offered to pay for electrical wiring and lights in the chicken coop and to install a burglar alarm. He again closed asking McLaughlin to visit him "before my family goes to Newport."[9]

The issue of the noise of the barking dogs was soon succeeded by the ringing of the bell of the parish church. On October 5, 1934, Havemeyer wrote to McLaughlin, "This morning, at 6:15, whoever was delegated to ring the bell certainly put enough vim into it to wake the dead." He offered to pay the cost of a "smaller knocker" that would produce a softer sound. McLaughlin offered to look into the matter.[10]

McLaughlin was very patient with Mr. Havemeyer. Havemeyer occasionally sent letters denouncing various Catholic priests, ranging from the liberal Father John A. Ryan to the very conservative Father Charles E. Coughlin. Both he considered as "socialistic" and partisans of "King Roosevelt." Together with his letters, he sent the rector pamphlets and copies of speeches. To each, McLaughlin replied at length, comforting Havemeyer with this theological assurance: "You need have no fear that the Catholic Church as such will ever become Communistic or Socialistic. First of all, the protection of the Holy Ghost will prevent It falling into error of this kind, since genuine socialism involves a philosophy at variance with Catholicity as the Popes have constantly pointed out."[11]

The relationship between the seminary and Havemeyer prospered. In 1936, McLaughlin gave Havemeyer permission to tap into the seminary water line when his became contaminated.[12] However, the bells of the Darlington parish church again would cause a problem, almost a crisis.

A rapid exchange of letters shows McLaughlin trying to be humorous, thereby making the situation worse.

On May 5, 1937, Havemeyer wrote to Demjanovich and to McLaughlin about the bells, which he described as "loud enough to almost wake the dead." He asked Demjanovich to be "neighborly in the matter and give consideration to this annoyance." Again he offered to pay for a "smaller knocker" or to have the present knocker covered with leather. He criticized the altar boys for ringing the bell as loudly and as long as they possibly could. An astute and efficient businessman, he kept records (shown below) that counted the number of rings for each of the early Masses for three successive Sundays. Perhaps Havemeyer and McLaughlin got along because both were sticklers to detail.

	6:45 A.M. MASS	7:45 A.M. MASS
	Number of rings	Number of rings
April 17	21	34
April 24	18	28
May 2	21	32[13]

McLaughlin told Havemeyer that to muffle the bells would create a mournful sound akin to the tolling of bells at a funeral, and that the Sunday ringing was to be joyous. He made the mistake of writing that the sound of the bells was just "faintly heard."[14] Havemeyer replied that "the reason you do not hear the church bell, as we do, is because the seminary is at least 3 times further away from the church than we are; secondly, because the hill that rises abruptly in the back of the church cuts off some of the sound from the seminary, and acts as a sounding board to direct the sound to us."

McLaughlin replied, "Even Longfellow in the 'Golden Legend' refers to the function of the church bell 'I praise the Lord, I call the people, I assemble the clergy, I bewail the dead, I disperse storm clouds, I do honor to feasts!' In Tennyson's 'In Memoriam' there are several happy allusions to the sound of the village church bell."[15]

Havemeyer was hurt by what he perceived as glib remarks, wondering if they were intended as a reflection on his faith. He saw the letter as "a very unkind and unjust accusation on your part." Pained, he closed with the words, "With the kindest personal regards and regretting that you should have seen fit to rebuke me, pains me very greatly, who, since I had the pleasure of knowing you, have always held you with the highest regard and in a plane far above any other priest or bishop I have ever had the pleasure of knowing."[16]

McLaughlin's successors would have the pleasure of receiving missives from Mr. Havemeyer, but never enjoyed the relationship that McLaughlin had with the gentleman. Havemeyer complained to Bishop Griffin concerning the dumping of refuse on his property during the construction of the new seminary in 1938; Griffin hastened to assure him that the situation would immediately be remedied.[17]

Poor Bishop Boland received the strongest complaint from Havemeyer, together with an unusual package. In 1942, Havemeyer implied that fires had been caused by careless seminarians trespassing on his property. He also objected to seminarians cutting down trees on his land and skating on his reservoir: "This winter, your seminarians had the practice of skating in my reservoir, and were told by my superintendent, that this was not permitted, yet they continued to do so, and not only that, but lit fires and left the refuse on my reservoir bank, which I am sending to you, in a separate package."[18] One wonders what was in the package.

Dealing with the rich is never easy.

Chapter Twenty-five

Day-to-day Life of the Faculty

It was not just the seminarians who were under a strict regimen. The faculty had their days regulated as well. Shortly after the move to Darlington, McLaughlin announced to the faculty members that, at "the direction of the Right Reverend Bishop . . . in all matters of an ecclesiastical or scholastic character, the priests of the household are subject [to the rector] in all matters as to their pastor." In other words, he was in charge.

He then informed them that they would take turns conducting High Mass and vespers "in the descending order of seniority by ordination," and established the schedule for daily Masses during the school year. During the summer, all priests were to take turns at duty with the seminarians for disciplinary purposes and to provide Mass in the various chapels. During the vacation period "two priests will be expected to remain on duty to sleep in the main house and provide Mass there and in the sisters' house." Except on their day off, faculty members were to secure the approval of the rector in case of absence.[1]

In addition to their seminary duties, the priests served the parish at Darlington. In 1928, shortly after the seminary moved to Darlington, Bishop Walsh established the parish of the Immaculate Conception, on property adjoining the seminary land. The rector of the seminary was named pastor, and the priests of the seminary served the parish. Deacons were assigned to preach, many delivering their first sermon to the local congregation.[2] Services were conducted in an old carpenter shop.

A parochial school was started in 1929. In 1931, the property was separately incorporated. A stone church and school were constructed in 1932.[3] In 1933, the school had 140 students, and about 400 attended Sunday Mass.[4] In 1939, the parish of St. Paul's, in Ramsey, New Jersey, was separated from the Darlington parish and the rector named administrator of that as well.[5] Faculty members also assisted at Sunday Masses in Paterson and Nutley, New Jersey. In the neighborhood they offered Mass at the Boy Scout camp and the Civilian Conservation Corps Camp.[6] Continuing the custom of Seton Hall, half of their Mass stipends were given to the seminary.

Bishop Griffin

When the new building opened, Bishop William Griffin, McLaughlin's successor, became McLaughlin's equal in issuing directives that ordered the lives of faculty, students, and employees. He assigned specific faculty members to live in the student residence. Father Donnelly, vice rector, and Father McCarthy, spiritual director, were assigned because of their offices, a custom that would continue for almost the entire time the seminary remained at Darlington. Other priests were assigned to the student residence as well.

The priests living in the student residence were told to "exercise a general supervision" over the discipline in the immediate neighborhood of their rooms. Griffin instructed, "This supervision need not be of such a character that it would interfere with the hearing of confession by priests other than Father Donnelly."

Only the vice rector and the spiritual director were directed to eat with the seminarians, at a "high table" set on a platform. The faculty was to dine together in the Crocker Mansion. Exceptions were made. Priests residing in the new building were allowed to take their meals in the seminarians' dining room "if the weather be inclement or if the priest be indisposed."[7]

The Lay Staff and Employees

Griffin outlined his regulations for the staff and employees in a forthright manner.

> The rector's policy in all matters of business is strictly objective that is, he is concerned only with the welfare of the seminary and its progress and with the high purpose it must achieve under his direction and administration. In the formulation and execution of this policy, sentimentality or friendship has no part whatsoever. A person is engaged only for the service he can render and for which he will be paid a just wage. He will be wise therefore to keep this objective policy always in mind. It will save himself or herself, as well as the officers and rector of the seminary considerable annoyance and will make for better understanding all around.[8]

He then gave very specific instructions. The men working in the boiler room were not to leave the boiler room without the permission of the rector or vice rector. They were to bring their lunch with them since "henceforth nothing will be served them from the kitchens of the seminary buildings." To keep staff isolated from the seminarians he ordered, "The girls working in the seminary office are henceforth to confine themselves to that territory. . . . Each girl has an hour for lunch and she may go home for lunch or bring her lunch." Like the boiler men, they were to receive no food from the seminary kitchen. All workers were directed to enter and leave the administration building by the front door only.

Griffin closed by saying that all he desired was "an open, honest and cooperative spirit." However, he announced that "anyone with the contrary spirit" will be dismissed "as an obstacle to the wholesome and healthy progress of seminary administration." In case anyone misunderstood, he ended his memorandum to the staff with the words "Let the policy of the rector prevail as already expressed, above, and to be expressed."[9]

While a strict disciplinarian, Griffin also was concerned about the welfare of the seminary workers. Eight families were living in old houses near the entrance to the seminary. These houses were without running water and utilized "primitive outhouses," and he asked the deputies to provide better quarters.[10]

Griffin was adamant about keeping expenses down and, like McLaughlin, worried about the "excessive" laundry bills incurred by the seminarians. Father Charles visited the Sisters of the Good Shepherd in Morristown, New Jersey, whose charges did the laundry, and obtained a reduced rate of 75 cents per week per seminarian. Any costs above that would be charged to the individual seminarian.[11]

Bishop Griffin's tenure was cut short by his appointment as bishop of Trenton on May 22, 1940. He remained as rector until July 22, the day before his installation in Trenton. On that day, the reins of seminary administration were assumed by Reverend Doctor Ahr, as acting vice rector, exercising "all the authority of the rector."[12] His tenure was quite short as the Most Reverend Thomas Aloysius Boland, the new auxiliary bishop of Newark, was appointed rector on the day of his episcopal consecration, July 25.[13]

Boland had been a member of the faculty—resident at first, non-resident since 1938—since his appointment to Seton Hall in 1923. From April 12 to May 9, 1938, between McLaughlin's departure and Griffin's appointment as rector, Walsh had named him as "Administrator pro tempore of our Major Seminary."[14] As rector, he would teach pastoral theology and liturgy, and lecture on the archdiocesan statutes.

A quiet and shy man, Boland possessed a wry sense of humor. Shortly after he had been informed of his appointment as auxiliary bishop, but before the announcement, Father Boland said Mass at a convent. After Mass, the sister superior told him, "It is a shame you have not been named a monsignor." He replied with a knowing smile, "Sister, I never will be a monsignor."[15]

Having served as Walsh's chancellor, Boland knew that the archbishop was a stickler for form and detail. One wonders what went through his mind when he wrote the following letter on chancery letterhead.

> April 5, 1940
> Rev. Thomas A. Boland, Chancellor
> Archdiocese of Newark,
> 31 Mulberry Street, Newark, N.J.
>
> Dear Father Boland:
>   His Excellency, the Most Reverend Archbishop,
> has appointed you extraordinary confessor to the Sisters
> of Our Lady of Lourdes Convent, 102 Palisades Avenue,
> Union City. His Excellency also desires that you give
> a conference once a month to the sisters at this convent.
> Please arrange with the Sister Superior as to the day and
> hour most convenient for them and for you.
>
> With all good wishes, I remain
> Sincerely in Christ,
> [s] Thomas A. Boland
> Rev. Thomas A. Boland,
> Chancellor[16]

Nine years earlier, he wrote to Father John G. Delaney, Walsh's secretary, requesting permission to use an automobile so he could fulfill his responsibilities as a teacher in the various catechetical centers in the diocese. He noted that to go from Darlington to Elizabeth, he had to take a taxi, the Erie Railroad, and Newark and Elizabeth buses, a two-and-a-half-hour journey. These travels followed a full Saturday morning of teaching. After his catechetical lectures he had to repeat the journey to go directly to Nutley for his Sunday Mass duties.[17] Father Delaney replied that the bishop had granted the permission, but that Boland's permission to use an automobile was restricted to going to teach catechetical courses.[18] Although Walsh was loath to give permission for priests in the 1930s to drive automobiles, he himself enjoyed motoring. At his death, his estate included a Cadillac, a Packard, and a Rolls-Royce.[19]

Boland became a patriarchal figure to the priests of Newark. After serving 24 years as faculty member, confessor, and rector, he would leave Darlington to succeed Bishop McLaughlin in Paterson in 1947, only to return as archbishop of Newark from 1953 to 1974. Generations of priests would know him in one or many of his roles, and he knew them as well. Shortly before Boland's death, Monsignor Walter G. Jarvais would remember "our professor of moral theology and our most popular confessor in front of whose door confessional lines formed early and often. While the seminarians had nicknames for all of the other teachers, he was always 'Father' Boland to us. And he was a father indeed."[20]

Quiet and unassuming, although always conscious of his position, he was a marked and, to many faculty and students, welcome contrast to McLaughlin. In a variety of responsible posts, he played a major part in the seminary at Seton Hall and at Darlington. As archbishop too, he was a strikingly different personality from his colorful predecessor, Archbishop Walsh. He would preside as archbishop over the peak years of seminary enrollment in the 1950s and early 1960s, as well as during the turbulent years that followed the Second Vatican Council (1961–1965).

Chapter Twenty-six

Goodbye to the Cows

Just before the United States entered World War II, a seminary institution, begun at South Orange by Father Bernard McQuaid, came to an end at Darlington. The cow farm was discontinued. The buildings were in a dilapidated state and the alternative was to build a new modern facility. The barns were abandoned, the cows sold to other farms, and the seminary began to buy milk from Blom's Dairy in Midland Park at eight cents per quart. The seminary consumed 212 quarts per day.[1]

Blom's was giving Darlington a bargain. Seven years earlier, the seminary charged Seton Hall almost 13 cents per gallon for 35,000 gallons of milk per year. Father Monaghan, president of Seton Hall, cancelled the contract when he got a much better deal, less than 10 cents a gallon, from Borden's Dairy. Monaghan took the opportunity, as he dropped the seminary contract, gently to remind McLaughlin of advice he had given him when he turned over the administration of Seton Hall to him: "You can see, Monsignor, I am trying to follow the advice you gave me when . . . you said: 'Watch the money; that is the principal thing. Watch the collection and disbursement of it.'"[2]

World War II

The unsettled situation in Europe first affected Darlington in 1938. Father Albert Hammenstede, O.S.B., S.T.D., one of the three Benedictines serving the seminary, was a German citizen. He experienced passport difficulties in November 1938. This necessitated his return to Germany on January 29, 1939, but he was able to resume his duties at Darlington by April 29, 1939.

In Austria, the closing of the Jesuit faculty at Innsbruck by the Nazis forced Father George Shea to move with the Jesuits to Switzerland to finish his doctorate. He returned to Darlington in the summer of 1939.[3]

Father Henry Beck had gone to Rome to pursue a doctorate degree in 1938 and returned during the summer of 1939. War broke out on September 1, 1939. When Beck sought to return to Rome, he discovered that the United States government refused to revalidate passports for travel to Europe due to the outbreak of war. Archbishop Walsh was anxious that Beck complete his studies but required that he sign a statement, witnessed by the vicar general and the chancellor, that he went "of my own free will, with full knowledge of the possible dangers."[4] Even before the heyday of tort litigation, Walsh covered all bases.

On October 6, Walsh wrote to President Franklin Delano Roosevelt, asking him to intercede to obtain a revalidation of Beck's passport.[5] Walsh's friend, James A. Beha, a prominent member of the New York Democratic Party, also contacted Alice Tully, Roosevelt's secretary.[6] On October 13, the president replied, stating that he could not intervene but noting that the policy was being reviewed every two weeks and he had "asked the Department of State to bear in mind Father Beck's desire and the request of Your Excellency with a view to validating Father Beck's passport just as soon as it is possible to do so."[7] Good news soon arrived and Beck sailed for Italy on October 23 on the Italian liner *Conte di Savoia*.[8] The following June, the Vatican Archives in Rome closed. Father Beck, who had just completed his licentiate in Church history, returned to Darlington in the summer of 1940. He would complete his doctorate after the war ended.

Father John Dougherty, who earlier had completed his doctorandus year for the doctorate in sacred scripture, likewise was forced to defer the completion of his doctoral work until the late 1940s. In an action not related to the war, Father Aloysius Welsh had returned home in 1939 after completing third theology. The closing of the North American College in Rome, in June 1940, brought Newark seminarians John J. Cain and John F. O'Brien home, together with former Darlington students John J. Duffy of Camden, New Jersey, and Robert L. Nealon of Scranton, Pennsylvania.[9] Both Cain and O'Brien were sent to the Catholic University of America, where they completed their seminary studies and obtained the S.T.L. Welsh, who had returned earlier, stayed on for two years and obtained the S.T.D. in 1942. Both O'Brien and Welsh joined the seminary faculty in 1942.

Reverend John F. O'Brien, affectionately known as "O'B," would serve on the seminary faculty until his retirement in 1991. Over the years he shared with students his reminiscenses of the death of Pius XI and the election of Pius XII, and tales of Mussolini's Rome in the last days before World War II. He recounted how the North American College students were told by the American embassy that they had to leave the country as soon as possible after the college closed. The embassy officials assured the American students that the sea journey would be safe, but "O'B" told several generations of Darlington seminarians that, during the entire Atlantic crossing, he could see submarine periscopes "everywhere, everywhere!"[10] Fortunately, he and the other evacuated seminarians returned home safely.

Faculty Chaplains

Soon after the outbreak of the war, Archbishop Walsh issued a call for chaplains. Fathers Shea, Meehan, and Beck volunteered. Shea and Meehan were accepted as chaplains in the navy; Beck was rejected because of a physical ailment. It is a sign of Walsh's patriotism and the mood of the country at the time that, after so many years of preparing priest professors, he would allow them to volunteer for service. Fathers Shea and Meehan departed in February 1942 and their classes were taken over by their colleagues.[11]

Many seminary alumni served as chaplains. One, Father John Patrick Washington, ordained in 1935, was immortalized as one of the heroic "Four Chaplains" who surrendered their life preservers to soldiers on the USS (USAT) *Dorchester*.[12] A commemorative stamp was issued in their honor and they were given a unique Congressional Medal of Valor. Another, Father Thomas Reardon, served as a navy and marine chaplain during the invasion of Guadalcanal. In the movie *Guadalcanal Diary*, the role of the chaplain, played by Preston Foster, was based on the exploits of Father Reardon. During the Guadalcanal fighting, Reardon was ordered by a colonel not to go forward with the marines. He replied, "My duty, sir, requires me to do anything that may help my men."[13]

The War Effort

Rationing was a part of the war effort and the seminary did not escape the common difficulty of securing foods and other commodities, but according to Bishop Boland, the rector, "Father Charles has been vigilant and alert in this regard, and we can thank him that we have suffered no real hardship . . . the food is substantial and sufficient, and no one has been hungry."[14] Meat was the scarcest commodity so each week the seminary observed one or two "civic ember days." Steel was in short supply, delaying the reconstruction of the library until late 1942.[15]

Seminarians were exempt from the universal conscription, which might cause some to look upon them as "shirkers" or "draft dodgers." To avoid this perception, the seminary took part as much as possible in the war effort. This involved a greater opening to the local community than was the custom. The seminary infirmary was used as a "base hospital" for local air raid drills, with the "wounded" being brought in from outside. The third theology class took first aid classes and received Red Cross certification. More than 100 seminarians and faculty members gave blood in the Red Cross drives in 1942 and 1943, and "the officials not only expressed their gratitude, but also their admiration for the conduct of the students while waiting." In 1943, the Red Cross gave the seminary a certificate for "eminent service."

Father Tierney served as collector for the Red Cross drive for funds, and also for the sale of war bonds. Two faculty members served as air raid wardens. Another served as secretary to the "Local Defense Council." A shrewd Bishop Boland wrote, "Although our motive is patriotic in accepting these appointments, we also feel that it is a measure of self-protection, so that we will always know what is being planned, and, consequently, have a sympathetic voice in the deliberations."[16]

This may sound strange, but Boland was referring to the local attitudes, which occasionally bordered on hostility to the seminary. The seminary was a Catholic island in the largely Protestant sea of affluent northern Bergen County. When, on November 16, 1944, the *Ramsey Journal* wrote, "The Immaculate Conception Seminary of Darlington saved the day for the blood bank when 75 theological students reported to donate blood. The Theological Seminary always heeds the call when the mobile units visit Ramsey," Boland reported to the deputies that the article showed "how far our efforts to aid in civic affairs have helped to break down the hostility manifested to us at the beginning."[17]

In all fairness, although anti-Catholicism was a real issue, the presence of so many draft-exempt men in the small town of Mahwah caused special problems. All seminarians were registered with the local draft board and this disproportionate number of exempt men caused almost all of the local eligible men to be called up in the draft. This did not endear them to the local population.[18]

While Father McQuaid would have been saddened by the demise of the cow farm, he would have rejoiced at the inauguration of a 30-acre "Victory Garden." "With the approval of the Most Reverend Archbishop," more than 80 seminarians helped care for the garden, under the direction of the dean of discipline.[19]

Acceleration

The Selective Service Board determined that all students who enjoyed deferments were required to accelerate their coursework on a 12-month basis. Archbishop Walsh was "extremely loathe [sic] to introduce a system of acceleration which would drastically disrupt the curriculum and present cycle of the seminary which after long years of striving we have finally reached in our seminary."[20] The seminary began the acceleration program in the summer of 1944. Accelerated classes began on July 24, 1944. The first term continued until Christmas, with a recess early in September to allow for the retreat of the Trenton priests. The second term extended from January 2, 1945, until May 5, 1945.

The mid-term recess at home was not permitted, as the Selective Service required that the time off from school should not exceed the 30-day yearly furlough granted to soldiers and sailors. The week between Christmas and New Year's Day was granted as a rest from class but the students did not go home.

Walsh was consoled by Boland's report that "although there was acceleration, there was no curtailment of the curriculum and the full number of school hours for each student was given."[21] In order to conform to Selective Service regulations, Walsh ordered that "all divinity students of eighteen years or over at Seton Hall [be] put in residence to ensure the perfect conformity with Selective Service regulations and to avoid embarrassment."[22]

While acceleration continued through the summer of 1945, the seminary found a way to advance Walsh's desire to develop some priests who later could teach at Seton Hall and in parochial high schools. The focus now was on science. The liberal arts curriculum followed by seminarians in college did not allow for many hours of science courses. Due to lack of proper credits, they were handicapped when they sought to pursue graduate degrees in the sciences, and had to complete many hours of undergraduate requirements before they could qualify for admission.

Under the direction of Dr. Elliott, director of studies of Seton Hall extension programs, a survey or screening course was developed that would be given to all seminarians in the summer of 1945. The survey, in mathematics, chemistry, physics, and biology, was gauged to discover the students with special aptitudes for the different sciences and also what work they already had done in these fields. The tests given afterward were standardized tests distributed by the Carnegie Foundation. Those students who showed proficiency and interest were allowed to take science courses at Darlington that were accredited by Seton Hall Extension School with the approval of the Middle States Association.[23] The acceleration requirement was dropped by the Selective Service in October 1945.[24]

Post-war Adjustments

In the immediate post-war years, the seminary, like the rest of the nation, experienced numerous inconveniences due to shortages caused by interruptions of production and delivery due to labor unrest. Father Demjanovich, the procurator, responded like so many other of his fellow citizens, by hoarding. He stored electrical equipment, plumbing and heating supplies, bed linens, table linens, paints, chemicals, and other scarce items.[25] Food, especially meat, was difficult to find, especially enough to feed more than 200 hungry young seminarians. Demjanovich made trips to Newark and Jersey City to purchase food and bring it back to the seminary.[26]

Since its move to Darlington, the seminary either administered the Darlington and Ramsey parishes or assisted them in various ways. To cut costs, in 1948, it ceased providing free bus service for the Darlington parish school as well as free housing for the sisters who taught there.[27]

The seminary managed to function by continuing to depend on the archdiocese for funding. The archdiocese, on its part, depended on the annual seminary collection taken up in the parishes. The budget for 1949–50 was $314,000. The seminary's income from tuition and burse endowment was a mere $24,000. The diocese paid the difference of $290,000.[28] Two years later the budget had crept up to $389,000, with an income of $38,000, leaving $351,000 to be "provided by the chancery office."[29]

This expanding deficit forced the seminary to raise the tuition for seminarians from suffragan dioceses from $500 to $700 per year, still below actual costs. The seminary and the archdiocese continued to subsidize the "sending dioceses."[30] In future years, finances would once again become a critical issue.

At the same time, Darlington was experiencing difficulties finding and retaining lay employees. To make employment more attractive, it enrolled the lay employees in Blue Cross–Blue Shield health insurance in 1948 and continued planning for better housing. By 1953, it had completed a low-cost housing unit of 10 houses and two eight-room dormitories located adjacent to Maryrest Cemetery adjoining the seminary property.

The same year it began preparations to enroll the lay employees in the Social Security system.[31] The board of deputies and the archbishop took great interest in the salaries being paid to the lay employees and often mentioned the importance of Catholic institutions observing the precepts of social justice.[32]

As the post-war years blended into the 1950s, sisters were becoming scarce. For almost a century the Sisters of Charity of St. Elizabeth of Convent Station, New Jersey, had provided sisters to supervise the cooking and housekeeping, as well as the infirmary, at the seminary. But by 1960, the number of sisters at Darlington was only six. In spite of repeated appeals from the rector, the congregation was unable to provide any additional sisters.[33]

Farewell to Schlitz

Bishop McLaughlin, the first rector of Darlington, died on March 17, 1947. He was eulogized at the next meeting of the seminary deputies as a figure "so intimately associated" with the seminary who "so wholeheartedly [devoted] his great talents and Christ-like zeal to its administration."[34] His combination of determination and hard work made the creation of Darlington possible, yet his personal style always was a cause of comment among seminarians and priests.

The seminarians rarely dared to provoke him. However, when Prohibition ended, they could not resist. They posted on the bulletin board a full-page advertisement from one of the local newspapers that announced in large type: "Schlitz Is Back Again!" It quickly disappeared.[35]

After he left the seminary, McLaughlin continued to behave in a manner that can only be described as aristocratic. As bishop of Paterson, he required his secretary to genuflect and kiss his ring each time she entered his office. As time passed, the poor woman developed arthritis in the knees. She explained to the bishop that her malady made it painful for her to genuflect. McLaughlin graciously replied that henceforth, upon entering his office, she could simply bow before kissing his ring. Henry Beck well described him as "grandiose, yet warm, abrupt or charming in manner as the mood took him, Bishop McLaughlin might well have graced the 18th century."[36]

Doctor Ahr

On June 21, 1947, Darlington's rector, Bishop Boland, was named as McLaughlin's successor in Paterson. He was installed on September 18. The Reverend

Dr. George W. Ahr became rector on the day before Boland's installation in Paterson. He already had served 14 years on the faculty and, since 1941, had served as vice rector. Invested as a domestic prelate in 1948, his would be a brief tenure. Scarcely more than two years later, on January 28, he was named bishop of Trenton and consecrated on the following March 20.

Ahr was a quiet, direct, and no-nonsense man. In 1948, in response to an offer to donate a television to the seminary, he said that he did not see a need for a television set at the seminary "now or in the foreseeable future."[37] Late in life Ahr was asked why he was sent to study in Rome, and he simply answered, "I was told to go."[38] Replying to a question posed in 1978 about his goals as a young priest, he said, "When I was ordained we didn't have this 'goal-setting' nonsense. We felt we were ordained to do the work of a priest, as designated by the bishop."[39]

He was a demanding teacher. One of his former students recalled him ". . . as the toughest teacher we ever had. Rigid beyond belief; we claimed that he had embalming fluid in his veins from his father [who was a funeral director], instead of blood."[40]

But there was more to Ahr than the tough professor. He was respected by Archbishop Walsh for his intricate knowledge of episcopal ceremonies. Walsh, who occasionally would mutter in an audible voice at his masters of ceremonies, "You stupid fool!,"[41] trusted Ahr. According to diocesan lore, Ahr, when he felt the loquacious archbishop had talked too long, would place the miter on Walsh's head, thus signaling the end of the sermon, and he got away with it.[42]

As rector, his apparent harshness was tempered; he showed a fatherly side to the seminarians, earning him the affectionate nickname "Doc Ahr." For the Italian-American seminarians, who sometimes felt that they were a neglected minority in the Irish-dominated seminary, Ahr was a font of understanding.[43] This may have resulted from his being a minority himself, born of parents of German origin. According to his biographer, "His exterior was a cover for his shyness; if any seminarian . . . had a problem or difficulty, and went to him, he would bend over backwards to help him."[44]

As rector he dealt with the dislocations in the faculty resulting from the postponement of doctoral studies by several faculty members. Just before and during the war years, Father Tierney had fulfilled all the requirements for the doctorate in canon law, Father Shea had obtained the doctorate in sacred theology at the Canisianum in exile in Switzerland, Father Welsh received the doctorate in sacred theology from Catholic University, and Father Cassels the master of arts degree in speech from Columbia University.

Now, following Archbishop Walsh's directives that the seminary and college faculty achieve appropriate graduate degrees, Fathers Beck and Dougherty returned to Rome during the summer of 1947 to complete their studies in ecclesiastical history and scripture. In 1948, Reverend Joseph Przezdziecki began a four-year doctoral program in philosophy at the Pontifical Medieval Institute in Toronto, Canada.[45]

The following year, Father Walter Curtis went to CUA to complete his doctorate.[46] Father John Koenig was appointed to the seminary that year, and Father William Ludlum was assigned temporarily to fill Father's Beck's Church history classes.[47]

In 1949, Reverend Stanley J. Adamczyk, S.T.L., and Reverend William F. Hogan, S.T.L., were added to the faculty. Father Hogan would serve as director of discipline until 1954, teach dogmatic and oriental theology, and eventually become spiritual director and finally rector of the seminary. Father Adamczyk, usually called "Father Stanley," would serve as professor of Latin and English. He succeeded Reverend Dr. Joseph Christopher, who returned to the Catholic University of America. In Henry Beck's words, with Dr. Christopher's departure, "a bit of Darlington migrated to the Potomac."[48]

Dr. Christopher was a revered character who possessed a fine wit and a keen sense of the ridiculous. During long sermons or speeches, he often would mutter in a stage whisper, *Tandem aliquando!*, or in the vernacular, "Enough already!" A seminary classmate and confidant of Cardinal Spellman, he occasionally would let slip to seminarians information concerning future episcopal appointments. In 1960, he returned to Seton Hall, where he taught Latin to the college seminarians until his death in 1964.

Ahr saw the realization of the long-delayed plans to provide suitable housing for seminary employees. These buildings, planned by McLaughlin and authorized in 1942 under Boland's rectorate, were brought to fruition in June 1950, shortly after Ahr left for Trenton. [49] Called Marycourt, located on the outskirts of the seminary grounds, these comfortable dwellings provided homes for the various maintenance and support staff. Many of these folks were poor and had been refugees from Europe.

When Monsignor Ahr took office, in September 1947, the number of students had decreased from 236 in 1945 to 195. The number was almost the same when he transferred to Trenton in March 1950, having increased only to 204.

Farewell to a Legend

Seminarians of the 1930s and 1940s have many memories of Archbishop Walsh. In particular, they remember his "state visits" to Darlington. Walsh justly was proud of his achievements during his almost quarter-century episcopacy, and Darlington was his proudest achievement. He did not frequently visit the seminary but always was there for the annual meeting of the board of deputies in May. On the appointed day, the seminarians were assigned to gather in the roadway leading to the Crocker Mansion where the meeting was held. There they awaited his arrival.

As soon as his Rolls-Royce brougham appeared, they began to cheer and to applaud. A few brave souls would yell "*Viva il Papa!*" Both the car and the archbishop were impressive sights. The brougham was a regal model that had an open seat in front for the chauffeur and an enclosed cabin for the passengers. Walsh was dressed in cassock, sash, and cross with a magenta cape over his shoulders. He wore the Roman *galero*, a wide-brimmed hat with gold and purple trim. He would acknowledge his seminarians with a smile and a wave.

Before entering the mansion, he briefly addressed the assembled throng and then, with a twinkle in his eye, he gave them his "special" blessing. "This blessing," he would tell them, "goes five generations into the past and five generations into the future; it goes five degrees collaterally and five degrees laterally."[50] What this meant no one knew; but some seminarians wondered why the archbishop gave them a blessing that extended five generations into the future. No one, of course, dared to ask him.

At the May 19, 1952, deputies' meeting, Archbishop Walsh spoke of the need for priestly spirituality and waxed nostalgic. According to the minutes of the meeting, Walsh "recalled the history of the new seminary building and the difficulties encountered in its construction and the hope and foresight used in placing the seminary at Darlington. The archbishop then gave thanks to God for our great major seminary, unique in the fact that the whole faculty and administration is composed of diocesan priests, a fact that cannot be duplicated in the United States. He declared that he was pleased that the rector and faculty stressed to the seminarians the paramount importance of spirituality in their training for the priesthood and as spirituality is the object of the faculty so should it be the object of all our prayers."[51] He died the following June 6.

At his arrival in Newark in 1928, the diocese had a Catholic population of almost 705,000, served by 710 priests in 276 parishes and missions in the seven northern counties of New Jersey.[52] At his death in 1952, he left an archdiocese, much smaller in area, consisting of four counties. In this reduced see, the Catholic population had reached more than 1.1 million, with 893 diocesan and religious congregation priests and 223 parishes.[53]

In 1953, Thomas Aloysius Boland returned to Newark. Having served as seminary and college professor, rector, auxiliary bishop, and bishop of Paterson, he became the second archbishop of Newark.

Chapter Twenty-seven

The Good Times

The post-World War II years, and especially the 1950s, were a time of optimism and expansion for the Catholic Church in the United States. In 1953, religious sociologist Will Herberg wrote:

> Catholicism in America today stands at its highest
> point of prestige and spiritual power. It is not hard
> to see why this should be so in this country as elsewhere
> in the Western world. In an age when the vacuities of
> "rationalism" and unbelief have become so painfully
> evident, Catholicism presents the picture of a dynamic
> faith sure of itself and capable of preserving its substance
> and power despite elaborate institutionalization. In an
> age of spiritual chaos and disorientation, Catholicism
> stands forth as the keeper of an enduring tradition that
> has weathered the storms of the past and stands
> unshaken amidst the disasters of our time.[1]

During the middle years of the twentieth century, the Church in New Jersey continued to grow in numbers and institutions. Seminary enrollment skyrocketed, new parishes opened in ever-expanding suburbia, Catholic schools burst at the seams. At Darlington, the spirit was equally optimistic. The future was limitless. Therefore, there was no need to change anything at the seminary.

However, no time is devoid of its anxieties. The Korean War, the Cold War, the threat of nuclear warfare, the forced integration of schools in Little Rock, Arkansas, and the Suez Crisis attest to that fact. John Tracy Ellis, looking back at this period, wrote, "Yet by comparison with what was to follow, the 1950s now seem a period of relative calm and general contentment for most Americans."[2]

Student Life after World War II

Daily life for seminarians after World War II was not markedly different than before. The horarium and the rule remained essentially the same. The greatest disruption to life was the suspension of classes in Fall 1949 due to the failure of the existing water supply system.[3]

However, societal changes began to affect the institution. In 1950, the students were enrolled in Blue Cross medical insurance at a premium of $13 per year.[4] Personal finances were not a burden. Until the 1970s, the seminarians were not charged tuition but, upon ordination, took out a 20-year life insurance policy that totaled $700 for each year in the seminary.[5] Each student ordained for the archdiocese of Newark also was directed to offer two Masses per year on behalf of the donor of a specified burse.[6]

Following Archbishop Walsh's plans to train priests in the sciences, selected seminarians spent the weekdays of the summer at Seton Hall taking science courses.[7] When this program was discontinued in 1956, Archbishop Boland remarked that "the original program began in war-time and was useful for keeping the students busy."[8] This was not an entirely accurate assessment. Walsh wanted priests trained in the various sciences to provide professors at Seton Hall and in the diocesan high schools. The war had little to do with the project.

Students also were kept busy in the summer with manual labor. After the old greenhouse in the rear of Walsh Hall was dismantled, the seminarians landscaped the grounds. They also assisted in the renovation of the speech laboratory.[9]

The growth of the seminary population and its characteristic enclosed monastic way of life caused it to develop a rather complicated internal structure so that it could function in an orderly manner separated from the outside world.

The complexity of organization is illustrated by the 43-page *Customs of the Seminary of the Immaculate Conception Darlington, N.J. –November 20, 1954*.[10] The following "Index of Customs" is overwhelming in itself.

HOUSE OFFICERS

Officers
Seniority
Time of Appointment

DEPARTMENTS

Barbershop
Bedellus
Bookstore
Ceremonies
Chant
Darkroom
DeSales Union
    Candy
    Ice Cream
    Soda
    Bookkeeping
    Records and Concerts
Home Study
Infirmary
    Infirmary
    Infirmarians
Library
    Library
    Book Bindery
    Mimeograph
Missiology
Organist
Prefect
Refectory
Sacristy
Speech
    Master of Reading
    Auditorium
    Laboratory
    Dramatics
    Movies
    Orchestra
    Entertainments

SPECIAL EVENTS

Al Fresco
Athletic Events
Christmas Arrangements
Christmas Eve
Deacon Farewell
Entertainments (cf. Speech)
Graduation (Senior)
Junior Arrival
Oriental Rite Mass
Quartet Contest
Reunion
St. Patrick's Night

PERMISSIONS

Home
    Family Matters
    Parish Affairs
    Deaths
    Not Permitted Items
    Late Orders
    Meditation and Rosary Outside
    Parties Permitted
    Shopping
    Smoking
    Visiting Rooms
    Visitors
        Clerical
        Lay
        Religious Sisters

INTERNAL AFFAIRS

Absence from Class
Athletic Competition (Outsiders)
Basement Areas
Blood Donations
Bus Trips
Care
Catholic Action Groups
Clothing Collection
Collections
    College Graduates
    Community Mass
    Convent
    Deacon Privileges
    Deacon Publicity
    Elevator
    Examinations
    Grove Care
    Holy Week
    Junior Philosopher Activities
    Laundry
    Locker and Shower Room Care
    Mail
    Mass for Deceased Faculty
       Members
    Medical Arrangements
    Moving Day
    Newspapers
    Orders
    Outings to Seminary
    Recreation Rooms
    Refectory
    Room Care
    Schedule
    Senior Man
    Spiritual Exercises
    Study Group
    Telegrams
    Telephone

Tradesmen
Vacations
Workshop
X-Rays (Bergen Cty. TB Assn.)

Student Officers

There were 13 student officers of the seminary, appointed by the rector on the recommendation of the director of students (director of discipline), by various professors, or by student officers. Amazingly, for the era, there was a certain amount of consultation in the appointment process. The positions are described in the table below.

OFFICERS	RECOMMENDED TO THE RECTOR BY:
First Prefect	Director of Students
Sacristan	*Faculty Sacristan
Master of Ceremonies	*Faculty Master
Infirmarian	Director of Students
Bookstore Manager	Director of Students
Librarian	*Faculty Librarian
Master of Speech	*Professor of Speech
Mimeograph Department Manager	*Faculty Librarian
Organist	*Professor of Music
Master of Chant	*Professor of Music
Master of Refectory	Director of Students
Master of Auditorium	*Professor of Speech
Book-Bindery Manager	*Faculty Librarian

*From names submitted to him by student officers. Faculty member may veto any name offered.[11]

First Prefect

Some of these positions entailed rather significant responsibilities. The most important was the first prefect. His duties were extensive and detailed.

> The first prefect is the liaison between faculty and students. As senior deacon it is his duty to report to the director of students and/or the rector on any problem of morale affecting the student body as a whole or any individual student. The first prefect alone may request a late order or any other permission which would affect the entire student body. (He is not obliged to channel every request made to him by other students to the authorities; he may use his judgment as to the suitability of requests).
>
> The prefect rings all bells in Walsh Hall (the Angelus excepted). He signals start of prayers in chapel, signals end of meditation and of thanksgiving after Mass.

He checks infirmary daily to learn names of those confined. He accepts money orders from the students and delivers them to the procurator's office. He assigns reader for chapel prayers. He assists the director of students when the junior philosophers enter the seminary in July, prepares chapel and refectory seating plans for them, explains arrangements for reception of Holy Communion. He prepares chapel seating for entire house. He makes arrangements (approved by director of students) with dry cleaner and shoemaker. When director of students is not available, students may report to prefect when they return from any journey (prefect notifies director of students later). He reports any unauthorized collections or spiritual bouquets to the director of students.

He was accorded special privileges.

The first prefect may visit rooms without permission on necessary business. He may visit the infirmary, except during evening study time. With permission he may address student body on necessary business. In the absence of the director of students, he may give permission to use the telephone in emergencies. He may use the telephone on necessary business.[12]

Privileges also were given to those in charge of major departments. They were exempted from waiting on tables and were allowed to visit rooms without permission on official business, but not to enter them.

The customs were quite detailed and covered almost any eventuality. Certain frail seminarians were placed on the "milk list" by the director of students. The milk list, like everything else in the seminary, was subject to detailed regulation.

Milk list permits glass of milk at 4:15 p.m. to 4:45 p.m. (and at 9:05 p.m. when special permission is given). Permission to be on milk list cannot be given by anyone except the DIRECTOR OF STUDENTS. Those advised to take this milk must confer with the director of students and may not presume permission. On Wednesday and Saturday afternoon, time is 4:00 to 4:30 p.m.[13]

Permissions

Permission to leave the seminary grounds, although relaxed a bit, continued to be rather stringent through the 1950s. For all circumstances, the details of any permission were quite restricted. Seminarians might go home from noon to 9 p.m. of the following day for these occasions:

- Parents' silver wedding anniversary Mass
- Brother either entering service or going overseas
- Wedding of brother or sister
- Religious investiture of sister or brother
- Religious profession of sister or brother
- Serious illness or operations
- Brother's priesthood ordination
- Baptism and/or confirmation of brother or sister
- Prolonged family illness

However, if the wedding was not at a Nuptial Mass, the seminarian was allowed only to go from noon until 9 p.m. of the wedding day. Permission was also granted to attend various parish anniversaries and anniversaries of pastors. When death occurred in a family, the rules were governed by the closeness of the relative. For parents, brothers, sisters, or grandparents, the seminarian could attend the wake and the Mass, and remain home for two additional days. For aunts, uncles, brothers-or sisters-in-law, he might only attend the Mass and return by 9 p.m.

Should his pastor or a curate in his home parish die, the seminarian was allowed to attend the funeral Mass and return by 9 p.m. as well. Five seminarians were allowed to attend the funeral of another seminarian's family member and a few could attend the wake if driven by a faculty member. These were the only occasions on which permission to visit home might be granted.[14]

Visitors not only were discouraged but, with few exceptions, forbidden. If a seminarian's brother was home from the military, he was allowed to visit, as were priests. However, in all cases, visits were to be conducted in the parlors on the first floor and no visitor was allowed above the first floor.[15]

Bookstore, infirmary, and library officers could use the elevator when on official business. But other seminarians were not permitted to use the elevator without the permission of the director of students. This usually was granted only when a seminarian had sprained or broken a limb.[16]

Mission Academia

Among student activities of the 1940s and 1950s, some of the most significant were the Mission Academia, the DeSales Union, the Home Study Course, and the entertainment department.

In spite of the many restrictions of the rule, outside contacts slowly began to develop. Not surprisingly, they took on apostolic and charitable themes. The mission department, called the Mission Academia, met monthly and provided guest lecturers on missions and directed several other activities. They supported an array of projects. Their Propaganda Department brought lecturers on mission activities to the seminary several times each year. Often, these lecturers were from Maryknoll. Maryknoll's headquarters were not far from Darlington and, over the years, a fraternal relationship developed between the two institutions.

The Mission Academia was an efficient fund-raiser. In a typical year, 1956, it contributed over $1,000 to the Propagation of the Faith. Through the Academia, seminarians contacted physicians in northern New Jersey, asking them to donate sample medicines sent to them by pharmaceutical companies.

The size of the collections was remarkable. One year the retail value of medical supplies shipped overseas reached $60,000.[17] These supplies always were sent to the needy overseas since federal law prohibited free distribution of medical supplies in the United States without the authority of a physician. They also collected religious articles and reading materials and distributed them to hospitals and prisons. In 1956, they distributed almost 1,400 pounds of these materials.[18]

After the end of World War II, the seminarians directed their charitable efforts toward assisting the needy in Europe. Each year they sponsored a clothing collection. The clothing was provided by families and friends, alumni, and parishioners from their home parishes. From these collections, they put together packages for the international aid organization C.A.R.E. They raised money to pay for shipping and for modest financial donations.

Initially these packages were sent to needy priests and seminarians in Germany. As the international situation changed, the object of the seminarians' charitable concern altered as well. In 1950, the seminarians assisted the cloistered Carmelite sisters of Lisieux with money and goods.[19] In the early 1950s, as a result of the Korean War, many packages were sent to Korea. In 1954, money and clothing were sent to Vietnamese refugees streaming south after the Communist takeover of the north.

By the end of the decade, the seminarians' charitable attention focused on the home front, and clothing packages were sent to the poor in local cities. Food drives for the needy of Newark and Jersey City were an annual event in the weeks preceding Christmas.

The magnitude of this charitable work is a tribute to the generosity and initiative of the seminarians. In 1954, they contributed $1,500 and sent 6,000 pounds of clothing.[20] The next year the clothing totaled 8,000 pounds.[21] The seminarians corresponded directly with the various relief agencies. In 1952, Reverend Wilson E. Kaiser, the Berlin representative of the War Relief Services of the National Catholic Welfare Conference, complimented them on their generosity and thanked them for their shipments of clothing. He apprised the seminarians of the desperate situation of their fellows in the Soviet-occupied zone of Germany and asked them in particular to send cassocks, surplices, Latin textbooks, rosaries, and copies of the *Liber Usualis*.[22]

In addition to direct contributions to the Propagation of the Faith, the Academia sent modest individual gifts to needy missionaries throughout the world. Through these individual gifts and the various food and clothing drives, the seminarians established and maintained contact with local parishes and with distant churches. They gave spiritual and financial support to missionaries and the needy at home. For them it was a valuable opportunity to participate in missionary and pastoral activity while in the cloistered confines of the seminary.

DeSales Union

The DeSales Union was the most significant student organization. [23] It had been established while the seminary was still at Seton Hall. Its purpose was to foster a spirit of unity, fraternity, and good sportsmanship among the seminarians; to provide suitable relaxation for mind and body; and to render recreational periods both pleasant and profitable.

The union sponsored numerous activities. For many years, it hosted an annual al fresco summer picnic to which all priest alumni were invited. *Al fresco* simply was Italian for "in the fresh air." The name probably came from the more Italianate of the Rome-trained faculty. The picnic included a softball game between priests and seminarians. Older seminarians would try to convince the newly arrived junior philosophers that the picnic was an event in honor of a deceased seminarian named Al Fresco.

The union also sponsored an annual "all-star" football game on Thanksgiving Day morning, and a swimming meet during the summer. It oversaw the decoration of the chapel, refectory, foyer, and recreation rooms for Christmas. It arranged for Christmas Eve carols after dinner. This featured each language group from the Master School singing carols in the language of study. The Christmas festivities were a major event of the seminary year. Students spent many hours gathering pine branches and cones on the spacious seminary grounds and assisting in the decorating. Christmas Eve was made even more memorable for it was, except for special dinners and anniversaries, a singular occasion on which the faculty dined with the seminarians.

A special feature of the evening was the arrival of Santa Claus, who greeted all the junior philosophers and presented them with gifts. However, the *Customs* note that "the text of Santa Claus should be prudent and in good taste." Even Santa Claus was "under the rule."

The union maintained a photographic darkroom, the swimming pool, a nine-hole golf course, a remnant of the "glory days" of the Crocker Mansion, a toolshed for voluntary work on the grounds, and a workshop for carpentry and repair work. It organized and provided equipment for softball, handball, basketball, and volleyball leagues, winter sports, and indoor recreation. For those so inclined, it also featured a weight-lifting room. All of its activities were financed by the annual dues of $1, by the profits from the candy store, donations from priest alumni, and occasional fund-raising events. [24]

Chapter Twenty-eight

Entertainment and Recreation

Although isolated, with contact to the "outside" world restricted, the seminarians were not without recreation and entertainment. Besides hiking, the outdoors provided other opportunities for recreation. In the fall and spring, there was tennis, handball, football, and baseball. A somewhat riskier diversion was tobogganing. The hill sloping down to the baseball and football fields was an ideal site. There was one peril. The cesspools, known as the "honey pots," were located there. Before descending, alert seminarians checked to ensure that the area had frozen over. A mistake could be catastrophic.

Indoor entertainments provided needed breaks from the routine as well. The Darlington Dramatic Society staged at least one play each year. Among them were *Arsenic and Old Lace*, *A Christmas Carol*, *The Tell-tale Heart*, *Down at Kitty's Saloon*, and *Daddy Misbehaves*. A major event each year was the "Deacon Farewell," a night of entertainment honoring the departing deacon class.[1]

Every week or two a movie provided entertainment. All were cleared with the latest edition of the Legion of Decency's approved list. Many had a religious or sports theme. In the 1950s the fare included *Ireland: Land of Welcome*, *Green Bay Packer Highlights*, *King Richard and the Crusades*, *Report on Fatima*, *The Steel Trap*, *The Wilson Story*, *The Story of Pope Pius XII*, *Bringing the Cross to Africa*, and *How to Build a Pipe Organ*.[2]

Milestones of the faculty, priesthood anniversaries, and papal honors were celebrated with formal but simple dinners. Departures of faculty similarly were observed. Often the programs for these events were rather elaborate. The May 22, 1949, return of Father Joseph P. Christopher to the Catholic University of America after 11 years on the faculty featured a seminarian choral group singing both the

"Marseillaise" and "The Rose of Tralee," while soloists performed "Una furtiva Lagrima" and "Torna a Sorrento."[3]

It was a simpler time in many ways. Gone were the elaborate dinners of years gone by. However, when Bishop Curtis left Newark in 1961 to take up his duties as bishop of Bridgeport, the menu appeared to be in the spirit of the Gilded Age.

Tomatoes au Jus
Cotes de Boef, a L'Americaine—Aus Jus
Puree de Pomes de Terre
Petits Pois au Beurre
Salade de Laitue
Queen Olives
Concombres a L'Allemonde de Douceur
Petits Pains—Buerre
Gateau aux Fraises
Café
Pastilles de Menthe—Assortment Noisett

The many grammatical and spelling mistakes can be excused when we consider that the dinner was simply tomato juice, roast beef, mashed potatoes, lettuce salad, rolls, strawberry cake, coffee, mint candies, and nuts.[4]

Almost every observance ended with the hymn, "A Priestly Heart." Brought from Innsbruck many years earlier by Monsignor McLaughlin, it remained a fixture of Darlington life until the late 1960s.

A PRIESTLY HEART

A priestly heart the Sacred Heart
For sins of men the burden bearing
Seeks everywhere in loving care
To bring back home the sheep when erring

O Sacred Heart with love benign Make of our hearts Thy altar shrine
May we always with hearts like Thine be holy priests Oh Heart Divine
May we always with hearts like Thine be holy priests Oh Heart Divine

A priestly heart the Sacred Heart
Its heavy cross a sad life story
It takes the weight of human guilt
And gives in turn celestial glory[5]

Lectures

The seminary routine occasionally was broken by an "outside lecturer." This venerable tradition, dating back to the nineteenth century, continued as a way of acquainting the seminarians with prestigious scholars and keeping them abreast of important issues.

Among the speakers were Monsignor Patrick W. Skehan of Catholic University on "The Dead Sea Scrolls"; Douglas Hyde on "The Nature and Dangers of Communism"; Reverend Thurston N. Davis, S.J., editor of *America*, on "Catholic Education"; Romeo Maione, President of the International Jocists, member of the Papal Commission for the World Lay Apostolate, on "Social Action"; and Dr. John G. Novak on "The Priest and Psychiatry." Because of the Holy See's concern about this sensitive issue, Novak's audience was restricted to the deacon class.[6]

Home Study Course

A further step in seminarian outreach began in 1953, when a home study course was initiated under the direction of Reverend Aloysius Welsh. It was a correspondence course in Catholic teachings run by the seminarians. Publicized in the parishes and through the diocesan newspaper, the course drew well over 100 inquirers each year. In 1957, the greatest number of inquirers was recorded, 268.[7] Between 1953 and 1964, the seminarians contacted and instructed almost 1,500 persons through this course.[8]

The correspondents followed a course prepared by Father Welsh in which they were given reading assignments, and sent in short essays and responses to questions. These were graded and returned by the students. The inquirers also could send in their own questions to which the seminarians would give responses.[9]

Father Welsh's innovative program gave the seminarians a window into the minds and hearts of Catholics and non-Catholics seeking to grow in the faith and provided an outlet for their creative talents.

Religious Vacation School

A major innovation in seminary routine and life came in 1954 with the introduction of the Religious Vacation School. Since the move to Darlington in 1927, summers were spent at the seminary, in accord with the Roman desire to keep seminarians "out of the world" to avoid the temptations of summer life. Archbishop Boland was more willing than his predecessor to adjust this policy and to give the students some experience in the parishes.

The Religious Vacation School was the beginning of what would evolve into the "apostolic activities" programs of the 1960s, which, in turn, eventually became a full-fledged pastoral formation program. Under the supervision of Father Walter Curtis, seminarians began to teach in the parish Religious Vacation Schools of the Confraternity of Christian Doctrine of the archdiocese of Newark and the diocese of Paterson.

Before venturing out into the world, the students were trained at a study week at the seminary two weeks before the start of the school. They were given instruction in the teaching of religion, in religious arts and crafts, and in supervising recreation. The Newark seminarians taught in 19 parishes, one orphanage, two CYO day camps, and in New Jersey's Boystown. A total of 72 seminarians from the archdiocese were assigned to this work. Happily, Monsignor Thomas H. Powers, Bishop Ahr's successor as rector of Darlington, noted that "reports made by the pastors of the vacation school parishes showed a universal approval for the activities of the seminarians. No difficulties with priests or with laity were reported."[10]

The program was a success. The next year 115 seminarians participated, and Powers proudly informed the deputies that "in this coming summer [1955] so great will be the demand for the services of seminarians that it will be necessary to limit the number to be sent to each parish."[11] Bishop Walter Curtis,[12] the program director, enthusiastically stated that "the experience acquired by the seminarians in this summer time program continues to be valuable for them and serves as an influence which tends to deepen their maturity and zeal."[13]

The seminary was beginning, little by little, to emerge from its isolation. But a practical question soon arose. Could the seminarians be paid for their services? Archbishop Boland settled the matter with a succinct comment: "They have all their expenses paid."[14]

The Cold War

As the Cold War intensified, the seminary became involved in Civil Defense activities. In the fall of 1950, at the request of the local Civilian Defense unit, all first-year theologians were given first-aid instructions by Father Thomas Smith of Good Counsel Parish, Newark. All students were assigned duties in case of an emergency. As they had during the war, students annually gave in significant numbers to the Red Cross blood drive.[15]

In 1954, the Cold War broke into the neighborhood with a vengeance. That year the Department of Defense took over 30 acres of seminary property for the installation of a Nike ballistic missile base. Nike Battery NY-93/94 was connected to a radar installation atop Campgaw Mountain in Franklin Lakes. One of 14 Nike sites in New Jersey, Battery 93/94 contained both Nike Ajax and Nike Hercules missiles.[16] The base adjoined the seminary property near the south gate.

Designed to shoot down attacking aircraft, the Nikes were deployed at sites that completely encircled major metropolitan areas, such as New York, with overlapping fields of fire, providing a line of defense against an attack by air. The presence of the base made the seminary a potential target for any nuclear attack. Civil Defense activities in the area naturally increased.[17]

Seminarians were ordered not to approach the fenced missile base while on their walks. Some could not resist rattling the cyclone fence and watching the barking guard dogs hurl themselves against it. They would quickly leave the scene before the human guards arrived. They were more afraid of being reported to the seminary authorities than of being taken prisoner by the army's military police.[18]

Eventually, Walsh and O'Connor Halls were designated as fallout shelters. These soundly constructed buildings were considered to be the only structures in the area suitable to serve this purpose. The Civil Defense authorities announced that the seminary buildings would, in case of atomic attack, accommodate 1,800 persons![19] Emergency food rations, medical supplies, and water containers for that many people were stored in the basements of the two buildings. Among the supplies were thousands of pounds of food biscuits and carbohydrate supplements, as well as water drums, sanitation kits, and medical kits.[20]

To assure communications in case of atomic attack, the Federal Communications Commission trained and licensed two seminarians to operate two short-wave radio receivers and transmitters supplied by the Civil Defense Communication Network.[21] They were assigned official military radio call letters, and the seminary was designated by the Mahwah division of Civil Defense and Disaster Control as "Unit Three Mike Delta (3MD)."[22] Two other seminarians were trained as radiological technicians in the use of Geiger counters to detect radiation. Each month these technicians were obliged to check their instruments and also to determine ambient radioactivity.[23]

"Jackson Whites"

In some ways, living at Darlington was similar to living in a national park. Until 1972, the seminary grounds encompassed almost 1,500 acres of the scenic Ramapo Valley. Other than the 20 acres or so around the buildings and the access roads, it was "unimproved" land. Before hiking during deer season, seminarians were warned to take extra care due to the inevitable poachers on the property. From time to time they would come upon a gutted deer carcass.

Their hikes took them past rivers and falls and natural and man-made lakes. The land truly was beautiful and unspoiled. From Lookout Point, the highest place on the property, they could enjoy a breathtaking view of the towers of Manhattan in the distance.

Occasionally during a hike, seminarians would meet gentle, dark-skinned people. Very poor, they lived in small houses and trailers, and often appeared unkempt. Some regularly came to the seminary seeking leftover food. Older students often warned new seminarians that these people might be dangerous.

They were known to the seminarians as the "Jackson Whites." According to local legend, they were descendants of runaway and freed slaves, called "Jacks," and whites. It was said that their ancestors included Dutch settlers and Hessian soldiers, who had supported the English during the American Revolution, and were forced to flee to the mountains after the end of the war.[24]

This is possible. In the turmoil following the Revolution, loyalists were hunted down and often tarred and feathered. Many African-American slaves in New Jersey escaped from their masters and fought for the British crown, relying on promises of freedom proclaimed by several generals in the name of King George III. Some engaged in guerilla warfare against the supporters of independence. After the war, they went into hiding, fled to another state, or emigrated, many to Nova Scotia and Sierra Leone.[25]

New Jersey historian David Cohen has written that many of the stories about these Ramapo Valley people are legends, not history. He states "it became increasingly obvious that, not only was the legend untrue, it was also the continuing vehicle for the erroneous and derogatory stereotype of the Mountain People."

The name Jackson Whites and its associated legends are rejected as pejorative by the members of the Ramapough Lenape Nation, who today describe themselves as the descendants of the Lenape and Munsee peoples, with varying degrees of African, Tuscarora, Dutch, and other ancestry. The Ramapough also claim common ancestry with other aboriginal American tribes in the north and west. The Ramapough assert that their ancestral language was Munsee, but the community was known to have spoken English and Dutch in the past, and speaks English today.

The state of New Jersey recognizes the Ramapough Lenape as an American Indian tribe, although the federal government does not.[26]

Hints of Change

In 1958, liturgical life at Darlington was enhanced with the introduction of the "Participation Mass" allowed by a decree of the Sacred Congregation of Rites of September 3, 1958. The entire congregation recited in unison all the parts of the Mass that formerly had been restricted to the altar boys.[27] A significant step in the renewal of the liturgy had been taken.

On October 28, 1958, Cardinal Angelo Roncalli, the patriarch of Venice, was elected Pope John XXIII. Less than three months later, he announced his intention to summon an ecumenical council. Cardinal Giovanni Battista Montini, later Pope Paul VI, remarked to a friend that "this holy old boy doesn't realize what a hornet's nest he's stirring up."[28]

Chapter Twenty-nine

The "Friendly Honest Man"

Henry G. J. Beck so described Monsignor Thomas H. Powers, Bishop Ahr's successor as rector of Darlington. Ordained in 1927, Powers was immediately assigned to the Seton Hall faculty. From 1940 until his appointment to Darlington, he was rector of Seton Hall Divinity School, the formal name for the minor seminary program that encompassed freshman and sophomore years at the college. At Seton Hall he taught Latin and took great pride in having his students read entire plays of Terence and Plautus.[1] On March 20, 1950, the day of Bishop Ahr's consecration as bishop of Trenton, Powers was named rector.[2] An easygoing and engaging person, Powers did not consider his position too lofty to prevent him from playing cards with seminarians and joining them on their walks.[3] As rector, he taught pastoral theology and Latin. On April 23, 1955, Powers accepted the pastorate of Immaculate Conception Church, Montclair.[4] He died in 1962.

During Monsignor Powers' rectorate, a familiar face left the seminary. Father Demjanovich, "Father Charles," known to the seminarians as "Charlie D," accepted the pastorate of St. Mary's, Rutherford, New Jersey. He was the last of the faculty who had served at the seminary at Seton Hall. He was the first to move to Darlington. He had served as procurator from 1923 to 1951, an amazing 28 years.

Monsignor Brady

Powers' successor could not be described as easygoing. Ordained in Rome on December 21, 1929, Father Joseph H. Brady received his doctorate in theology the following July. During his 25 years at Seton Hall, he earned a Ph.D. in history at Columbia University. Brady's appointment was the closest the seminary came to a "dynasty" in the office of rector. His sister was married to the brother of his predecessor, Bishop Ahr.

Brady devoted what free time he had to preparation of a history of the diocese and archdiocese of Newark for the diocesan centennial in 1953. Sadly, he never accomplished this task. Health problems may have been the reason. During the very hot summer of 1951, he suffered a severe heart attack, followed by another attack two years later. From that time on, he relied on digitalis to relieve angina attacks. He never was without his vial of pills. Seminarians, who love to imitate the mannerisms of their superiors, often mimicked Brady's not-infrequent passing of his right hand over his mouth. They did not know that he was taking medication.[5]

He was the first rector who had no classroom responsibilities. Beck describes Brady's rectorate as "devoted to administration . . . characterized by an almost mathematical attention to detail, yet it was broad and kindly and stamped with a constant willingness to seek counsel."[6]

Brady described the goals of seminary training in traditional terms. He wrote that "the seminarian must grow each day in charity, the essence of Christian perfection. He must grow each day stronger in character; he must acquire and deepen true and worthy ideals, acquire and strengthen proper habits, a strong will, and emotional stability [and] each day, move closer . . . to a manly spirituality."[7]

Like his predecessors, Brady emphasized the importance of obedience and docility as exemplified through fidelity to the seminary rule. For Brady, obedience was "more than order imposed from without; it is self-control, under the guidance and direction of authority." Fidelity to the rule and customs of the seminary is "an instrument of perfection."[8] For Brady, obedience was to be cultivated "for its own sake and as a means of sanctification, rather than from fear of reprimand or punishment."[9]

He summed up the goals of seminary spiritual formation in few words: "The spiritual life of the seminarians continues to be centered about three basic elements: a special love of Christ in the Eucharist, a filial devotion to Our Blessed Lady; and obedience to the rule and to superiors as manifestations of the divine will."[10]

Brady's approach to spirituality appeared to many to have a rather gloomy cast. Reporting to the deputies, he recounted two funerals that had taken place during the previous year in terms that showed his very serious nature and his understanding of the power of the Almighty.

> The seminarians were allowed to participate in the fullest possible measure in the requiem services for Monsignor Tierney (died December 22, 1955) and for their fellow-student, Mr. Harold J. O'Neill. They would derive therefrom, it was felt, valuable lessons on the brevity of life and the inevitability of death. They gave, at the time and since, every indication of having been properly and profitably impressed.

> One devotion in particular seems to deserve comment.
> By a system administered by the seminarians themselves,
> each student is assigned one day of reparation each
> month, on which regular and special prayers and acts
> of virtue are offered up to appease the Divine Majesty.[11]

As maudlin as this might appear, it was written by a man who knew every day that it could be his last. He died of a massive heart attack on July 3, 1961, almost exactly ten years after his first seizure. When he was found, his digitalis pills were scattered at his side.[12]

Faculty

For the first time, in 1956,[13] the rector's report included lengthy comments on outside faculty activities and scholarship. This was an innovation of Monsignor Brady, a former university professor who undoubtedly saw the value of such activities. It also was the fruit of Archbishop Walsh's plan to have a highly educated, professionally trained faculty who would be scholars as well as teachers.

Archbishop Boland supported the faculty in their scholarly activities and remarked that "they are the means of keeping the seminary before the world as a scholarly institution."[14]

In 1956, Brady singled out Father John Dougherty's radio and television appearances on "Look Up and Live," "Town Meeting of the Air," and the "Catholic Hour," in addition to his articles in the *Catholic Biblical Quarterly* and *America*. Later Dougherty would become a familiar television personality, narrating the prize-winning television film "Eternal Rome" and receiving the Catholic Arts Award from the National Council of Catholic Men.

Dougherty's theatrical skills were honed in the classroom. Not only did he reject manual-based lectures, he rejected the manuals themselves. He provided four volumes of his own notes for the students.[15] His teaching style can only be described as engaging. On one occasion, as Brady passed by Dougherty's classroom, he heard sounds that appeared to be laughter. "Father Dougherty," he intoned, "are you teaching or are you entertaining?" Came the response, "Monsignor, I am trying to do both!"

Father George Shea was cited for an article on "The Assumption" and a lecture on "St. Thomas Aquinas and the Papacy" at Fordham University. Father Przezdziecki contributed to *Nine Mediaeval Thinkers* and *A Tribute to Etienne Gilson*, published by the Pontifical Institute of Mediaeval Studies, while Father Curtis published a book entitled *The Simplification of the Rubrics*, and Father Welsh contributed an article to the *Homiletic and Pastoral Review*.

Father Przezdziecki, affectionately known as "Joey Prez" or "Prezzy," went beyond the boring manuals to engage the seminarians in the study of philosophy.

He gave the seminarians a "sense of reading the actual texts of the great philosophers." With his unique intonation, he "would read a text from Aristotle or Aquinas, and then proceed to march back and forth in front of the classroom reflecting on or wrestling with the position enunciated in the text."[16]

Subsequent years[17] would find numerous faculty articles and books published and faculty participation in a wide variety of scholarly and pastoral activities. They also assumed leadership positions in national and international learned societies. Father Shea served as president of the Catholic Theological Society of America, delivering the significant presidential lecture on "Theology and the Magisterium." Father Cassels was elected president of the Catholic Homiletic Society. Father Dougherty was appointed to the International Congress of Pastoral Liturgy at Assisi and the Pontifical Commission on Radio and Television. Father Beck was named to the International Society for Comparative Church History and served as an editor of the *American Catholic Historical Review*. Meanwhile, Father Welsh directed the Pope Pius XII Institute of Industrial Relations.

Among books published by faculty were Father Hogan's *Augustine Bonetty and the Problem of Faith and Reason* and *The Redemptive Sacrifice of Christ*. Father Dougherty published *Searching the Scriptures*. Over the years, Father John Koenig published a well-received series of children's books called *Stories for God's Little Ones*. In 1961, Monsignor Beck published *The Centennial History of Immaculate Conception Seminary—Darlington, New Jersey.* He undertook the seminary history "under obedience and without any enthusiasm,"[18] but produced an excellent work.

Beck, like Dougherty, was a highly regarded teacher, although his style was quite different. Like Dougherty, he despised manuals. Often, he brought a pile of books to class, placed them on the desk, and spent the hour analyzing the varying approaches of the authors to a particular topic. His students thereby understood that many issues could be regarded from different perspectives.

Faculty contributed to *Theological Studies*, the *Catholic Historical Review*, *Homiletic and Pastoral Review*, *Encyclopedia Britannica*, *Junior Encyclopedia Britannica*, *Encyclopedia Americana*, the *New Catholic Encyclopedia*, *Ave Maria*, and *America*. They were members of the Catholic Theological Society of America, the American Mariological Society, the American Catholic Philosophical Society, the American Catholic Historical Association, and the Canon Law Society of America.

In addition to scholarly activities, the faculty of the 1940s and 1950s continued to be involved in various diocesan projects such as the preparation of sermon outlines for the parishes and outlines of the monthly conferences given to the sisters and nuns of the archdiocese. They also served as visitors, supervising catechetical work for the Confraternity of Christian Doctrine, or the C.C.D.,[19] and as members of the Marriage Tribunal and the Liturgical Commission. Among Father Welsh's appointments was that of archdiocesan director for Social Action.[20]

Several faculty members were assigned as confessors in convents and orphanages. Outside the diocese, faculty members taught at St. John's University, St. Joseph College in Connecticut, and Ladycliff College. Some filled civic responsibilities, Father Tierney acting as the local agent for the Red Cross blood drive, and Father Demjanovich as a member of the board of trustees of the North Bergen Nursing Service.

There was need for continual renewal of the faculty. In the mid-twentieth century, it was the custom in the Newark archdiocese to assign priests as pastors according to a seniority system. When their time came, they assumed a pastorate. This system was adjusted according the ethnic background of the priest. Normally, someone of German, Italian, or Polish background would be assigned to a national parish. These parishes moved along on a separate list from the territorial parishes. Priests assigned to the seminary therefore often "moved on" to a parish when their "time came up." Occasionally, depending on the seminary's needs, they would remain a few years longer.

This remained the practice even though, since the Roman educational reforms of the 1930s, it meant the loss of professionally trained educators after a comparatively short tenure. The large number of priests and seminarians, at home and overseas, allowed this policy to continue without disruption to the seminary. New professors often were selected while still in seminary studies and sent to graduate school immediately after ordination.

In 1958, Reverend Joseph Manz succeeded Reverend Thomas Carey as procurator. The same year Fathers Leo O. Farley and Carl D. Hinrichsen were sent for higher studies in moral theology and Church history.[21] The following year Monsignor Dougherty left Darlington to assume the presidency of Seton Hall University, and Fathers Russell G. Ruffino and Robert E. Hunt were appointed to the faculty and sent for higher studies in philosophy and dogmatic theology.[22]

Spiritual Life

After World War II and through the 1950s there was little change in the seminary rule, horarium, and spiritual exercises. It was a time of calm and perhaps of complacency, characteristic of the nation at large. Monsignor McCarthy continued as spiritual director until his appointment as pastor of Our Lady of Sorrows in South Orange in 1953. He was named auxiliary bishop of Newark in 1954 and became bishop of Camden in 1957. He died two years later in 1959. He was succeeded as spiritual director by Monsignor George Baker.[23]

Typical of the rector's reports was the comment that "Monsignor McCarthy is pleased with the sincerity of the students in striving for priestly perfection."[24] The spiritual director's role did not change. He attended all the spiritual exercises of the seminarians and set a schedule for spiritual visits. He remained available for individual consultation and gave regular conferences to the seminarians.[25]

Regarding devotional life, particular emphasis was "always placed on devotion to Jesus Christ in the Holy Eucharist and to His Blessed Mother."[26] However, the seminarians did take some initiative, but always within the boundaries of approved devotions. The administration was pleased with "the growth of a sense of personal responsibility in the spiritual life as manifested by the private and voluntary devotions of the students—visits to the Blessed Sacrament, the Stations of the Cross, the private recitations of the Breviary before the Blessed Sacrament."[27]

In 1947 and 1948, the seminarians addressed the crucial elections in Italy by organizing a novena in honor of Our Lady of Fatima for the successful outcome of the election and for the protection of the Holy Father. With the permission of the rector "they wrote to all the Seminaries in the country inviting the seminarians to join them in this crusade of prayer. They received favorable replies from seminaries across the country to California."[28]

The authorities were quite happy. In 1950, Monsignor Dauenhauer, deputy for discipline, reported to the board in utopian terms that "discipline and spirituality were better than anywhere in the world." This report drew from Archbishop Walsh appreciation for the work of the "super-expert deputies."[29]

In this period, discipline and spirituality were closely linked. Discipline and the following of the rule through habitual fidelity to the spiritual exercises were seen as the mechanism to produce a strong spirituality. Repetition would produce habits that would remain with the priest for a lifetime. Fidelity to the rule and the spiritual exercises was the basis for evaluating the fitness of a seminarian for ordination. Canon law therefore prescribed a deputy for discipline, whose charge logically included the spiritual life of the seminary.

As the seminary enrollment continued to grow and, by the late 1950s, to approach 300, it became evident that one spiritual director could not adequately address the needs of such a great number of seminarians. He did receive some assistance from the faculty. In 1955, Brady reported that "in addition to the spiritual director . . . the seminarians may consult any other members of the faculty on spiritual matters."[30]

This was not enough. In 1958, Father William F. Hogan, who had served as a professor and as director of discipline, was appointed as assistant spiritual director to assist Monsignor Baker. Hogan devoted himself principally to the philosophy students, although he was available to all. The philosophers were now separated from the theologians for their spiritual conferences as well as under a separate spiritual director. Hogan also established "a system of individual conferences, by which he sees each student several times during the year."[31]

Brady's remark and Hogan's subsequent appointment indicated a serious underlying problem. The seminary had grown so large that it was impossible for the faculty, who were not specifically charged with the evaluation of seminarians for ordination, adequately to know the students. It became evident in the evaluation process. Hogan complained to Brady that there was a "traditional ignorance of the students on the part of a segment of the faculty."

The "professionalization" of the faculty and their subsequent scholarly pursuits, in Hogan's words, made "gaining of knowledge of the students outside of class and confession…a luxury." He suggested that future faculty should be chosen with "an eye to their general balance as well as to their intellectual competence." He also urged that the seminary ask the archdiocese to limit the "outside work" often assigned to faculty, and that the faculty be substantially enlarged. He realized that the institution could not simply increase the responsibilities of the existing faculty, while asking them to maintain the professional engagement necessary for academic competence.[32]

Discipline

Just as the spiritual life was seen as leading to development of virtues of docility and obedience, discipline was considered a means to advance in the spiritual life. In 1954, Father Hogan was succeeded as director of discipline by Reverend John M. Mahon, who served until 1957, when he was replaced by Reverend Robert G. Gibney. In 1961, he, in turn, was replaced by Reverend James J. Finnerty.[33]

In Fall 1950, the rule was simplified but the changes were minor.[34] As in the past, the rector and the director of discipline explained the rule and the reasons for its observance in periodic conferences.[35]

The seminary continued to seek to impress on the students the need for a spiritual motive for observing the rule. Seminarians were urged "to look upon the regulations as necessary for the common good and a means of personal spiritual progress."

Monsignor Powers saw the rule not only as a means of developing "prompt obedience" and docility, but also as an aid in the spiritual development of the seminarian by cultivating habits of piety and devotion. In turn, this spiritual development would be of benefit to the people whom the future priest would serve.[36] Faculty members made "every effort to have the rule observed from a spiritual, supernatural motive, and to impress upon them that a mere external conformity or 'eye-serving' will be of little advantage in developing disciplined, manly character necessary for the priesthood."[37]

Observance of the rule also was seen as a way of developing self-discipline and self-reliance. It was meant to develop habits of will and ready acquiescence to duty that would carry the priest over many great difficulties in his later life.[38]

Each year, through the 1940s and 1950s and into the 1960s, the deputies expressed continued satisfaction with the discipline of the seminary. They based their reports on interviews with the director of discipline and the deacon prefect, and occasionally other seminarians. Archbishop Walsh took their tasks seriously. One year Monsignor Dauenhauer missed a deputies' meeting, and a report from the director of discipline and the first prefect was submitted. Walsh ordered Dauenhauer to come to the seminary and to make a definite investigation personally and not to get his information only from the director of discipline.[39] The next year, Dauenhauer carefully prefaced his report noting that he based it "not only on personal observation but gleaned from tactful questioning of seminarians who are his parishioners, and from the young curates assigned to him—graduates of the seminary."[40]

Despite an occasional rebuke from the archbishop, a deputy's duties were hardly taxing. Invariably they found the seminarians "happy and satisfied"[41] and thought the "spirit to be excellent."[42] In 1954, when Monsignor Corr was named to succeed Monsignor Dauenhauer as deputy for discipline, Monsignor Powers, in a light mood, wrote to him that "this duty should not cause you too much stress. I know you want to live a few more years so the report had better be good."[43]

Only in 1960 did difficulties begin to appear. Brady attributed the "increasing strain" on the director of students, as the director of discipline had been renamed, not on any changes in the student body but on the "size of the house," now almost 300, which made the maintenance of "adequate supervision" difficult.[44]

Chapter Thirty

A Coat of Arms

Like every good historian, Monsignor Brady was interested in heraldry. He commissioned William F. J. Ryan, America's foremost ecclesiastical heraldic expert of the time, to design a coat of arms for the seminary.[1]

In 1955 Ryan provided an appropriate, heraldically correct coat of arms.

THE COAT OF ARMS OF
IMMACULATE CONCEPTION SEMINARY

Blazon

DESCRIPTION OF THE ARMS

Argent, four bars wavy azure, over all the Chi-Rho and in flanks thereof the Greek letters Alpha and Omega gules, on a chief of the last, a crescent between two trefoils of the field. Crest: On a wreath of the colors a crown fleury or. Motto: *Dispensatores Mysteriorum Dei.*

Four wavy blue bars on a silver background, superimposed a red Chi-Rho, on either side of the Chi-Rho, the Greek letters Alpha and Omega in red. In an upper compartment, on a red background, a silver crescent with a silver shamrock on both sides. Crest: A gold fleur-de-lis crown on a wreath of silver and blue.

SIGNIFICANCE

The principal elements of the coat of arms, composed of the arms of the archdiocese of Newark in their entirety, identify Immaculate Conception Seminary as under the auspices of the archdiocese of Newark.

The wavy blue and silver bars are derived from the coat of arms of Newark in Nottinghamshire, England. These arms were granted by Dethick, Garter King of Arms, on December 8, 1561. On the archdiocesan arms they recall that Newark, New Jersey, was named after Newark in England. In 1666, a band of about 30 Puritans from Milford, Connecticut, led by Captain Robert Treat, settled at Four Corners. They were joined the next year by another group equal in number from Branford and Guilford, Connecticut. The name of the settlement was chosen in honor of their pastor, Reverend Abraham Pierson (1608–1678), who came from Newark-on-Trent, England.

To difference the English coat and make the arms peculiar to the see of Newark, a red chief (upper compartment) was added that it might bear the lunar symbol of the Immaculate Conception, the title under which Our Lady is Patroness of the United States of America and of the archdiocese of Newark. It is a happy coincidence that the arms of the city of Newark, granted during the reign of Elizabeth I, were bestowed on the feast of the Immaculate Conception. The crescent is accosted on either side by two shamrocks, known as trefoils in heraldry, to honor Saint Patrick, the titular or patron of the pro-cathedral of Newark.

To permit the arms of the archdiocese to refer specifically to the seminary, the monogram of Christ, the Greek Chi-Rho flanked by the Greek letters, Alpha and Omega, have been emblazoned in a form similar to that found on the coins of Constantius (Emperor Flavius Julius Constantius, 337–361, son of Constantine the Great and Fausta).

As in the Cross, early Christian writers recognized in the Chi-Rho the mystical seal alluded to by the Prophet Ezekiel (Ezekiel 9:4, 6) and in the Apocalypse or Book of Revelation (Revelation 7:2, and 14:1); Tertullian (born 160) and St. Clement of Alexandria (died c. 215), both allude to it; Origen (185–253) and

Epiphanius (died 403) explain it as symbolical of Christ's two-fold nature. There are many varieties of the Chi-Rho monogram in early Christian art in the catacombs and in the first Roman Churches.

The Chi-Rho, the symbol of the High Priest of the New Testament who offered the bloody sacrifice of the Cross for the redemption of mankind, is indeed an appropriate charge for the shield of a seminary that trains *Alteri Christi* to offer the Eucharist, the unbloody sacrifice commanded by Jesus Christ in commemoration of the sacrifice of the Cross. It is an equally appropriate symbol for those who seek to serve Christ in various ministries of the Church and in the study of Catholic theology.

The Alpha and Omega have been cryptically significant of the divinity and infinity of Christ since the writing of the Book of Revelation. "I am the Alpha and the Omega," says the Lord God, who is, who was, and who is to come, the Almighty (Revelation 1:8). Another reference in Revelation to these letters is, "I am the Alpha and the Omega, the beginning and the end. I will give water from the well of life to anybody who is thirsty (Revelation 21:6)." As Alpha, God is the beginning of all things at the creation in Genesis; as Omega in Revelation, He is the consummation of all things. Commenting on the words quoted above from Revelation, the Venerable Bede (672–735) wrote: "I am the Alpha and the Omega, the beginning and the end, says the Lord God. The beginning without predecessor; the end without royal successor. He who is, and who was, and who is coming, the Almighty."

On a wreath of silver and blue a golden crown is displayed as a crest above the shield. The origin of this wreath, or torse, is interesting. In the tournament, or joust, the knight, as he passed his lady in the arena, received at times a token or favor from her; this usually consisted of a handkerchief or some other fabric in the metal and color of her family arms—in the livery colors, as they are called. The knight took this and wound it like a wreath around the base of the crest, where it joined the top of his helmet. The wreath has now become but a stand for the crest; it is always in the principal metal and color of the shield, and the metal must be the first of the six pieces.

Fortunately, but happily, the principal tinctures of the shield of the archdiocese of Newark are silver and blue, the Marian colors. These are the tinctures that must be used for the wreath. In this instance the wreath stands for the seminarian's esteem for the Immaculate Virgin, and is, therefore, a most appropriate foundation on which to place the crown that symbolizes Mary as Queen of Heaven. In the year of the establishment of this coat of arms for Immaculate Conception Seminary (1955), Pope Pius XII instituted the feast of the Queenship of Mary for the Universal Church.

The motto *Dispensatores Mysteriorum Dei* is taken from St. Paul's First Letter to the Corinthians: "People must think of us as Christ's servants, stewards entrusted with the mysteries of God" (1 Corinthians 4:1). These same words also occur in the Roman Pontifical in the Rite for the Ordination of a Priest.[2]

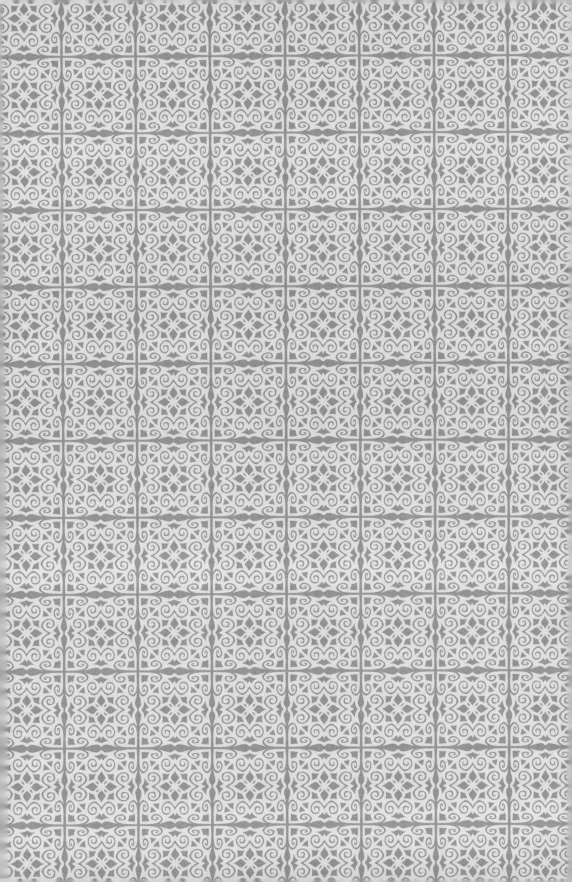

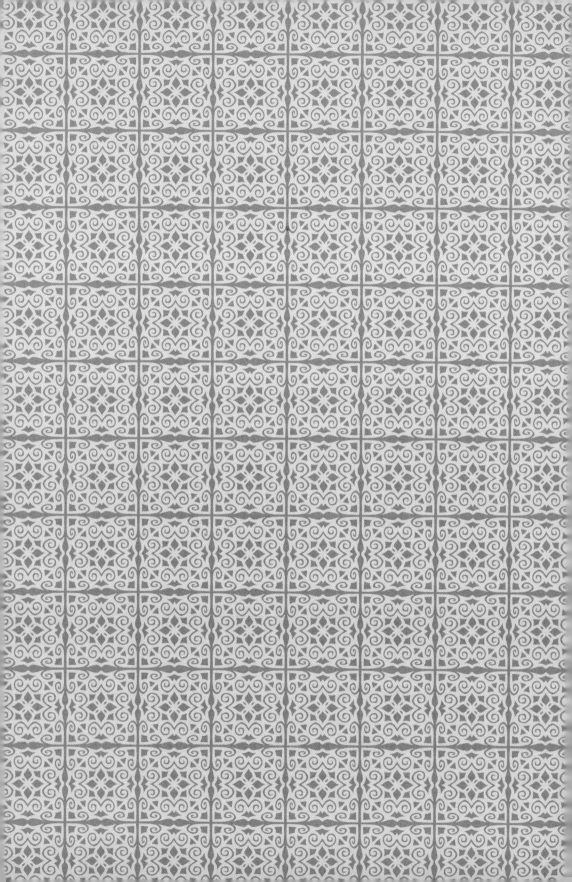

The Major Archdiocesan Philosophical-Theological Seminary
of the Immaculate Conception at Darlington, New Jersey

Crisis and Change

1961–1982

Chapter Thirty-one

Pope John XXIII

As the 1960s began, the seminary shared the optimism of the Church and of the nation. The papal conclave of 1958 brought to the throne of Saint Peter the jovial and charismatic John XXIII. Now Blessed Pope John, the pontiff caught the imagination of the world with his friendly, informal, and open style. The press reported every incident that showed his humanity. When his family visited him in the Vatican, Pope John's sister, Assunta, fearing that her beloved brother might not be properly cared for in the Vatican, brought along a homemade salami.

Pope John even left the confines of the Vatican, journeying to the shrine of Loreto by train, obviously enjoying the trip. He visited Rome's *Regina Coeli* prison, where he told the inmates that he too was a prisoner who could not go where he wished when he wished. To the shock of the papal courtiers, he recounted that an uncle had once been jailed for poaching.

But Pope John's most exciting act was summoning an ecumenical council, the first in 90 years. He declared that his council would not issue censures and condemnations but be a "pastoral council" that would bring the Church "up to date" by going back to its roots. He gave theology two new words: *aggiornamento* and *resourcement* as the touchstones of his vision.

Seminary faculty members joined in the enthusiasm, giving talks and lectures on the possibilities that might be opened by the council. Probably the most enthusiastic was Monsignor Beck, who lectured widely on the history of previous councils and the potential of Pope John's initiative.

Some American bishops did not think much would come of the council. An issue that engaged many was a "vernacular" liturgy. To the surprise of many, "Doc Ahr," now bishop of Trenton, saw little difficulty with such an idea. Visiting Darlington a year before the council opened, he dined with the seminarians from

Trenton and shocked them when he said that if a vernacular liturgy would help the people understand the Mass better, he was in favor of it.[1] Ahr's reputation as a theologian led his colleagues to elect him as the head of the bishops' committee on doctrine. His opinion of his colleagues was not very complimentary. After the first session of the council, Ahr, always the scholar and theologian, privately expressed his opinion of the American bishops at the council. He put it simply, as was his wont: "They don't know what they are talking about."[2]

Archbishop Boland was of a different mind regarding vernacular liturgy. Interviewed in Rome during the second session of the council in 1963, he pointed out that in New York and in New Jersey, where so many nationalities attend Mass together, "Latin has many advantages." Boland was very impressed by new religious communities he encountered in Rome. He singled out the Little Sisters of Jesus: "They wear simple blue denim dresses, bandana headdresses, sandals on bare feet. They work with nomad tribes in North Africa, on barges in canals in Holland, in small factories in depressed areas, in European slums. They are doing marvelous work and they make many of us—consecrated for religious missions—ashamed."[3]

Bishop James A. McNulty of Paterson rather colorfully described the work of the council as "a positive work—to remove any of the symptoms of Godlessness which seems to grow around Catholic life and to infect it. The bark of Peter has been picking up barnacles—the work of the Council will be to remove them."[4] Among the symptoms of Godlessness, he pinpointed growing Catholic sympathy for abortion, contraception, and divorce.

Archbishop Boland's New Jersey

The state of New Jersey in 1960 had a population of 5.2 million, compared with 4.2 million at the end of World War II in 1945. Catholics, numbering over 1.3 million, made up 31 percent of the total population in 1945. They had grown to 2.3 million in 1960, 43 percent of the total population.[5] While the general population had increased, the decline of the cities had begun during the Depression of the 1930s and the population of Newark had shrunk from 442,000 in 1930 to 405,000 in 1960.[6] Jersey City, Paterson, Trenton, and Camden experienced similar losses. A Newark city commissioner lamented the trend, writing that a "large number of outstanding citizens . . . have moved to the suburbs."[7] The Garden State was becoming the "Suburban State."

Archbishop Boland, who had succeeded Archbishop Walsh in 1953, spent much of the first decade of his time as archbishop presiding over unprecedented growth in the archdiocese of Newark, which included Bergen, Union, Hudson, and Essex Counties. The weekly archdiocesan newspaper, *The Advocate*, chronicled this expansion, including an annual "construction issue." Almost every month it carried a picture of Boland, in cope and miter, wielding a shovel as he broke ground or a trowel as he blessed the cornerstone of a new church, school, rectory, or convent.

This growth began after the end of World War II and continued into the 1960s.

In 1960, Catholics in the archdiocese of Newark had grown to 1.4 million, constituting almost 50 percent of the population of the four counties. There were 239 parishes served by 1,151 priests, 758[8] of whom were diocesan, 393 religious. The 218 elementary schools and 52 high schools[9] were staffed by 3,321 sisters and 102 brothers. Seton Hall University, the Jesuit Saint Peter's College in Jersey City, and the Dominican Sisters' Caldwell College for Women, which together had 12,572 students, added to the Catholic educational spectrum.

The seminary was crowded and plans were made for a new building to house the philosophy students. Although seminary enrollment throughout the United States continued to rise in the post-war years, the ratio of seminarians to the growing Catholic population had been slipping since 1944, a sign of slow-but-steady changes in the attitudes of Catholics.[10]

Immigration Restrictions

The development of mid-twentieth century American Catholicism partly was a result of a series of restrictive immigration laws. The 1921 Emergency Quota Act limited immigration from any country to three percent of the number of people from that country residing in the United States in 1910. The 1924 Johnson-Reed Act reduced the number to two percent of a nationality's population in the United States in 1890, and the Oriental Exclusion Act prohibited most immigration from Asia.

Before these restrictions, hundreds of thousands of Catholics annually entered the United States. They sparked an unprecedented growth in Church membership. The American Catholic Church met this challenge with a proliferation of institutions and the development of religious communities to serve them. These waves of immigrants and their children filled the seminaries and convents.

With the immigration restrictions in place, the Church was given time to consolidate its gains and improve its parochial and educational structure without the challenge of providing for waves of new arrivals every year. As generations passed, Catholics assimilated into the political, social, and economic structure of the nation, some achieving great success and affluence.

In New Jersey, the growth and the euphoria that surrounded the Church's expansion masked underlying developments that provide a fuller, although not as optimistic, picture.

Suburbanization

The completion of the New Jersey Turnpike in 1952 and the Garden State Parkway in 1957 linked the northern and southern portions of the state and provided easy access to the New Jersey shore. East-west Interstate Highways 78 and 80, completed in the 1970s, provided similar access to the western parts of the state.

Suburban growth and concurrent urban decline began in the 1930s but escalated after World War II. The G.I. Bill provided low-rate home loans to returning veterans, many of whom eschewed the urban lifestyle of their parents and chose to reside in the suburbs. The archdiocesan growth of this period was in the suburbs of Bergen County and western Essex and Union Counties. The surrounding dioceses of Paterson and Trenton experienced similar, if not greater, growth.

The suburban expansion of the archdiocese of Newark was not without a price—the decline of the urban parishes. Several government policies propelled this transition. Beginning in the 1930s but increasing after World War II, federal and state authorities, seeking to end urban "blight," bulldozed entire city blocks. The homes on these blocks, mostly row houses, were replaced either with housing projects or with government and educational buildings.

In the name of progress and urban renewal, numerous city parishes were decimated. The New Jersey Turnpike, the Garden State Parkway, and the interstate highways literally drove through neighborhoods and replaced thousands of homes with six-to-eight lanes of highway. These depressed highways splintered parishes and dispersed parishioners. Tens of thousands of parishioners left the cities, especially Newark, Jersey City, Orange, East Orange, and Elizabeth. Many relocated in Bergen County and in other suburban areas, but large numbers relocated outside the archdiocese. As they left, a rich heritage of urban life and ethnic communities disappeared.

Urban renewal and highway construction left behind shattered neighborhoods that no longer were attractive and thus the exodus continued. Suburban Catholic growth had a dark side: the collapse of urban Catholic life and of urban parishes. For a century, the urban parishes had provided most of the vocations in the archdiocese of Newark. Their demise and the events of the 1960s would bring that phenomenon to an end.

Migration and Immigration

The ethnic makeup of the population was changing as well. Most of the emigration from the archdiocese was composed of Catholics of European heritage—Irish, Italian, Polish, German, and Slovak. At the same time, the cities experienced the influx of large numbers of African Americans who were leaving the southern states in search of a better life. Very few were Catholic. The "new" Catholics in northern New Jersey were mostly from Puerto Rico. As citizens, they were not subject to the restrictive immigration laws enacted in the 1920s. In the early 1960s, after the Communist revolution of Fidel Castro in Cuba, refugees from that unfortunate island flocked to New Jersey, most settling in Hudson County.

The new migrations and immigrations foreshadowed the radical ethnic transformation of the archdiocese of Newark that would take place in the closing decades of the twentieth century after the passage in 1965 of the Hart-Celler Immigration and Nationality Act.

Expansion and Debt

The increased prosperity of New Jersey Catholics fueled the institutional expansion of the early Boland era. In 1960, Catholic elementary schools in New Jersey counted almost 128,000 pupils, Catholic high schools almost 21,000.[11] It is not surprising that Church leaders saw a limitless future. No one could imagine what lay ahead.

Everything appeared positive. The archdiocese had foreseen the suburban expansion and had purchased land for churches and schools. These were constructed with breakneck speed as the new parishioners arrived in the burgeoning suburbs. The swift character of the expansion unfortunately resulted in churches that must be described as no more than adequate, especially in comparison to the majestic ecclesiastical edifices left behind in the cities.

While Catholics moved to the suburbs, they wanted to retain the Church institutional services they had grown accustomed to in the cities. The archdiocese decided to provide them.

In 1960, the archdiocese of Newark announced an ambitious expansion program. A capital campaign was initiated that would have as its goal the collection of $30 million. These funds would provide for the construction of eight high schools, two in each of the archdiocese's four counties; four homes for the aged, one in each county; and a philosophy house for the seminary to house 250 seminarians.

The goal of the campaign was not reached, and unforeseen increases in construction costs forced serious cutbacks. Six of the high schools were completed. One, in Hudson County, never opened as a high school, but was transformed into a parish church and elementary school. None of the homes for the aged was built. The story of the philosophy house will be part of our narrative.

Not only were the planned buildings not constructed, the high schools were plagued with large deficits. The post-conciliar flood of departures from the priesthood and from religious life resulted in hiring lay teachers at much higher cost. The archdiocese for many years subsidized these new institutions and its debt mushroomed.[12] At the same time, the "flight to the suburbs" had destabilized many city parishes that now clamored for aid from the archdiocese. This uncontrolled, ever-increasing debt would have an impact on the seminary and radically change its future.

Chapter Thirty-two

The Seminary and Psychology

In 1930, the Sacred Congregation of the Sacraments, concerned over an increasing number of requests for declarations of nullity of ordinations due to outside pressure, issued the instruction *Quam ingens Ecclesiae*.[1] In 1955, marking the twenty-fifth anniversary of that instruction, it sent a confidential circular letter[2] to bishops that reflected the congregation's continuing concern over this matter. Archbishop Boland sent the letter to Monsignor Brady on May 9, 1957, telling him that he would "find the Latin refreshingly classical at times."[3]

The congregation lamented that there was no letup in requests for nullifications of ordinations with the result that many "are compelled, alas, to remain in their unhappy state for the remainder of their lives, content at most with a simple reduction to the lay state while the obligation of keeping sacred celibacy continues intact." While the congregation expressed sympathy for these men, it went on: "The common good, serving as the bulwark upon which the law was enacted must prevail over the private convenience of a few."

It considered that lack of application of the instruction of 1930 was responsible for this state of affairs, allowing that the dislocations caused by World War II might have prevented proper application of the canonical norms. The congregation outlined the principal complaints it received. They included: 1) ignorance of the 1930 instruction, 2) lack of sufficient realization of the duties of the priesthood, 3) encouragement by superiors that they would receive sufficient grace for their duties, 4) undue influence of parents and relatives, and 5) candidates being "timorous by nature, anxious, doubtful, troubled by scruples, entirely incapable of making a decision of any importance" together with their fear that they would be "abandoned to the world . . . devoid of any skill or profession" and even fear of the "punishments of hell" were they to "depart from the clerical state."

The "richest source" of complaint was from those who contended that they "suffered from psychological illnesses of a sexual nature, which they called psycasthenia, neurosis, or psychosis. They represent themselves as invincibly . . . prone to lust . . . and incapable of preserving chastity." In spite of various penances and austerities, including hairshirts, they were unable to control their impulses.

In order to address this continuing problem, the congregation repeated the order that the 1930 instruction be read to all seminarians each year and that retreat masters and spiritual directors discuss these issues in their conferences.

More significantly, the congregation added that the investigation into the fitness of candidates might include a psychological assessment utilizing "contemporary scientific research in psychiatry and biology, provided this research is entirely free from the taint of rank materialism."

The congregation added that "very special observation must be given the student who suffers perhaps from psychopathy or sexual hyper aesthesia, namely, one who must be reckoned in the number of those whom psychiatrists call neurotics, the scrupulous, those affected by aboulia, the hysterical and generally all those afflicted with abnormal physiological or psychological deficiencies of a sexual nature, or with some mental defect (schizophrenics, paranoiacs, etc.)."

The congregation advocated that questionable candidates be "thoroughly examined" by a "psychiatrist commended for the task by his skill, good morals, religious convictions; a man of advanced age, and unaffected by materialistic ideas." For the first time, seminaries were urged to utilize the psychological sciences in the determination of a candidate's fitness for entry and of fitness for ordination.

The seminary moved swiftly to implement the intentions of the letter. In 1960, with the endorsement of the archbishop of Newark and the bishops of Paterson, Trenton, and Camden, it "inaugurated a psychological testing program for all applicants for admission to the Seminary."[4]

In order to provide a baseline for the testing program, a preliminary study of 43 second-year theology and 43 fourth-year theology students was conducted in July 1960. They were given a battery of tests: the College Qualification Test, the Minnesota Multiphasic Personality Inventory, the Religious Behavior Inventory, the Bender-Gestalt test, and the Rotter Incomplete Sentence Blank.

The psychologists who administered the tests reported that the tests gave a good picture of the characteristics of the seminarians and that they would be useful in filtering out those maladapted to seminary life. They also noted that the group was above average in intelligence, and below average only in the scientific tests.[5]

The seminary proceeded to administer the tests to the Seton Hall candidates in 1961. That summer, the Supreme Sacred Congregation of the Holy Office issued a *monitum*, or warning, that put in an unfavorable light the use of psychoanalysis and psychological testing. Paragraph 4 of the monitum rejected the opinion that "psychoanalytical examination is definitely necessary" before admission to the seminary or before reception of Holy Orders.[6]

Opponents of psychological testing immediately questioned its use in seminaries. However, other analysts noted that the remarks about psychiatry were commentary and not central to the monitum, which focused on the imputability of human acts. They noted, "By no means has the Holy Office directed a condemnation toward the psychological testing of candidates for the priesthood and the religious life." Rather, the monitum rejected the opinion that psychoanalytical processes are absolutely necessary to ascertain the aptitude for priesthood. Therefore, they argued that to affirm that psychoanalysis and psychological testing could be helpful in such discernment was not disapproved.[7]

Following the Holy Office monitum, issues regarding psychological testing were discussed at a symposium conducted by the American Catholic Psychological Association at Fordham University on August 31, 1961. The most serious question raised by psychological testing concerned the privacy of the individual with regard to his moral conscience. The symposium concluded that "the desired end of knowing the complete picture about a man does not justify the means of an obligated revelation of moral conscience in psychological testing programs or the revelation of moral conscience in the external forum."[8] However, it noted that the candidate or seminarian might willingly permit information gleaned from psychological testing or counseling to be revealed.

The symposium also discussed the negative and positive value of psychological reports and the proper authority of psychological reports. It concluded, "The direction and attitude of the Holy See are quite clearly in favor of this development of the seminary program."[9]

The seminary quickly moved from psychological testing for applicants to provision of psychiatric services for seminarians. Faculty members could arrange for a seminarian to be interviewed by a psychiatrist. If the process extended beyond four visits, the rector was notified. If therapy was indicated, the seminarian was required to take a leave of absence until the therapy was completed. The seminarian would be permitted to return to the seminary only if the therapist stated that the seminarian might safely be advanced to the priesthood. The seminarians were informed of this policy so that they would be aware that embarking on diagnostic testing might lead to therapy that would bring their situation into the external forum.[10] While Archbishop Boland approved, he urged caution on the use of psychiatrists for treatment of seminarians.[11]

The seminary continued to apply the testing program but noted in 1963 that it was "still too early . . . to be able to evaluate the worth of this program."[12]

Rejection of Candidates—A Crisis Ensues

As the years passed, the seminary more and more viewed psychological testing and evaluation in a positive light. The faculty supported this policy and urged the rector to give even "greater weight" to psychological assessment as an admissions criterion.[13]

One of the effects of this testing was the rejection of an increasing number of candidates from the Seton Hall Divinity School for admission to Darlington. In 1965, the parents of a number of rejected candidates protested their sons' rejection to Monsignor George Shea, rector of Darlington, indicating that they believed advancement from Seton Hall to Darlington was practically automatic. Shea asked Bishop Dougherty, president of Seton Hall, to initiate a policy, "instantaner, instantium, instantissime," whereby divinity students would sign a statement acknowledging that acceptance into the divinity school did not commit the major seminary to accept them.[14]

This provoked a contretemps between the seminary and the university. The university professors who had recommended the candidates were quite upset by the number of rejections, in particular those based on psychological assessment. Apparently, they were not as convinced of the validity of these assessments as were the seminary authorities and the archbishop. Archbishop Boland, who signed off on all acceptances and rejections, expressed surprise at the attitude of the parents and saw no reason why the students should not be required to sign a statement such as Shea desired.[15]

Two years later, in 1967, the same issue arose, with greater intensity. Dougherty wrote Boland an impassioned letter protesting the "unprecedented rejection of so many applicants for Darlington," telling the archbishop the action had been "most disturbing to me and the priests of Seton Hall." Dougherty did not question the "basic validity of psychological testing," but wondered why "suddenly it has been given new and heightened importance in decision making."[16] Individual priests of Seton Hall also directly addressed protests to Boland.[17]

Shea was not to be moved. In a 10-page letter to the archbishop, copied to Dougherty, he addressed each case in detail. He explained that the seminary had been using psychological testing on an experimental basis since 1961, but now the "experimental period was over" and that "our cumulative experience with the entrants from 1961 on had been such, that, as a general rule, henceforth it would be wise to rely heavily on the psychologist's reports and recommendations."

Monsignor Shea told the archbishop, "The quality of the general run of applicants in recent years" had been "in steady decline" since 1961. He added that this was the experience of all the seminaries on the eastern seaboard.

He explained that "during the trial period, when screening applicants, we in large measure disregarded the adverse reports and recommendations of the psychologists. But, knowing what we now know about the usefulness of such warnings, surely it would be folly to continue to disregard them in large measure, and to rely instead on the judgments of the SHU Divinity School Faculty . . . who do not have access to the psychologists' findings."[18]

Immaculate Conception Seminary, at a very early time in comparison to many United States seminaries, was and remained convinced of the value of psychological assessment in screening candidates.

The Faculty's Changing Role

The difficulty of providing spiritual guidance for and evaluating a seminary population of almost 300 had caused Father Hogan, the spiritual director, to ask Monsignor Brady to enlist the teaching faculty more directly in these tasks. Brady appointed a group of faculty to address this issue and the faculty's role as confessors in the seminary. The report they compiled revealed tensions within the faculty and disagreement regarding their role.

The report was written in a very legalistic style. This is not surprising as the chairman of the committee was Reverend Donald Zimmermann, a faculty member regarded as a brilliant canon lawyer. It cites the appropriate canons and commentaries and draws several conclusions. Its first conclusion, that the "only task assigned by law to the professor of a seminary is to teach," appears to rule out any other role for faculty. It recognized that the rector is "commanded by law" to consult all professors before advancing a student to Holy Orders, but emphasized that this was a consultative role and professors had the right to abstain whenever they wished.

Regarding confession, it notes the hesitancy of the Holy See in many documents to allow the professors to become involved in the spiritual sphere of the seminary. Specifically, in diocesan seminaries, faculty never may be ordinary confessors, only extraordinary confessors, and to be such requires an appointment.

The report states that a faculty member may be named to a disciplinary post to assist in evaluation of students, but such a post requires an official appointment and is not part of one's responsibility as a professor. Moreover, such appointments are "not encouraged certainly since all the official statements on the subject urge that the professors be free from any distracting task."[19]

The committee recommended that entirely separate and well-defined spheres of activity and influence be maintained: 1) spiritual direction and confessional work, 2) discipline, and 3) teaching. It stated that the "talents and energies of each faculty member should be so utilized that he will be enabled to become a specialist and primary responsible agent in one and only one of the . . . spheres of activity."[20]

In order to lighten the load on the spiritual directors they recommended the appointment of at least four additional ordinary confessors and the appointment of four or five of the professors to act as extraordinary confessors.

While this addressed the problem of confessions, it did not solve the problems regarding evaluation of candidates for Holy Orders. The faculty committee held that the "evaluation of the characters of students with an eye to their advancement or dismissal is essentially a disciplinary matter and is therefore the responsibility primarily of the rector, vice rector, and the director of students."

They reported that the "primary duty of a professor is to make himself truly skilled and learned in the field in which he teaches . . . [and] no professor could be expected to achieve, without detriment to his primary obligation, sufficient knowledge of even a notable number of the seminarians which would enable him to cast any sort of deliberative or responsible vote in any but a very limited number of cases."[21]

To assist in the task of evaluation, they recommended the creation of an advisory council of professors. To maintain the inviolability of the sacramental forum, they urged that none of the faculty who were confessors serve on the council.

Essentially, the committee made clear that the teaching faculty by law had no role in student evaluation. It stated that professors should not "be expected to know seminarians to the extent required for intelligent voting for advancement to Orders since sufficient personal contact is impossible in the vast majority of cases." A reason proffered for this is that professors whose classes are conducted as lectures alone have "no personal contact with the students on a daily basis." Indeed, the customs of the seminary in the early 1960s required that the faculty dine in a formal dining room in the Crocker Mansion. Only the spiritual director, the director of students, and the priest "on duty" ate with the seminarians, and then at a separate and elevated table.

This situation was a culmination of an evolution in the role of a seminary professor over the past century. In the nineteenth and early twentieth centuries, the professor was a "jack of all trades." Trained as a generalist theologian, he taught a wide variety of subjects—scripture, canon law, theology, Church history. The professor served as confessor and spiritual counselor, and occasionally as disciplinarian, as well. The rector also served as spiritual counselor, professor, and disciplinarian.

From the late nineteenth century, the Holy See had expressed concern over the maintenance of the internal forum in seminaries. Faculty members who served as confessors also voted on the fitness of candidates for ordination, leading to possible conflicts in this area. After the proclamation of the Code of Canon Law in 1917, a spiritual director was appointed to oversee all aspects of spiritual formation. The hearing of confessions was restricted to the spiritual director and confessors who were not on the faculty.

As far back as 1838, the Sacred Congregation for the Propagation of the Faith had issued the instruction *Quae a praesulibus*, directing that the seminary "professor be free of all other duties, lest being distracted by these other obligations, he find himself unable to devote his most diligent effort to that task which is of so great an importance, i.e., teaching."[22]

In 1931, *Deus scientiarum Dominus* required that seminary professors have professional training equal to the standards of the world's universities. As a result, by the 1960s, seminary professors no longer were generalists but professional specialists in distinct fields of academe. The scholarly credentials and publications of the Darlington faculty annually were presented to the board of deputies as proof of the seminary's academic excellence.

It is not surprising that what might be described as a change in the professor's "job description" was not met with unalloyed enthusiasm. The result of the committee's work was the compromise establishing the faculty council that assisted in evaluation. It would last just a few years until the entire seminary program was turned upside down.

Faculty Transition

As the "job description" for faculty was changing, so was the faculty itself. In 1960, Reverend James J. Finnerty replaced Reverend Robert G. Gibney as director of students and professor of college religion. Father Russell G. Ruffino joined the faculty, having earned his Ph.D. in philosophy at the Gregorian University, together with Reverend Carl D. Hinrichsen, who had completed four years of study in Church history at the Catholic University of America. In the next three years they would be joined by Father Anthony T. Padovano, who, after completing the S.T.D. at the Gregorian University, taught dogmatic theology; Reverend Edward J. Ciuba, who earned the S.S.L. degree after studies at the Pontifical Biblical Institute in Rome and the École Biblique in Jerusalem; and Reverend Frank J. McNulty, who taught moral theology after obtaining the S.T.D. at Catholic University.[23]

The most significant change was the appointment of Monsignor George W. Shea as rector on September 21, 1961, succeeding Monsignor Brady. In the interim, Father John O'Brien had served as acting rector. Shea, born in 1910, was ordained at Innsbruck in 1936. He returned to Innsbruck for doctoral studies that were interrupted by the Nazi annexation of Austria and the relocation of the Jesuit theological faculty to Switzerland. Completing his doctoral studies in 1939, he returned to teach at Darlington.

At the outbreak of World War II, he volunteered for military chaplain service and served in the United States Navy in the South Pacific. Returning to the seminary, he developed a reputation as an excellent theologian. He served as president of the Catholic Theological Society of America from 1956 to 1957. During the 1950s he engaged in a theological disagreement with Reverend John Courtney Murray, over Murray's opinions regarding church-state relations. Murray's views eventually were vindicated at the Second Vatican Council.

Shea was most at home engaging in scholarly research and writing. He never appeared comfortable in social settings. Perhaps he was shy. He did not know the students well; but there were over 300 of them. Honest to the core, when he encountered an unfamiliar seminarian, he would bluntly ask, "Who are you?"[24] It is fair to say he never anticipated becoming rector and viewed the administrative tasks and necessary personal interaction with faculty and students as a burden.

He attended the Second Vatican Council as Archbishop Boland's personal theologian, and was named a *peritus* (theological expert) of the council. He also was a member of a team that briefed the press after the council sessions. The press never got much real news from Monsignor Shea.

Early in 1963, Dr. Hans Küng traveled in the United States delivering a lecture entitled "The Church and Freedom." At the close of his tour, the lecture was published in *Commonweal.* Shea was enraged at Küng's lecture, considering it an attack on the Church, poor theology, and a misrepresentation of the Second Vatican Council, then in progress. From July to September 1963, he published a series of

10 articles, "Replying to Hans Küng," in the Newark archdiocesan newspaper, the *Advocate*. In these, Shea critiqued the "young Tübingen sage" as a "Professor of Wild Generalizations."[25]

Reaction to Shea's articles was as intense as it was unexpected. The newspaper was deluged with hundreds of letters, some in support and many in opposition. They published several dozen of them. The editor of the *Advocate* noted that "reader reaction was such . . . that we've had to sidetrack comment on some other issues."[26] Seminarians believed that some of the negative letters postmarked in nearby Suffern, New York, which were signed by a variety of women with Irish surnames, actually were written by seminary professors.[27]

It is arguable whether George Shea's time as rector, or that of his successor, William Hogan, was the most turbulent period in the history of Immaculate Conception Seminary.

Chapter Thirty-three

The Calm Before the Storm

The year 1961 was one of great optimism. Pope John's council was on the horizon; a Catholic was in the White House; the seminary was celebrating its centennial. There were 291 seminarians at the beginning of the academic year. The budget was $533,000.[1] The archbishop and the deputies were pleased to hear that "the seminarians continue to be edifyingly docile, pious, and studious,"[2] that student morale was high, and that there seemed to be "no great problems among them."[3]

There was little to indicate that the growth and progress of the seminary would not continue unabated. In fact, new and positive initiatives were evident. In 1961, the seminarians, together with the faculty, had initiated an in-house literary and theological review, entitled *Encounters*. Its goal was to encourage scholarship, inspire interest in theological and spiritual matters, and contribute to the development of the students' skills in writing and expression. It disappeared by the mid-1960s.[4]

That same year, the seminary hoped to begin construction of a new philosophy house. Plans called for a structure in the form of a *T*, with the chapel projecting beyond the crossbeam. It would contain classrooms, a dining room, a kitchen, a library, recreation rooms, an auditorium-gymnasium, and accommodations for 252 students, eight faculty members, and one guest. The cost of the building was projected to be $4 million.[5]

However, the whole project came to a standstill with the publication, in July 1961, of a proposal by the Governor's Passaic Valley Flood Control Committee. The committee proposed to convert the Ramapo River Valley, from Oakland to Mahwah, into a flood-detention basin, which would adjoin the proposed site of the new building.

Anticipating enrollment that would stretch beyond the 295-room capacity of Walsh Hall, the administration planned to press into service four rooms in the infirmary wing in Walsh Hall, place two to three students in each of the eight rooms of the former servant quarters on the third floor of the Crocker Mansion, and, if necessary, transform a recreation room in Walsh Hall into a dormitory for up to 10 students.[6] In Fall of 1962, with an enrollment of 307, the servant quarters hosted the excess seminarians.[7] This was the highest enrollment in the history of the seminary.

Centennial

In correspondence with Archbishop Boland, Monsignor Brady had established 1961 as the most appropriate date to observe the seminary's centennial. He disproved the common misapprehension that the seminary and Seton Hall College concurrently were founded in 1856.[8] The centennial would recognize 100 years of the teaching of theology, initiated in 1861.

In January 1961, Boland asked Brady to consult with his faculty and to propose an "ecclesiastical celebration" to mark this milestone.[9] Brady suggested that the observances open with a Solemn Pontifical Mass celebrated by Boland at the seminary on December 8, 1961, followed by an "in house" dinner, and close with a Mass at Sacred Heart Cathedral on December 8, 1962. In between, Brady suggested that, in September 1962, the planned philosophy house be formally dedicated. He also proposed that the observance include a public lecture on theology by a nationally known theologian and the publication of a brief history of the seminary that he was working on.

Brady's death in June 1961 meant that the centennial plans would be carried through by his successor, Monsignor Shea. Circumstances would alter the proposed schedule. Construction on the philosophy house was postponed, so there would be no dedication. The Second Vatican Council kept Archbishop Boland in Rome past December 8, so the closing Mass in Sacred Heart Cathedral was moved to September 15, 1962.

The centennial opened according to Monsignor Brady's plan with the Mass in the Seminary Church of Christ the King. The "in house" celebration included most of the New Jersey bishops, the seminary deputies, and the consultors of the archdiocese. The faculty and students took the occasion to re-dedicate themselves to the task of seminary formation. The simple mimeographed program states in its dedication:

> Mindful, however, that we have reaped where others
> have sown, we undertake with quiet determination
> to maintain our sacred heritage of steadfast loyalty
> to the Church and of single-minded dedication to
> the supreme task of forming priests after the mind
> of Christ, who shall ever savor the things of God
> and not the things of men.[10]

On April 3, 1962, the centennial lecture was delivered by Reverend Cyril Vollert, S.J., of St. Mary's College, Kansas. The year before, Father Vollert received the Cardinal Spellman Award for Theology,[11] the highest award for scholarship of the Catholic Theological Society of America. At a convocation at Seton Hall, Father Vollert addressed the topic "The Ecumenical Spirit and the Catholic Attitude."

The closing ceremony was a Solemn Pontifical Mass in Sacred Heart Cathedral on September 15, 1962. Archbishop Boland presided, Archbishop Egidio Vagnozzi, the apostolic delegate, celebrated the Mass, and Bishop Ahr preached.

The date was the Feast of Our Lady of Sorrows, and the seminary choir planned according to the liturgical requirements of that feast.

Not surprisingly, the planned program called for a rousing, polyphonic *Ecce Sacerdos Magnus* to accompany Archbishop Vagnozzi's procession. According to the program, the Introit, *Stabat juxta crucem,* followed; and shortly thereafter, the Gradual, *Dolorosa et lacrimabilis es.* The entire *Stabat mater* would also be sung. The program was already in rehearsal when somebody noticed that these chants, which focused on the sorrows of the Blessed Virgin at the crucifixion of Christ, her Son, did not convey the joyful and celebratory tone of the observance of the seminary centennial. The Mass of the day was replaced with the Votive Mass of the Holy Spirit, the chants of which were much more apropos.[12]

More than 2,000 attended, including 350 priests.[13] The Mass was followed by dinner for 850 at Seton Hall University. Although the program was a multi-colored masterpiece of the engraver's art, the dinner was rather prosaic: prime ribs of beef, Idaho potato, string beans, ice cream. Gone were the gustatory delights of past years. Dinner was accompanied by an eclectic music program that included "Pomp and Circumstance," "Echoes of Ireland," "Ave Maria," selections from *The Merry Widow* and *The Student Prince,* and, as the finale, "The Priestly Heart."[14]

The dinner at Seton Hall was for priests, religious, and laity. For the seminarians, there was no room in the inn. They were bused to Thomm's Restaurant in Newark for dinner.

Those attending the Mass and dinner received copies of *The Centennial History of the Immaculate Conception Seminary—Darlington, New Jersey*, which was composed for the occasion by Monsignor Henry G. J. Beck. The history includes a short letter of congratulations to the seminary from President John F. Kennedy, received after "considerably less-than-encouraging responses from the president's staff."[15]

The Cuban Missile Crisis

In October 1962, during the Cuban Missile Crisis, the seminary was at full alert under the supervision of the acting rector, Monsignor John F. O'Brien (with Shea absent at the council session). Air-raid drills were taken quite seriously. The basement windows of Walsh Hall were covered with sandbags. As seminarians filed down the stairways during air-raid drills, faculty members were stationed at strategic points to give general absolution.[16]

Monsignor O'Brien promulgated detailed air-raid instructions. He gave specific directives for those who might be outside enjoying recreation when the siren sounded:[17] "Proceed to nearest building. Run like mad!"

A student of the time recalls, "At the sound of the air raid sirens, we were ordered into the basement and told to sit on the floor and cover ourselves with our zimarras. Father Finnerty would inspect us and to anyone not properly covered, he would shout: 'You're dead!'" Soon after, someone discovered that black absorbed radiation. The zimarras were black. The seminarians' instructions were changed and thereafter they protected themselves from atomic bombs with their white bed sheets.[18]

At the height of the crisis, Monsignor O'Brien telephoned the regional Civil Defense headquarters and was told the office was closed for the weekend.[19]

Death of a President

On November 22, 1963, at 1 p.m., the seminarians were in the chapel for nave choir practice. This weekly event, during which hymns and chant were practiced, was among the least favorite of seminary activities. A few minutes after the hour, Father Finnerty, the director of students, entered the chapel. He did not come to the middle of the chapel but stood in the corner. In a halting voice, he announced that the president had been shot and it was not known whether he was alive or dead. He turned and departed in silence.

The choir director stood frozen on his podium. After about 10 seconds, seminarians, one after another, began to leave the chapel. Once they exited, they ran to the two recreation rooms where there were television sets. The almost 300 students jammed into these two rooms. In about an hour, Walter Cronkite told them that President Kennedy was dead. Dazed, some wept, some left and wandered on the grounds, some stayed to continue to watch the television.

The shock was such that no one noticed that everyone had violated at least one or more rules at once. Perhaps no one cared. Those walking on the grounds noticed that someone had lowered the flag to half-staff.[20] Later that afternoon, at evening prayer, Father Finnerty announced that classes would not be held on Saturday and the seminarians could watch the ongoing television news coverage. On Saturday morning, a solemn requiem Mass was held in the seminary chapel. It proved to be one of the last of its genre. It was complete with a catafalque covered with a black pall, surrounded by six towering unbleached candles.

Students and faculty passed through Sunday in a daze. On Monday, they joined the rest of the nation as they watched President Kennedy's funeral on television. Tuesday classes resumed with most, although not all, of the professors speaking about the late president. Father Ruffino was so overcome that he called for John F. Kennedy's immediate canonization, together with that of Pope John XXIII. One seminarian challenged him on the propriety of such an instant declaration of sanctity. Ruffino heatedly defended his proposal.[21]

Fire

In November 1964, the seminary was threatened by a forest fire that flamed out of control for several days. The smoke approached the seminary and there was concern that it might have to be evacuated, either due to the smoke or to the fire itself.

As more than 500 acres were being consumed by fire,[22] the state called for help and many seminarians volunteered. Monsignor O'Brien, vice rector, again was in charge in the absence of Monsignor Shea at the Second Vatican Council. He was not enthusiastic about allowing seminarians to leave the grounds to fight the fire but as it drew nearer, he relented. However, he allowed only deacons to enter the fight. The reason for this restriction eluded the students. They wondered why he would risk those on the brink of priesthood after spending almost six years of study to put their lives at risk. Surely the junior philosophy students were more expendable.

Upon inquiry of professors, they were told that Monsignor O'Brien considered the deacons more mature and expected that they would comport themselves better than the younger seminarians and thereby be a credit to the seminary.

Monsignor O'Brien did not have great affection for the younger seminarians of those years. The class that entered in 1962 was the largest in Darlington history, 72. They called themselves the "72 Disciples." Monsignor O'Brien called them many things, but not disciples. On one occasion, he called the class into the chapel for a special *lectio*, or conference. He enumerated their many transgressions and warned them that the Church's need for priests would not cause the seminary to lessen its demands on them. If they did not "shape up," he threatened them with a mass expulsion that would result in the 72 being reduced to so few that "your class will be ordained in a broom closet!"[23]

Entertainment, Generosity, and Apostolic Activities

The various seminary organizations continued to provide for sports and other activities and services. Student plays were a central activity that drew wide participation. Overseeing thespian activities was Father John Cassels, professor of speech. Cassels made it clear that he preferred the more archaic title "professor of sacred eloquence."[24] The rector's report of 1962 noted that Father Cassels had assumed the oversight of student theatrical activities with the title of "director of entertainment."

This was an appropriate title for Cassels. He often had a dour mien, which resulted in the seminarians giving him the nickname "Jolly Jack," or simply "Jolly." In fact, he possessed a keen sense of humor, which, together with his great compassion and empathy, induced a very large number of seminarians to choose him as their confessor.

Seminarians continued to be very generous to the missions and to various local charities, in a typical year sending 2,500 pounds of clothing and $6,000 in medical supplies to the missions, while contributing over $1,500 to the Propagation of the Faith. The Mission Academia continued its work of communication with and support of overseas missions. Occasionally, they would receive poignant pleas for help. Father Ed Moffett, a Maryknoll missionary in the Sochung Islands of South Korea wrote:

> Last nite's [sic] typhoon ruined us. . . .
>
> Waves like stone mountains pounded our 20 ton boat till the hull cracked. Now I'm cut off—from my people on all the beaches of my other fishing villages. I can't get supplies to my little Korean Sisters on the other islands. I can't answer sick calls.
>
> It's hardly dawn but I'm running this SOS off to you to beg for help. The weekly Air Force plane to the radar station here is due today, if it can land on the beach, I'll post this and you'll have it Monday morning.[25]

Moffett had done two years of philosophical studies at Darlington from 1939 to 1941.[26] The seminary responded with a generous check of $175.[27] Father Moffett told the seminarians, "The infant church here in the ocean is growing rapidly—sacrifices like yours keep it from sinking in a crisis."[28]

The Mission Academia began publication of a newsletter, *By Hook and by Crook,* in 1962. It contained articles written by seminarians on various mission topics and apostolic activities. Like *Encounters*, it lasted only a few years.[29]

Outside apostolic activities continued with seminarians serving summer religious vacation schools in parishes, CYO day camps, orphanages, and at New Jersey's Boystown. Deacons continued to preach in neighboring parishes, and seminarians began to work in Catholic charities.[30]

A new apostolic opportunity came to the deacon class in 1963 when St. Agatha Home for Children in Nanuet, New York, asked the rector to allow seminarians to visit the institution's 400 dependent children, largely Puerto Rican and African American, from New York City. Shea asked the deacon class for volunteers and all volunteered to take turns visiting the institution daily throughout summer session.

The St. Agatha authorities reported that the seminarians had a tremendous impact on the children, and literally transformed the spirit of all at the institution, including the lay personnel. The sister superior lauded the seminarians, telling Shea that "I have never known a group to so completely win the respect and admiration of everyone here: Sisters, staff, and children."[31] The children also sent Shea a letter thanking him "for letting your seminarians come to this home" and hoping that "they will be able to come back when they are priests."[32]

The experiment was altogether positive. Sister Cecilia, the superior, told Shea that he was blessed "to have young men who represent the Church be so fine, so interested, so human." In her opinion, they gave the children at St. Agatha's "a better image of the Church than they have ever had before."[33] Shea believed that the seminarians themselves tremendously benefited from this experience and was pleased that they kept in touch with the youngsters by correspondence and by visits during vacations. For most of the deacons, this was their first encounter with non-whites.

More Hints of Change

In the 1962-1963 academic year, a new trend appeared. In the past no more than six or seven students would leave the seminary in any given year. That year, 19 left, "most of their own accord."[34] The next year, "20 left; 12 of own accord; 3 dismissed; 5 on leave."[35]

The administration was not concerned. In 1964, Monsignor Shea told the deputies that "the number dropping out of Darlington is much less than other seminaries." Archbishop Boland was equally unconcerned, remarking that "the dropouts will vary from year to year." One of the deputies, Monsignor William Furlong, suggested that more freedom might encourage seminarians to stay. Archbishop Boland countered with the rather oblique reply that "the lack of more freedom may be the cause of more not leaving."

The deputies were comforted by Shea's assurance that the "seminarians continue to be docile, faithful to studies, and progressive in spirituality."

> By and large, our seminarians have remained free
> from the spirit of unrest, not to say rebellion, which
> has manifested itself in varying degrees at some other
> seminaries. The spiritual directors, the director of
> students, the vice rector and the rector have taken
> particular pains this past year to inculcate a proper
> respect for authority and for the virtue of obedience.
> In homilies delivered on Holy Thursday and on World
> Vocation Sunday (April 12), the rector emphasized the
> fact that a priest owes his priestly powers to his bishop
> and should exercise them in loyal submission to the
> will of the bishop.[36]

Regarding admissions, Shea reported that 47 Newark candidates and 12 Paterson candidates at the Seton Hall University Divinity School had applied for admission to Darlington, but quite likely some of these applications "will have to be rejected."[37] He did not inform the deputies that the rejections would be based on the psychological testing program.

Doubts about the feasibility of the philosophy house surfaced at the 1964 deputies meeting. The flood control program for the Ramapo Valley was still under discussion and its outcome uncertain. New Jersey Governor Richard Hughes had told Boland, "You may take a calculated risk and build." The governor's comment was hardly reassuring or encouraging. Boland also was concerned about announced plans by the Paterson and Camden dioceses to build minor seminaries. Boland wondered, if this transpired, "Would we need a philosophy house?" He also noted that smaller enrollments in Catholic grammar schools might foretell a leveling or a drop in future vocations. With these factors in mind, the deputies voted to postpone the building program "for the time being."[38]

The faculty continued to be renewed. In 1964, Reverend George M. Keating was appointed assistant spiritual director; Reverend Gene A. Herbster was assigned to studies in Church history; and Reverend Stephen S. Feehan and Reverend Richard M. Liddy to studies in philosophy. There were now 21 resident and 12 non-resident faculty at Darlington. In early 1965, Monsignor Henry G. J. Beck, who had served at Darlington for his entire priesthood, except for his time in graduate studies, was appointed pastor of Sacred Heart Parish in Lyndhurst, New Jersey.[39] Beck remained as a non-resident professor, but his departure was a sign that the old order was passing.

The Seminarians Do a Lot of Reading

In May 1965, 17 students had resigned during the previous academic year, and five were on leaves of absence. There were 281 seminarians, significantly down from the peak of 307 in 1962.

Archbishop Boland, apparently more concerned than he had been the year before, asked the reason for the dropouts. Shea replied, "It is a phenomenon going on all over the country." He attributed it to contemporary students of college age finding it difficult to decide what to do in life. He also blamed a general unrest occasioned by the Second Vatican Council and exaggerated criticism of the Church that weakened the convictions of seminarians.

One of the deputies, noting that most of the seminarians left over the summer, wondered if "the summer program be a strong reason for dropouts because of the loss of the spiritual life and program due to working?" His question went unanswered.

The 1965 rector's report and the minutes of the deliberations of the board of deputies are significant both for what they contained and what was missing. The standard "boilerplate" of decades that "the seminarians continue to be edifyingly docile, pious, and studious" is nowhere to be found and never appeared again. There was uncertainty in the air.

Monsignor Shea told the deputies that "the seminarians do a lot of reading and in that way get ideas and become dissatisfied with the seminary program." He remarked that the faculty had urged a reevaluation of the seminary program, and wanted participation from the seminarians in the process. He clearly was not pleased with the suggestions offered so far by the students: "The seminarians have handed in a program but from some of their statements it is obvious that some have confused renewal with self-indulgence!" He must have been impassioned as the secretary recorded an exclamation point in the minutes.

Shea acknowledged that "some good suggestions" were in the student report but these were ones "which the faculty already had in mind." An example was the expanded program of apostolic activities going into effect in the upcoming summer and school year. However, he clearly lacked enthusiasm. He remarked that the faculty was seeking to form a realistic seminary training program based on the urged "renewal," a word that he often put in quotation marks. In spite of these concerns, the deputies for discipline believed "that discipline and morale among the students was very good."

Archbishop Boland commented that many books were being written on seminary training and acknowledged that "some are good." However, he lamented the "great deal of criticism of the church in publications today" and their negative influence on seminarians. He emphasized that seminarians must realize that "their training is a two fold process: one of education and the other formation, which includes humility and docility." Boland closed the discussion of seminarians with a typically serene and simple remark: "These are not easy times; we have difficulty too with college students."

Boland also was concerned about seminary finances. The budget was increasing. The last year had brought word of possible minor seminaries in Camden and Paterson that would draw students from Darlington, at least from its philosophy program. He told the deputies that "the future revenue from suffragan dioceses will provide less money towards the cost of running the seminary each year, as Bishop Ahr is thinking of starting his own major seminary, and the Paterson diocese may do the same. . . . There is still room for outside students, but we cannot depend on them."

An apparent decline in vocations, the possible loss of students from the suffragan dioceses of New Jersey, and rising building costs made a new philosophy house less of a priority. Boland closed the meeting with the remark: "If any building is contemplated, the size must be reconsidered. However, before any construction takes place, we will have to wait until the Council ends because its decisions may affect our program."[40]

Chapter Thirty-four

Revolutionary Years

The years after the close of the Second Vatican Council in December 1965 brought new and unexpected challenges to the Church and its seminaries. The seminaries, which had for centuries existed in splendid isolation in an atmosphere of unquestioned discipline and authority, were asked to radically reform every aspect of their programs. At the same time, the United States was going through a severe crisis in its national culture, a crisis that would have a deep impact on the Church and on the seminaries.

Catholics of the early 1960s could not foresee the storms to come. The Second Vatican Council had lifted their spirits and given their imaginations new visions of the Church of the future. In the seminary world, the council's call for personal and group responsibility would unleash tensions and conflicts among rectors and archbishops, faculty members and seminarians.

The descendants of the pioneer immigrant Catholics were now part of the American mainstream, for better or for worse. Completely unexpected was what John Tracy Ellis described as "the rise of unrealistic expectations on the part of certain progressive elements regarding reforms and innovations in the wake of the ecumenical council, a mentality that was counter-balanced at the opposite end of the spectrum by those who refused to accept changes introduced by the council's actions and directives." For Ellis, a dangerous development was "the succumbing of an increasing number of Catholics to those aspects of the national ethos . . . that have seriously undermined the moral and spiritual ideals of the body politic in the United States."[1]

Throughout the 1960s and into the 1970s, moral and social structures that had been presumed to be perennial fell one after the other. Some of these changes were positive; others were not. The civil rights movement for equality of all citizens, regardless of their color, forced the Church to address discrimination within its own structures and within its own heart. The women's liberation movement had repercussions within the Church, forcing it to address the role of women in its schools, its colleges, its parishes, and its sanctuaries. Various "sexual liberation" movements rejected the Church's teachings regarding sexual morality and considered concepts such as clerical celibacy hopelessly outdated.

The prolonged American war in Vietnam brought many Catholics, who considered that they had "arrived" on the political scene with the election of John F. Kennedy in 1960, into unimagined conflict with their government.

Divergent and often confused feelings regarding the Vietnam War were brought into sharp focus at the seminary with the death of an alumnus. Father Charles J. Watters, ordained in 1953, and a chaplain in the United States Army, was killed on November 29, 1967, while rescuing wounded men during the battle of Dak To. Father Watters was posthumously awarded the Congressional Medal of Honor for his "unyielding perseverance and selfless devotion to his comrades." He is one of only seven chaplains to have received the nation's highest award for valor on the battlefield.[2]

Anger over the Vietnam War, the "Pentagon Papers" scandal, and then the Watergate debacle destroyed the respect that many Americans felt for their government and its institutions, and replaced it with mistrust and cynicism. Such disenchantment also entered the Church.

Within the Church, many theologians challenged traditional understandings of the Church and its moral teachings. The achievements of the Second Vatican Council were marred by calls by some for reforms not intended by the council and by widespread misinterpretations of the "spirit of the council." The loss of respect for authority in the civil arena was mirrored by a similar diminution of respect for Church authority. This was exemplified by the public rejection of Paul VI's encyclical *Humanae vitae* (Of Human Life) by large numbers of Catholic theologians. Darlington's faculty, on the other hand, issued a statement of unanimous support for the encyclical.[3]

The enthusiasm of the various civil movements and the inherent American concept of democracy encouraged many seminarians to demand at least a consultative voice in their formation. Some went even further. In these demands, seminarians often were supported by many of the seminary faculty. In the theological confusion of the time, it was not unusual for seminarians to lose respect for authority and to believe that the Church's discipline regarding priestly celibacy was certain to be changed.

Seminarians and priests also were dismayed by the sudden increase of resignations from the priesthood beginning in the mid-1960s and extending into the 1970s. In the early 1960s, the archdiocese of Newark masked this reality by reporting that priests who had actually resigned or taken leaves of absence had been "assigned to further studies." This deception soon was abandoned. The wave of departures from the priesthood could not but negatively affect the morale of seminarians and discourage potential candidates from entering the seminary. The resignations from the priesthood of several seminary faculty members contributed to a malaise not unique to the seminary at Darlington.

The same issues were troubling every seminary in the United States. After the June 1966 meeting of the Eastern Conference of Major Seminary Rectors, the president of the organization outlined the following categories of common interest:

1. The openness of the American seminary today
2. Personal responsibility and freedom
3. Methods of communication between students and faculty; also between seminaries and hierarchy
4. Liturgical renewal
5. Apostolic activities
6. Seminary community life
7. Prayer life
8. Curriculum[4]

This list included every aspect of seminary life, which was in flux nationally and at Darlington.

Renewal or Meltdown?

In the 1965–66 school year, changes came to Darlington at a rapid pace—frequent concelebration, Mass facing the people, increased singing at Mass, occasional group Masses.[5] They were welcomed with enthusiasm by most faculty and students. Apostolic activities were expanded and, during the summer, each student was assigned to eight weeks of apostolic work. Although the seminarians of the day were very different from a generation ago, their morale remained "good" and they were "generally docile."[6]

The Darlington summer program for juniors, seniors, and deacons remained for a time. In 1967, Monsignor Shea asked Archbishop Boland to allow the senior philosophers to do apostolic work rather than attend the summer session. His reasons showed the strains the seminary was experiencing. The seniors had become "unreceptive and disgruntled" and were exercising a negative influence on the new junior philosophy students, "wising them up" and counteracting the efforts of the faculty.

While advocating this change of policy, Shea correctly foresaw that it would lead to agitation from the deacons to be released from "Darlington summer" as well.[7] Boland granted the request and the Darlington summers, an institution since the move from Seton Hall and an American version of the Italian "villegeatura," disappeared.

To enlarge the deacon preaching program, the archbishop decided to confer diaconate at the beginning of the summer instead of in the fall. Numerous changes in the horarium were proposed and several effectuated: greater flexibility in recreation and study time, extended use of libraries, and lights out at 11 p.m. Major changes in the curriculum and the program of spiritual formation were under study.[8]

In sum, the changes in the regimen of the seminarians involved a reduction of the formal rules of the seminary, and placing of some aspects of the routine in the categories of regulation and custom. The goal of the changes was to give the seminarian greater latitude in decisions concerning his use of time and greater freedom of movement within the seminary. In the mind of the faculty, the purpose of the changes was neither to make the life of the seminarian easier nor to make concessions to what some considered "the limitations of a softer generation,"[9] but to place a greater degree of responsibility on the individual seminarian.

This was done by taking away, to some degree, the support that the individual receives from the group when the group does everything together. Each one is then thrown on his own resources and forced to make decisions for which he is responsible and with which he has to live. This, it was hoped, gave the seminarian the opportunity to mature and to know himself better in relation to the demands of the priesthood. It also enabled the faculty to know the seminarian better.

Among the changes was a much later "lights out." Archbishop Boland was concerned whether the seminarians could get by with less sleep. Shea assured him that seminarians could go to bed at 9:30 p.m. if they wished, and "this greater freedom will eventually disclose those who are not reliable on their own, so that they can be removed as candidates." When asked by one of the deputies if the students were satisfied with the program, Shea responded that there was general acceptance, but noted that "there is an occasional note of dissatisfaction."

He was accurate. An anonymous letter signed by "a sincere seminarian" informed Boland that there was "unrest and tension here at the seminary" and that while the seminarians had proposed many changes, a scant few had been implemented. He asked for the end to the long monastic grace before meals, the angelus, and Sunday vespers. He also wanted the *Martyrology* in English, an occasional evening Mass, and making Stations of the Cross and Benediction optional.[10] In retrospect, these changes hardly were radical and many soon were implemented.

Another seminarian sent Boland a very different letter: "Dear Archbishop Boland: Yippee—thanks a lot!! I want to express my thanks to you for approving the various changes at the seminary." After enumerating several of the reforms, he closed: "So, for all that has come so far, and also for all that is yet to come, THANK YOU, thank you very much."[11] One only can wonder what response such a letter would have drawn from Boland's predecessor, Archbishop Walsh. Boland filed it without a response.

A Simpler Schedule

The revisions to the day of the seminarian are clear in the new horarium.

6:50 a.m.	Rising
7:10 a.m.	Morning Prayers
7:30 a.m.	Breakfast
8:20 a.m.	Class or Study
9:10 a.m.	Class or Study
10:00 a.m.	Recreation
10:10 a.m.	Class or Study
11:00 a.m.	Class or Study
11:50 a.m.	Return to Walsh Hall
12:07 p.m.	Spiritual Reading
12:30 p.m.	Angelus; Lunch; Recreation
1:30 p.m.	Class or Personal Initiative Time
4:30–4:55 p.m.	Meditation
5:00 p.m.	Community Mass; Personal Reflection and Thanksgiving
5:45 p.m.	Dinner; Recreation
7:15 p.m.	Night Prayers, followed by Study
9:30 p.m.	Recreation
10:00 p.m.	Night Silence
11:30 p.m.	Lights out

Those whose apostolic or other assignments on a particular weekday will prevent their attending the regular Community Mass at 5:00 p.m. on that day will follow the schedule given hereunder:

6:25	Morning Prayers
6:35	Mass; Personal Reflection and Thanksgiving
7:05	Meditation
7:30	Breakfast

Normal schedule thereafter, until apostolic or other assignment begins.

While this still is a rigorous schedule, many of the activities no longer required that the seminarian remain in his room for extended periods of time. For example, he was now allowed to take study time in the library. The introduction of apostolic activities already had a strong impact. For the first time in the seminary's history, students no longer were united daily at community Mass. Seminarians were beginning to develop "customized" schedules. This necessarily had an impact on the community life of the institution and on many aspects of the program.

In a very practical vein, apostolic activities inevitably caused increased expenditures for transportation and other expenses incurred by seminarians in the course of these activities. The 1967 budget had grown to $670,000, including $15,000 for the purchase of two Volkswagen buses, travel, and meals.[12] While Boland had ruled out remuneration for seminarians for their efforts, this question would arise again.

While all this was transpiring, the archdiocesan chancery office expressed concern about a planned Girl Scout camp adjoining the seminary property.[13] Monsignor O'Brien, vice rector, calmed the waters, informing the vicar general, Monsignor Hughes, that "no access roads run from our property to the section where they plan to build."[14] A Girl Scout camp would prove to be the least of the seminary's problems.

What a Difference a Year Makes

Significant changes had been made, in particular in the horarium and in the required spiritual exercises. Morning prayers were now in silence, allowing the recitation of Lauds in private and time for preparation for Mass. No longer was there a particular examination of conscience at noon. Instead the seminarians were urged to spend 15 minutes reading the scriptures in chapel or in their rooms. Before the evening meal, a half-hour was set aside for meditation, again in chapel or in the rooms. Evening prayers were replaced by Vespers in common.

Rosary, spiritual reading, particular examination of conscience, Stations of the Cross, and First Saturday devotions were all left to the seminarians to perform on their own. October and May devotions, as well as First Friday devotions, were reduced and simplified. Novenas were abandoned, with the exception of the novena to the Holy Spirit. Visits to the Blessed Sacrament were now, like so many other devotions, the responsibility of the seminarians. The reading of the *Martyrology* was abandoned and short English prayers replaced the extensive monastic grace before and after meals.[15]

The responsibility for the implementation of this program fell to confessors and spiritual directors, who were responsible to ascertain whether seminarians were faithful to the variety of exercises that they were called on to engage on their own responsibility.

A radical transformation of seminary life, especially its spiritual life, was under way but it did not solve the tensions in the seminary. The pace was too slow for many, including an increasingly disgruntled faculty. Shea complained, "There would appear to be some discontent among members of the faculty and, I am told, among seminarians that it is taking so long to effect changes in our program for the seminarians' spiritual life."[16]

Enrollment continued to decline. In the course of the 1966-1967 academic year, six seminarians were dismissed, 17 resigned, and two took leaves of absence. In his report to the deputies on May 18, 1967, Monsignor Shea expressed his frustration and dissatisfaction with the attitude of the seminarians.

> Within a few days, at the end of the semester, I expect to dismiss 6 Newark and 2 Paterson and 1 Trenton candidate; to grant a leave of absence to 4 Newark candidates; and to accept the voluntary resignation of 1 Trenton candidate.
>
> A year ago I was able to report to the board of deputies that, in the main, our seminarians were docile, their spirit and morale good. Since then this happy state of affairs has deteriorated quite perceptibly. As had already happened in many other seminaries, the student body had grown more restive and demanding, more impatient of control, despite the introduction, last September, of changes in the rules and in the spiritual exercises, which changes will be spoken of later. To judge from some of their demands, complaints and requests over the past year, many of them would like to be able to determine, among other things, who will be ordained, when they will be ordained, where they will be ordained, by whom they will be ordained, what the curriculum will be, what the rules and the measure and manner of their enforcement should be.[17]

A New Rule

At the same time, a new seminary rule was promulgated.[18] Many of the changes were made necessary by the apostolic program that required the seminarians periodically to leave the seminary to go to the sites of their assignments. Instead of a list of 77 rules, the violation of almost any of which could result in dismissal, the new rule was composed of 11 "formative directives," 12 "specific regulations," and lengthy "seminary customs" that were contained within numerous regulations. One of the directives sounded a familiar tone: "Failure to observe faithfully the directives and customs of the seminary shall render the seminarian liable to dismissal."

The "formative directives," addressing areas such as "community life," "fraternal charity," "spiritual life," and "academic life," were exhortations to seek ideals in each area. The customs actually were rules under a different name but not as restrictive. Seminarians now were allowed to use time not devoted to class or chapel exercises as they wished. This time was called "personal initiative time."

Seminarians still were forbidden to use the elevators or to enter the room of another seminarian. In their own rooms, they now were permitted to have a typewriter, family photos, a transistor radio, a tape recorder, and extra blankets. Appliances other than electric razors were forbidden, but students could store small amounts of food in their rooms.

The rules and customs surrounding meals were significantly changed. No longer did seminarians march as a unit to the refectory for each meal and leave afterward in the same style reciting the *Benedicite*. Breakfast and lunch were buffet style; only dinner remained a community event from opening to closing prayers. Faculty members occasionally joined them at dinner.

Visitors still were prohibited and seminarians urged to restrict their communication with employees and sisters. They could leave the grounds for apostolic activities but otherwise were restricted to the property of the seminary.

The Law of Unintended Consequences

Some of the changes in the rule were a result of the "law of unintended consequences." During Fall 1967, several newly arrived junior philosophers innocently asked permission to take a once-a-week night class at Seton Hall. A highly skeptical John Flesey, the *bedellus*, set up an appointment with Shea. Shea was ill and received the seminarians in bed in his bedroom. Perhaps due to his fever, Shea granted permission. Flesey was shocked and within 24 hours there was a parade of seminarians asking similar permission.

Flesey then had to go back to Shea to tell him that, in order to go to class at Seton Hall, the seminarians needed to maintain cars at the seminary, and Shea gave permission for cars. That snowballed into the expansion of the parking lot, and ultimately the seminary paying the seminarians' mileage expenses for using their own cars for apostolic assignments. So much for Boland's denial of any payment.

Just one year later there occurred what was later named the "night of the fog." One Sunday afternoon the seminary hosted a conference for all the Newman Clubs in the state of New Jersey. During the day such a dense fog set in that no one could safely leave and many of the faculty could not return from their weekend assignments. The rector was forced to call Boland to obtain permission for the Newman Club students to stay at the seminary overnight. About half of these college students were women![19]

"How Will It End?"

The new rules did not bring peace. In 1967, a frustrated Shea told the deputies, "The changes were made in accordance with the letter and the spirit of the relevant documents of Vatican II, but, as has already been intimated, they were not as fully appreciated and as loyally responded to by the student body as we had hoped."

Shea's report produced consternation. The enrollment had fallen to 211, the lowest since the 1940s.[20] The deputies for discipline, Monsignors William Furlong and Francis X. Coyle, expressed shock and anger. Coyle questioned Shea on the benefits of the changes in the horarium and the rules. Shea defended the rules as "moderate and not nearly as relaxed as in some seminaries" but added that the seminarians were far from satisfied and wished to have more personal "say" in the running of the seminary.

With Boland's permission, the seminary had instituted a faculty-student conference of administrators, professors, and elected student representatives to establish better communication and give the students a means of expressing their opinions. Shea indicated that this had helped somewhat to ease the tension and agitation of the past year.[21]

The archbishop expressed surprise and some annoyance that he had received many "extraordinary requests" from the seminarians, and had rejected them, including a request from the deacon class for a "more open and relaxed" retreat. This he could not grant as the Holy See insisted on a "closed" retreat before ordination to priesthood. Boland added, "The problem with vocation students is not localized as most of the seminaries and sister novitiates throughout the country are having problems."

Clearly dismayed, the deputies ended the discussion and their minutes unhappily concluded with the words: "Who knows how and when and where it will end?"[22]

There was more to come.

Chapter Thirty-five

Seminarians, Unite!

Seminarians, hitherto docile and pious, now were enthusiastically embracing activism. One sought permission to submit for publication an article entitled "Black Power: The Answer to a Two Hundred Year Old Problem." Shea told Boland that he had no quarrel with the article other than its "sophomoric, poorly argued and written character" and asked Boland to grant permission.[1]

Shea also gave permission for several seminarians to attend a conference at Maryknoll, "Theological Students for Viet Nam Peace Talks." However, he conditioned his approval, warning them, "No publicity is to be given to the fact of your attendance; none of you is to join the committee; and none of you is to commit himself to cooperation in further activities or projects of the committee."[2]

Darlington's seminarians joined forces with others. As the Second Vatican Council was nearing its end, a group of American seminarians, responding to the council's call for more participation by all people in the life of the Church, organized the Northeast Seminarians Study Conference. The conference received the support and patronage of Cardinals Francis Spellman, Richard Cushing, and Lawrence Shehan.

In August 1964, 10 Darlington seminarians attended the conference, meeting at Maryknoll, New York. In 1965, Monsignor Shea granted them permission to join the group. The seminarians sent copies of the group's material to Archbishop Boland in December of that year.[3] The Darlington seminarians were very well organized and oversaw the publication of the *NSSC Newsletter* in 1966. That journal included an article by Reverend Anthony Padovano of the seminary faculty, "Celibacy and the Church's New Generation." In this article, Father Padovano defended celibacy and wrote, "The priest sees in celibacy not only something which imitates the celibate public ministry of the Lord but which reaches the mystery of the cross in a unique way."[4]

The Darlington seminarians became very active in the organization and, in 1966, received permission from Boland and Shea to host the August 25–27, 1967, Northeast Seminarians Study Conference at Seton Hall University. The topics of the conference and the speakers changed as planning went on, but the seminarians kept the rector and the archbishop informed at all times. Reflecting the era's concern for the inner city, the title of the conference was "The Witness of the Church in Megalopolis."

Shea recommended approval of the speakers: "I cannot personally vouch for all who are on the list; on the other hand, I know no reason why any of them would be unacceptable."[5] Boland had "no objection to any of them."[6] The archbishop even approved an early list of alternate speakers that included such disparate individuals such as William F. Buckley, Jr. of the *National Review* and the Jesuit theologian Charles Davis, who would leave the Church later that year amid great notoriety.[7]

Ultimately, the speakers of the conference were Bishop John Dougherty, Harvey Cox of *The Secular City* fame, Reverend Anthony Padovano of the Darlington faculty, civil rights leader and St. Francis College alumnus Cyril Tyson, Rev. William Lynch, S.J., of Saint Peter's College in Jersey City, and author William Stringfellow.[8] The list was impressive and a tribute to the leadership and organizing skills of the seminarians. The problems that ensued would not come from the speakers or the program as it was planned.

The archdiocese cooperated at every stage of the preparations, granting permissions for concelebrated Masses in various rooms of the university complex, small-group liturgies, and the use of guitars. Preaching faculties also were granted to priests from other dioceses.[9]

The Ivory Tower Crumbles

The conference opened on August 25, 1967, with Archbishop Boland celebrating the opening Mass. Almost immediately, it exploded into the press with banner headlines. "Seminarians Want Optional Celibacy," "Seminarians, Sisters Take Anti-war Stands," "Seminarians in Rumble: Ivory Tower's Crumbling" were among the many local and national headlines. Naturally, they drew the attention of Church authorities on both sides of the Atlantic.[10]

The *Newark Evening News* outlined the resolutions passed by the 410-member conference. The resolutions urged that:

- The National Conference of Bishops examine "with renewed energy" the possibility of making clerical celibacy a matter of individual choice.
- Seminaries be liberalized to the "standard of study, research and questioning which mark the great educational centers of this country."
- Experimental ministries be established in the urban centers to aid the problems of the "alienated masses."
- Non-Catholic Christians be permitted to take part in Catholic Communion Masses during Church Unity Week the following year.

- The bombing of North Vietnam be stopped and a massive peace effort launched to end the war altogether.
- All discriminatory practices in housing be abolished.
- The Church affirm its support for the efforts of minority groups "to determine with dignity their own social, political and economic destiny."
- The dioceses not purchase any products from firms which discriminate.

A statement by the president of the conference, Darlington seminarian Patrick Brannigan, attempted to alleviate the controversial nature of these resolutions. Brannigan, surprised by the resolutions, told the press that the conference was "not speaking for seminarians in the country" and that the resolutions "do not necessarily reflect the thoughts of the staffs of the respective seminarians, or of Seton Hall University."[11] As sincere as Brannigan was, the damage was done.

Shea summoned the Darlington seminarians involved with the conference. He told them that they were very naïve in their dealings with the press and in their assumption that the press would not sensationalize the resolutions. He considered the behavior of the conference immature and self-important. However, he did not put blame entirely on the seminarians. He told Boland, "In their new-found self-importance, seminarians of today often mistake their immaturity for maturity, and unfortunately their feeling of self-importance has been fed by statements, sometimes from high ecclesiastical levels, to the effect that 'the youth of today have much to tell us and we should listen to and learn from them.'" He never identified the "high ecclesiastical levels" to which he was referring.

Shea informed Boland that the rectors of the seminaries in the region were equally dismayed at the outcome of the conference. He closed his nine-page letter of explanation with the words, "With genuine sorrow that the NSSC proved so unworthy of Your Excellency's trust in and hospitality toward that organization, and with sincere apologies for those of the Darlington seminarians who may have had a part in that cavalier treatment, I am, filially yours in Christ."[12]

A sidelight to this imbroglio is the invitation of the NSSC leadership to visit the apostolic delegate, Archbishop Egidio Vagnozzi. The year before the Seton Hall conference, several Darlington seminarians visited Washington and, while there, contacted Monsignor Harold P. Darcy, a Newark priest who was secretary at the apostolic delegation. Darcy arranged for the delegate to invite the NSSC officers for a chat. The delegate phoned Darlington to extend the invitation.

Monsignor O'Brien knocked on the door of seminarian Patrick Brannigan.

"Brannigan, what are you up to?" O'Brien queried.

"Magnum silentium," Brannigan replied.

"No," responded O'Brien. "You are up to something, I know it, the apostolic delegate wants to talk to you, telephone him!"

"I don't have a phone," Brannigan meekly replied.

"Use the house phone!" was O'Brien's shouted retort.

The seminary simply was not accustomed to a personage as august as the Holy Father's representative calling and asking to talk to a lowly seminarian. Brannigan recalls a friendly meeting in Washington that ended with the delegate saying, "Thank you for coming. I have to go to lunch now." No invitation to join him was extended. Post-conciliar cordiality still only went so far.[13]

In December 1967, Shea received a letter from the new apostolic delegate, Archbishop Luigi Raimondi. Raimondi informed him:

> There has been a reply from the Sacred Congregation for Seminaries with regards to the August convocation of the Northeast Seminarians Study Conference. You will recall the various resolutions that were passed and publicized on that occasion.
>
> This Congregation wishes to assure you that it has been well informed on the matter and that in no way are you considered responsible or culpable. I thought you would want to have this information.[14]

Monsignor Shea certainly did not consider himself culpable but was pleased to know that Rome did not either. No matter what Rome said or thought, George Shea was at the end of his rope. The NSSC, like so many other organizations that sprang up immediately after the Second Vatican Council, soon passed into oblivion.

Monsignor Shea Bids Farewell

It may be an understatement to say that Monsignor Shea was not at all pleased with the direction of seminary reform. In a letter to Archbishop Boland on May 6, 1967, forwarding the details of the deacon class's requests for changes in their upcoming ordination retreat, he clearly expressed his dissatisfaction.

> After glancing at the proposals, I remarked that, like the generality of changes proposed by students in the name of "aggiornamento," they were strongly in the direction of relaxation and self-convenience, etc. [e.g., the request for permission for organized sports], and that I was much disturbed and distressed by this tendency and by the failure ever to petition for something that would involve added obligation and self-denial.
>
> Organized sports during the retreat are, I said, out of the question. Others of their proposals moved me to remark that it seems the young men of today always have to be talking to one another, whereas traditionally

retreats, especially retreats before Orders and above all
before ordination to the priesthood, are a time for the
individual to talk to God—"you have been talking to one
another for six years; surely now in the precious last days
of preparation for the priesthood you should prize and
use every opportunity to talk with God."[15]

On May 31, 1967, two weeks after the meeting of the deputies, Shea again
wrote to Boland.

> It is my considered opinion—the fruit of earnest
> pondering these past few months, and of prayerful
> reflection during the retreat now ending—that the
> seminary would benefit by a change of rectors, and that
> it is my duty in conscience to make this opinion known
> to Your Excellency.
>
> In arriving at this opinion I have honestly striven
> to view the matter solely on the basis of what is best
> for the seminary, not allowing personal preferences
> to move me one way or another.
>
> I appreciate beyond words Your Excellency's
> unfailing confidence in, and patience with, my efforts
> to discharge faithfully the duties of rector these past
> six years; but I feel it would be a betrayal of that
> confidence, and an abuse of that patience, if I failed
> to write this letter.[16]

Shea felt himself estranged from the faculty. In August, one day after the
close of the NSSC meeting at Seton Hall, he wrote to Boland regarding the report
of the faculty committee on discipline and the horarium. He reminded the archbishop
he had given him a copy at a recent priests' study day and remarked that on that
occasion "Monsignor Koenig and Father Keating petitioned that Your Excellency
discontinue the requirement that Darlington seminarians attend two Masses on
Sunday." Implied was his consternation that communication on seminary issues was
not going through normal channels. Both faculty and seminarians were lobbying
the archbishop! Regarding the proposals of the committee, he told Boland, "I am not
particularly keen on some of the proposed innovations, but I have no violent objections
against any of them, and I must confess that I feel the new school year would get off
to a better start if we had at least some of these changes to offer as further evidence
of continuing updating of the seminary."[17] On this letter, the archbishop wrote,
"Answered by phone. Go with few changes. 9/31/67 +TAB."

Not receiving a reply regarding his desire to resign, Shea again addressed the archbishop on October 23, 1967. It is a poignant letter. Shea's exhaustion, frustration, anger, and anguish are palpable.

> Some months ago I informed Your Excellency of my
> considered opinion that the seminary would benefit
> by the appointment of a new rector.
>
> I am still of that opinion—indeed, it has grown
> into a conviction. The war of attrition (euphemistically
> called "aggiornamento") carried on in seminaries these
> last five or six years against rectors by students and
> by some faculty members has ground me down to the
> breaking point. I no longer have the self-confidence
> or the stamina to cope with the relentless pressures
> and endless problems of present-day seminary life.
>
> In short, I have outlived my usefulness at
> Darlington, and it is therefore incumbent upon me
> in conscience to request Your Excellency to accept
> my resignation from the seminary.
>
> With prayerful good wishes, and also with heartfelt
> thanks for the honor of having been allowed to serve
> as rector this long, I am . . .[18]

On February 17, 1968, Monsignor George W. Shea was named pastor of Our Lady of Sorrows Parish in South Orange, New Jersey. He died in 1990.

Chapter Thirty-six

Sudden Departures

Monsignor William F. Hogan succeeded Shea as rector on February 8, 1968.[1] Hogan possessed the finest credentials. Appointed to the seminary in 1949, he had served as professor of dogma, director of students, spiritual director, and academic dean. Unlike Shea, Hogan embraced the post-conciliar reforms in seminary training.

In 1966, Fathers Robert Hunt, professor of dogmatic theology, and Leo Farley, professor of moral theology, left Darlington to teach at the Catholic University of America.[2] In 1967, Father Russell Ruffino was released to join Hunt and Farley at CUA. The loss of these popular professors was keenly felt among the faculty and students. These three priests were young; it was expected that they would serve many more years on the faculty. The careful plans of faculty renewal, set in place long ago by Archbishop Walsh and continued by Archbishop Boland, were unraveling—and it would worsen.

Just before Hogan assumed the office of rector in 1968, Darlington continued to experience further transition in the faculty. Monsignors Cassels and Manz accepted pastorates, and Father Finnerty was named an assistant pastor. Monsignors Manz and Cassels were senior faculty members, and their "seniority" entitled them to pastorates, so this was a natural transition. Father Finnerty, like his predecessors as director of students, was of the "junior clergy" and his transition also was not unexpected.

Coming to the faculty were Reverend Edward G. Price as procurator, Reverend Joseph F. Flusk as director of students and professor of music, Reverend Philip D. Morris, a doctoral candidate at Catholic University who became professor of homiletics, and Reverend Richard M. Liddy, who returned from doctoral studies at the Gregorian University in Rome to teach philosophy.

Three other priests were in doctoral studies preparing to teach at the seminary: Fathers Stephen S. Feehan, studying philosophy at St. Louis University; Chester J. Miros, working in moral theology at the Alphonsianum in Rome; and Charles W. Gusmer, pursuing studies in liturgy at the University of Trier.

In a major innovation, beginning in 1967, women taught at the seminary. Sisters Mary Aloysius, Anne Gertrude, and Rose Anita, all Sisters of Charity, and Sister Regina Celeste, M.S.B.T., taught English, Spanish, and catechetics.

During Monsignor Hogan's rectorate, faculty involvement in archdiocesan activities continued. Six of the seminary priests were elected to the senate of priests. Others were appointed to the personnel board, the ecumenical commission, the liturgical commission, the music commission, and the Confraternity of Christian Doctrine. Father Price served as the director of continuing education for priests and Father Zimmermann as defender of the bond and in other capacities in the chancery office.

Seminary Life Is No Longer Tidy

Hogan displayed a much more positive attitude toward post-conciliar reforms than did his predecessor. He believed that morale had improved and attributed the improvement to the student-faculty dialogues that had gone on during the year.

In his evaluation, the initial reaction of the seminarians to change was "chaotic," as many of them felt that "all restraints had been removed." However, in his opinion, their tone changed as they realized that self-discipline was necessary in the new regime. Hogan admitted that mistakes had been made but emphasized that strong efforts were under way to correct them.

A positive aspect of the new system was that individual characteristics of the seminarians emerged more clearly, thereby giving the faculty a better opportunity to know a student's assets and liabilities. These perceptions would enable them to make a more perceptive judgment on worthiness for Holy Orders.

In spite of these benefits, Hogan acknowledged that the transition had put a great strain on the faculty members, who were accustomed to a very different style of seminary life. Constant involvement in the daily lives of seminarians was a new experience for them. Their preparation had been exclusively academic and now, in addition to their academic responsibilities and duties within the archdiocese, they were charged with "getting to know" the seminarians as individuals whose fitness they would judge for orders. This responsibility previously had been the almost-exclusive preserve of the rector, vice rector, and director of students.

The frustration of the faculty deepened as the years went on. This chiefly was due to the continuing alteration of their "job description" to include duties for which they were not prepared. A few years earlier the faculty members had very strongly affirmed their responsibilities to be limited to teaching. Now they were spending "innumerable hours counseling confused seminarians, dialoguing with impatient seminarians, and supporting wavering seminarians." They also were saddled with endless meetings, including weekly faculty meetings. Faculty members served as moderators of 20 "small groups" into which the seminary student body was divided. These groups had the general purpose of discussing, reflecting on, and praying over the priestly life.

In a great understatement, Hogan told the deputies at their 1968 meeting that seminary life was "no longer as tidy and as predictable as it used to be" and admitted that "it would be naïve in the extreme to say that these experiments have been an unqualified success." However, he hoped "that the venture that this experiment represents has been successful to a reasonable degree and that we are at least on the way to constructing a strong and viable preparation for the priesthood."[3]

Hogan was optimistic but realistic. He knew that the transition taking place in seminary life would not be an easy journey. He explained this to the deputies and asked for their patience.

> When it is said that morale has improved, it is not meant that the seminarians at Darlington have managed to escape the tensions and insecurities that characterize their generation. These are very evident and will probably pose a problem for the foreseeable future. The improvement in morale probably is made up of equal parts of student objectivity about their problems and faculty recognition that there are real problems which have no simple answer and which must be dealt with patiently.[4]

Frustrated, Restless, and Discontented

The next year, 1969, Hogan was much less upbeat. He reported, "The word that comes to mind in trying to describe and evaluate the average seminarian is discontent. He is restless and uneasy with authority, with his peers, with himself, with his education, with his prospects." The situation was "not something that can be dispelled by a new program or by a tightening or loosening of regulations. It forces those charged with educating him to be sensitive to his needs and to be engaged in a constant evaluation of the quality of seminary life. At this time, there is no solution at hand."[5]

Hogan saw seminary unrest as part of the general post-conciliar destabilization in the Church. He wrote of the unrest, confusion, and impatience that characterized seminarians. He told the deputies that his report would not be precise because the situation was "difficult to assess in terms of specific accomplishments" and admitted that the faculty members were frustrated.[6]

He did have some good news. The seminary faculty, in August 1968, publicly and unanimously had supported Pope Paul VI's encyclical *Humanae vitae.*

We, priests of the Immaculate Conception Seminary at Darlington, wish to affirm our acceptance of Pope Paul's decision. . . . We believe that the developing consensus in the Church in support of this decision is an indication that Paul has spoken not only in virtue of his office but on behalf of the Church at large.[7]

A major source of seminarian discontent and faculty concern in 1969 was the failure of one major experiment. The attempt to establish student government, as suggested by the American bishops, "collapsed completely." The inability of the seminarians to agree on even the most general terms revealed deep divisions among them. The faculty was surprised at the depth of the divisions and spent much of the year attempting to address them in many group discussions. While Hogan wondered whether these myriad and lengthy meetings would "contribute much or anything," he had no choice but to soldier on.

Divisions within the seminary community were a new phenomenon. While administration assumed all changes, in particular those lessening the obligations of the rule, would universally be welcomed by the students, they were mistaken. Many of the divisions, focused on liturgical change, foreshadowed future divisions in the Church.

The number of seminarians had dipped to 199, and would shrink even more as the philosophy classes were transferred to Seton Hall over the coming years. At the same time, expenses were increasing, partly due to new costs involved with the various apostolic programs, as well as capital improvements to a facility now 30 years old. The seminary budget for 1969–70 was $756,000. Of this sum, $638,000 was to be "raised by the chancery."[8] The seminary was also burdened with property-tax hikes on sections of its 1,400 acres that were not exempt. With rising property values, Mahwah sought to raise the seminary's tax bill from $12,000 to $61,000—more than 500 percent. The archdiocese appealed the judgment.[9]

A Revolution Has Taken Place

Hogan was well aware of the many criticisms leveled at the seminary. He wrote that "the seminary can be badly misjudged. . . . Patience can look like weakness. Willingness to listen can look like indecision. Experiment can look like drift." He lamented that "at this time the seminary is a very uncomfortable place."

Hogan's 1970 report was short, less than one-quarter the length of his previous reports. He was more optimistic, telling the deputies that "this year I would like to be less grim, if not quite cheerful, about our prospects." He cited a reduction in tension among the seminarians and "a dramatic improvement in their involvement in prayer." He saw no substantive changes for the next year and believed that the seminary was evolving in accord with the wishes of the Second Vatican Council and the standards of the American bishops.[10] Hogan's main concern was the seminary's inability to grant degrees.[11]

The apostolic program was experiencing serious difficulties. Assessment was difficult, seminarians were using it as an outlet and their academic work was suffering. Practically, transportation was a problem. Seminarians also complained that they did little in the parish and they were being used in "baby-sitting" situations.[12] Hogan recommended the appointment of a full-time faculty member to oversee the program.

Unity in the seminary had been a given in pre-conciliar years. The faculty followed the rector; the seminarians followed the rule. The faculty fulfilled their assigned roles, the seminarians theirs. While not all were always happy and satisfied, all went along or they went away. The assigned roles of faculty and seminarians now radically had changed, and the relationship between the two groups as well. The rector also had a new role; he was to "build community."

Building the seminary community, Hogan told the deputies, "depends on the development of faith and love in the group, on the building of mutual respect and trust, on the willingness of all to share their talents, insights, time and energy, and on the ability to live with and respect the individuality of others."[13] To the deputies, senior priests trained in a very different era, these words bordered on incomprehensible.

Hogan believed the seminary was moving in this direction and resisting "a tendency toward disintegration that has characterized many other seminaries." It forced responsibility on the seminarians and allowed the faculty to see "them as they really are." However, this goal of "building community make[s] frequent contacts between the priests and the seminarians necessary. To insure these contacts, we have begun, this year, to assign each student to a faculty member who will be his mentor. They must meet once a month and during their meeting discuss the whole range of the student's activities, his understanding of the priesthood and the progress he is making as a priestly person."[14]

Hogan closed his 1971 report with the words: "Even a cursory reading of the bishops' program leads one to the conclusion that a revolution has taken place in seminary education. That revolution is now an accomplished fact and has been legitimated by the program."[15] This did not please the deputies.

In his last report as rector, in 1972, Hogan outlined two further changes that altered the seminary program at Darlington.

In recent years, the deacons had spent their eighth and last semester in residence at a parish, their deacon internship. Beginning in Fall 1972, deacons remained in residence in their assigned parishes for all of their fourth year. During the fall, they returned to the seminary two days a week to complete required courses. During the spring, they were required to take part in seminars, pastoral in nature, in the area in which they were assigned.[16] Effectively, four years of the theological program were reduced to three.

As he closed what would be his last year as rector, Hogan was honest in his appraisal of the situation and did not mince words.

The morale of the students cannot be said to be good. At the same time, it seems to be better than the morale of most seminaries in this part of the country. As was indicated in last year's report, the students seem to be experiencing many tensions among themselves. Some of them make strong efforts to relieve the tensions and eliminate the hostilities. But such efforts are sporadic, and on the whole, unsuccessful.

This is a constant source of worry to the faculty. The situation is unfamiliar to us. At this point, however, it can be debated whether or not this distress is completely bad. It may be that tension and distress are normal in real life, and, that experiencing them from here, while under supervision and with help at hand, the seminarians are making a painful entrance into adulthood. On the other hand, it can be urged that the seminarians are coming from backgrounds unfamiliar to us, are subjected to outside stresses unprecedented in the Church and consequently are not as deeply affected by spiritual direction as we would hope.

The matter of morale has been a problem for more than a decade. Substantive successes have been gained, but much remains to be done. It is hoped that the deputies will be sympathetic to whatever honest efforts are made to this end.[17]

His hope for the sympathy of the deputies was in vain.

Chapter Thirty-seven

Hogan Under Fire

Shortly after Monsignor Hogan took office in 1968, he was interviewed in the *Record*. During and after the Second Vatican Council, the press, especially what many Church leaders quaintly called the "secular press," took an ever-increasing interest in Catholic affairs. He told the *Record* that he would be "more concerned with the examination and evaluation of changes already made in the seminarians' training program than with making any more changes." He explained, "We have had some pretty radical changes in the last few years, and we are now in the process of evaluating them."[1]

His opinions were echoed by other seminary leaders. Monsignor George Mulcahy, former rector of Mount St. Mary's Seminary in Emmitsburg, Maryland, wrote in 1970, "Many people are realizing that the period of experimentation in seminaries soon will have to come to a stage of honest evaluation. The good that has been learned will be made available to all. The good lightly discarded will be restored. The mistakes made will be acknowledged courageously and corrected."[2]

But Hogan was not to be allowed this luxury for long. For better or for worse, the lifestyle of the seminary had changed. The atmosphere was different. The guidelines approved by the American bishops mandated many things that would not have been tolerated five years before. Obvious to all, dress codes were changing. The cassock, biretta, and zimarra were disappearing. Many seminarians wore jeans, sport shirts, sneakers, long hair—and beards. A few continued to wear the cassock. The change was so sudden that a deacon in 1973 recalled that he and his classmates, when recalling to new seminarians the dress codes in place in their first year, 1967, were stunned that the new men did not even know the names of the various pieces of abandoned apparel.[3]

Informality characterized the relations between seminarians and faculty, a striking contrast to the rigidity that prevailed just a few years before. Rector and faculty mingled with and—*quelle horreur!*—occasionally ate with seminarians. Faculty members even were asked to treat seminarians with openness and trust. This new way of life was more of a drain on faculty energies than the old system ever was.

Seminarians often expressed radical views with serious theological and pastoral ramifications. A seminarian at Washington's Theological College in 1970 mused:

> Most guys and faculty aren't sure what a seminary should be. We've had a firm structure for years and suddenly we've realized it's inadequate. There must be a period of questioning and wondering—a period of transition. Right now I'm not sure exactly what a seminary should be doing. But I think it should be an environment forcing you to raise questions such as: What is a priest? What special witness does he offer? What should he be doing in the world? How much of a role does private, interior prayer play in the life of a priest?
>
> As for celibacy, I think it should be optional. I also think that a priest should not have to be ordained for life. He should have the option of perhaps being a priest for 20 years and then leaving if he desires, without any stigma being attached to his leaving.[4]

Such radicalism was, by no means, universal. A Darlington seminarian was much more traditional in an article he wrote for the *Record*.

> I think a person chooses the priesthood because he sees the meaning of this life, because he sees a greater good, in fact, the greatest good—a man in union with his God.
>
> There is an old saying that it is enough for a priest to be ordained, save one soul, and then die. This might sound sophomoric in these days of mass production, but I think it still holds.[5]

Boland Under Siege

Seminarians continued to write to Archbishop Boland on a variety of topics and to ask him to support a diverse range of causes. Among them, they asked him to issue a statement in support of the California migrant farm workers' boycott of lettuce[6] and to set aside a day of prayer in protest of the United States' invasion of Cambodia.[7] The seminarians took these issues very seriously. During the time of the bombing and invasion of Cambodia, many spent their lunchtimes fasting and praying in the chapel.[8]

While these missives did not disturb Boland's equilibrium, others did. "A concerned parent" of a seminarian complained that the seminary was lacking in "honesty, integrity, and compassion with a faculty whose teaching border [sic] on the radical."[9] Another signed letter asserted that the quality of young priests had declined and that "their obvious lack of self-discipline" was a result of the "decline in the quality and dedication of a number of faculty members," whose views were "not in agreement with Catholic doctrines."[10] An angry lay woman from South Orange sent a four-page letter protesting the annual seminary collection for an institution that had "so few attending."[11] While some of these letters came from cranks, the very fact that lay persons were complaining to the archbishop about the seminary was an unpleasant novelty.

On the other hand, letters from members of the board of deputies and prominent priests of the archdiocese caused serious disquiet to the archbishop. In August 1970, Monsignor Francis X. Coyle, a member of the seminary board of deputies, phoned the archbishop with his numerous concerns. Some of them were based on an "informant" who gleaned his information from conversations with seminarians during their apostolic programs as well as from a "group of priests."

Coyle reported to Boland that there was concern among many priests regarding the "defections of young priests and the lack of spirituality among those who remain." They traced the situation to "the seminary and the lack of training that is received." Specifically, they alleged that often scheduled classes were not held and the "seminarians were left to their own devices."

Their strongest attack was against a seminary professor, Father Anthony Padovano, who, they claimed, based on articles in the conservative newspaper *The Wanderer*, was "guilty of heresy." Coyle acknowledged that much of this was "gossip" and not "the result of investigation,"[12] but he nevertheless reported it.

Boland, not in good health and approaching the mandatory retirement age of 75, was dealing with other major difficulties. In 1968, a group of Newark priests organized a protest against what they termed the "institutionalized racism" of the archdiocese of Newark. Not surprisingly, as the press reported the story, the implication was that they had personally accused Archbishop Boland of racism. The youth of many of these protesting priests, some of whom were recently ordained, increased the cry among the archdiocesan clergy, "What is going on at the seminary?" The protesters soon became known as the "Newark Twenty," perhaps in imitation of the "Catonsville Nine," a group, including several Catholic clergy, that had destroyed draft records in the Selective Service office in Catonsville, Maryland.

The pressure also was affecting Hogan's health, and he was hospitalized during the summer of 1970.[13] In 1970, Father Padovano published a paper entitled "Ecclesial Authority and the Senate of Priests" in *Chicago Studies*. In this article, Padovano argued that the senate of priests had more than advisory power.

Padovano was a nationally known theologian who had done major work in the composition of two recent pastoral letters of the United States bishops. He also served on the National United States Dialogue Group for Lutheran-Catholic Theological Conversation. A few months earlier, as a member of that group, he stated that he accepted the validity of the Lutheran ministry and Eucharist.

In Fall 1970, the senate of priests of the archdiocese of Newark discussed the adoption of Padovano's article as a basis for dialogue with Boland on expanding the senate's role. Monsignor Shea, the former seminary rector, rebutted Padovano's arguments in a 42-page paper, heavily documented with citations from the Second Vatican Council, arguing that priest senates are strictly advisory groups.

Boland warned the senate that any change in its advisory function would result in its "self-liquidation." The senate wisely acknowledged that it did not intend to change its advisory function by any action, thereby avoiding self-liquidation. Nevertheless it endorsed Padovano's article by a vote of 28 to 13.

Boland could not have been pleased that among the priest senators who voted to adopt Padovano's position were the rector, Monsignor Hogan, and Fathers McNulty and Ciuba of the seminary faculty. Monsignor Henry G. J. Beck, former seminary Church history professor, together with Reverend Victor Yanitelli, S.J., president of Saint Peter's College, also voted for Padovano's position.[14]

Twelve of the 13 priest senators who voted "no" issued a rebuttal, criticizing "a small group of senators" for presuming "to speak for all archdiocesan priests without consulting them." Monsignor Shea criticized the senate's action, telling the press, "At best, priest senates are not centers for theological matters. The senate role is primarily a pastoral one, having to do with parish matters. Although it may include theologians within its membership, it should not assume the role of theological authority."[15]

While the criticisms of the seminary from deputies and others arrived on his desk, and the senate votes caused consternation concerning the attitudes of some of the seminary professors, Boland received a rather positive letter from Monsignor John P. Hourihan, director of the apostolate for the deaf of the Mount Carmel Guild. Hourihan recently had begun to teach sign language at Darlington.

Hourihan told Boland that there were rumors among the priests that the deputies were "so critical [of the seminary program] that Monsignor Hogan offered to resign." Hourihan praised the seminary faculty for introducing "a program of training that is striving to meet the needs of the young men who are products of a new age and a changing culture." He recommended that the deputies and concerned pastors enter into dialogue with the seminary administration and faculty "to determine where their value system differs with that of the faculty."[16]

Boland, on the advice of his vicar general, Bishop Joseph Costello, disregarded Hourihan's suggestion about initiating a dialogue between the deputies and the faculty. Costello thoroughly misunderstood the situation and thought the deputies were not "very critical" of the seminary.[17]

Hogan Resigns

At their May 1971 meeting, the deputies charged that seminarians did not attend class regularly and that there was no discipline in the institution.[18] They had a lengthy and heated discussion regarding many negative reports circulating throughout the archdiocese about the seminary. These accusations vigorously were denied by the rector and the vice rector.[19]

In Spring 1972, an exhausted Monsignor Hogan resigned. Boland called a special meeting of the board of deputies and the archdiocesan consultors to discuss the seminary. The deputies and the consultors offered stinging criticism of the changes that had taken place in the seminary. They called for the revision of the deacon internship program and much more supervision of deacons. They criticized the seminary program as providing only "minimal discipline, if indeed there is any discipline at all." Specifically, they charged that seminarians absented themselves overnight from the seminary without permission and cut classes.

They asked that "discipline be restored," and that "if the director of students cannot fulfill, or chooses not to fulfill, his assigned tasks as disciplinarian, that he be asked to resign and another appointed in his stead." The spiritual program was indicted as "obviously minimal" and should be replaced by "a formal program of spiritual direction and spiritual exercises supervised by the spiritual director[s]." Apparently, the deputies and consultors nostalgically yearned for the era of "manual theology," as they also asked for the end of note-taking and reading lists and for the assignment of "official texts" to be "used by professors and seminarians alike."

This would remedy their belief that seminarians could not distinguish between the opinions of their professors and the official teaching of the Church and often neglected their obligation to "teach the public doctrine of the Church." The relaxed rule, in their opinion, also resulted in tensions between pastors and recently ordained priests, since the seminarians "were being trained for a type of life that pastors are not prepared to provide."

While the board members accepted dialogue and consultation among the faculty, they urged that "the rector should . . . rely on his own judgment in great measure in that ultimately decisions would be his in most instances and his responsibility. Lastly, they asked that the new rector initiate a self-evaluation of the seminary to be followed by a formal visitation of the seminary.[20]

The seminary faculty was enraged by these criticisms and blamed them on misconceptions and misunderstandings that came from priests who were "ill-informed, mis-informed, and un-informed." They believed that the seminary had made the post-conciliar transition "more successfully and with less stress than almost any other seminary in the United States." They resented the attacks as impugning their own personal integrity.

The faculty particularly were angered that the criticisms came from consultors and deputies that "have shown nothing more than perfunctory interest in the seminary." They accurately noted that the deputies visited the seminary only once a year for their meeting and never engaged in conversation with the faculty except within their official meeting. They were correct; however, in fairness, no one ever asked the deputies to do more.

The faculty believed that the deputies and consultors simply wished a return to the *status quo antea*, which would be in direct conflict with the interim guidelines on seminary formation issued by the American bishops. Finally, they strongly expressed their ire at the "pejorative reflections on the administrative and personal integrity of Monsignor Hogan."

> Monsignor Hogan's leadership, theological acumen and spiritual strength . . . saved the seminary when it was in deep trouble. Without his guidance and inspiration the seminary could easily have collapsed in disarray. The restoration of morale and the strengthening of the entire program are traceable to his unsparing efforts and his always perceptive response to the needs of the Church. To see his administration denigrated by the charges veiled as recommendations is a sorry reward for the lifetime he gave to the seminary.[21]

The faculty's opinion of Hogan was shared by many seminarians. One recalls that "for the guys of my time, Hogan was something of a mystical, suffering servant."[22]

Signs of the Times

Amid this turmoil, a sign of the times for the seminary and the Church was the end of a relationship that had endured for more than a century. The Sisters of Charity were leaving. For so many years, they had supervised the household tasks and the food service of the seminary, first at Seton Hall, then at Darlington.

Hogan, battered on every side, was unable to lament the end of this era of noble service. He told Boland, "This move should not cause any great inconvenience to the seminary. One sister is in charge of housekeeping in Walsh Hall and we will have to recruit a lay person to replace her. The other two sisters can be replaced by lay persons already employed there. Should the convent be vacated . . . I think it can best be used as a center for the continuing education of priests."[23]

John Petrone, M.D., who had served as seminary physician for 35 years, resigned in August 1970.[24] He was not replaced, as the new schedule allowed seminarians time and freedom to consult with their own physicians in time of illness.

In 1972, the archdiocese sold 624 acres of undeveloped seminary property on the west side of Route 202. The land had become a liability due to frequent trespassing and poaching resultant from the increasing development of the neighborhood. There also were disconcerting reports of "skinny dipping" in the lake by students of nearby

Ramapo College.[25] It was, after all, the "Age of Aquarius." The property was sold to Bergen County for $1.5 million to be used as a wildlife park.[26]

On the occasion of Monsignor Hogan's resignation, the seminary faculty took the unprecedented step of submitting names to the archbishop for consideration as his successor. Quoting the newly issued *Program of Priestly Formation*, which urged bishops to "seek the advice . . . especially [of] the faculty" in such appointments, they submitted three names for Boland's consideration in order of preference. They were Reverend Frank J. McNulty, Monsignor Donald B. Zimmermann, and Monsignor John M. Smith.[27] McNulty and Zimmermann were faculty members, Smith was a chancery official. They noted that Monsignor John O'Brien's name originally appeared second on the list, but he asked that it be withdrawn.[28]

A month later, the archbishop acknowledged the faculty letter "with appreciation." Boland was especially pleased that the faculty had assured him that "whomsoever is ultimately selected for the position of rector, he will be warmly received by the members of the faculty and be accorded the utmost cooperation of all." He told the faculty that he consulted many in the process of choosing the new rector, and that the final choice was "made with the unanimous approval of the archdiocesan board of consultors and the seminary deputies, as well as many others whom we have consulted on an individual basis."[29]

In the past, bishops either consulted a few advisers concerning such an appointment, or simply made the appointment *motu proprio*. The situation at the seminary was deemed so critical that Boland expanded the circle of consultation and sought unanimous approval before moving forward. On July 17, 1972, two days after his letter to the faculty, he appointed Monsignor Harold P. Darcy as rector.

Boland wanted an "outsider." He was concerned about the situation at the seminary and under pressure from the deputies. The involvement of seminary faculty with the vote endorsing Padovano's article on the inherent authority of priest senates, as well as the criticism of the faculty from some priests of the archdiocese, caused him to shy away from the candidates proposed.

Chapter Thirty-eight

Academic Reform

During the tumult of the late 1960s and early 1970s, the spiritual life, the rule, and the horarium were not the only aspects of seminary life in transition. In Fall 1967, class hours were shortened with the goal of the students doing more work on their own. Additional reading requirements were instituted, term papers required, and seminars introduced. The seminary abandoned the reliance on manuals and classroom lectures that had characterized its pedagogy since its foundation. Over the previous two decades, individual professors had been moving in this direction, but now the new style was formalized.[1] A minimum of 15 books was required for outside reading, a major shift in an institution that in the recent past had restricted access to the library.

One innovation was the combining of the theological, liturgical, and canonical aspects of sacramental theology into one five-hour course, replacing individual courses that consumed nine hours. Another was in homiletics. Lay persons from neighboring parishes were invited to the seminary to listen to and critique homilies, quite different from the custom of seminarians listening to their peers.

The faculty expressed satisfaction with these innovations but was less content with the introduction of seminars. The seminars were inhibited by the large size of some of the classes, in particular the remaining "cycle" classes. They advocated the final elimination of all "cycle" classes.[2]

By the 1970–71 year, the seminary completely had re-aligned its entire curriculum and confirmed the new directions in pedagogy that had been under way. Hogan described the new curriculum in this way:

or "church students," they completed their freshman and sophomore college years at Seton Hall before going on to the major seminary. While at Seton Hall, they constituted the "Divinity School," and followed a course of studies leading to the B.A. degree with a major initially in Latin, and later in classical languages.

The policies of Archbishops Walsh and Boland concerning residence on campus for these church students varied from year to year. Even when required to live on campus, students had no special residence building designated for them and they followed a very simple and undemanding rule. Little more was expected of them than daily attendance at Mass and weekly conferences. Academically, the order of courses for church students was coordinated with the program at Darlington. While at Seton Hall, their concentration was in classical languages; at Darlington, in philosophy.

A Joint Committee

As the 1960s progressed, both Seton Hall and Darlington were changing their curricula without reference to the other. During this decade, various forces would lead to further separation as well as unexpected coordination.

Middle States was forthright in its criticisms, and gave rather good advice. In particular, they criticized the concentration of all philosophy courses in the junior and senior years at Darlington, without any supervision by the university. They noted that, in spite of the great number of philosophy courses, the seminarians received a B.A. in classical languages, to no one's satisfaction.[9] They also raised the issue that the philosophy faculty at Darlington, while it was officially linked to the university, was not under any university supervision.

The Middle States visitors offered several possible solutions to the problem. One was to build the proposed philosophy house on the South Orange campus. Another was to divide the philosophy classes between Seton Hall and Darlington. A third was to offer the seminarians a choice of major. At the same time Middle States was making its recommendations, Darlington was reviewing its entire program, thereby providing an opportunity for the exploration of creative solutions.

In 1967, responding to these pressures, the seminary and the university established a joint committee to review academic matters. The committee's goals were to improve the education of the philosophy students through a cooperative effort of both institutions and to explore the feasibility of the seminary becoming an integral part of the university.[10]

Criticism from the Middle States Association was not the only factor encouraging change in the seminary educational system. Seminaries had long felt pressure to conform to the American system of four years of college at one institution rather than the six-year program of philosophy and theology at one school. Further, judging from the reports that the joint committee generated, the "closed" atmosphere of seminaries was viewed as restricting the maturation of high school and college students.

A College Seminary

Less than a year later, on April 10, 1968, the committee submitted its final report. It recommended that 1) seminarians complete their college education at Seton Hall before proceeding to theology at Immaculate Conception Seminary; 2) seminarians be allowed to choose their own majors within the B.A. program and be required to take advanced Latin and Greek courses; and 3) seminarians be required to reside on campus only for their junior and senior years. They further recommended that the junior and senior seminarians reside in the general residence halls of the university in small groups of six or seven under the direction of a priest counselor.[11]

In coming to these conclusions regarding the establishment of what would become a "college seminary" at Seton Hall, the committee believed that "two more years on the campus of the university should hasten the intellectual and emotional maturity of the students . . . [and that] contact with and competition with the secular students would contribute to the maturing process."[12]

The committee consulted a group of psychologists who were opposed to a separate residence for college seminarians. The psychologists believed that community life in a separate residence would provide "support for inadequate personalities," "not necessarily lead to deep convictions," and not "help in making a mature and enduring commitment." They believed that life in the general campus population would provide an "atmosphere more conducive to emotional and intellectual growth" and better prepare the priesthood candidate for his lifelong commitment.

The seminary representatives, Monsignors O'Brien and Hogan, agreed to a college seminary program that did not place seminarians in a separate living facility.[13] The seminary faculty endorsed this policy, believing that the isolation of the divinity students from the general population of the student body had encouraged the immaturity that they noted in recent seminarians.[14] Following the recommendations of the joint committee, in July 1968, Archbishop Boland approved the plan to have seminarians complete their entire college course of studies at Seton Hall.[15]

To plan for the college seminary, Bishop John Dougherty, president of the university, reconstituted the joint committee.[16] The discussions concerning the establishment of a college seminary dragged on for four more years. They focused on the curriculum to be followed by the college seminarians and often included heated discussions on the status of the proposed college seminary within the university structure or independent of it, on the content of the courses, and on the teachers of the undergraduate theology and philosophy courses.

In 1970, Archbishop Boland delayed implementation of the plan to transfer philosophical studies to Seton Hall. Seton Hall was undergoing a difficult time. Campus disturbances in recent years caused many to question its suitability as a site for priestly formation. Several of the priests of the department of theology resigned from the priesthood, adding to the uncertainty.[17] However, in December 1971, Middle States reiterated its concern that the program of taking philosophy at Darlington did not meet its norms.

Meanwhile, the seminary was committed to the elimination of philosophical studies at Darlington. The situation possessed its own momentum. Finally, in April 1972, Archbishop Boland approved the elimination of junior-year philosophy at Darlington. The next year, the senior year was eliminated and the College Seminary was established at Seton Hall.

By 1973, the property of St. Andrew's Episcopal Church on Centre Street, not far from the campus, was purchased as the site of what would be known as the College Seminary—St. Andrew's Hall.

The Possibility of Affiliation

The joint committee also discussed but made no final recommendation on the possibility of Darlington granting its own degrees. It suggested the consideration of two possibilities, the same that the seminary faculty earlier had advocated. The first was affiliation with Seton Hall through which the seminary would share in the university's accreditation, allowing it to grant both bachelor's and master's degrees. The seminary, under this plan, would have "quasi-independent status" similar to the law and nursing schools.

The second alternative was for the seminary to obtain its own licensure from the state of New Jersey and accreditation from the Middle States Association, thereby allowing it to confer degrees in its own name. Under this second suggestion, the seminary could pursue a relationship or affiliation of some form with Seton Hall.[18]

Monsignor Hogan wished to pursue the second course. He informed Archbishop Boland that he was "increasingly uncomfortable operating in the academic shadows of Seton Hall and Catholic University."[19] He believed it was "urgent" that the seminary be capable of granting degrees since most seminaries did so and the priests of the archdiocese were desirous of having some recognition of their four years of theological study.

Monsignor Hogan's hesitancy regarding a link of the theology department with Seton Hall was driven by developments at the university that were changing its Catholic character. Like many Catholic universities, Seton Hall was moving toward a rather "neutral" stance regarding its Catholic heritage.

In October 1967, a group of Catholic university leaders gathered at Land O'Lakes, Wisconsin, to discuss ways in which Catholic universities could participate in the renewal sparked by the Second Vatican Council.[20] They issued a statement[21] that, in its first paragraph, called for "true autonomy and academic freedom in the face of authority of whatever kind, lay or clerical, external to the academic community itself." They also called for experimentation to achieve a university that would be true to Catholic heritage and to the idea of the university.

Most Catholic universities, including Seton Hall, took this challenge to heart and embarked on a series of reforms and changes in governance and administration that led in many different directions. Although parts of the statement appeared radical to many, the Land O'Lakes Statement insisted that not only did theology belong on campus, but that theology provided the defining element of Catholic university identity.

"The Catholic university," the statement read, "must be an institution, a community of learners or a community of scholars, in which Catholicism is perceptibly present and effectively operative." Catholicism was to be made "perceptibly present and effectively operative . . . first of all and distinctively by the presence of a group of scholars in all branches of theology." It further insisted that "theological disciplines are essential to the integrity of any university."[22]

While Seton Hall embraced the elements of the Land O'Lakes Statement regarding freedom from ecclesiastical "control," it ignored the statement on the centrality of theology at a Catholic university.

By 1973, the theology department, initiated in 1960, had disappeared, replaced by a religious studies department. Religious studies is devoted to a multi-disciplinary and secular study of religion. As such it is quite distinct from theology, which normally is confession-based and, in the Roman Catholic tradition, linked to the service of the Church. With the demise of the Seton Hall theology department, there was no longer an undergraduate component with which the Darlington graduate theology department could relate.

The Middle States Association noted the weakening of Seton Hall's Catholic identity in its 1973 report, pointing out that "when the core curriculum was sharply reduced, much that would have identified it as specifically Catholic was eliminated." The report concluded that it is "fair to say that, except for the presence of a scattering of religious on the campus and the effective presence of the president, there is little a visitor would notice to distinguish Seton Hall from a secular university."[23]

Expenses Rise, Enrollment Slips

While expenses were rising and enrollment was slipping, the seminary eliminated one-half of its program. The junior and senior years of philosophy moved to Seton Hall; and fourth-year theology moved to the parishes. The resulting lower enrollment figures would cause more troubles for the seminary and exacerbate criticisms of the seminary within the archdiocese of Newark.

Hogan was concerned over a "recruiting war taking place among the seminaries of the east coast due to declining enrollment across the board." The result was that "Darlington has been virtually cut off from candidates from the other dioceses of the state." In addition, he feared that the flow of candidates for the archdiocese was "drying up." These grim realities led him to conclude that "for the first time the Darlington enrollment is reaching a dangerously low level." The academic year 1971–72 opened with an enrollment of 163 and was expected to begin the next year with 132 [24]

Hogan renewed his call to the archbishop for incorporation and accreditation. It was clear to him that, with declining enrollment, the facilities of Darlington would not be fully utilized in the foreseeable future. To address this, he urged that the seminary be developed as a theological center for the archdiocese that could serve the religious of the area, the religion teachers of the archdiocesan school system, and the priests of the archdiocese.

Incorporation

How had this situation come about? Why did the seminary have no academic charter or licensure and no corporate existence as an institution? From 1860 to 1927, it was part of Seton Hall College, enjoying the degree-granting powers of its charter and sharing its corporate identity. After the move to Darlington, its theology department remained for a time an integral part of Seton Hall and continued to grant the master's degree in Seton Hall's name until 1932. Even after that, its philosophy department continued to be a part of Seton Hall, which granted the B.A. degree to the senior philosophy seminarians. Moving the philosophy department to Seton Hall made the seminary consider various alternatives so that it would have degree-granting status.

From its foundation, the seminary possessed separate canonical status, even after the separation from Seton Hall. However, within the realm of civil law, after 1927, it became part of the civil corporation of the archdiocese of Newark. Without its own civil incorporation, the seminary could not apply for state licensure and eventual accreditation. In spite of Hogan's entreaties, Boland did not move to have the seminary civilly incorporated.

Each year, Hogan lamented the seminary's inability to grant degrees. This was a very serious matter as it affected the seminary's ability to attract students from other dioceses. No longer could Darlington rely on nearby bishops for students. The other dioceses in New Jersey were allowing seminarians to choose their seminary, and Hogan feared Darlington would lose the competition among seminaries. With enrollment slipping and philosophy moving to Seton Hall, recruitment was crucial, and the ability to grant degrees was crucial to recruitment.[25]

Hogan repeatedly brought up the issue at meetings of the deputies.[26] The newly formed senate of priests also pushed the issue with the archbishop, and Boland promised the senate that the seminary would be incorporated "by the beginning of Lent" 1971. When that date passed, he promised the incorporation would be accomplished "by July 1" of the same year.[27] A year after that date had passed, at the deputies meeting in May 1972, Hogan brought the matter up again, but Boland gave no positive response.

Three weeks after the deputies meeting, a committee of seminary faculty members presented the archbishop with a lengthy memorandum outlining the necessity of incorporation as soon as possible so that licensure could be pursued. They were quite forthright in their language, telling the archbishop that "the bare fact of the matter is that for three years the seminary's efforts to achieve legal status have been fruitless. The academic faculty is appalled and gravely concerned about the procrastination in this matter."

The committee "viewed with alarm" the declining number of students at Darlington and told the archbishop that dioceses were unwilling to send seminarians to an institution that did not grant degrees. Their language was not very diplomatic. They declared that they saw no "indication that the matter was being seriously considered," that they intended "to pursue it until the matter is properly resolved," and they would "tolerate no further delay."[28]

Monsignor O'Brien, the vice rector, upbraided the committee for their actions and their language. He told them that their actions did not represent the faculty, and worked against the efforts of the seminary administration. "If TAB [Archbishop Boland] is moved by these implied threats, I'll wager he moves 'with all deliberate speed.'"[29]

He did, but only after he appointed a new rector.

Chapter Thirty-nine

The Darcy Interlude

Harold P. Darcy was born in 1929 and ordained in Rome in 1954. He received the S.T.L. from the Gregorian University in 1955 and the J.C.D. (doctor of canon law) from the Gregorian in 1960. From 1961 to 1971, he served at the apostolic delegation in Washington, D.C. After his return from Washington, he was named pastor of St. Vincent DePaul Church in Bayonne, New Jersey. After serving from 1972 to 1974 as rector of Darlington, he became rector of the Pontifical North American College in Rome from 1974 to 1979. Thereafter he served as pastor of Notre Dame Church in North Caldwell, New Jersey, and later as minister to the priest community of Seton Hall University and chaplain of the Seton Hall law school. He died in 1997.

Monsignor Darcy took the reins as rector of Darlington at a crucial time. The enrollment was dropping. Two rectors in succession had resigned, one in despair, one under attack. The deputies had lost confidence in the institution. The faculty was perceived by senior pastors as "liberal." The attitudes and behavior of recently ordained priests were causing dissension with pastors. The seminary's relationship with the Seton Hall Divinity School, the seminary's "major feeder," had deteriorated.

Over the previous six years, following the guidelines issued by the Holy See and the National Conference of Catholic Bishops, the formation and academic programs had not only been revised, but radically restructured, their final form still unclear.

Darcy addressed a list of unfinished business. The swift incorporation, licensure, and accreditation of the seminary, long desired by the administration and faculty and inexplicably delayed by Archbishop Boland, now were crucial for the future.

Harold Darcy proved to be the perfect man for the job. He possessed a fine sense of humor, a necessary ingredient for a seminary rector at any time. His manner, always bluff and often pontifical, exuded confidence. Most importantly, he possessed the confidence of the aging Archbishop Boland.

In contrast to the utterly frank rector's reports of preceding years, his first report to the seminary deputies described his first year as an "invigorating and personally rewarding experience." His enthusiasm extended to the seminarians: "Young men today tend to be anxious but their altruism and generosity make them, in general, an unusually attractive group of people with whom to work and to live."[1]

Mindful of the criticisms of deputies and pastors in recent years, Darcy assured the deputies that "the traditional elements of seminary prayer life are maintained: the usual spiritual exercises, morning and evening prayer, daily community celebration of the Eucharist, conferences by the rector and spiritual directors, days of recollection . . . and the annual house retreat."[2]

In his second and last report to the deputies in 1974, he remained positive, but noted that "despite some problems, pains, and anguish, frustrations and disappointments, a successful year emerged."[3]

Civil Incorporation

One of the first orders of business was the civil incorporation of the seminary. Boland had dragged his feet on this issue for many years. In June 1969, he received a draft of incorporation papers from the archdiocesan attorney.[4] He asked for several redrafts in 1970 and in August of that year received one ready for signature. He took no action.[5] Finally, on August 23, 1972, a month after Darcy's appointment, the seminary incorporation documents were signed and notarized.[6]

Although officially incorporated, the seminary did not receive a certified copy of the incorporation document for almost two years. Thomas Gassert, the archdiocesan attorney, sent the certified copy to Darcy with the message, "I had to personally go to Trenton and have a deputy attorney general help me find this certificate buried on the desk of a clerk of the Department of Institutions and Agencies and then hand carry it to the secretary of state. God bless bureaucracy!"[7]

A Board of Trustees

The new board of trustees included the archbishop, vicar general, and rector as "ex officio" members. Boland appointed the deputies, who remained the canonical board, consisting of Monsignors Coyle, Fronczak, Furlong, and Holmes, to the new board. He then added Auxiliary Bishop John J. Dougherty; Monsignor O'Brien, vice rector; and Reverend Frank Maione, business manager. Darcy informed O'Brien and Maione rather casually of their appointments. O'Brien recounted that "Harry [Darcy], while walking up the stairs, appointed Frank and me as trustees, and me as secretary! If that means I'm the one to go to jail, I resign!"[8]

Boland was careful not to allow the seminary to stray in the slightest degree from episcopal oversight. The seminary property did not devolve to the new corporation but remained the property of the archdiocese of Newark.[9] Over the coming years, the authority of the board of trustees would develop under the leadership of a new archbishop and a new rector.

Darcy also established the Rector's Advisory Board.[10] This board was drawn from the broader academic community and various professions. It had no deliberative power but was designed to give counsel to the rector. As the board of trustees evolved and grew, the Rector's Advisory Board was abandoned.

Licensure

With incorporation in hand, the seminary could proceed to the next step before accreditation, licensure by the state of New Jersey. In 1972 and 1973, Darcy had several meetings at the Department of Higher Education in Trenton. The seminary went through the tedious process of gathering the requisite documentation for the state.

In order to meet state requirements, the curriculum again was revised. Although the focus of the seminary's mission remained the formation of priests, it was decided to admit students who would not be candidates for the priesthood. The students would be offered two degree programs: the master of divinity (M.Div.) and the master of arts in theology (M.A.). The M.Div. program offered the basic professional degree for students who successfully complete a four-year program that combines academic formation and pastoral formation.

While a four-year program was envisioned, it would be shorter for a time. In 1971, Archbishop Boland had authorized a deacon internship program. Henceforth, immediately after diaconate ordination, deacons were assigned to an eight-week summer parish residency. They returned to the seminary for the fall semester of residence and full-time academic work. The spring semester encompassed full-time assignment and residence in a parish.[11]

In 1972, the program was further modified. Newly ordained deacons were assigned to full-time residence in parishes for the entire year of what once was fourth-year theology. They returned to the seminary during the fall semester for two successive days of classes each week to complete their academic requirements. During the spring semester, work was continued in "action-training seminars and special question seminars under seminary auspices both at Darlington and at convenient locations elsewhere."[12]

The seminary program was now a three-year program. This change was intended to "provide an effective blending of academics and the ministry of service."[13]

The M.A. program offered concentration in a specific area of theology and was designed to give the necessary background for further graduate-level work beyond the M.A. degree.[14]

A team from the New Jersey Department of Higher Education visited Darlington from February 3 to 5, 1974. The team had reviewed the three sizeable volumes of documentary material provided by the seminary and conducted extensive interviews with administration, faculty, staff, and students. Licensure and degree-granting authority for the master of divinity and master of arts degrees were granted to Immaculate Conception Seminary by the state of New Jersey on April 19, 1974. Usually, the state granted initial licensure for a period of three years, but Darlington was granted a preliminary licensure of five years. The visitors must have been impressed.[15]

A feature of the arrangement with the state allowed the seminary retroactively to grant degrees to alumni. This gave the seminary the opportunity to validate the four-year theology course that so many priests had successfully completed without the credential of a degree.

The Mission Expands

The cloister surrounding Darlington had begun to open in the late 1960s. The seminarians were able to leave the premises on a regular basis, often as part of the field education program. At the same time, "outsiders," whom in previous years either were discouraged or forbidden to enter the sacred precincts, arrived in droves.

Priests' retreats, study days, and recollection days were a long-time feature of the Darlington scene. Now, laity and groups of laity were invited to use the Darlington facilities. The period after the Second Vatican Council had witnessed an explosion of "continuing education" and "adult education" programs. Beginning in 1973, Darlington offered an excellent Lenten lecture series called Darlington Institute for Continuing Education, or DICE.

The faculty contributed their professional services and DICE drew a large number of participants. During Lent 1974, 251 lay persons, mostly from nearby towns in Bergen County, attended the series.[16] The *Record* hailed this innovative program with a lead story headlined "You don't have to be a seminarian to study theology at Darlington," praising the seminary professors as "the powerhouse of adult religious education for Bergen County's Catholics."[17]

In addition to the DICE program, the seminary welcomed 52 groups, totaling almost 1,500 persons, during the 1973–74 academic year. They included the Confraternity of Christian Doctrine Congress; days for shut-ins; recollection days and retreats for parishes, sisters, and laity; vocation retreats; marriage encounters; and cursillos.

While expanding the seminary's mission, these events brought in needed revenue. However, the annual subsidy from the archdiocese of Newark increased from $598,000 to $678,000 from 1973 to 1974. The decreased seminarian enrollment and the increasing expenses resulting from funding new programs, such as field education, were fueling the increases.

In addition to seminarian students, the academic year 1973–74 included 54 priests and 14 religious sisters in the classes. Darcy encouraged the opening of the seminary to priests, sisters, and laity: "In the Christian dispensation we know that it is God who calls and man responds to that call. This call may be to the ordained ministry or it may be to the priesthood of the laity."[18] With the advent of licensure and the prospect of accreditation, these numbers would increase.

Immaculate Conception Seminary entered a new educational world. Priests, sisters, and laity from 1974 onward shared its classrooms and its resources. In 1975, the summers would once again be utilized for various activities. However, the summer program no longer was to keep seminarians off the streets and safe from temptation, but to house the Darlington Summer Institute that attracted a wide variety of students over the next decade.

Seminarians of the Seventies

Monsignor Darcy believed that the seminarians of the 1970s differed from their predecessors in several significant ways. He was concerned that they had little interest in theology, seeing it as of little or no practical value. As a result, they devoted little time to studies.

He also observed in many seminarians a fear of commitment that made a peaceful vocational decision quite difficult. Darcy attributed this to spiritual immaturity. He found this spiritual immaturity most evident in new seminarians who had not gone to a college seminary and who had no formal training in the spiritual life.

The fear of commitment noted by Darcy had begun to spread throughout American society in the 1960s and 1970s. It is not surprising it affected priesthood candidates. In fact, it probably had more of an impact on them than on many others. These years were the ones when the largest number of priests left the active ministry.

The seminary was no exception. Between 1968 and 1974, six faculty members resigned from the priesthood. Fathers Russell Ruffino and Robert Hunt, who had become professors at the Catholic University of America in 1966 and 1967, shortly thereafter left the priesthood. Between 1968 and 1974, Fathers Chester Miros, professor of philosophy, Gene Herbster, professor of Church history, Joseph Fitzpatrick, professor of moral theology, and Anthony Padovano, professor of dogma, left the active ministry.[19]

The departure of these young, well-trained, highly skilled, and well-regarded priests left deep scars at Darlington. Not only did their departures shred the careful plans of many years to continually renew the faculty, their resignations destabilized the confidence of the seminarians preparing for the vocation they had abandoned. One of these priests taught only one day. He entered the class and put the course outline on the board. He then left the classroom, the seminary, and the priesthood.

Welcoming new seminarians who had no previous training in the spiritual life was a new phenomenon. Heretofore, only candidates who had been divinity students at Seton Hall were admitted to the philosophy section of the seminary. The seminary then addressed the specific spiritual formation of these young seminarians and they had time to progress before entering the theology department. Now candidates were admitted to the first year of theology either with the minimal spiritual formation provided at Seton Hall or with no spiritual formation at all.

The seminary sought to address this deficit by devoting the first year of theological studies to an "intense" spiritual program. Time for reflection groups, recollection days, and class retreats was found by eliminating field education from the first year.[20]

Field education needed additional attention. Darcy noted that there was a lack of supervision at the field education sites. In order to provide for trained supervisors, he arranged for Reverend Thomas O'Leary to be appointed to the seminary as full-time director of field education. One of O'Leary's responsibilities would be to train supervisors at the various sites.[21]

The new realities and challenges of the years after the Second Vatican Council meant that the seminary no longer could depend on its entering candidates to possess the personal and spiritual qualities that were assumed in the past. The situation further was complicated by the shortened formal seminary program. Less than a decade earlier, the seminary had six years to provide spiritual formation to prospective ordinands. With the elimination of the philosophy department and the shortening of the theology program to three and a half years, and later to three years, the seminary had half this time. In addition, the candidates were arriving at the seminary with a host of personal issues resulting from changes in society.

In his inimitable style, Darcy described the goal of the program.

> It is absolutely essential that our men be men of decision. Commitment to Christ is complex and so is discernment of the call to the priesthood, and both come hard. Commitment to the priesthood requires the development and the support of a determined and tough attitude; it cannot be sustained by a careless indifference. Dishonesty kills it; self-indulgence contradicts it; a kind of agnosticism or a lazy and careless minimalism aborts it. We are preparing men to give creative pastoral leadership not only to meet the needs of today but the people of tomorrow and surely we must have the wisdom and the experience to know that from the blood, sweat, and tears of extraordinary effort flow happiness and joy.

"Seminary Adopts Freer Life-Style"

As the program changed year by year, it was necessary continually to revise the seminary rule. Already gone was the comprehensive rule of the past, replaced in the 1960s by directives and regulations. In July 1972, new regulations were added, reflecting changes in seminarian behavior that had to be addressed as well as practical concerns.

Seminarians were told not to absent themselves overnight without authorization under pain of dismissal. Were seminarians not doing so, there would have been no need for this rule. The new guidelines noted that parking regulations would strictly be enforced. Monsignor O'Brien faithfully roamed the parking lot, noting cars, and therefore seminarians, absent without a reason. Seminarians, who just a few years previously could not step off the grounds, now had their own automobiles.

Seminarians, who once were forbidden to have any cutlery and could only keep minimal food in their rooms, now were told that they must purchase their own "knives, forks, pitchers, spoons, cups, saucers, etc." The previous rule forbidding the introduction of any furniture, even one's own holy pictures, had disappeared. Seminarians now could paint and furnish their own rooms as they pleased, "subject to inspection," of course. The present writer remembers a seminarian in the early 1980s who painted his entire room, walls and ceiling, black. Fortunately, he chose not to pursue a priestly vocation.[22]

With an "open seminary" and visitors and seminarians constantly coming and going throughout the day and into the night, security became a problem. The doors now were locked throughout the day and keys given to the seminarians.

The *New York Times* rather simplistically summed up all these changes in an article titled "Seminary Adopts Freer Life-Style."[23] The "newspaper of record" recorded that "in the past, there were about 75 strict rules. Now, the present student body . . . has just six basic regulations to observe." In the article, seminarian Bill Schladebeck told the *Times'* readers that "life used to be regimented and structured here, getting up at 6:30 in the morning and lights out and in bed by 10:15. But now we have the mentor program and it comes down to basic honesty with your self and your mentor."

The mentor program, implemented gradually in the 1970s, ensured that seminarians were speaking with a responsible person in addition to their confessor and their spiritual director. It provided an opportunity to address openly and honestly various issues in the external forum and also served as a forum in which the mentor could offer practical advice and encouragement.

Part and parcel of this "freer life-style" was openness to dialogue hesitantly begun in the 1960s. A feature of this was the "speak-out." Faculty and seminarians would join in an open discussion of a wide range of topics. Their goal was to create an atmosphere of trust and openness between seminarians and faculty members. While the speak-outs could be heated on both sides, they eventually produced an honest dialogue.

Pay As You Go

     The cost of seminarian education continued to rise. The archdiocese was experiencing financial problems. The seminary made what economies it could. In 1971, the subsidy for laundry service was discontinued. Hereafter, seminarians had to take care of their own laundry requirements.

     Laundry was the least of the problems. The seminary's sewage system, the legendary "honey pots," was beyond repair. The rector advised the archbishop that the cost of a new system would be in excess of $100,000. Boland authorized the expenditure, noting on the rector's letter that "money can be borrowed from the escrow account on the Phil. House Chapel."[24] This comment of the archbishop indicates the rickety finances of the archdiocese and the lack of financial planning and controls that would plague Boland's successor.

     In 1971, the annual board and tuition cost per year for one seminarian was $4,200. Each seminarian was charged $1,500 toward his archdiocesan insurance policy. This policy was paid through semi-annual installments over a 20-year period, payable upon death.[25] However, this was not enough. On July 30, 1973, Monsignor Darcy informed seminarians that the archdiocesan insurance payment plan was discontinued and hereafter seminarians studying for the archdiocese of Newark would be required to pay $1,800 annually for their board and tuition. This did not represent anything near the entire cost of their education, but indicated that some of the rising costs would be borne by seminarians. They were advised to take out state and federal student loans for this purpose.[26]

     A month later, in August 1973, Archbishop Boland rejected plans ranging from $50,000 to $125,000 for the renovation of the seminary chapel as too costly. He allowed the seminary to restructure the chapel arrangements but on a modest scale utilizing present materials and seminary staff carpenters.[27]

     This renovation, which took place several years later, resulted in a new configuration of the worship space. A wooden altar was placed to the left of the central part of the nave. The pews were set in a semicircle around it. The Blessed Sacrament was reserved in the original marble altar in the sanctuary.

Commencement

     Now licensed to grant degrees, Immaculate Conception Seminary held its first commencement on June 7, 1975. Ninety-eight degrees were conferred, 77 of which were granted retroactively to alumni in accord with agreements with the Association of Theological Schools and the Middle States Association.

     That year, the seminary awarded an honorary doctoral degree to Monsignor Thomas Fahy, president of Seton Hall University. Later honorary degree recipients included Frank Sheed,[28] Monsignor John Tracy Ellis,[29] Reverend Edward A. Synan,[30]

Reverend Raymond E. Brown, S.S.,[31] Reverend Bruce Ritter, O.F.M.,[32] Dr. Monika Helwig,[33] and Reverend David Stanley, S.J.[34] In 1983, the seminary's last year as an unaffiliated institution, it awarded an honorary doctorate to Reverend Theodore Hesburgh, C.S.C.[35]

Chapter Forty

Archbishop Gerety

On April 2, 1974, Archbishop Boland's resignation was accepted by the Holy See. He had submitted it three years earlier when he reached the age of 75. On the same day, Most Reverend Peter Leo Gerety, bishop of Portland, Maine, was named archbishop of Newark. He was installed in a sweltering Sacred Heart Cathedral on June 24, 1974.

Born in Shelton, Connecticut, on July 19, 1912, Peter Leo Gerety was the first of nine sons of New Jersey natives Peter Leo and Charlotte Daly Gerety. His father was an industrial engineer and a leader in the business community of Connecticut. Archbishop Boland's future successor entered St. Thomas Seminary in Bloomfield, Connecticut, and was chosen for study at St. Sulpice Seminary in Issy-les-Moulineaux, France. After ordination in 1939, his first assignment was St. John the Evangelist in New Haven, Connecticut. In 1942, he established an interracial center that later became St. Martin de Porres Parish. For a quarter-century he energetically shepherded a growing African-American Catholic community. In 1966, he was appointed coadjutor bishop of Portland and succeeded to the see three years later.

As archbishop, Gerety faced numerous challenges, not the least of which was the burden of enormous debt. During the Boland years, the Catholic population of the archdiocese reached its highest point, numbering over 1.5 million. During the Gerety years, the archdiocese continued to welcome new waves of immigrants from Latin America, Asia, the Pacific Islands, Africa, and Eastern Europe. An already diverse population now was a mirror of the entire Catholic world.

Gerety was a great contrast to his predecessor. After two decades of the mild and quiet style of Archbishop Boland, the archdiocese of Newark had an energetic and outspoken shepherd with strong opinions who delighted in facing and overcoming challenges.[1]

The Archbishop's Dilemma

The history of the archdiocese of Newark explains some of the challenges Archbishop Gerety faced in 1974. When created in 1853, the diocese of Newark comprised the entire state of New Jersey. In 1881, the southern 14 counties became the diocese of Trenton, with Newark retaining the northern seven. When Newark became an archdiocese in 1938, Camden was created out of the southern six counties of Trenton, and Paterson was carved out of the western three counties of Newark.

When you look at a map, the Newark-Paterson division does not make much sense. Newark consists of four small counties in the northeast corner of the state. The see city of Paterson is in the eastern extremity of the diocese, bordering on the archdiocese of Newark. It was an ecclesiastical gerrymander, complicated by the county boundaries of New Jersey, themselves the result of classic political gerrymandering.

Proposals for the division of Newark, which went back to the early twentieth century, suggested that a smaller diocese of Newark be comprised of Hudson, Essex, Union, and Morris Counties. This would give Newark greater territory and a balance of urban, suburban, and rural counties. However, by the time Rome made a decision, Immaculate Conception Seminary was located in Bergen County, which, under the old plan, would have become part of the Paterson diocese. Archbishop Walsh was not about to give up his seminary.

So the lines were redrawn, giving rural Morris to Paterson and smaller, suburban Bergen to Newark. Thus, Newark became the smallest archdiocese in area in the United States. At the time of the split in 1938, the four counties had a Catholic population of 645,000. When Gerety arrived in 1974, it had increased to 1.5 million.

During the previous two decades, great population shifts had taken place in the archdiocese. The move by many Catholics out of the cities to the suburbs had a massive impact. The construction of the George Washington Bridge, which opened in 1931, brought great numbers from New York. They generally settled in Bergen County. New parishes were established in increasingly affluent suburbs, while the city parishes lost Catholic population.

The new folks in the city parishes, many of whom were recent arrivals from Latin America, and later from Asia and Africa, were generally quite poor and found it difficult to maintain their institutions without assistance from the archdiocese. These city parishes also tried to meet the social and educational needs of many African Americans, recently arrived from the South, the majority of whom were not Catholic.

Unprecedented Debt

After taking on the reins of the archdiocese, Archbishop Gerety quickly became aware of an unsecured debt of $24.5 million. Through a committee of lay and clerical advisers, he quickly consolidated the debt with five banks. Through stringent economies, the unsecured debt was reduced to $21.5 million by mid-1977. This did not include an additional $13.4 million in mortgages and deposit and loan debt. Interest costs on this debt exceeded $1.8 million annually.

The massive debt principally arose from the operations of the regional high schools and the Mount Carmel Guild, a social services organization, during the approximately 10 to 15 years prior to 1976.

In 1961, the archdiocese conducted a development campaign to raise funds over a five-year period for the construction of regional high schools and other institutions, including a philosophy house for the seminary. As related earlier, approximately $24 million was raised. However, the cost of the schools alone exceeded $32 million.

Construction costs had been greatly underestimated. Eight high schools were planned; six were built. Four homes for the aged were envisioned; none materialized. The philosophy house for the seminary was designed; its construction never began. These unfulfilled promises left bad feelings among many contributors.

Due to the departure of teaching sisters and brothers, the cost of maintaining the high schools skyrocketed. The method of collecting tuition from pastors of the students failed. By the end of 1976, the cumulative operating costs had exceeded tuition and other revenues by $26 million for the previous 10-year period.

The Mount Carmel Guild expanded in the 1960s as the needs in the archdiocese, and particularly in the inner cities, increased. By 1976, the guild had an accumulated deficit of almost $14 million.

In the late 1950s, Seton Hall entered into an agreement to utilize facilities owned by Jersey City and located its dental and medical school there. Seton Hall made certain leasehold improvements and purchased necessary furniture and equipment. The operation of the school caused significant cash drain and in May 1965, the school was sold to the state of New Jersey. The state purchased the leasehold improvements, furniture, and fixtures at book value. Seton Hall then paid off the bank loans incurred in connection with the school, which resulted in a loss of more than $3.5 million. This loss was absorbed by the university and seriously weakened the institution, which incurred increasing debt over the next decade.

Addressing the Problem

The financial problems of the archdiocese required major attention by the summer of 1976. That year, in May and June, the archdiocesan campaign, called "Lifeline," failed to reach its goal of $6 million. By July, Gerety ordered an immediate review of the budgets of archdiocesan offices. It resulted in drastic cuts.

The school office, for instance, was cut from a staff of 16 people to only seven, and new educational programs under consideration had to be abandoned. Another casualty was the Institute for Social Justice and Peace, which was closed entirely, thus ending an office that began in the 1950s as the Institute of Industrial

306

Relations. Nearly every office had to do more work with curtailed staffs and reduced budgets.

Cutting budgets and offices is always unpleasant. Archbishop Gerety gathered together the heads of the various archdiocesan offices and explained the situation. He told them that the cutbacks were absolutely necessary. He said, "There's going to be some blood on the floor around here, but we can't help it."

Gerety looked for new ways to fund archdiocesan agencies. Most Catholics looked upon their parish as their sole financial priority. Many were disillusioned by the failure of the development campaign in the 1960s that did not deliver the facilities promised. People did not realize that many parishes were having difficulty making ends meet and were seeking subsidies from the archdiocese.

The annual Lifeline program was discontinued, and the Archbishop's Annual Appeal was inaugurated with a lower and more realistic goal of $3 million. It was launched in May 1977 and successfully met its goal. The revenue from the appeal was intended to fund archdiocesan services such as Catholic Community Services and education, and to service the debt. Revised parish assessments aimed to finance the administrative offices of the archdiocese.

Despite the success of the first of the annual appeals, it remained a high priority to hold spending down. Auxiliary Bishop Joseph Francis chaired the archdiocesan plans and programs committee that reviewed agency budget requests. Through 1977 and 1978, archdiocesan expenditures remained about the same despite an inflation rate of five percent.

Gerety established a lay finance council and initiated a formal process of examining all areas of the archdiocese to find suitable candidates for the boards of institutions affiliated with the archdiocese such as Seton Hall University, Catholic Community Services, and the seminary.

Seton Hall was on the verge of bankruptcy, operating on a $5 million line of credit that was almost exhausted. Catholic Community Services, the successor to the Mount Carmel Guild, was mired in debt. The seminary was drawing an annually increasing subsidy.

Reorganization of Seton Hall

Gerety reorganized the structures of some institutions by giving them a two-tier structure. The first tier was the level of the corporation itself. It would consist of a handful of members, but in such fashion that the archbishop would be in complete control. Then the corporation would elect members to become the working board, or the board of trustees or regents, as it might be called. They were empowered to carry on the affairs of the institution but, with the two-tier structure, the authority of the archdiocese would not be compromised.

An example of the financial morass was the situation in Seton Hall University. When Archbishop Gerety asked for a financial statement, he received several yellow legal-sized sheets of paper, on which the university's financial officer had written what he called a summary of the finances of the institution.

The archdiocese's historic responsibility for Seton Hall University at South Orange took new directions in the early 1980s. The university had passed through a troubled period in the 1970s. An operating deficit of $1 million in 1972 grew to $7 million by 1979.

Through these years, the university experienced a substantial turnover in its central administration that detracted from its ability to engage in effective planning for the future. Monsignor Thomas G. Fahy, president since 1969, died suddenly in 1976. The following year leadership passed to Seton Hall's first lay president, Robert Conley, who struggled with financial difficulties until his resignation in 1979. Reverend Laurence Murphy, M.M., took the presidency from August 1979 until August 1980, when poor health forced his resignation. Executive Vice President Edward R. D'Alessio was named president in June 1981.

After studies by the committee of the laity, important changes were made in the university's governing arrangements. In 1980, its governing bodies were restructured so that the board of trustees would remain the legal incorporators though reduced in number and function. The new board of regents, a majority of whom were lay people, was responsible for the entire management of university affairs, including the power to appoint the president and other officers as well as faculty and staff. The archbishop of Newark remained president of the board of regents. Reverend John J. Petillo, co-chancellor of the archdiocese, was appointed chairman of the board of regents.

Controlling Spending

The success of the Archbishop's Annual Appeal had to be balanced with the continuing challenge to hold spending down. A committee, under Bishop Joseph Francis, reviewed the budgets of 48 archdiocesan offices, agencies, and institutions. It was necessary to fashion an austerity budget. A major expense continued to be debt service, which took 55 cents of every dollar of income from assessment and the appeal.

It was imperative that a new financial strategy be adopted to deal with the load of debt. The chief architect of the fiscal program was Joseph Nehila, Gerety's chief financial officer. In May 1978, a major reform was introduced in budgeting and reporting procedures for archdiocesan agencies and offices. Offices and agencies of the archdiocese of Newark had been operating without much internal budget control. They, including the seminary, now were required to follow stringent accounting and budget procedures.

Negotiating with the Banks

Efforts to improve the archdiocese's financial situation were bedeviled by the interest payments on its debt. The 1976 loan agreement with the consortium of banks set the interest rate at one percent above the prime rate. This rate rose through 1978 to reach 11.25 percent by October. A large portion of the archdiocese's loan payments was going to interest, and only a slight amount to paying off the principal. Thus debt liquidation appeared to be postponed indefinitely.

The burden of debt service made it difficult to fund much-needed and long-postponed programs for educational and pastoral services in the archdiocese. Gerety wrote to the bankers to inform them that there had to be a renegotiation and described the interest payments as "unconscionable." The banks had a good thing going. They continued to collect interest, and with so little being paid on the principal, they could look forward to years of interest income.

Gerety appointed a committee consisting of John W. Culligan, president of American Home Products Corporation; Milton F. Lewis, vice chairman of Howard, Weil, Labouisse, Friedrichs, Inc., a brokerage firm in New York; and Father John Petillo, co-chancellor, to negotiate a new agreement with the consortium of banks. They began to do so in October 1978.

In order to strengthen the archdiocese's financial position in negotiations with the banks and to raise revenue, the archdiocese adopted a cash management program of grouping the weekly parish revenues in a common pool of funds. The parishes could thereby earn a higher rate of interest than they could by having separate accounts. At the same time, they would still be able to pay ordinary parish expenses. The plan also demonstrated to the creditor banks that the archdiocese was serious about meeting its goal of repaying the loan.

Key to success was the cooperation of the pastors. Gerety had several meetings with them and elicited their support. He told the pastors of the very tense situation in the negotiations and described to them how his efforts to settle had so far been rejected. He wanted the pastors to know this information since they had accounts with these same banks. Gerety got the pastors stirred up. After all, pastors could move their accounts to other banks. Sometimes they got a bit over-enthusiastic. At one meeting, Father John Maloney, pastor of St. Patrick's Pro-Cathedral, stood up and, waving his hands, shouted, "We'll kill the banks. We'll kill the banks."

The negotiations continued through November and December 1978 in an atmosphere of increasing urgency. There was a possibility that the bankers might declare the archdiocese in default at the end of December. Of course, the bankers did not want the archdiocese to go into bankruptcy. Bad debts, especially of this size, would not look good as they closed their books at year's end.

A Cold Meeting

Just before Christmas, on December 23, 1978, the committee and the bankers met in the Mount Carmel Guild building next to the chancery. John Culligan chaired the meeting, which he described, in his typical gentlemanly fashion, as one of "intensive negotiations." Gerety did not attend. He went upstairs to his office in the nearby chancery to wait for news. It was a very cold day, the temperature in the mid-teens.

The bankers complained about the cold in the building. Culligan told them, "We don't have any money for heat." The bankers didn't like that. Everybody was very uncomfortable. In spite of the cold weather, the meeting was heated. Culligan demanded that the bankers choose a spokesman. They resisted but finally agreed and Malcolm Wilson was chosen. The bankers threatened to "blow the whistle," to foreclose. Milton Lewis asked, "Do you want the cathedral or the cemeteries?" This infuriated the bankers. The committee persisted. It was two days before Christmas and everybody wanted to get out of that frigid room.

Finally, the committee and the bankers reached an agreement in principle for a new loan whose interest would be fixed at seven percent firm. They completed the negotiations and settled it with a handshake. John Culligan later confessed to Gerety that the reason that the building was so cold was that somebody had mistakenly put on the air-conditioning rather than the heat. Years later, Gerety innocently recalled, "No one knows how this happened. We had no money for heat, but we had air-conditioning in mid-teen weather. That is a great ploy for negotiations!"

The loan agreement was finally signed on March 28, 1979, and provided for a fixed interest rate of seven percent over the next five years until January 1, 1984. The 1984 deadline would have significant impact on the future of the seminary. As a major archdiocesan institution, as the institution that drew the largest subsidy from the archdiocese, Immaculate Conception Seminary, in the short term and in the long term, would be greatly affected by the debt crisis of the archdiocese.

Only months after the new loan agreement was signed, the positive effects of the new agreement became evident. By July 1979, the archdiocese applied $250,000 to the reduction of principal and thereby lowered the monthly interest payment by $2,000 to $156,000. In Fall 1979, the sale of the property of the closed St. Mary's Orphanage in the Vailsburg section of Newark and the sale of Archbishop Boland's house in West Orange enabled the archdiocese to apply a lump sum of $1 million directly to reducing the principal.

The debt was now under control, but financial troubles continued for the archdiocese. Given the fiscal arrangements in place, they would have a serious impact on the seminary.

Chapter Forty-one

Choosing a New Rector

In Spring 1974, Monsignor Darcy was appointed rector of the Pontifical North American College in Rome. Two years earlier, upon the resignation of Monsignor Hogan, the seminary faculty sent a letter to Archbishop Boland containing recommendations for the office of rector and asking a part in the selection process. Boland declined their request and rejected their recommendations.

Upon Darcy's departure, Monsignor O'Brien once again assumed the role of acting rector. Unlike Boland, Archbishop Gerety asked the seminary faculty to submit recommendations for a new rector. Darcy confidentially informed Gerety that he believed that his successor should be selected from the seminary faculty. He told Gerety that the seminary would soon embark on the complicated and exhaustive process of applying for accreditation from both the Middle States Association and the Association of Theological Schools. For this reason, an outsider might require time to acclimate himself to the situation and valuable time would be lost.

Darcy also felt that it would be a "jolt to the morale" of the faculty if twice in succession a rector was chosen from outside. He recommended Father Ciuba be chosen as rector.[1] On September 9, the faculty recommended *ex aequo*[2] Reverend Edward Ciuba and Reverend Frank McNulty. Both had joined the seminary faculty in 1963—McNulty as professor of moral theology, Ciuba as professor of sacred scripture. Both were young: McNulty was 48, Ciuba was only 39.

Gerety moved quickly and summoned the new seminary board of trustees to a special meeting at Darlington on September 13, 1974. For the first time, a rector would be chosen with input from the faculty and after deliberation by a board. The members of the board were Archbishop Gerety as chairman, Bishop John J. Dougherty, Bishop Joseph A. Costello, and Monsignors William F. Furlong, Francis X. Coyle,

Richard D. Holmes, Harold P. Darcy, John F. O'Brien, acting rector, and Reverend Francis T. Maione, business manager. Monsignor Alexander W. Fronczak was absent.

Before proceeding to a discussion of the candidates, Gerety asked the board to set the term of rector at five years, with the possibility of three one-year renewals. He wanted this so that frequent change "would insure bringing new vision to the office."[3] The meeting was not entirely amicable. Some of the board complained that the seminary faculty was too liberal and that its attitude toward the Seton Hall divinity program was patronizing. Archbishop Gerety directed that matters between the seminary and Seton Hall be worked out. Gerety found "labels more divisive than helpful" and felt that "a faith-filled intellectual experience should make them unnecessary." He was not concerned about controversy, believing that "tensions are not necessarily unhealthy and can lead to a fruitful exchange of ideas."

A turning point had been reached. Those trustees who also served on the board of deputies were the same who severely criticized the seminary two years earlier, precipitating Monsignor Hogan's resignation. Even together with Bishop Costello, they now were outnumbered. Not only were they outnumbered, they did not have the support of the new archbishop, who endorsed the direction in which the seminary faculty wished to move.

Regarding the appointment of the new rector, Bishop Costello and his allies did not give up. Costello maintained that what was needed was a rector who would "shake up the seminary." He cited stories of a faculty member refusing to read the United States bishops' letter on abortion, of faculty members espousing controversial positions and persons, citing the invitation to Father Charles Curran to speak at the seminary. He insisted that the new rector have extensive parish experience and that he have the confidence of the pastors.

Bishop Dougherty emphatically disagreed, rejecting the idea of a rector without previous seminary experience in view of the monumental administrative tasks ahead. Monsignor O'Brien angrily rebutted Bishop Costello's call for a "shake-up" of the seminary. Gerety then added that "actually our parishes may need a shaking up." Darcy also vigorously defended the seminary and its faculty against Costello.

Finally, Gerety placed the names of Fathers Ciuba and McNulty on the table. As a last-ditch effort, Monsignor Coyle, in the name of the absent Monsignor Fronczak, nominated four other priests. The minutes state that "no support was forthcoming for any of them." After discussion of the two candidates, filled with encomia for both, Monsignor Coyle formally moved that Father Ciuba be selected as rector, and the motion unanimously was passed.

Actually, the chief officer of Immaculate Conception Seminary now had a new title—"president/rector." Incorporation and licensure provoked the new designation. Monsignor Darcy, a stickler for protocol, surprisingly did not use the title, although he was entitled to it, simply signing his last report to the trustees as "rector." Father Ciuba thus became the first, and would be the only, president/rector.

Before the meeting closed, a few other items were resolved. Archbishop Gerety had established a priest personnel board to advise him on appointments. Bishop Costello asked that the board be consulted on the appointment of the new rector. Costello remarked that the board was miffed that it had not been consulted by the archbishop when he appointed his secretary and chancellor. Gerety immediately responded that these appointments did not fall within the competence of the personnel board and announced that he would inform Father Ciuba of his appointment as soon as the meeting adjourned.[4]

Father Ciuba

Reverend Edward J. Ciuba was ordained in Rome in 1959. He served as assistant pastor of St. Ann's Polish Parish in Jersey City for one year before returning to Rome for biblical studies. In 1963, he received the licentiate in sacred scripture from the Pontifical Biblical Institute. After an additional year of higher studies in Jerusalem he was designated Élève Titulaire de l'École Biblique de Jérusalem and returned to join the seminary faculty at Darlington in 1964.[5]

Father Ciuba's colleagues held him in the highest esteem. They described him as "young, affable, interested in the students and their problems . . . a fine scholar, a balanced personality, able to bridge the old and the new, not afraid to take a stand, knows the value of a dollar." They recognized his "leadership ability" and "strong Christian commitment" and considered him a "good representative of the theological community in the United States," a person who "has the pulse of the Darlington community and of the current movement of the Church in the United States."[6]

An Optimistic Rector

The seminary entered an entirely new era with a new rector and a new archbishop. Father Ciuba began what would become a tumultuous tenure with great optimism, a quality that never deserted him. He saw the seminary as having a "new role in the contemporary Church . . . a theologically and spiritually vigorous resource center to which the priests, sisters, and laity of the province of Newark look for creative leadership and sound preparation for ministry today."

In his first year as rector, 1974–75, a total of 215 students were enrolled in the seminary. Of them, 91 were seminarians, but only 70 were in full-time residence; the others were deacon interns. They were different from Darlington seminarians of the recent past. Few came from the Seton Hall Divinity School. Most had completed college and had pursued careers in the business world. They ranged in age from 21 to 65. The varied backgrounds of seminarians brought problems and challenges of their own, never before encountered.

Students of the 1970s at Darlington included seminarians from the archdiocese of Newark and the dioceses of Paterson, Trenton, and Camden, as well as Augustinian, Capuchin, and P.I.M.E. (Pontifical Society for Missionary Extension) fathers.[7]

In the coming years, the seminary would welcome a new student population, Latinos. In the beginning, there were tensions created by the variety of national and cultural backgrounds among the Latino seminarians themselves.[8] The seminary often stumbled in serving this new constituency. Believing that these men would prefer separate reflection groups, they immediately were informed by the Latino seminarians that they did not want to be set apart in any way whatsoever.[9]

To increase enrollment Ciuba embarked on a program that Immaculate Conception Seminary never needed before, recruitment of seminarians. He named Reverend Stephen Feehan, professor of philosophy, as director of student development, charged with recruiting seminarians through contacts with bishops and vocation directors. The seminary, once filled to capacity with seminarians from Newark and Paterson, along with a few from Trenton and Camden, now depended on the good will of other dioceses and religious communities to provide students.[10]

Ciuba was aware of emerging divisions among the seminarians, some of whom welcomed the changes in the seminary, others who did not. He saw a "seeming lethargy and occasional petulant criticism" among the resident students and regarded it as a "disturbing but not a threatening problem."[11]

He immediately instituted several changes in the rule. He abolished the decades-old ban on all alcoholic beverages that "is not now—and never has been—honored." He also changed the dress code that unofficially had been evolving. The clerical collar was restricted to deacons and seminarians on pastoral assignments. Seminarians were to wear "neat, clean, socially acceptable attire." Recognizing that this would annoy some of the seminarians, he allowed cassocks and black shirts with collar "because of long-standing tradition at the seminary."[12] Cassocks soon disappeared.

In the 1975 fiscal year, the seminary's financial statement revealed that although its total expenditure was over $960,000, its subsidy from the archdiocese was $621,000, almost $85,000 less than the previous year. This rather positive state of events was due to new income from the various revenue-generating conferences and other activities, as well as from strict economies.[13]

Father Ciuba's Darlington

The seminary buildings looked the same but their functions were quite different. The old Crocker Mansion was officially O'Connor Hall, in honor of Bishop O'Connor, who moved the seminary from Seton Hall to Darlington. The great hall, or *Magna Aula*, which had served as chapel and as the setting for the "cycle" courses, was the main reading room of the library. The Gold Room, divided by partitions, held the offices of the rector and the business manager. Rooms formerly used as classrooms housed parts of the library collection. The rector and several faculty members still lived on the second and third floors.

The residence building remained Walsh Hall, but its libraries were classrooms. The first- and fourth-floor recreation rooms also were used for classes and meetings. The second-floor recreation room was a student lounge, complete with tables and chairs under the aegis of the student council. The bookstore occupied three rooms in the first-floor corridor of Walsh Hall. The fourth-floor library served as the homiletics classroom, equipped with videotape equipment.

The old convent had gone through several reincarnations, first as the speech laboratory, then as a seminar building; and it continued to serve as a conference building. It was used by study, prayer, and reflection groups, many of them sponsored by archdiocesan continuing education programs and other pastoral projects.

There had been no Sisters of Charity at Darlington since 1971. The convent, built in 1952, was called Boland Hall, in honor of recently retired Archbishop Boland. Boland Hall was used for a variety of pastoral purposes, retreats, recollection days, marriage encounters, and programs focused on the continuing education of priests.

The seminary property west of Route 202 was now owned by the Bergen County Park Commission. It remained pristine, and Darlington students were welcome to utilize it for recreation.[14]

Seminary and More

Under Father Ciuba, the seminary continued to expand its already varied ministerial education programs and its utilization as a conference and resource center. During his first year, more than 4,500 people came to Darlington for one or more of its activities. These activities included continuing education for priests, retreats, recollection days, study days, ecumenical meetings, marriage encounters, retreats for sisters, retreats for collegians, vocation retreats, search weekends, charismatic prayer groups, and events for senior citizens and groups of handicapped.[15]

Full- and part-time graduate students included clergy alumni, brothers, women religious, and lay men and women, most of whom were involved in ministerial activities. Archbishop Gerety enthusiastically endorsed the seminary as the "locus" where training for emerging ministries should take place.[16]

Summer sessions were an extremely successful innovation at Darlington. The 1977 session enrolled 165 students. They represented a widening constituency of students, often attracted by the seminary's national advertising program, which drew students from the entire eastern seaboard, the Midwest, and Canada.

Ciuba considered the summer students an "exceptionally loyal" group that viewed the seminary as "a place of renewal, of spiritual, academic, pastoral and personal growth . . . a place of faith and hope." For him, the successful summer sessions were "a clear and exhilarating realization of our cherished ideals and goals."[17]

An Increasingly Diverse Student Body

In the 1977–78 academic year, the seminary enrolled 117 seminarians and an equal number of non-seminarians, 117. The seminarians included 10 from Camden, one from Charleston, two from Hartford, 54 from Newark, 10 from Paterson, 14 from Trenton, 14 Capuchins, three Augustinians, two Carmelites, two Benedictines, and four Franciscans, one of whom was from Puerto Rico. The number of Latino seminarians was rising; that year there were seven: two Cubans, two Puerto Ricans, two Spaniards, and one Costa Rican.

The non-seminarian population was similarly diverse: 12 lay men, 28 lay women, 16 diocesan priests, 10 priests from religious orders, 44 women religious, three brothers, two permanent deacons, and two non-Catholic ministers, one of whom was a woman. The religious communities of men included Carmelites; Capuchins; Augustinians; Franciscans; Marists; Xaverians; and the P.I.M.E. Fathers. In addition, there were various communities of women religious: Sisters of Charity; Felician Sisters; School Sisters of Notre Dame; Sacred Heart Sisters; Cenacle Sisters; Dominicans; Sisters of Compassion, of the Sacred Heart, of the Holy Child, of St. Dorothy, of Mercy, of St. Joseph; and Parish Visitors.

Self-Study, Evaluation, and Accreditation

On May 30, 1975, Immaculate Conception Seminary was given "candidate for accreditation" status by the Middle States Association and the Association of Theological Schools (ATS).[18]

The year 1977 was a year of intense self-study and evaluation. Reverend Philip Morris, professor of homiletics and dogma, oversaw this complex project.[19] The Middle States and the ATS accreditation teams visited Darlington from March 6 to 9. Two weeks later, the visitation team of the Bishops' Committee on Priestly Formation arrived from March 27 to 30. Each visit had its difficulties.

Although the seminary received accreditation from Middle States and the ATS, there was argument over the report's statement concerning seminary finances. Given the struggles of the previous years, this should not have been startling.

Of greater concern was the bishops' committee report. In the preliminary draft there were some surprises. It contained sections on community life and discipline that had not been part of the final oral debriefing. Both Ciuba and Gerety sent letters objecting to the contents, stating, "The section referred to was flawed by demonstrable errors of fact relating to the structure of community life and governance and was marred by references and unwarranted inferences concerning the theological stance of some faculty members and the climate of student life."[20] After several communications with the visiting team, the report was revised to the satisfaction of the seminary.

Chapter Forty-two

Cannons on the Right!

In the words of John Tracy Ellis, "Never before in the nearly 190 years since the church was formally organized in this country had Catholics experienced anything comparable to the unsettling events that overtook them in the post-conciliar age."[1] Ellis wrote:

> In all that pertains to change in traditional patterns of thought or behavior, most human beings will demonstrate what may be called a left wing that welcomes it and a right wing that deplores it. By the late 1960s such a division had sharply split the unity of Catholic Americans as never before. Neither wing was free of extremists who, on the one hand interpreted the council's decrees beyond their true intent, and on the other hand entrenched themselves in the past and all but defied change of any kind. The consequence was deep ideological differences that led in some instances to angry confrontations, in the process of which scarcely a diocese, a religious community, a seminary, college, or university in the land escaped the menace of a 'house divided against itself.'"[2]

The growing polarization in the Church after the Second Vatican Council had ramifications at Darlington. During the 1975–76 school year, several seminarians and priests from the nearby P.I.M.E. house of formation charged that the theology taught at Darlington lacked "a Catholic sense." They accused several faculty members of not being faithful to the Church's magisterium in their class lectures.

Reverend James M. Fannon, a P.I.M.E. father and a member of the Darlington adjunct faculty, brought these charges to his American provincial, Reverend Charles Minck, who accepted them as accurate, and to his major superiors in Rome as well. The P.I.M.E. students and priests residing in nearby Oakland, New Jersey, were split on the matter and some of them protested to Father Minck.[3]

Fannon brought his charges to his superiors without informing either the archbishop or the rector of the complaint, let alone discussing it with them. Archbishop Gerety was informed of the matter by Father Ciuba, who had already registered vigorous objections with the P.I.M.E. congregational superiors.

The archbishop wrote to Minck, telling him that he had no question about the orthodoxy of the seminary faculty. Gerety was angered at the nebulous character of the complaints and the lack of specificity, which did not give him an opportunity to reply to what was being said.[4]

Meanwhile, at a meeting in Detroit, 90 percent of the P.I.M.E. congregation in the United States voted to remain at Darlington.[5] But, in the end, even after investigation proved the charges groundless,[6] the P.I.M.E. seminarians transferred to the Catholic Theological Union in Chicago.[7]

There were ideological strains among some of the diocesan seminarians as well.[8] Father Ciuba was aware that some Seton Hall Divinity School students, "perhaps aided by our own seminarians," expressed reservations and apprehension about the "ideological climate" at Darlington.[9]

This was not a phenomenon unique to Darlington. Matthias Neuman, O.S.B., of St. Meinrad Seminary, in his article "Seminaries and the New Conservatives," in *America* magazine, discerned a new "devotionalism" in many seminarians. He attributed this to a desire to preserve a "religious space" in a secular culture. Neuman believed that these men had been turned off by the social action phase in religious education of the late 1960s and were more interested in focusing on individual faith and personal prayer than on social involvement. He believed that this "new conservatism" would grow in the future.[10]

Ciuba was concerned that some seminarians hid behind a façade while in the seminary and, upon ordination, became very critical of the seminary and of new programs in the archdiocese. Gerety also was disturbed by this phenomenon, and was perplexed that at a Mass in the cathedral, only one seminarian took Communion in the hand.[11]

There was general agreement among the archbishop, the trustees, and Ciuba that these attitudes came from a "lack of personal development, maturity and vision which, coupled with an overclericalized vision of the Church, could produce candidates who may be unable, or unwilling, to function in the church of today and tomorrow."[12]

318

The seminary appealed the recommendation, which also included a $100,000 reduction in the seminary subsidy to the plans and programs committee of the office of research and planning. Father William Linder, the chairman, was unsympathetic. He criticized the seminary's mission statement as not dealing with the urban character of the archdiocese and as "culture-bound." He also expressed "concern over the overall direction of preparation programs for pastoral ministry."[28]

Father Ciuba regarded Linder's comments as filled with "prejudice, unfounded criticisms, accusations of middle-class attitudes and insensitivity to urban needs." Linder appeared to be unaware that the seminary was "involved in ministerial activity in practically every agency and project in the archdiocese."

Ciuba was angered that Linder did not recognize that the seminary was actively concerned for the urban, cultural, and ethnic realities of the archdiocese. Characterizing Linder's memorandum as reflecting "a total misunderstanding and lack of knowledge," he was incensed that the seminary was criticized for an "individual-centered" formation program because such was precisely the spiritual and personal formation called for by the bishops.[29]

Ciuba's memorandum to Linder rejected most of his premises and severely censured the office of planning and research. Responding to remarks that the seminary was "culture-bound," Ciuba responded, "In the laudable attempt to effectuate a redress of the neglectful attitude and lack of attention given to the ethnic and urban, others should not be denigrated. The total setting and context of the archdiocese should be seen in an interlocking and mutually supportive relationship in any planning and organizational policies."[30]

Ciuba equally was unhappy with the power given to the research and planning office, writing that "there is a centralization of power with respect to the pastoral activities of the archdiocese. An inordinate amount of that power lies in a review board whose membership is not determined by the people of the archdiocese and whose knowledge and competency in making fair and objective judgments upon the pluriformity and intricacy of so many programs is questionable. There is a danger here of a monolithic use of power, a practice which generally results in tragic and disastrous consequences."[31]

He was equally scathing regarding the office's style: "Might I add that the office of research and planning should try to simplify and clarify its documents which are frequently couched in management jargon and opaque terminology, which, however familiar to office personnel, is confusing in the extreme and produces more derision than decision."[32]

Ciuba undoubtedly chuckled a few months later when he submitted an evaluation of seminary programs to the office. He wrote that "all criteria indicate substantive progress toward the intrinsically elusive objectives."[33] Perhaps he was trying to prove that he was as adept in the use of jargon as the planning office was.

Even more infuriated was Monsignor O'Brien, who called Linder's comments "flawed and misleading,"[34] reflecting ignorance of the United States bishops' seminary program and norms. Monsignor Hogan, now on the seminary board, quietly noted that Father Linder appeared to be asking the seminary to solve problems for which there may be no solution.

Linder apparently was unaware, among other things, that the seminary had successfully integrated Latino students into community life while respecting and strengthening their identity, and required non-Latino students to take courses in Spanish. The seminary also held regular liturgies in Spanish.[35]

Archbishop Gerety tried to smooth things over by stating that the problem was one of "communication." He said that Father Linder wanted to "unsettle things, raise questions, and bring the problems into sharper focus." He directed that the "seminary and the board must find ways of communicating the realities to Father Linder and his office." He "was delighted with Father Linder's memo because it stirred up problems existing here at the seminary, introduced questions that are being asked about the seminary, legitimate questions . . . the criticism may not be based on a totally accurate picture of the facts, but the questions are legitimate."[36]

Father Linder's commitment to the inner cities and their poor cannot be underestimated. He went on to found the New Community Corporation that built housing for the poor, brought the first supermarket into Newark in decades, opened a wide variety of social services, and was awarded a MacArthur Prize in 1991. He donated the proceeds of the prize to the various inner-city projects.

Communication continued to be a problem. Informed by Sister Mary George O'Reilly, of the archdiocesan office of administration, that a $16,000 deficit in the seminary budget was "unacceptable,"[37] Ciuba told the sister that the budget, with the deficit, had been approved at a board of trustees meeting with Archbishop Gerety presiding.[38] Such contretemps were more and more frequent in the highly charged atmosphere of financial crisis. The seminary had to deal with several bureaucratic levels and often was frustrated. The archbishop was hesitant to overrule the officials he had charged with maintaining the financial stability of the archdiocese and this caused hard feelings at the seminary.

The Archbishop Is Candid

In 1976, Gerety bluntly told the trustees that the archdiocese is "in a financial crisis but there are a lot of people in the archdiocese who really don't believe that . . . questions are being asked about the very existence of the seminary . . . we have to face it . . . we will have to cut severely."[39]

Part of the reality was that seminary tuition was among the lowest in the country and the seminary effectively was subsidizing the suffragan dioceses and the religious congregations. Getting bishops to pay the real cost of seminary education was, in Gerety's frank words, "easier said than done." As a first step, the seminary raised its tuition from $1,800 to $2,100, then to $2,500 in 1979. Non-Newark students were charged an additional $400.[40]

Not surprisingly, the archbishop dominated the meeting and Gerety's words demonstrate his firmness and his own tension.

> Your first obligation is to help the archdiocese pay off its debt. In all seriousness, everything here is very academic. We have to have a serious reevaluation of what the seminary is doing and we must justify it. We have all sorts of problems in the area of how much resources will be devoted to the seminary. There is criticism that we have taken no action on getting rid of this very large tract of land that we don't need. A second question is whether we need a seminary. My feeling is that there is no way we are going to dispose of this until we know how we can do it, hire a planner, and then decide on the action.
>
> The archdiocese remains in crisis and we only have a certain amount of money. The seminary is requesting a large slice and we should examine it carefully. We need outsiders to look into this. We have to do something about this; we are in a very serious crisis. Every department comes in with a blown up budget which we cannot afford. That is the why of coordinating relationships, to pull this in somehow, otherwise we won't have a seminary. After clarifying where we are, then we decide how much it will cost to do it.[41]

At the end of the day, the $700,000 subsidy requested by the seminary was first reduced to $600,000, then reduced again to $500,000, out of a total budget of $936,000. The cuts again were accomplished mainly by the postponement of needed capital repairs. Father Maione, business manager, created a bare-bones budget. The budget reflected new realities. Tuition and fees in fiscal year 1976–77 represented 20 percent of income as compared to 16 percent the previous year. The chancery subsidy dropped from 71 percent to 57 percent of income. In the past it had been as high as 79 percent.[42] This was accomplished by fund-raising and fees for services and activities. The revenue from retreats and other meetings rose from nine percent to 16 percent of income.[43] But would these efforts be enough to save the institution?

The resulting tension affected Father Ciuba's health. Overworked and tired, he was hospitalized with what he referred to as "executive's cramps,"[44] which forced him to take a welcome few days of rest and recuperation.

A New World

The seminary and the archdiocese entered into a new and unprecedented relationship. For the first time, the seminary had to justify its programs and its cost to archdiocesan offices and to the presbyterate. Its existence was at stake. Seminary administration and faculty were concerned about this new relationship. Some anger was inevitable.

While understanding the general frustration caused by the magnitude of the financial crisis, Father Ciuba resented the "apparently basic ideological opposition" of the director of the office of research and planning, Father Linder. He was further disconcerted by Linder's "intransigent attitude in the face of clear proof to the contrary." He attributed the attitude of some of the presbyterate to a "visceral reaction against newer theological currents."[45]

Monsignor O'Brien, never one to mince his words, criticized a "certain prelate," obviously Archbishop Gerety, for reducing the problems with the office of research and planning to a simple failure of communication. He denounced Father Linder as an "intransigent opponent who had publicly vowed to 'close the seminary.'"[46]

The board itself was feeling the strain. At the June 14, 1976, meeting, Gerety felt it necessary to assure Sister Patricia Aidan, a member of the board, that regarding seminary property, there was no adversarial position between the archdiocese and the seminary. He also assured the board that he had stopped suggestions emanating from the archdiocesan fixed assets committee to sell the entire property, considering these ideas to be "deleterious," conceding that the financial crisis in the archdiocese was reflected in a very serious crisis in the seminary.[47]

Benedict Harter, a trustee, maintained a dignified sense of humor through all the interactions with the chancery. He remarked that a meeting with archdiocesan officials, "after penetrating the purple persiflage, could be considered 'Much Ado About Nothing' or struggling with gnats." Harter always was candid and asked that his "frontal approach" be excused, noting that "from a business point of view we cannot waste time on trivia," adding wittily, "although from a religious point of view, I can see how sometimes we must."[48]

Monsignor Hogan criticized the seminary for allowing its mission statement to be overly influenced by the "sociological thrust" of the office of research and planning, rather than reflecting the "theological basis and Gospel context" of the mission. But even the outspoken Monsignor O'Brien asked that the statement not be tinkered with in view of the strained relationship with the office of research and planning.[49]

Seminary finances were further complicated by its lack of corporate identity until 1972. After incorporation, the seminary property remained the property of the archdiocesan corporation. Donations to the seminary routinely were sent to the chancery office. While this may appear to violate the intentions of the donors, the funds were channeled to the seminary through the annual subsidy. By the mid-1970s, the seminary held notes receivable from the chancery of over $1 million. In 1977, the archbishop agreed to pay the seminary three percent interest on these notes, which amounted to $30,000 per year.[50] In June 1979, the board voted to forgive the note receivable.[51] The archdiocesan subsidy over two years was used to liquidate the debt, but this essentially was a "paper transfer."

Financial Crisis Looms

Financial problems and criticism would not go away. In 1979, Auxiliary Bishop Joseph Francis, a member of the board of trustees, voiced opinions similar to Father Linder's. In Francis' opinion, Darlington was "isolated from reality, not applicable to the social situation, [and] perhaps unwittingly destined to discourage seminarians from working in Newark." He "wondered whether seminarians should be resident in the cities," rather than in the suburbs. His fellow trustees strongly disagreed and argued that geography did not preclude an atmosphere sensitive to social issues and objected to the idea that "the seminary could fulfill its mission properly only in an urban setting."[52]

Archbishop Gerety continued to emphasize the archdiocesan crisis and the cost of the seminary. In 1979, he supported another increase in tuition but let the board know that this also increased the archdiocese's costs, since it paid the tuition for the Newark seminarians.[53] At the March 5, 1979, meeting of the trustees, the archbishop asked the board to analyze the use of facilities. O'Connor Hall, he noted, was over 70 years old, and expensive to maintain. Could, he asked, the seminary consolidate its activities and produce savings? Dismayed by declining enrollment, Gerety, for the first time, questioned the continuation of the archdiocese's financial responsibility for the seminary.[54]

Chapter Forty-three

Public Relations

In 1978, the seminary established a newsletter, *South Gate,* for alumni and supporters. It was so successful that its initial run of 800 was expanded to 2,300 for the second issue.[1] It used this medium to inform its public, and its critics within the archdiocese, of its many academic and pastoral activities.

To improve communication with the Newark presbyterate, the seminary invited priests to visit the seminary and, in some cases, involved them in development and growth programs for seminarians.[2] As a further step, an alumni association was formed in 1978.[3] The association sponsored recollection days and social gatherings for the priest alumni at the seminary.[4]

The Darlington Institute for Theological and Pastoral Renewal, a program of mini-sabbaticals for priests, brought many alumni back to the seminary. However, enrollment never was high and it was reduced from a semi-annual to an annual program in 1977.[5]

In its reports to the office of research and planning, the seminary emphasized the use of its facilities. This not only indicated its involvement in the life of the archdiocese, but produced income that helped bridge the gap between the archdiocesan subsidy and the actual operating budget. In one year, 1976–77, 188 activities, attended by over 10,000 people, were held at Darlington.

Ciuba emphasized to the critics of the seminary's "isolation" that these persons covered the entire spectrum of ethnic, social, and economic life in the archdiocese. He specifically noted that of 50 parish groups using the seminary's facilities, more than half were from inner-city parishes. Among the activities were workshops, retreats, and days of recollection. The Darlington Institute for Continuing Education (DICE) alone drew 350 attendees.[6] In the 1978–79 school year, the number of persons using Darlington's facilities would more than double to over 21,000.[7]

The seminary welcomed and sought press attention. On Sunday, November 24, 1974, the New York *Daily News* published a multi-page article, "Sign of Times: Few Called, Fewer Chosen." Although the report was fair and balanced, it did not please all of the seminary's constituents, especially those who yearned for the seminary life of the past. It informed readers that things clearly had changed.

> A recent visitor to Darlington found some seminarians with long hair, beards and mustaches and some with short hair and clean shaven faces. Some had their rooms heavily decorated and some filled them only with essentials. Some had cars, televisions and stereos. Some were outspoken and some introspective.[8]

Ciuba told the reporter:

> It's very hard to draw up a profile of a seminarian. In days gone by, I guess you can say that most of them were All-American boys. But today they represent a real cross-section of society. We have men who are robust athletes; we have men who are soft and sensitive; we have men who are given to the arts; we have men who need self-affirmation, and we have men who are poised and developed. The men, I suppose, are just a reflection of all men in their age of society.[9]

Monsignor O'Brien used the opportunity of an interview in the *Record* to emphasize the wide influence of the seminary faculty and its activities. After reviewing the seminary's programs for an article headlined "Seminary Serves 6,000," O'Brien stated that "we are not only a theological and spiritual center where people can come; our faculty also reaches out into almost every area and parish. Our priests not only celebrate mass in parishes over the weekend, but they give lectures, serve as consultants or retreat masters. What happens here goes out in concentric circles, affecting thousands. These statistics are impossible to compile."[10]

The archdiocesan newspaper, the *Advocate,* offered many articles on the seminary, and highlighted the new academic programs for lay students in the article "Darlington's Open Door: Men and women of all ages seek degrees at seminary."[11]

Fund-raising

In 1978, the seminary established Cornerstone, a group of lay men and women who raised funds through a variety of efforts much like those in parishes: book sales, bake sales, garage sales, a "Treasures from the Darlington Attic" sale, and other activities. A garage sale netted over $4,500,[12] and, in its first year, Cornerstone raised almost $8,000.[13]

The same year, the board of trustees, under the direction of George Keenan, established the Darlington Fund, an annual drive to raise money to offset the archdiocesan subsidy. In its first year, it raised $51,000.[14]

The seminary applied for and received a $50,000 grant from the Lilly Endowment for trustee development and to establish a development office. It was necessary to give the office a different name, the office of "planning and resources," so as not to conflict with the archdiocesan offices of "research and planning" and of "development."

This legerdemain was necessary given the continual turf wars between the archdiocesan offices and what were considered independent seminary activities.[15] Ciuba jokingly referred to the seminary development office as "a name used intra house but avoided in all publicity and fundraising."[16] Ciuba kept Gerety informed of all these activities.[17]

Planning

In 1977, the seminary embarked on an ambitious planning program under the aegis of the Center for Applied Research in the Apostolate (CARA). The program was directed by Father Cassian Yuhaus, C.P.

CARA also provided a study of the archdiocese that confirmed the seminary's direction for developing, in Gerety's words, "a broad approach to ministry rather than just priestly ministry." Gerety wished to move "on all fronts to coordinate the various areas of the apostolate" through a formation for ministry task force that dealt with the seminary, permanent diaconate, lay ministry, and other forms of ministry.[18]

It was a daunting task but Ciuba wanted to formulate goals and objectives that would closely be coordinated with the archdiocese's office of research and planning that was in the process of refining the archdiocese's mission statement.

Faculty

In 1976, Reverend Stanley J. Adamczyk, left the faculty after 26 years of service. Monsignor Walter G. Jarvais retired as spiritual director but continued to live at Darlington, remaining very active and a sought-after counselor, confessor, and preacher. The legendary Monsignor Jarvais died at age 98 in 2003. Renowned as a saintly priest, he had a keen wit. At a convocation of archdiocesan priests, he remarked, "I've run into several priests I thought were dead."[19]

In spite of financial and other crises, the faculty continued to be renewed and the seminary rejoiced to receive five-year accreditation from the Middle States Association and the Association of Theological Schools in 1977. The previous year Reverend Joseph Kukura returned from studies to teach moral theology and Reverend Arthur Serratelli returned to teach scripture, having obtained both the S.T.D. and S.S.L. degrees. That summer, Reverend Robert J. Wister was assigned to the seminary and left for Rome for doctoral studies in Church history.[20] In 1977, Father Leo Farley and Father Philip Morris left the seminary for pastoral work. Father Frank Maione left to become vicar for the Hispanic apostolate and was succeeded by Reverend Joseph P. Masiello. Father George Keating resigned as spiritual director and entered the hospital apostolate.[21] Keating was replaced as spiritual director by Reverend Richard M. Liddy. Added to the faculty was Reverend John Kakolewski, who was assigned to begin studies in spiritual theology.

In 1978, the first full-time woman faculty member was appointed when Sister Agnes Mallner, O.S.U., was named to serve as a spiritual director and to teach spiritual theology.[22] Sister Agnes, an Ursuline nun, had served as a missionary in Venezuela and held an M.Div. from Weston School of Theology. [23]

In 1980, Reverend Richard Liddy left Darlington to become spiritual director of the North American College in Rome. He was succeeded by Reverend George Reilly. At the same time, Reverend Michael Alliegro, of the Trenton diocese, was named director of pastoral theology programs.[24]

Seminarian Finances

Priests recently ordained began to experience serious financial difficulties. The archdiocese had ended its policy of financing their education through an insurance program taken out after ordination. They were expected to pay their own tuition or take out government loans. The payments on the loans were extremely burdensome and much higher than the insurance premiums.

The finance committee of the board of trustees was concerned. There was an element of fairness involved. Other dioceses either assumed the entire cost or assisted their seminarians in other ways. [25] The contrast was not only sharp; it also was damaging. Newark candidates were beginning to look to other dioceses that were more generous.

Realizing that this incipient migration did not augur well for the archdiocese, Archbishop Gerety remarked, "We have to plan how to enable our boys to get out of debt."[26] In 1978, Gerety approved a program through which the archdiocese would subsidize 80 percent of the cost of Newark seminarians and reimburse those who had incurred significant debt in the immediately preceding years.[27]

Ciuba Renewed

In 1979, Father Ciuba's term of office was renewed for three more years. As he began the year, the seminary had 102 seminarian students and 145 lay men and women. The entering candidates that year varied widely in ages—21 to 52—and in background—a widowed deacon with six children, a former seminarian returning after 20 years and a successful career as a speech therapist, the head of an established law firm, a former Salvatorian brother, and five from Seton Hall's divinity school. Six seminarians were Latinos.[28]

Due to pressures of office, Ciuba appointed Father Kukura to serve as executive assistant for development to represent him in areas of development and

Father Feeehan as director of admissions for ordination candidates to give relief in interviewing prospective candidates.[29]

Ciuba presided over a seminary that had embraced a three-fold mission. It was composed of concentric circles: the innermost defined the seminary as a center for the preparation of candidates for the ordained priesthood of the Roman Catholic Church; the next outer circle encompassed the preparation of individuals for other ministries in the Church; and the outer circle embraced the seminary's role as a center for the theological and spiritual enrichment of God's people.[30]

Ciuba continued to be optimistic but realistic as he spoke of "great hope" mingled with "some concern." His concern stemmed from the crisis in vocations to the priesthood and "from the financial uncertainties which beset all theological institutions."[31]

To help address the financial issues, the board of trustees established a task force to study space utilization and energy conservation, as Archbishop Gerety had suggested. They further endorsed a plan to put 300 acres of seminary property on the market, reserving more than 100 acres surrounding the seminary buildings.[32]

Finances Lead to New Options

In 1980, the financial situation continued to be alarming, to say the least. The finance committee of the trustees appointed a task force to address a two-fold question: "How can the seminary's mission be conducted in the most economically efficient manner at Darlington?" and "Where can the seminary's mission be conducted in the most economically efficient manner?"[33] A preliminary report was set for March 31, 1981. Why did the board move in this direction at this time?

CARA, financed by the Lilly Endowment, conducted a national study of seminary finances and provided the trustees with a report specifically focused on Darlington, its mission, and its finances. The CARA report studied Darlington's enrollment and finances, its revenues and its operating costs, the amount of the annual archdiocesan subsidy, its reliability in the future, and the income derived from the use of seminary facilities. The trustees concluded that a further study should be undertaken to determine the best way to operate the seminary at an acceptable cost while accomplishing its stated mission.

Leonard Miraglia, the chairman of the board's finance committee, remarked that it was clear: "We cannot go on the way we are." Father Ciuba recognized the situation as very serious, noting that the national seminary situation was not positive and Darlington's was "not bright . . . even with forward steps being made by development and board of trustees." Trustee David Toomey noted that the seminary was not a self-supporting organization, since it received 50 percent of its funds from the archdiocese. He concluded, "It is important firstly, to determine a more economic way that the mission of the seminary can be executed here. Secondly, where else can the same mission be executed."[34]

Archbishop Gerety emphasized that the board must examine "exactly what type of facility we want to have given the present situation in the church. You do need some sort of academic and spiritual location . . . however, unless we examine all of these things it is difficult to justify the subsidy with the archdiocese. The national report says seminaries have to be changed. We have to do it in a very positive spirit, and have one of the best faculties."[35]

Gerety also rejected any idea of regionalization. He was concerned with the overload of the faculty with the many new initiatives Darlington had created over the previous decade and called for a focus on priestly formation and lay ministerial formation.

Trustee Bishop Frank Rodimer of Paterson cut to the chase when he said, "You can't ask question one without asking question two." In other words, "Should the seminary remain at Darlington?"[36]

Chapter Forty-four

Affiliation with Seton Hall Emerges

The meeting of the trustees' corporate membership on May 19, 1981, could not be described as serene. The task force had recommended that the seminary contract its operations into Walsh Hall, closing O'Connor Hall (formerly the Crocker Mansion) and that it embark on a series of energy-saving initiatives. Father Petillo, the archdiocesan co-chancellor for administration, informed the board that the contraction of the seminary into Walsh Hall as recommended by the task force was acceptable, but the cost must come from the current budget.

Trustee Leonard Miraglia was very annoyed that the archbishop had not formally replied to the task force report submitted at the end of March. Bishop Francis defended the archbishop's lack of response as due to the pressure of work, but Miraglia countered that there was much pressure on the task force members to complete the report in the allotted time. He further said that the absence of a response gave rise to suspicions that matters regarding the seminary buildings and property may be moving ahead without consultation with the board of trustees. A response came two days later, simply affirming Petillo's remarks.

For the first time, the possibility of affiliation with Seton Hall was raised. When George Keenan noted that affiliation had not been brought into the discussion heretofore, Ciuba admitted that he had conducted some informal conversations with Dr. D'Alessio, the president of Seton Hall, on the possibility but nothing substantive resulted.[1]

When the full board met on June 1, 1981, the gathering was even less tranquil. Gerety surprised the trustees by showing them a letter he had received that day from Ramapo College offering to purchase the seminary buildings and 75 acres of seminary property. He asked what the seminary would do if the archdiocese sold the property on which the seminary buildings rested. He then raised the possibility of the seminary becoming the graduate school of theology of Seton Hall University and said that the possibility merited consideration.

Gerety went on to say that the advantages to the university were clear, for it would acquire a recognized and respected school of graduate theology and a distinguished faculty. The seminary could be reestablished as a house of formation on the model of the North American College in Rome. He told the board to consider what steps should be taken, given the possibility of affiliation with Seton Hall University. He also indicated that the board should take minimal steps toward implementation of the task force report until it had given serious consideration to this new possibility.[2]

Miraglia raised several questions, specifically whether there would be any savings resulting from an affiliation with Seton Hall. He noted that no one had studied how much operating costs would be under this new proposal when compared with the operating costs projected in the recently completed task force report.

For Archbishop Gerety the controlling question was the advantages and disadvantages of affiliation. The archbishop clearly believed that Immaculate Conception Seminary and Seton Hall University should affiliate, whether the seminary moved or stayed at its present location. Affiliation, he said, would strengthen the university, in particular its Catholicity, about which he was very concerned, and he directed Ciuba to discuss affiliation procedures with the president of the university.

The feasibility of a move to the overcrowded South Orange campus was questioned by several trustees. Sister Patricia Aidan wondered whether Seton Hall University was financially sound and whether it would be in the future. Gerety answered that steps were being taken to improve the university's financial situation. He also suggested that the seminary's affiliation with the university could lead to mutual benefits not easily discerned at the present moment.

David Toomey, clearly unhappy with this new turn of events, was concerned that the discussion on affiliation had indicated only the benefits to the university and the benefit of the sale price to the archdiocese. He wished to know how the seminary would benefit from affiliation.

Gerety summed up his views: "Unless seminaries have a support system they will just disappear. If we must move, I think we should affiliate. One of the great concerns in this archdiocese is Seton Hall University. There is grave concern regarding Catholicity. I don't think that affiliation is that difficult. CARA says that if a seminary of this nature continues to be free standing, and if it does not regionalize or become associated with stronger institutions, it would be locked up."[3]

Survival of the Mission

Miraglia felt that a study should be made, with the seminary's mission in mind, to ascertain the benefits of affiliation. He reiterated that affiliation was not a guarantee of reduced costs.

Gerety emphasized that the seminary's mission establishes levels of priority, the first being preparation of candidates for priesthood. He felt that a university setting would permit this to be done much more effectively and would permit the other facets of the seminary's mission to be continued as well. He added that Seton Hall planned to purchase land that would permit this expansion.

Bishop Francis stated that he had never been comfortable with the seminary's essential statement. He said that the basic mission was training for priesthood and that he did not believe that the training of any but priesthood candidates should be part of the seminary's mission.

Sister Patricia Aidan thought that location was important and that the board always maintained the necessity of preparing candidates for other ministries: "If we just talk about priestly formation we have countless alternatives and it would be much cheaper" to relocate "in the inner city."[4]

Miraglia interjected that all this had been discussed when the board determined the seminary's essential mission statement, and any change now would require a change in the mission statement. He said that the board felt that preparation for lay ministry was important, wanted it continued, and felt what was being done at Darlington in this area was significant. Archbishop Gerety said that affiliation with Seton Hall would permit these efforts to continue.

Toomey asked that the archbishop be frank with the board: "You have the key to the place and the check book in the other pocket; we need you to be open and candid."[5] The archbishop assured the board that the only firm contact the archdiocese had was the letter he received that day from Ramapo College. In the end, Ciuba was empowered by the board to open discussions with the university.

The Trustees Are Angry

David Toomey made clear that the task force question regarding cost-effective operation had been answered, and the mission of the seminary could be conducted efficiently without affiliation. In his opinion, the seminary was a better seminary than the university was a university. Bishop Dougherty quietly remarked that the six schools of the university were of unequal quality. Bishop Francis then declared that the question was whether the seminary could survive without the university. The tension was palpable.

At this point, Archbishop Gerety left the meeting. Ciuba, blindsided and annoyed, told the trustees that he had no idea the archbishop was going to present the Ramapo College offer or bring up possible affiliation with Seton Hall. Sister Patricia was quite irritated. She declared that the situation violated justice to the seminary and its constituencies. She was angry that the board had not been given all the facts, and wondered how much input and influence the board could have. Monsignor Kenneth Lasch, a priest of the diocese of Paterson, opined that there were two agendas in play and a hidden planning cycle operating. Frustrated, he asked how the board could get a sense of direction if the archbishop did not make the members privy to the information it needed.

Bishop Dougherty, trying to calm the waters, suggested that, in view of the confused situation, the board should hold all things in abeyance. Monsignor Lasch concluded that, prior to any decision by the board of trustees, the exploratory talks with the university must determine whether the seminary's essential mission would be maintained if affiliation occured. Only then could the board make a decision.

Mr. Miraglia said the task force report, if implemented, could result in $200,000 in savings. Bishop Francis then stirred the waters, commenting that he felt other economies could be effected by a more careful sense of stewardship. Miraglia replied that frugality had been employed, and Monsignor O'Brien angrily commented that criticism of the seminary's stewardship in this matter was unwarranted. Monsignor Ciuba entered a demurrer in a similar vein.

In the end, the board decided to address the energy conservation measures of the task force report immediately and leave the second part of the proposal, the move to Walsh Hall, to a later date.

Events Move Rapidly

Ciuba and D'Alessio met with officials of the Catholic University of America to discuss the arrangements between the theological school and the university in Washington. Both recognized that it was necessary to produce a clearly defined and specified contractual relationship between the seminary and the university. Tentatively, they determined on a facility for 120 students on or near the Seton Hall campus.[6]

The board was not pleased with the fast pace of events and decisions. Miraglia made his feelings clear: "As a trustee I feel an obligation to review and to be sure that the mission of the seminary be maintained. If something like this is to be decided by the archbishop, he really doesn't need a board." Bishop Francis tried to cool him down: "I think the leadership [Archbishop Gerety] says, 'I want to see this done—now help me to do this.'" Admitting that there would be "more advantages to Seton Hall at the beginning," Miraglia, however, was convinced that "for the seminary it was a matter of survival."[7]

On September 28, 1981, Gerety met with the seminary faculty and informed them of the plans for affiliation with Seton Hall. The same day he announced to the trustees that he had received two serious offers for the property, but had informed the prospective buyers that he required a two-year wait before they could take ownership. He then spoke of affiliating the seminary with Seton Hall University. He said that the archdiocese was the umbrella under which the university, the College Seminary, and the seminary at Darlington all rested. He reiterated his statement that he did not want to see the seminary destroyed and his conviction that it would disappear unless it affiliated with Seton Hall.

> It has been previously mentioned if the archbishop
> would only be frank. What further can I do to be frank?
> I have continually said I do not want to destroy the
> seminary and I believe it will be destroyed if we do
> not affiliate. . . . We are dreaming if we think we can
> continue this seminary the way it is being done. . . .
> This seminary is worth millions of dollars. The fact
> of the matter is that the archdiocese had a tremendous
> argument with banks. On January 1, 1984, I have to face
> the banks again. We have been supporting this seminary
> over $600,000 a year. This cannot go on. A couple of
> years ago I served notice that the large subsidy has to
> come to an end. . . . The decision to sell is not within
> the purview of the board. The archdiocese owns it.
> The property is valued at millions of dollars.[8]

Monsignor Ciuba reported that, on the basis of his discussions at Catholic University, he believed that the university would be greatly strengthened by the affiliation of the seminary with its prestigious theological faculty. The affiliation would also bolster the university's Catholic identity. From the seminary's standpoint the affiliation would bring advantages such as access to major library resources and interaction with the other schools and colleges on the university campus. This would widen the dimensions of the school of theology and give it an increased ability to attract scholars.

Ciuba also believed that the financial dimension of affiliation also must be recognized. He noted that the CARA/Lilly fiscal study bore witness to the fact that unless seminaries regionalized or amalgamated, they could not survive, even with increased enrollment. He was now convinced that unless the seminary moved, the years ahead would be very difficult, if not impossible. Ciuba found D'Alessio to be cordial and easy to deal with and described the initial meetings as very positive. He admitted that a move from Darlington, or even a move to Walsh Hall, would circumscribe the seminary's mission to some extent. However, the third facet of the seminary's mission, a spiritual center for theological and pastoral renewal, could be pursued in collaboration with the university.

Gerety mentioned that Seton Hall needed more land and the seminary site was yet to be determined. He admitted that "many of these things have been happening so fast that a lot of these details have not been straightened out."[9]

This clearly was the feeling of the board as well. In response to Miraglia's intervention that the seminary's identity and mission must be maintained and strengthened, Gerety responded, "I would never want the seminary to become just a part of Seton Hall University."[10]

After long discussions of the possibility of affiliation, of the value of affiliation to each institution, and of the need to preserve the seminary's identity and mission, the board on motion of Monsignor Hogan, seconded by Bishop Dougherty, unanimously resolved to pursue affiliation with Seton Hall University.

Ciuba suggested an affiliation committee be composed of three seminary representatives, three Seton Hall representatives, and one representative of the archdiocese. The committee would report to the board at its meeting on January 25, 1982. Hogan summed up the feelings of many of the board: "I don't think that we have come to a decision that this is a good idea. I don't think we have any other option."[11]

Chapter Forty-five

A Joint Committee

On October 1, 1981, Archbishop Gerety established a joint committee
to study affiliation of Immaculate Conception Seminary and Seton Hall University.
Monsignor Ciuba, Mr. Keenan, and Father Francis DeDomenico, academic dean,
represented the seminary. Mr. Daniel O'Brien, co-chancellor of the archdiocese, was
the archdiocesan representative on the committee and served as its chairman. Seton
Hall's president, Dr. D'Alessio; the vice president for planning, Dr. Nicolas DeProspo;
and Brother Leo Ryan, C.S.V., of the board of regents represented the university.

The joint committee met three times, on October 19 and November 9,
1981, and on January 11, 1982. It sent representatives to visit seminaries affiliated
with universities. They also visited several potential sites for the seminary. In addition
the committee brought in as consultants Monsignor William Baumgaertner of the
seminary department of the National Catholic Educational Association and Reverend
Ronald Anderson of the National Conference of Catholic Bishops.

Although public statements always spoke of cordiality and occasionally
"spirited" discussions, these meetings underlined differences that would cause great
difficulty in the future. Dr. D'Alessio wanted a clear "distinction between the academic
mission of the school of theology and the formational mission of the 'seminary.'"
Stating that the term "rector" was obsolete, he also demanded that both "the school
of theology and the formational program . . . be under the auspices and jurisdiction of
the president of the university."[1] Eventually conceding on the title, he objected to the
chief officer of the seminary reporting to anyone outside the university structure, in
other words, to the archbishop. He was concerned about "priests running to another
authority to solve their problems."[2] Throughout the meetings, he continued to emphasize
that the "seminary must become an indistinguishable part of the university."[3]

Another issue that caused much "spirited discussion" was the ownership of the seminary facility. It was to be paid for with archdiocesan funds, but the university demanded that it be owned by the university. Ciuba advocated archdiocesan ownership so that the archbishop's jurisdiction would be clear and the identity and integrity of the seminary more easily maintained.[4] If ownership was not vested in the university, D'Alessio threatened to suspend all discussions of affiliation. The archdiocese agreed to university ownership of the seminary facility.[5]

Finances were discussed but not clearly resolved, leaving a confusing situation that would vex both seminary and university for decades. The status of the faculty was another question not resolved in these discussions. Ciuba emphasized the necessity of some faculty having both academic and formational roles, and the professional status of those who had entirely formational responsibilities.[6] Eventually, the faculty would receive non-tenure appointments,[7] but that would change shortly after the seminary moved to the campus and provoke much dissension. The committee reached the consensus that affiliation of the seminary and university was feasible and advisable.

The committee agreed in principle to recommend affiliation and appointed a sub-committee to consider the format of that affiliation. During the meetings, Baumgaertner emphasized that in professional theological education, the academic and formational programs must be integrated into a coherent whole. He affirmed the necessity of one person being accountable for both the academic and formational aspects of the program and of professional status being granted to formation personnel.[8]

Although disagreements remained, both Ciuba and D'Alessio reported to Gerety that affiliation was feasible and advisable, and that the relocation of the seminary should be on or near the Seton Hall campus.[9]

Decision to Move

The seminary trustees were under tremendous pressure to move swiftly. The affiliation negotiations were in process. There were several offers for the Darlington property and the banks had agreed that $3 million could be withheld by the archdiocese to finance relocation. These early offers for the property came to naught.

Daniel O'Brien, co-chancellor of the archdiocese, informed the Seton Hall board of regents of the possibility of affiliation on December 10, 1981, and the regents responded positively. Several of the regents, including the influential John Culligan, insisted that the seminary be located on campus, not at a satellite location.

At the executive committee of the seminary board, meeting on December 15, 1981, trustees complained that the board was treated like a "stepchild" and that they were not "taken seriously." In order to ensure board approval of affiliation, they urged that the full board be given all the facts before the executive committee recommended approval of affiliation to the full board.[10]

Father Petillo, attending an executive committee a week later, asked the executive committee to set a target date of September 1, 1982, for affiliation.[11]

Vote to Affiliate

When the full board of trustees met on December 21, 1981, the trustees reacted positively to the proposed affiliation. However, there were concerns. Bishop Rodimer continued to be anxious about priestly formation on the campus. Leonard Miraglia emphasized "the proposed affiliation should insure the seminary's continued growth, not merely the continuing existence of the seminary." He also demanded that the entire affiliation should be spelled out and committed to writing before any formal agreement.[12] Unfortunately, this did not occur.

Agreement on numerous serious issues still had not been reached. The idea at the initial stage was for the seminary to continue at Seton Hall as a house of formation. The school of theology would be integrated into Seton Hall University in some as yet undetermined manner. However, Baumbaertner's insistence that one person be accountable for both the academic and formational aspects of the program soon moved discussions in another direction.

Location also was still to be decided. Although there had been some tentative efforts to find a site similar to the Darlington campus near the university, this had not been pursued. The trustees favored an on-campus location, as did the Seton Hall regents. Sister Patricia Aiden believed such a location would "get the seminarians in touch with the real world."[13]

Archbishop Gerety made it clear that the affiliation and relocation, although it would bring financial benefits, was dictated by "more significant academic and pastoral considerations."[14] He expounded on this theme, reiterating his concern about the Catholic character of Seton Hall.

> I don't see how it will be possible for the archdiocese
> to furnish a seminary faculty by itself ten years from
> now. . . . My concern is about the Catholicity of
> Seton Hall University. It seems to me that to have the
> seminary, with the scholars that are now on the faculty,
> immediately puts us in a position to have influence
> on the university scene.[15]

He saw the seminary presence as a catalyst for "attracting distinguished scholars, bringing new theological offerings to the university students, influencing the entire university scene, and contributing to the Catholicity of the university." He also noted that the bishop regents, when told of the affiliation proposal, seemed interested, thereby raising hopes of increased seminary enrollment.[16] This was a vain hope.

The trustees voted that the affiliation of Immaculate Conception Seminary and Seton Hall University at a site on or near the university campus be pursued.[17]

Tensions Beneath the Surface

Now that affiliation was decided, the details had to be worked out. As in all things, "the devil is in the details." It was no different for the seminary and the university. Ciuba was positive, feeling at these early stages that "the university has given us much more than we anticipated." D'Alessio was not as upbeat, and accused DeProspo of "selling out to the seminary." One of DeProspo's crimes was that he had shared revised drafts of the affiliation models with the archdiocesan representative against D'Alessio's orders.[18]

The university made it clear that it didn't "want anything to do with a house of formation," but the structure of the school of theology was still a matter of contention. The trustees were concerned about the relation of the rector to the school of theology. Recalling that Monsignor Baumgaertner said it was essential that the institution have one head, not two, the trustees were adamant that one person hold the offices of rector and dean. On the other hand, Bishop Francis' main concern was that "the academic integrity of the university be protected."[19]

Some trustees were concerned that the seminary, especially when viewed as a place of priestly formation, had to be different from other colleges of the university. Others were aware that as a school of theology the seminary would have to abide by academic requirements proper to all graduate schools on campus. The challenge was to fit the seminary into the university structure without doing violence to the university structure and without weakening the identity and integrity of the seminary as a place of preparation of men for the priesthood and of other ministries in the Church.

When the board met on January 25, 1982, the committee on affiliation finally had decided that the seminary's rector would retain responsibility for all formational and academic aspects of the seminary program. In academic and administrative matters he would be dean and would have the same responsibilities as other deans within the university structure.

The board discussed possibilities of collaboration with the university's department of religious studies, but Gerety made it clear that all formal discussion of working collaboratively with the university undergraduate departments would wait until the affiliation and the relocation were completed.

Bishop Rodimer reiterated his concern that the crowded university campus could not provide a site that would guarantee the peace, quiet, and prayer needed for a house of formation.[20] Cutting to the bone, Rodimer told the trustees he could not "understand exactly how this will remain a seminary and still be part of the university."[21]

Sister Patricia Aiden was not very worried about losing a quiet ambience. Her congregation was "moving in the opposite direction—for noisy contemplation.

That is the thrust of congregations in general."[22] She believed that a person in a busy environment can learn to create the desired interior environment, and that the seminarians' training must involve life situations and a challenge to move into contemplative experiences.

Archbishop Gerety did not envision the seminarians being in isolation on campus, but he believed that in their lives there should be some silence, some place apart. He summed up, stating, "My feeling is that we have to make sure that we are transferring Immaculate Conception Seminary over to Seton Hall University and keeping it substantially as it is."[23] His view was quite different from Dr. D'Alessio's view of the matter.

Moving Along, Full Speed Ahead!

Discussions continued. There were proposals for offering joint programs with the department of Judaeo-Christian studies, creating consortia relations with Drew and Princeton seminaries, and creating an institute for theological studies. These all were put aside so that the committee drafting a model for affiliation could focus on the more immediate issues.[24]

A model for affiliation was presented to the executive committee of the trustees on April 23, 1982,[25] and to the full board three days later. According to the model, the seminary would continue to prepare candidates for the priesthood and prepare men and women for other ministries in the Church. Its integrity as a seminary would be maintained, and the rector would be a university dean. It would offer the same three degree programs it was licensed to grant. The university would own the seminary building. Finally, the name of the seminary was to be "Darlington Seminary of the Immaculate Conception Graduate School of Theology and Pastoral Ministry of Seton Hall University."[26] No one thought how such a cumbersome title would fit on letterhead. In 1986, the name was simplified to "Immaculate Conception Seminary School of Theology."[27]

At this late stage, to everyone's surprise, Archbishop Gerety told the trustees he had not yet seen the affiliation document. This added to David Toomey's worries. "I, for one, am seriously troubled by this proposal. There is really not an affiliation but an absorption into Seton Hall. It seems to me there is no reason why the seminary as an institution could not be transferred intact. I think that this proposal has unraveled the fiber of the seminary."[28] Ciuba's comments that the agreement would be subject to annual review and formal review after the third year failed to mollify him.

The board members discussed the question at some length and with somewhat divergent views on the viability and/or wisdom of the affiliation document as submitted. Eventually it was agreed that the meeting of June 9 would be used to discuss the proposal submitted by the joint affiliation committee.

Before the meeting closed, at Archbishop Gerety's motion, the board voted to extend Monsignor Ciuba's term (about to expire) through the transition with a vote of wholehearted confidence in his stewardship.[29] A year earlier, Ciuba alerted Gerety that he was beginning the last year of his eight-year term as rector. In what may have been a Freudian slip, he wrote to Gerety that he was beginning his "eighty" year as rector, and asked to resign in September 1982.[30] He would remain as rector for several more years.

The Board Weighs In

Board members submitted written observations over the next few weeks. They were concerned about details and ambiguities in the document. Bishop Dougherty, former president of Seton Hall, made it clear that he preferred autonomy for the rector/dean and asked for a careful spelling out of that relationship. The bishop also was troubled about a lay vice president for academic affairs overseeing a "graduate program of *theological* education." He equally was anxious about the preponderance of lay persons on the proposed seminary board and their lack of familiarity with "theological education, Roman statements on priestly formation, and bishops' guidelines."[31]

Leonard Miraglia believed that it was essential for the seminary to "maintain its separate identity and integrity." In his opinion, the model for affiliation did "not maintain the identity and integrity of Immaculate Conception Seminary" and he refused to approve it unless changes were made. He suggested that the seminary move to the proposed site on Seton Hall's campus "while maintaining its current corporate and operating structure."[32]

David Toomey simply stated that he "respectfully decline[d] to support the model that has been presented to the board," and instead suggested a loose "alliance" with Seton Hall.[33]

Monsignor Hogan was not concerned, writing that he did not "think that the seminary will lose its identity and integrity unless the seminary administration gives them away in the future."[34]

The consensus of the seminary faculty was that, in general, the model was a realistic basis for affiliation. However, they were concerned that in some areas the language of the document was not precise and did not reflect the requirements either of the National Council of Catholic Bishops' *Program of Priestly Formation* or of ecclesiastical law. In particular, they noted that there was a reference to the university's president being consulted concerning the spiritual and formational administration of the seminary. It was, in their opinion, more than "debatable that the university president can be given this role." The faculty also expressed dismay at the phrase "optimum utilization" referring to the seminary facility. They emphasized that use of the facility for undergraduate students must be ruled out completely.[35]

Revisions were made to the April draft in preparation for the June 9, 1982, trustees meeting. This draft received serious criticisms as well. David Toomey repeated his concerns, emphasizing that the draft weakened the authority of the ordinary, and that it did not preserve the integrity or the separate identity of the seminary.[36]

Leonard Miraglia echoed Toomey and was especially concerned about university authority over formation, and the dilution of the authority of the board in the new structure. He criticized the document as too vague and asked, "Is this affiliation document specific enough since the leadership of the diocese, Seton Hall, and the seminary could change at any time?"[37]

When the June 9, 1982, trustees meeting opened, Archbishop Gerety announced that the affiliation document had been examined and unanimously approved by the board of regents of Seton Hall University.

The seminary board continued to be concerned with lines of authority in the document. George Keenan suggested that the board accept the affiliation document submitted by the committee. Toomey remained concerned about the integration of the seminary into the Seton Hall structure and preferred it remain intact.

Gerety replied that there was provision for revision within the document: "I want to assure you that if there are any revisions here they can be taken care of. If I ask for it they will do it."[38] Finally, Keenan suggested that the board approve the document as submitted, with the understanding that the university board of regents would examine the areas of concern and clarify the lines of authority as deemed necessary. The board approved the document of affiliation on June 9, 1982.[39]

Gerety was good to his word. When the trustees met for their final meeting on September 22, all the changes requested had been made.[40]

The Rector's Summary

Ciuba summarized the reaction to the affiliation in his report of June 24, 1982.

> The spirit in the seminary is good. It survived the initial shock and subsequent anxieties following the announcement of the renewed affiliation with Seton Hall University and of the anticipated transfer of site.
>
> The news was received by bishops and vocation directors with varying degrees of concern. There may be some erosion of support for the seminary from the suffragan sees.
>
> Alumni reaction to the anticipated change was generally favorable and supportive. Obviously there was a touch of sadness and nostalgia, but the prevailing view was that it was a wise and necessary move which would benefit both seminary and university.
>
> It is significant that the priest alumni supported the Darlington Fund in greater numbers than in any of the preceding years.

The New Jersey bishops were open to the affiliation, at least on the surface. However, their true feelings and concerns became clear in the summer of 1982, when the other four dioceses of New Jersey sent only two seminarians to Darlington.[41]

Life Goes On

Indeed, life went on. Ciuba reported that ATS had granted the seminary 10-year accreditation, and the seminary was waiting for final action by Middle States. Looking to the future, he announced that Reverend Thomas Guarino was appointed to the faculty effective July 1, 1982, and Reverend Robert Harahan would be in residence by 1983. On the other hand, Reverend Michael Alliegro resigned to return to the new diocese of Metuchen, New Jersey. Ciuba acknowledged that a decline in overall enrollment seemed inevitable, at least until the transition was completed.[42]

At the trustees meeting on June 28, 1982, Archbishop Gerety asked why the personnel and the offices presently located in O'Connor Hall could not be moved to Walsh Hall, as had been recommended a year earlier. Ciuba responded that the suggested move would not result in any appreciable saving, given the fact that the seminary was to relocate within a relatively short time.

Leonard Miraglia told Archbishop Gerety that a move to Walsh Hall would involve the cost of renovations needed to accommodate the offices and personnel being relocated. David Toomey confirmed that the special task force had determined that the suggested move was not economically feasible in the short run. Gerety said that he wondered how accurate that judgment was. Miraglia, referring to the report, responded that the relocation costs had been indicated, and that the cost of the move would far exceed any savings that could be anticipated by moving. He noted that the major expense of any move to Walsh Hall would stem from the relocation of the library.

The board formally approved the affiliation agreement with one change designed to protect the canonical authority of the archbishop of Newark: "The board of overseers for the seminary would be responsible for overseeing the seminary subject to the authority of the ordinary of the archdiocese of Newark."[43]

Ciuba announced that the goal was to move to Seton Hall by January 1984 at the earliest. Gerety announced that the sale of the property was delayed by disagreement among prospective buyers about the uses to which the property will be put and zoning issues. He added that the banks had agreed that $3 million of the proceeds from the sale of the Darlington property could be put toward the construction of the new seminary building.

The Last Trustees Meeting

The Board of Trustees of Immaculate Conception Seminary met for the last time on September 22, 1982. They approved a budget of almost $1.4 million, including a $616,000 subsidy from the archdiocese. The board then authorized whatever legal steps must be taken to transfer authority from the seminary board of trustees to the Seton Hall board of regents and the new seminary board of overseers. The meeting adjourned. On this day, less than one year after Archbishop Gerety appointed the affiliation committee, the affiliation of Immaculate Conception Seminary and Seton Hall University went into effect.[44]

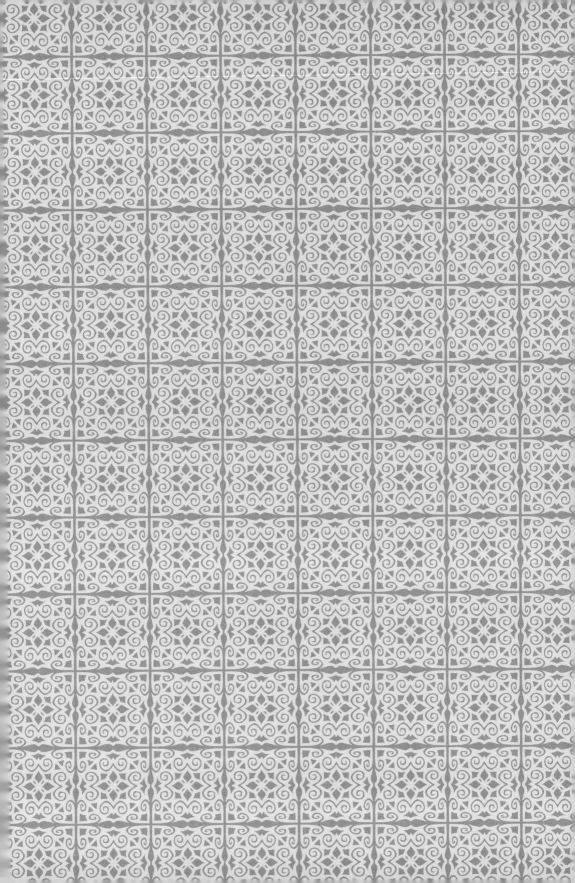

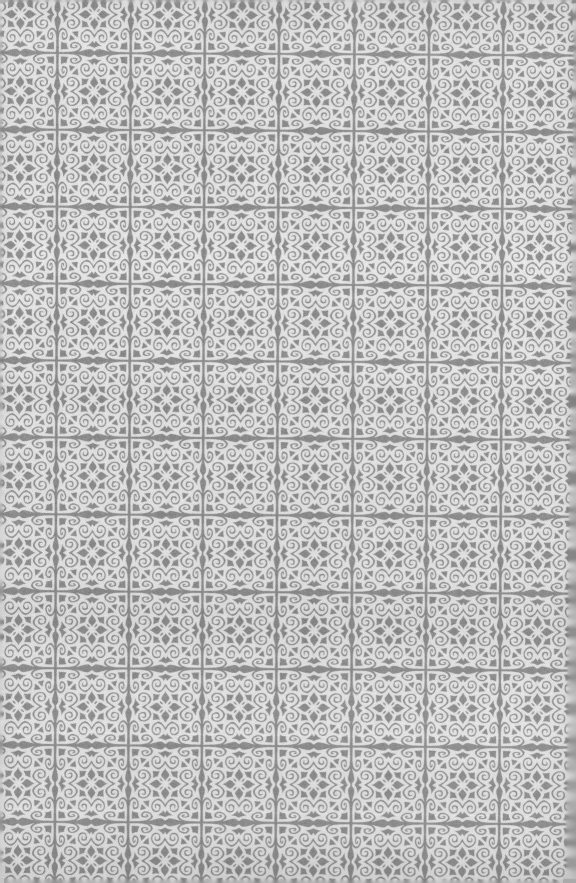

Immaculate Conception Seminary School of Theology,
Seton Hall University

Affiliation and Relocation

1982–2010

Chapter Forty-six

Sale Completed

With affiliation accomplished, the transition from Darlington to South Orange proceeded apace. Rumors abounded that the seminary was closing,[1] forcing Ciuba to issue what were now "boiler plate" statements regarding the affiliation. Gerety met with the seminary faculty to assure them of his support.[2] In a letter to the priests of the archdiocese, Ciuba began, "A word of reassurance! The seminary is not closing nor will it!"[3]

The sale of the seminary property moved along a bumpy road. Several offers did not materialize.[4] Zoning problems[5] also slowed the sale of the property. Meanwhile, on January 4, 1984, the final $14 million of the archdiocesan debt to a consortium of banks was paid.

The sale of the property to Darlington Associates finally was completed on December 23, 1985.[6] Three million of the $8.6 million realized from the sale was assigned to the cost of construction of the new seminary facility. The remaining $5 million of construction costs came from an archdiocesan capital campaign for the purpose.

The more than $5 million remaining from the sale of Darlington was used to establish an endowment to fund retirement of archdiocesan priests.[7] At the time, there was no money in the retirement fund. For years, the priests' pensions had been paid out of current income.

Business as Usual

In 1972, the seminary had reduced the on-campus program of theological studies to six semesters, changed to seven semesters in 1977. In each case, the program had, in addition, a one-year supervised deacon internship. After Archbishop Gerety's *ad limina* visit and submission of his quinquennial report, Cardinal William

Moving Out

In 1983, as the seminary was preparing to move, it enrolled 100 seminarians, resident and non-resident, and 80 non-seminarians, of whom 59 were female. These numbers reflected a small drop in the number of seminarians from a high of 114 in 1977, and a significant drop in non-seminarians from a high of 137 in 1978.[29]

Moving from Darlington after almost 60 years was a mammoth project. It was complicated by the tight financial situation. No money had been allocated for the furnishing and decoration of the new facility at Seton Hall. It was necessary to move desks, chairs, beds, and other furniture from Darlington to South Orange. These furnishings were old and had been designed for the Darlington buildings. Often they did not fit well in the new building, and many were rather worn.

Monsignor Ciuba appointed several committees to oversee the move. They were charged with chapel furnishings, artistic and heritage items, and general furnishings. It was a complex operation. The terms of the sale dictated that items such as stained glass and the chapel organ remain at the site. However, with the permission of the archdiocese and the buyers, chapel statues and some movable chapel furnishings were transferred to South Orange and installed in the new seminary building.

Moving Days

The seminary opened at Darlington for orientation on August 26, 1984. Classes were held from September 6 through September 28. From September 29 through October 12, caravans of moving vans moved the furniture and the library to South Orange. Careful planning ensured that almost everything was delivered to the proper place. Classes resumed, now at Seton Hall, on October 15.

On October 12, Ciuba wrote to Gerety:

> On April 17, 1927, Msgr. Thomas McLaughlin, the rector of the seminary at South Orange, recorded the following in his diary:
> "Took all seminarian registers and documents pertaining to seminary and new seal to Darlington, thus closing seminary at South Orange after 66 years in that spot. May God bless the seminarians and successors in new home."
> As I close this seminary at Darlington, on October 12, 1984, I too am taking all seminarian registers and documents pertaining to the seminary, thus closing the seminary at Mahwah, N.J. after 57 years in that spot. May God bless the seminarians, faculty and staff in our new home on the campus of Seton Hall University.[30]

The construction crews were still working as the materials and the people arrived. The building was complete—almost. The workers would remain for weeks finishing up. The first evening the faculty gathered in their lounge. Monsignor James Turro, always a man of few words, entered. He said, "I am not an angel." No one knew what this meant. Turro was revered as a spiritual director and as an excellent homilist who could compress complex ideas into a few short sentences. Finally, he explained that the designers or the construction workers must have assumed that he was an angel, as the bathroom in his apartment had not been furnished with a toilet. The laughter that followed reduced the tension in the room.

Covering the Walls

No funds were allocated for the decoration of the new building. It was bare. There was not even a cross on the outside to indicate it had a religious function. There was no choice but to use ingenuity, lest the seminarians and faculty live in a totally beige environment. A few items were allowed to be moved from Darlington. A copy of Andrea DelSarto's "*Disputa* on the Trinity" graced a wall in the entry lobby, as did the seminary coat of arms.

The long corridors received some color from a collection of posters a faculty member had brought on his return from Rome. There was no money for framing, but Monsignor Ciuba allowed the sale of a number of inexpensive "commemorative chalices." They were of no artistic value but had silver cups and in the inflated silver market of the day, they brought enough to pay for framing.

Little by little, statues from the Darlington chapel migrated to Seton Hall. The four evangelists graced the entry to the chapel; St. Peter and St. Paul stood guard at the entrance to the administration wing. Other statues found their way to Seton Hall. St. John Vianney and St. Thomas Aquinas eventually were placed in front of the seminary building, St. Francis DeSales alongside the classroom building. Others appeared here and there on the campus.

Making a Home

The seminarians took to their new lodgings with rather good humor, occasionally complaining of problems with the plumbing and incessant hammering as the building was finished. However, they quickly found the local pizzerias and enjoyed the athletic facilities of the campus.

The rector and the faculty did their best to mitigate the strain of the transition. The chapel was not ready for a few weeks, so Mass and common prayer took place in the student lounges. Here the liturgy was celebrated with much less solemnity than usual. At the Halloween and other community celebrations, the seminarians took the opportunity to lampoon their new surroundings and many of the campus personalities with whom they were becoming acquainted. By Christmas, all were settled in.

Dedication

In the presence of 15 bishops and Milton and Rita Lewis, the benefactors after whom the new building was named, Archbishop Pio Laghi, apostolic pro-nuncio, dedicated the new home of Immaculate Conception Seminary on April 10, 1985. At the dedication, Archbishop Gerety remarked that the seminary had returned to the university "because the university is where the action is." He added, "We are in a new age in history, so how could it be that the training of priests has not changed drastically from the style determined four centuries ago?"

Archbishop Laghi praised Gerety's courage in undertaking the construction of the new facility and the relocation of the seminary. "When Archbishop Gerety informed me he was about to make this decision," the papal representative said, "I expected a kind of reaction and letters pouring into my office." This, he added, did not occur.

Monsignor Ciuba, universally praised at the ceremony, told the gathering the dedication was not the celebration of a new residence but a "celebration of a recommitment to priestly formation in a new and rich environment."[31]

The new facility contained 101 seminarian rooms and 15 faculty suites as well as a refectory, two student lounges, and a faculty lounge.

Portents of Impending Difficulties

Although the seminary board of trustees approved the relocation and affiliation, some of them clearly were not enthusiastic. A year after the move to Seton Hall, former trustee George E. Keenan resigned in frustration from the new board of overseers. He felt "no sense of accomplishment" as an overseer and regarded his new role as "totally ineffectual."[32]

Seton Hall was trying to get its financial house in order. Monsignor Petillo, the new executive chancellor, had a proven track record as a financier from his work as co-chancellor for administration in the archdiocese and as chairman of the board of regents of the university. Among the budget constraints he advocated was the elimination of all classes that failed to enroll 12 or more students. Even before the move to South Orange, Ciuba told Petillo that such a policy would severely constrain the seminary, which often had small numbers in some classes.[33]

Such unilateral decisions made without any consultation increased tensions between the seminary and the university. The faculty took great care to keep the serious problems of adjusting to the university from the seminarians, but, of course, the seminarians were aware.

Chapter Forty-seven

Changing of the Guard

After 11 years as president/rector and rector/dean, an exhausted Monsignor Edward Ciuba left the seminary in 1985 for a sabbatical.[1] He needed and deserved a rest.

In his final report as rector to the board of overseers, Ciuba presciently outlined future areas of conflict. He was apprehensive that, in the rush to affiliation and relocation, basic questions remained unanswered. Among them, a foundational issue: "How is the seminary an entity of the university and what makes the seminary distinctive and different from other entities on the university campus?" He was troubled that the university regarded the seminary as just another school.

He summarized his concerns in his concluding statement to the overseers.

> One of the key features of short and long term planning
> will be the issue of seminary integrity on the campus
> of the university. To be true to its nature and to the
> recommendations of the Program for Priestly Formation,
> how does the seminary relate to the university
> administration and to the ordinary of the archdiocese?
>
> The role of the chancellor of the seminary should
> be correctly defined so that all parties concerned will
> understand clearly the proper lines of authority and
> communication between the chancellor, the rector and
> the ordinary of the archdiocese. An initial step in that
> direction should be the re-examination of the document
> of affiliation between the university and the seminary
> which calls for an annual review.

A dialogue between the chancellor and the rector and seminary faculty should also take place. When the role of the chancellor vis-à-vis the seminary is properly defined and agreed upon by the ordinary of the archdiocese, it should be communicated to the rector and faculty so that there is one common understanding had by all. Such a commonly accepted understanding is vital before the Vatican Visitation team comes for the three-day visit in February, 1986.[2]

On July 1, 1985, Father Richard Liddy was appointed as Ciuba's successor. Liddy was born in 1938. Ordained in Rome in December 1963, he was assigned to the seminary upon his return to the United States in June 1964. He returned to Rome the following fall and obtained the doctorate in philosophy from the Gregorian University in 1970. From 1970 to 1980, he served as professor of philosophy and as spiritual director from 1976. In 1980 he returned to Rome as the spiritual director of the North American College until recalled to accept the office of rector/dean.

Other administrative changes followed swiftly. Father DeDomenico accepted a parish assignment and was succeeded as associate dean by Reverend Robert Wister. Father Masiello also left for a parish assignment, leaving the office of vice rector vacant. Reverend James M. Cafone, spiritual director of the College Seminary, was named director of formation and eventually vice rector. Reverend William Harms joined the faculty to oversee a new program in church management.[3] The new administrators quickly discovered that the concerns of the former rector and board of trustees that the affiliation agreement was defective and lacking in important details were quite valid.

During Liddy's tenure, the seminary reflected the changing character of the archdiocese and of the Church in the United States. The seminary also reached out to assist missionary dioceses through scholarships to several seminarians. In 1986, there were 60 seminarians in residence or on deacon internships. Approximately half the seminarians were studying for the archdiocese of Newark. Other dioceses represented were Worcester, Massachusetts; Rochester; Albany; Bridgeport; Camden; Green Bay; Halifax in Nova Scotia; Paterson; Scranton; Trenton; and Wilmington, Delaware. Seven members of religious communities participated in the academic program, coming from the Capuchins, Benedictines, and Vocationists.

The average age of the students was 26. Among them were several older students who had significant life experience in other walks of life. However, there were also a number who entered the seminary immediately after college, a few of them from a college seminary.

Many of the seminarians, although not all, came from traditional Catholic families and had attended Catholic schools and colleges. The seminary had a distinctly international flavor. This was a trend that would continue. Students came from Vietnam, Zaire (Congo-Kinshasa), Haiti, Peru, Bolivia, and Canada. The Latino presence was significant and would continue to grow in the future.[4]

Demotions

Despite public statements that the affiliation was proceeding smoothly, the mood of the faculty quickly turned to wariness and anger. In June 1984, without any previous knowledge, faculty members had received "letters of release" from Archbishop Gerety, and letters of appointment to the seminary from Monsignor Petillo. Even more surprising, these appointments were for three-year terms. They were informed in these letters that letters of appointment to the school of theology would be forthcoming from the chancellor of Seton Hall University. These letters were not forthcoming.

The only indication of an appointment was a vague letter to the rector from the vice president for academic affairs appointing seminary faculty "to the university faculty."[5] At the same time, the faculty verbally was informed of new ranks that would be effective with this appointment. Three faculty members, not one of whom was consulted, were reduced in rank from associate to assistant professor. They were told that their seminary ranks did not conform to the requirements of the Seton Hall faculty guide. These demotions violated normal academic procedures and rights of due process. The seminary faculty legitimately had received their ranks under the terms and criteria of the 1981 seminary faculty guide, and assumed they would be respected in the affiliation.

Despite repeated requests, the Seton Hall administration never gave the professors involved reasons in writing for their reduction in rank. These professors were neither given an opportunity to appeal this decision, nor to file a grievance following normal due process procedures existing at the university.

This action, which initiated the new relationship with the university, contributed to a growing suspicion of the motives of the university administration on the part of the seminary faculty. Monsignor Ciuba protested these actions as "arbitrary" and "needlessly raising bad feelings," but to no avail.[6] The situation only grew worse after Ciuba's departure.

The university held that the seminary faculty guide had lapsed with affiliation. In June 1984, the seminary presented to the chancellor and the vice president for academic affairs a new edition of the seminary faculty guide. It had been prepared at the request of the university administration. It was assumed by the seminary faculty that it would become the school's governing document. It never was officially acknowledged by the university.

On Track or Off Track

The seminary faculty knew that accommodations were necessary in their new situation. The seminary recognized the university's oversight over academic programs and had allowed its licensure to lapse lest it conflict with the Seton Hall charter.

After the seminary faculty were released for three-year, non-tenure-track terms, but never formally assigned to the school of theology faculty, the university shifted gears. It initiated moves to put the faculty on tenure track and place them under the university faculty guide. Those few professors whom the university ranked as associate or full professors automatically would be tenured. Others would go on tenure track. This decision was made unpalatable by the previous reduction in rank of several professors who, after more than the required seven years of teaching, would now go through a tenure process.

This decision to reduce professors in rank came as a surprise to all. In July 1984, Ciuba had been informed of the plan to change the faculty status to tenure, a question that had been debated during the affiliation process. However, Dr. Richard Connors, the vice president of academic affairs, assured him that campus policy was that anyone who held the rank of associate or full professor for three years acquired tenure. In addition, Seton Hall had awarded tenure to assistant professors who had taught continuously for seven years and a "similar accommodation would be made for members of the seminary faculty."[7] This raised the possibility of "grandfathering" senior seminary faculty into tenure.

On November 8, 1985, a few months after Ciuba's departure, at the university administration's request, the affiliation agreement was amended to place the seminary faculty on tenure track.[8]

Why Tenure?

Father David Bossman, O.F.M., who replaced Connors in the new post of university provost in fall 1985, now quickly moved to place the members of the school of theology faculty on tenure track. While, in accord with the affiliation, all faculty members had been appointed to the seminary, academic appointments had to be made separately. Up to this time the only academic appointments made to the school of theology had been those of Father Liddy and Reverend Robert Lorenzo, who never came to the seminary.

Bossman determined to implement a plan to grant tenure to the remaining few who still held the rank of professor or associate professor after the demotions. Those who were assistant professors or had been reduced to the rank of assistant professor would go through the university tenure process, normally six years. However, the provost wanted all to apply for tenure review within two years.

Liddy protested that two years was unfair and violated the university's own procedures. He informed Bossman that "only gradually has it been revealed to me that the administration of the university wants the seminary professors on the tenure track." Liddy believed that the seminary needed a "period of institutional stability with changes that are organic and incremental." Instability would damage the seminary's ability to recruit students. He reminded Bossman that the Middle States had called the affiliation "a merger," suggesting a smaller entity that was "swept into and swamped by a larger one."[9]

In the tenure-track discussions, it became clear to the rector and the faculty that the university administration had an agenda of its own. At best, the administration understood theology simply as religious studies totally divorced from the Church, and wished to pursue policies that, if adopted, would seriously compromise the mission of the seminary. In Liddy's opinion, the only agenda of the university administration was complete control of the seminary.[10]

It was increasingly apparent that there were very deep differences between the university administration and the seminary. Seminary faculty members unanimously affirmed their connection to the archbishop and the local church as essential to their identity. Further, they believed that theology as a discipline is internal to the Church and is, of its nature, related to the ecclesiastical magisterium. As a practical expression of this belief, the faculty contributed significant services to the archdiocese and to the national and universal Church.

The provost made matters worse when he informed the faculty that service to the archdiocese and the wider Church would not be considered as "community service" and was therefore not credited for tenure review. If that was not enough, he also rejected participation in priestly formation as irrelevant to tenure review.

The role of formation was a major point of contention. Formation activities necessarily consumed a large portion of faculty time and energy, requiring course-load reductions. The seminary administration proposed that these activities be considered for tenure purposes as "professional training" analogous to such training in the other professional schools. This proposal was rejected out of hand by university administration, quite often in terms denigrating to the entire concept of priestly formation. Seminary officials responded that, regardless of the university's opinion of formation, it was a central part of their mission and faculty members dedicated a very significant portion of their time and effort to this central task.

As a part of these discussions, the school of theology faculty met with the provost. This only made matters worse. The provost declared that he, and only he, would determine course-load reductions that would allow seminary faculty to take part in formation. He rejected without reading a written proposal made by the faculty to define formation and academic roles. The faculty again asked that service to the Church in various forms be considered within the parameters of "community service." This he again rejected out of hand.

The rector and the faculty tried to inform the administration that the character of the seminary required that most academic faculty members be involved in formation. This, however, would become impossible if formation as well as Church service were to be rejected as irrelevant to the tenure process. The result would be that any academic faculty members who wished to be involved in formation would find it impossible to obtain tenure, due to the increasingly complicated and time-consuming role of priestly formation. Thus, they either would leave formation or be rejected for tenure. The seminary proposal also included, for some faculty members, a completely academic track without formational responsibilities, something the provost wanted.

This meeting further was aggravated by the provost's assertion that the main reason to seek tenure was to "free oneself" so that one could write whatever one pleased, even if in conflict with the Church. He remarked that Catholic universities had escaped from the "Catholic ghetto" and this was the seminary's chance to do the same.[11] The faculty was shocked and viewed the provost's comments with abhorrence. Such statements demonstrated that the university and the seminary had basic differences regarding the relationship of theology and theologians to the Church, and the Catholic character of the university. The seminary faculty members believed that the university administration wanted to impose its diluted definition of Catholicism on the seminary. So much for academic freedom.

The seminary faculty had no objection to the idea of tenure as such. The atmosphere, however, was such that it was not possible to engage in a mutual dialogue on issues or rights. Effectively disenfranchised by the three-year appointments, the entire faculty was at the mercy of the whims of the university administration. After several meetings with Father Wister, the new associate dean, the provost relented on only one issue. He allowed that assistant professors could wait up to six years to apply for tenure, something that was already their right according to university standards, and which had been demanded by Liddy.[12]

Confusion was compounded as the university administration and university faculty negotiated revisions of the university faculty guide. When Wister asked Bossman whether it was the university's intention that the school of theology be a part of this guide, he was informed that "other arrangements" would be made. No details of these "other arrangements" were ever forthcoming. Bossman added that there was no need for school of theology faculty membership on the committee revising the university faculty guide.

In all of these actions, the school of theology faculty members were being subjected to various procedures in which they had no participation. Further, they were being subjected to arbitrary interpretations of guides and policies that did not officially apply to them. Throughout this sorry affair, "university policy" was cited as the determining norm. When university administrators were asked to present a compendium of such policies, the request was ignored. Apparently, these "policies" were whatever was said at the moment. A priest on the university faculty sagely remarked during these disputes, "University policies are written in sand at low tide."

On numerous occasions, the chancellor and the provost made it clear to the associate dean that the goal was the separation of the school of theology from the seminary. The school would be fully integrated into the university. To symbolize this separation, Father Wister twice was asked to move his office from the seminary building. Twice he refused.

The university also asked the seminary to absorb the Judaeo-Christian studies department. The department's deficit budget would put an additional financial burden on the school. The seminary refused to cooperate. The atmosphere had become poisonous.[13]

Chapter Forty-eight

Apostolic Visitation

After tumultuous, often-bitter negotiations, the university prepared to appoint the seminary faculty members to tenure-track positions. However, these appointments were to be linked to the university faculty guide, a guide from the recent revision and ratification of which they had been excluded.[1] The Vatican visitation mandated by Pope John Paul II for all U.S. seminaries was near, and the university wanted to have all in order for the representatives of the Holy See.

The apostolic visitation of the seminary took place February 17–27, 1986. Bishop George Wirz, auxiliary of Madison, Wisconsin, headed the team. The other members were Reverend Cornelius McRae of St. John's Seminary, Boston; Reverend William J. Fay of Mount St. Mary's Seminary, Emmitsburg, Maryland; Reverend Paul Harman, S.J., of the Jesuits' New England province; and Reverend Charles Froehle of St. Paul Seminary, St. Paul, Minnesota.

The visitors were very positive, lauding the spirit of the seminarians and faculty. They noted the academic credentials of the faculty and their many contributions to the archdiocese and to the theological academy. They described the faculty as "not simply academicians but deeply concerned with the overall formation of seminarians." They commended the faculty members for their "availability, fraternity, patience, joy, and industry." The faculty members were definitely available and, in confidential interviews with the visitors, expressed their dissatisfaction with the seminary's relationship with the university.

However, the visitors were uneasy about several matters. Their concerns mirrored the anxieties expressed during the affiliation process by the seminary trustees and administration. Not surprisingly, they focused on the affiliation document, faculty participation in formation, and the tenure situation.

They were unhappy that, while the affiliation document generically asserted the rights of the Church and the ordinary, "the present formulation of the document does not clearly accomplish this goal." They particularly were distressed over the method of appointment of seminary faculty. The visitors recommended that the "archbishop of Newark appoint all faculty . . . upon recommendation of the rector/dean," and that the "office of rector and dean always reside in the same person who is a Roman Catholic priest of the archdiocese of Newark."

Not surprisingly, the visitors addressed the integrity of the seminary formation program. They recommended a review of the faculty's status to guarantee that academic faculty members could participate in priestly formation without jeopardizing their employment in the seminary school of theology.

The visitation team also addressed tenure procedures. The visitors recommended that tenure should never be offered without the recommendation of the rector/dean, that retention of tenure "be subject to the review of the archbishop of Newark," and that the tenure policy should encourage "the real integration of academic study and priestly formation." They criticized the tenure policy as not adequately addressing "the question of promoting excellence in the work of priestly formation," and recommended that it be reviewed "in order to guarantee that the work of priestly formation is seriously promoted."

They specifically urged that since "the time consumed in spiritual direction, counseling, role modeling, informal contact with seminarians, participation in liturgy, and other forms of liturgical prayer, and pastoral work are so crucial to seminary life . . . [these factors] should be serious considerations in any question of rank or tenure."[2]

All such apostolic visitations end with a meeting between the visitation team, the diocesan bishop, and the seminary administration. In this case, university administrators also were present. Monsignor Liddy described the meeting in an eloquent and honest summary.

> My most prominent memory of the "conflict" aspect of those times was the "Showdown at the OK Corral" breakfast where we met with the Vatican Visitation team, Archbishop Gerety, and John Petillo. Gerety began the breakfast by saying: "Bishop [Wirz], we are going to do everything you say! We are going to follow your recommendations to a 'T'!" That breakfast was a turning point for me. I remember telling the seminarians afterwards that I never saw so clearly the power of "the word," that is, meanings expressed in Church documents and shared by others in the Church. Of course, John Petillo tried one last time to have his way—resulting in that traumatic meeting with Archbishop McCarrick, but that was Petillo's last gasp.[3]

After the Visitation

The overseers and regents accordingly revised the affiliation agreement on March 29, 1986. The revised document clearly stated that the rector/dean was to be appointed by the archbishop and the faculty by the rector/dean. The faculty remained on tenure track. The revision also included a phrase requested by the seminary faculty: "All faculty of this seminary and school of theology recognize that the archbishop of Newark is the ultimate interpreter of Roman Catholic doctrine and teaching for this seminary and school of theology."[4]

Yet two months later, Petillo asked Gerety to "release" Fathers Flesey and Coleman for him to appoint to the seminary faculty.[5] Liddy quickly told Petillo that the method of appointment had been changed, as it was "contrary to process recommended by the Vatican visitation and incorporated in the March 29, 1986 revision of the affiliation agreement." Liddy emphasized that "the underlying issue is the canonical autonomy of the seminary vis-à-vis the university and the right of the rector/dean to have direct access to the archbishop for approval of priest personnel changes."[6] Liddy was worried that, with the Vatican visitors safely away, the university might try to reassert its direct control over the seminary.

A Surprise to All

On June 3, 1986, the apostolic pro-nuncio released the official announcement that Archbishop Gerety's request to retire had been accepted and Bishop Theodore Edgar McCarrick of Metuchen had been named archbishop of Newark. This was a great surprise, since Archbishop Gerety was 74 years old, and the mandatory retirement age was 75.

Gerety believed that, in view of his expected resignation at 75, it was unrealistic to preside over the direction of new plans for the archdiocese and unfair to commit his successor to any new and ambitious programs. Gerety immediately released a statement explaining his early retirement.

> The reasons for my action in submitting my resignation are very simple. It is well known that a bishop must resign at the age of 75. I will be 74 years old next month and I told the Holy Father in my letter of resignation that, 'For the good of God's Church, and for my own peace of mind and relief, I believe it is time for a younger man to take over the reins of office here in Newark. . . . I see no point in delaying this step. Another year would only put off certain necessary plans for the future of this archdiocese.[7]

Among his final acts as archbishop, Gerety appointed Reverend James M. Cafone as vice rector of the seminary and named Reverend Robert F. Coleman to the faculty as professor of canon law.[8] The reestablishment of the office of vice rector and the appointment of a full-time professor of canon law were among the recommendations of the Vatican visitation.

A Peripatetic Ordinary

Theodore Edgar McCarrick was born in New York City on July 7, 1930, where he attended Catholic elementary school and Fordham Preparatory School. After studies at St. Joseph's Seminary in Yonkers, New York, Cardinal Francis Spellman ordained him to the priesthood on May 31, 1958, in New York City. He went on to earn a master's degree in social sciences and a Ph.D. in sociology from the Catholic University of America.

Father McCarrick was named president of the Catholic University of Puerto Rico in Ponce in 1965. Cardinal Cooke recalled Monsignor McCarrick to New York to serve as associate secretary for education and then as the cardinal's secretary from 1971–77. In 1977, Pope Paul VI named McCarrick auxiliary bishop of New York. In 1981, Pope John Paul II appointed him the first bishop of Metuchen, New Jersey. He was installed as the fourth archbishop of Newark on July 25, 1986. He was transferred to Washington, DC, on November 21, 2000, elevated to the College of Cardinals on February 21, 2001, and retired as metropolitan ordinary on May 16, 2006.

Throughout his years as archbishop of Newark, McCarrick would take a direct role in the seminary and be a frequent visitor, often presiding at liturgies and being present at seminary activities.

Continuing Revision of Affiliation

Monsignor Petillo appointed a committee of university and seminary officers to review the seminary arrangements in the light of the Vatican visitation. The seminary faculty was very concerned about the implications of tenure at Seton Hall. While appreciating the idea of tenure per se, they believed it was of little or no advantage to them at Seton Hall. The shifting from three-year appointments to tenure track while demoting long-serving faculty did not encourage the seminary faculty to place any trust in the university administration.

This belief was heightened by the denial of tenure to two priests serving on the university faculty. In one case, the chair of the department had written that the priest spent too much time on his priestly duties.[9] One of the priests resigned from the priesthood; the other sued the university and won his tenure. This did not encourage confidence in the fairness of the tenure process at the university. In addition, the departures of Monsignor Ciuba and Fathers Kukura, DeDomenico, and Masiello soon after relocation made some faculty members wonder how much time they had left. On the other hand, the university did not welcome the visitation team's recommendations regarding ecclesiastical safeguards in the tenure system.

Archbishop McCarrick energetically participated in all seminary matters and required that all of the Vatican visitation recommendations be meticulously implemented. Consequently, the affiliation agreement again was amended, eliminating tenure and returning the seminary faculty to a contract system. This took place on October 28, 1986. The seminary faculty had been on tenure track less than one year. In faculty appointments, the role of the university chancellor was reduced to "concurrence."[10]

Working Out the Contracts

The board of overseers immediately appointed a committee to work out the new contract system. Representing the university were Dr. Nicolas DeProspo and Reverend Richard Nardone, chair of the religious studies department. Fathers Cafone, Serratelli, and Wister represented the seminary. Reverend Daniel Degnan, S.J., dean of the Seton Hall law school, and Reverend Charles Kavanagh, director of the seminary department of the National Catholic Educational Association, served as advisers.

The committee worked out a system in which faculty would be appointed by the archbishop after appropriate searches and would receive seven-year contracts. In the sixth year, the faculty member was to be evaluated in a process identical to tenure review, before receiving another seven-year contract.

The committee also proposed revisions to the affiliation agreement that would give the rector/dean control over class size and apportionment of teaching responsibilities. The faculty believed that such a system preserved the integrity of the seminary, affirmed faculty members' ability to engage in priestly formation, and ensured academic rigor and accountability. It would, of course, require another revision of the affiliation agreement.

The university administration was not pleased with the proposed arrangement. In February 1987, the rector, Monsignor Liddy, and the associate dean, Father Wister, were summoned by the academic committee of the board of regents, in the presence of the new provost, Dr. Bernhard Scholz. Father Bossman had left the office of provost in June 1986, after less than one year. The academic committee, led by Brother Leo Ryan, expressed grave displeasure that the seminary had not apprised them of the Vatican visitation. Liddy responded that the chancellor, the provost, and other university officers were involved in the visitation and that it was the responsibility of the chancellor to have notified them.

The committee then scolded Liddy and Wister for proposing term contracts and rejecting tenure. Wister asked why they were talking about proposals that still were under discussion, and remarked that it was inappropriate for the board even to have copies of the drafts. Wister also implied that the board was exercising undue interference in administrative and faculty matters, and that the regents properly could only consider a final draft. The academic committee insisted that all faculty appointments be approved by the provost. The seminary refused to agree.

The meeting did not end happily, but all agreed that the affiliation agreement again needed revision.[11]

A continuing issue was the role of the university executive chancellor. The chancellor of Seton Hall was the chief executive officer of the university. It was the only American university where this title was used in such a manner.

Further, the role of the university chancellor as chancellor of the seminary remained obscure. He was sometimes referred to as the chief executive officer of the seminary, but what did that mean? What then was the position of the rector? Monsignor Donald Zimmermann, seminary professor of canon law, often noted that there could be no intermediary between the rector and the archbishop. However, the chancellor insisted on playing an active role in the appointment of seminary officers and faculty.[12]

McCarrick wanted matters settled and was anxious to preserve the integrity of the seminary, but he had to tread carefully, respecting the autonomy of the university. He suggested that Liddy and Wister consult with Bishop Adam Maida of Green Bay and Monsignor George Kelly at St. John's University.[13] Maida supported the contract system as opposed to the possible difficulties resulting from tenure. He suggested that the contract-signing authority of the provost not be surrendered but delegated to the rector/dean,[14] a system used in many colleges and, until recently, at Seton Hall.

Liddy, a gentle and quiet man, was suffering under the strain of continual confrontation. After receiving a lengthy and lecturing memorandum from provost Scholz together with an even lengthier and testier one from Professor John Mitchell of the religious studies department,[15] he expressed his frustration to McCarrick in a frank critique of the motives of the university administration.

> I was shocked. At times I wonder whether we're not "straining at gnats" in straightening out these legal arrangements; but the present communiqué and especially the paper of John Mitchell convinces me that the people we are dealing with are not friends of the Church.
>
> What stings one's pride the most is his frequent reference to "respect within the community of colleges and universities in the United States." The seminary received a most favorable accreditation from Middle States and the Association of Theological Schools in 1982; which is more than the university received in her recent Middle States accreditation. The issue of academic excellence is, I believe, a smoke-screen to cover an anti-Church bias.[16]

Liddy proposed a looser affiliation with the university, one similar to that between the St. Paul Seminary and the University of St. Thomas in St. Paul, Minnesota, wherein the rector is a vice president of the university. Liddy stated, "The problem, it seems to me, arose when the seminary was just plopped down on the campus of Seton Hall and stripped of its independence without any awareness of the dangers to either side. A first step should have been a genuine affiliation, rather than as the chairman of the Middle States board called it, 'a takeover.'"[17] This idea was greeted with a singular lack of enthusiasm by the university.

The entire seminary faculty, and also others involved with the affiliation, shared Liddy's analysis. Monsignor Baumgaertner, who had served as an adviser to the original affiliation committee, remarked that the result was "a shotgun wedding, and both barrels were shot right at you guys." Reverend James Coriden of Catholic University recalled that he had told the seminary administration that "the arrangement violated canon law regarding the archbishop." Monsignor Charles Froehle, a member of the Vatican visitation team, recalled that the team "saw that your situation couldn't work, so we chose a stronger position."[18]

Liddy maintained close communication with McCarrick, lamenting the "impotence" of the board of overseers as it was structured within the university bureaucracy. He worried that the "Holy See's desire for a free-standing and autonomous seminary" would soon be lost.[19]

"It Ain't Over 'til It's Over"

Yogi Berra's words of wisdom well describe the first four years of the seminary at Seton Hall. Meetings continued between the rector, the associate dean, the provost, and the chancellor.

The seminary faculty was in constant agitation. Among other things, they were irritated by the lack of offices. The original plans called for seminary faculty offices in the "academic wing," now called Alfieri Hall. However, when plans for this building were scaled down, the seminary faculty offices disappeared and the university was deaf to requests to rectify the situation.

While internal peace of mind was hard to find, external peace and quiet came under attack. In March 1987, with no notice to the seminary, the university redesigned the courtyard area between the seminary and Presidents Hall, and the chancellor[20] made it clear that it would be open to the entire university community, destroying the one remaining quiet area on the campus. Part of the redesign included a gazebo to be used for wedding pictures and other social events.

Liddy alerted the archbishop[21] and protested to Petillo, calling the plans a symbol "of a disregard for the seminary in the administrative circles of the university." He reminded McCarrick that Gerety had told everyone at the seminary dedication a year before that the courtyard "belonged to the seminary."[22]

The university backed down, denying that there were any plans for a gazebo, although a seminary faculty member was shown the gazebo by friends in the university physical plant department. Eventually, the courtyard was sealed with a locked gate.

Less than a month later, in April 1987, the chancellor, without any warning, announced that the seminary as a house of formation would be separated from the university and the school of theology completely integrated into the university. Those school of theology faculty members who so desired would be allowed to remain as university faculty while the seminary's relation would be clarified later.

The seminary and school of theology faculty strenuously objected to this plan and met with the archbishop over the issue. Archbishop McCarrick was very upset and quite angry. The faculty was in a state close to revolt, and many told McCarrick they would resign rather than be a part of the chancellor's plan. McCarrick also was concerned because Seton Hall was to host a meeting of all American seminary rectors and their ordinaries in two months' time. If the situation was not resolved, the fallout would be most embarrassing to all. The seminary faculty was aware of this fact and pressed the archbishop very hard.

McCarrick asked the seminary faculty members what was going on, telling them, "I want to be your friend, don't make me your enemy."[23] After more than an hour, the meeting ended with a stunned archbishop saying that he would see to it that the situation was resolved in a positive manner. McCarrick had been archbishop of Newark less than a year and he was faced with a seminary that was unraveling.

Chapter Forty-nine

The Act of Settlement

At Archbishop McCarrick's behest, Petillo appointed yet another committee to settle matters. They were charged to develop a revised affiliation agreement and a faculty guide for the seminary separate from the university faculty guide. This committee was composed of Monsignor Liddy, Father Wister, and Father Guarino. Over the next year they produced the *Affiliation Agreement Between the Archdiocese of Newark, Seton Hall University and Immaculate Conception Seminary (1988)* and the *Faculty Guide of ICS School of Theology of SHU (1988)*. These documents, approved by the faculty, the board of overseers, and the board of regents, institutionalized the changes the seminary faculty had requested. They remain, with some changes, the constitutional and governing documents of Immaculate Conception Seminary School of Theology.

Although seminary faculty had, from the beginning of affiliation, been members of the faculty of the university, it was only after these documents were ratified that they were placed on the university faculty mailing lists with faculty rank added to their names. From this time on, they served on all university committees except for rank and tenure.

The revisions to the affiliation agreement and the ratification of the separate seminary faculty guide by the Seton Hall board of regents ended five difficult years of adjustment for the seminary to its new situation as a constitutive school of the university. Those years were marked not only by tension, but occasionally by acrimony. The underlying reasons for the many disagreements were fundamentally different definitions of the institution itself as well as occasional clashes of personalities.

Officials of the university viewed the seminary simply as another academic unit. They were indifferent to its particular mission as a place for the formation of priests with a canonical connection to the archbishop. This may have been due to efforts on the part of some university officials, like many of their contemporaries at other Catholic colleges at the time, to loosen ties with ecclesiastical authorities. The seminary and its faculty, however, were unwilling to make any concessions that would weaken its essential mission. Therefore, they were willing to sacrifice such academic privileges as tenure.

Two events ended this stalemate: the Vatican visitation and the appointment of Theodore E. McCarrick as archbishop of Newark. The visitation's legatine authority ensured that its recommendations regarding the relationship of the seminary to the archbishop and the preservation of the essential formational role of the faculty would be followed. Archbishop McCarrick was swift to prevent the university administration's last-ditch attempt to separate the academic and formational aspects of the seminary. McCarrick, trained by Cardinals Spellman and Cooke, did not hesitate to act behind the scenes to enforce his will and to obtain a positive outcome, always with a smile.

As the year progressed, Monsignor Liddy expressed optimism about the future. In 1988, he wrote, "All in all, this was a prosperous year for Immaculate Conception Seminary and we look forward to continuing prosperity in the future."[1] In reviewing the previous four years since the seminary's return to Seton Hall, he praised the completion of the faculty guide, the establishment of a church management program in 1985, the creation of the pre-theology program in 1987, a 40 percent increase in overall enrollment since 1984, the refinement of the lay ministry programs, the new institute for the continuing education of priests, and the seminary's contributions to strengthening the Catholic identity of the university.[2]

Liddy was correct in his assessment. The seminary now was able to settle into its new home and to continue and expand its mission without the distractions of continual strife with the university administration. Of course, there would be occasional tensions but these revolved around issues that were part and parcel of daily university life—turf, facilities, and funding struggles.

A Shock

In November 1988, Reverend Richard Asakiewicz, who had succeeded Father Wister as associate dean the previous July, became seriously ill. Father Asakiewicz, who was a popular and energetic professor of Christology and ecclesiology, was well known in ecumenical circles and for many years chaired the Archdiocesan Commission for Ecumenical and Interreligious Affairs. His sudden death on November 26, after several days of hospitalization for heart failure, shocked the seminary community.[3] His funeral was memorable in many ways. Several seminarians noted afterward that Father Richard, as he was known, would have chuckled at the discomfiture of the other faculty members who endured a homily that lasted almost three-quarters of an hour. The funeral was so lengthy that the archbishop almost missed a flight from Newark Airport.[4] Father Asakiewicz was succeeded as associate dean by Reverend William Harms.

Moving on Through the Nineties

In December 1989, Monsignor Petillo announced his resignation as chancellor and, shortly after, his resignation from the priesthood. In January 1990, Monsignor Liddy took over the reins of the university as interim chancellor. He would hold this post until July 1990, when he was named university professor of Catholic studies. Liddy later remarked, "In relation to being rector, being acting chancellor of the university was a breeze."[5]

Reverend James Cafone, vice rector, was immediately named acting rector. Father Cafone had served as parish priest, university professor, and spiritual director of the College Seminary before assuming the post of vice rector. A gregarious and outgoing man who loved to laugh, he possessed a fine singing voice that often was heard throughout the seminary and above the entire congregation in the chapel. In the few months he served as acting rector, he earned the respect and affection of seminarians and faculty alike—no easy task.

During his brief tenure, he worked with determination and success to rectify the academic rank of several faculty members. This resolution smoothed relations with the university immeasurably. He also addressed a neuralgic internal issue. There was general dissatisfaction among students and faculty regarding the arrangement of the chapel, in particular, the Eucharistic shrine. In 1988, it was extensively renovated under Cafone's direction and the Eucharist placed in a central position.[6]

A faculty search committee presented three names to Archbishop McCarrick for consideration for rector/dean: Father Cafone; Reverend Robert Harahan, professor of moral theology; and Reverend James Sullivan, former rector of the College Seminary and former director of the seminary department of the National Catholic Educational Association.[7] Father Harahan was chosen and was installed as rector/dean on September 30, 1990.[8]

Father Harahan also had a fine sense of humor, a requirement for seminary rectors. His memos to the seminary community were anticipated both for content and style. Reporting on Reverend John Flesey's successful defense of his doctoral dissertation, he wrote, "Needless to say he is thrilled; the *Cloud of Unknowing* [the topic of his dissertation] has become 'cloud nine' for him."[9] On an occasion when leaks in the basement had filled the entire seminary building with noxious odors, he announced to the community, "Since the door to the tomb has been opened and the stench of Lazarus has greeted us, the seminary has responded by informing physical plant to take appropriate action."[10]

In 1992, the renovation of the seminary refectory and the resultant dislocation of the seminarians from their accustomed dining room brought forth his finest memo: "Lest you forget and 'your tongue cleave to your palate,' please know you are free to return to the refectory. . . . There is still some work that needs to be done and some furniture to be ordered. I will keep you informed of progress. Thank you for your gracious good spirit during our exile. No longer a need to 'hang up your harps,' Pharaoh's coupons are now surpassed with gifts of a more plenteous redemption."[11]

Although the major issues of the seminary's relationship with the university had been settled, the various minor inconveniences of institutional living remained problems and irritants for the rectors. Security was a case in point. Father Arthur Serratelli once entered his room to find an intruder. Father Wister entered the faculty lounge to find a thief handing the VCR out the window to a confederate. In the second case, the miscreant was a member of the university security staff. Campus security was improved during Harahan's tenure and the more serious problems disappeared. Probably a sign of the times, from then on the building was locked when there was no one at the reception desk, and seminarians were warned not to allow strangers into the building and to report suspected intruders.[12]

Like all contemporary educational institutions, the seminary required additional administrators and administrative coordination. Harahan hired a professional business manager, Sister Ann McManamon, to assist Father Stanley Ortyl, the vice rector, in this area of his responsibilities. Father Ortyl, very popular among the seminarians and highly regarded by the faculty, served as vice rector from 1990 to 1996. He died suddenly in 1999.

In 1992, the university asked to revisit the affiliation agreement in order to further "integrate" the seminary into the university structure. One of Harahan's concerns was that the seminary committee or board of overseers was not living up to its potential. He obtained a grant from the Lilly Endowment to address the situation. At an all-day meeting of the board of overseers, the various issues involved were addressed by Sister Katarina Schuth, noted writer on seminary issues; Father William Harms of the Seton Hall planning office; and Father Robert Wister, then executive director of the seminary department of the National Catholic Educational Association. While no major changes were made to the structure of the board of overseers in the aftermath of this meeting, no significant alterations were made to the affiliation agreement either.[13]

The improvement of the seminary's relationship with the university also was due to the university's efforts to reclaim its Catholic identity. Father Thomas Peterson, O.P., succeeded as chancellor in 1990 after Monsignor Liddy briefly held the post following Monsignor Petillo's resignation. Peterson previously had served as president of Providence College. During his five years as chancellor and as chancellor/president, he undertook efforts to advance the Catholic mission of the university. After Monsignor Robert Sheeran became president in 1995, a number of more substantive initiatives emerged. A Center of Catholic Studies was founded in 1997 under the direction of Monsignor Richard Liddy, former rector of the seminary. The G. K. Chesterton Institute for Faith and Culture came to the campus in 1999, and a university office of mission and ministry was established in 2001.

After five years as rector, Monsignor Harahan took a well-deserved sabbatical, after which he was named pastor of St. Theresa's Parish in Summit, New Jersey.

He was succeeded in 1995 by Father John Flesey, the seminary spiritual director. A deeply spiritual and very serious man, Flesey accepted the appointment as a duty but grew to enjoy his role as rector. To most, he seemed to possess a dry, even droll sense of humor. Students were unaware of his talents as a mimic and impressionist. It is just as well that he limited the enjoyment of these talents to the faculty, as he was a master in imitating seminarians. His imitation of W. C. Fields was of a truly masterful level and rivaled those on the professional stage. He did not limit himself to actors. If one listened at the door of the faculty lounge, one might think a high-ranking prelate was present, even the highest-ranking one of all.

The tasks of a seminary rector are daunting; they are manifold and very time-consuming. Monsignor Flesey kept assiduous records of the various items that required his attention. His methodology was simple and straightforward. On his desk there always was a black and white composition book, similar to those used in schools many years ago. In this book he enumerated his "to do" items. He listed them numerically. As he was writing during a meeting, his visitor asked what the number of the current item was. He replied, "You are numbers 634 and 635. By the way, I began this book less than three months ago."[14]

Upon completing his term as rector, Flesey wrote, "Hidden in these five years have been difficulties and challenges, but also innumerable blessings."[15] Among the difficulties, challenges, and blessings, he recalled that the major blessing was the faculty itself, whom he described as "an incredibly dedicated and talented group of scholars and mentors." He deeply appreciated the support of Father Peterson, the university chancellor and president, who always was available for advice and assistance, and whose presence at many seminary events gave a priestly example to the seminarians. Flesey found maintaining a balance of formation activities and academics a challenge due to the "packed" schedule of the seminary.

While he enjoyed working with the other deans of the university, he thought that often there were competing values at play in the discussions. In a practical vein, he found that development activity was a great frustration since there was competition to balance the development goals of the archdiocese and the university with those of the seminary. In other words, the seminary was not allowed to "poach" on special donors.[16]

The Very Involved Archbishop

Archbishop McCarrick became involved in all aspects of seminary life. He frequently visited and presided at the liturgy. During his many visits, scheduled and unscheduled, he made himself available to faculty and seminarians alike. His informal style and dress confused some of the workers who occasionally mistook him for "just another visiting priest" or, on one occasion, as a member of the cleaning staff.

For his convenience during longer visits, a suite was reserved for him. It remains today the Archbishop's Suite. His schedule was like a marathon race.

While he spent quite a bit of time at the seminary, sometimes his visits were cut short by the need to rush to the airport to catch a plane to one quarter of the globe or another. He did not like to waste a minute or to have an idle moment. It was his custom to do the formal "call to orders" at the seminary before morning prayer. Morning prayer was at 6:45 a.m. This required that his first appointment could be as early as 4:30 a.m. It did not bother him in the slightest, but often he called a sleepy seminarian to orders.

McCarrick took an interest in the minutiae of the seminary's daily life and administration. A stickler for detail, he checked and sent corrections to drafts of minutes of the board of overseers and offered suggestions regarding every topic the board discussed. Often he expressed concern about the "lack of precision," in particular regarding official documents.[17] On one occasion he added, "It is not a major point, but I send it in the interest of perfection!"[18]

Archbishop McCarrick was very "well connected" with Church leaders throughout the world. Soon after his arrival, a stream of high-level hierarchical visitors arrived at the gates of the seminary. Over the years they included Cardinals William Baum, Carlo Martini, Stephen Kim, Bernard Law, Dominic Ekadam, Francis Arinze, Paul Poupard, Edward Cassidy, Antonio Quarracino, Nicholas Lopez-Rodriguez, Henryk Gulbenowicz, Joseph Glemp, and Basil Hume, and Patriarchs John Peter XVIII Kasparian and Ignatius Anthony II Hayek, to mention but a few. In addition, there were countless archbishops and bishops who graced the seminary with their presence.[19]

The archbishop took a serious interest in the physical health of the seminarians. He sent the seminary a treadmill, noting, without additional comment, that "some of the men could profit from it."[20] Always trim, McCarrick was quite concerned about obesity among the seminarians. He supported the establishment of an Overeaters Club and paid for a scale to inspire the club members to even greater achievements.[21]

Little known was McCarrick's keen interest in liturgical music. He continually sent memos to rectors asking them to include various hymns that he recently had heard and liked in the seminary repertoire. These hymns included "God, We Praise You," "We Walk by Faith," "As We Gather at Your Table," "Praise to You, O Christ Our Savior," "Sing of the Lord's Goodness," "Center of My Life," and "I Heard the Voice of Jesus Say," among many others.[22]

McCarrick often required the presence of the seminarians at events at the cathedral. For the seminarians, one of the most interesting occasions at which their attendance was mandated was the transfer of the mortal remains of Bishop Wigger, the third bishop of Newark, to Sacred Heart Cathedral in 1987. Winand Michael Wigger died in 1901 and was buried in Holy Sepulcher Cemetery in East Orange, New Jersey. Several priests thought he deserved a "more exalted" resting place. They raised the money necessary to exhume his body, place it in a new casket, and move it to the crypt of the bishops and archbishops beneath the sanctuary in Sacred Heart Cathedral. When they dug poor Wigger up, there was not much to move. His skull remained, together with a few fragments of bones, and some shreds of his vestments. His cross and ring, made of gold, also survived. The fragments of Wigger's remains were placed in the new casket, but McCarrick deposited the cross and ring in the archdiocesan treasury. He occasionally wore the cross.

All seminarians were ordered to attend these unusual obsequies, which included the celebration of Mass. Faculty members were not very interested in going—most thought the entire project a bit bizarre—so Monsignor Liddy sent them the following plea: "I am looking for faculty volunteers (sacrificial lambs) to accompany the seminarians."[23] A luncheon followed the ceremonies. A wonderful time was had by all.

A Darlington Postlude

Archbishop McCarrick never hid the fact that he was unhappy with the sale of the Darlington property. He considered the loss of the facilities as tragic. Less than six months after his installation, he made inquiries regarding the possibility of purchasing the former seminary buildings and 30 to 50 surrounding acres. This opportunity arose because Darlington Associates, the purchasers, were having difficulties obtaining the zoning changes necessary for their development plans from the township of Mahwah.

Responding to rumors of the interest of the archdiocese in reacquiring the property, C. Nevins McBride, a Bergen County developer, contacted McCarrick's office in early December 1986, offering to approach Darlington Associates.[24] As far back as 1984, McBride had urged the archdiocese to try to regain the seminary buildings and surrounding acreage.[25] It quickly became apparent that this would be an expensive project. Not only would the price be high, but the archdiocesan finance office estimated that the buildings would require at least $1.5 million to $2 million for repairs.[26] McBride approached the developers with an offer to reduce the original purchase price, which was to be paid over nine years, by $500,000 and consider the return of the property as a tax-deductible contribution of $2.5 million to $3 million to the archdiocese. The initial reaction of the new owners was that this was an insult.[27]

A few weeks later McBride told McCarrick that the developers continued to have zoning problems with the township of Mahwah and "things aren't as dead as we might have thought." In addition to zoning issues, the town fathers were not happy that filming had taken place in the chapel and dogs were being trained in the convent, both violations of the residential, not commercial, zoning status of the property. The town quickly shut down these operations.[28] McBride also suggested that the archbishop "sweeten the deal" by raising an additional $500,000 from a group of wealthy Catholics.[29]

All seemed to be over when, on January 27, 1988, Darlington Associates informed McBride that they had "never offered the former seminary buildings for sale or charitable contribution" and had "no interest in the contribution or sale of these buildings."[30] McCarrick was "not happy" that this appeared to end any chances to "get some of that seminary back into archdiocesan hands."[31] However, McBride did not give up. The developers, in addition to continuing zoning problems, had to deal with legal problems as well.[32]

In late July, McCarrick asked McBride to form an "informal committee" together with business executives John Culligan and William Boyle to continue to investigate the possibilities of reacquiring the Darlington property. McCarrick seriously wanted the property, mentioning that he would even settle for only 10 acres around the buildings.[33] His letter to Culligan and Boyle shows the depth of his feeling on the issue.

> You and I have chatted from time to time about my
> lingering hope that something might make it possible
> for us to reacquire part of the Darlington property
> once again.
> You know that the loss of the seminary buildings
> and chapel is still a great sadness for all of us and I am
> very sensitive to the great desire of so many priests to
> reacquire the place where they had their formation for
> the ministry in the archdiocese of Newark.[34]

Boyle offered his assistance but had little hope of success, telling the archbishop that the purchasers had informed him that they would not consider selling the seminary property.[35]

There was no movement for almost a year. Behind the scenes, the township still was reluctant to agree to all of the developer's desires. Some of the local officials supported the return of an archdiocesan presence to the area. The archdiocese considered the possibility of utilizing the former Walsh Hall as a retreat center and the convent as a priest retirement home.

Rumors flew left and right about what might be going on behind the scenes. One rather outlandish rumor circulated that the archdiocese wanted to convert Walsh Hall into a retirement home for 300 priests. The purveyors of this rumor probably confused the 300 small seminarian rooms without full bathroom facilities with retirement suites. Or, perhaps, it was a scare tactic. Darlington Associates said the archdiocese's $2 million offer—it had been raised[36]—for the buildings and surrounding acreage was "ludicrous" and added that an old-age retirement home was not appropriate in the midst of multi-million-dollar homes.[37]

McCarrick was angered that "they misinterpreted our desire to use the property for the wrong reason. I could see it used as a retreat center, as a spiritual life center, or as a number of things, but I do not see it as a residence for 300 priests."

With his usual wit, he added, "The plumbing needs to equip it for that would be extraordinarily expensive."[38] Unfortunately, for the archdiocese, the courts ruled in favor of the developer in its conflicts with Mahwah.[39]

There remained a glimmer of hope. A few years earlier, on October 19, 1987, the Dow Jones Industrial Average dropped more than 22 percent. This had a devastating effect on the real estate market, and sales of Darlington Associates' multi-million-dollar homes dropped almost 85 percent in 1989.[40] The developer began to experience cash-flow problems. John Mavroudis of Darlington Associates, who had dismissed early offers from the archdiocese as "insulting" and "ludicrous," had a payment of $3 million due to the archdiocese on December 23, 1990. He now asked the archbishop for an extension of the loan "because of the severe restriction of real estate financing by lending institutions." With prescience of McCarrick's later elevation to the College of Cardinals, he asked to meet with the archbishop "if this is acceptable to your eminence."[41]

Darlington Associates still would not entertain an offer for the property. The archdiocese allowed an extension to Darlington Associates on interest payments favorable to the archdiocese. The matter was closed. The archdiocese was moving on and facing increasing financial needs to fund weak parishes and various retirement plans.

However, Nevins McBride still tried to capitalize on the weak financial condition of Darlington Associates. He wrote to McCarrick in late 1992, asking to reopen attempts to acquire the buildings and the property. McBride never gave up but he died on May 13, 1993, at age 85.[42] Any hope of the archdiocese reacquiring the Darlington property was now gone. Mega-mansions, many of them rather vulgar, continued to sprout up here and there on the old seminary campus, and Walsh Hall was eventually converted into condominiums.

The final chapter of the Darlington saga was written on September 25, 2008, when the 75-room Crocker Mansion was purchased for $8.8 million by businessman Ilija Pavlovic. A few years before, Darlington Associates unsuccessfully tried to sell the mansion and 12.5 surrounding acres for $25 million.[43]

Chapter Fifty

Enrollment[1]

During the 1980s, seminarian and lay student enrollment remained rather steady, with the exception of a short-term drop in numbers in the years immediately following the move to Seton Hall. In the 1990s, enrollment gradually increased among both seminarians and lay students.

Throughout the last two decades of the twentieth century, seminarians represented almost 20 dioceses. In addition to Newark, these included Albany, Bridgeport, Burlington (Vermont), Camden, Green Bay, Hartford, Manchester (New Hampshire), Metuchen, Portland (Maine), Scranton, Springfield (Massachusetts), Trenton, Wilmington, Worcester, Taipei (Taiwan), Manono (Congo-Kinshasa), and two Eastern Rite dioceses.

Religious communities continued to send seminarians as well. Among them were Adorno Fathers, Augustinian Recollects, Benedictines, Capuchin Franciscans, Carmelites, the Incarnatio Consecratio Institute, Oratorians, Pallotines, Pauline Fathers, Salesians, the Society of Jesus Christ the Priest, and the Vocationists.

The Neocatechumenal Way

The Neocatechumenal Way was founded in Madrid in 1964 by Kiko Arguello and Carmen Hernandez. Based on the catechumenate of the early Church that prepared converts for Baptism, it provides a post-baptismal catechumenate to adults who are already members of the Church. The Neocatechumenate is implemented in small parish-based communities. There are approximately 20,000 such communities worldwide embracing nearly 1 million members.

The statutes of the Neocatechumenal Way were approved *ad experimentum* in 2002 and given definitive approval by the Holy See in 2008.

The seminary chose to utilize the Institute for Clergy Formation as a vehicle to attain this goal. The summer program provided lectures and discussions on various areas of priestly life and spirituality led by prominent theologians, psychologists, and pastoral experts in a relaxed, oceanside atmosphere. The seminarians attended selected lectures under the supervision of seminary faculty and were held accountable for their participation through reflection papers and examinations.

In 1996, the seminary initiated an intensive Summer Spiritual Institute within the structure of the Institute for Clergy Formation at Long Branch. Its purpose was to provide "a reflective atmosphere in a recreational setting: thereby allowing for human, academic, spiritual and pastoral renewal."[18] The format allowed the seminarians to take credit-bearing courses in spiritual direction, psychology, and homiletics. This had the added advantage of lightening their credit load during the school year, thereby providing more time to focus on formational issues.

Over the course of the first summer, the seminarians attended lectures by Fathers Avery Dulles, Eugene LaVerdiere, Roland Murphy, Paul Cioffi, Peter Cameron, and Benedict Groeschel. Monsignor Cusack, together with Fathers Flesey and O'Brien of the seminary faculty, assisted the seminarians in integrating the lectures with their studies. The program exposed the seminarians to recognized leaders in their fields and afforded them the opportunity to mingle with the many priests attending the institute from around the world.

At the same time, ordination to diaconate, which had taken place at various times over the previous two decades due to a constantly changing seminary program, returned to the traditional time of the end of the third year of theology.[19]

In 2001, the seminary added an even more intensive program. The program offered by the Institute for Priestly Formation (IPF), at Creighton University in Omaha, Nebraska, was chosen. Newark seminarians completing first-year theology were required to participate.

Finances

Although essentially of a spiritual nature, these additional programs all came with a price tag. Tuition, room, board, and fees for seminarians rose above the $10,000 mark in 1991.[20] This created a long-term burden for seminarians. The majority had little or no savings and very few had significant financial support from families. This especially was true for foreign-born men who, in many cases, were penniless. As a result, even though the archdiocese required that they reimburse the archdiocese for only 20 percent of the costs their training incurred, they carried a heavy load of debt since their financial situation required them to take out substantial loans during their years of seminary training.

Each diocese had its own method of financing the training of their seminarians. The stewardship policy of the archdiocese of Newark, formally enunciated in 1995, stated in its preamble that ". . . the financing of a candidate's education and formation is identified as a joint commitment and investment by the Church of Newark and by the individual candidate." Its stated intention was to relieve the seminarian of financial cares that could place stress on him during the period of formation.

> This philosophy presumes that the candidate will commit himself to the spiritual, academic, pastoral, and practical preparation required for a life of service to the Church while placing the highest priority on discerning the call of the Lord which is so central to this journey. Thus, the candidate is to be free of undue financial concerns and, simultaneously, responsible and accountable for the use of all resources.[21]

While this was a great improvement over recent programs, it did not achieve the laudable goal of freeing seminarians from financial concerns, since it did not take into consideration the level of debt that was growing and the difficulty of paying it off while living on a priest's very small salary.

The seminary had been aware of these difficulties for many years. Cornerstone provided support to seminarians for books, medical care deductibles, and other necessities. The Judge Breslin Fund provided financial aid, in particular in cases of urgent need.[22] In addition to loans, the archdiocese also provided grants to needy Newark seminarians. The Knights of Columbus, as usual, were extraordinarily generous to the seminarians. The expenses of the Clinical Pastoral Experience (CPE) were borne by the archdiocese, which, in addition, provided seminarians with $100 per week during the program. Health insurance also was paid by the archdiocese. In addition, during the academic year, seminarians could earn additional money by participating in work-study programs within the seminary and in other units of the university.

To make ends meet, fund-raising was essential. Fortunately, seminary fund-raising was quite successful. The $52,000 raised in 1985 grew to $185,000 in 1989.[23] In 1999, it reached $608,000. That year, Monsignor Flesey took great pride that the seminary raised more money than the Seton Hall law school, whose alumni enjoyed incomes far in excess of seminary alumni.[24] Two years later, fund-raising efforts surpassed $874,000.[25]

The Holy See had declared the year 2000 a year of jubilee. In the spirit of a biblical jubilee, Archbishop McCarrick included the seminarians and recently ordained in an archdiocesan-wide debt-forgiveness program. He told the happy recipients, "I am pleased to announce a Jubilee Debt Reduction Program for the parishes, schools and institutions within the archdiocese. I am pleased to advise your remaining seminary personal loan obligations have been completely forgiven." The amounts forgiven ranged from $1,000 to $12,000.[26]

Technology

During the 1990s, Seton Hall University embarked on an ambitious program to integrate technology into academics. The university was rated among the nation's "most wired" many years in a row. Not content to rest on those laurels, it soon became one of the most "wireless." This transition indicates the rate of progress in technology.

Technology affected every area of seminary life. In the 1980s, immediately after the move to Seton Hall, seminary administrators hotly debated whether seminarians could have private telephones in their rooms. A major concern was the noise that ringing phones would cause. Phones were allowed but the bells inside the instruments were disconnected. In the 1990s phones were not an issue. Seminarians had beepers and cell phones. By the next decade, many had upgraded to Palm Pilots and then to BlackBerry smartphones and iPhones.

Email changed the culture of communication. Mentors and seminarians set appointments electronically. Seminarians who were ill were required to email their professors explaining their absence from class. Professors evaluated drafts of term papers over the Internet. Technology entered the classroom. Software programs like Blackboard contained course assignments, readings, PowerPoint presentations, videos, and a variety of other course materials. By 1997, all of the course offerings of the Church history department were available electronically.[27]

Laptops appeared in the classroom. The evolution was fascinating. In the mid-1990s, tech-savvy professors instructed students on how to access various materials and sources on the Internet and how to utilize the newly available technology. By the middle of the next decade, the students were far more technologically sophisticated than the professors.[28]

Chapter Fifty-one

Tragedies and Scandals Usher in the Third Millennium

The third millennium opened with deceptive serenity. Fears that "Y2K" would cause severe communications difficulties proved false. In early January, the Spring 2000 semester began normally. Less than two weeks later, disaster struck.

Around 4:30 a.m. on Wednesday, January 19, 2000, when most on campus were asleep, a fire began in Boland Hall, an undergraduate student residence. It spread rapidly across three couches in the third-floor lounge in less than five minutes. Most students on the third floor evacuated using the staircases; a few jumped more than 40 feet to the ground. Sleeping seminarians were awakened by the screaming sirens of approaching fire trucks. Cell phones started to ring. In the space of only a few minutes, the entire campus was a scene of pandemonium.

Seminary faculty members and students rushed from their rooms to see what was happening. All on campus tried to assist students fleeing Boland Hall and to give first aid to the injured. Seminarians brought blankets and coats for the freezing students who had fled from Boland Hall. Initially few were aware of the magnitude of the tragedy. The injured were rushed to nearby hospitals, and priest faculty members followed to provide assistance and comfort to the injured and their families.

By mid-afternoon, it was clear that the entire university community had suffered devastating losses. Three undergraduate students were lost. Aaron Karol and Frank Caltabilota died of thermal injuries, and John Giunta died due to smoke inhalation. Fifty-eight students and firefighters were injured, four seriously enough to require lengthy hospital stays and rehabilitation.

Less than two years later, Tuesday, September 11, 2001, began peacefully. Morning prayer and Mass were followed by breakfast. Classes started at 8:30. By 9 a.m., a strange unease was apparent. A few seminarians who had their laptops in class noticed instant messages appearing. Of course, they were not permitted to open these during the lectures. Most classes took a short break at about 9:30. Word spread rapidly. Something had happened in New York City, at the World Trade Center. The seminary is only 16 miles from Manhattan, and smoke could be seen in the distance.

The long day that would become known as "9/11" had begun. Classes throughout the university immediately were cancelled. Seminarians and faculty members, together with the entire university community, were in a state that can only be described as extreme shock. Those from New Jersey, particularly, were worried about the fate of relatives and friends who worked in the Twin Towers. A long vigil began. Phone communication was spotty at best. Many mobile phones did not function. Land lines were jammed.

Students, faculty members, and staff went to the top floors of various buildings on campus to look across New Jersey cities and towns to watch the smoke that for weeks would rise from lower Manhattan. Some faculty and students cannot forget standing at a window in Xavier Hall and watching the North Tower burn as the South Tower was struck, and then witnessing first the South Tower collapse, followed by the North Tower.[1] The seminary community joined in the many impromptu prayer services that sprang up spontaneously across the campus. By the end of the day, it became clear that relatives, friends, and associates were victims of the disaster. Four Seton Hall graduate students and numerous alumni died that day. For weeks, the daily liturgy was marked by prayers for those who had lost their lives and those who had lost their loved ones.

Fewer than two hours had passed between the first plane attacking the towers and the collapse of both. But those two hours left searing scars on all who witnessed the terrorist assault. One faculty member recalls attending nine funerals during the weeks after the attack. Four of these took place with empty caskets or caskets containing memorabilia of a loved one whose remains could not be found.[2] The archdiocese of Newark gave permission for funeral Masses to be said under these doleful conditions.

Before the impact of these tragedies even slightly waned, the scandal of sexual abuse of minors by clergy broke into the press. The scandals were deeply felt by the seminarians, though the impact varied. Most told Monsignor Flesey, then spiritual director, that they remained unshaken in their conviction that they were called to the priesthood. However, many found that their vocation was challenged by their family and friends. They were urged to leave the seminary and asked why they would "join an organization" that allowed such flagrant abuse to occur. It is not possible to determine whether any seminarian left formation due to the negative impact of the scandals, but the records show that very few left the seminary during this time.

Following the fire, 9/11, and the scandals, an atmosphere of trauma and loss did not quickly dissipate. Flesey reminded the seminarians that they should not allow the situation to interrupt their formation. Rather, the experience of these tragedies contributed to their training. The disruptions to the normal schedule, the feelings of sadness, the need to minister to one another and to the campus community were all part of their formation as priests. He told the seminarians that, in reality, this was what they would encounter as priests, caring for one another and, in spite of one's own feelings, ministering to God's people.

In working through the issues resulting from these events, the seminarians greatly were assisted by the counseling staff, veteran counselor Father John Balweg and Livvy Dinneen. Flesey recalled that he took great satisfaction in having recruited Ms. Dinneen for the seminary counseling staff.[3]

Changes at the Helm

Upon completion of his five-year term in June 2000, Monsignor Flesey took a sabbatical and then returned to his post as spiritual director. Monsignor Robert F. Coleman, vice rector and professor of canon law, assumed the post of rector/dean on July 1, 2000.[4] Not finding such a combined title to his liking, he immediately demonstrated his independence and attention to detail by changing his title to "Rector and Dean." Monsignor Coleman had been at the seminary for a decade, interrupting his service to direct the planning and execution of the visit of Pope John Paul II to Newark.

As vice rector, Coleman had made his mark on the seminary in a substantive manner. When Lewis Hall opened in 1984, there was no money available for furniture. The furniture from Darlington was moved to the new facility. In many instances, it simply did not fit, and the desks and beds now were 60 years old. As vice rector, he raised funds to renovate the seminarian rooms and to provide new furnishings of an appropriate size and style. Coleman accomplished this in a way that demonstrated his patient but determined administrative style. Unable to raise sufficient money to fix all rooms at once, he took a gradual approach. Each year he raised sufficient funds for 20 or 25 rooms and renovated them, repeating the process until all were completely refurbished.

Coleman projected an austere and reserved demeanor that masked a subtle wit. He was greatly amused by the manner in which letters from the Association of Theological Schools addressed him. In spite of continued attempts at correction, the association habitually addressed its correspondence to "Ronald Coleman." Although flattered to be mistaken for the actor, upon receipt of these letters, Robert Coleman casually remarked, "He's dead, you know."

Devoted to the liturgy, he insisted that it always be celebrated with the dignity and attention to detail it deserved. A lover of music who possessed what has been described as an almost perfect Irish tenor voice, he worked as vice rector to create a *schola cantorum* that was able to perform many of the most complicated Latin motets with skill and precision. This project required that he spend many hours instructing the singers in the proper pronunciation of Latin. As rector, his interest in liturgical music continued and he found a receptive audience among the seminarians.

Monsignor Coleman took his role as rector very seriously. Seminarians and faculty members quickly learned that he said what he meant and he meant what he said. In matters regarding discipline, he was eminently fair and always acted without bias or prejudice. Much to everyone's surprise, he gave unfailing and enthusiastic support to the seminary soccer team. No one had ever accused him of being a sports fan. Yet, he attended almost every soccer game against other seminaries, both home and away. While he refused even high-ranking visiting prelates the privilege of granting a day off from classes, he pledged that when the seminary soccer team won the Rectors Cup, the trophy awarded to the championship team among the northeastern seminaries, he would grant a full holiday from class.

On November 21, 2000, before Coleman was able to settle into his new position, Archbishop McCarrick was transferred to the archdiocese of Washington, DC.

All the Way from Peoria

On July 22, 2001, John J. Myers, the bishop of Peoria, Illinois, was named as McCarrick's successor. On October 9, Myers was installed as archbishop of Newark; he remains archbishop as of the writing of this book.

Appointed coadjutor bishop of Peoria at 45 years of age, Myers had attended the North American College as a seminarian and earned a doctorate in canon law from the Catholic University of America, on whose board of trustees he has also served for years. His time in Peoria was marked by intensive recruitment of seminarians and a deep interest in university campus ministry, two traits that he would bring to Newark.

On the day of his appointment, shortly after the customary press conference, he drove to the Seton Hall campus to meet with the priest community. In informal conversations that day, he made it clear that the university and the seminary would be very high priorities for him. He has lived up to that promise.

Although he speaks of himself as a "farm boy from Illinois," Myers adapted very quickly to urban New Jersey. For anyone, a move from the farms of the Midwest to the parkway and turnpike interchanges of "Jersey" might prove traumatic, but the new archbishop adapted very quickly to the congested cities and suburbs of his new see.

Soon after his installation, he became a regular presence in the seminary. His visits normally combine an afternoon Eucharist with a homily followed by dinner. At the dinner, the archbishop always sits at a table of seminarians. Some seminarians are a bit nervous but quickly are put at ease by Myers' relaxed manner. On some occasions, the archbishop delivers the Sunday evening conference. The seminarians enjoy these visits, especially since they always guarantee a meal of higher quality than the daily fare.

The archbishop also hosts barbeques for all the archdiocesan seminarians. These events include the men from Emmaus House of Discernment, the College Seminary, Redemptoris Mater, and Immaculate Conception Seminary. He also is unfailingly present at the annual cookout for seminarians at the College Seminary. Myers does not limit his presence to these occasions. He has initiated a Holy Hour at the seminary for ordinands and their families on the day before priestly ordination. On the morning of ordination, he gathers with the ordinands at the cathedral rectory for prayer and the recitation of the rosary.

For Archbishop Myers, Monsignor Coleman restored an old Darlington custom from the days of Archbishop Walsh. When the archbishop arrives, the seminarians crowd the stairs and the lobby and, as he leaves his car, they burst into spontaneous applause. Myers is as amused by this custom as are the seminarians. Occasionally, he responds with a pontifical-style wave that encourages some seminarians to call out *Viva il Papa!,* as their predecessors did for Archbishop Walsh over a half-century ago. Myers has not indicated that he has heard these cheers.

In addition to providing a social and spiritual presence, the archbishop has supported the seminary and seminarians in a variety of ways. To the joy of the seminarians and the recently ordained, he announced "that the archdiocese's subsidy of seminary tuition (including room and board) will increase from 80 percent to 100 percent effective immediately. I have also approved a $250 per semester personal allowance for each seminarian."[5] The post-ordination burden of debt was significantly lightened. Although an individual might have taken out loans during his time in the seminary, his financial situation was greatly eased. This was extremely important as the number of students from outside the United States, who often had little or no financial resources, increased.

Strengthening the Structure of the Seminary

Archbishop Myers directed that the affiliation agreement between the seminary and university, last revised in 1995, be updated. A committee consisting of Monsignor Coleman, representing the seminary, Father Michael Andreano, vice chancellor, representing the archdiocese, and Sister Paula Buley, I.H.M., executive vice president of the university, labored for almost two years on the document. Most of the adjustments reflected new financial arrangements. However, the description of the seminary as a "graduate school" of the university was changed. The word "graduate" was eliminated, reflecting the introduction of new seminary programs. The majority of the changes were modest but the financial arrangements were finally clarified.[6]

Through the almost two decades of its existence, the seminary board of overseers had not reached its potential. Harahan had tried to enhance its role but was given little support. Myers made it very clear to the seminary that he wanted a stronger board of overseers. The board was expanded to include some of the bishops who sent students to the seminary as well as laity whose expertise would help in the area of seminary development.[7]

The archbishop supported a revision of the university board of trustees, which also served as the seminary's corporate board. The result was a stronger board with enhanced authority in overseeing the Catholic mission of the university. The changes also included clarifying the seminary board's name. Up to this point, reflecting the 1983 affiliation, it sometimes had been called the seminary committee of the board of regents; other times it was referred to as the seminary board of overseers. It now became officially the board of overseers. The change in nomenclature signaled a more significant role for this group.

Archbishop Myers also brought the Fellowship of Catholic University Students (FOCUS) to the campus. Myers knew this group well from his years as bishop of Peoria, where the fellowship was a presence at the University of Illinois. Founded by Curtis Martin, FOCUS is an organization of college students who devote several years of their lives to serve as missionaries on college campuses. Through personal interaction with their peers, they draw university students to prayer groups, scripture study, and involvement with the poor. In their own words, "FOCUS helps college students to allow Jesus Christ to be the Lord of their lives—including their studies, social life, dating relationships, and major life decisions."[8] The interaction between these highly motivated young people and the seminarians has proven to be mutually beneficial. The FOCUS missionaries find support from the commitment of the seminarians, and the seminarians draw encouragement from the zeal and dedication of lay women and men of their own age.

The Quiet Rector Makes Changes

One of Coleman's first projects was a complete overhaul of the administrative structure of the seminary. The structure in place since affiliation in 1983 had been adjusted and augmented over the years, but there had never been a systematic evaluation of its efficiency or its adequacy. Concurrent with the administrative reorganization, the administrative wing in Alumni Hall was gutted and replaced with an attractive reconfiguration of offices that allowed for more expeditious and professional service.

With a new rector came a new administrative staff. Reverend Thomas Nydegger was appointed vice rector on November 4, 2000.[9] In 2002, Reverend Joseph Chapel succeeded Father Anthony Ziccardi as associate dean. Reverend Lawrence Porter followed Monsignor James Turro as seminary librarian in 2004. Dr. Dianne Traflet, named an assistant dean in 1999, succeeded Dr. Zeni Fox as director of lay ministry in 2001, and was named an associate dean in 2004.

In 2002, Monsignor Nydegger succeeded Monsignor Cusack as director of formation. Nydegger, with his typical energy, analyzed and restructured the priestly formation program. After an extensive consultation with faculty members, the newly ordained, and the seminarians, a new schedule was created, many more presenters were recruited, and a different format was established, incorporating a more scriptural and spiritual foundation.[10]

In 2004, Monsignor Cusack died suddenly. He had been in ill health for several years but his death came as a surprise. His tall presence and always windblown, white hair had become fixtures at the seminary. His wisdom and counseling skills and his role as director of formation had made him a popular confessor and adviser for almost 17 years at the seminary.

The current formation program as developed by Nydegger retains some aspects of the previous program but its substance is dramatically changed. It incorporates a different format, a different approach, and a different implementation. (It is described in Chapter 52.)

In the 2002–2003 academic year, the seminary undertook an exhaustive self-study chaired by Monsignor Wister, in preparation for ATS reaccreditation. All parts of the seminary community participated. The self-study raised several neuralgic and continuing issues, many revolving around the lack of adequate facilities. Paramount was the lack of faculty and adjunct faculty office space and the continued use of the chapel for lectures and conferences. The loss of guest rooms also was a major concern.

The reaccreditation visit in 2004 by the Association of Theological Schools of the United States and Canada and the Middle States Association was an unqualified success. The seminary received reaccreditation for 10 years by both agencies. In conjunction with this process, the seminary also participated in the university's program review, which also had a positive outcome.

Programs for the Third Millennium

The Vatican visitation team in 1986 made several recommendations regarding the College Seminary. The visitors' principal recommendations reflected their perception that the integration of the various elements of the program was weak. In particular they believed that philosophy, one of the most important parts of the College Seminary program, was not an "integral" part of the students' education. They were concerned that students rated the philosophy department as a "very weak element in their education," and they also were troubled that no priests taught in the department. They commented on the need for the rector of the College Seminary to work more closely with the faculty of the philosophy department .[11]

Unfortunately, the seminary had long ago determined that the course offerings of the university's philosophy department did not meet all of the requirements of the *Program of Priestly Formation*. In 1987, the seminary began to offer the required undergraduate courses in philosophy that the bishops' program mandated. The fifth edition of the *Program*, promulgated in 2006, was even more extensive and explicit in its enumeration of courses in philosophy and undergraduate theology that would be required for college seminary and pre-theology programs.

After discussions with the university's departments of philosophy and religious studies, the seminary—under the leadership of Father Joseph Chapel, associate dean, and Father Douglas Milewski—went through the laborious process of developing and obtaining university approval for a new program, a bachelor of arts in Catholic theology. This program was approved and opened in Fall 2007. It serves both the pre-theology and College Seminary programs, and is open to all university undergraduates. Its 10 courses (30 credits) in philosophical theology and its five courses (15 credits) in Catholic theology fulfill the spirit and letter of the fifth edition of the *Program of Priestly Formation*. Although the seminary anticipated that the bachelor's degree program would be successful, no one was prepared for the amount of interest that it provoked. In its second academic year, 2009–10, it counted 85 majors. It soon became necessary to hire two additional philosophy professors and two additional undergraduate theology professors to meet the demand for courses.

Vatican Visitation

In 2002, the cardinals and the chief officers of the United States Conference of Catholic Bishops, after a meeting with Pope John Paul II concerning the sexual abuse crisis in the U.S. Church, concluded that it would be helpful to have a visitation of the seminaries and religious houses of formation. This visitation would focus on formation for celibate chastity and the teaching of moral theology. Edwin O'Brien, archbishop of the Military Services, was appointed coordinator of the visitation. In February 2005, he informed the seminary rectors that the visitation would take place during the 2005–2006 academic year.[12]

The visitation of the seminary took place from October 23 to October 28, 2005. The chairman of the visitation was Charles Chaput, O.F.M. Cap., archbishop of Denver. The members of the visitation team were Michael Burbridge, auxiliary bishop of Philadelphia, Reverend Michael Glenn of St. John Vianney Theological Seminary of Denver, Reverend Gabriel Cingolani, C.P., of St. Augustine's Seminary of Toronto, and Monsignor Robert Zapfel, S.T.D., of the diocese of Buffalo. The resource person for the visitation was Dr. Alfred V. Hanley of St. Charles Seminary in Philadelphia.[13]

The visitors faced an exhausting task. In a period of fewer than five days, they interviewed all administrators and faculty of the seminary as well as all resident seminarians. In addition, they examined seminary documents such as student and faculty handbooks, evaluation handbooks, admissions criteria, sex-abuse policy, policies on the Internet and its monitoring, pastoral policies and boundary issues, catalogues, course syllabi, rules of life, and any other documents relating to priestly formation.

Three years later, the seminary was pleased to hear that "the visitors found this to be a healthy institution, which is providing a solid formation for the priesthood." After congratulating the archbishop and the seminary faculty for their "good work," Cardinal Zenon Grocholewski, prefect of the Congregation for Catholic Education, added, "The doctrine on the priesthood presented by the seminary is solidly based on the Church's magisterium, and both faculty and seminarians accept this teaching. . . . A sound understanding of the priesthood is taught in the academic courses and reflected in the programs of spiritual and pastoral formation."

The cardinal lauded the faculty members as "well-qualified men who are dedicated to their ministry. There is a spirit of harmony and ecclesial communion among them, and they show a sincere *sentire cum Ecclesia*. They most definitely give a good example of priestly living. . . . The seminary program offers a sound program of spiritual formation, which meets the expectations of the Church for candidates to the priesthood. The seminary has a rhythm of life that supports a prayerful atmosphere, with a balance between liturgical life and private prayer. Spiritual direction is fostered as an essential element of priestly formation. . . . All in the seminary understand the theological motivation of the Church's law on celibacy. Integration of the human and spiritual dimensions of formation, above all in the area of celibate chastity, is facilitated by the conversations of the seminarians with their spiritual directors and with their priest mentors. . . . The visitors affirmed that the institution pays great attention to this crucial aspect of priestly formation."[14]

The seminary was quite pleased by this very strong affirmation from the Holy See and moved toward its one hundred fiftieth anniversary with confidence.

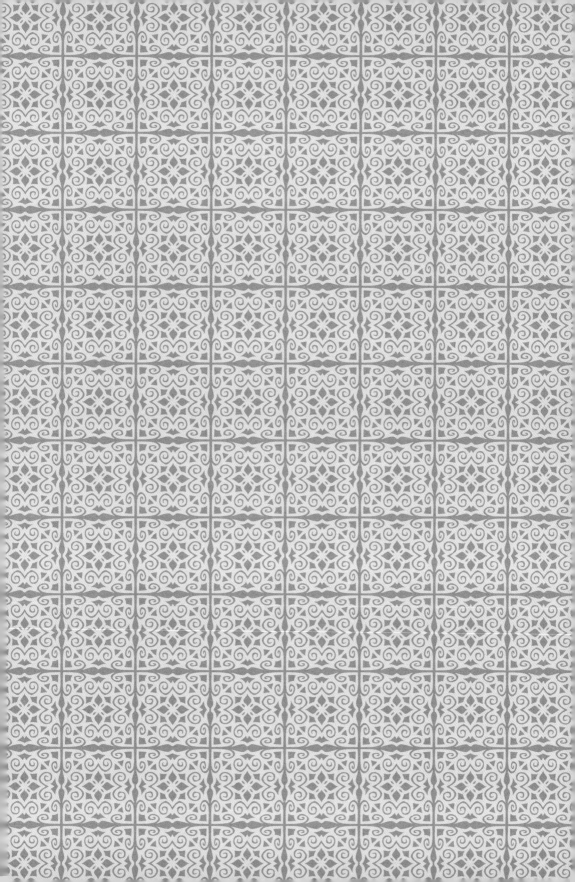

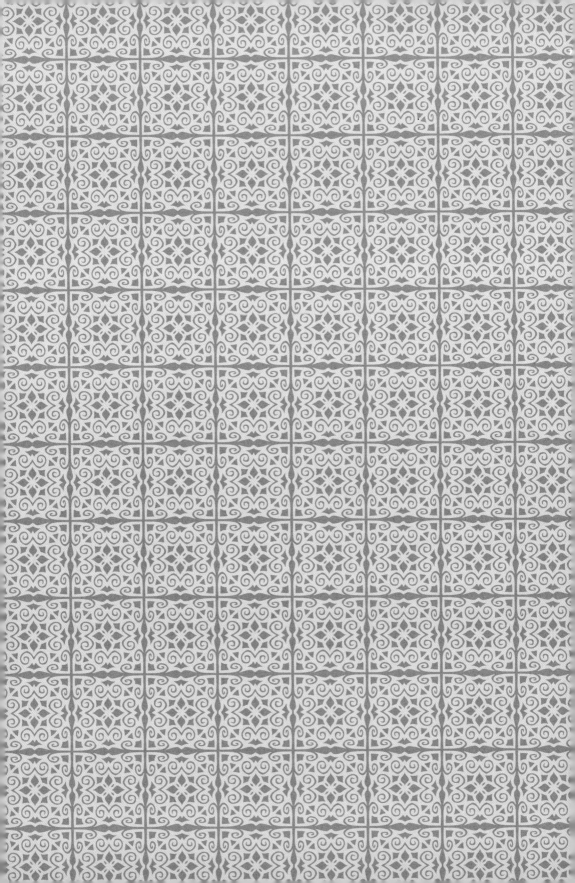

Immaculate Conception Seminary School of Theology,
Seton Hall University

Moving into the Future

2010

Chapter Fifty-two

The Seminary Today

A decent respect for the curiosity of future generations requires that we present a detailed description of Immaculate Conception Seminary in its one hundred fiftieth year.

Immaculate Conception Seminary School of Theology is one of the nine schools that make Seton Hall a "university," and the presence of the seminary at the heart of the university community strengthens Seton Hall's Catholic identity.

Indeed, the university's own mission statement, approved by the board of regents on June 6, 1996, indirectly reflects many of the strengths of Immaculate Conception Seminary School of Theology. While the university insists upon "ethical development" and "values-centered curricula," it is precisely *faith*, and the moral imperatives and human values that spring from it, that is the very foundation upon which the seminary stands.

The seminary of 2010 can be further identified through its own mission statement.

> Immaculate Conception Seminary is a House of Formation for the Roman Catholic Priesthood and the School of Theology of Seton Hall University.
>
> As a House of Formation, the Seminary offers men preparing for the priesthood the personal, academic, ministerial and spiritual formation essential for conversion to Jesus Christ and for their commitment to a life of service to the Church.

As a School of Theology, the Seminary provides:
a theological foundation and a pastoral and spiritual
formation for men and women preparing for ministries
among the people of God; a theological foundation for
men and women desiring to pursue doctoral studies; and
varied opportunities for continuing theological education.

The mission statement provides a succinct summary of the work
of the seminary and infers unique constituencies within the overall seminary
community. Essentially, there are five distinct groups of students comprising
the total student population.

Resident seminarians are the largest group. These men, preparing for
the diocesan priesthood, currently represent the archdiocese of Newark and various
sending dioceses.

Seminarians living at Redemptoris Mater Archdiocesan Missionary
Seminary are another group preparing for the diocesan priesthood. These men
are members of the Neocatechumenal Way, preparing for service as priests of the
archdiocese of Newark. They also may devote some years to missionary service.
The seminary provides their academic formation and collaborates with Redemptoris
Mater in their pastoral formation.

Religious seminarians are students preparing for ordination in various
religious orders and communities. For these students the seminary provides academic
formation and the pastoral practica found within the M.Div. program.

Non-seminarians include priests, permanent deacons, religious sisters and
brothers, and laity pursuing studies in theology or pastoral ministry. Among these
students are a number of non-Catholics and non-Christians. While the totality of
their formal formation may be provided by the seminary, it differs in both depth and
degree from that required of candidates for priestly ordination. Most of this group
enrolled in the M.A. in theology program avail themselves only of the academic
program, although they may participate in other aspects of seminary life.

Undergraduate students are the newest addition to the seminary community.
The bachelor of arts in Catholic theology program includes diocesan seminarians
living at the College Seminary and seminarians from religious communities. It also
includes undergraduate students who are not in a seminary formation program.

In Fall 2009,[1] there were 122 graduate seminarians and 87 graduate
non-seminarians registered.

Total graduate seminarians	122
Resident seminarians	73[2]
Non-resident seminarians	51
Redemptoris Mater	34
Salesians	3
Society of St. Paul	1
Adorno Fathers	4
Augustinian Recollects	1
Carmelites	4
Oratorians	2
Capuchins	2
Graduate non-seminarians	87
Priests	7
Deacons	10
Brothers	1
Sisters	3
Lay women	35
Lay men	31
Total graduate students	209
Undergraduate seminarians	65
Undergraduate non-seminarians	16
Total undergraduates	81
Total graduates and undergraduates	290

As Pope John Paul II made clear in his apostolic exhortation *Pastores dabo vobis*, the formation of priests—whether initial or ongoing—involves four principal areas: the human, spiritual, intellectual, and pastoral pillars of priestly life and ministry. Proper attention must be given to the candidates themselves, their formators, the community these persons create, and the environment in which that community dwells.

As the pope and the bishops have made clear, priestly formation is a holistic process, involving the integration of a deep-rooted spirituality, well-developed intellect, and dedicated pastoral concern in a healthy, charitable, psychosexually mature individual. The seminary, then, is neither merely place, nor process, nor even experience. It is, rather, a way of life leading the seminarian and the lay student more deeply into the company of Jesus Christ and more intimately into personal commitment, which is the individual's response to the vocation to the service of Christ's Gospel and his people.

The seminary also bears a special responsibility toward its non-seminarian students seeking to prepare for apostolic service to the Church. The cooperative and complementary nature of the relationship between priests and laity in fulfilling their respective roles in the apostolate requires high-quality formation experiences for all concerned. This is especially critical for those lay people who will engage in the tasks of evangelization and the teaching of theology.

The seminary also welcomes persons of other faiths who wish to avail themselves of its programs of study. Attracted by the seminary's foundation in faith and its atmosphere of welcome and respect, they are an important part of the seminary community and enrich the seminary with their presence and their insights.

In serving these varied constituencies, the seminary maintains the integrity of a priestly formation program as a house of formation, serves other communities of men preparing for priesthood by providing the academic component of their formation, engages in the preparation of lay ministers, and opens the riches of theological education to all qualified persons.

Seminary students have access to all the services of the university, including the university library, recreational facilities, and academic and cultural events on the campus. They also may avail themselves of the health and counseling services when appropriate.

As part of the university, the seminary has integrated information technology into its daily life, both inside and outside the classroom. The university supplies a laptop computer to each undergraduate student and insures that all undergraduates are computer literate and are employing technology in their learning. Many graduate students utilize laptops in the classroom and all classrooms are wireless. Computer labs are available to the graduate students and most professors utilize information technology in the classroom. The seminary building has wireless computer access as well as ethernet connections in each room.

Bringing from its storeroom the best of the old and the new, Immaculate Conception Seminary School of Theology is very much online and quite plugged-in to technology.

A Global Community

The seminary boasts a widely diverse student body, with students hailing from North and South America, from Europe and Asia, and from Africa and Oceania. The seminary is a global community. Students are prepared for leadership in a culturally and ethnically diverse northeastern United States and for leadership in missionary service around the world. In Fall 2009, there were students from

31 nations represented in the graduate and undergraduate divisions of the seminary. The dioceses represented in the seminarian student body reflect this same diversity.

2009 Nations of Origin

Argentina	1
Bahamas	1
Brazil	4
Cambodia	1
Canada	2
Chile	1
Colombia	39
Costa Rica	1
Croatia	4
Cuba	2
Dominica	1
Dominican Republic	5
Ecuador	2
El Salvador	4
Guatemala	1
Haiti	2
India	2
Italy	6
Korea	3
Mexico	8
Nicaragua	3
Nigeria	2
Paraguay	2
Philippines	15
Poland	8
Portugal	2
Puerto Rico (U.S. Territory)	3
Spain	1
Trinidad and Tobago	1
Venezuela	1
Vietnam	6
Total Students	134
USA	156
Grand total	**290**

Day-to-Day Life

The integral nature of the priestly formation program—encompassing spiritual, academic, human, and pastoral needs—fulfills the mission of the seminary to prepare candidates for priesthood. This is exemplified most clearly in the program for resident seminarians. In varying ways, this fidelity to the mission is maintained as the seminary enables non-resident seminarians and lay students to achieve their academic and ministerial goals.

Fidelity to the mission and the achievement of the goals of the seminary requires fidelity to the authority of the Catholic Church as it is expressed in directives from the Holy See, the bishops of the United States, and the archbishop of Newark. The development of the seminary's formation programs demonstrates its reflection on and application of these directives over the last decade.

Human Formation

The formation program of Immaculate Conception Seminary responds to Pope John Paul II's 1992 apostolic exhortation, *Pastores dabo vobis*, and the 2006 edition of the *Program for Priestly Formation*.

Friday mornings are exclusively dedicated to formation. To meet the particular needs of the fourth-year theologians, who have weekend duties in parishes and are preparing for priesthood ordination, Thursday evening is reserved for their formation sessions. Sunday is dedicated to fostering a greater sense of community among the seminarians.

In order to facilitate the human formation and affective growth of each seminarian, two licensed psychotherapists, one a priest and one a layperson, each holding master's degrees in both theology and psychology, are available to the seminarians for counseling. Human formation for non-resident seminarians is the responsibility of their religious community or house of formation.

The primary goal in the human formation of the priestly candidate is affective integration, enabling the candidate to bring to his relationships a strong and lively love for Jesus Christ that overflows into a spirit of dedication and respect for others.

Although a celibate commitment requires abstinence from both sexual activity and exclusive intimate relationships, the seminarian remains a sexual person who is expected to develop mature expressions of chaste love and caring. Consequently, the need for a human integration of affectivity is especially important. As the seminarian gradually internalizes his celibate commitment, his sexuality is directed toward a more vibrant spiritual life and a caring priestly ministry.

Without affective integration, some life experiences may give rise to debilitating depression or destructive anger. Affective maturity involves a process of growth in personal freedom. With the help of God, the seminarian devotes himself to the struggle against selfishness in all its forms. Affective maturity flows from the depths of one's personality. It is expressed in a refinement of personal conscience and obedience to moral obligation.

The specific means of human formation are embodied in the events, resources, and programs of Immaculate Conception Seminary. The seminary program of spiritual, personal, and academic formation focuses on developing healthy relationships, awareness of human intimacy, and formation of conscience. This calls on the individual to grow and commit to the dignity of the human person and to the common good. As such, it requires healthy psychological growth, sociological awareness, and cultural evangelization.

On this journey toward a mature and responsible freedom, the community life of the seminary provides an indispensable context. The seminary provides opportunities for one-on-one dialogue that includes both informal discussions between seminarians and faculty, and formal professional counseling that can address specific issues. Throughout the seminary program, the resident seminarian is called upon to discuss human growth issues in regular meetings with his mentor and spiritual director.

The call to celibacy is a spiritual summons to offer the whole of one's love and care to Jesus Christ and to his Church. To respond fittingly to the gift of celibacy, seminarians need to be educated in the Christian understanding of human sexuality—its essential goodness derived from the goodness of creation and its place in God's plan for humanity. Properly understood, human sexuality is a dimension of the whole person that fosters and facilitates the sincere self-giving that constitutes the essence of human love.

To give oneself in love to another implies that one has a self to give. Attention to self-mastery and growth in affective maturity are essential prerequisites to responsible human love. To embrace fully the gift of celibacy, seminarians need an intensive and comprehensive formation in celibate chastity. This is understood as the spiritual virtue that enables one to see others as icons of God. It frees one's love from selfishness and aggression, often expressed as manipulation and control.

A primary academic vehicle for growth in chaste, responsible love and for a deeper appreciation of celibate love is moral theology. At the seminary, sexual morality is taught from the perspective of the universal human vocation to holiness. Such holiness is essentially a grace-filled growth in charity designed to permeate the depths of our being and extend fully into our relationships with others. For the celibate priesthood candidate, such charity will engender and form the virtues of prudence, continence, modesty, and chastity, which are necessary to live a celibate life in loving service to God and neighbor.

In addition, the seminary offers many other academic venues to develop the necessary cognitive and affective skills for growth in chaste, responsible love. These include courses that explore the dimensions of the human person. In both academic theology and spiritual direction, the aspects of divine providence and sacramental grace are examined. This includes the human and theological dynamics of life in marriage and in priesthood. During these courses, attention is given to developmental issues of human growth and relationships.

For the past four decades, the bishops of the United States have urged the use of psychological testing and counseling in seminary admissions processes and in the course of seminary training. Such testing helps to identify suitable candidates. Counseling assists in addressing life issues and should be reinforced by the experience of community life and spiritual direction.

Professional counselors are available to resident seminarians. Counseling staff members periodically make presentations to the seminarians on the counseling and developmental issues that they are likely to encounter in themselves as well as in their ministry.

Seminarians are encouraged to avail themselves of this professional assistance in the area of personal growth and development. In correct perspective, counseling plays a supportive role in formation. Proper psychological insight into complex and delicate issues is important for individuals who will themselves offer pastoral counseling. The overall goal of the counseling program is to help the seminarians fully develop the human potential that will help them to be better and more effective priests.

Community life in the seminary helps the candidate to achieve the balance, strength, and freedom necessary for pastoral responsibilities. The *Program of Priestly Formation* notes the significant role community life plays in the growth of a seminarian. Active and honest participation in community life helps each seminarian to understand himself better.

Seminary life is community-oriented by nature. For example, the regular weekly schedule includes daily liturgical worship and common meals. Each Thursday evening is reserved for recreation in common, except for fourth-year theologians who have their formation sessions then. The Sunday schedule includes liturgical worship, recreation, dinner, and a presentation on priestly life. These communal events constitute not only formation in priestly living but also opportunities to reflect on the total educational process. In other words, this regular schedule of community events complements formation in the field and the classroom.

The community life of the seminary also includes activities that are not part of the weekly cycle. Several special events take place annually, such as the March for Life each January in Washington, DC. Spiritual events are also scheduled to coincide with yearly milestones in priestly formation. For example, every class makes a weekend spiritual retreat, with priest faculty leadership, at one of several nearby retreat centers. In addition, as seminarians progress through the ministries of lector and acolyte leading to ordination, they attend, as a class, a spiritual reflection in community. Other events that take place once every three to four years include the seminary choir tour to Italy and the seminary pilgrimage abroad.

While the community life of the resident seminarians is necessarily a major concern of the seminary, it also seeks to provide a vibrant community in which non-resident seminarians and lay students can participate.

Spiritual Formation

The entire seminary program of spiritual direction is supervised by the spiritual director of the seminary.

Every seminarian chooses a spiritual director from a list of priests approved by the archbishop of Newark. As his life of prayer unfolds, the seminarian inevitably faces challenges and receives consolations that he needs to understand. It is the responsibility of the individual spiritual director to assist the seminarian in the process. Of its very nature, spiritual direction requires a great deal of trust on the part of the seminarian who is invited to share with his director the deepest secrets of his heart. On the part of the director, spiritual direction requires a great deal of wisdom.

Ordinarily, the director and the seminarian meet once every three weeks or more frequently if needed. The priest director is considered a spiritual father for the seminarian. He strives to help the seminarian develop the interior freedom necessary to live out his vocation in the joy of the Holy Spirit.

Each seminarian is required to make two retreats a year. The first retreat is conducted over a weekend. Depending on the number of seminarians, two or three priests accompany each retreat group. The second retreat takes place over five days immediately following the conclusion of the academic year in May. Those who are to be ordained deacons make their retreat together. This retreat concludes with ordination to diaconate. The next week those to be ordained priests go on retreat. Their retreat concludes with ordination to the priesthood. Seminarians in pre-theology, first-year theology, and second-year theology are required to make an annual five-day retreat.

Liturgical formation is an important part of spiritual formation. The primary aspect of spiritual formation is daily participation in the Mass, central to Catholic life. The seminarian also participates in the Liturgy of the Hours, in common, at both morning and evening prayer. This practice gives the seminarian the *habitus* of praying the universal prayer of the Church that is central to the spiritual life of every priest.

Newark seminarians completing first-year theology are required to participate in the Institute for Priestly Formation at Creighton University in Omaha, Nebraska, during one summer. This institute offers opportunities for spiritual development of diocesan priests and seminarians that complement and deepen existing programs of spiritual formation. Based on the *Spiritual Exercises of St. Ignatius*, the institute invites priests and seminarians into a depth of prayer not easily attained in regular seminary formation, and provides assistance for the integration of this life of prayer into the active lives of diocesan priests.

Newark seminarians take part in Seton Hall's Institute for Clergy Formation during the summer following first-year and third-year theology. Formation faculty priests provide a special program in worship and spiritual direction.

Spiritual formation also is required for lay students enrolled in the master of arts in pastoral ministry (M.A.P.M.) or master of divinity (M.Div.) programs. There are three essential components of their program: foundational spiritual experience, spiritual direction, and an extended retreat experience.

The foundational spiritual experience is an eight-month program offered to students early in their course of theological study. Once a month students spend an evening together with a time for liturgy, quiet prayer, a meal, instruction, and faith sharing.

Pastoral Formation

Pastoral formation assignments form a substantial part of the preparation of the resident seminarians for ministry. The supervisor's written evaluation provides significant information for the evaluation of resident seminarians. These evaluations are given considerable attention, since pastoral formation is one of the four principal pillars of priestly formation. With field education so crucial to pastoral formation, candidates for ordination participate in a two-year, 12-credit program that provides a variety of ministerial experiences. Each aspect of the program is overseen by the director of pastoral education.

Theological reflection takes place during the two academic years of field education. To encourage a wide range of discussion, reflection sessions include resident seminarians, lay students, and non-resident seminarians, under the direction of a faculty member. Exploring theological dimensions of field assignments, the sessions integrate spirituality, pastoral ministry, and academic coursework. Seminarians in fourth-year theology who are deacons are assigned to area parishes each Sunday.

All lay students in the M.A.P.M. and M.Div. programs are required to participate in an external field education program, as well as in theological reflection with the seminarians.

Institute for Christian Spirituality

In the 1970s, the seminary opened its doors to non-seminarian students. Initially, the majority of students were sisters seeking theological renewal in the years following the Second Vatican Council. By the mid-1980s, the majority were lay men and women. They came for a variety of reasons. Some were teachers pursuing an academic master's degree in theology, some were parish ministers studying for the master's degree in pastoral ministry, and others simply wanted to increase their knowledge of the faith.

In the 1990s, an increased interest in spirituality was seen throughout the United States. In the survey done as part of the 2002–2003 planning for ATS reaccreditation, a great number of respondents, both seminarian and lay, asked for more courses and programs in spirituality.[3]

Seeking to provide true Catholic spirituality and spiritual experiences to a broad sector of people, Dr. Dianne Traflet, associate dean, applied for a $2 million grant from the Lilly Endowment's "Making Connections" initiative. The grant application was successful and the full amount was received in 2005. As a result of the grant, the seminary established the Institute for Christian Spirituality. The institute reaches out to the archdiocese of Newark and to neighboring dioceses by means of a number of initiatives aimed at encouraging the development of spirituality among the laity.

The central component of the institute is the STEPS (Seminary's Theological Education for Parish Services) program. This program, which can lead to a certificate or a master's in theology, is located at Our Lady of Mount Carmel Parish in Ridgewood, New Jersey. In addition to the academic program, the students participate in retreats and spiritual conferences that complement their theological education. They also engage in volunteer work, assisting the Missionaries of Charity at the organization's soup kitchen in Newark.

The institute goes beyond the academic. It sponsors retreats with speakers that include seminary faculty and staff, lay leaders, and students of the STEPS program. An example is the retreat entitled "Beholding the Face of God," given on February 10, 2008, at Mallinckrodt Convent in Mendham, New Jersey.

A popular initiative of the institute is its Great Spiritual Books program. This "book club" reaches an audience that is not able or perhaps inclined to participate in a full schedule of academic classes, but which has an interest in Catholic spirituality and spiritual reading. The presenters normally are experts in the particular author under discussion. The books discussed include classics such as Thomas Merton's *Seven Storey Mountain*, Dorothy Day's *The Long Loneliness*, and various works of C. S. Lewis. Occasionally, the book discussed is of a more esoteric nature. In November 2008, the book club discussed "Perceiving the Imperceivable in Russian Orthodox Spirituality, and Icons in St. Seraphim of Sarov's *On the Acquisition of the Holy Spirit*."

One of the most successful programs that the institute sponsors is a series of ongoing conferences entitled "Finding the Work You Love." These meetings are led by Julie Burkey, M.A.P.M., and feature a variety of witness speakers. They apparently have tapped into a feeling among many professionals that their careers lack a spiritual dimension and that this emptiness may be related to their profession.

The institute connects with young Catholics through a high school essay contest. Appropriately named to attract youthful participants, the 2008 theme was "Believing and Seeing in *The Chronicles of Narnia: Prince Caspian* by C. S. Lewis." Each year nine to 10 high school students from among almost 100 participants are honored for their contribution to the contest.[4]

Chapter Fifty-three

Academics Today

The academic component of formation at the seminary flows from its mission statement. The intellectual mission of the seminary is inextricably linked with other aspects of formation for all its students and especially for its seminarians.

The seminary offers four degree programs: the graduate degrees of master of arts in theology (M.A.), master of arts in pastoral ministry (M.A.P.M.), and master of divinity (M.Div.), and the undergraduate degree of bachelor of arts in Catholic theology (B.A.).

Master of Divinity

The M.Div. program is the first professional degree providing theological training for those preparing to undertake ministry in the Roman Catholic Church, primarily through ordination to the priesthood. On occasion, with the approval of the rector and dean, qualified students who do not seek ordination are admitted to the M.Div. program.

The M.Div. curriculum is arranged as follows:

- Coursework—72 credits
  Biblical studies—12
  Church history—6
  Moral theology— 6
  Pastoral theology—27
  Systematic theology—21
- Field education—12 credits, and theological reflection—Two semesters
- Spiritual formation
- M.Div. comprehensive project as part of the six-course pastoral sequence

Academic Program for Priesthood Candidates

The 126- to 132-credit academic program for priesthood candidates is the prescribed curriculum for all seminarians seeking ordination to the Roman Catholic priesthood. It complies with the requirements of the *Program of Priestly Formation*. This program includes all the requirements of the M.Div. program. It is extended over four years and includes courses and credits in addition to those required by the M.Div.

The requirements of the priesthood curriculum are:

- Coursework—126 to 132 credits
    Biblical studies—18
    Church history—12*
    Moral theology—15*
    Systematic theology—36*
    Pastoral theology—45 to 51**
 *Includes one elective; **6 credits in Spanish as required*
- Spiritual formation
- M.Div. comprehensive project as part of the six-course pastoral sequence

Master of Arts in Pastoral Ministry

The master of arts in pastoral ministry program prepares students for competent leadership in a specialized ministry in the Catholic Church: youth ministry, Christian spirituality, and health care ministry. The degree also may be pursued through the Great Spiritual Books program and the Seminary's Theological Education for Parish Services (STEPS) program. The M.A.P.M. program provides students with both a basic core of theological knowledge and specialized training in the chosen field of ministerial engagement.

The M.A.P.M. program consists of four components:

- Coursework—39 credits
    Core theological curriculum—27 credits
    Area of specialization—12 credits
- Field education—6 credits, and theological reflection—10 hours
    Two one-semester field experiences of six to eight hours weekly in a supervised setting, or
    Clinical Pastoral Experience (CPE), or
    Other means approved by the associate deans
- Spiritual formation
    Foundational spiritual experience, and
    Spiritual direction, and
    Retreat of several days
- Integration Seminar/final comprehensive project—3 credits

At the end of each year, he presents a draft evaluation of each seminarian in his charge regarding the four areas of priestly formation as delineated by the *Program of Priestly Formation* (intellectual, spiritual, human, pastoral). His evaluation is based on his meetings, academic performance of the seminarian, the written and oral comments of fellow faculty, and other contacts with the student, both formal and informal. After discussion of the evaluation at a faculty meeting toward the end of each year, the mentor revises it in accord with the observations of fellow faculty members. Faculty members who are not mentors may offer input on the seminarians.

Faculty members also serve on standing and ad hoc committees both in the seminary and in the university. In May of each year, all faculty members attend an annual assessment and planning session to discuss the previous year and to make plans for the upcoming year.

Faculty members serve as advisers to the archbishop of Newark and the United States Conference of Catholic Bishops on various theological and ethical issues. Currently, faculty members serve as members of the theological faculty of the Pastoral Provision (with one serving as chair), and on numerous boards and commissions of their respective dioceses and communities, including the College of Consultors, the Vocation Board, and the Commission for the Ecclesiastical Patrimony. Many serve as *censores librorum* and as theological consultants to their ordinaries and superiors. They also belong to a significant number of learned societies.[1]

Faculty members have been active in scholarly and academic service, offering dozens of presentations, interviews, retreats, and speeches every year. Faculty members have conducted workshops, performed volunteer work, and appeared as guest panelists and commentators on numerous television programs. They also have accepted invitations nationally and internationally to speak on current issues, bioethics, cloning, spirituality, and the papal election of 2005.

Faculty members also support the campus community and the Catholic mission of the university through service in a variety of ways, including serving on the Seton Hall University board of trustees and on university committees. They often preside at university chapel liturgies and work with campus ministry, the Institute of Christian Spirituality, the Institute on Work, and the Rite of Christian Initiation for Adults.

In addition to serving in academic, formational, and service capacities, priest faculty members serve as spiritual directors for the seminarians, subject to approval by the archbishop of Newark. Faculty members, both lay and ordained, may also assist with the spiritual needs of other students. Priest faculty members provide a variety of other services: celebration of the Eucharist, Liturgy of the Hours, individual celebration of the sacrament of reconciliation, and other liturgical and sacramental celebrations within and outside the seminary.

Significant time is spent serving students outside the classroom, giving spiritual direction, guidance, counseling, and directing M.A. theses. Members of the priest faculty, as well as many members of the lay faculty, work weekends giving retreats, assisting in parishes, and performing other services for the Church and the community.

Chapter Fifty-four

The Administration
of the Seminary

The seminary makes every effort to serve well and faithfully its dual population of seminarians and lay students. Firmly committed to ecclesiastical authority, the seminary is closely attentive to the directives of the Code of Canon Law. It follows the directives of Pope John Paul II's 1992 apostolic exhortation on seminary formation, *Pastores dabo vobis*, and assiduously adheres to the fifth edition of the *Program of Priestly Formation* of the United States Conference of Catholic Bishops, issued in 2006. It observes the norms of *Lay Ecclesial Ministry: The State of the Question*, a reflection on the ministries of the laity published by the National Conference of Catholic Bishops in 1999. Throughout its programs, the seminary also seeks to respond to the concerns of the dioceses and religious orders that send candidates for theological education.

The authority of the seminary to function as a house of formation for ordained and non-ordained ministers derives from its foundation by the archdiocese of Newark for this purpose. The seminary's authority to function as an educational institution of theology derives from its status as Seton Hall University's School of Theology, from the charter granted to the university by the state of New Jersey, and from its continuing accreditation by ATS and Middle States.

The structure of the seminary's authority and whence it is derived is detailed in the chart on page 424–425, illustrating that the ecclesiastical authority of the archbishop of Newark is exercised through and with the governing board, which is the board of overseers. The archbishop is chairman of the university board of trustees, president of the university board of regents, and chairs the seminary board of overseers, which also is a standing committee of the board of regents. The trustees of the university are members of the seminary corporation, the legal "owners" of Immaculate Conception Seminary. The rector and dean is an *ex officio* member of the board of trustees of the university and the board of overseers of the seminary.

The rector and dean of the seminary is responsible, as rector, directly to the archbishop for all matters pertaining to the formation of candidates for the priesthood and to the preparation of others for various ministries in the Church, as outlined specifically by the Code of Canon Law, the *Program of Priestly Formation*, and other regulatory ecclesiastical documents.

The rector and dean is responsible, as dean, to the provost of the university for all academic matters in the School of Theology. The rector and dean is also responsible to the board of overseers for the overall direction of the seminary and its programs.

To assist him in each of his primary functions, the rector and dean relies upon three key administrators: the vice rector and the associate deans, respectively responsible for the temporal administration and the academic programs of the seminary.

Temporalities

Financial processes and budget development are conducted in accordance with the university's policies, procedures, and oversight. The business manager and the business office of the seminary work in cooperation with the office of the provost and the budget office of the university to construct the annual budget of the seminary. The business manager, in consultation with the office of the associate dean of the seminary and the office of the provost of the university, projects the revenue side of the budget based on credits anticipated. The business office of the seminary, in consultation with the other offices of the seminary and the office of the provost, projects the expense side of the budget, based on recent history and any anticipated needs for the seminary in the upcoming year. Once the budget is completed, it goes before the university board of regents for final approval.

Development

The development office solicits donations from various benefactors for the Darlington Fund and the Judge Breslin Fund. Contributions to the Darlington Fund are generated by phone solicitation and extensive mailings under the supervision of the director of development. The Judge Breslin Fund is supported by benefactors through an annual golf outing.

The Father Gavin Fund is a restricted fund that was donated to the seminary for a clearly defined purpose: to address financial concerns of the resident seminarians of the archdiocese of Newark. This fund and all these different resources provide assistance to the students and contribute to the overall financial health of the seminary.

Reflection

Immaculate Conception Seminary today continues the mission entrusted to it by Bishop Bayley 150 years ago. It has expanded that mission to serve a Church community that Bayley could not have envisioned. It has been true to the motto of the Seton family, *Hazard Zet Forward* (which, translated, means: "Whatever the hazard, move forward), and continues confidently to move forward regardless of any hazards as it prepares men to be "Stewards of the Mysteries of God" and lay men and women to serve God's Church.

To be continued . . .

Immaculate Conception Seminary
School of Theology Organizational Chart

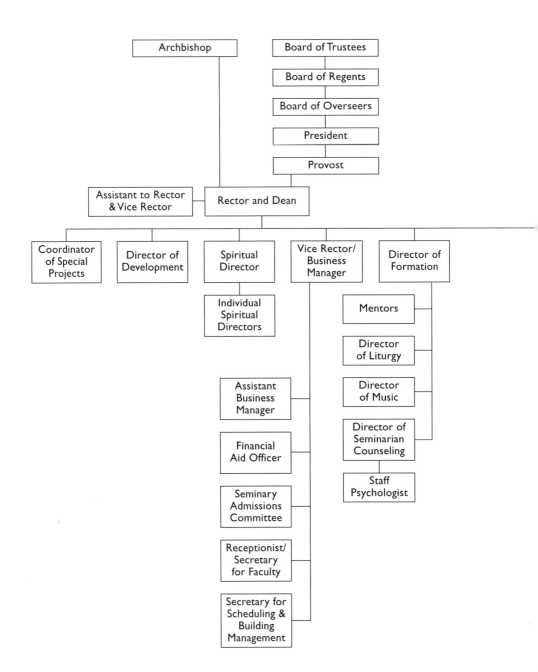

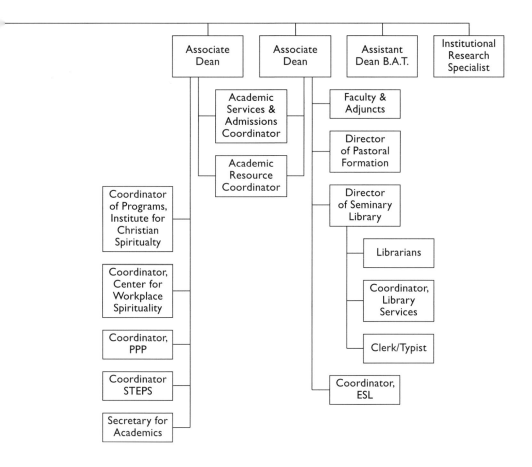

Endnotes

Chapter One

1 James Roosevelt Bayley (1814–1877), first bishop of Newark (1853–1872), eighth archbishop of Baltimore (1872–1877).

2 Kupke, Raymond. "James Roosevelt Bayley," in *The Encyclopedia of American Catholicism*, Michael Glazier and Thomas J. Shelly, eds., Collegeville, MN: 1997, 130–31.

3 *Freeman's Journal*, November 2, 1853, in Yaeger, Sister Hildegard M. *The Life of James Roosevelt Bayley, First Bishop of Newark and Eighth Archbishop of Baltimore 1814–1877*, Washington, DC: 1947, 96.

4 Bernard J. McQuaid (1823–1909), first president of Seton Hall College (1856–57, 1859–68), first bishop of Rochester (1868–1909).

5 Flynn, Joseph M. *The Catholic Church in New Jersey* (Morristown, NJ: 1904), 271–73.

6 Zwierlein, Frederick J., *The Life and Letters of Bishop McQuaid*, I (Rochester, NY: 1825), 293–95.

7 Ibid.

8 Zwierlein, I, 297.

9 The statistics vary. At one point Bayley estimated there were 50,000 to 60,000 Catholics in New Jersey.

10 Knapp, Charles Merriman. *New Jersey Politics during the Period of the Civil War and Reconstruction* (Geneva, NY: 1925), 2, cited in Yaeger, 157n.

11 Flynn, 61, names the first church in Trenton "St. Francis." Murray, Regina W., Joseph C. Shenrock, and James O'Neill, in *Upon This Rock: A New History of the Trenton Diocese* (Trenton, NJ: 1993), 358, 360, state that the original church in Trenton was named St. John's. When the parish moved to a larger building in 1851, the original building was purchased by a German congregation and renamed St. Francis.

12 Flynn, 68–69.

13 *The Metropolitan Catholic Almanac and Laity's Directory 1854* (Baltimore: 1854).

14 Bayley to Society for the Propagation of the Faith, June 1854, in Flynn, 275.

15 Bayley to Cardinal Prefect, June 8, 1854, in AAN R.G. 3 Accession # AND 8–88, Quinquennial Reports.

16 Bayley to Society for the Propagation of the Faith, July 1856, in Flynn, 282.

17 Bayley, *Circular Letter*, Sept. 1, 1860, in AAN 1.2.2.

18 Bayley to Corrigan, Paris, September 17, 1869, in AANY, C-2, cited in Yaeger, 245.

19 Bayley to Corrigan, Rome, February 25, 1870, in AANY, C-2, cited in Yaeger, 245.

20 "When Seton Hall became a university in 1950, the inscription on the seal was changed from *Collegium Setoniense* to *Universitas Setoniana*. This change provided an opportunity to correct an error in the Latin inscription. *Setoniensis, -e* is an adjectival form of the name Seton, but is a "locative" form used to refer to a place name, as if Seton were the name of the town in which the university was located. The correct form, the simple adjective *Setonianus, -a, -um*, was adopted to modify the now appropriate word *Universitas*. According to tradition, this correction was made by Rev. Joseph P. Christopher, Ph.D., then professor of Classical Languages at The Catholic University of America and later professor at Seton Hall." in Wister, Robert J., "Saints, Monsters, Bishops and Seton Hall: The Presidential Medallion, in http://pirate.shu.edu/~wisterro/Medallion/index.htm.

21 Marshall, William F. *Seton Hall College Catalogue*, 1895, 2, in AHSU 1.1.1.

22 Bayley to Society for the Propagation of the Faith, August 1855, cited in Flynn, 277.

23 McNamara, Robert. "Bernard Joseph McQuaid," in *the Encyclopedia of American Catholicism*, 895.

24 Joseph Flynn. *The Catholic Church in New Jersey*, 270.

25 Flynn, 146.

26 Marshall, 2.

27 Beck, Henry G. J. *The Centennial History of the Immaculate Conception Seminary—Darlington, N.J.* Privately printed: 1961, 4.

28 *The Metropolitan Catholic Almanac and Laity's Directory 1854* (Baltimore: 1854).

29 Marshall, 14.

30 Marshall, 15. Beck notes that the house alone had originally cost $40,000.

31 Beck, 5.

32 Bayley, *Register*, I, 83, in AAN 1.1.2.

33 Bayley, *Register*, I, 85, in AAN 1.1.2.

34 Bayley, *Circular Letter*, May 16, 1860, in AAN 1.2.2.

35 Ibid.

36 Digest of Bishop Bayley's letter of August 1860 to the Lyons Society for the Propagation of the Faith, cited in Beck, 4. Beck references "AAN, Bayley: Memorandum, 1859–72, p. 14." This cannot be found.

Chapter Two

1 Beck, 5–6. Beck bases this conclusion on the research of Monsignor Joesph Brady.

2 William McNulty to Bayley, Madison, NJ, August 27, 1860, in AICS 17, Early Dimissorials.

3 Diocesan Reports to the Holy See, February 5, 1862, in AAN, R. G. 3, Acc.AAN 8–88, Quinquennial Reports.
"seminarium habet duobus abhinc annos institutum . . . decem juvenes ibi alunitur, studiis vacant quae in omnibus fere Europae seminariis vigent . . . collegium diocesanum habet in eadem parte ac seminarium, illique adjunctum ad hoc praeparatum ut 80 alumnos contineat, qui quidem numerus hoc anno integer existit."

4 *Seton Hall College Catalogue* 1861–62, in ASHU 1.1.1.

5 *Sadlier's Catholic Almanac and Ordo, 1865.*

6 *Sadlier's Catholic Directory, Almanac, and Ordo, 1872.*

7 Beck notes, in AICS 1.2.2.1.

8 The writer owes a great debt to Henry G. J. Beck, author of the seminary's centennial history. Beck's painstaking detective work in several scattered archives established the foundation of the seminary in 1860 and the beginning of the teaching of theology in 1861. All previous works presumed the foundation of the seminary as coterminous with that of Seton Hall College in 1856. This myth was perpetuated in Seton Hall and seminary catalogues and in a variety of historical works and newspaper reports throughout the decades. In his research, Beck undoubtedly relied on the notes of Monsignor Joseph Brady. Brady's research on the history of the diocese of Newark included a study of the origins of the seminary. This is clear from two letters Brady sent to Archbishop Boland in 1958, outlining the rationale for the dating of the seminary's foundation. Brady to Boland, January 17, 1958, and January 30, 1958, in AICS 3.6.5.

9 Bayley, *Register*, I, 99, in AAN 1.12; Seton Hall *Register*, 75, in AAN 10.2.

10 Flynn, 146.

11 Seton Hall Charter, http://provost.shu.edu/charterday/charter.htm

12 *Seton Hall College Catalogue* 1861–62, in ASHU 1.1.1.

13 McQuaid to Bayley, South Orange, June 26, 1862, in Zwierlein, Frederick J., *The Life and Letters of Bishop McQuaid*, I (Rochester, NY: 1925), 327.

14 Crowe, Michael J. *The Extraterrestrial Life Debate, 1750–1900*, 1999, 454–56.

15 Brann to R. E. Burke, October 31, 1911, reproduced in Burke's *The Bishop's Bill and Setonia Bards* (Englewood, NJ: 1913), 380–86, cited in Beck, 9.

16 Kennelly, Edward F., *A Historical Study of Seton Hall College,* submitted in partial fulfillment of the requirements for the degree of Doctor of Education in the School of Education of New York University, 1944, 114, unclassified, in ASHU.

17 Unclassified, in AAN 1.42, Bayley Papers.

18 http://www.onehda.com/

19 http://www.onehda.com/ourhistory.php

20 Brann, Henry. "Seton Hall from 1862 to 1864, in Burke, Robert E. *The Bishops' Bill and Setonia Bards* (Englewood, NJ: 1913), p. 380–86, typescript in notes of Carl Hinrichsen, in ASHU, unprocessed note file.

21 Bayley, *Register*, I, 57, 103, in AAN 1.12.

22 McQuaid to Bayley, September 1862, in Zwierlein, I, 328.

23 Bayley to McCloskey, July 18, 1864, in Bayley, *Letterbook*, I, 175. Cited in Beck, 11.

24 Brann to M. A. Corrigan, June 8, 1875, in AAN, R. G. 12, Accession 10–89, Other Bishops and Priests, Box 12, Brann file.

25 Brann to Bayley, October 8, 1867, in AAN, R. G. 12, Accession 10–89, Other Bishops and Priests, Box 12, Brann file.

26 Brann to Corrigan, October 27, 1873, in AAN, R. G. 12, Accession 10–89, Other Bishops and Priests, Box 12, Brann file.

27 Ibid.

28 Brann to Corrigan, March 12, 1875, in AAN, R. G. 12, Accession 10–89, Other Bishops and Priests, Box 12, Brann file.

29 Ibid.

30 Ibid.

31 Brann to Corrigan, January 26 and January 29, 1875, in AAN, R. G. 12, Accession 10–89, Other Bishops and Priests, Box 12, Brann file.

32 Brann to Corrigan, October 27, 1873, in AAN, R. G. 12, Accession 10–89, Other Bishops and Priests, Box 12, Brann file.

33 Brann to Bayley, October 8, 1867, in AAN, R. G. 12, Accession 10–89, Other Bishops and Priests, Box 12, Brann file.

34 Corrigan to Brann, July 25, 1878, in AAN, R. G. 12, Accession 10 – 89, Other Bishops and Priests, Box 12, Brann file.

35 Brann, Henry. "Seton Hall from 1862 to 1864," in Burke, *Bishops' Bill and Setonia Bards*, 380–86, typescript in notes of Carl Hinrichsen, in ASHU, unprocessed note file.

36 Brann, Henry, "Seton Hall from 1862 to 1864," 380–86.

37 Bayley to Bennett, February 30, 1862. This correspondence was provided in photocopy to Beck by All Hallows and is cited in Beck's unpublished notes. Beck's notes to his centennial history of Immaculate Conception Seminary can be found in AICS 1.2.2.1.

38 *Seton Hall College Catalogue,* 1862, 5.

39 Zwierlein, I, 328.

40 McQuaid Circular Letter, May 24, 1862, in AAN "Marriage Tribunal" unprocessed material.

41 Seton Hall *Register,* 5, in AAN 10.2.

42 Seton Hall *Register,* 75, in AAN 10.2; Bayley *Register,* I, 89, in AAN 1.12. According to the Seton Hall *Register,* Bayley confirmed 11; according to Bayley's *Register,* he confirmed 12.

43 *Seton Hall Catalogue,* 1861–62, in ASHU 1.1.1.

44 Curran, Robert Emmett. *Michael Augustine Corrigan and the Shaping of Conservative Catholicism in America, 1878–1902* (New York: 1978), 27.

45 *Seton Hall Catalogue,* 1861–62, in ASHU 1.1.1.

46 Brann, Henry, "Seton Hall from 1862 to 1864," 380–86.

47 Ibid.

48 *Seton Hall Catalogue,* 1861–62, in ASHU 1.1.1.

49 Ibid.

50 Marshall, 18.

51 Brann, Henry, "Seton Hall from 1862 to 1864," 380–86.

52 Marshall, 24.

53 Beck, 11.

54 *Seton Hall College Catalogue,* 1862, 5, in ASHU 1.1.1.

55 Marshall, 19.

56 Brann, Henry, "Seton Hall from 1862 to 1864," 380–86.

57 Beck, 10. Beck's notes ascribe this story to the remembrances of Doctor Brann in a letter to R. E. Burke, dated October 31, 1911, which is reproduced in Burke's *The Bishop's Bill and Setonia Bards* (Englewood, NJ: 1913), 380–86.

58 Brann, Henry, "Seton Hall from 1862 to 1864," 380–86.

Chapter Three

1 McQuaid Circular Letter, May 24, 1862, in AAN "Marriage Tribunal" unprocessed material.

2 Bayley, Circular, May 1, 1863, in AAN 1.22.

3 Thomas Preston, vicar general of New York, cited in Yaeger, 470.

4 AANY, E-b, Copy of letter to Reverend John Kelly, Jersey City, June 3, 1863, cited in Yaeger, 471.

5 Bayley *Register,* I, 108, in AAN 1.12.

6 Flynn, 604.

7 Wister, Robert J. *Immaculate Conception Chapel—Seton Hall University,* http://theology.shu.edu/chapel/.

8 Wister, Robert J. *Immaculate Conception Chapel—Seton Hall University,* http://theology.shu.edu/chapel/. The chapel continues to serve as the chapel of Seton Hall University.

9 *Newark Daily Advertiser,* February 7, 1870.

10 Beck, 10–11.

11 Marshall, 24.

12 Zwierlein, I, 347–48; Bayley, *Register,* I, 92, in AAN 1.12.

13 Mooney, Joseph A., *Memorial of the Most Reverend Michael Augustine Corrigan, Third Archbishop of New York* (New York: 1902), 5 ff; Curran, Robert Emmett, *Michael Augustine Corrigan and the Shaping of Conservative Catholicism in America, 1978–1902* (New York: 1902), 26–29.

14 Curran, 28.

15 McCloskey to M. A. Corrigan, Rome, September 7, 1865, in AANY, cited in Curran, 40.

16 McCloskey to M. A. Corrigan, Rome, March 3, 1865, in AANY, cited in Curran, 41.

17 Mooney, *Memorial of the Late Most Reverend Michael Augustine Corrigan,* 16; *Seton Hall College Catalogue,* 1864–65 to 1868–69, in ASHU 1.1.1.

18 *Seton Hall College Catalogue,* 1864–65, in ASHU 1.1.1.

19 Marshall, 25.

20 Bayley *Register,* I, , 135, in AAN 1.12.

21 Marshall, 25. Bayley *Register*, I, 142, in AAN 1.12; *Seton Hall Catalogue*, 1865–66, 23–26, in ASHU 1.1.1.

22 Marshall, 25. Bayley *Register*, I, 142, in AAN 1.12; *Seton Hall Catalogue*, 1865–66, 23–26, in ASHU 1.1.1; *Newark Daily Advertiser*, January 29, 1866.

23 George Hobart Doane (1830–1905). Doane was the son of George Washington Doane, Episcopal Bishop of New Jersey. After ordination to the diaconate in the Episcopal Church, he converted to Catholicism and was ordained a priest by Bishop Bayley. He served as pastor of St. Patrick's Cathedral as well as chancellor and vicar general.

24 Marshall, 25–26.

25 Bayley, *Circular Letter,* January 31, 1866, in AAN, 1.2.2.

26 Ibid.; McQuaid, *Circular Letter,* in *Seton Hall College Catalogue,* 1865–66, 23–26, in ASHU 1.1.1.

27 Marshall, 26–29.

28 *Seton Hall College Trustees Minutes,* 14–18, in ASHU 4.6.1.

29 Bayley to Society for the Propagation of the Faith, March 8, 1862, in Flynn, 287, writes that "My college, seminary, and the different missions of the Sisters of Charity are all doing well, and my only fear is our immense debt."

30 Beck, 12.

31 *Seton Hall College Catalogue,* 1865–66, frontispiece, in ASHU 1.1.1.

32 Marshall, 29–30.

33 Wister, Robert J., "Seton Hall Chapel," in http://theology.shu.edu/chapel/.

34 J. H. Corrigan, *Circular Letter,* June 18, 1885, interleaved in *Seton Hall College Catalogue,* 1885, in ASHU 1.1.1.

35 J. H. Corrigan, *Circular Letter,* June 18, 1885, interleaved in *Seton Hall College Catalogue,* 1885, in ASHU 1.1.1.

36 Leroy McWilliams with Jim Bishop. *Parish Priest* (New York: McGraw-Hill, 1953), 45. McWilliams was in the seminary during World War I, but seminary life had not changed much from the 1860s.

37 *Seton Hall College Catalogue,* 1864–65, 1868–69, in ASHU 1.1.1.

38 Bayley *Register,* I, 152, 154, in AAN 1.12.

39 Bayley *Register*, I, 155, in AAN 1.12; Zwierlein, II, 1–2.

40 Marshall, 33.

41 Zwierlein, II, 3.

42 Letter to Cardinal Barnabo, Rochester Copy, 1867, in BCA, 43A-R-4, cited in Yaeger, 235.

43 J. H. Corrigan to Wigger, Rochester, August 25, 1885, cited in Beck, 13.

Chapter Four

1 *Seton Hall College Trustees Minutes,* 20, in ASHU 4.6.1.

2 *Seton Hall College Trustees Minutes,* June 23, 1869, in ASHU 4.6.1

3 Bayley *Register*, I, 160, in AAN 1.12.

4 Beck, 13.

5 Beck, 14 Völker's principal task was instruction in the college department.

6 Joseph M. White. *The Diocesan Seminary in the United States: A History from the 1780's to the Present* (Notre Dame, IN: 1989), 131.

7 *Registrum Alumnorum et Ordinatorum ex almo Seminario sub titulo Immac. Conc. B. V. M.*, 2–4, in AICS B.4.

8 *Seton Hall College Catalogue,* 1862, 8–9, in ASHU 1.1.1.

9 Michael A. Corrigan, 1876 Quinquennial Report, December 13, 1876, in AAN, R. G. 3, Accession # ADN 8–88, Quinquennial Reports.

10 *Seton Hall College Catalogue,* 1870, in ASHU 1.1.1.

11 Brady to Boland, January 30, 1958, in AICS 3.6.5. Monsignor Joseph Brady carefully analyzed the early Seton Hall College catalogues and concluded that, based on class lists and other evidence, the theological program was a four-year program.

12 *Seton Hall College Catalogue,* 1870, in ASHU 1.1.1.

13 Beck, 15.

14 White, 134.

15 Examples in collection of Archives of Seton Hall University.

16 Marshall, 32, 43.

17 Corrigan, *Register,* II, 87, in AAN 2.11.

18 Kennelly, Edward F. *A Historical Study of Seton Hall College,* unpublished Ed.D. thesis from New York University, 1944, 83.

19 *Seton Hall College Catalogue,* 1869–71, in ASHU 1.1.1.

20 Ibid.

21 White, 132.

22 *Seton Hall College Catalogue,* 1864–65, in ASHU 1.1.1.

23 McCloskey to Michael Corrigan, September 7, 1865, NYAA, C-5, McCloskey, cited in Beck, 16.

24 White, 128.

25 Wister, Robert J., *Immaculate Conception Chapel—Seton Hall University*, http://theology.shu.edu/chapel/.

26 Marshall, 21–22.

27 Flynn, 529.

28 Corrigan *Register,* I, 327, in AAN 1.12.; M. A. Corrigan, 1876 Quinquennial Report, December 13, 1876, in AAN, R. G. 3, Acc. AAN 8–88, Quinquennial Reports.

29 This schedule is based on a summary of the horarium of the period in White, 128–30; and on records in the *Seton Hall Register* and Bishop Bayley's *Register* which record ordinations.

30 *Seton Hall College Catalogue,* 1870–72, 1872–73, in ASHU 1.1.1.

31 Program interleaved in *Seton Hall College Catalogue*, 1871, in ASHU 1.1.1.

Chapter Five

1 White, 48–86.

2 *Seton Hall College Catalogue*, 1867–68, in ASHU 1.1.1.

3 Burse Ledger, in AICS 6.3.1.

4 Beck, 16.

5 A dollar in the 1860s and 1870s would be worth $25 to $30 in 2009. All such figures are approximations cf. http://www.halfhill.com/inflation.html.

6 Bayley, Circular Letter, September 4, 1865, in AAN 1.2.2.

7 Bayley, Circular Letter, September 8, 1870, in AAN 1.2.2.

8 Bayley, Circular Letter, October 30, 1871, in AAN 1.2.2.

9 Bayley, Circular Letter, September 12, 1872, in AAN 1.2.2.

10 Doane, Circular Letter from Bishop's Secretary, undated, in AAN 1.2.2.

11 Corrigan, Circular Letter, December 1, 1876, in AAN 1.2.2.

12 *Sadlier's Catholic Directory, Almanac, and Ordo 1876* (New York: 1876).

13 Bayley to Corrigan, May 22, 1872, in AAN 1.32.

14 *Seton Hall College Trustees Minutes,* 21, 28, in ASHU 4.6.1.

15 *Seton Hall College Catalogue*, 1871–72, in ASHU 1.1.1.

16 J. H. Corrigan's circular of June 18, 1885, is interleaved in *Seton Hall College Catalogue*, 1885–86, in ASHU 1.1.1.

17 Wilson, Harold F. *Outline History of New Jersey* (New Brunswick, NJ: 1950), 124, cited in Hinrichsen, 43.

18 *Seton Hall College Trustees Minutes,* June 23, 1869, 29, in ASHU 4.6.1.

19 Bayley to M. A. Corrigan, February 20, 1869, in AANY, C-2, Bayley, cited in Beck, 17.

20 McQuaid to M. A. Corrigan, September 30, 1870, in Zwierlein, III, 368.

21 Bayley to M. A. Corrigan, Paris, September 17, 1869, in AANY, C-2, cited in Yaeger, 256.

22 J. H. Corrigan to Bayley, October 23, 1870, in AAN 1.42, Bayley Papers.

23 Galishoff, Stuart, *Newark: The Nation's Unhealthiest City 1832–1895* (New Brunswick, NJ: 1988).

24 J. H. Corrigan to Bayley, October 23, 1870, in AAN 1.42, Bayley Papers.

25 McQuaid to M. A. Corrigan, September 30, 1870, in Zwierlein, III, 368.

26 *Seton Hall Trustees Minutes*, June 20, 1870, in ASHU 4.6.1.

27 J. H. Corrigan to Wigger, May 15, 1882, in Beck unpublished notes, in AICS 1.2.2.3.

28 McQuaid to M. A. Corrigan, March 15, 1886, in Zwierlein, I, 318.

29 M. A. Corrigan to McQuaid, September 18, 1868, in Zwierlein, Fredrick J. *Letters of Archbishop Corrigan to Bishop McQuaid and Allied Documents,* I (Rochester, NY: 1946), 1.

30 *Concilii Plenarii Baltimorensis II., in Ecclesia Metropolitana Baltimorensi . . . Decreta* (Baltimore: 1868), 228.

31 McQuaid to John J. Williams, April 13, 1885, in ADR McQuaid Copybook, 187–88, cited in Ellis, *The Formative Years of the Catholic University of America* (Washington, DC: 1946), 143.

32 M. A. Corrigan to Orestes Brownson, April 12, 1871, in AUND, Brownson Papers, cited in Beck, 17.

33 Beck, 18.

34 Obituary of Archbishop Michael A. Corrigan, *New York Times*, May 6, 1902, cited in Curran, 42n.

35 Reverend William McNulty to McQuaid, April 26, 1871, in ADR, McQuaid Papers, cited in Beck, 18.

36 M. A. Corrigan to Orestes Brownson, April 21, 1871, in AUND, Brownson Papers, cited in Beck, 18.

37 *Seton Hall Trustees Minutes*, June 21, 1877, 43, in ASHU 4.6.1.

38 Bayley, *Circular Letter*, August 31, 1871, in AAN 1.2.2.

39 Bayley to Corrigan, Newark, September 16, 1871, in ASHU, Letter File, 1872, cited in Yaeger 117–19, note 71.

40 Bayley to Corrigan, February 25, 1870, in AANY, C-2, cited in Yaeger, 245.

41 Yaeger, 246.

42 Bayley *Register,* I, 141, 150, 159, 160, 165, 171, 194, 198, 200, in AAN 1.12.

43 Bayley to Corrigan, December 18, 1865, in AANY, Corrigan Papers, C-2, Bayley, cited in Beck, 15.

44 *Seton Hall College Catalogue*, 1870, interleaved invitations, in ASHU 1.1.1.

45 Bayley *Register,* I, 174, in AAN 1.12.

46 Curran, 42.

47 Bayley, *Letterbook,* 193, in Beck, 19.

Chapter Six

1 Marshall, 5.

2 Edward F. Kennelly, *A Historical Study of Seton Hall College* (unpublished doctoral dissertation, New York University, 1944), 84, cited in Hinrichsen, 39.

3 Bayley to Corrigan, Baltimore, December 21, 1872, In AANY C-1, cited in Curran, 43.

4 Bayley to Corrigan, Baltimore, August 19, 1873, in AANY, C-1, cited in Curran, 43n.

5 Bayley to Corrigan, Baltimore, August 19, 1873, in AANY, C-1, cited in Curran,, 47.

6 Corrigan to McQuaid, Newark, April 15, 1873, in ADR, cited in Curran, 47.

7 McQuaid to Corrigan, Rochester, April 6, 1873, in AANY, C-1, cited in Curran, 47.

8 Beck, 14.

9 Corrigan to Seton, January 1, 1878, in AUND, Seton Papers, cited in Curran, 48.

10 Corrigan Diary, 1872–73, October 10, 1872, in AANY, cited in Curran, 48.

11 J. H. Corrigan, Circular Letter, September 8, 1877, interleaved in *Seton Hall Catalogue*, 1878, in ASHU 1.1.1.

12 M. A. Corrigan, August 28, 1877, Circular Letter, cited in Beck, 21.

13 M. A. Corrigan to McQuaid, August 23, 1878, in ADR, McQuaid Papers, cited in Beck, 21.

14 M. A. Corrigan to McQuaid, undated, in Zwierlein, *Letters of Archbishop Corrigan to Bishop McQuaid and Allied documents,* I (Rochester, NY: 1946), 13.

15 Beck, 21.

16 *Seton Hall College Catalogues*, 1877, 1878, 1879, 1880, in ASHU 1.1.1.

17 J. H. Corrigan to Wigger, May 14, 1882, in AAN 3.3.

18 J. H. Corrigan, *Circular Letter,* June 18, 1885, interleaved in *Seton Hall Catalogue* 1885–86, in ASHU 1.1.1.

19 *Seton Hall College Trustees Minutes,* 46, 49, 51, 54, in ASHU 4.6.1.

20 Corrigan, *Register,* II, 187, in AAN 2.11.

21 J. H. Corrigan to Wigger, May14, 1882, in AAN 3.3.

22 M. A. Corrigan, Circular Letter, March 27, 1875, interleaved in *Seton Hall College Catalogue*, 1875, in ASHU 1.1.1.

23 Isaac A. Nichols, Health Physician, Newark, N.J. to President of Seton Hall College, April 10, 1875, interleaved in *Seton Hall College Catalogue*, 1875, in ASHU 1.1.1.

24 M. A. Corrigan, Circular Letter, March 27, 1875, interleaved in *Seton Hall College Catalogue*, 1875, in ASHU 1.1.1.

25 Corrigan *Register,* I, 288–91., in AAN 1.12.

26 J. H. Corrigan to Parents of Students, December 11, 1880, interleaved in *Seton Hall College Catalogue*, 1880, in ASHU 1.1.1.

27 *Seton Hall College Catalogue*, 1898, 53, in ASHU 1.1.1.

28 Josephine Tardis to Bernard McQuaid, September 11, 1865, in ASHU, R.G. 3.1, Box 1.

29 *Seton Hall College Catalogue,*1877–78, in ASHU 1.1.1.

30 Marshall, 39.

31 McNamara, Robert. *The American College in Rome, 1855–1955* (Rochester, NY: 1956), 715–16, n 37; Flynn, 612–13.

32 Marshall, 35–42.

33 Leslie, Shane, ed., *Memories of Many Years (1839–1922)by Archbishop Seton* (New York: 1923), 18.

34 William McCloskey to M. A. Corrigan, September 15, 1884, in AANY, C-5, M, cited in Beck, 24.

35 Leslie, Shane, ed., *Memories of Many Years (1839–1922)by Archbishop Seton*, New York: 1923, 184.

36 Ibid., 11.

37 Ibid., 154.

38 Ibid., 159–61.

39 Ibid., 161.

40 Leslie, Shane, ed., *Memories of Many Years (1839–1922)by Archbishop Seton*, New York: 1923, 190.

41 *Dictionary of American Biography,* under the auspices of the American Council of Learned Societies (New York: 1924–44), xvi, 597–98.

42 Marshall, 59–60, photo on 60.

43 M. A. Corrigan to Gibbons, April 28, 1884, Private, in AAB, 78-1-5, cited in Hinrichsen, 208.

44 Ellis, John Tracy, *The Life of James Cardinal Gibbons*, II, 423.

45 Leslie, 227–30.

46 Beck, 20.

47 Marshall, 46.

48 Ibid., 44.

49 Ibid., 46.

50 Beck, 21.

51 *Seton Hall College Catalogue*, 1878, 43, in ASHU 1.1.1.

52 Marshall, 6.

53 Helene DeBarberey, *Elizabeth Seton*, 499, cited in Kennelly, 33.

54 Beck, 22.

Chapter Seven

1 Program interleaved in *Seton Hall College Catalogue*, 1881, in ASHU 1.1.1.

2 J. H. Corrigan, *Circular Letter*, interleaved in *Seton Hall College Catalogue*, 1878.

3 Corrigan *Register*, I, 164, 166, 167, 187, in AAN 1.12.

4 Hinrichsen, Carl D. *The History of the Diocese of Newark, 1873–1901* (Ann Arbor, MI, 152–53.

5 APF, Acta, v 249, f 257r.

6 Hinrichsen, 154.

7 McQuaid to Corrigan, May 27, 1881, in Ellis, *Formative Years*, 75–76.

8 Hinrichsen, 155.

9 Archives of the Sacred Congregation for the Evangelization of Peoples, or *de Propaganda fide*, Acta, 1881, v 249, f. 262v (orig. Italian), hereafter ACPF, Acta.

10 DeConcilio to Cardinal Simeoni, January 25, 1881, in ACPF, Scritture Originali Riferite nelle Congregazioni Generali, 1622–1892, hereafter ACPF, SOCG, 1881, v 1013, f 923r-924v. (orig. Italian).

11 Smith to Cardinal Simeoni, January 30, 1881, in ACPF, SOCG, 1881, v 1013, f 928r-929v. (orig. Italian).

12 ACPF, Acta, 1881, v. 249, f 260r (orig. Latin).

13 McQuaid to Corrigan, July 29, 1881, cited in Hinrichsen, 169.

14 Corrigan to McQuaid, July 30, 1881, in ADR, cited in Hinrichsen, 169.

15 Hinrichsen, 170.

16 Flynn, 478.

17 Hinrichsen, 171n.

18 Ibid., 169.

19 Seton to Edwards, March 18, 1893, in AUND, Edwards papers, cited in Hinrichsen, 168n.

20 Seton to Edwards, August 30, 1907, in AUND, Edwards Papers, cited in Hinrichsen, 168n.

21 Hinrichsen, 159n.

22 Ibid., 158.

23 Wigger, *Register*, III, 99, in AAN 3.1.1.

24 Hinrichsen, 158.

25 Ibid., 160.

26 Ibid., 173.

27 *Freeman's Journal*, October 22, 1881, cited in Hinrichsen, 175.

28 Secretary of Congregation to Wigger (draft), in ACPF, Lettere e Decreti, 1886, 240, April 20, 1886.

29 Flynn, 211.

30 Yaeger, 144.

31 Hinrichsen, 182–83.

32 Denis J. McCartie (secretary to Bishop Wigger), Circular Letter, December 10, 1881, cited in Beck, 23.

33 Hinrichsen, 183–84.

34 Ibid., 184n.

35 Messmer to Wigger, March 8, 1883, in AAN 3.36.

36 Wigger *Register*, II, 226, in AAN 2.11.

37 *Freeman's Journal*, March 31, 1883, cited in Hinrichsen, 185.

Chapter Eight

1 *Freeman's Journal*, November 3, 1883.

2 Marshall, 61.

3 Beck, 28.

4 W. J. Schickel to Wigger, September 22, 1883, cited in Beck, 28.

5 Marshall, 61–62

6 Ibid., 62.

7 Seminarians of the Immaculate Conception Seminary, Circular Letter to the Clergy, March 1, 1887, interleaved in bound *Seton Hall College Catalogues*, 1893–1903, in ASHU 1.1.1.

8 Marshall, 63–64.

9 M. A. Corrigan to McQuaid, January 18, 1881, in ADR, McQuaid Papers, cited in Beck, 29.

10 Seton Hall *Trustees Minutes*, August 25, 1882, 56–57.

11 J. A. Corrigan to Wigger, May 14, 1882, in AAN 3.36.

12 Ibid.

13 M. A. Corrigan to McQuaid, November 20 and November 22, 1882, in ADR, McQuaid Papers, cited in Beck, 29.

14 McQuaid to Corrigan, November 23, 1882, in AANY, C-2, cited in Hinrichsen, 265.

15 Boniface Wimmer to Alexius Edelbrock, November 27, 1882, in Jerome Oetgen, (ed.), *The Letters of Boniface Wimmer, Volume III, 1872–1887*, Draft 2000, 390. I am grateful to Dr. Dermot Quinn for providing me with his research on this question.

16 Hinrichsen, 265–66.

17 Wigger, *Register,* II, 230, in AAN 2.11.

18 *Seton Hall College Trustees Minutes*, May 1885, 62, in AAN 4.6.1.

19 Wigger, *Circular Letter*, August 15, 1885, in AAN R.G. 3.32.

20 *Concilium Plenarium Baltimor. III, Acta et Decreta* (Baltimore: 1886), 182–84.

21 Spalding, John Lancaster, *Lectures and Discourses* (New York: 1882), 151; also in Ellis, *Formative Years,* 77.

22 http://tour.cua.edu/heritage/biographies/marycaldwell.cfm;
http://www.schenectadyhistory.org/families/hmgfm/caldwell-1.html

23 New York *Sun,* December 11, 1884, in Ellis, *Formative Years*, 116.

24 Spalding to Ryan, February 8, 1885, in Minutes of the meeting of the university committee, Monday–Tuesday, January 26–27, 1885, New York City, in ACUA, cited in Ellis, *Formative Years*, 127.h

25 Ibid.

26 Wigger to M. A. Corrigan, January 15, 1885, in AANY, C-2, cited in Beck.

27 Minutes of the meeting of the university committee, January 26–27, 1885, in Ellis, *Formative Years*, 124.

28 *New York Times*, February 3, 1885.

29 Gibbons to John Farley, March 3, 1885, in AAB, Letterbook of Archbishop Gibbons, p. 145, cited in Ellis, *Formative Years*, 132.

30 M. A. Corrigan to Gibbons, March 25, 1885, in AAB, 79 H3.1, cited in Ellis, *Formative Years*, 136.

31 Ibid.

32 Gibbons to Corrigan, April 1, 1885, in AANY C-2, cited in Curran.

33 Spalding to Gibbons, April 21, 1885, in AAB 79-J-12, cited in Hinrichsen, 265.

34 *Sadlier's Catholic Directory*, 1884, 383; 1885, 265–66.

35 J. H. Corrigan, *Circular Letter*, June 18, 1885, Private. Not to be communicated to the Press or the Public, interleaved in *Seton Hall College Catalogue*, 1885–86, in ASHU 1.1.1.

36 Marshall, 65.

37 Kennelly, 98. Flynn, 619.

38 *Newark Daily Advertiser*, March 9, 1886, 2.

39 Ibid.

40 Ibid.

41 Marshall, 68.

42 J. H. Corrigan, *Circular Letter*, March 23, 1886, interleaved in Seton Hall Catalogue, 1885–86, in ASHU 1.1.1; Marshall, 66.

43 *Seton Hall College Trustees Minutes*, 69, in ASHU 4.6.1.

44 J. H. Corrigan, *Circular Letter*, March 23, 1886, interleaved in Seton Hall Catalogue, 1885–86, in ASHU 1.1.1; Marshall, 66.

45 Wigger *Register*, III, 5, in AAN 3.11; Seton Hall Trustees Minutes, 65–67, in ASHU 4.6.1; Marshall, 68.

46 *Seton Hall College Trustees Minutes*, 70, 73, in ASHU 4.6.1.

47 *Seton Hall College Trustees Minutes*, 65–67, 75, 107, in ASHU 4.6.1.

48 Wigger *Register*, III, 242, in AAN 3.11.

49 Wigger to J. H. Corrigan, January 3, 1888, in AAN 3.31, Letterbook, v.2, 289.

50 Flynn, 610.

51 Marshall, 70.

52 Ibid., 89

53 Kennelly, 114.

Chapter Nine

1 Beck, 23–26.

2 Marshall, 93.

3 J. H. Corrigan to Wigger, February 14, 1882, in AAN 3.36.

4 J. H. Corrigan to Wigger, May 14, 1882, in AAN 3.36

5 Robert Seton to Wigger, November 24, 1883, in AAN 3.36.

6 Robert Seton to Wigger, January 10, 1884, in AAN 3.36.

7 Robert Seton to Wigger, November 24, 1883, in AAN 3.36.

8 Hinrichsen, 207–9.

9 Shane, 197.

10 *Concilium Plenarium Baltimor. III, Acta et Decreta* (Baltimore: 1886), 135–93.

11 Wigger *Register,* II, 287, in AAN 3.11.

12 White, *Diocesan Seminary in the United States*, 244.

13 *Minutes of the Diocesan Council,* 1887–1912, 1, September 22, 1887, in AAN 3.1.

14 Beck, 28.

15 *Seton Hall College Catalogue* 1885–86 *Supplement*, 3, in ASHU 1.1.1.

16 *Seton Hall College Catalogue*, 1878, in ASHU 1.1.1.

17 *Seton Hall College Catalogue,* 1898, 69–70, in ASHU 1.1.1.

18 *Registrum Alumnorum,* 48, in AICS B. 4.

19 *Seton Hall College Catalogue*, 1873–74, ASHU 1.1.1.

20 *Seton Hall College Catalogue*, 1898, 56–57, ASHU 1.1.1.

21 Ibid., 69–70."

22 *Seton Hall College Catalogue*, 1898, 6970; 1926–27, 60, in ASHU 1.1.1.

23 White, *The Diocesan Seminary in the United States*, 249.

24 Ibid.

25 Adolphe Tanquerey to Thomas McLaughlin, Jan. 21, 1931, in AICS, 3.1.9.3.

26 Beck, 27–28. Beck compiled the list of texts from the Seton Hall catalogues that listed the texts used in philosophy and from analysis of seminary library holdings and interviews with alumni.

27 Wigger *Register*, III, 8, 31, in AAN 3.11.

28 Wigger *Register*, II, 208, 229, 252, in AAN 2.11; III, 21, 27, 286, 315, in AAN 3.11.

29 J. H. Corrigan to Wigger, April 28, 1882, in AAN 3.3.

30 J. H. Corrigan to Wigger, April 19, 1882, in AAN 3.3.

31 Beck, 26.

32 Spalding, John L., "The Higher Education," in *Means and Ends of Education* (Chicago: 1895), 212–13, cited in Ellis, *Formative Years*, 100.

33 McCartie to Wigger, October 7, 1890, in AAN 3.36.

34 M. A. Corrigan to Cardinal McCloskey, April 28, 1876, in AANY A-30 A, cited in Beck, 24.

35 Beck, 24.

36 Marshall, 42–43.

37 Ibid., 43.

38 Flynn, 614.

39 Beck, 25.

40 Wigger, *Register,* 252, in AAN 3.1.

41 Flynn, 259.

42 Kennelly, 118.

43 Flynn, 621.

44 Marshall, 86.

Chapter Ten

1 Beck, 25, Kennelly, 120.

2 *Hoffmann's Catholic Directory 1898.*

3 Wigger, *Register*, III, 277—78.

4 Wigger, *Register*, II, 271, in AAN 2.11.

5 Wigger, *Register*, III, 325, in AAN 3.11.

6 Beck, 31.

7 Wilson, Harold F. et al., *Outline History of New Jersey* (New Brunswick, NJ: 1950), 187.

8 Ibid., 124–25, 128, 138–40, 186

9 Third Plenary Council of Baltimore, 1884, Title ii.

10 ACPF, Acta, v 272, f 345v; Flynn, 552.

11 ACPF, Acta, v 272, f 345v, 348r, 350v.

12 Wister, Robert J. *The Establishment of the Apostolic Delegation in the United States: The Satolli Mission, 1892–1896* (Rome: 1981), 271–72.

13 ACPF Acta 1901, v 272, f345r-351r, 351r.

14 Wister, *Establishment of the Apostolic Delegation*, XVII, XXI.

15 *Newark News*, July 25, 1901.

16 Flynn, 554.

17 Unidentified clippings in McLaughlin Library and *Seton Hall Clippings, 1901–1906,* cited in Beck, 32.

18 Beck, 32.

19 Ibid., 32.

20 Flynn, 554.

21 *The Catholic Directory 1902* (Milwaukee: 1902).

22 Program "Greetings of the Seminarians and Students of Seton Hall to their Honored Alumnus and Beloved Bishop, Rt. Rev. John J. O'Connor, D.D., on the Occasion of the Silver Jubilee of His Priesthood," in AAN 4.41, O'Connor Papers.

23 *Newark Evening News*. March 19, 1903.

24 John O'Connor, *Pastoral Letter*, November 1, 1902, in Flynn, 555-560.

25 O'Connor, *Circular Letter*, October 1, 1903, in Flynn, 561-563.

26 Beck, 33.

27 Flynn, 563, 565.

28 Ibid., 565.

29 Analysis of *Registrum Alumnorum et Ordinatorum ex almo Seminario sub titulo Immac. Conc. B. V. M.*, 76–77, in AICS B.4.

30 Hinrichsen, 300.

31 *Newark Evening News*, May 4, 1904.

32 AAN, 4.80, O'Connor Papers.

33 *Newark Evening News*. March 19, 1903.

34 *Newark Evening News,* October 20, 1904.

35 Beck, 33.

36 Interview with Alan Delozier, archivist of Seton Hall University, January 9, 2009.

37 Seton Hall Clippings 1901–6, in archives, cited by Beck, 33.

38 Stafford to O'Connor, January 13, 1905, in AAN 4.42, O'Connor Papers.

39 Beck, 34.

Chapter Eleven

1 Wister, Robert, *Immaculate Conception Chapel Seton Hall University: The Story of its Interior Design,* http://theology.shu.edu/chapel/SHU_Chapel/interior_page_04.htm.

2 Wister, Robert, *Immaculate Conception Chapel Seton Hall University: The Story of a Venerable Building,* http://theology.shu.edu/chapel/SHU_Chapel/chapel_page_01.htm.

3 *The Newark Daily Advertiser*, June 12, 1906.

4 *Seton Hall Catalogue 1906,* 77, in ASHU 1.1.1.

5 Wister, Robert, *Immaculate Conception Chapel Seton Hall University: The Story of its Interior Design,* http://theology.shu.edu/chapel/SHU_Chapel/interior_page_04.htm.

6 Beck, 34; *Newark Sunday Call*, June 3, 1906; *Newark Evening News,* June 13, 1906.

7 O'Connor, Circular letter, August 22, 1905; February 4, 1906.

8 Stafford to O'Connor, January 13, 1905, cited in Beck, 34.

9 Beck, 34.

10 Kennelley, 128–29.

11 Beck, 37. Beck bases his information on interviews with senior priests of the 1960s who attended Seton Hall during Mooney's tenure as rector. They were Monsignors James Owens, John Clark, and George Baker.

12 *Seton Hall College Catalogue*, June 1910, 29–30, in ASHU 1.1.1; *Catholic Directory*, 1910, 5-7-508.

13 Beck, 37.

14 Ibid.

15 *Acta Apostolicae Sedis*, I, 1909, 532.

16 Beck, 36.

17 Beck, unpublished notes in AICS 1.2.2.1.

18 *The Independent*, New York, LXXVII, n. 3173, September 23, 1909, 714–716.

19 McNamara, Robert F., "Archbishop Hanna, Rochesterian" in *Rochester History*, XXV, n. 2, April 1963, 14–17.

20 Beck, 37.

21 McWilliams, LeRoy, with Bishop, Jim, *Parish Priest* (New York: 1953), 50.

Chapter Twelve

1 Recollections of Jersey City lore by the author.

2 McWilliams, LeRoy, with Jim Bishop, *Parish Priest* (New York: 1953), 38–39.

3 Joseph O'Toole to Thomas McLaughlin, February 24, 1931, in AICS 3.7.1.D.

4 McLaughlin to O'Toole, March 7, 1931, in AICS 3.7.1.D.

5 Durant, Will, *Transition: A Sentimental Story of One Mind and One Era* (New York: 1927), Foreword.

6 http://www.willdurant.com/bibliography.htm

7 Buckley, William F., "Will Durant, RIP," *National Review*, January 22, 1982, 20.

8 Durant, Will and Ariel, *Will and Ariel Durant: A Dual Autobiography* (New York: 1977), 30.

9 Ibid., 30–31.

10 Ibid., 24.

11 Ibid., 32.

12 Ibid., 32–33.

13 Ibid., 34.

14 Durant, *Transition*, 60.

15 Ibid., 51.

16 Ibid., 51.

17 Ibid., 111–112.

18 Ibid., 112.

19 Durant, Will and Ariel, 35.

20 Durant, *Transition*, 124.

21 *Registrum Alumnorum et Ordinatorum ex almo Seminario sub titulo Immac. Conc. B. V. M.*, 76–77, in AICS B.4. Those who entered that day were John James Clark, Timothy Joseph Hanley, John Clarence McClary, William James Durant, Thomas Joseph Herron, Thomas Francis Maher, and William Joseph Caffrey. In his autobiography, Durant dates his entry into the seminary as September 1908. Records show it to be September, 1909. He also dates his departure as 1910; records show it to have been Feb. 1, 1911.

22 Durant, Will and Ariel, *Will and Ariel Durant*, 36.

23 Durant, *Transition*, 111.

24 McWilliams, 45.

25 Ibid., 42.

26 Durant, *Transition*, 124-128; McWilliams, Leroy, 44-45.

27 McWilliams, 46.

28 Durant, *Transition*, 124–28.

29 McWilliams, 38–39.

30 Durant, *Transition*, 124–28.

31 Ibid., 127-128.

32 McWilliams, 38–39.

33 Ibid., 40.

34 Ibid., 40.

35 Durant, *Transition*, 124–28.

36 McWilliams, 38–39.

37 Ibid., 42.

38 Durant, *Transition*, 130–131.

39 McWilliams, 44.

40 O'Connor, Quinquennial Report, 1914, in AAN, R. G. 4, Acc. 8–88, Quinquennials.

41 McWilliams, 47.

42 Ibid., 48.

43 *Seton Hall College Catalogue*, 1908, in ASHU 1.1.1, notes that there is a private retreat in December for those to be ordained priests that month, and another retreat in June for those to be ordained then.

44 Durant, Will and Ariel, *Will and Ariel Durant*, 36.

45 Durant, *Transition*, 141.

46 Ibid.

47 Durant, Will and Ariel, *Will and Ariel Durant*, 38.

48 *Newark Evening News*, January 19, 1912, 1.

49 Schroth, Raymond A., "The Rise, Fall and Rise Again of Will Durant, Truth-Seeker," *New York Times*, December 8, 1985, sec. 11, p. 40.

50 Durant, *Transition*, 45–46.

51 McWilliams, 49–50.

Chapter Thirteen

1 *Newark Evening News*, March 28, 1909, p. 4.
2 Kennelley, 132.
3 Durant, *Transitions*, 133.
4 Ibid., 134.
5 *Newark Evening News*, March 28, 1909, p. 4.
6 Kennelley, 133.
7 *Seton Hall College Trustees Minutes*, April 5, 1909, in ASHU 4.6.1.
8 Kennelley, 133.
9 Durant, *Transition*, 133–34.
10 O'Connor *Circular Letter*, July 13, 1911.
11 *Seton Hall College Trustees Minutes*, June 11, 1919, in ASHU 4.6.1.
12 O'Connor, *Quinquennial Report, 1914*, in AAN, R. G. 4, Acc. 8-88, Quinquennials. "Novo aedificio tamen opus est ut dioceseos indigentiis provideri possint. Nam numerus alumnorus quovis anno crescit. Novum aedificium anno proximo incepturi sumus quod pro numero alumnorum sat amplo sufficient."
13 *Seton Hall College Trustees Minutes*, June 9, 1920, in ASHU 4.6.1
14 *Seton Hall College Trustees Minutes*, June 15, 1921, in ASHU 4.6.1.
15 Ibid.
16 Kupke, Raymond, *Living Stones: A History of the Catholic Church in The Diocese of Paterson* (Clifton, NJ: 1987), 221–22.
17 Photograph Collection in ASHU.
18 McLaughlin, *Circular Letter*, undated, under cover letter of Bishop O'Connor, April 20, 1923, in AAN, 4.20.
19 Field, William N. "Thomas Aloysius Boland," in *The Bishops of Newark* (South Orange, NJ: 1978), 125–146, and Catholic Hierarchy http://www.catholic-hierarchy.org/bishop/bbolandt.html .
20 Upon episcopal ordination, bishops assume the honorary degree of doctor of divinity, placing the letters "D.D." after their names. The degree of doctor of sacred theology, "S.T.D.," is an earned degree and cannot simply be assumed.
21 Notebook, probably of House Prefect, 1924–25, in AICS 12.1.1.
22 Beck, 43.
23 McLaughlin *Memorandum 1924–1927*, in AICS 3.1.9.1.
24 McLaughlin to Mestice, March 6, 1929, in AICS 3.7.1.M.
25 Mestice to McLaughlin, March 8, 1929, in AICS 3.7.1.M.
26 Notebook, probably of House Prefect, 1924–25, in AICS 12.1.1.
27 McLaughlin, *Memorandum 1924–1927*, in AICS 3.1.9.1.
28 Notebook, probably of House Prefect, 1924–25, in AICS 12.1.1.

Chapter Fourteen

1 *Seton Hall College Trustees Minutes*, June 15, 1921, in ASHU 4.6.1.
2 *Seton Hall College Trustees Minutes*, June 10, 1925, in ASHU 4.6.1.
3 Beck, 35.
4 Ibid., 39.
5 *Pastor Aeternus*, ch.3, p. 2, July 18, 1870.
6 White, 268.
7 Ibid. Joseph White gives an excellent description of the growth of Roman authority over seminaries, 267–92.
8 *Acta Sanctae Sedis* 38 401f. Decrees of the Sacred Congregation of the Council.
9 *Sacrorum antstitum*, in *Codicis iuris canonici fontes,* cura Petri Cardinalis Gasparri editi (Typis polyglottis Vaticanis, 1933), III, 774–90.
10 *Acta Apostolicae Sedis*, I (1909), 7 –19.
11 *Acta Apostolicae Sedis* 7 (1915), 493–95; White, 269.
12 White, 270.
13 Fumasoni-Biondi, Pietro, "Copy of Letter Addressed to All the Ordinaries of the United States by Order of the Sacred Congregation for Seminaries and Universities," May 26, 1928, in AICS 3.2.2.
14 An excellent summary of the seminary legislation of the 1917 *Code of Canon Law* is found in White, 269–71.
15 White, 273; AAS 22 (1930), 146–48.
16 White, 273.
17 Fumasoni-Biondi, "Copy of Letter Addressed to All the Ordinaries of the United States."

18 Ibid.

19 Ibid.

20 White, 275.

21 Ibid.

22 Ibid, 462, n. 23.

23 Ibid., 312.

24 McLaughlin, "Proposal," in ASHU 3.9, presidential papers.

25 Crawley, F. M. to McClary, V. G., March 23, 1936, cited in Beck, 39.

26 McCabe, L. R., "Darlington, A Jacobean Manor in New Jersey," in *The Architectural Record* XXXII (July–December, 1912), 497, in AICS 9.2.1.2.

27 Ibid., 502.

28 *Newark Evening News*, November 8, 1924, in AICS 9.2.1.2.

29 Russo, Michael, "Darlington: An Estate in the Ramapo Valley, 1871–1914," New York University, unpublished seminar paper in AICS 9.2.1.2, provided the information about the history of the estate. Documents relating to the country club, including promotional brochures, in AICS 9.2.1.2.

30 "Brief History of the Immaculate Conception Major Diocesan Seminary of the Diocese of Newark, New Jersey—1937," in AICS 1.2.1.3. This was composed to be placed in the cornerstone of the seminary. No author is indicated on the copy in the archives.

31 Minutes of the Board of Consultors, 1926–35, cited in Beck, 39.

32 *Seton Hall College Trustees Minutes*, June 9, 1926, in ASHU 4.6.1.

33 Financial Report ICS, July 1926–December 17, 1928, in AAN, ICS file, cited in Beck, 39.

34 Vicar General to Fumasoni-Biondi, June 4, 1926, in AAN, R.G. 3,4,5,6, Acc. 8-88, 2—Apostolic Delegate.

35 "Brief History of the Immaculate Conception Major Diocesan Seminary of the Diocese of Newark, New Jersey—1937," in AICS 1.2.1.3.

36 Thomas McLaughlin, Appointment Books, in ASHU, 2.9.1.1, Presidential Papers.

37 *Newark Ledger*, October 13, 1926, cited in Beck, 40.

38 McLaughlin notes cited in "Brief History of the Immaculate Conception Major Diocesan Seminary of the Diocese of Newark, New Jersey—1937," in AICS 1.2.1.3.

Chapter Fifteen

1 McLaughlin *Memorandum 1924–1927*, in AICS 3.1.9.1.

2 Ibid.

3 Ibid.

4 "Recall Early Darlington Days," in *The Advocate*, July 4, 1958.

5 See McLaughlin *Memorandum 1924–1927*, in AICS 3.1.9.1.

6 "Brief History of the Immaculate Conception Major Diocesan Seminary of the Diocese of Newark, New Jersey—1937," in AICS 1.2.1.3.

7 The location of the rooms is based on the recollections of Msgr. John McHenry, as recorded in the unpublished notes of Henry G. J. Beck, in AICS 1.2.2.1.

8 List of professors in Beck, 43.

9 *Constitutiones Seminarii Majoris Dioceseos Novarcensis*, Darlington, NJ, 1929, in AICS 1.3.1; *Immaculate Conception Seminary Rules and Regulations for Seminarians*, c. 1936, in AICS 1.3.1. The citations are taken from these two documents.

10 McLaughlin *Appointment Books*, in ASHU 2.9.1.1, Presidents' Papers.

11 Ibid.

12 "How good and joyful it is to live as brothers together."

Chapter Sixteen

1 Cicognani to Your Excellency, May 5, 1935, in AICS 3.2.2.

2 Walsh to Cicognani, May 14, 1935, in AICS 3.2.2.

3 Fenlon to Curley, March 13, 1934, in Sulpician Archives, Baltimore, RG 13, Box 14, cited in White, 280.

4 Recollections of this writer. These devotions continued until 1967.

5 Fumasoni-Biondi, "Copy of Letter Addressed to All the Ordinaries of the United States ."

6 Form letter of acceptance, June 1942, in AAN R.G. 6, Acc. 2-89, Series 1.

7 Ibid.

8 *Benedicite Dominum*, or the Canticle of the Three Young Men is taken from the Old Testament book of Daniel (Dan. 3, 57–88; 56).

9 A serious demeanor.

10 Fumasoni-Biondi, "Copy of Letter Addressed to All the Ordinaries of the United States . "

Chapter Seventeen

1 *Fifteenth Census of the US—1930—Population*, vol 1, 713.

2 *Official Catholic Directory 1929;* Beck, 31.

3 *Official Catholic Directory 1929.*

4 Reilly, George A., "Thomas J. Walsh," in *The Bishops of Newark 1953–1978*, (South Orange, NJ: 1978), 98–105.

5 "Brief History of the Immaculate Conception Major Diocesan Seminary of the Diocese of Newark, New Jersey—1937, in AICS 1.2.1.3. This was composed to be placed in the cornerstone of the seminary. No author is indicated on the copy in the archives.

6 *Minutes of Council of Deputies—Darlington—Immaculate Conception Seminary (1927–1968)*, May 24, 1928, in AICS 2.1.1.

7 Immaculate Conception Seminary File, Report of December 17, 1928, cited in Beck's unpublished notes in AICS 1.2.2.1.

8 McLaughlin to Walsh, December 14, 1929, in AAN R.G. 5, Walsh, Box 7.

9 Pledge, June 1935, in AICS 4.3.3.1.

10 *Minutes of the Board of Deputies*, May 12, 1932, in AICS 2.2.1.

11 Report of the Rector of the Immaculate Conception Major Diocesan Seminary at Darlington, presented to the Annual Meeting of the Board of Deputies held at the Seminary, May 13, 1937, in AICS 2.2.1.

12 McLaughlin to Walsh, June 24, 1933, in AAN R.G. 5, Walsh, Box 7.

13 *Minutes of the Board of Deputies*, May 17, 1934, in AICS 2.2.1.

14 The titles "Most Reverend" and "Excellency" were introduced for Roman Catholic bishops in 1931. Previously Roman Catholic bishops were "Right Reverend" and addressed in the English style as "Your Lordship."

15 "A Seminarian" to Walsh, January 5, 1991, in AAN R.G. 5, Walsh, Box 7.

16 Walsh to McLaughlin, January 7, 1931, in AAN R.G. 5, Walsh, Box 7.

17 McLaughlin to Walsh, February 18, 1931, in AAN R.G. 5, Walsh, Box 7

18 Walsh to McLaughlin, February 24, 1931, on McLaughlin to Walsh, February 18, 1931, in AAN R G. 5, Walsh, Box 7.

Chapter Eighteen

1 *Statement of Rt. Rev. Msgr. Thomas H. McLaughlin, P.A., V.G., S.T.D., Rector of Seminary, concerning the relations of Joseph Sanford Shanley, of Newark, architect and the project of new building for Immaculate Conception Seminary, at Darlington,* March 11, 1935; McLaughlin to Walsh, December 17, 1931, both in AICS 9.2.2.1.

2 Shanley to McLaughlin, November 12, 1929, in AICS 9.2.2.1.

3 *Minutes of the Board of Deputies*, June 8, 1936, in AICS 2.1.1.

4 McLaughlin to Walsh, draft, December 20, 1930, not sent, together with notation regarding conversation with Walsh, in AICS 9.2.2.1.

5 *Minutes of Council of Deputies—Darlington—Immaculate Conception Seminary (1927–1968)*, May 21, 1931, in AICS 2.1.1.

6 McLaughlin to Walsh, December 3, 1927, in AICS 9.2.2.1.

7 *Minutes of Council of Deputies—Darlington—Immaculate Conception Seminary (1927–1968)*, May 12, 1932, in AICS 2.1.1.

8 *Statement of Rt. Rev. Msgr. Thomas H. McLaughlin, P.A., V.G., S.T.D., Rector of Seminary, concerning the relations of Joseph Sanford Shanley, of Newark, architect and the project of new building for Immaculate Conception Seminary, at Darlington,* March 11, 1935; McLaughlin to Walsh, December 17, 1931, both in AICS 9.2.2.1

9 Shanley to Walsh, February 19, 1935; Shanley to Cicognani, August 1, 1935; October 14, 1935, receipt "Paid in full," in AICS 9.2.1.1; also in *Minutes of the Board of Deputies*, note dated October 14, 1935, in AICS 2.2.1.

10 John A. Duffy, Affidavit, undated, in AAN R.G. 6, Acc. AAN 4-89, Box 3 of 4.

11 John C. McClary, Chancellor, Circular Letter, May 1, 1929, in AAN R.G. 6, Acc. AAN 4-89, Box 3 of 4.

12 Program and Invitation, Conferral of Papal Honors, October 30, 1929, in AAN R.G. 6, Acc. AAN 4-89, Box 3 of 4.

13 Thomas J. Maloney account, in AAN R.G. 6, Acc. AAN 4-89, Box 3 of 4.

14 Pius XI to Walsh, August 1, 1929, in AAN R.G. 6, Acc. AAN 4-89, Box 3 of 4.

15 *Jersey Journal*, August 18, 1934.

16 Definitive Financial Report, New Seminary Campaign, December 8, 1941, covering Nov. 19, 1936, to November 19, 1941, in AICS 14.2.1.1.2.4.

17 *Minutes of the Board of Deputies*, June 6, 1935, in AICS 2.1.1.

18 *Minutes of the Board of Deputies*, June 8, 1936, in AICS 2.1.1.

19 *Minutes of the Board of Deputies*, June 6, 1935, in AICS 2.1.1.

20 Note of January 27, 1936, in *Minutes of the Board of Deputies*, June 6, 1935, in AICS 2.1.1.

21 Wister, Robert, *History of St. Patrick's Pro-Cathedral, Newark, NJ,* in
http://pirate.shu.edu/~wisterro/hoc/Architecture_page.htm.

22 Walsh, "Address Delivered By His Excellency, The Most Reverend Thomas Joseph Walsh, S.T.D., J.C.D.,
At The six Banquets In His Honor," in AICS 9.2.2.4, same as Walsh, Radio Address, November 8, 1936,
in AICS 14.2.1.1.

23 Letters to McLaughlin, in AICS 3.1.9.3.

24 James A. McNulty to Thomas A. Boland, January 10, 1939, in AICS 14.2.1.2.

25 Thomas A. Boland to William A. Griffin, January 10, 1939, in AICS 3.2.4.

Chapter Nineteen

1 Walsh, Radio Address, November 8, 1936, in AICS 14.2.1.1.

2 Financial Report, New Major Seminary Campaign Fund, November 19, 1936 to November 19, 1941,
in AICS 14.2.1.1.2.4.

3 Walsh to McLaughlin, January 27, 1937, in AICS 3.1.9.3.

4 "Text of the announcements by his Excellency, The Most Reverend Thomas Joseph Walsh, S.T.D., J.C.D.,
Bishop of Newark, made at the Session of the Diocesan Conference held at St. Patrick's Cathedral Hall,
Newark, on Wednesday, November 17, 1937," in AICS 14.2.1.1.2.1.

5 J. C. McClary to Reverend dear Father, November 19, 1937, in AICS 14.2.1.1.2.1.

6 Theodore Kaczmarek to McClary, November 23, 1938, in AICS 9.2.2.2.4.2.

7 B. Marcilla to McClary, November 23, 1938, in AICS 9.2.2.2.4.2.

8 Ladler Kiczek to McClary, November 29, 1938, in AICS 9.2.2.2.4.2.

9 Walsh to McLaughlin, November 22, 1937, in AICS 3.1.9.3.

10 "Returns from Mayor Hague," in AICS 14.2.1.2 "Mayor Hague" file.

11 Harry A Delaney to John C. McClary, June 15, 11939, in AICS 14.2.1.2.

12 Walsh, "Text Of The Address Of His Excellency, The Most Reverend Thomas Joseph Walsh, S.T.D., J.C.D.,
Bishop Of Newark, On The Occasion Of The Laying Of The Cornerstone Of The Seminary Chapel Of
Christ The King And Of The Seminary Edifice Of The Immaculate Conception For The Major Newark
Diocesan Philosophical-Theological Seminary, Darlington, N.J., On Sunday Afternoon, September 26,
1937 A.D., Radio WOR," in AICS 9.2.2.3.1.

13 Beck, 46–47. Paterson was created by papal letter, "*Recta cuiusvis,*" December 9, 1937, AAS 30 (1938),
253–56. Newark raised to metropolitan status by papal letter, "*Quo utilius,*" April 10, 1937, in AAS 30
(1938), 258–60. Newark enthronement and Paterson installation, *Newark Evening News*, April 27, 1938;
Paterson Evening News, April 28, 1938. Bishop Griffin consecration, *Newark Evening News*, May 2, 1938.

14 *Official Catholic Directory 1939.*

15 Report of the Rector of the Immaculate Conception Major Diocesan Seminary at Darlington, presented
to the Annual Meeting of the Board of Deputies held at the Seminary, May 13, 1937, in AICS 2.1.2.

16 Walsh, Sermon, Immaculate Conception Seminary Dedication and Consecration of Chapel, 12/8/38,
in AICS 9.2.2.3.1.

17 "Program—Solemn Consecration of the Chapel of Our Lord, Jesus Christ the King, and Solemn Dedication
of the Major Seminary of the Immaculate Conception of the Blessed Virgin Mary at Darlington, New Jersey,
December 8, 1938, A.D.," in AICS 9.2.2.2.4.2.

18 Report of the Rector of the Immaculate Conception Major Diocesan Seminary at Darlington, presented
to the Annual Meeting of the Board of Deputies held at the Seminary, May 25, 1939, in AICS 2.1.2.

Chapter Twenty

1 AAS 17 (1925), 593–610.

2 AAS, 20 (1928), 1650178.

3 White, 276.

4 AAS 23 (1931), 120–29.

5 White, 277.

6 Ibid.

7 AAS 23 (1931), 263–80. White, in note 35 on page 277, refers to Markham, James J., *The Sacred
Congregation of Seminaries and Universities of Studies* (Washington, DC: Catholic University of
America, 1957), especially pages 47–101, which contain an extended exposition of the provisions
of the apostolic constitution.

8 White, 278.

9 Canon 1366, para. 3, *Code of Canon Law (1917)*.

10 AAS 28 (1936) 6–53.

11 Cicognani to "Your Excellency," February 12, 1936, in AAB, Curley Papers, cited in White, 281.

12 Cicognani to "Your Excellency," August 20, 1938, in AAB, Curley Papers, cited in White, 281.

13 Fenlon to Pierre Boisard (vice superior general of the Society of St. Sulpice), October 6, 1938, in Sulpician Archives Baltimore, RG13, Box 1a., cited in White, 282.

14 White, 282.

15 *Seton Hall Catalogue*, 1865–66, 1866–67, in ASHU 1.1.1.

16 *Seton Hal College Trustees Minutes,* 287–89, in ASHU4.6.1.

17 *Seton Hall Catalogue*, 1932, in ASHU 1.1.1.

18 McLaughlin to Adam Leroy Jones, September 23, 1926, in ASHU 3.1, Accreditation.

19 Adam Leroy Jones to McLaughlin, November 18, 1925, November 30, 1925, in ASHU 3.1, Accreditation.

20 George Gailey Chambers to McLaughlin, May 21, 1932, in ASHU 3.1, Accreditation. Also see *Catalogue of the Immaculate Conception Seminary 1930–1931,* in AICS 1.5.

21 Undated, in ASHU 3.1, Accreditation.

22 McLaughlin to George Gailey Chambers, May 24, 1932, in ASHU 3.1, Accreditation.

23 Adam Leroy Jones to McLaughlin, June 16, 1932, in ASHU 3.1, Accreditation.

24 *President's Report*, in *Seton Hall College Trustees Minutes*, May 25, 1933, 358, in ASHU 4.6.1.

25 George Gailey Chambers, Report of Visit to Seton Hall College on November 4, 1932, George Gailey Chambers to McLaughlin, November 9, 1932, in ASHU 3.1, Accreditation.

26 McLaughlin to Adam Leroy Jones, August 25, 1932, in ASHU 3.1, Accreditation.

27 George Gailey Chambers, Report of Visit to Seton Hall College on November 4, 1932, George Gailey Chambers to McLaughlin, November 9, 1932, in ASHU 3.1, Accreditation.

28 McLaughlin to George Gailey Chambers, November 14, 1932, in ASHU 3.1, Accreditation.

29 Adam Leroy Jones to McLaughlin, November 25, 1932, in ASHU, 3.1, Accreditation.

Chapter Twenty-one

1 AAS 23 (1931), 263–80. White, in note 35 on page 277, refers to Markham, James J., *The Sacred Congregation of Seminaries and Universities of Studies* (Washington, DC: 1957), especially pages 47–101, which contain an extended exposition of the provisions of the apostolic constitution.

2 McLaughlin to Walsh, August 15, 1932, in AAN R.G. 5, Walsh Papers, Box 7.

3 News Release, ASHU, R.G. 2.9.2.4.

4 Beck, 46.

5 Beck, Unpublished notes, in AICS 1.2.2.1.

6 Walsh to Hayes, October 11, 1938, in AICS 3.4.10.

7 Report of the Rector of the Immaculate Conception Major Archdiocesan Seminary at Darlington, presented at the Annual Meeting of the Board of Deputies held at the Seminary, Thursday, May 25, 1939, in AICS 2.1.2.

8 Walsh, Decree, "Constitution of a Special Academic Commission in Seton Hall College," July 13, 1943, in AICS 3.1.10.

9 Walsh, Decree, April 16, 1943, in AICS 3.1.10.

10 Ibid.

11 *Minutes of the Council of Deputies—Darlington—Immaculate Conception Seminary (1927–1968),* June 10, 1943, in AICS 2.1.1.

12 Walsh Decree to Frank J. Monaghan, January 8, 1936, in AICS 3.1.9.3.

13 *Minutes of the Board of Deputies*, June 8, 1936, in AICS 2.1.1.

14 Ibid.

15 Wister, *St. Patrick's Pro-Cathedral,* http://pirate.shu.edu/~wisterro/hoc/History_page5.htm.

16 Beck, 45.

17 Ibid., 48.

18 The minutes of the four meetings of the committee and a digest of its deliberations are found in AICS 5.1.15.

19 Report of the Rector of the Immaculate Conception Major Archdiocesan Seminary at Darlington presented at the Annual Meeting of the Board of Deputies held at the Seminary, Thursday, May 25, 1939, in AICS 2.1.2.

20 Beck, 49.

21 *Immaculate Conception Seminary Bulletin of Information 1961–1962*, in AICS 1.5.

Chapter Twenty-two

1 *Minutes of the Board of Deputies*, June 2, 1938, in AICS 2.1.1.

2 Burke to McLaughlin, December 21, 1932, in AICS 3.4.10.

3 Notes and correspondence regarding the affiliation are found in AICS 5.8.1.

4 Decree of Sacred Congregation of Seminaries and Universities, December 23, 1947, in AAN R.G. 6, Acc. 8-88, Walsh and Boland Subject Files, Rome.

5 Rescript of Sacred Congregation of Seminaries, December 23, 1947, Rescript 1580/38/13,cited in Beck, 49.

6 Report of the Rector of the Immaculate Conception Major Archdiocesan Seminary at Darlington presented at the Annual Meeting of the Board of Deputies held at the Seminary, Thursday, May 25, 1939, in AICS 2.1.2.

7 Report of the Rector of the Immaculate Conception Major Diocesan Seminary at Darlington, presented to the Annual Meeting of the Board of Deputies held at the Seminary, May 29, 1941, in AICS 2.1.2.

8 Beck, 50

9 Ibid.

10 Beck unpublished notes, in AICS 1.2.2.1.

11 Note of Rev. Gerard Sloyan, Ph.D., to author, April 13, 2007.

12 Board of Deputies Special Meeting held at the Immaculate Conception Seminary, Darlington, NJ, Thursday, May 18, 1939, in AICS 2.1.2.

13 Report of the Rector of the Immaculate Conception Major Diocesan Seminary at Darlington, presented to the Annual Meeting of the Board of Deputies held at the Seminary, May 9, 1940, in AICS 2.1.2.

14 Note of Rev. Gerard Sloyan, Ph.D., to author, April 13, 2007.

15 "The Canonical Visitation of The Immaculate Conception Seminary, Archdiocese of Newark, Darlington, N.J., by His Excellency, Most Reverend Amleto Giovanni Cicognani, Apostolic Delegate," report to Archbishop Walsh, Griffin to Walsh, December 29, 1938, in AICS 8.3.1.

16 Note of Rev. Gerard Sloyan, Ph.D., to author, April 13, 2007.

17 Martin W. Stanton was consecrated auxiliary bishop of Newark on September 24, 1957. He died on October 1, 1977.

18 Report of the Rector of the Immaculate Conception Major Archdiocesan Seminary at Darlington presented at the Annual Meeting of the Board of Deputies held at the Seminary, Thursday, May 25, 1939, in AICS 2.1.2.

19 Ibid.

20 Pizzardo to Walsh, July 17, 1941, in AICS 8.3.1.

21 Ibid.

22 Compiled from statistics in Visitation Report, *Visitatio Apostolica Seminariorum—1938*, in AICS 8.3.1.

Chapter Twenty-three

1 Donnelly to Boland, December 20, 1938, "Information for Catholic Directory," in AICS 3.2.4.

2 Digest of the Deliberations of the Archbishop's Committee on the Co-ordination of Curricula of Seton Hall College and the Immacualte Conception Seminary, August 1938, in AICS 5.1.15.

3 Visitation Report, Visitatio Apostolica Seminariorum—1938, in AICS 8.3.1.

4 Boland memorandum, September 14, 1943, in AICS 5.1.1.

Chapter Twenty-four

1 Havemeyer to McLaughlin, July 13, 1928, AICS 9.2.3.

2 Walsh to McLaughlin, January 31, 1929, in AICS 9.2.3.

3 McLaughlin to Walsh, February 15, 1929, in AICS 9.2.3.

4 Havemeyer to McLaughlin, May 7, 1930, in AICS 9.2.3.

5 Walsh to Havemeyer, July 3, 1935, in AAN, R. G. 5, Acc. 8-88, Series 1.

6 Apostolic Brief, Pope Pius XI to "Our Beloved Son, the Ordinary of Newark," August 1, 1929, in AAN, R. G. 5, Acc. AAN 8-88, Series 1.

7 Hamill to McClary, May 9, 1933, in AICS 9.2.3.

8 McLaughlin, Memorandum, undated, 1933, in AICS 9.2.3.

9 Havemeyer to McLaughlin, June 19, 1930, in AICS 9.2.3.

10 Havemeyer to McLaughlin, October 5, 1934, in AICS 9.2.3.

11 Havemeyer to McLaughlin, November 23, 1934; McLaughlin to Havemeyer, November 21, 1934, November 27, 1934, in AICS 9.2.3.

12 Havemeyer to McLaughlin, August 22, 1936, McLaughlin to Havemeyer, August 24, 1936, in AICS 9.2.3.

13 Havemeyer to Demjanovich, May 5, 1937; Havemeyer to McLaughlin, May 10, 1937, in AICS 9.2.3.

14 McLaughlin to Havemeyer, May 11, 1937, in AICS 9.2.3.

15 McLaughlin to Havemeyer, May 17, 1937, in AICS 9.2.3.

16 Havemeyer to McLaughlin, May 23, 1934, in AICS 9.2.3.

17 Havemeyer to Griffin, October 31, 1938; Griffin to Havemeyer, November 3, 1938, in AICS 9.2.3.

18 Havemeyer to Boland, April 30, 1942, in AICS 9.2.3.

Chapter Twenty-five

1 McLaughlin to Boland, September 5, 1928, in AAN R.G. 5 Walsh, Box 7.

2 Sermon Topics, 1927–38, in AICS 3.6.8.

3 "Souvenir of Dedication, Immaculate Conception Church and School, Darlington, New Jersey, September 11, 1932," in AICS 1.2.1.2.

4 McLaughlin, Memorandum, undated 1933, in AICS 9.2.3.

5 Decree of establishment of St. Paul's Parish, January 26, 1939, in AICS 3.6.8.

6 *Minutes of Council of Deputies—Darlington—Immaculate Conception Seminary (1927–1968)*, June 8, 1936, in AICS 2.1.1.

7 Griffin, "Priests Residing in New Residence," September 21, 1938, in AICS 3.1.10.

8 Griffin, Notice, November 9, 1938, in AICS 3.1.10.

9 Ibid.

10 Report of the Rector of the Major Archdiocesan Seminary of the Immaculate Conception at Darlington, presented at the Annual Meeting of the Board of Deputies held at the Seminary, Thursday, May 9, 1940, in AICS 2.1.2.

11 Board of Deputies, May 25, 1939, in AICS 2.1.2.

12 Griffin to Ahr, July 19, 1940, in AICS 3.1.10.

13 Walsh to Boland, July 25, 1940, in AAN R.G. 6, Acc. 2-89, Series 1, Boland.

14 Walsh to Boland, April 12, 1938, in AAN R.G. 6, Acc. 2-89, Series 1, Boland.

15 Interview with Rev. Peter Lennon, July 7, 2006.

16 Boland to Boland, April 5, 1940, in AAN R.G. 6, Acc. 2-89, Series 1, Boland.

17 Boland to Delaney, October 2, 1931, in AAN R. G. 6, Acc. 2-89, Boland.

18 Delaney to Boland, October 9, 1931, in AAN R. G. 6, Acc. 2-89, Boland.

19 Thomas J. Walsh, Estate Inventory, in AAN, unfiled.

20 *Advocate,* September 29, 1977.

Chapter Twenty-six

1 "Report of the Rector of the Immaculate Conception Major Diocesan Seminary at Darlington, presented to the Annual Meeting of the Board of Deputies held at the Seminary, May 9, 1940, and May 21, 1942, in AICS 2.1.2.

2 Monaghan to McLaughlin, November 27, 1933, in AICS 3.4.1.

3 Beck, 52.

4 Beck to Walsh, September 20, 1939, in AAN, Priest files, Beck, Henry G. J.

5 Walsh to Roosevelt, October 6, 1939, in AAN, Priest files, Beck, Henry G. J.

6 Beha to Walsh, October 13, 1939, in AAN, Priest files, Beck, Henry G. J.

7 Roosevelt to Walsh, October 13, 1939, in AAN, Priest files, Beck, Henry G. J.

8 Walsh note, in AAN, Priest files, Beck, Henry G. J.

9 Boland to Hayes, April 4, 1941, in AICS 3.4.10.

10 Recollections of the author.

11 Beck, 54.

12 http://www.fourchaplains.org/

13 *CYO News*, Vol. I, No. 6, March, 1943, 5.

14 Report of the Rector of the Immaculate Conception Major Diocesan Seminary at Darlington, presented to the Annual Meeting of the Board of Deputies held at the Seminary, June 10, 1943, in AICS 2.1.2.

15 Beck, 54.

16 Report of the Rector of the Immaculate Conception Major Diocesan Seminary at Darlington, presented to the Annual Meeting of the Board of Deputies held at the Seminary, June 10, 1943, in AICS 2.1.2.

17 Report of the Rector of the Immaculate Conception Major Diocesan Seminary at Darlington, presented to the Annual Meeting of the Board of Deputies held at the Seminary, May 15, 1945, in AICS 2.1.2.

18 E-mail from Peter Ahr, August 6, 2006.

19 Report of the Rector of the Immaculate Conception Major Diocesan Seminary at Darlington, presented to the Annual Meeting of the Board of Deputies held at the Seminary, May 25, 1944, in AICS 2.1.2.

20 Minutes of Council of Deputies—Darlington—Immaculate Conception Seminary (1927–68), May 25, 1944, in AICS 2.1.1.

21 Report of the Rector of the Immaculate Conception Major Diocesan Seminary at Darlington, presented to the Annual Meeting of the Board of Deputies held at the Seminary, May 15, 1945, in AICS 2.1.2.

22 Minutes of Council of Deputies—Darlington—Immaculate Conception Seminary (1927–68), May 15, 1945, in AICS 2.1.1.

23 Report of the Rector of the Immaculate Conception Major Diocesan Seminary at Darlington, presented to the Annual Meeting of the Board of Deputies held at the Seminary, May 15, 1945, in AICS 2.1.2.

24 NCWC to Bishops and Rectors, October 29, 1945, in AICS 4.3.10.

25 Rector's Report, May 14, 1948, in AICS 2.1.2.

26 Rector's Report, June 5, 1946, in AICS 2.1.2.

27 Rector's Report, May 14, 1948, in AICS 2.1.2.

28 Minutes of the Board of Deputies, May 25, 1950, in AICS 2.1.2.

29 Board of Deputies Minutes, May 19, 1952, in AICS 2.1.2.

30 Rector's Report, May 19, 1952, in AICS 2.1.2.

31 Rector's Report, May 22, 1953, in AICS 2.1.2.

32 Board of Deputies Minutes, May 14, 1959, in AICS 2.1.2.

33 Rector's Report, May 19, 1960, in AICS 2.1.2.

34 Minutes of Council of Deputies—Darlington—Immaculate Conception Seminary (1927–68), May 22, 1947, in AICS 2.1.1.

35 E-mail from Peter Ahr, August 2, 2006, story told to him by Bishop George Ahr.

36 Beck, 55.

37 Ahr to Vito F. Daidone, February 27, 1948, in AICS 3.7.1.

38 Toborowsky, Jonathan, "To Teach, To Rule, To Sanctify: The Life of Bishop George William Ahr," Mount St. Mary's Seminary, October 7, 1997, 3.

39 Ibid., 8.

40 Ibid.

41 Interview, Msgr. Emmanuel M. Capozzelli, May 10, 2008.

42 Toborowsky, 12–13.

43 Interview with Msgr. Emmanuel M. Capozzelli, May 10, 2008.

44 Toborowsky, 14.

45 Beck, 56.

46 Rector's Report, June 2, 1949, in AICS 2.1.2.

47 Rector's Report, May 14, 1948, in AICS 2.1.2.

48 Beck, 57.

49 Rector's Report, May 10, 1951, in AICS 2.1.2.

50 Interview with Rev. Peter Lennon, July 6, 2006.

51 Board of Deputies Minutes, May 19, 1952, in AICS 2.1.2.

52 *The Official Catholic Yearbook 1928.*

53 *The Official Catholic Directory 1954.*

Chapter Twenty-seven

1 Herberg, Will, "A Jew Looks at Catholicism," in *The Commonweal*, LVIII (May 22, 1953), 174.

2 Ellis, John Tracy, "American Catholicism, 1953–1979: A Notable Change," in *Thought*, v. 54, n. 213 (June 1979), 114.

3 Rector's Report, June 2, 1949, in AICS 2.1.2.

4 Rector's Report, May 10, 1951, in AICS 2.1.2.

5 Minutes of the Board of Deputies, May 19, 1966, in AICS 2.1.2.

6 Rector's Report, May 22, 1947, in AICS 2.1.2.

7 Rector's Report, May 29, 1952, in AICS 2.1.2.

8 Board of Deputies Minutes, May 17, 1956, in AICS 2.1.2.

9 Rector's Report, May 22, 1953, in AICS 2.1.2.

10 *Customs of the Seminary of the Immaculate Conception—Darlington, N.J.,* in AICS 1.1.3.

11 Ibid., 1.

12 Ibid., 20.

13 Ibid., 13.

14 Ibid., 30, 31.

15 Ibid., 33.

16 Ibid., 37.

17 Mission Academia Report, 1986, in AICS 12.2.8.

18 Rector's Report, May 27, 1956, in AICS 2.1.2.

19 Rector's Report, May 25, 1950, in AICS 2.1.2.

20 Rector's Report, May 19, 1954, in AICS 2.1.2.

21 Rector's Report, May 18, 1955, in AICS 2.1.2.

22 Kaiser to Powers, March 5, 1952, in AICS 3.7.1.I.

23 *Customs*, 26, 27.

24 DeSales Union Report, May 16, 1965, in AICS 12.2.4.

Chapter Twenty-eight

1 Programs, in AICS 12.4.1.

2 Stage Crew Record Book, in AICS 12.2.5

3 Program, in AICS 12.4.1.

4 Ibid.

5 http://midihymns.homestead.com/King.html

6 Rector's Report, May 16, 1958, in AICS 2.1.2.

7 Rector's Report, May 16, 1957, in AICS 2.1.2.

8 Records of Home Study Program, in AICS 12.2.7.

9 Rector's Report, May 19, 1954, in AICS 2.1.2.

10 Ibid.

11 Rector's Report, May 18, 1955, in AICS 2.1.2.

12 Walter W. Curtis was consecrated auxiliary bishop of Newark on September 24, 1957, in http://www.catholic-hierarchy.org/bishop/bcurtis.html.

13 Rector's Report, May 16, 1958, in AICS 2.1.2.

14 Rector's Report, May 18, 1961, in AICS 2.1.2.

15 Rector's Report, May 10, 1951, in AICS 2.1.2.

16 http://alpha.fdu.edu/~bender/NYmsg.html.

17 Rector's Report, May 19, 1954, in AICS 2.1.2.

18 Personal recollections of the present writer.

19 Rector's Report, May 15, 1964, in AICS 2.1.2.

20 John Glasgow to B. W. Gorcyca, copy, November 24, 1964, in AICS 12.2.1.

21 Memorandum, Civil Defense and Disaster Control, Mahwah Division, May 6, 1965, in AICS 12.2.1.

22 Memorandum, Civil Defense and Disaster Control, Mahwah Division, May 18, 1966, in AICS 12.2.1.

23 Memorandum, Civil Defense and Disaster Control, Immaculate Conception Seminary, May 9, 1964, in AICS 12.2.1.

24 Recollections of the present writer.

25 Schama, Simon, *Rough Crossings—Britain, the Slaves and the American Revolution* (New York: 2006), 109–16.

26 http://en.wikipedia.org/wiki/Ramapough_Mountain_Indians.

27 Rector's Report, May 14, 1959, in AICS 2.1.2.

28 George Weigel, "Thinking Through Vatican II," review of Giuseppe Alberigo's *History of Vatican II*, in *First Things*, June/July, 2001.

Chapter Twenty-nine

1 Correspondence from Rev. Gerard Sloyan, Ph.D., April 13, 2007.

2 Beck, 58.

3 Interview with Rev. Peter Lennon, July 10. 2006.

4 Beck, 61.

5 Interview with Peter Ahr, August 3, 2006.

6 Beck, 61.

7 Rector's Report, May 18, 1955, in AICS 2.1.2.

8 Ibid.

9 Rector's Report, May 14, 1959, in AICS 2.1.2.

10 Rector's Report, May 16, 1957, in AICS 2.1.2.

11 Rector's Report, May 17, 1956, in AICS 2.1.2.

12 Interview with Peter Ahr, August 3, 2006.

13 Rector's Report, May 17, 1956, in AICS 2.1.2.

14 Board of Deputies Minutes, May 17, 1956, in AICS 2.1.2.

15 Dougherty notes, in AICS 10.2.3.

16 Richard Liddy, *Startling Strangeness—Reading Lonergan's Insight* (New York: 2007), 18.

17 Rector's Reports, 1957 to 1961, in AICS 2.1.2.

18 Conversation of the author with Henry Beck many years ago.

19 Rector's Report, June 6, 1946, May 22, 1947, in AICS 2.1.2.

20 Rector's Report, May 14, 1959, in AICS 2.1.2.

21 Rector's Report, May 16, 1958, in AICS 2.1.2.

22 Rector's Report, May 14, 1959, in AICS 2.1.2.

23 Beck, 58 ss.

24 Rector's Report, June 5, 1946, in AICS 2.1.2.

25 Ibid.

26 Rector's Report, May 25, 1950, in AICS 2.1.2.

27 Rector's Report, June 2, 1949, in AICS 2.1.2.

28 Rector's Report, May 14, 1948, in AICS 2.1.2.

29 Board of Deputies Minutes, May 25, 1950, in AICS 2.1.2.

30 Rector's Report, May 18, 1955, in AICS 2.1.2.

31 Rector's Report, May 14, 1959, in AICS 2.1.2.

32 Hogan to Brady, March 1, 1958, in AICS 3.1.16.

33 Beck, 59, 62.

34 Rector's Report, May 10, 1951, in AICS 2.1.2.

35 Rector's Report, May 16, 1957, in AICS 2.1.2.

36 Rector's Report, May 25, 1950, in AICS 2.1.2.

37 Rector's Report, June 5, 1946, in AICS 2.1.2.

38 Rector's Report, May 22, 1947, in AICS 2.1.2.

39 Board of Deputies Minutes, June 2, 1949, in AICS 2.1.2.

40 Board of Deputies Minutes, May 25, 1950, in AICS 2.1.2.

41 Board of Deputies Minutes, May 17, 1956, in AICS 2.1.2.

42 Board of Deputies Minutes, May 16, 1957, in AICS 2.1.2.

43 Powers to Corr, January 25, 1954, in Rector's Report, May 19, 1954, in AICS 2.1.2.

44 Rector's Report, May 19, 1960, in AICS 2.1.1.

Chapter Thirty

1 Rector's Report, May 17, 1956, in AICS 2.1.2, and in AICS 1.4.4.

2 This description was written by the designer of the coat of arms, William F. J. Ryan, in 1955. It was slightly revised in 2005 by the present writer.

Chapter Thirty-one

1 Peter Ahr, e-mail to author, August 2, 2006.

2 Ibid.

3 *Advocate*, November 8, 1963.

4 *Advocate*, October 4, 1963.

5 *The Official Catholic Directory 1946, 1960.*

6 http://www.wnjpin.net/OneStopCareerCenter/LaborMarketInformation/lmi01/poptrd6.htm

7 Jackson, Kenneth T., *Crabgrass Frontier: The Suburbanization of the United States* (New York: Oxford University Press, 1987), 277.

8 *The Official Catholic Directory 1960.* This includes 30 priests active outside the diocese and 15 retired, sick, or absent.

9 School totals include diocesan, parochial, and private schools.

10 Analysis of statistics in *The Official Catholic Directory* from 1940 to 1990.

11 *The Official Catholic Directory 1960.*

12 Unpublished memoirs of Archbishop Peter L. Gerety.

Chapter Thirty-two

1 AAS 23 (1931), 120–29.

2 Masella to Excellentissime ac Reverendissime Domine, Sacred Congregation of the Sacraments, Confidential Circular Letter to Bishops, December 27, 1955, in AICS 3.2.1. (orig. Latin).

3 Boland to Brady, May 9, 1957, in AICS 3.2.1.

4 Rector's Report, May 18, 1961, in AICS 2.1.2; Rigney to Brady, January 5, 1961, Ahr to Brady, January 4, 1961, McNulty to Brady, January 3, 1961, in AICS 3.6.13.

5 Jeanne G. Gilbert, Ph.D., and Frank L. Catalano, Ph.D., "Preliminary Study of Students in Immaculate Conception Seminary," undated, in AICS 3.6.13.

6 Holy Office, *Monitum*, July 15, 1961, in AICS 3.6.13.

7 Commentary on Holy Office *Monitum* on July 15, 1961, Anonymous, in AICS 3.6.13.

8 Notes taken at a symposium conducted by the American Psychological Association at Fordham University on August 31, 1961. Participants: Bro. Austin Dondero, F.S.C., LaSalle College, Philadelphia, Pennsylvania; Rt. Rev. Msgr. Francis Reh, Rector of Saint Joseph's Seminary, Yonkers, New York; Rev. Bernard Ristuccia, C.M., Mary Immaculate Seminary, Northampton, Pennsylvania, in AICS 3.6.6.

19 Dates are recollection of Msgr. Francis Seymour, January 25, 2007.

20 Rector's Report, June 20, 1974, in AICS 2.1.2.

21 Ibid.

22 O'Brien to Seminarians, Memorandum, July 25, 1972, in AICS 4.13.

23 *New York Times,* March 11, 1973.

24 Hogan to Boland, September 28, 1971, in AAN, R.G. 2.8, Series 2, Box 2 of 3.

25 Hogan to Seminarians, Memorandum, August 9, 1971, in AICS 3.9.

26 Darcy to Seminarians, July 30, 1973, in AICS 6.12.

27 Costello to Darcy, August 23, 1973, in AAN R.G. 2, R.G. 2.8, Series 2, Box 2 of 3.

28 Catholic author and publisher.

29 Historian of the American Catholic Church, professor at the Catholic University of America.

30 Alumnus and president of the Pontifical Institute of Medieval Studies in the University of Toronto.

31 Scripture scholar, professor at Union Theological Seminary, New York.

32 Founder of Covenant House.

33 Theologian and professor at Georgetown University.

34 Scripture scholar and former member of the Pontifical Biblical Commission.

35 President of the University of Notre Dame.

Chapter Forty

1 The majority of the material in this chapter is drawn from the unpublished memoirs of Archbishop Peter Leo Gerety. Some of the recollections herein included are based on interviews with John Culligan and Joseph Nehila.

Chapter Forty-one

1 Darcy to Gerety, September 6, 1974, in AICS 2.1.2.

2 O'Brien to Gerety, September 9, 1974, in AICS 2.1.2.

3 Board of Trustees Minutes, September 13, 1974, in AICS 2.2.1.

4 Ibid.

5 Priest Records in AAN; courtesy of Msgr. Francis Seymour, archivist of the archdiocese of Newark.

6 O'Brien to Gerety, Confidential, September 9, 1974, in AICS 2.1.2.

7 President's Report, January 29, 1976, in AICS 2.2.1.

8 President's Report, June 8, 1978, in AICS 2.2.1.

9 Board of Trustees Meeting, verbatim, June 12, 1978, in AICS 2.2.1.

10 President's Report, June 3, 1975, in AICS 2.2.1.

11 Ibid.

12 Ciuba to Faculty, July 15, 1975, in AICS 3.1.18.9.

13 Immaculate Conception Seminary, Statement of Current Funds, Revenues, Expenditures, and Transfers, Years ended June 30, 1975 and 1974, in AICS 2.2.1.

14 *The South Gate,* v. 1, n. 1, March 1975.

15 President's Report, June 3, 1975, in AICS 2.2.1.

16 President's Report, January 29, 1976, in AICS 2.2.1.

17 President's Report, October 31, 1977, in AICS 2.2.1.

18 President's Report, January 29, 1976, in AICS 2.2.1.

19 Liddy to Wister, August 8, 2007.

20 President's Report, May 27, 1977, in AICS 2.2.1.

Chapter Forty-two

1 Ellis, "American Catholicism, 1953–1979" 121.

2 Ibid., 122.

3 President's Report, June 14, 1976, in AICS 2.2.1.

4 Gerety to Minck, June 14, 1976, in AICS 3.1.18.18.

5 Board of Trustees Minutes, June 14, 1976, in AICS 2.2.1.

6 Board of Trustees Minutes, October 25, 1976, in AICS 2.2.1.

7 Minck to Ciuba, August 12, 1976, in AICS 3.1.18.18.

8 President's Report, May 27, 1977, in AICS 2.2.1.

9 Board of Trustees Minutes, June 16, 1976, in AICS 2.2.1.

10 Neuman, Matthias, "Seminaries and the New Conservatives," *America,* September 10, 1977.

11 Board of Trustees Minutes, verbatim, March 6, 1978, in AICS 2.2.1.

12 Board of Trustees Minutes, October 30, 1978, in AICS 2.2.1.

13 Board of Trustees Minutes, verbatim, June 11, 1979, in AICS 2.2.1.

14 President's Report, June 11, 1979, in AICS 2.2.1.

15 President's Report, June 8, 1978, in AICS 2.2.1.

16 Board of Trustees Minutes, verbatim, October 30, 1978, in AICS 2.2.1.

17 Petillo to Ciuba, February 5, 1976, in AICS 3.1.18.25.

18 Ciuba to Petillo, March 25, 1976, in AICS 3.1.18.25.

19 President's Report, January 29, 1976, in AICS 2.2.1.

20 Ciuba to Harrold Murray, January 6, 1976, in AICS 3.1.18.25.

21 Board of Trustees Minutes, May 14, 1976, in AICS 2.2.1.

22 Ciuba to Board of Trustees, Memorandum, May 10, 1976, in AICS 2.2.1.

23 Board of Trustees Minutes, June 13, 1977, in AICS 2.2.1.

24 Board of Trustees Minutes, May 14, 1976, in AICS 2.2.1.

25 Board of Trustees Minutes, October 31, 1977, in AICS 2.2.1.

26 *Record*, December 17, 1978.

27 Department of Vocational Ministry, Memorandum, undated, in Board of Trustees Meeting, May 14, 1976, in AICS 2.2.1.

28 Linder to Gerety, May 12, 1976, in AICS 2.2.1.

29 Board of Trustees Minutes, verbatim, October 30, 1978, in AICS 2.2.1.

30 Ciuba to Linder, August 5, 1976, in AICS 3.1.18.25.

31 Ibid.

32 Ibid.

33 Ciuba to Linder, January 31, 1977, in AICS 3.1.18.25.

34 Board of Trustees Minutes, verbatim, October 30, 1978, in AICS 2.2.1.

35 Ibid.

36 Ibid.

37 O'Reilly to Ciuba, June 30, 1978, in AAN 7.2.4.1, 1978, Box 18 of 24.

38 Ciuba to O'Reilly, July 7, 1978, in AAN 7.2.4.1, 1978, Box 18 of 24.

39 Board of Trustees Minutes, May 14, 1976, in AICS 2.2.1.

40 Board of Trustees Minutes, March 5, 1978, in AICS 2.2.1.

41 Board of Trustees Minutes, verbatim record, June 14, 1976, in AICS 2.2.1.

42 Board of Trustees Minutes, February 28, 1977, in AICS 2.2.1.

43 Budget 1976–77, in AICS 2.2.1.

44 Ciuba to Costello, February 16, 1976, in AAN R.G. 2, R.G. 2.8, Series 2, Box 2 of 3.

45 President's Report, June 14, 1976, in AICS 2.2.1.

46 O'Brien to Morris, June 30, 1976, in AICS 2.2.1.

47 Board of Trustees Minutes, June 14, 1976, in AICS 2.2.1.

48 Harter to Ciuba, March 9, 1979, in AICS 2.2.1.

49 Board of Trustees Minutes, October 25, 1976, in AICS 2.2.1.

50 Board of Trustees Minutes, February 28, 1977, in AICS 2.2.1.

51 Board of Trustees Minutes, June 11, 1979, in AICS 2.2.1.

52 Board of Trustees Minutes, March 5, 1979, in AICS 2.2.1.

53 Ibid.

54 Ibid.

Chapter Forty-three

1 Board of Trustees Minutes, October 30, 1978, in AICS 2.2.1.

2 Board of Trustees Minutes, verbatim, June 13, 1977, in AICS 2.2.1.

3 President's Report, June 8, 1978, in AICS 2.2.1.

4 Kavin and Ruane to Dear Father, September 17, 1979, in AAN, R.G. 2.8, Series 2, Box 2 of 3.

5 Board of Trustees Minutes, June 13, 1977, in AICS 2.2.1.

6 President's Report, May 14, 1977, in AICS 2.2.1.

7 President's Report, June 11, 1979, in AICS 2.2.1.

8 New York *Daily News*, November 24, 1974.

9 Ibid.

10 *Record*, July 9, 1976.

11 *Advocate*, July 10, 1975.

12 Board of Trustees Minutes, verbatim, October 30, 1978, in AICS 2.2.1.

13 President's Report, June 11, 1979, in AICS 2.2.1.

14 President's Report, June 11, 1979, in AICS 2.2.1.

15 Board of Trustees Minutes, October 30, 1978, in AICS 2.2.1.

16 Board of Trustees Minutes, verbatim record, October 30, 1978, in AICS 2.2.1.

17 Ciuba to Gerety, September 11, 1978, in AAN, R.G. 7.2.4.1, 1978, Box 18 of 24.

18 Board of Trustees Minutes, verbatim record, October 30, 1978, in AICS 2.2.1.

19 Recollections of the author.

20 President's Report, June 14, 1976, in AICS 2.2.1.

21 President's Report, May 27, 1977, in AICS 2.2.1.

22 President's Report, June 8, 1978, in AICS 2.2.1.

23 Board of Trustees Minutes, verbatim record, June 12, 1978, in AICS 2.2.1.

24 President's Report, May 28, 1980, in AICS 2.2.1.

25 Board of Trustees Minutes, June 13, 1977, in AICS 2.2.1.

26 Board of Trustees Minutes, verbatim record, June 13, 1977, in AICS 2.2.1.

27 Draft Statement, April 18, 1978, in AAN, R.G. 2.8, Series 2, Box 2 of 3; Board of Trustees Minutes, June 12, 1978, in AICS 2.2.1; *Advocate,* June 8, 1978.

28 President's Report, October 15, 1979, in AICS 2.2.1.

29 Ibid.

30 Board of Trustees Minutes, March 10, 1980, in AICS 2.2.1.

31 President's Report, May 28, 1980, in AICS 2.2.1.

32 Board of Trustees Minutes, Verbatim report, June 2, 1980, in AICS 2.2.1.

33 Board of Trustees Minutes, October 5, 1980, in AICS 2.2.1.

34 Board of Trustees Minutes, Verbatim report, October 5, 1980, in AICS 2.2.1.

35 Ibid.

36 Ibid.

Chapter Forty-four

1 Minutes of Board of Trustees Corporate Membership, May 19, 1981, in AICS 2.2.1; Gerety to Ciuba, May 1, 1982, in AAN, R.G. 7.2.4.1, 1981, Box 9 of 24.

2 Board of Trustees Minutes, June 1, 1981, in AICS 2.2.1.

3 Board of Trustees Minutes, June 1, 1981, verbatim report, in AICS 2.2.1.

4 Ibid.

5 Ibid.

6 Board of Trustees Executive Committee Minutes, September 14, 1981, in AICS 2.2.1.

7 Board of Trustees Executive Committee Minutes, September 21, 1981, in AICS 2.2.1.

8 Ibid.

9 Ibid.

10 Ibid.

11 Ibid.

Chapter Forty-five

1 D'Alessio to Ciuba, August 4, 1981, in AICS 3.8.2.

2 Affiliation Study Committee Minutes, February 24, 1982, in AICS 3.8.2.

3 Affiliation Study Committee Minutes, January 11, 1982, in AICS 3.8.3.

4 Ciuba to O'Brien, February 17, 1982, in AICS 3.8.2.

5 O'Brien to Ciuba, February 23, 1982; Affiliation Study Committee Minutes, February 24, 1982, in AICS 3.8.2.

6 Affiliation Study Committee, January 11, 1982, in AICS 3.8.3.

7 Model for Affiliation, June 9, 1982; March 8, 1984, in AICS 3.8.3.

8 Ciuba, Chronicle of Events, December 17, 1981, in AICS 3.8.2.

9 Board of Trustees Special Meeting Minutes, December 21, 1981, in AICS 2.2.1.

10 Board of Trustees Executive Committee, verbatim, December 15, 1981, in AICS 2.2.1.

11 Board of Trustees Executive Committee, Minutes, verbatim, December 21, 1981, in AICS 2.2.1.

12 Board of Trustees Minutes, December 21, 1981, in AICS 2.2.1.

13 Ibid.

14 Board of Trustees Minutes, December 21, 1981, in AICS 2.2.1.

15 Board of Trustees Minutes, verbatim, December 21, 1981, in AICS 2.2.1.

16 Board of Trustees Minutes, December 21, 1981, in AICS 2.2.1.

17 Ibid.

18 Ciuba to O'Brien, January 5, 1982, in AICS 3.8.3.

19 Board of Trustees Executive Committee Minutes, verbatim, January 19, 1982, in AICS 2.2.1.

20 Board of Trustees Minutes, January 25, 1983, in AICS 2.2.1.

21 Board of Trustees Minutes, verbatim, January 25, 1982, in AICS 2.2.1.

22 Ibid.

23 Ibid.

24 Progress Report on Affiliation, January 22, 1982, in Board of Trustees Minutes, January 25, 1982, in AICS 2.2.1.

25 Board of Trustees Executive Committee Minutes, April 23, 1982, in AICS 2.2.1.

26 Board of Trustees Minutes, April 26, 1982, in AICS 2.2.1.

27 Petillo to Liddy, November 20, 1986, in AICS 3.18.18.17.

28 Board of Trustees Minutes, verbatim, April 26, 1982, in AICS 2.2.1.

29 Board of Trustees Minutes, April 26, 1982, in AICS 2.2.1.

30 Ciuba to Gerety, September 17, 1981, in AAN, R.G. 7.2.4.1, 1981, Box 9 of 24.

31 Dougherty to O'Brien, April 30, 1982, in AICS 2.2.1.

32 Miraglia to Ciuba, May 10, 1982, in AICS 2.2.1.

33 Toomey to Ciuba, May 10, 1982, in AICS 2.2.1.

34 Hogan to O'Brien, May 7, 1982, in AICS 2.2.1.

35 Faculty Opinions Summary, undated, in AICS 2.2.1.

36 Toomey to Ciuba, undated, in AICS 2.2.1.

37 Miraglia to Petillo, June 1, 1982, in AICS 2.2.1.

38 Board of Trustees Minutes, verbatim, June 9, 1982, in AICS 2.2.1.

39 Ibid.

40 Memorandum, Ciuba to Board of Trustees, August 26, 1982, Final Draft of the Model for Affiliation Between Immaculate Conception Seminary and Seton Hall University, in AAN, R.G. 7.4.2.1, 1984, Box 9 of 18.

41 Ciuba to Gerety, July 2, 1982, in AAN, R.G. 7.2.4.1, 1982, Box 7a of 18.

42 President's Report, June 24, 1982, in AICS 2.2.1.

43 Board of Trustees Minutes, June 27, 1982, in AICS 2.2.1.

44 Board of Trustees Minutes, September 22, 1982, in AICS 2.2.1.

Chapter Forty-six

1 *Star Ledger*, August 11, 1981.

2 Ciuba to Gerety, September 14, 1981, in AAN, R.G. 7.2.4.1, 1981, Box 9 of 24.

3 Ciuba to Fellow Priests, January 13, 1982, in AAN, R.G. 7.2.4.1, 1982, Box 7a of 18.

4 News Release, Archdiocese of Newark, February 26, 1982, in AAN, R.G. 7.2.4.1, 1982, Box 7a of 18.

5 *Star Ledger*, January 24, 1984.

6 Casale to Executive Finance Committee, December 23, 1985, in AAN, R.G. 7.2.4.1, 1985, Box 7 of 13.

7 *Star Ledger*, January 24, 1984.

8 Baum to Gerety, October 16, 1981, in AAN, R.G. 7.2.4.1, 1981, Box 9 of 24.

9 Ciuba to Gerety, March 23, 1981, in AAN, R.G. 7.2.4.1, 1981, Box 9 of 24.

10 Ciuba to Gerety, February 29, 1984, in AAN, R.G. 7.2.4.1, 1984, Box 9 of 18.

11 Ciuba to Gerety, June 4, 1982, in AAN, R.G. 7.2.4.1, 1982, Box 7a of 18.

12 Ciuba to Gerety, July 6, 1982, in AAN, R.G. 7.2.4.1, 1982, Box 7 of 18.

13 Gerety to Ciuba, July 6, 1982, in AAN, R.G. 7.2.4.1, 1982, Box 7 of 18.

14 Ciuba to O'Brien, January 25, 1983, in AICS 3.8.2.

15 Laghi to Ciuba, November 21, 1983, in AAN, R.G. 7.2.4.1, 1983, Box 10 of 23.

16 Ciuba to Gerety, August 13, 1984, in AAN, R.G. 7.2.4.1, Box 9 of 18.

17 Gerety to file, December 2, 1981, in AAN, R.G. 7.2.4.1, 1981, Box 9 of 24.

18 Gerety to file, February 25, 1982, in AAN, R.G. 7.2.4.1, 1982, Box 7a of 18.

19 Secretary to Gerety, Feb. 1, 1983, in AAN, R.G. 7.2.4.1, 1983, Box 10 of 23.

20 *Star Ledger*, January 27, 1982.

21 *Sunday News*, January 9, 1983.

22 LeMay to Gerety, January 9, 1983, in AAN, R.G. 9.2.4.1, 1983, Box 10 of 23.

23 *Advocate*, June 15, 1963.

24 *Star Ledger*, January 31, 1984.

25 Gerety to Ciuba, July 20, 1984; Casale to Gerety, July 20, 1984, in AAN, R.G. 7.2.4.1, 1984, Box 9 of 18.

26 *Record*, November 6, 1984.

27 Gerety to file, December 13, 1984, in AAN, R.G. 7.4.2.1, 1984, Box 9 of 18.

28 Rector/Dean's Report to Board of Overseers, April 18, 1985, in AAN, R.G. 7.4.2.1.

29 Board of Overseers documentation, June 13, 1984, in AAN, R.G. 7.4.2.1, 1984, Box 9 of 18.

30 Ciuba to Gerety, October 12, 1984, in AAN, R.G. 7.2.4.1., 1984, Box 9 of 18.

31 *Star Ledger*, April 10, 1985.

32 Keenan to Gerety, October 7, 1985, in AAN, R.G. 7.4.2.1, 1985, Box 7 of 15.

33 Ciuba to Petillo, in AICS 3.8.3.

Chapter Forty-seven

1 In 1987, Ciuba was appointed pastor of Notre Dame Parish in North Caldwell, NJ. He retired in 2009.
2 Rector/Dean's Report to Board of Overseers, April 18, 1985, in ADN 7.4.2.
3 Ciuba to Petillo, June 3, 1985, in AICS 3.18.18.17.
4 Report of the Vatican Visitation Team, February 17–27, 1986, in AICS 8.3.1.
5 Connors to Ciuba, August 9, 1984, in AICS 3.8.20.
6 Ciuba to Petillo, June 15, 1984, in AICS 3.18.18.17; Ciuba to Connors, August 9, 1984, in AICS 3.8.20
7 Connors to Ciuba, July 11, 1984, in AICS 3.8.20.
8 Affiliation Agreement, Nov. 8, 1985, in AAN, R.G. 2.8, Series 2, Box 3 of 3.
9 Liddy to Bossman, December 8, 1985, in AICS 3.8.20.
10 Liddy notes with Liddy to Wister, August 4, 2007.
11 Letter from Reverend Thomas Guarino, May 16, 2007.
12 Liddy to Bossman, December 8, 1985, in AICS 3.8.20.
13 Notes and recollections of the present writer.

Chapter Forty-eight

1 Wister to Stetar, January 16, 1986, in AICS 3.8.4.
2 Report of the Vatican Visitation–1986, in AICS 8.3.1.
3 Liddy to Wister, August 4, 2007.
4 Affiliation Agreement, 1986 (revised March 1991), in AICS 3.8.4.
5 Petillo to Gerety, May 29, 1986, in AICS 3.8.4.
6 Liddy to Petillo, June 6, 1986, in AICS 3.8.4
7 Gerety statement to press, in AAN, R.G. 7.2.4.1.
8 Gerety to Liddy, May 27, 1986; Gerety to Liddy, May 28, 1986, in AICS 3.8.4.
9 Chu to Scholz, October 24, 1984, in AAN, R.G. 2.8, Series 2, Box 3 of 3.
10 Affiliation Agreement, October 28, 1986, in AICS 3.8.4.
11 Recollections of the author, confirmed by Monsignor Richard Liddy.
12 Wister to Liddy, January 1, 1987, in AICS 3.8.4.
13 McCarrick to Liddy, February 20, 1987, in AAN, R.G. 2.8, Series 2, Box 3 of 3.
14 Liddy to McCarrick, February 24, 1987, in AAN, R.G. 2.8, Series 2, Box 3 of 3.
15 Scholz to Liddy, February 23, 1987; John J. Mitchell to Scholz, Memorandum, November 24, 1986, in AAN, R.G. 2.8, Series 2, Box 3 of 3.
16 Liddy to McCarrick, February 24, 1987, in AAN, R.G. 2.8, Series 2, Box 3 of 3.
17 Liddy to McCarrick, March 5, 1987, in AAN, R.G. 2.8, Series 2, Box 3 of 3.
18 Wister to Liddy, April 4, 1987, in AAN, R.G. 2.8, Series 2, Box 3 of 3.
19 Liddy to McCarrick, March 30, 1987, in AAN, R.G. 2.8, Series 2, Box 3 of 3.
20 Cafone to Liddy, March 30, 1987, in AAN, R.G.2.8, Series 2, Box 3 of 3.
21 Liddy to McCarrick, March 30, 1987, in AAN, R.G. 2.8, Series 2, Box 3 of 3.
22 Liddy to McCarrick, April 7, 1987, in AAN, R.G. 2.8, Series 2, Box 3 of 3.
23 Recollections of the present writer, confirmed by conversations with Monsignor Richard Liddy and Reverend Thomas Guarino.

Chapter Forty-nine

1 Liddy to Scholz, May 26, 1988, in AICS 2.3.1.
2 Rector/Dean's Report to Board of Overseers, September 28, 1988, in AICS 2.3.1.
3 Liddy to Scholz, January 22, 1989, in AICS 2.3.1.
4 Recollections of the present writer.
5 Liddy to Wister, August 4, 2007.
6 Liddy to Faculty, March 10, 1988, in AICS 3.1.19.1.
7 Serratelli to McCarrick, February 23, 1990, in AAN, R.G. 2.8, Series 1, Box 22 of 75.
8 Annual Report 1990–91, in AICS 3.1.20.8.
9 Harahan to Seminary Community, April 4, 1990, in AICS 3.1.20.1.
10 Harahan to Seminary Community, April 2, 1990, in AICS 3.1.20.1.
11 Harahan to Seminary Community, March 19, 1992, in AICS 3.1.20.4.
12 Recollections of the present writer.
13 Harahan to Dykstra, October 27, 1992, and Harahan to Board of Overseers, April 1, 1993, in AICS 3.1.20.3.
14 Recollections of the present writer.
15 Flesey to McCarrick, June 30, 2000, in AAN, R.G. 2.8, Series 1, Box 74 of 75.
16 Interview with Most Rev. John Flesey, November19, 2008.

17 McCarrick to Harahan, January 24, 1994, in AICS 2.3.1.
18 McCarrick to LoBalbo, March 2, 1992, in AAN, R.G. 2.8, Series 1, Box 32 of 75.
19 List of Visitors, in AAN, R.G. 2.8, Series 1, Box 48 of 75.
20 McCarrick to Liddy, January 19, 1989, in AAN, R.G. 2.8, Series 1, Box 23 of 75.
21 Harahan to McCarrick, March 20, 1991, in AAN, R.G. 2.8, Series 1, Box 32 of 75.
22 Memoranda to Liddy, Harahan, and Flesey, in AAN, R.G. 2.8, Boxes 22, 23, 32, and 48, of 75.
23 Liddy to Resident Faculty, October 29, 1987, in AICS 3.1.19.1.
24 Nehila to Gedrich, December 5, 1986, in AAN, R.G. 2.8, Series 1, Box 16 of 75.
25 McBride to Petillo, February 28, 1984, in AAN, R.G. 2.8, Series 1, Box 16 of 75.
26 Murray to McCarrick, December 29, 1986, in AAN, R.G. 2.8, Series 1, Box 16 of 75.
27 McBride to McCarrick, January 2, 1987, in AAN, R.G. 2.8, Series 1, Box 16 of 75.
28 Gedrich to McCarrick, February 26, 1987, in AAN, R.G. 2.8, Series 1, Box 16 of 75.
29 Gedrich to McCarrick, March 5, 1987, in AAN, R.G. 2.8, Series 1, Box 16 of 75.
30 Mavroudis to McBride, January 27, 1988, in AAN, R.G. 2.8, Series 1, Box 16 of 75.
31 McCarrick to McBride, January 30, 1988, in AAN, R.G. 2.8, Series 1, Box 16 of 75.
32 McBride to McCarrick, February 5, 1988, in AAN, R.G. 2.8, Series 1, Box 16 of 75.
33 McCarrick to McBride, July 30, 1988, in AAN, R.G. 2.8, Series 1, Box 16 of 75.
34 McCarrick to Culligan and Boyle, July 30, 1988, in AAN, R.G. 2.8, Series 1, Box 16 of 75.
35 Boyle to McCarrick, August 10, 1988, in AAN, R.G. 2.8, Series 1, Box 16 of 75.
36 McBride to McCarrick, March 17, 1989, in AAN, R.G. 2.8, Series 1, Box 16 of 75.
37 *Sunday News,* March 19, 1989, and *Sunday Post,* March 25, 1989.
38 McCarrick to Trabold, March 29, 1989, in AAN, R.G. 2.8, Series 1, Box 16 of 75.
39 McBride to McCarrick, May 16, 1989, in AAN, R.G. 2.8, Series 1, Box 16 of 75.
40 McBride to McCarrick, February 13, 1990, in AAN, R.G. 2.8, Series 1, Box 16 of 75.
41 Mavroudis to McCarrick, November 26, 1990, in AAN, R.G. 2.8, Series 1, Box 16 of 75.
42 *New York Times*, May 14, 1993.
43 *Record*, September 25, 2008.

Chapter Fifty
1 Statistics in AICS 2.3.1, AICS 3.1.20.8, and ASHU R.G. 2.20.
2 http://www.camminoneocatecumenale.it/en/index.asp and
  http://en.wikipedia.org/wiki/Neocatechumenal_Way .
3 Annual Report, July 3, 1997, in AAN, R.G. 2.8, Series 1, Box 48 of 75.
4 Ziccardi to McCarrick, September 19, 2000, in AAN, R.G. 2.8, Series 1, Box 74 of 75.
5 Guarino to Harahan, April 1, 1990, in AICS 3.1.20.4.
6 Board of Overseers Meeting, May 16, 1991, in AICS 2.3.1.
7 Cf Self-Study 1993–94, in AICS 2.3.1.
8 Porter to Scholz, September 3, 1992, in AICS 3.1.20.8.
9 Harahan to Scholz, November 30, 1990, in AICS 2.3.1.
10 Harahan to Scholz, February 24, 1992, in AICS 2.3.1.
11 Summer Program 1993, in AICS 2.3.1.
12 Self-Study 1993-1994, in AICS 2.3.1.
13 Seminary Committee Minutes, October 15, 1991, in AICS 2.3.1.
14 Self–Study 1993–94, in AICS 2.3.1.
15 Liddy to Faculty, August 19, 1987, in AICS 3.1.19.1.
16 Cusack to McCarrick, March 11, 1988, in AAN, R.G. 2.8, Series 1, Box 16 of 75.
17 The present writer's recollections of conversations with Monsignor Andrew Cusack.
18 McCarrick to Your Excellency, March 20, 1996, in AAN, R.G. 2.8, Series 1, Box 48 of 75.
19 Flesey to McCarrick, February 5, 1996, in AAN, R.G. 2.8, Series 1, Box 48 of 75.
20 Overseers Report, May 7, 1992, in AICS 3.1.0.
21 Seminary Stewardship Policy, August 17, 1995, in AAN, R.G. 2.9, Box 24 of 31. A similar version of the
   policy dated 1991 can be found in AICS 3.2.20.1.
22 Administrative Committee Minutes, March 9, 1992, in AICS 3.1.0.
23 Monthly Reports in AICS 3.1.0.
24 Flesey to McCarrick, May 5, 2000, in AAN, R.G. 2.8, Series 1, Box 74 of 75.
25 Coleman to Myers, January 24, 2002, in AAN, R.G. 2.9, Series 1, Box 31 of 32.
26 McCarrick to individual seminarians, July 21, 2000, in AAN, R.G. 2.8, Series 1, Box 74 of 75.
27 Annual Report, July 3, 1997, in AAN, R.G. 2.8, Series 1, Box 48 of 75.
28 Recollections of the present writer.

Chapter Fifty-one

1 Recollections of the present writer.
2 Recollections of the present writer.
3 Interview with Most Rev. John Flesey, November 19, 2008.
4 McCarrick to Coleman, June 27, 2000, in AAN, R.G. 2.8, Series 1, Box 74 of 75.
5 Myers to Coleman, May 28, 2002, in AAN, R.G. 2.9, Series 1, Box 24 of 32.
6 Peterson to McCarrick, July 17, 1995, in AAN, R.G. 2.9, Series 1, Box 24 of 32.
7 Coleman to Myers, December 10, 2003, in AAN, R.G. 2.9, Series 1, Box 20 of 21.
8 http://www.focusonline.org
9 McCarrick to Nydegger, September 25, 2000, in AAN, R.G. 2.8, Series 1, Box 74 of 75.
10 Annual Report 2003, in AAN, R.G. 2.9, Series 1, Box 20 of 21.
11 Visitation Report of February 16–19, 1987, in Marshall to McCarrick, February 5, 1988, in AAN, R.G. 2.8, Series 1, Box 23 of 75.
12 O'Brien to Rectors/Presidents, February 11, 2005, in files of the rector of Immaculate Conception Seminary.
13 O'Brien to Coleman, August 11, 2005, in files of the rector of Immaculate Conception Seminary.
14 Grocholewski to Myers, August 25, 2008, in files of the rector of Immaculate Conception Seminary.

Chapter Fifty-two

1 Statistics are as of October 16, 2009.
2 Two resident seminarians are undergraduate students.
3 Self-Study 2002–3, in AICS 8.6.
4 *Stirrings*, vol. 3, issue 2, fall 2008. *Stirrings* is the newsletter of the Institute for Christian Spirituality.

Chapter Fifty-three

1 Faculty members currently are members of the following organizations: American Association of University Professors, American Academy of Religion, American Catholic Historical Association, American Catholic Historical Society of Philadelphia, American Catholic Philosophical Society, American Historical Association, American Society of Church History, British Catholic Theological Association, Canon Law Society of America, The Catholic Biblical Association of America, The Catholic Theological Society of America, Great Britain and Ireland, Centre for Faith and Culture, National Catholic Educational Association, Carl Menninger Institute, Catholic Psychologist-Psychiatrists, Fellowship of Catholic Scholars, Metaphysical Society of America, National Association for Lay Ministry, Society of Biblical Literature, Society of Catholic Social Scientists, Society of Old Testament Scholars, University Faculty for Life, and the Venerable John Henry Newman Association.

Bibliography

Archives

AAB – Archives of the Archdiocese of Baltimore, Baltimore, MD.

AAN – Archives of the Archdiocese of Newark in Special Collections of Walsh Library of Seton Hall University, South Orange, NJ.

ACPF – Archives of the Sacred Congregation for the Evangelization of Peoples, or *de Propaganda fide*, Rome, Italy.

ADR – Archives of the Diocese of Rochester, Rochester, NY.

AICS – Archives of Immaculate Conception Seminary in Special Collections of Walsh Library of Seton Hall University, South Orange, NJ.

ASHU – Archives of Seton Hall University in Special Collections of Walsh Library of Seton Hall University, South Orange, NJ.

Books

Athans, Mary Christine, *To Work for the Whole People: John Ireland's Seminary in St. Paul*, Mahwah, 2002.

Beck, Henry G.J. *The Centennial History of the Immaculate Conception Seminary – Darlington, N.J.*, privately printed: 1961.

Bleichner, Howard. *View from the Altar: An Insider's Look at the Changing Catholic Priesthood*, New York: 2004.

"Brief History of the Immaculate Conception Major Diocesan Seminary of the Diocese of Newark, New Jersey – 1937," composed to be placed in the cornerstone of the seminary. No author is indicated on the copy in the archives.

Brann, Henry. "Seton Hall from 1862 to 1864, in Burke, Robert E. *The Bishops' Bill and Setonia Bards*, Englewood, NJ: 1913, p. 380-386.

Carey, Patrick W. and Muller, Earl C., eds., Theological *Education in the Catholic Tradition: Contemporary Challenges*, New York: 1997.

Ciccarino, Christopher. *Seeds of Faith, Branches of Hope: The Archdiocese of Newark, New Jersey*. Strasbourg, France: 2003

Concilii Plenarii Baltimorensis II., in Ecclesia Metropolitana Baltimorensi…Decreta, Baltimore:1868.

Crowe, Michael J. *The Extraterrestrial Life Debate, 1750-1900*. Mineola, NY: 1999.

Curran, Robert Emmett. *Michael Augustine Corrigan and the Shaping of Conservative Catholicism in America, 1878-1902*, New York: 1978.

Dictionary of American Biography, under the auspices of the American Council of Learned Societies, New York: 1928-44.

Dougherty, John J. *The Bishops of Newark, 1853-1978 : the first 125 years of the Archdiocese of Newark as seen through the lives and administrations of the seven men who have been its leaders,* prepared under the direction of the New Jersey Catholic Historical Records Commission, John J. Dougherty, chairman, South Orange, NJ: 1978.

Durant, Will. *Transition: A Sentimental Story of One Mind and One Era*, New York: 1927.

Durant, Will and Ariel. *Will and Ariel Durant: A Dual Autobiography*, New York: 1977.

Ellis, John T. *Formative Years of The Catholic University of America,* Washington: 1946.

Ellis, John T. *The Life of James Cardinal Gibbons, Archbishop of Baltimore, 1834-1921*, Milwaukee: 1952.

Flynn, Joseph M. *The Catholic Church in New Jersey*, Morristown, NJ: 1904.

Galishoff, Stuart. *Newark The Nation's Unhealthiest City 1832-1895,* New Brunswick, NJ: 1988.

Hinrichsen, Carl D. *The History of the Diocese of Newark, 1873-1901*, Ann Arbor, MI: 1963.

Jackson, Kenneth T. *Crabgrass Frontier: The Suburbanization of the United States*, New York: 1987.

Knapp, Charles Merriman. *New Jersey Politics during the Period of the Civil War and Reconstruction*, Geneva, NY: 1925.

Kupke, Raymond. "James Roosevelt Bayley," in *The Encyclopedia of American Catholicism*, Michael Glazier and Thomas J. Shelly, eds., Collegeville, MN:1997.

Kupke, Raymond. *Living Stones, A History of the Catholic Church in the Diocese of Paterson*, Clifton, NJ: 1987.

Leslie, Shane, ed. *Memories of Many Years (1839-1922) by Archbishop Seton*, New York: 1923.

Liddy, Richard. *Startling Strangeness – Reading Lonergan's Insight*, New York: 2007.

Mahoney, Joseph F. and Wosh, Peter J., eds. *The Diocesan Journal of Michael Augustine Corrigan, Bishop of Newark, 1872-1880*, Newark, NJ: 1987.

McNamara, Robert. "Bernard Joseph McQuaid," in *the Encyclopedia of American Catholicism*, Michael Glazier and Thomas J. Shelly, eds., Collegeville, MN: 1997.

Marshall, William F. *A Sketch of Seton Hall College*, South Orange, NJ: 1895.

McWilliams, Leroy with Bishop, Jim. *Parish Priest*, New York: 1953.

Mooney, J. A. *Memorial of the Most Reverend Michael Augustine Corrigan, Third Archbishop of New York*, New York: 1902.

Murray, Regina W., Shenrock, Joseph C., and O'Neill, James. *Upon This Rock: A New History of the Trenton Diocese,* Trenton: 1993.

Reilly, George A. "Thomas J. Walsh," in *The Bishops of Newark 1953-1978*, South Orange, NJ: 1978.

Schama, Simon. *Rough Crossings – Britain, the Slaves and the American Revolution,* New York: 2006.

Spalding, John Lancaster. *Lectures and Discourses*, New York: 1882.

White, Joseph M. *The Diocesan Seminary in the United States: A History from the 1780's to the Present*, Notre Dame IN: 1989.

Wilson, Harold F. *Outline History of New Jersey,* New Brunswick, NJ: 1950.

Wister, Robert J. *The Establishment of the Apostolic Delegation in the United States: The Satolli Mission, 1892-1896*, Rome: 1981.

Wister, Robert J., Augenstein, John, and Kauffman, Christopher, eds., *One Hundred Years of Catholic Education: Historical Essays in Honor of the Centennial of the National Catholic Educational Association,* Washington, DC: 2003.

Yaeger, Sister Hildegard M. *The Life of James Roosevelt Bayley, First Bishop of Newark and Eighth Archbishop of Baltimore 1814-1877*, Washington, DC:1947.

Zwierlien, Frederick J. *The Life and Letters of Bishop McQuaid*, I, Rochester, NY: 1925.

Journals, Chapters, and Articles

Acta Apostolicae Sedis

Acta Sanctae Sedis

Balcerak, Cal, "What's Happening to Seminaries?", in *Columbia*, August 1970.

Buckley, William F., "Will Durant, RIP," in *National Review*, January 22, 1982.

Ellis, John Tracy, "American Catholicism, 1953-1979: A Notable Change," in *Thought*, v. 54, n. 213 (June 1979).

Herberg, Will, "A Jew Looks at Catholicism," in *The Commonweal*, LVIII (May 22, 1953).

McCabe, L.R., "Darlington, A Jacobean Manor in New Jersey," in *The Architectural Record* XXXII (July-December, 1912).

McNamara, Robert F., "Archbishop Hanna, Rochesterian" in *Rochester History*, XXV, n. 2, April 1963.

Neuman, Matthias, "Seminaries and the New Conservatives," in *America*, September 10, 1977.

Weigel, George, "Thinking Through Vatican II," review of Giuseppe Alberigo's *History of Vatican II*, in *First Things*, June/July, 2001.

Wister, Robert J. "American Catholic Seminaries: Three Decades of Change," in *Fede e Libertà: Scritti in onore di p. Giacomo Martina, S.J.* a cura di Maurilio Guasco, Alberto Monticone e Pietro Stella, Brescia 1998.

Wister, Robert J. "The Effects of Institutional Change on the Office of Rector and President in the Roman Catholic Theological Seminaries, 1965-1994," in *Theological Education*, v xxxii (Supplement I) 1995.

Wister, Robert J. "Ministerial Formation in the American Catholic Church," in *Ministerial Formation* (a Journal of the World Council of Churches), 70, July 1995.

Wister, Robert J. "The Seminaries and NCEA," in Robert J. Wister, John Augenstein and Christopher Kauffman, eds., *One Hundred Years of Catholic Education: Historical Essays in Honor of the Centennial of the National Catholic Educational Association*, Washington, DC: 2003.

Wister, Robert J. "Theological Education in Seminaries" in Patrick W. Carey and Earl C. Muller, eds., *Theological Education in the Catholic Tradition: Contemporary Challenges*, New York: 1997.

Directories

Catholic Directory

Fifteenth Census of the US – 1930

Hoffmann's Catholic Directory 1898

The Metropolitan Catholic Almanac and Laity's Directory 1854, Baltimore: 1854.

Immaculate Conception Seminary Bulletin of Information 1961-1962

The Official Catholic Directory

Sadlier's Catholic Directory, Almanac, and Ordo

Seton Hall College Catalogue

Dissertations and Papers

Kennelly, Edward F., *A Historical Study of Seton Hall College,* Submitted in partial fulfillment of the requirements for the degree of Doctor of Education in the School of Education of New York University, 1944.

Russo, Michael, "Darlington: An Estate in the Ramapo Valley, 1871-1914, New York University, unpublished New York University seminar paper.

Toborowsky, Jonathan, "To Teach, To Rule, To Sanctify: The Life of Bishop George William Ahr," Mount St. Mary's Seminary, unpublished essay.

Newspapers and Periodicals

The Advocate (later *The Catholic Advocate*) – Official Newspaper of the Archdiocese of Newark

The Bergen Record (later *The Record*)

South Gate (Immaculate Conception Seminary newsletter)

Cornerstone (Immaculate Conception Seminary newsletter)

Freeman's Journal

Newark Daily Advertiser

Newark Evening News

The Newark Star Ledger (later *The Star Ledger*)

Newark Sunday Call

Stirrings (newsletter of the Institute for Christian Spirituality of Immaculate Conception Seminary)

The New York Sunday News

The New York Sunday Post

The New York Times

Electronic Sources

Bob Wister's Homepage: http://pirate.shu.edu/~wisterro

Boston College: http://www.bc.edu

Catholic Hierarchy: http://www.catholic-hierarchy.org

The Catholic University of America: http://tour.cua.edu/heritage/biographies/marycaldwell.cfm

Fairleigh Dickinson University: http://alpha.fdu.edu

Focus: http://www.focusonline.org

The Four Chaplains Memorial Foundation: http://www.fourchaplains.org

Holy See: http://www.vatican.va

Immaculate Conception Seminary: http://theology.shu.edu

Neocatechumenal Way: http://www.camminoneocatecumenale.it

Oneda Vineyard: http://www.onehda.com

Ramapough Mountain Indians: http://en.wikipedia.org/wiki/Ramapough_Mountain_Indians

Schenectady Digital History Archive: http://www.schenectadyhistory.org/families/hmgfm/caldwell-1.html

State of New Jersey: http://www.wnjpin.net

Tom's Inflation Calendar: http://www.halfhill.com/inflation.html

Will Durant Foundation: http://www.willdurant.com/bibliography.htm

Index

Appendix I

Appointed bishop of Trenton, NJ: May 10, 1918
Consecrated bishop: July 25, 1918
Installed bishop of Trenton, NJ: July 31, 1918
Appointed bishop of Newark, NJ: March 2, 1928
Installed bishop of Newark, NJ: May 1, 1928
Appointed archbishop of Newark, NJ: December 10, 1937
Installed archbishop of Newark, NJ: April 27, 1938
Died: June 6, 1952

Thomas Aloysius Boland[7]
Born, Orange, NJ: February 17, 1896
Ordained priest of diocese of Newark, NJ: December 23, 1922
Appointed auxiliary bishop of Newark, NJ and titular bishop of Hirina:
    May 21, 1940
Consecrated bishop: July 25, 1940
Appointed bishop of Paterson, NJ: June 21, 1947
Installed bishop of Paterson, NJ: September 18, 1947
Appointed archbishop of Newark, NJ: November 15, 1952
Installed archbishop of Newark, NJ: January 14, 1953
Retired archbishop emeritus of Newark, NJ: April 2, 1974
Died: March 16, 1979
Council Father: Second Vatican Council

Peter Leo Gerety[8]
Born, Shelton, CT: July 19, 1912
Ordained priest of diocese of Hartford, CT: June 29, 1939
Appointed coadjutor bishop of Portland, ME and titular bishop
    of Crepedula: March 4, 1966
Consecrated bishop: June 1, 1966
Appointed apostolic administrator of Portland, ME: February 18, 1967
Succeeded bishop of Portland, ME: September 15, 1969
Appointed archbishop of Newark, NJ: April 2, 1974
Installed archbishop of Newark, NJ: June 28, 1974
Retired archbishop emeritus of Newark, NJ: June 3, 1986

Theodore Edgar McCarrick[9]
Born, New York, NY: July 7, 1930
Ordained priest of archdiocese of New York, NY: May 31, 1958
Appointed auxiliary bishop of New York, NY and titular bishop of Rusibisir:
    May 24, 1977
Ordained bishop: June 29, 1977
Appointed bishop of Metuchen, NJ: November 19, 1981
Installed bishop of Metuchen, NJ: January 31, 1982
Appointed archbishop of Newark, NJ: May 30, 1986

Installed archbishop of Newark, NJ: July 25, 1986
Appointed superior of Turks and Caicos, Antilles: October 17, 1998
Appointed archbishop of Washington, DC: November 21, 2000
Installed archbishop of Washington, DC: January 3, 2001
Elevated to cardinal priest of Ss. Nereo e Achilleo: February 21, 2001
Retired archbishop emeritus of Washington, DC: May 16, 2006
Participated in conclave: 2005

John Joseph Myers[10]

Born, Ottawa, IL: July 26, 1941
Ordained priest of diocese of Peoria, IL: December 17, 1966
Appointed coadjutor bishop of Peoria, IL: July 7, 1987
Ordained bishop: September 3, 1987
Succeeded bishop of Peoria, IL: January 23, 1990
Appointed archbishop of Newark, NJ and superior of Turks and Caicos,
    Antilles: July 24, 2001
Installed archbishop of Newark, NJ: October 9, 2001

Bishops Affiliated with Immaculate Conception Seminary and Seton Hall University

George William Ahr[11]

Born: Newark, NJ: June 23, 1904
Ordained priest of diocese of Newark, NJ: July 29, 1928
Appointed bishop of Trenton, NJ: January 28, 1950
Consecrated bishop and installed bishop of Trenton, NJ: March 20, 1950
Retired bishop emeritus of Trenton, NJ: June 23, 1979
Died: May 5, 1993
Council Father: Second Vatican Council

David Arias Pérez, O.A.R.[12]

Born, Mataluenga, Spain: July 22, 1929
Ordained priest of Order of Augustinian Recollects: May 31, 1952
Appointed auxiliary bishop of Newark, NJ and titular bishop of Badiae:
    January 25, 1983
Ordained bishop: April 7, 1983
Retired auxiliary bishop emeritus of Newark, NJ: May 21, 2004

Reginald Arliss, C.P.[13]

Born, East Orange, NJ: September 8, 1906
Professed member of the Congregation of the Passion: August 15, 1928
Ordained priest of the Congregation of the Passion: April 28, 1934
Appointed titular bishop of Cerbali and prelate of Marbel, Philippines:
    November 18, 1969

Consecrated bishop: January 30, 1970
Retired prelate emeritus of Marbal, Philippines: October 1, 1981
Died: April 26, 1996

Paul Gregory Bootkoski[14]
Born, Newark, NJ: July 4, 1940
Ordained priest of archdiocese of Newark, NJ: May 28, 1966
Appointed auxiliary bishop of Newark, NJ and titular bishop of Zarna:
    July 7, 1997
Ordained bishop: September 5, 1997
Appointed bishop of Metuchen, NJ: January 4, 2002
Installed bishop of Metuchen, NJ: March 19, 2002

Vincent DePaul Breen[15]
Born, Brooklyn, NY: December 24, 1936
Ordained priest of diocese of Brooklyn, NY: July 15, 1962
Appointed bishop of Metuchen, NJ: July 8, 1997
Ordained bishop and installed bishop of Metuchen, NJ: September 8, 1997
Retired bishop emeritus of Metuchen, NJ: January 4, 2002
Died: March 30, 2003

Joseph Arthur Costello[16]
Born, Newark, NJ: May 9, 1915
Ordained priest of archdiocese of Newark, NJ: June 7, 1941
Appointed auxiliary bishop of Newark, NJ and titular bishop of Choma:
    November 17, 1962
Consecrated bishop: January 24, 1963
Died: September 22, 1978
Council Father: Second Vatican Council

Manuel Aurelio Cruz[17]
Born, La Habana, Cuba: December 2, 1953
Ordained priest of archdiocese of Newark, NJ: May 31, 1980
Appointed auxiliary bishop of Newark, NJ and titular bishop of Gaguari:
    June 9, 2008
Ordained bishop: September 8, 2008

Walter William Curtis[18]
Born, Jersey City, NJ: May 3, 1913
Ordained priest of diocese of Newark, NJ: December 8, 1937
Appointed auxiliary bishop of Newark, NJ and titular bishop of Bisica:
    June 27, 1957
Consecrated bishop: September 24, 1957
Appointed bishop of Bridgeport, CT: September 23, 1961
Installed bishop of Bridgeport, CT: November 21, 1961

Retired bishop emeritus of Bridgeport, CT: June 28, 1988
Died: October 18, 1997
Council Father: Second Vatican Council

Edgar Moreira da Cunha, S.D.V.[19]
Born, Riachão do Jacuípe, Brazil: August 21, 1957
Professed member of Society of Divine Vocations: February 11, 1975
Ordained priest of Society of Divine Vocations: March 27, 1982
Appointed auxiliary bishop of Newark, NJ and titular bishop of Ucres:
June 27, 2003
Ordained bishop: September 3, 2003

Nicholas Anthony DiMarzio[20]
Born, Newark, NJ: June 16, 1944
Ordained priest of archdiocese of Newark, NJ: May 30, 1970
Appointed auxiliary bishop of Newark, NJ and titular bishop of Mauriana:
September 10, 1996
Ordained bishop: October 31, 1996
Appointed bishop of Camden, NJ: June 7, 1999
Installed bishop of Camden, NJ: July 22, 1999
Appointed bishop of Brooklyn, NY: August 1, 2003
Installed bishop of Brooklyn, NY: October 3, 2003

Gaetano Aldo (Thomas) Donato[21]
Born, Jersey City, NJ: October 3, 1940
Ordained priest of archdiocese of Newark, NJ: May 29, 1965
Appointed auxiliary bishop of Newark, NJ and titular bishop of Jamestown:
May 21, 2004
Ordained bishop: August 4, 2004

John Joseph Dougherty[22]
Born, Jersey City, NJ: September 16, 1907
Ordained priest of diocese of Newark, NJ: July 23, 1933
Appointed auxiliary bishop of Newark, NJ and titular bishop of Cotenna:
November 17, 1962
Consecrated bishop: January 24, 1963
Retired auxiliary bishop emeritus of Newark, NJ: September 18, 1982
Died: March 20, 1986
Council Father: Second Vatican Council

Michael Joseph Dudick[23]
Born, Saint Clair, PA: February 24, 1916
Ordained priest of apostolic exarchate of United States of America, Faithful
of the Oriental Rite (Ruthenian): November 13, 1945

Incardinated priest of eparchy of Passaic (Ruthenian), NJ: July 6, 1963

Appointed eparch of Passaic (Ruthenian), NJ: July 29, 1968

Consecrated bishop and enthroned eparch of Passaic (Ruthenian), NJ: October 24, 1968

Retired eparch emeritus of Passaic (Ruthenian), NJ: November 6, 1995

Died: May 30, 2007

John Aloysius Duffy[24]

Born, Jersey City, NJ: October 29, 1884

Ordained priest of diocese of Newark, NJ: June 13, 1908

Appointed bishop of Syracuse, NY: April 21, 1933

Consecrated bishop: June 29, 1933

Installed bishop of Syracuse, NY: July 11, 1933

Appointed bishop of Buffalo, NY: January 5, 1937

Installed bishop of Buffalo, NY: April 14, 1937

Died: September 27, 1944

John Walter Flesey[25]

Born, Jersey City, NJ: August 6, 1942

Ordained priest of archdiocese of Newark, NJ: May 31, 1969

Appointed auxiliary bishop of Newark, NJ and titular bishop of Allegheny: May 21, 2004

Ordained bishop: August 4, 2004

Joseph Abel Francis, S.V.D.[26]

Born, Lafayette, LA: September 30, 1923

Ordained priest of Society of the Divine Word: October 7, 1950

Appointed auxiliary bishop of Newark, NJ and titular bishop of Valliposita: May 3, 1976

Ordained bishop: June 25, 1976

Retired auxiliary bishop emeritus of Newark, NJ: June 25, 1995

Died: September 1, 1997

Joseph Anthony Galante[27]

Born, Philadelphia, PA: July 2, 1938

Ordained priest of archdiocese of Philadelphia, PA: May 16, 1964

Appointed auxiliary bishop of San Antonio, TX and titular bishop of Equilium: October 13, 1992

Ordained bishop: December 11, 1992

Appointed bishop of Beaumont, TX: April 5, 1994

Installed bishop of Beaumont, TX: May 9, 1994

Appointed coadjutor bishop of Dallas, TX: November 23, 1999

Installed coadjutor bishop of Dallas, TX: January 14, 2000

Appointed bishop of Camden, NJ: March 23, 2004

Installed bishop of Camden, NJ: April 30, 2004

Robert Francis Garner[28]

Born, Jersey City, NJ: April 27, 1940

Ordained priest of archdiocese of Newark, NJ: June 15, 1946

Appointed auxiliary bishop of Newark, NJ and titular bishop of Blera:
May 3, 1976

Ordained bishop: June 25, 1976

Retired auxiliary bishop emeritus of Newark, NJ: June 11, 1995

Died: December 25, 2000

William Aloysius Griffin[29]

Born, Elizabeth, NJ: November 20, 1885

Ordained priest of diocese of Newark, NJ: August 15, 1910

Appointed auxiliary bishop of Newark, NJ and titular bishop of Sanavo:
February 26, 1938

Consecrated bishop: May 1, 1938

Appointed bishop of Trenton, NJ: May 21, 1940

Installed bishop of Trenton, NJ: July 23, 1940

Died: January 1, 1950

George Henry Guilfoyle[30]

Born, New York, NY: November 13, 1913

Ordained priest of archdiocese of New York, NY: March 25, 1944

Appointed auxiliary bishop of New York, NY and titular bishop of
Marazane: October 17, 1964

Consecrated bishop: November 30, 1964

Appointed bishop of Camden, NJ: January 2, 1968

Installed bishop of Camden, NJ: March 4, 1968

Retired bishop emeritus of Camden, NJ: May 13, 1989

Died: June 11, 1991

Thomas A. Hendrick[31]

Born, Penn Yan, NY: October 29, 1849

Ordained priest of the diocese of Rochester: June 7, 1873

Appointed bishop of Cebu, Philippines: July 17, 1903

Consecrated bishop of Cebu, Philippines: August 23, 1903

Died: November 29, 1909

Edward Thomas Hughes[32]

Born, Lansdowne, PA: November 13, 1920

Ordained priest of the archdiocese of Philadelphia, PA: May 31, 1947

Appointed auxiliary bishop of Philadelphia, PA and titular bishop of Segia:
June 14, 1976

Ordained bishop: July 26, 1976

Appointed bishop of Metuchen, NJ: December 11, 1986

Installed bishop of Metuchen, NJ: February 5, 1987

Retired bishop emeritus of Metuchen, NJ: July 8, 1997

Dominic Anthony Marconi[33]

Born, Newark, NJ: March 13, 1927

Ordained priest of archdiocese of Newark, NJ: May 30, 1953

Appointed auxiliary bishop of Newark, NJ and titular bishop of Bure:
  May 3, 1976

Ordained bishop: June 25, 1976

Retired auxiliary bishop emeritus of Newark, NJ: July 1, 2002

Justin Joseph McCarthy[34]

Born, Sayre, PA: November 26, 1900

Ordained priest of diocese of Newark, NJ: April 16, 1927

Appointed auxiliary bishop of Newark, NJ and titular bishop of Doberus:
  March 27, 1954

Consecrated bishop: June 17, 1954

Appointed bishop of Camden, NJ: January 27, 1957

Installed bishop of Camden, NJ: March 19, 1957

Died: December 26, 1959

Charles James McDonnell[35]

Born, Queens, NY: July 7, 1928

Ordained priest of archdiocese of Newark, NJ: May 29, 1954

Appointed auxiliary bishop of Newark, NJ and titular bishop of Pocofeltus:
  March 15, 1994

Ordained bishop: May 12, 1994

Retired auxiliary bishop emeritus of Newark, NJ: May 21, 2004

James Augustine McFaul[36]

Born, Larne, Ireland: June 6, 1850

Ordained priest of diocese of Newark, NJ: May 26, 1877

Appointed bishop of Trenton, NJ: July 20, 1894

Consecrated bishop and installed bishop of Trenton, NJ: October 18, 1894

Died: June 16, 1917

James Thomas McHugh[37]

Born, Orange, NJ: January 3, 1932

Ordained priest of archdiocese of Newark, NJ: May 25, 1957

Appointed auxiliary bishop of Newark, NJ and titular bishop of Morosbisdus:
  November 20, 1987

Ordained bishop: January 25, 1988

Appointed bishop of Camden, NJ: May 13, 1989
Installed bishop of Camden, NJ: June 20, 1989
Appointed coadjutor bishop of Rockville Centre, NY: December 7, 1998
Succeeded bishop of Rockville Centre, NY: January 4, 2000
Died: December 10, 2000

Thomas Henry McLaughlin[38]
Born, New York, NY: July 15, 1881
Ordained priest of diocese of Newark, NJ: July 26, 1904
Appointed auxiliary bishop of Newark, NJ and titular bishop of Nisa in Lycia:
    May 18, 1935
Consecrated bishop: July 25, 1935
Appointed bishop of Paterson, NJ: December 16, 1937
Installed bishop of Paterson, NJ: April 28, 1938
Died: March 17, 1947

James Aloysius McNulty[39]
Born, New York, NY: January 16, 1900
Ordained priest of diocese of Newark, NJ: July 12, 1925
Appointed auxiliary bishop of Newark, NJ and titular bishop of Methone:
    August 2, 1947
Consecrated bishop: October 7, 1947
Appointed bishop of Paterson, NJ: April 9, 1953
Installed bishop of Paterson, NJ: May 20, 1953
Appointed bishop of Buffalo, NY: February 12, 1963
Installed bishop of Buffalo, NY: May 1, 1963
Died: September 4, 1972
Council Father: Second Vatican Council

Bernard John Joseph McQuaid[40]
Born, New York, NY: December 15, 1823
Ordained priest of diocese of New York, NY: January 16, 1848
Appointed bishop of Rochester, NY: March 3, 1868
Consecrated and installed bishop of Rochester, NY: July 12, 1868
Died: January 18, 1909
Council Father: First Vatican Council

Sebastian Gebhard Messmer[41]
Born, Goldach, Switzerland: August 29, 1847
Ordained priest: July 23, 1871
Appointed bishop of Green Bay, WI: December 14, 1891
Consecrated bishop: March 27, 1892
Installed bishop of Green Bay, WI: April 7, 1892
Appointed archbishop of Milwaukee, WI: November 28, 1903

Installed archbishop of Milwaukee, WI: December 10, 1903
Died: August 4, 1930

Francis Joseph Monaghan[42]
Born, Newark, NJ: October 30, 1890
Ordained priest of diocese of Newark, NJ: May 29, 1915
Appointed coadjutor bishop of Ogdensburg, NY and titular bishop of Mela:
     April 17, 1936
Consecrated bishop: June 29, 1936
Installed coadjutor bishop of Ogdensburg, NY: July 8, 1936
Succeeded bishop of Ogdensburg, NY: March 20, 1939
Died: November 13, 1942

Robert Edward Mulvee[43]
Born, Boston, MA: February 15, 1930
Ordained priest of diocese of Manchester, NH: June 30, 1957
Appointed auxiliary bishop of Manchester, NH and titular bishop of Summa:
     February 15, 1977
Ordained bishop: April 14, 1977
Appointed bishop of Wilmington, DE: February 19, 1985
Installed bishop of Wilmington, DE: April 11, 1985
Appointed coadjutor bishop of Providence, RI: February 9, 1995
Installed coadjutor bishop of Providence, RI: March 27, 1995
Succeeded bishop of Providence, RI: June 11, 1997
Retired bishop emeritus of Providence, RI: March 31, 2005

Andrew Pataki[44]
Born, Palmerton, PA: August 30, 1927
Ordained priest of apostolic exarchate of United States of America, Faithful
     of the Oriental Rite (Ruthenian): February 24, 1952
Appointed auxiliary bishop of Passaic (Ruthenian), NJ and titular bishop
     of Telmisus: May 30, 1983
Ordained bishop: August 23, 1983
Appointed eparch of Parma (Ruthenian), OH: June 19, 1984
Enthroned eparch of Parma (Ruthenian), OH: August 16, 1984
Appointed eparch of Passaic (Ruthenian), NJ: November 6, 1995
Enthroned eparch of Passaic (Ruthenian), NJ: February 8, 1996
Retired eparch emeritus of Passaic (Ruthenian), NJ: December 6, 2007

Jerome Arthur (Gerolamo) Pechillo, T.O.R.[45]
Born, Brooklyn, NY: May 16, 1919
Ordained priest of the Third Order Regular of St. Francis of Penance:
     June 10, 1947

Appendix II

Seton Hall College/ University President		Immaculate Conception Seminary Director/Rector/President/Dean	
Bernard McQuaid	1856-1857		
Daniel J. Fisher	1857-1859		
Bernard J. McQuaid	1859-1868	Bernard J. McQuaid	1860-1862
		Henry Brann	1862-1864
		Michael A. Corrigan	1864-1868
Michael A. Corrigan	1868-1877	James H. Corrigan	1868-1873
		William Salt	1873-1890
James H. Corrigan	1877-1888		
William Marshall	1888-1897	John J. O'Connor	1890-1895
Joseph Synnott	1897-1899	Joseph Synnott	1895-1899
John Stafford	1899-1907	John Stafford	1899-1907
James Mooney	1907-1922	James Mooney	1907-1922
Thomas McLaughlin	1922-1933	Thomas McLaughlin	1922-1938
Francis J. Monaghan	1933-1936		
James Kelley	1936-1949	William Griffin	1938-1940
		Thomas Boland	1940-1947
John McNulty	1949-1959	George Ahr	1947-1950
		Thomas Powers	1950-1955
John J. Dougherty	1959-1969	Joseph Brady	1955-1961
		George Shea	1961-1968
		John O'Brien (Acting Rector)	Sept.-Dec. 1962,1963 1964,1965
		William Hogan	1968-1972
Edward Fleming (Acting President)	1969-1970		
Thomas Fahy	1970-1976	Harold Darcy	1972-1974
		Edward Ciuba	1974-1985
John Cole (Acting President)	1976-1977		
Robert Conley	1977-1979		
Lawrence T. Murphy	1979-1980		

Appendix II continued

Seton Hall College/ University President		Immaculate Conception Seminary Director/Rector/President/Dean	
Edward D'Alessio	1980-1984		
John Petillo (Chancellor)*	1984-1989	Richard Liddy	1985-1990
Dennis Mahon (Acting Chancellor*)	1988		
Richard Liddy (Interim Chancellor*)	1990	James Cafone (Acting Rector)	1990
Thomas Peterson (Chancellor*; Chancellor* and President; Chancellor)	1990-2000	Robert Harahan	1990-1995
Robert Sheeran	1995-2010	John Flesey	1995-2000
		Robert Coleman	2000-

*Executive Chancellor. For almost one year Monsignor Petillo served as Executive Chancellor and CEO while Dr. D'Alessio remained as president. With the retirement of Father Peterson and the restoration of the office of president, the office of chancellor fell into desuetude.

Appendix III

Faculty 1950-1984[1]

Adamczyk, Rev. Stanley S.T.L., The Catholic University of America Ph.D., Fordham University	Latin Greek Patristics English Dean of Studies Academic Dean
Alliegro, Rev. Michael J. D.Min., Drew University	Pastoral Theology Director of Lay Ministries
Asakiewicz, Rev. Richard V. Ph.D., University of Louvain	Systematic Theology
Baker, Right Rev. Msgr. George J. A.M., Seton Hall University	Ascetical Theology Pastoral Theology Spiritual Director
Barbieri, P.I.M.E., Rev. Amedeo L. S.S.L., Pontifical Biblical Institute	Sacred Scripture
Beck, Rev. Msgr. Henry G. J. Hist.Eccl.D., Pontifical Gregorian University	Church History Oriental Theology Logic
Brady, Right Rev. Msgr. Joseph H. S.T.D., Pontifical Urban College de Propaganda Fide Ph.D., Columbia University	Rector
Carey, Rev. Thomas J. A.B., Seton Hall University	Procurator
Cassels, Very Rev. Msgr. John J. S.T.L., The Catholic University of America M.A., Columbia University	Sacred Eloquence Homiletics English
Cerna, S.C., Sister Rose Anita A.M., Fordham University	Spanish Hispanic Studies
Ciuba, Rev. Msgr. Edward J. S.T.L., Pontifical Gregorian University S.S.L., Pontifical Biblical Institute Élève Titulaire de L'École Biblique de Jérusalem	Sacred Scripture Hebrew Rector President/Rector

Appendix III continued

Faculty 1950-1984[1]

Curtis, Most Rev. Walter W.[2] S.T.L., Pontifical Gregorian University S.T.D., The Catholic University of America	Moral Theology Canon Law Religion Sacristan
Darcy, Rev. Msgr. Harold P. S.T.L., Pontifical Gregorian University J.C.D., Pontifical Gregorian University	Canon Law President/Rector
DeDomenico, Rev. Francis A. S.T.L., Pontifical Gregorian University S.T.D. (cand.), University of Ottawa	Systematic Theology Academic Dean
Demjanovich, Right Rev. Charles C. A.M., Seton Hall University	Procurator
Dougherty, Most Rev. John J.[3] S.T.L., Pontifical Urban College de Propaganda Fide S.S.D., Pontifical Biblical Institute	Sacred Scripture Hebrew Greek German Librarian
Farley, Rev. Leo O. S.T.D., The Catholic University of America	Moral Theology
Feehan, Rev. Stephen S. Ph.D., St. Louis University	Philosophy Theology
Fitzpatrick, Rev. Joseph S.T.L., The Catholic University of America	Moral Theology
Finnerty, Rev. Msgr. James J. A.B., Seton Hall University	Religion Director of Students
Flusk, Rev. Joseph F. A.B., Seton Hall University	Sacred Music Director of Choir
Gibney, Rev. Robert G. A.B., Seton Hall University	Religion Director of Students
Guarino, Rev. Thomas G. S.T.D., The Catholic University of America	Systematic Theology

Appendix III continued

Faculty 1950-1984[1]

Gusmer, Rev. Msgr. Charles W. S.T.D. and Liturgisches Diplom, University of Trier	Sacramental Theology Sacramentology Liturgy Systematic Theology
Harahan, Rev. Msgr. Robert E. S.T.D., Academia Alfonsiana	Moral Theology
Herbster, Rev. Gene A. S.T.L., Pontifical Gregorian University Hist.Eccl.L., Pontifical Gregorian University	Church History Oriental Theology
Hinrichsen, Rev. Msgr. Carl D. Ph.D., the Catholic University of America	Church History
Hogan, Rev. Msgr. William F. S.T.D., The Catholic University of America	Ascetical Theology Spiritual Theology Dogmatic Theology Oriental Theology Director of Discipline Dean of Studies Spiritual Director Rector
Hunt, Rev. Robert E. S.T.D., Pontifical Gregorian University	Dogmatic Theology
Jarvais, Right Rev. Msgr. Walter G., P.A. A.M., Seton Hall University L.H.D., Bloomfield College	Ascetical Theology Spiritual Director
Kakolewski, Rev. John A. M.Div., Immaculate Conception Seminary	Spiritual Theology
Keating, Rev. George M. S.T.L., The Catholic University of America	Ascetical Theology Spiritual Director
Kirby, S.C., Sister Margaret M.A., Manhattan College	Director of Lay Ministry
Koenig, Very Rev. Msgr. John H. S.T.L., The Catholic University of America A.M., University of Notre Dame	Liturgy Philosophy Metaphysics Ethics Religion

Appendix III continued

Faculty 1950-1984[1]

Kukura, Rev. Joseph W. M.A., University of Louvain S.T.D. (cand.), The Catholic University of America	Moral Theology Christian Ethics Executive Assistant for Development
Leiken, O.S.B., Rev. Joel M.A., Seton Hall University	Homiletics
Liddy, Rev. Msgr. Richard M. S.T.L., Pontifical Gregorian University Ph.D., Pontifical Gregorian University	Philosophy Systematic Theology Theology Spiritual Director
Mahon, Rev. John M. A.B., Seton Hall University Director of Students	Religion Liturgy
Maione, Rev. Francis T. M.A., University of Louvain Hispanic Studies	Procurator/Business Manager Director of Hispanic Studies
Maleski, Alice M.M., D.M.A. (cand.) Manhattan School of Music	Sacred Music Director of Choir
Mallner, O.S.U., Sister Agnes M.Div., Weston School of Theology	Spiritual Theology Assistant Spiritual Director
Manz, Very Rev. Msgr. Joseph C. A.B., Seton Hall University	Procurator
Masiello, Rev. Msgr. Joseph P. S.T.L., Pontifical Gregorian University	Pastoral Theology Procurator/Business Manager
McCarthy, Most Rev. Justin J. S.T.L., Pontifical Urban College de Propaganda Fide[4]	Ascetical Theology Religion Spiritual Director
McGrath, R.S.M., Sister Eileen B.A., Georgian Court College	Pastoral Theology
McNulty, Rev. Frank J. S.T.D., The Catholic University of America	Moral Theology Christian Ethics Pastoral Theology Pastoral Ministry

Appendix III continued

Faculty 1950-1984[1]

Miros, Rev. Chester J. S.T.B., A.M., University of Louvain	
Morris, Rev. Msgr. Philip D. S.T.D., The Catholic University of America	Systematic Theology Ecumenical Theology Theology Homiletics Communications Arts Assistant Academic Dean
O'Brien, Very Rev. Msgr. John F. S.T.L., The Catholic University of America	Philosophy Catechetics Education Metaphysics Dean of Studies Executive Assistant to the Rector Vice Rector Vice President/Vice Rector Acting Rector
O'Leary, Rev. Msgr. Thomas M. S.T.L., The Catholic University of America	Field Education Pastoral Ministry Director of Field Education Director of Students Dean of Students
Padovano, Rev. Anthony T. S.T.D., Pontifical Gregorian University	Dogmatic Theology
Powers, Right Rev. Msgr. Thomas H. A.M., Seton Hall University	Pastoral Theology Latin Rector
Price, Rev. Edward G. A.B., Seton Hall University	Procurator
Przezdziecki, Very Rev. Msgr. Joseph J. L.M.S., Pontifical Institute of Medieval Studies Ph.D., University of Toronto	Philosophy History of Philosophy Metaphysics Fundamental Theology
Reilly, Rev. George M. M.Div., Immaculate Conception Seminary	Spiritual Director

Appendix III continued

Faculty 1950-1984[1]

Rispoli, Angelina A. M.A., St. John's University	Sacred Music Director of Choir
Ruffino, Rev. Russell G. S.T.L., Pontifical Gregorian University Ph.D., Pontifical Gregorian University	Philosophy
Serratelli, Rev. Msgr. Arthur J.[5] S.S.L., Pontifical Biblical Institute S.T.D., Pontifical Gregorian University	Biblical Studies
Shea, Right Rev. Msgr. George W. S.T.D., Royal Imperial University of Innsbruck Fundamental Theology	Sacramental Theology Special Dogmatic Theology German Librarian Rector
Tierney, Very Rev. Msgr. John J. S.T.L., Propaganda College, Rome J.U.L., Pontifical University of the Lateran	Canon Law Ethics
Turro, Rev. Msgr. James C. S.S.L., Pontifical Biblical Institute Ph.D., New York University	Sacred Scripture Biblical Studies New Testament Greek Hebrew German English History of Philosophy Librarian Director of Libraries Director of Library Services
Welsh, Right Rev. Msgr. Aloysius J. S.T.D., The Catholic University of America	Moral Theology Sociology English Education

Appendix III continued

Faculty 1950-1984[1]

Wister, Rev. Msgr. Robert J. S.T.M., Union Theological Seminary Hist.Eccl.D., Pontifical Gregorian University	Historical Studies Church History
Zimmermann, Very Rev. Msgr. Donald B. S.T.L., Pontifical Gregorian University J.C.D., Pontifical Gregorian University	Canon Law Moral Theology

1 The professors are listed with the ecclesiastical title they possessed either while at the seminary or after their departure from the seminary. The ecclesiastical titles were changed in 1968, eliminating the terms "Right" and "Very" before "Rev. Msgr." I have left the original form in most cases. The catalogues also were not clear in designating departments so the references are as appear in the successive catalogues. It is interesting to note that faculty often taught in a variety of areas.

    In this chart the administrative titles change as well. The appendix covering faculty since 1984 will note changes in administrative titles as well as further changes in academic nomenclature.

    The chart does not include adjunct faculty. All listed are designated as "faculty" or "full-time faculty" in the catalogues. However, the catalogues 1974-1975 and 1975-1976 list all faculty members, full-time and adjunct without distinction. I have culled the full-time from these lists.

    Early catalogues do not have clear departmental divisions, therefore, in some cases, the catalogue refers to a general area or a specific course or discipline. The nomenclature for areas of teaching changes over the years and is reflected in this list.

2 Consecrated auxiliary bishop of Newark on September 24, 1957. Appointed bishop of Bridgeport on September 23, 1961.

3 President of Seton Hall University 1959-1969. Consecrated auxiliary bishop of Newark on January 24, 1963.

4 Consecrated auxiliary bishop of Newark on June 11, 1954. He was appointed bishop of Camden on January 27, 1957.

5 Ordained auxiliary bishop of Newark on September 8, 2000; installed bishop of Paterson on July 6, 2004.

Appendix IV

Faculty since Affiliation in 1984

Asakiewicz, Rev. Richard V. Ph.D., University of Louvain	Systematic Theology
Bico, Rev. Antonio I. S.T.D., University of St. Mary of the Lake	Systematic Theology Assistant Spiritual Director
Blumenfeld, Rev. Donald Ph.D., Graduate Theological Foundation	Director of Field Education Director of Pastoral Education
Bracken, C.P., Rev. W. Jerome Ph.D., Fordham University	Christian Ethics Moral Theology
Cafone, Rev. James S.T.D., The Catholic University of America	Pastoral Theology Vice Rector Director of Formation Acting Rector
Chapel, Rev. Msgr. Joseph R. S.T.D., Accademia Alfonsiana	Moral Theology Associate Dean
Ciccarino, Rev. Christopher S.S.L., Pontifical Biblical Institute S.T.D., Pontifical Gregorian University	Biblical Studies
Ciuba, Rev. Msgr. Edward J. S.S.L., Pontifical Biblical Institute Elève Titulaire de L'École Biblique de Jérusalem	Biblical Studies Rector/Dean
Coleman, Rev. Msgr. Robert F. J.C.D., Pontifical Gregorian University	Canon Law Vice Rector Rector and Dean
Cusack, Rev. Msgr. Andrew T. Ph.D., St. John's University	Pastoral Theology Staff Psychologist Director of Continuing Education Director of Formation
DeDomenico, Rev. Msgr. Francis A. S.T.L., Pontifical Gregorian University Ph.D. (cand.), University of Ottawa	Systematic Theology Associate Dean
Donato, Most Rev. Thomas A.[1] M.Div., Immaculate Conception Seminary	Spiritual Director

Appendix IV <small>continued</small>

Faculty since Affiliation in 1984

Donohue, Rev. Patrick M.Div., Immaculate Conception Seminary	Director of Field Education Business Manager
Figueiredo, Rev. Anthony J. S.T.D., Pontifical Gregorian University	Systematic Theology Spiritual Theology
Fleming, Rev. Msgr. Edward J. S.T.L., The Catholic University of America Ph.D., St. John's University L.H.D., Seton Hall University	Director of Development
Flesey, Most Rev. John W.[2] S.T.D., Pontifical University of St. Thomas (Angelicum)	Pastoral Theology Spiritual Theology Spiritual Director Rector/Dean
Fortin, Timothy P. Ph.D., Pontifical University of the Holy Cross	Philosophy
Foster, David Ph.D., The Catholic University of America	Philosophy
Fox, Zeni V. Ph.D., Fordham University	Pastoral Theology Director of Lay Ministry Program
Fuhrman, Rev. Msgr. Robert M.Div., M.A., Immaculate Conception Seminary	Vice Rector Director of Formation
Gadenz, Rev. Pablo T. S.S.L., Pontifical Biblical Institute S.T.D., Pontifical Gregorian University	Biblical Studies
Glazov, Gregory Y. D.Phil., Oxford University	Biblical Studies
Grimm, Rev. John S. S.T.L., Pontifical Faculty of the Dominican House of Studies, Washington, DC J.D., Widener University School of Law	Moral Theology
Grondelski, John M. Ph.D., Fordham University Moral Theology	Associate Dean
Guarino, Rev. Thomas G. S.T.D., The Catholic University of America	Systematic Theology

Appendix IV continued

Faculty since Affiliation in 1984

Gusmer, Rev. Msgr. Charles W. S.T.D. and Liturgisches Diplom, University of Trier Sacramentology	Liturgy
Harahan, Rev. Msgr. Robert E. S.T.D., Academia Alfonsiana	Christian Ethics Rector/Dean
Harms, Rev. Msgr. William M.C.R.P., Rutgers University M.Div., Immaculate Conception Seminary	Pastoral Theology Associate Dean
Hart, Rev. John M.A., Immaculate Conception Seminary	Director of Field Education
Johnston, Eric M. Ph.D., The Catholic University of America	Theology

Kukura, Rev. Joseph W.
M.A., University of Louvain
S.T.D. (cand.), The Catholic University
   of America
	Moral Theology
	Christian Ethics
	Executive Assistant
	   for Development

Kulig, Rev. Anthony A.B., Seton Hall University M.Div., Immaculate Conception Seminary	Formation Mentor
Liddy, Rev. Msgr. Richard M. S.T.L., Pontifical Gregorian University Ph.D., Pontifical Gregorian University	Spiritual Theology Rector/Dean Interim Chancellor
Lucey, Rev. Walter D. A.B., Ramapo State College M.Div., Immaculate Conception Seminary	Formation Mentor
Mallner, O.S.U., Sister Agnes M.Div., Weston School of Theology	Assistant Spiritual Director
Maluf, Leonard S.T.D., Pontifical Gregorian University S.S.L., Pontifical Biblical Institute	Biblical Studies
Masiello, Rev. Msgr. Joseph S.T.L., Pontifical Gregorian University	Pastoral Theology Vice Rector Business Manager

494